Fortresses
of the
Knights

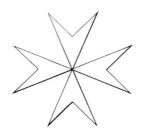

AIR MALTA

With Compliments

Fortresses
of the
Knights

Stephen C. Spiteri

Book Distributors Limited

Malta

First Published 2001

Fortresses of the Knights is a new, revised, and abridged version of *Fortresses of the Cross: Hospitaller Military Architecture*, first published in 1994.

Copyright Stephen C. Spiteri 2001

Book design and layout by the author
Setting and production by Gutenberg Press, Hal Tarxien, Malta
Cover design by Patrick Fenech
Published by Book Distributors Limited, 32 St Vincent Street, Hamrun, Malta
Printed by Gutenberg Press, Hal Tarxien, Malta

All drawings of fortifications reproduced in this book, unless where specifically stated, were produced by the author.

Cover illustration: Couvre Porte and the Birgu Fortifications.

ISBN 99909-72-06-0

Other books by the same author:

Discovering the Fortifications of the Knights of the Order of St John in Malta (Malta,1988)
The Knights' Fortifications (Malta, 1989)
The British Fortifications (Malta, 1991)
Fortresses of the Cross: Hospitaller Military Architecture (Malta, 1994)
British Military Architecture in Malta (Malta, 1996)
The Palace Armoury: A Study of a Military Storehouse of the Knights of the Order of St John (Malta 1999)
The Fougasse: The Stone Mortar of Malta (Malta, 1999)

*For my Mother and Father
and my wife, Marthy*

Contents

Introduction

The history of the knights of the Order of St John of Jerusalem, Rhodes, and Malta, better known as the Knights Hospitallers, is a constant source of fascination to a wide range of audiences. This appeal stems primarily from the all-pervading link with crusading warfare, for the Order of Hospitaller knights, a religious-military institution first conceived in the Holy Land as a direct consequence of the Crusades, was one of the most formidable and feared fighting machines in Christendom. Even after the loss of the Latin East, the knights continued to nourish their crusader traditions with another four hundred years of warfare against their Muslim enemies, operating first from Rhodes and then from the tiny island of Malta. The Order's survival as a military organization throughout nearly six centuries was as much the result of the bravery and fighting prowess of the knights as their unceasing ability to invest in formidable works of fortification.

Fortresses of the Knights is a work which is dedicated to the study of these military works. Not that Hospitaller fortifications have failed to attract attention. On the contrary, Crac des Chevaliers, the fortress of Rhodes, and the fortifications of Malta have been the focus of various masterly studies. What has not been forthcoming, however, despite the vast literature on the Order's military works, has been a comprehensive attempt to explain and assess the total Hospitaller achievement in the construction of fortresses, one that takes into consideration not only the world-famous architectural landmarks such as Crac, the city of Rhodes, and the Laparelli enceinte of Valletta, but also the multitude of other less familiar, though nonetheless important, fortifications built, or adapted, by the knights to protect their far-flung interests. Many of these gaunt but romantic strongholds and towers, standing in bleak vigilance on the borders of what were once Hospitaller outposts on the frontiers of Christendom, far away from normal and easily accessible routes, have attracted very little attention.

This book seeks to make amends. It attempts to reveal both the outstanding extent of the Hospitaller contribution to the art of fortification and to draw attention to the varied individual works themselves. It is a book, which is totally devoted to the study of the development of military architecture as expressed by the Hospitaller knights.

In *Fortresses of the Knights* attention has been focused on the *materia prima* and the method consisting of a systematic compilation of the numerous military works; an attempt not only to record but also to explain the pattern of development in order to enable a better understanding of the nature and extent of the Hospitaller contribution to the art of fortification. Given the stated focus of this study, the book is not concerned with the wider political, diplomatic, social, and economic aspects of the Order's history. For a fuller appreciation of this military institution and its wider background, the reader is directed to consult other scholarly and detailed historical works, many of which are listed in the bibliography.

Indeed, in writing this book I have had to work in the shadow of many masterly historians such as Riley-Smith, Deschamps, Rossi, Gabriel, Luttrell, Hughes, Hoppen, and Pringle, all of whom have contributed much to our understanding of the history of the Order of St John and to the study of its fortifications. I have relied heavily on their works but, frequently, there was no beaten track to follow and I have had to undertake considerable research myself in the archives of the Order in Malta, and various other libraries and archives abroad wherever such material is carefully conserved, together with numerous field trips to the many castles and fortified sites themselves. I also invested considerable time and energy in creating a comprehensible visual medium.

As in all my previous publications, the method adopted here relies on a graphical approach, making use of my own drawings, many now revised, which first appeared in my earlier publications, although, a few have been specifically executed for this edition. I have also made extensive use of photographs of original plans, many in colour, rather than the photocopies or tracings in the original edition, for these capture better both the details of construction and the graphic style of the period. In describing and illustrating the individual forts, I have purposely sought to focus mainly on the salient and characteristic features of each work, in order to avoid a monotonous and repetitive exposition. My principal aim all along has been to synthesize the vast amount of existing information.

Surely, the production of this publication would have been much more easier, and quicker, had I just opted to follow the staple formula adopted by many authors of works on fortification. But simply reproducing a number of old plans and photographs, as a mere backdrop to a ponderous text would surely not have made the subject any more comprehensible. Like any technical subject, the art of fortification needs to be translated into more digestible terms to be more widely understood. Art, the universal language, is perhaps the best medium for the job. Pietro Cataneo, in his *Quattro primi libri di architettura,* stated that one of the two main prerequisites in architecture, both civil and military, is *disegno.* Since any study of fortification must, at the end of the day, reduce itself to one of military architecture, and architecture, in turn, is fundamentally the study of shape and form, *disegno* remains the basic tool in any study of fortification.

Hence, it is primarily through *disegno* that the nature, extent, and development of Hospitaller fortifications are explained and described in this book. Shape and design, however, can only be interpreted with the help of the third dimension, a concept, which was well understood by the mapmakers of old who sought to produce bird's eye views of entire cities. Furthermore, given that the subject of fortification tends to suffer from all the limitations affecting the understanding of historical structures surviving in part or in ruins, or in other uses, almost inevitably, a degree of reconstruction is always necessary to enable some form of understanding of what the original structures must have looked like. Here again *disegno* comes to the rescue, enabling many a graphic reconstruction of the defensive works throughout various stages in their history based on archaeological, documentary, and historical evidence.

The reconstruction drawings and aerial views illustrating this publication endeavour to reach an acceptable solution between the inanimate simplicity of plans and the confusing detail of modern aerial photographs by capturing the essence of the fortifications under review: their design, technicalities, and texture, features that are unique to each and every fortress.

Fundamentally, *Fortresses of the Knights* is but a second edition of my earlier work, *Fortresses of the Cross: Hospitaller Military Architecture (1136-1798),* first published in 1994. In reality, however, the original book has been totally revised, rewritten, and redesigned to present practically a new book. The unwieldy 700 pages of the original publication have now been draconically reduced into a more handy 400-page layout. The new version is also more attractively produced and bound, with much more use of colour, enabling a more faithful reproduction of old plans and my own drawings. To achieve this, however, a considerable amount of material had, inevitably, to be omitted. Among the sections which were left out, or severely cropped, are those on the coastal fortifications of the Maltese islands, the Hospitaller garrisons and armed forces, building methods and techniques, and the illustrated glossary. It is my intention, however, to develop and expand further some of these themes in separate publications. The glossary, for example, is being built into an illustrated dictionary of military architecture that will hopefully be published in coming years.

The main reason behind this drastic restructuring has been to produce a book that serves more effectively as an introduction to the subject for, despite its bulkiness, the original publication was still little more than a guidebook to many of the forts and fortresses, for not all of the fortifications described therein were treated in the same depth and detail. Discussion of the armament of forts, their garrisoning, and the internal arrangement and structures within them was likewise limited. As with any other book of its type, which tries to encompass a vast field of study, the work merely touches the fringes of the subject and can serve no more than a mere introduction to the military architecture of the knights of St John. At best it is a general survey of the works of fortification erected by the knights across the shores of the Mediterranean but it is hoped, now even more in its new edition, that it will continue to serve as a stepping stone from which the growing band of students and researchers may continue to develop our knowledge of the past defences to greater effect.

In the many years of research, travels, and study which it has taken to produce this book, I have realized that each fort mentioned here deserves a detailed study in its own right. The subject is vast and large quantities of material still lie largely untapped for future researchers to investigate with profit. As such, it makes little sense to cram too much information into any one book. In this respect, therefore, I believe *Fortress of the Knights* to be much more effective than its predecessor, for in its new format it provides the reader with a sharper and more focused overview of Hospitaller fortifications and their development through the ages.

To achieve this, the new edition has been divided into two major sections. The first provides the overall historical context and the second is a sort of illustrated gazetteer arranged in chronological order, and subdivided into three sections representing distinct theatres of war in which the Order had established its Convent (i.e., its headquarters), beginning with the Holy Land and the Latin East, then going on to Rhodes and the Dodecanese, and ending with Malta and the central Mediterranean.

In architectural terms, each of these epochs covers essential developments. The initial period in Outremer is important because it witnessed the rapid development of the medieval castle, from the simple Norman keep down to the successive enceintes of mighty concentric fortresses. The Rhodian defences, on the other hand, are significant because they illustrate an embryonic and transitional form of early gunpowder fortifications, while the Maltese defences display a rich and concentrated collection of the bastioned form in its various styles, as introduced and perfected by the Italians in the sixteenth century, up to its apogee, including even the beginning of its demise in the emergence of the polygonal manner of fortification.

It is important to point out here that this study is mainly concerned with the direct Hospitaller involvement in the building of fortifications and not with buildings which were the product of other cultures and were simply occupied by the knights, as was the case in Latin Morea and Spain. This explains why the book may appear weighted in favour of the later works. But this is also borne from the fact that it becomes increasingly more difficult to trace the older structures since most have disappeared with the passage of time or have survived as sparse ruins and archaeological sites. In the Latin

East, to give just one example, a large number of Hospitaller strongholds were demolished by Saladin after 1187. On the other hand, the numerous commanderies and priories throughout mainland Europe, frequently fortified, and the Hospitaller castles of the *Reconquista* in Spain, do not fall within the scope of this book.

Another important element of Hospitaller fortifications which is not treated in this study is the religious. Most of the knights's fortifications, given the religious, conventual, and Hospitaller nature of the Order, had their own church, chapel, or, as in the case of the major fortresses, even cathedrals, convents, and hospitals. The study of Hospitaller religious architecture, however, is a specialized discipline in its own right and does not fit within the scope of this study.

Even so, this still leaves a considerable corpus of fascinating, complex, and varied buildings to be explored and studied, many of which, as will be shown in the following pages, are amongst the most outstanding examples of military architecture in the world. Crac des Chevaliers, Marqab, Rhodes, Bodrum, and Valletta, together with all other Hospitaller fortresses knit of dressed stone and virgin rock, stand monument not only to a bygone age of chivalric élan but also to the immense energy, ingenuity, and single-mindedness of purpose of so small, yet so formidable, a band of warriors drawn together in defence of a common ideal.

Photographic Acknowledgments

Plans of fortifications
National Library of Malta, Valletta
National Museum of Archaeology, Valletta
National Museum of Fine Arts, Valletta
Vatican Library, Rome

Old views of Malta
National Museum of Archaeology, Valletta

Prints
Clerkenwell Library, St John Gate, London
BBC Hulton Paul Picture Library
Déparment des Manuscrits, Bibliothèque nationale de France

Acknowledgments

It is a pleasure, as well as duty, to express my gratitude to all those who have made this work possible. I can only name the leading ones without forgetting those many others who encouraged me to carry on. To begin with, I am most grateful to Mr Anthony Gatt for his unstinting support and encouragement, and for giving me the opportunity to see this work once again in print. I am also particularly indebted to the Sovereign Military Order of Malta for its assistance during the preparation of the first edition which enabled me to visit most of the foreign places described in this book. In this respect, I am indebted to His Excellency, the Prince and Grand Master, Frà Andrew Bertie and to Mr Roger de Giorgio KM for their personal interest and encouragement. I am also most grateful to Professor Quentin Hughes with whom I have had several opportunities to discuss this work and learn from his observations as well as to receive his constant encouragement. Especially in the preparation of this new edition, I would like to thank Dr Michael Losse for his advice and assistance on various aspects of the fortifications of Rhodes which had to be updated. I am similarly indebted to Mr Louis Scerri for his comments and advice on the layout and setting of this publication.

I would also like to express my thanks to the staffs of the various libraries, archives, and museums where I had the pleasure of working, particularly those of the National Library at Valletta and Clerkenwell Museum, St John Gate, London. I thank, too, the Director of Museums for his permission to reproduce many old photographs of the fortifications of Malta. Likewise, I thank the many fellow researchers and historians who kindly provided me with all types of useful information, from plans and photographs, to books and copies of old documents.

Surely, not least, I am greatly indebted to my father who instilled in me a love for drawing, architecture, and all things beautiful.

The
Historical
Context

The Hospitaller War-Machine

'We and our brethren, mixing knighthood with religion, sweat in the unending toil of defending [the Holy Land]. We do not refuse to spill our blood as we resist the enemies of the Cross of Christ and we make greater expenses than ever before in its defence ..'

Letter from Master Gilbert d'Assailly to the Bishop of Trani

The Military Orders of knighthood which came into existence during the Crusades can all be said to have evolved in response to the exigencies of Christian pilgrims in the Holy Land. The Hospitaller Order of St John, in particular, began as a charitable institution based upon the founding of a hospital in Jerusalem for the care of pilgrims and even when its brethren eventually took up arms, they did so as an extension of their eleemosynary activities in order to protect pilgrims on the dangerous insecure routes leading to and from Jerusalem. Together with the Templars, they soon began to participate in the military affairs of the kingdom and eventually developed into an effective and feared military organization, one that combined the concepts of knighthood and monasticism to ensure a single-mindedness of purpose that anchored their Order in the forefront of the Christian struggle against the infidel in a kind of holy war.

The heart of this war machine, like that of any other military organization with its origins deeply rooted in the medieval world, were the knights, an élite corps of feudal warriors drawn from among the noble families of Europe. Unlike their secular counterparts, however, the Hospitaller *milites* were warriors bound by religious vows of poverty, chastity, and obedience to an organization devoted towards furthering the aims and ambitions of the church. This did not make them the less militant. On the contrary, it only served to reinforce their role as the soldiers of Christ. In all the theatres of war in which the Order established its convent, the Hospitallers followed an unremitting aggressive policy of offensive actions - the *chaveaux* in the Holy Land and the naval *corso* in Rhodes and Malta. This continual belligerency inevitably roused heavy retaliation from their Muslim enemies. In effect, the Hospitallers' survival throughout nearly six hundred years of warfare was as much a result of their daring, bravery, and fighting prowess as it was due to their unceasing efforts in strengthening and building fortifications. Their ability to survive on the border outposts of Christendom in the face of ever-growing Muslim

Hospitaller brethren giving alms to the poor and sick, from Caoursin's *Stabilimenta.*

power was largely possible only because of the possession of formidable fortresses.

It can thus be said that the history of the Hospitaller knights is in many ways a history of fortifications. For it begins in the Holy Land with the gift of the castle of Bait Gibrin from King Fulk of Jerusalem in 1136, and ends with the surrender of the Maltese islands to Napoleon Bonaparte in 1798. In between, there were nearly six centuries of incessant warfare, sieges, and fortress-building spread across the shores of the Mediterranean. Six centuries that saw the evolution of the art and science of fortification from the medieval castle at one end, down to the polygonal gun forts at the other. Crac des Chevaliers, Marqab, the fortresses and castles of Rhodes and the Dodecanese islands, and the bastioned enceintes and towers of Malta, are amongst the most outstanding examples of military architecture in the world and all stand monument to the extraordinary effort which the knights of St John invested in the design and construction of their fortifications in an unending struggle to redress the odds stacked against them.

For the moment the Hospitaller brethren took up arms, fortified strongholds became an indispensable tool of their crusading *métier*. The importance of these fortifications and their role in the continued existence of the Order becomes all the more clear when one appreciates the comparative smallness of the Hospitallers' military organization, which never amounted to more than a few hundred brethren backed by a few thousand men, the latter generally mercenaries or native militia recruited from the Order's territories. Stacked against them, however, was the might of the Muslim world, and on many occasions this was unleashed with great fury. With shortage of manpower being a constant feature of the Order's existence, it was inevitably the stone walls which had to make up for the lack of warriors 'in the permanent and arduous task of defence.' Frequently, the formula worked well and the knights owed much of their fame to a succession of epic sieges, notably those of Rhodes in 1480 and Malta in 1565, in which they successfully resisted considerably larger Turkish armies. And even where it failed, as at Acre in 1291and Rhodes in 1522, the knights were able to extract some glory from their defeats. Charles V's well-worn comment that nothing was ever so well lost as Rhodes was inspired by its surrender to Sultan Suleiman after a 5,000-strong Christian force led by Grand Master L'Isle Adam held out for six months against a Turkish army of 200,000 men.

In all the theatres of war in which the Order established its military base - the Latin East, Rhodes, and Malta - the knights' fortifications served primarily as the eastern bulwarks of Christendom. Their strongholds functioned both as frontier marches guarding against Muslim incursions into Christian territory and as military bases spearheading raiding expeditions into enemy lands. Twice the Hospitaller knights were forced to withdraw from their position under the heavy blows of the mighty Turkish war machine as it forced its way westward towards Christian lands, first at Acre in 1291 and then Rhodes in 1522, and each time the Order had to seek a new base and adapt itself to continue its struggle. Perhaps the most significant factor that was to influence the nature of the fighting tradition of the Hospitaller knight was the Order's transformation

into a naval force for, with the loss of Acre in 1291, the Hospitaller knights had no other option but to trade their chargers for galleys in order to retain their crusading *métier*, going on to fight most of their battles at sea, preying on Turkish shipping from their island bases of Rhodes and, later, Malta.

Although with the acquisition of its territorial possessions, particularly the islands of Rhodes and Malta, the Hospitaller Order acquired the trappings of an independent sovereign state, it remained intrinsically an international force which, whenever the need arose, could draw upon huge resources from those European nations represented in its organization. At the head of this brotherhood stood the grand master, who was elected for life by the senior members of the Order. The grand master, however, was subject to the Hospitaller statutes and was expected to govern with the advice of the council. His actual power was circumscribed by the chapter general, the supreme legislative authority. This assembly comprised all the senior brethren of the Order and was convened occasionally to enact laws and impose taxes. The day-to-day administration of the government of the Order was performed by the *Gran Consiglio*, the council or *conventus*, which was presided over by the grand master himself and involved the senior knights, the grand priors and bailiffs, residing at the convent, the Order's headquarters.

Grand priors, bailiffs, or piliers *(pillerii)*, the heads of the various nationalities making up the Order, were responsible for administering the Order's vast territorial properties. The various nationalities, known as tongues, langues or languages, were in effect based on the geographical groupings of such territorial possessions, known as priories. Each priory was itself subdivided into basic administrative units known as commanderies, governed by a commendator. Those commanderies crucial for the defence of the Order were known as castellanies and fell under the jurisdiction of a castellan. The grand priors actually residing in the convent, the conventual bailiffs, held the important posts in the government of the Order. These responsibilities were established according to strict and elaborate rules intended to guarantee that political power within the Order was not concentrated into the hands of any one faction. Thus, second in rank to the master, came the grand commander *(magnus commendator)*, a post always occupied by the pilier of the langue of Provence. His role was to control the common treasury. The pilier of Auvergne served as the grand marshal, the senior military commander. France supplied the grand hospitaller who administered the hospital, Italy the admiral in charge of the Order's naval forces, and Aragon, the conservator, who was responsible for the upkeep of charitable foundations. The pilier of England, the grand turcopolier, controlled the native militia. With the demise of the English langue in the mid-sixteenth century, this duty was delegated to the seneschal. The pilier of Germany held the title of *magnus praeceptor* and was entrusted with the command of the military outposts.

It was the *Gran Consiglio* which was directly concerned with the overall management of fortifications. It delegated such tasks, however, to commissions of knights assisted by competent military engineers. In 1475, for example, a commission of two knights was set up to inspect and record, every two years, the state of the towers and castles of Rhodes. A competent 'Commissario delle Fabriche e fortificationi, e le munitione' during that period was the knigh Frà Filippo di Giudone. Grand master d'Aubusson, prior to his being elected to his magistracy in 1476, held the post of 'Provediteur des Fortifications'. After the mid-seventeenth century these commissions were institutionalized into permanent sub-committees of the council, known as the congregation of war and fortification. By the late eighteenth century, these came to be composed of the marshal, four commissioners, the seneschal, the resident military engineer, the ordinary commissioner of fortification, the commander of artillery, and the commanders of the regular regiments. The member of the congregation most directly in control of the fortifications, however, was the resident engineer, the *Ingeniere della Religione,* who was employed specifically by the Order and entrusted with the supervision and maintenance of all fortified works. One of the earliest known engineers who operated in such a capacity was Bartholino de Castilione. He is known to have been employed at Bodrum and other islands in 1502. It is also in Rhodes that one first comes across the distinction between the ordinary resident engineer and the foreign military expert loaned by some European monarch to help design specific projects for the Order. Beneath the engineer came the master masons, skilled craftsmen and the native labourers. Slaves, too, were frequently put to work digging trenches and transporting earth.

Creating and maintaining a network of fortifications and outposts, an army, and after 1291, even a navy, demanded a good organizational framework and huge resources went into ensuring that the Order's armed forces, garrisons, and fleet of galleys were adequately supplied with the weapons and munitions necessary for war. The money which paid for all this military effort and kept the Order's war machine oiled came form various founts. A large part was derived from the commanderies which remitted, annually, a fraction of their incomes (fixed at one-third) to the central treasury of the Order. To this revenue was usually added the profits generated from the *spoglios,* the spoils of war and mortuaries (properties of knights which reverted to the Order on their death) but these funds merely helped pay the soldiers' wages and other current expenditures, and

A chapter general of the Order in session, from Caoursin's Stabilimenta.

were frequently insufficient to support the extraordinary outlays that accompanied military campaigns and large-scale building of fortifications. The bulk of the money to cover such enterprises generally came from donations and gifts made to the Order by European princes and monarchs, and, more frequently, by individual members of the Order itself, some of whom were considerably wealthy men in their own right.

Indeed, the Hospitallers were drawn from the noble aristocratic families of Europe and their nobility gave the Order direct access to the courts of many a European monarch. These connections also allowed the Order to tap the expertise of many of the leading military engineers employed in the warring armies of Europe. Their services ensured that Hospitaller military works remained within the stream of the latest developments in the art of fortifications. On many occasions, however, the Hospitaller knights and the engineers in their employ did not simply succeed in keeping abreast of the latest developments in the art of fortification, but were able, in the words of Prof. Quentin Hughes, 'to actually lead the field - they were early in the development of concentric defences, gun-powder artillery bastions, countermining, the caponier, the fougasse and polygonal forts. From the twelfth to the end of the eighteenth century, Hospitaller military architecture manifests nearly all the emerging devices of fortification which were to influence the nations of the West.'

Castellans of Outremer
Hospitaller Fortifications in the Latin East

'When I came into your land and asked at the castle to whom they belonged ... I could not find any castles which belonged to you, except three. But all belong to the religious Orders.'

Ruler of Armenia to King of Jerusalem - Livre au roi

The story of Hospitaller fortifications begins with the gift of the castle of Bait Gibrin to the Order by King Fulk of Jerusalem in 1136.[1] The fact that this important castle, one of three strongholds built by King Fulk to confine the Muslim port of Ascalon, was handed over to the Hospitallers does not simply reveal the Order's growing military importance and contribution to the defence of the Holy Land in the wake of the First Crusade but also the precarious nature of the Christian hold over the Latin East. For the four Crusader states - the kingdom of Jerusalem, the principality of Antioch and the counties of Tripoli and Edessa - were bordered by hostile Muslim emirates and weakened by the presence of Saracen strongholds within the areas they sought to control. To the north lay the

unstable kingdom of Armenian Cilicia and the Seljuks of Mas'ud while to the north-east lay the Danishmend emirate; in the east were the powerful Muslim cities of Aleppo, Damascus, Hama, and Hims and the threat from the Seljuks of Baghdad and the Fatmids of Fustat; to the south, the sultanate of Egypt.[2] The Byzantines, on the other hand, were careful not to allow the Crusader states from becoming all too powerful. In this situation, the survival of the Franks depended on the use of force but given the constant shortage of manpower in the Latin states, large forces could rarely be maintained except during the time of a Crusade. Castles and their garrisons, therefore, came to be the basis of Frankish defensive strategy. With time, however, even holding on to these strongholds became a problem and the secular rulers of the Latin states, like King Fulk, were increasingly forced to hand over the responsibility for these defences, particularly in the more exposed regions, to the military Orders. Such territorial donations were frequently accompanied by great privileges that made some of the acquired estates nearly independent territories that rendered profitable the Orders' military responsibilities. Bait Gibrin, for example, was accompanied by a large tract of surrounding territory including ten villages and this possession became the first great religious military lordship in the Holy Land, locally autonomous and controlled by the Hospitallers.[3]

Bait Gibrin was soon followed by the donations of other strongholds in south Palestine, namely Tamarin, situated a few kilometres north-west of Gibrin itself, and Bellfort, north of Jerusalem.[4] In the north, Count Raymond of Tripoli, perhaps influenced by King Fulk's gesture, and anxious to strengthen his own frontiers against the growing Atabeg power, gave the Order the castle of Hosn al-Akard, later known as Crac des Chevaliers, and Montferrand in 1142, knowing well that the Order, grown rich from the

Detail from a 13th-century map of Palestine by Matthew Paris showing some of the Crusader fortresses situated along the littoral planes.

many donations made to it in recognition of its hospitaller services, had ample funds with which to maintain and improve them.[5] Two years later, the Hospitallers again received from Raymond another three castles, Castellum Bochee, Felicium, and Lacum.[6] The count's anxiety to hand over the responsibilities for these frontier marches is clearly reflected by the fact that the Order was to owe no feudal obligations, unlike at Bait Gibrin, for the vast tract of valley at La Boquee. About the same time, the lord of Mares in the far north gave Platta to the Order on condition that it was to 'fortify the said place within a year' from the following Pentecost.[7] Similarly, the lord of Montreal, in 1152, gave the knights a tower and a barbican in the fortress of Kerak in Moab, while in 1153 the castle of Coliath was confirmed in the possession of the Order by Pope Eugene III.[8] The lord of Toron, in 1157, granted the Hospitallers half of Paneas and half of Chastel Neuf (Hunin) on condition that they would share the burden of the defence of Paneas.[9] In that same year the Order was given part of the castle and town of Subeibeh by Renier Brus but a relief force sent to occupy the place was ambushed and annihilated by Nur al-Din before it had time to reach its destination.[10]

Modern historians have shown that Hospitallers' military role during this initial phase should not be exaggerated as the fact that the Order was ready to give up Crac des Chevaliers to King Wladislas of Bohemia does seem to imply that there was no real heavy commitment to hold on to acquired castles.[11] It is only after 1160 that castles were acquired and bought by the Order of its own accord. For the mastership of Frà Gibert d'Assailly (1163-70) saw the limited and rudimentary military organization established by his predecessor Raymond du Puy develop rapidly to make possible participation in large-scale military activities. It is during d'Assailly's mastership, in fact, that one begins to read of Hospitaller castellans.[12] In 1163, the Order bought the castle of Le Sarc from William of Maraclea and, in 1168, that of Belvoir from Ivo Velos for the sum of 140 besants. By the end of that decade, it had also acquired, in the kingdom of Jerusalem, the castles of Belmont, Belveer, Emmaus, Turris Salinaru, and the castles of Belda, Shughr-Bakas, Rochefort, and Cavaea in the principality of Antioch, and perhaps Fonteines in the county of Tripoli.[13] The Hospitallers also laid claim to the castles of Apamee, Bokebais, Logis, Arcicant, Basarfut, and Locaba in the principality of Antioch - an impressive array of strongholds when compared to the seven castles which it had in its possession prior to 1160.

The Hospitallers went on to acquire even more strongholds during the course of the following decade. In 1170, while Count Raymond III was being held prisoner in Aleppo, King Amalric of Jerusalem granted them, on the count's

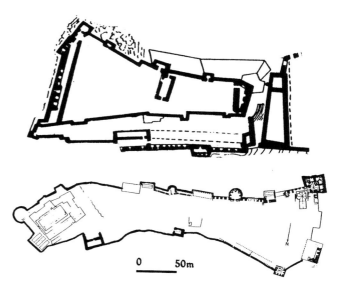

Plans of the Crusader fortresses of Kerak in Moab, top, and Banyas (Subeibeh).

behalf, the castles of Archas (Arqa) and Gibelcar (Akkar), which had been ruined by an earthquake.[14] Raymond, who owed his freedom in part to Hospitaller intervention, continued to delegate the responsibility of his frontiers to them. In 1180 he gave them the castle of Touban, north-east of Crac des Chevaliers and, in the following year, all the land to the south of this *seigneurie* together with the castle of Melechin.[15] Earlier in 1177, Raymond III of Tripoli conceded Castrum Rubrum (Qal'aat Yahmur) to the Hospitallers who were then obliged to pay its lord, Raymond of Montolif, 400 besants in 1178.[16]

Throughout the regency of Raymond of Tripoli, both the Hospitallers and Templars were given custody of royal castles.[17] With the renting of Marqab from Bertrand Le Mazoir in 1186, for an annual rent of 2,200 Saracen besants, the Order took over the defence of southern Antioch and northern Tripoli against the Assassins and other hostile Arabs.[18] With Marqab came the castles of Ericium, Brahim, and Popos and the coastal town of Valenia.[19] To these outposts around Marqab should be added Beuda and probably Karfis which was abandoned and sacked after the fall of Crac.[20] The Hospitallers were given the rights of liege-lordship over the knights in their fief and of conducting their own affairs with the Muslim neighbours, thus making Marqab the centre of a semi-independent palatinate.[21]

Saladin's invasion of the Latin states found the Order of St John in possession of some 27 castles - an impressive network of strongholds and accompanying territories that

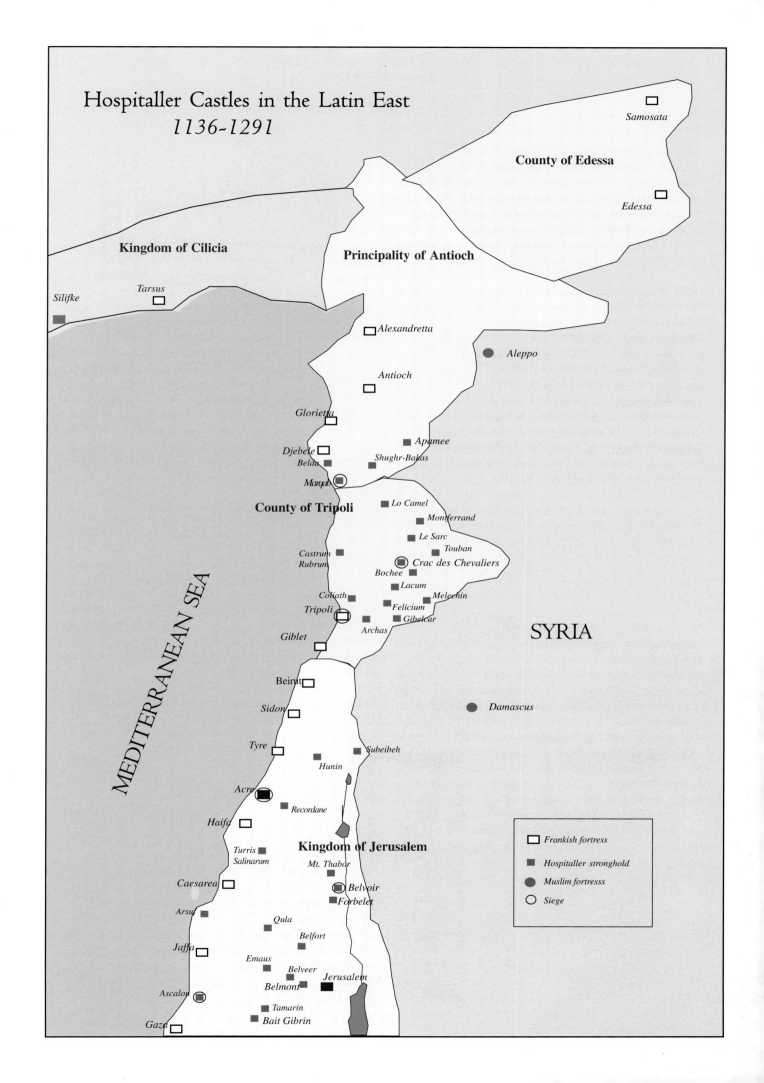

Hospitaller Castles in the Latin East
1136-1291

County of Edessa

Samosata

Edessa

Kingdom of Cilicia

Principality of Antioch

Silifke

Tarsus

Alexandretta

Aleppo

Antioch

Glorietta

Apamee

Djebele

Shughr-Bakas

Belda

Marqab

County of Tripoli

Lo Camel

Montferrand

Le Sarc

Touban

Castrum Rubrum

Crac des Chevaliers

Bochee

Lacum

Coliath

Melechin

Tripoli

Felicium

Archas

Gibelcar

Giblet

SYRIA

Beirut

Sidon

Damascus

MEDITERRANEAN SEA

Tyre

Subeibeh

Hunin

Acre

Recordane

Haifa

Kingdom of Jerusalem

Turris Salinarum

Mt. Thabor

Caesarea

Belvoir

Forbelet

Arsul

Qula

Belfort

Jaffa

Emaus

Belveer

Jerusalem

Belmont

Ascalon

Tamarin

Gaza

Bait Gibrin

☐ *Frankish fortress*

■ *Hospitaller stronghold*

● *Muslim fortresss*

○ *Siege*

rendered it a prime stakeholder in the military and political affairs of Outremer. The Hospitallers had surely come a long way from their humble beginnings under Brother Gerard. By 1186, they were feudal lords in their own right. In fact, the years just before Saladin's invasion mark the peak of the extent of the Order's possessions in the Holy Land. Thereafter the number of the Hospitaller strongholds declined abruptly.

Truly, not all of these forts were formidable castles of the type of Belvoir, with its two concentric *castra* strengthened by mural towers, or as impregnable as the fortress of Marqab. Even Crac des Chevaliers during this period comprised nothing more than a single turreted enclosure, but it must still have presented a formidable sight to have dissuaded Saladin from attacking it. The greater part were little more than towers or outposts of larger castles and many of these served mainly as administrative and policing centres within complex estates rather than military positions, although the weakness of the Latin East meant that in moments of crisis even these would have had to perform some sort of military role.

The Hospitallers grouped their possessions in Outremer into castellanies and commanderies. There appear to have been at least twenty such units though not all Hospitaller castles were governed by a castellan.[22] It is known, for example, that there was a castellan at Bait Gibrin in 1170, but this office disappeared with the surrender of the castle in 1187.[23] In 1170, there appeared a castellan of Belmont who administered important properties on the Jerusalem road (until 1187); a castellan of Belvoir (1173-89), whose *seigneurie* lay to the south; a castellany of Crac des Chevaliers with its own treasury and chancery; and, after 1186, a castellan of Marqab who controlled vast estates in Syria.[24] In 1186, there was a commander of Emmaus, and others for Bethany and Spina, the latter apparently responsible for the Order's estates between Jaffa and Caesarea.[25] By 1165, the estates in Galilee were administered by the commander of Tiberias. The city of Acre and its *seigneurie* were the responsibility of the commander of Acre while the commander of Tyre seems to have governed possessions in Beirut, Sidon, and Toron. The estates in the county of Tripoli were initially controlled by the prior of Mont Pelerin but, after 1182, this title was changed to that of commander of Tripoli.[26] The Hospital's possessions in Antioch were divided into two commanderies, those of Loadicea and Gibel controlled the southern estates, while the commander of Antioch administered the northern properties near Cilicia.[27] After the loss of Silifke in 1226, the Order founded the commandery of Armenia.[28] The acquisition of Mt Thabor in 1255, led to the establishment of the castellany there with possessions stretching into eastern Galilee.[29]

Above, 12th-century highly formalized plan of Jerusalem. Left,19th-century photograph showing Bordj-al-Laqlaq, the Tower of Storks, on the north-east ramparts of Jerusalem.

The Crusader Fortress
Castle Design in the Latin East

*'Now the castle had three lines of walls and three barbicans ... Muslim soldiers stormed
into the courtyard ... the last defenders took refuge in the great towers'*

The siege of Crac des Chevaliers - *Ibn Shaddad*

The Hospitaller involvement in the military struggle for the Latin East coincided with some of the most important developments in the art of fortification throughout the middle ages - developments which the Hospitaller knights themselves embraced and perfected in the design of their own strongholds. The story of this evolution begins with the territorial conquests of the First Crusade and ends, to a certain extent, with the loss of Acre, the last Christian outpost in the Holy Land, in 1291. Roughly two centuries marked by simple keeps at the earlier end and the enceintes of mighty concentric castles, such as Crac des Chevaliers, employing to perfection techniques of fortification, at the other.

Initially, the Crusaders in Outremer took over existing Byzantine and Muslim fortified sites in a hasty attempt to secure territorial acquisitions.[1] Their own requirements, however, were very different for they lacked the manpower to maintain large armies and garrisons; they needed, instead, castles which were stronger, quick to build, and easy to defend. The Crusaders' first reaction was to introduce their own style of fortification into the area. This was no more than a great rectangular tower, or *donjon* (now called the keep) of a type perfected by the Normans.[2] Such structures were either added on to the walls of existing fortresses, as at Anavarza in Cilicia and Sahyun in Syria, or else enclosed within an outer shell to form new castles as at Safita (Chastel Blanc), Qala'at Yahmur (Chastel Rouge), and Giblet.[3] Owing to the shortage of wood, crusader tower-keeps were constructed entirely of heavy masonry and were vaulted internally, making them squatter and shorter in appearance than their European counterparts. Their masonry and vaulted construction, however, rendered them much more resistant to fire and battering - both important military advantages in the struggle against Greeks and Arabs skilled in the use of combustibles and other sophisticated siege techniques.

Yet, although the rectangular keep offered great solidity, its plain and simple shape had defensive limitations which soon proved inadequate for the requirements of Outremer. Eventually it was discarded in favour of other forms of castle design. One of these was the *castrum* type of fortress which consisted of an enclosure fitted with corner towers and sometimes, such as at Belvoir and Coliath, with additional towers built in the middle of each wall. Rectangular *castra* were being erected by the Latins in Outremer by 1130. Modern scholars tend to reject the theory that these crusader *castra* were simply imitation of Byzantine and Muslim models since similar structures have been shown to have existed in western Europe well before the First Crusade. It is believed, instead, that the *castrum* form was dictated primarily by the exposed locations of many of the sites on which these were built and the need for rapid construction.[4]

Still, the influence of the local Byzantine and Muslim military architecture was instrumental in shaping crusader fortifications.[5] The Franks borrowed many ideas from their neighbours and opponents. Machicolations, for example, were certainly of Islamic derivation. These balcony-like projections allowed offensive materials to be dropped on attackers below through gaps in their floors. Buttress-machicoulis of the type found at Crac des Chevaliers already existed at the late eight-century Islamic palace-fortress of Ukhaidir. The box-type machicolation, the *saqqata*, such as found on the outer ward of Crac and at Qal'at al-Rum, existed on pre-Muslim architecture of the sixth-century Syrian watch-tower houses.[6] These are also found above the entrances to the eight-century Qasr al-Hair ash-Sharqi and on the walls of Cairo built by the Fatmids in 1090 to the design of Armenian architects from Edessa.[7]

Byzantine influences, on the other hand, are recognized in the two-tiered *chemin-de-rondes,* the shape of arrow-slits, and the frequent use of posterns.[8] Amongst various other ideas incorporated into the design of crusader castles was the use of mural towers to isolate whole sections of curtain walls, where each tower was made a self-contained unit of defence. The variety of towers encountered in Outremer make it difficult to schematize into date-tight compartments

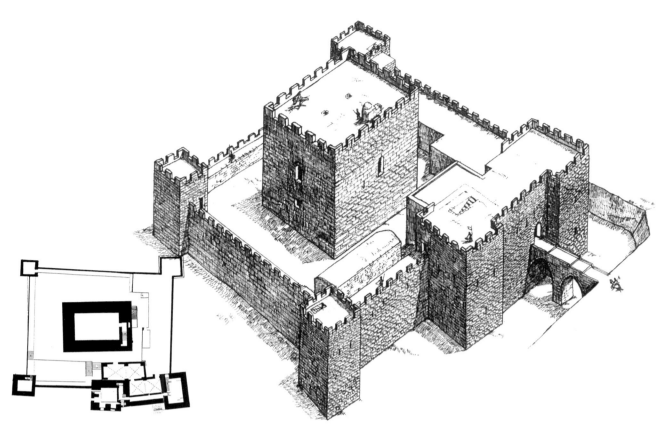

the development of these features and to lay any great significance on the distinction between square and round forms. The defensive merits of one type over the other lay in the extent to which a tower projected beyond the main wall and allowed for an active defence, and reduced the area of dead ground along its outer face. Towers of a bold projection held a wider flank and enabled better enfilading fire. The u-shaped and polygonal towers, such as built by the Hospitallers on the inner ward of Crac, were an attempt to combine the advantages of both curvilinear and rectilinear types in a single structure.

The Crusaders introduced their own style of fortification into Outremer. This was no more than a great rectangular tower-keep, or donjon, of a type perfected by the Normans. In the Latin East the keep was built of stone and vaulted internally and was either added on to the walls of an existing fortress or else enclosed within an outer shell to form new types of castles such as Safita (Chastel Blanc), right, and Giblet, above.

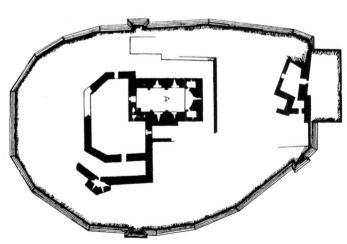

The military theorists of the late Roman world, like Vegetius, Vitruvius, and Philo of Byzantium were almost unanimous in recommending that towers should be of rounded or polygonal form, but in the Byzantine fortifications of Syria, where practical considerations of immediate importance ruled over abstract principles of fortification, nearly all wall-towers were built in square or rectangular plan.[9] The early crusader castles, too, employed mainly rectangular towers. Round towers, on the other hand, were ubiquitous in Muslim fortifications and the curvilinear plan eventually crept into crusader castle design, sparingly at first such as at Beaufort and Cursat, and than predominantly as at Crac and Marqab.

Other refinements included battlements fitted with arrow slits and loopholes. Some ramparts were given two rows of arrow-slits, an upper one placed in merlons along the *chemin-de-ronde*, and a lower one usually protected by vaulted recesses at ground level.[10] The arrow-slits themselves were splayed out at the base to enable the bowmen to cover the foot of the ramparts.[11] Towers and ramparts were frequently built to take siege engines - one mangonel was actually taken from Crac by Baybars who used it to attack Acre in 1291. The base of walls and towers were frequently given a talus or sloping plinth which increased their resistance to ramming and allowed offensive materials dropped from above to bounce out against the attackers. The gate, always the most vulnerable part of any castle, attracted particular attention. Initially gates were first placed in the flanks of towers. Gradually tower-gates evolved into the gate-houses, sometimes consisting of two mural towers placed together and a series of obstacles were developed to hinder the attacker's passage into the castle.

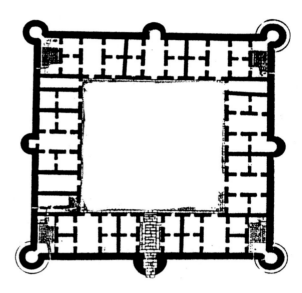

Plan of the Saracen desert fort of Atshan. It clearly follows the rectangular plan of the earlier Roman forts built in the East, the quadriburgum, *but with rounded wall-towers instead of rectangular ones as was generally employed on the Roman forts.*

The first was the use of the drawbridge. This spanned the main ditch and could be withdrawn to deny access. The Franks also added the bent entrance and the *porticullis*. Along the entrance passage, special holes in the vaulted ceiling called *meurtrieres* enabled the defenders to shower the attackers with missiles and combustibles. Gatehouses were sometimes protected further by a barbican, a form of

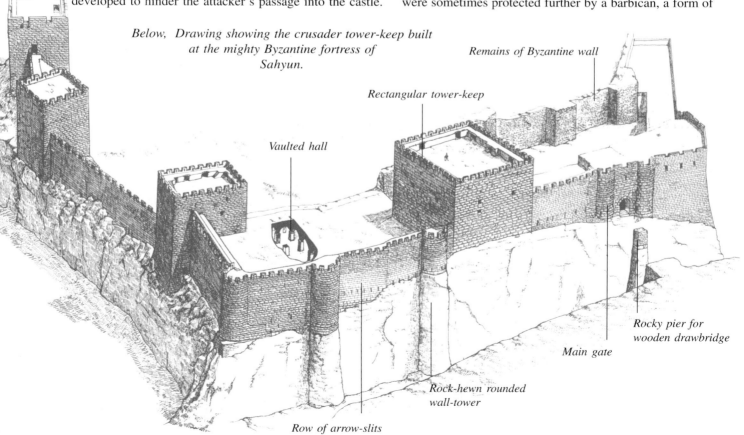

Below, Drawing showing the crusader tower-keep built at the mighty Byzantine fortress of Sahyun.

Remains of Byzantine wall

Rectangular tower-keep

Vaulted hall

Rocky pier for wooden drawbridge

Main gate

Rock-hewn rounded wall-tower

Row of arrow-slits

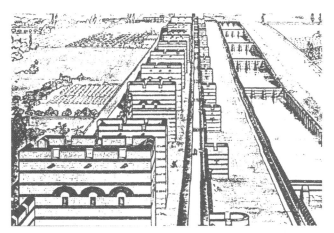

The walls of Constantinople built by Theodosius II showing the moat, berm, proteichisma (first wall), and the megateichos (second wall) with its large wall-towers (after Danzig Krischen).

outerwork consisting of a detached gatehouse or series of linked towers.

Undoubtedly, the most significant progressive feature introduced into the design of crusader fortifications in the twelfth century was the use of concentric defences, with castle wards set one inside the other, where the outer line of defence was supported by the inner one above it. The use of concentric defences had been employed in the fortifications of Constantinople by the Byzantines since the fifth century and was also found at Nicaea and in the Seljuk defences of Jerusalem in 1099.[12] By the middle of the twelfth century concentric castles became common in the crusader states and both Hospitaller and Templars built many of their strongholds on the concentric plan: Tortosa, Belvoir, Belmont, Marqab, Atlit, La Feve, and Crac des Chevaliers all illustrate this principle. The concentric castle was particularly well suited to serve the military orders. For, aside from providing a double line of defence, the inner enceintes also served as defensible *collachia*, separating the brethrens' quarters from those of the native levies and mercenaries forming the greater part of the garrison. Such an arrangement gave the Hospitaller brethren some degree of protection against a mutiny *en masse* and ensured direct control over the castle's military supplies.

Early historians of crusader castles, such as Rey and Lawrence, sought to distinguish between Hospitaller and Templar military architecture. Rounded towers and corbelled machicolations, for example, were believed to be the product of the Hospitaller 'school' inspired by French architecture, while Templar architecture, with its use of rectangular towers and rectangular *castrum* plan, was thought to be heavily influenced by Byzantine models.

Modern historians, however, tend to dismiss these distinctions as being merely illusory for there is very little to distinguish in any functional sense the Hospitallers' architecture from that of the Templars. True, rounded towers are found at Crac and Marqab, but these were also a common feature of Muslim forts and even the Templars, who generally employed rectangular types, did occasionally build them into the enceintes of their fortresses. Nor are rectangular towers to be found solely on Templar strongholds. The Hospitallers frequently built fortresses in this manner too, the best example being Belvoir.

The locations where castles were established in Outremer were diverse. The physical geography of the Holy Land provided defensible features in the form of spurs, separated from the neighbouring high ground on all sides by deep ravines except at the junctions which, however, were easily isolated by the provision of a fosse. Many of the castles, including Crac des Chevaliers and Marqab, took advantage of such features and were reinforced further by strong enceintes, becoming practically unassailable in the process. Where a rocky scarp could be utilized, castles such as Kerak in Moab, were built to fit the contours of the site but where the ground provided no defensive features, castles ware sometimes built on artificial earthen mounds, or tells, for added defence. Belvoir, which was built on a flat plateau was made defensible by a deep man-made ditch. Various strongholds, however, such as Bait Gibrin, were built without the added advantage of natural defences and illustrate the fact that castles could not always afford to be so inaccessible that their only function lay in defending their garrison.

Perhaps the castle which best epitomizes the achievements of the crusader military architecture in Outremer is Crac des Chevaliers as rebuilt by the Hospitallers around 1200. The master masons who designed and constructed it showed an extraordinary aptitude to bring together the main themes developed through nearly a century of castle-building and siege warfare, namely, the utilization of natural topographical defensive features to reduce the threat of direct assault, an increasing emphasis on the strength of the curtain wall to withstand ever more powerful mangonels and other siege weapons, the projection of towers beyond the main enceinte to provide archers with a field of fire along the face of adjacent curtains, and the addition of concentric wards. A direct assault against a fortress systematically employing all these means of defence had very little chance of success. The balance between siegecraft and fortification had shifted in favour of the latter. When a castle fell, as eventually did Crac des Chevaliers and all the other Hospitaller, Templar, and Frankish strongholds in the Latin East, it was usually for other reasons.

Knights and Mercenaries
The Garrison of a Hospitaller Stronghold

'Whoever shall surrender a castle to the Saracens without the permission of his superiors ... shall lose his habit.'

Statutes of Master Nicholas Lorgne - 1283

The donation of castles and territories to the Order and also their acquisition brought not only great privileges and wealth but also the responsibility of maintaining and defending these possessions. Initially, it seems that the Order fulfilled these duties merely by hiring mercenaries but soon a distinct class of brethren-knights was established to deal with the ever-increasing military obligations. The appearance of the office of marshal reveals that a military organization, modelled on that of the Templars, had been created by the 1160s.[1] Within this military framework, a Hospitaller castle fell under the command of a castellan, generally a senior knight and experienced warrior. Under the castellan's command was a small nucleus of fighting brethren, supplemented by vassals, lay European knights and sergeants serving for pay, mercenaries, and a large number of native levies. The Hospitaller military brethren were divided into knights and sergeants. The social and economic standing of Hospitaller knights distinguished them from sergeants, not only in their equipment but even in the number of mounts they were expected to have. This distinction was made even more clearly by the colours they wore over their armour, a black surcoat for the knights and a red one for the sergeants, though after 1278 all came to don a red surcoat with a white cross.[2]

The actual size of a Hospitaller garrison manning any one of the many castles in the Latin East, however, depended mostly on the strength, extent, and importance of the stronghold itself. Where recorded, garrison strengths were often substantial, though these were certainly mainly mercenary in composition, the proportion of fighting brethren of the Order being always very small, rarely consisting of complements of more than 40 to 60 men. When the castle of Marqab fell in 1285, for example, there were only 25 Hospitallers out of a force of some thousand men in that fortress.[3] Moreover, of these, only a maximum of 300 troops would have constituted the castle's permanent garrison. At Crac des Chevaliers there were 60 knights in

1255 while at Mt Thabor, there were forty. Such figures would imply that the Hospital had around a third of its knights in the East engaged in garrisoning Marqab and Crac des Chevaliers.[4]

The Hospitallers also devoted a large number of their brethren to the defence of coastal fortresses. Antioch, Tripoli, and Acre, being important centres, had their own convent and in those places the Order was actually responsible for manning and defending important sections of the fortifications. When Arsuf fell in 1265, some 90 Hospitaller brethren were killed or captured and later, at the siege of Tripoli in 1289, they again lost 40 of their brethren and 100 horses, this being considered so serious a toll that attempts were made to bring over reinforcements from Europe to make up for the loss.[5]

Paid troops were an increasingly important component in the Order's military forces both on campaign and in garrisoning castles.[6] Both Christian and native mercenaries were employed by the Hospitallers. Many of these would have accompanied the crusader armies - of the 4,000 crossbow-men who accompanied the Fifth Crusade, for example, nearly half are believed to have been mercenaries.[7] There were then the native troops. Amongst these were Syrian and Armenian auxiliaries and such was their importance that both the Hospitallers and Templars came to include the turcopolier amongst their most important officers.[8] The turcopolier was the commander of the turcopoles, the native lightly-armed Syrian mercenaries. During the 1160s, Master Gilbert d'Assailly was able to muster a large 'quigentos milites et totidem Turcopoles bene armatos' to assist King Amalric of Jerusalem in the invasion of Egypt.[9]

Another source of troops for the Order came from its vassals. As the owner of vast territorial possessions, the Order, like any other feudal lord, was itself owed *servitium debitum* by its vassals. The acquisition of Arsuf in 1261-65, for example, provided the Hospitallers with the service of six knights and 21 sergeants.[10]

Hospitaller garrisons, everywhere, were governed by strict discipline and regulations, regardless of their size, especially in those strongholds that were located close to enemy territory. Tight security was enforced at all times at gates and posterns, particularly at night when the castle gates were kept shut and the brethren were not allowed to leave.[11] Both the Hospitallers and Templars would dismiss a brother from their Order if he did not use the proper entrances and exits.[12] One traveller passing through Marqab in 1212 noted four Hospitaller knights and 28 soldiers posted on guard duty around that fortress. [13]

The castellan had also to ensure that his fortress was well supplied with the arms, munitions, and victuals necessary to withstand a siege. The survival of a stronghold depended not only on the strength of its defences but on its capacity to store sufficient quantities of water, food, and munitions. Every castle thus required large storerooms, mills, presses, and cisterns to enable the hoarding of adequate supplies. At Marqab, for example, the Hospitallers could stock enough supplies to sustain themselves for five years against a siege, even though, in the end, it only resisted for six weeks against Kalavun in 1285.[14] The fall of Crac des Chevaliers in 1271, on the other hand, is attributed by the Muslim chronicler Ibn Abd al-Zahir to the fact that food provisions which grew on its territories had been devastated by an enemy raid in the previous year.[15]

The greatest advantage held by Muslim armies over the Christian forces, however, was their access to larger manpower resources. Hospitaller garrisons, like most of the other Frankish forces in Outremer, were, in relative terms, generally inadequate when faced with massive armies sent to besiege them. Their survival depended for most of its part on the passive strength of the fortifications and their siting. Still, at times the knights showed both courage and ingenuity and were prepared to forgo the protection of their strongholds to face Muslim armies in the open. Despite being outnumbered by over ten to one, the Christians at Marqab, for example, sallied out and defeated a Muslim force which arrived to capture the castle in 1281. In attack, however, the Muslims would generally immediately press for a result and take the initiative, utilizing fully the vast quantities of manpower at their disposal. This usually meant that they were able to complete a siege in a matter of weeks. Crac des Chevaliers, in 1271, and later Marqab, in 1285, both succumbed after very short sieges lasting not more than six weeks. The effect of massive numbers is best illustrated in the siege of Acre in which the Muslims carried the city defences in a violent frontal

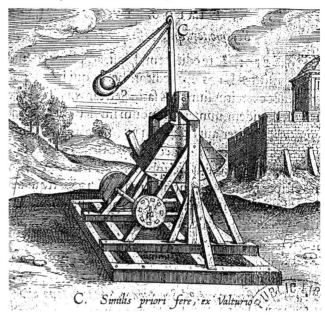

The tools of medieval siege warfare - a trebuchet (after Justius Lipsius, Poliocreticon).

assault, according to the author of *Gestes des Chiprois*, assailing the city from all sides in numbers which were beyond comprehension. [16]

Hospitaller manpower problems were complicated further by the Order's commitment to help defend the other great towns and castles which were not directly their own responsibilities. Although this initiative gave the knights greater political power, in military terms it reduced their ability to adequately man their own fortifications. At the siege of Arsuf in 1265, for example, the Hospitallers lost 90 brethren killed or captured.[17] Similarly, Hospitaller brethren were fighting in defence of the Templar fortress of Saphet when it fell to Baybars in the following year.[18]

Muslim siege armies also relied heavily on the power of their ballistic weapons, either as a prelude to assaults or to subdue the defences.[19] The principal engines in use in the twelfth and thirteenth centuries were the *ballista*, the mangonel, the petrarie, and the trebuchet, all stone-throwing weapons. The *ballista*, a kind of giant crossbow, worked by tension to propel a large bolt. The mangonel worked by torsion, that is, by twisting of the cords and ropes to produce force by which to propel the projectile. The trebuchet was worked by counterpoise and relied on the sudden release of heavy weights to generate force.[20] In the sieges of both Crac and Gibelcar, it was the impact of siege engines, coupled with the frontal assaults of the Saracen troops, that determined the outcome. Engines also played a significant role against Marqab in 1285, although it appears that these were placed too close to the fortress

A Hospitaller knight from the garrison of Crac des Chevaliers as he would have appeared around the beginning of the 13th century.

and the defenders were able to destroy a few with their own engines.[21] The same basic weapons were used by both Muslims and Christians for defence and attack. One Christian mangonel taken from Crac des Chevaliers was used in the siege of Acre in 1291.[22] The solid masonry construction of crusader castles, especially terraces of vaulted ranges and casemated ramparts, provided spacious and stable platforms for the deployment of artillery. Two other weapons which seem to have been peculiar to the Muslims during this period were the use of Greek fire, a highly inflammable mixture, and the *caraboha,* a hand-held sling.

Perhaps, the most effective siege technique for breaching a castle's walls was that of undermining the foundations and causing a section to collapse. The easiest way of achieving this was to dig a cavity which was shored up with timber and combustibles which, when fired, would burn through and collapse, bringing down a section of the rampart above. Mining operations were particularly effective when employed against the Order's fortress at Marqab in 1285.[23]

The Saracens dug a deep mine which, when fired, caused a breach in the walls but a tower which had also collapsed filled in the breach that had been made. The mine, however, had penetrated so deep into the fortress that the Hospitallers feared that the *Tour de l'Esperance,* a main tower, was about to collapse - they were thus obliged to surrender. Mines were again employed at the siege of Tripoli in 1289 and also at the siege of Acre in 1291, when they were directed against a number of towers.[24]

Even though the Hospitaller knights were constrained to operate their troops in a series of scattered garrisons, these were far from totally static forces. Contingents from these garrisons were frequently called to participate actively in most of the major battles, sieges, and campaigns that were fought in the Latin East from the mid-twelfth century onwards. The attack on Mt Thabor, the Fifth Crusade and that of Frederick II, the battle of Gaza, the invasion of Egypt, the assault of Paneas and the siege of Cacho, were some of the most important campaigns of the thirteenth century in which the Order of St John actively participated. In 1233, for example, the Hospitallers led a force of 500 knights, to which the Order contributed 100 *milites,* together with 400 mounted sergeants and 1,500 foot soldiers in an assault on Ba'rin.[25]

Frequently small parties were sent out on raiding expeditions into enemy territory. These raids, known as *chevauchée,* were not undertaken to make any permanent territorial gains but were intended mainly to inflict devastation and extract tribute, or else even as retribution. The strategically well-positioned strongholds of Crac des Chevaliers and Marqab enabled the Hospitallers to mount many effective raids into the very heart of Muslim territory in northern Syria. These two strongholds allowed the Hospitallers to dominate many of their surrounding Muslim neighbours, and enjoy a level of influence unparalleled anywhere else in the Latin East.

A Hospitaller contingent holding a fortress on the fringes of some Frankish territory was not solely concerned with the Muslim threat from outside but also with the possibility of an uprising of the native mercenary troops from within. For this reason there were certain provisions in a castle's design which were primarily concerned with internal security. Thus the Hospitaller brethren at Belvoir, Crac des Chevaliers, and Belmont were lodged either inside the inner wards, or shell-keeps, of these strongholds or, as at Marqab, within a citadel. These fortified cores, apart from acting as a second line of defence during a siege, served also as a kind of defensible *collachia* which set the

brethrens' quarters apart from those of the mercenaries. At Crac des Chevaliers the knights' quarters inside the large towers at the southern flank of the inner ward were protected further by a *saut-de-loup,* a gap which had to be crossed by a wooden bridge. This arrangement ensured considerable protection for the small contingent of Hospitaller brethren against a mutiny *en masse* or a *coup de main* in the form of night attack.[26]

The loss of a castle to the enemy generally meant not only the loss of a military position but also the loss of the income that was derived from its dependent territories. It was both a military and economic loss at the same time. Particularly unforgivable, however, was the surrender of a castle by its Hospitaller garrison - an act that was seen above all to tarnish the reputation of the Order itself. The statutes of the Order warned that whoever of the brethren surrendered a castle without the permission of his superiors, and all those advising that it be done, were to lose their habits. This could only be done, according to the statutes, with the knowledge of the master and his *prud'hommes.* Indeed, Arab historians recount that the garrison of Crac des Chevaliers only surrendered the castle to the Mameluke army after receiving a letter, supposedly from their Master, ordering them to do so. What they did not know, however, was that the letter was forged by Sultan Baybars himself.

Crusaders attacking a Saracen fortress with a siege-tower. Inset, Siege-tower with battering ram (after Lipsius).

Rearguard of the Crusades
The Loss of the Holy Land

'The Saracens took it by assault ... and many brothers of the Hospital of
St John were killed or taken.'

The fall of Tripoli in 1289 - al-Munsar Qalawun

The loss of Jerusalem to Saladin in 1187 marked a turning point in the fortunes of the Christians in the Holy Land. The Latin hold over the East, always difficult at the very best, became increasingly tenuous after the Frankish defeat at Hattin. A succession of Crusades launched to recapture the holy city either came to nothing or, at the most, only succeeded in prolonging the survival of the few Latin possessions penned to the coast. Saladin had shown that whenever the Muslims managed to muster their forces and unite under a single leader, there was very little that the Christians could do.

For the Hospitallers, Saladin's victory meant also the loss of many of their strongholds and territorial possessions and revenues that went with them, including their famous hospital in Jerusalem. Denuded of most of their garrisons, many Hospitaller castles such as Belmont, Bait Gibrin, and Forbelet, as did many Frankish fortified settlements on the coastal plains such as Tiberias, Acre, Jaffa, Sidon, Beirut, and Ascalon, quickly succumbed to the Saracen onslaught.[1] Most Hospitaller strongholds could offer little resistance.

Plan of the fortress of Antioch. The Hospitallers guarded the citadel of Antioch during the civil war that helped weaken that principality early in the 13th century.

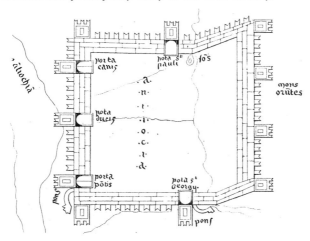

Bait Gibrin surrendered without a fight on the same terms as those accorded to the defenders of Jerusalem.[2] Belmont was abandoned by its garrison and was demolished on Saladin's orders in 1191.[3] Forbelet fell to Saladin's general Saif-ad-Din, who then occupied the castle.[4]

Only the mighty stronghold of Belvoir, amply provisioned and its garrison reinforced by the Hospitaller survivors who had fled from Hattin, was able to hold out heroically for almost a year until January 1189. Saladin descended on Belvoir with a well-equipped army but the rainy season and the nature of the terrain created great difficulties for the attackers. The Muslim army was forced to encamp close to the castle's walls within bow shot of the garrison but Saracen miners eventually breached the outer walls. This was immediately followed by a series of assaults under the cover of concentrated volleys of arrows and the outer enceinte fell into Saladin's hands. The knights retreated into the castle's inner ward but soon realized the hopelessness of their situation and offered to surrender if their lives were spared. Saladin agreed and the castle was occupied by his army.[5] Earlier, in 1188, Saladin appeared before Crac des Chevaliers but realized that his forces were not strong enough to capture this fortress even though it was then still a single-ward castle. At the time of the invasion, Maraclee was defended by Hospitallers but the city was ignored by Saladin who had set his eyes on Marqab farther north. The fortified town of Marqab with its formidable citadel, however, was too strong and well provisioned for Saladin's attack and his army encountered some difficulty in moving along the road beneath the fortress. The nearby Hospitaller town of Valenia, and a number of castles farther north, including Shughr-Bakas which fell on 12 August 1188, were captured or devastated.[6] Valenia was still in a state of desolation in 1212.[7]

The loss of Jerusalem to Saladin in 1187 meant above all the loss of the Order's famed hospital and headquarters - a vast compound of buildings adjoining the convent of St Mary of the Latins which, although primarily intended for the service of pilgrims was also capable, in 1172, according to the German pilgrim Theoderich, of housing 400 Hospitaller brethren-at-arms. With the help of the Third Crusade (1189-92), the Christians recovered some of the kingdom's lands they had lost but even after the Treaty of Jaffa in 1192, these possessions were for the most part limited to the coastal areas. Amongst the territories regained was the fortress of Acre which soon became the seat of the Order's convent in the Latin East. Acre held by far the largest of the Order's hospitals next to that of Jerusalem itself and although throughout most of the thirteenth century the Hospitallers' military activities were conducted mostly from Crac and Marqab in the north, it remained an important logistical base for the arrival of fresh recruits, supplies, and provisions from the West.

A period of relative peace followed until 1217, when the Fifth Crusade was launched partly as a consequence of the Muslim fortification of Mt Thabor which was seen to threaten Acre and the rest of the kingdom.[8] The Hospitallers took part in the attack on Mt Thabor, north-west of Belvoir, and later in the 1250s after petitioning the pope, they acquired the castle and its monastery.[9] A strong earthquake in 1196 caused considerable damage to Crac des Chevaliers, as a consequence of which the stronghold was rebuilt and enlarged. The knights continued to improve its fortifications until they lost it later in the century. Around 1207-08, the small castle of Coliath was destroyed by Adil. It was rebuilt in 1266 but was soon captured by Baybars.[10]

In 1207 Raymond Roupen of Antioch gave the Hospitallers the right of possession over Djebel and, in 1210, he re-confirmed his decision by granting them also Chateau La Vieille which, however, was still in Muslim hands.[11] Djebel was reoccupied by 1218 and the knights were receiving an annual rent of 2,000 besants from its cloth market alone but it was again lost to the Saracens in 1220.[12] When it was eventually reoccupied in 1261, half the town of Djebel was assigned to the Templars.[13]

The thirteenth century also saw the Hospitallers extend their influence into Armenia. In 1210 King Leo sought the Hospitallers' assistance during the wars of Antiochene succession and against the Seljuks. He created a Hospitaller march in western Cilicia and gave the Order 'Civitatem Seleph, castellum novum et Camardesium'.[14] The French summary from the *Inventory of the Charters* refers to the town of Seleck (Silifke) with its castle, Camerdes, and Chateau Neuf, together with rights over Karaman (Laranda).[15] The latter was a Byzantine fortress which was captured in the early twelfth century by the Danishmends and was temporarily held by Leon II in 1210.[16] Camardesium probably refers to Goumardias, north of Silifke. The castle of Silifke was held until 1226.[17]

Plan of the fortress of Caesarea (after Rey). Bottom, Plan of the Templar fortress of Tortosa (after Rey).

Besides manning their own strongholds, the Hospitallers knights also assisted in times of crises in the defence of the great towns of Frankish settlements. They helped defend the walls of Jerusalem and Tyre in 1187, and had erected a strong tower on the walls of Ascalon and another at Jaffa in 1194.[18] At Acre, after its reconquest by the Third Crusade, they were presented with a whole network of

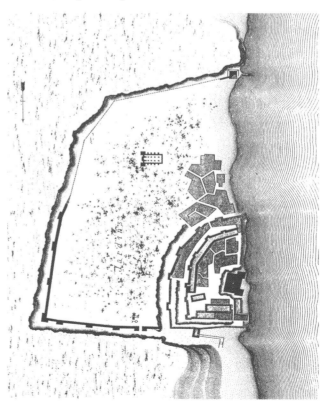

fortifications.[19] In Tripoli, they were assigned a gate to defend in 1196 and also possessed a 'forte et neuve' tower on its city walls in 1289.[20] In the early years of the thirteenth century they guarded the citadel of Antioch during the civil war that helped weaken that principality.[21] In 1218 the Order assisted in the fortification of Caesarea. Later in 1243, Emperor Frederick II entrusted Ascalon - which had been re-fortified by Richard of Cornwall in 1241 - to the Order and promised to refund the cost of its upkeep. The Hospitallers eventually took possession of Ascalon in 1244 until it fell to an Egyptian army in 1246.[22]

The Hospitallers, engaged in continual warfare against the Saracens, became acknowledged experts in the art of warfare and in the construction of fortifications. In 1251 Louis IX fortified Caesarea on their advice and, in 1253, they helped direct the siege of Paneas.[23] The Order continued to expand its possessions but, early in the thirteenth century, most of its responsibilities lay in the north. In 1262, the knights seem to have owned half of Loadicea and in the previous year they rented Arsuf from Balian of Ibelin for the annual sum of 4,000 Saracen besants.[24] Four years later, however, Arsuf fell to Baybars with the loss of a large number of brethren.[25] Hospitaller brethren were also present in the defence of the Templar castle of Saphet in 1266.[26] It appears that by 1242, the Sultan of Egypt had returned Bait Gibrin and Belvoir back to the Hospitallers.[27] Riley-Smith states that Belvoir was lost again in 1247 but there does not seem to be any evidence for Frankish reoccupation of this stronghold. Bait Gibrin, in 1250, once again formed part of Christian territory.[28]

The Mameluke invasion of Syria in 1260 saw the final phase in the Muslim recovery of the Holy land. The Latin settlements in the interior were reduced in quick succession beneath the powerful Egyptian armies of Sultan Baybars leaving the Franks penned in a few sites on the coast. By 1267, Marqab and Crac des Chevaliers in the north were being seriously threatened by Baybars. In 1269, he attacked Marqab, but the fortress held out.

The first Hospitaller fortress to succumb to the Mameluke war machine was the formidable Crac des Chevaliers, which was seized in 1271 after a brief but violent struggle. Baybars appeared before the fortress on 3 March with a mighty army composed also of contingents from Hama, Saone, and the Assassins. Heavy rains prevented the Saracens from setting up their siege batteries but the attackers were quick to overrun the *burgus* and a partially-built outerwork of the fortress. The sultan then set his miners to work on the walls of the castle and eight days later the southwest tower collapsed. Muslims troops then 'stormed their way into the castle, massacred the Hospitallers, took prisoner the mountaineers, but let the villagers go to keep up cultivation

in the country.'[29] The knights fell back into the stronghold's inner ward where they and held out for more than ten days before surrendering on being offered favourable terms. Arab sources record that the Baybars forged a letter to the castellan of Crac from his superior ordering him to surrender. The Hospitaller knights were allowed to retire to Tripoli.

With the fall of Crac des Chevaliers, Marqab remained the only important Hospitaller fortress in the region. The knights tried to buy time by making peace with the sultan, as a result of which they were obliged to evacuate Corveis and surrender the castle of Belda.[30] This truce, however, did not last long as the Hospitallers were soon raiding into neighbouring Muslim country. In 1279, the fortress was besieged by an army sent from Crac under the command of Balban al-Tabbakhi.[31] The Hospitaller garrison, however, made a sortie and drove off the attackers but the surrounding land had been laid waste. Two other attempts were made by the Muslims to reduce the place in 1281 and 1282 but even these proved unsuccessful. Finally, in April 1285, a large Mameluke army, well provisioned and supplied with siege engines, appeared off Marqab. Initially, the Muslim army could make little impression against the mighty fortress and its well-equipped garrison. The attackers' siege-engines were placed too close to the walls of the fortress and were destroyed by the defenders' own weapons but after a month Saracen engineers succeeded in driving a mine deep into the castle beneath the great round keep, bringing down in the process the *Tour de l'Esperance*. With their fortress so critically compromised, the Hospitallers were obliged to surrender. Twenty-five brethren, the full complement of knights engaged in garrisoning Marqab, were allowed to leave the castle with their arms.[32]

By that time, the Latin states had been reduced to a handful of sites, notably Chateau Pelerin, Acre, Beirut, Tyre, and Sidon. The port of Latakia, the last remaining possession in the pincipality of Antiokia, succumbed to a Muslim army in 1287. Tripoli, one of the most important coastal cities, met the same fate in 1289. A strong contingent of Hospitallers under the command of the marshal, Matthew de Clermont, fought bravely in its defence. The Christian defenders, however, were heavily outnumbered. Mameluke Sultan Al Mansur Qalawun, Baybar's successor, 'had so many men that every embrasure had twenty Saracen archers shooting at it.'[33] At Tripoli, the Order of St John lost 40 brethren and 100 horses and this was considered so serious a toll that attempts were made to bring adequate reinforcements from Europe to make up for the loss.[34]

In less than two years, however, the Mameluke army was on the march again - this time heading towards Acre - the

last major Frankish foothold in Outremer. The massive Muslim force, equipped with over a hundred siege engines, arrived before Acre in April 1291. The large fortress was defended by some 14,000 men. The Hospitaller and Templar knights were each assigned important sections of the city's ramparts; both fought fiercely in its defence and lost many of their brethren in the course of the two months of heavy fighting that ensued. The Hospitaller marshal, Matthew de Clermont, died fighting while the master of

A romantic 19th-century depiction of the crusader defence of Acre against the Saracen armies (BBC Hulton Picture Library).

the Hospital, John of Villiers, was gravely wounded. As the city fell to the Saracen hordes, he was carried away by his sergeants-at-arms and taken by boat to the island of Cyprus.[35] The presence of the Hospitallers in the Latin East had come to its end.

A New Role in Cyprus
The Hospitaller Search for a Military Base

'... the noblest of all islands ... well supplied with cities, castles and villages'
Ludolph of Sudheim, c.1340

With the fall of Acre in 1291, the Hospitallers lost not only their last foothold in the Holy Land but most of their brethren and military hardware. Only seven knights had managed to escape with their lives and even the master of the Order, John of Villiers, had to be carried away, badly wounded, by his men. The magnitude of this disaster can be gauged from the fact that for more than ten years later, the number of fighting brethren present in the convent at Cyprus was never greater than 80 men - a striking contrast when compared with the hundreds of knights who garrisoned the fortresses of Latin Syria.[1]

It was on Cyprus that the Order set about rebuilding its military strength and seeking new ways of continuing the struggle for the recapture of the Holy Land. Together with the Templars, they established their headquarters in the city of Limassol, on the south coast of Cyprus, where they already held some property. By 1300, the Hospitallers had established a preceptory of Limassol and a *baille* of Cyprus while the statutes of 1301 and 1302 laid down that 80 brethren-at-arms, of which 65 to 70 were to be knights, were to be present on Cyprus.[2] The Order held a strong tower on the walls of the fortress of Limassol and was also present at Nicosia. Nothing remains of the Hospitaller convent, or of the fortifications of Limassol today, since these were sacked by the Egyptians in 1417 and pulled down by the order of the Venetian senate in 1539 while Nicosia, on the other hand, was rebuilt in 1567 with bastions after the old medieval walls had been pulled down.[3]

A 16th-century engraving of the island of Cyprus, showing Nicosia, Famagusta, Limassol, and the Hospitaller commandery of Kolossi (Clerkenwell Library).

At first, the years spent on the Lusignan island were characterized by a loss of purpose and then by a growing realization that a military alternative still existed if the Order could develop from a land power into a naval one. As early as 1300, and acting in conjunction with the Templars, the Hospitallers dispatched a fleet from Famagusta with a small force which raided a number of coastal villages on the shores of Egypt and Palestine. These puny sea-borne raids, although relatively unimportant excursions, were the knights' first tentative step in the direction of what was to establish them as the most feared Christian corsairs in the Mediterranean. In 1301, the office of admiral appears for the first time in the organization of the Order, in reference to the small fleet raised the previous year. This fleet was mainly composed of transport vessels but later fighting ships, the galleys, were introduced.[4]

Still, in Cyprus, the Hospitallers' position was far from satisfactory for they were not allowed to act as they wished. The Lusignan king, Henry II, and his nobles were suspicious of the Order's military powers and forbade them from imposing taxes on their own properties, acquiring further properties or arming ships without royal licence.[5] Thus, unable to act freely as they were always accustomed to do, the Hospitallers were soon casting around for a new territorial base which they could call their own - one, however, that would enable them to continue with their crusading role.

They found it in the island of Rhodes. The opportunity presented itself in 1306, when the Genoese adventurer and pirate Vignolo dei Vignoli approached Master Foulques de Villaret with a proposal for the joint conquest of the Rhodian archipelago.[6] Rhodes and the other islands of the archipelago then formed part of schismatic Byzantium and papal approval for the project was not difficult to obtain. The Byzantine Governor of Rhodes had cast off his allegiance from Constantinople such that the island was effectively ruled as an independent state.[7] The Rhodian population, depleted by Turkish raids, had apparently been paying tribute to the Turks, some of whom even served in its defence against the Hospitallers, while Turkish pirates from Rhodes had raided Cyprus in 1303.[8] The Order was careful not depict the attack on the island as a crusade against the Greek Byzantine empire (the Latin kingdom of Constantinople had collapsed in 1261) and, early in 1307, the Hospitallers had even sent an embassy to Andronisus II offering to hold the island as his subjects.[9] The attack on Rhodes was envisaged as a preliminary step in the reconquest of the holy places. The island was nevertheless a Christian country of Orthodox Greeks but the pretext was good enough to justify a scheme which sought to take advantage of the Greeks' inability to withstand Turkish pressure. The Dodecanese islands, sited as these were on

the Levantine trade route, had been often disputed between the Venetian and the Genoese. In 1234, the Venetians had established a protectorate in Rhodes but were soon ousted by the Genoese fourteen years later. Inevitably, soon after their establishment at Rhodes, the Hospitallers were seriously clashing with the Venetians over some of these territorial possessions.[10]

On 27 May 1306, at a secret meeting held in Limassol, attended by the master, the marshal, admiral, drapier and other brethren, a notarized arrangement was drawn up between the Order and Vignolo.[11] It was agreed that the latter would assist the Order in the conquest of Rhodes and

A 15th-century woodcut showing the Hospitaller navy at Rhodes (Clerkenwell Museum).

the surrounding islands in return for a third of the rents and incomes of the lesser islands and the castle and *casale* of Lardos on Rhodes.[12] Subsequently, on 23 June 1306, a force of 35 knights, some Levantine horsemen and 500 soldiers, under the command of Grand Master Villaret left Limassol on two galleys and four other craft and, joined by other Genoese galleys, they sailed for the small island of Kastellorizo, where they waited while Vignolo went ahead to reconnoitre. Vignolo was nearly captured by the Greeks who seem to have been forewarned but succeeded in rejoining the main force which than proceeded to Rhodes, where a land and sea assault on the city failed to achieve its objective. The knights then set about capturing the island's castles. On 20 September, they took the castle of Philerimos situated on the west coast.[13] Later in November, they managed to capture the important fortress of

Philerimos, ten miles south of the city of Rhodes, through the treachery of one of the Greeks who opened a postern gate. The 300 Turks who were assisting the Greeks in the castle were all massacred. Early in 1307, a relief force of eight galleys sent by the Byzantine Emperor Andronisus II, compelled the Hospitallers to lift the siege after losing 10 knights and 80 men.[15] By October, however, they held the impregnable fortress of Lindos.[16] While the main force was employed in reducing the main strongpoints on Rhodes, smaller detachments were sent around the other islands. A small force of two knights and 50 men managed to capture by surprise attack the castle of Kos but were unable to hold it against the Greeks who garrisoned it for the emperor.[17]

The city of Rhodes, well fortified and amply garrisoned, however, refused to surrender. The long and unexpected resistance put up by the Rhodians placed a great strain on the Order's resources so that the knights were reduced to mortgaging their revenues to a Florentine money-lender by the name of Peruzzi. Two decades later, the Hospitallers were still paying off their debts.[18] In the end, the fortress fell to the Hospitallers not through military operations but through a stroke of luck. A relief force sent by the Byzantine emperor was carried off by a storm to Famagusta in Cyprus and the captain of the ship was forced by the Hospitallers to talk the Rhodian populace into surrender.[19] With their reinforcements gone and with adequate terms presented to them, the Rhodian garrison had no other option but to surrender and on 15 August 1309, the gates of the city were thrown open to the Hospitallers.[20]

With the island firmly in their hands, the Hospitallers transferred their Convent from Cyprus to Rhodes and set about securing a hold over the nearby islands. Cyprus itself, however, remained an important bailiwick and the Hospitallers continued to hold a number of important properties there right until the loss of the island to the Turks. Between 1312 and 1313, the Hospital received the bulk of the Templar's property in Cyprus after the Templar Order was dissolved by the pope.[21] Amongst these were the fortress of Gastra and the towers at Fermasoyia and Khirokitia.[22] By 1374, the Hospitallers possessed some sixty *casali* scattered around the island, remitting annually a sum of 10,000 florins to Rhodes.[23] The most important of these was the castle and 'casale quod dictur Colos', which had been granted to the Order by King Ugo I in 1210.[24] There the knights established an important sugar-producing industry which they continued to run until the island was lost in the fifteenth century.

Hospitaller knight of the late 15th century at the priory of England, Clerkenwell (Clerkenwell Museum).

Rhodes and the Dodecanese
An Island Kingdom

'In this way God ordained divine aid for the noble master and the valiant knights of the Hospital. They freely held a great franchise, and combined mastery of the seas with independence of any other authority.'

With the occupation of Rhodes, the Hospitallers did not only acquire a new base from where to organize their military activities but also a little island kingdom. For with Rhodes came the rulership of the surrounding islands of Nisyros, Symi, Halki, Alimonia, Telos, Kalymnos, and Leros. In 1313 the Order also took possession of the islands of Karpathos and Kassos, disturbing the rule of Andrea Cornaro who induced Venice to intervene.[1] Venice began lengthy lawsuits against the Hospital to repossess Kassos and Karpathos and in 1315, the Order was compelled to withdraw from these islands.[2] In 1314 the Hospitallers occupied Kos but their hold on this and the other islands was initially very fragile. Sometime before 1319, they lost Kos, which they did not recover until 1336; in 1319, they had to retake the island of Leros where the Greek inhabitants had revolted and massacred the Hospitaller garrison.[3] At some later date they also occupied the island of Astipalea.[4]

Not long after the transfer of the Order's convent from Cyprus to Rhodes, the Hospitallers were soon attracting Turkish attention and Osman, one of the Muslim princes on the Turkish mainland, unsuccessfully attacked their island base in 1310.[5] The Hospitallers, however, were quick to assert their naval control over the Aegean and, by 1320, they had won two important victories over the neighbouring Turkish emirates.[6] They even secured and temporarily held a small number of castles on the Anatolian mainland itself and for the next century Rhodes was able to prosper in relative peace.[7] Before 1306, Turkish razzias and slave-raiding had severely reduced the population of the Dodecanese islands. In Rhodes, an island 80 kms long and 38 kms wide, the number of inhabitants had dropped to well below 10,000 and much of the fertile lands had fallen out of cultivation. [8]

The Hospitallers' first task once they had taken control of the islands was to repopulate them with Latin settlers and develop their commerce and agriculture so that men and

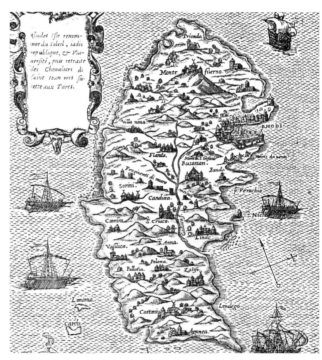

Map of Rhodes showing the principal settlements, fortresses and outposts in the early 16th century.

supplies would be available for the defence of Rhodes. Farms, mills, and agricultural estates were leased out in emphyteusis or in perpetuity.[9] In 1316 the fertile volcanic island of Nisyros was granted as a fief to the Assanti family of Ischia, for which they owed the service of a galley (an obligation which was later commuted for an annual sum of 200 florins in 1347) and in 1366, the islands of Kos and Telos were granted to Borrello Assanti, *burgensis* of Rhodes, on condition that he was to erect a watch-tower on the little island of Alimonia, near Halki.[10] Nevertheless, the number of men who actually settled down permanently on Rhodes, especially fighting men, remained small. In 1313 the Order

Map of the island of Rhodes (after Buondelmonte - De Insularis Archipelago). The small island of St Nicholas held a monastery that was fortified by Grand Master L'Isle Adam in 1522.

offered land and pensions to any westerners who would settle as soldiers or sailors in Rhodes.[11] The statutes of 1311 and 1314 projected a force of 500 cavalry and 1,000 foot soldiers to serve as a permanent garrison in Rhodes while the number of brethren in the East stood between

The Castles of Rhodes

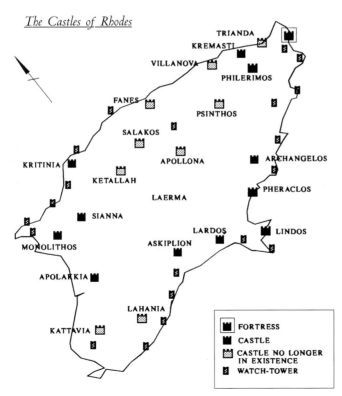

200 and 350.[12] The Greek inhabitants were also involved in the defence of the islands and had to perform servitude in the building of fortifications. On Kos, for example, the inhabitants were forced to fortify the *suburbium* in 1381.[13]

Each district, or *castellania,* had a castle under the command of a Hospitaller captain to which the rural population could retreat in times of danger, though most of the fortifications scattered around Rhodes and the neighbouring islands, with the exception of a few like Lindos, Pheraclos, Horio (Kalymnos), and Platanos (Leros) were neither powerfully built nor large enough to withstand determined attacks. Indeed, in times of crisis, many of these castles were actually abandoned and the inhabitants shipped off to the safety of Rhodes or the nearest impregnable fortress such as happened in 1470 and 1475, when the population of the islands of Telos and Halki were evacuated to Rhodes.[14] Similar evacuations occurred in 1461 (Kalymnos), 1462 (Kos), 1471(Nisyros), 1479 (Alimonia), and 1480 (Telos and Nisyros).[15] Many of the lesser islands were never allowed to prosper as they were continually subjected to corsair raids; Leros, for example, was attacked in 1457, 1460, 1477, 1502, and 1506 while Kalymnos was sacked in 1457.[16]

To ensure that Rhodes was governed effectively, it was divided into a number of castellanies.[17] The *Castellania* of the city of Rhodes included the strongholds and villages at Trianda, Psinthos, and Philerimos; the towers of St Etienne, Faliraki, Afandou, and Massari; the hamlets of Marista, Salia, Katangaro, Ermia, Eleoussa, Arhipolis, Platania, Malona, and Kamiro; and the fortified monasteries of Aghios Ilias and Tsambika.[18] The castles and villages of Koskinou, Archangelos, and Kremasti were autonomous and had to arrange for their own defence. In 1479 the castellany of Pheraclos was set up and it came to include properties which were formerly part of the castellany of Rhodes; the castles and villages of Pheraclos and, Archangelos, and some hamlets.[19] The castellany of Lindos consisted of the castle and *burgus* of Lindos, the castles and villages of Asklipion and Lardos, the towers of Pefka, Aghios Yorghios and Gennadion, and the hamlets of Pilona and Kalathos. In 1475 it was decreed that 'al Castello di Lindo ridurre si dovessero i Casali di Calatto, di Pilona, di Lardo, di Steplio (Asklipion) e di Ianadi (Gennadion).'[20] Askiplion was detached from the castellany of Lindos in 1479 and, together with the castle and village of Vathy, formed into a separate administrative unit.[21] The castellan of Lahania was responsible for the village and castle of Lahania, the towers at Aghia Marina, Cap Lahania, and Cap Vaglia together with the hamlets of Tararo, Tha, Defania, and Efgales. The castellany of Kattavia consisted of the village and stronghold of Kattavia and the hamlet of Messangros.[22] The castellan of Apolakkia governed the

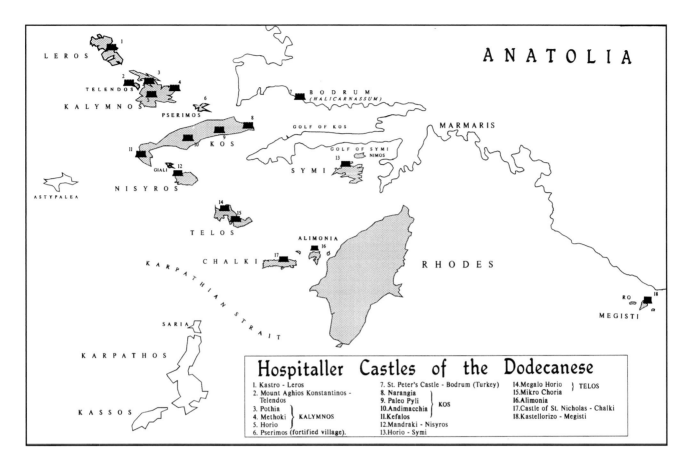

Hospitaller Castles of the Dodecanese

1. Kastro - Leros
2. Mount Aghios Konstantinos - Telendos
3. Pothia
4. Methoki } KALYMNOS
5. Horio
6. Pserimos (fortified village).
7. St. Peter's Castle - Bodrum (Turkey)
8. Narangia
9. Paleo Pyli
10. Andimacchia } KOS
11. Kefalos
12. Mandraki - Nisyros
13. Horio - Symi
14. Megalo Horio } TELOS
15. Mikro Choria
16. Alimonia
17. Castle of St. Nicholas - Chalki
18. Kastellorizo - Megisti

castle of Apolakkia and its village together with the other hamlets of Arnitha, Profilia, and Istrios.[23] In 1479 this district was amalgamated with that of Monolithos.

The castellany of Sianna consisted of the castles and villages of Sianna, Telemonias, and originally, even Monolithos and the towers of Glifada, Amartos, and Cape Armenistis.[24] The castles and villages of Salakos and Ketallah and the towers of Langonia and Cape Minas belonged to the castellany of Salakos.[25] The castellanies of Fanes and Villanova were attached to Rhodes in 1479, while that of Apollona, with the castles and villages of Apollona and Laerma (Laderma), gathered the sparsely-populated mountain districts on Mount Attavyros.[26] The strongholds and villages of the magistral isles of Halki, Alimonia, Tragousa, Strongilo, Makri, Nisso, and Aghios Theodoros were dependent on Rhodes.[27] In all, there appear to have been 20 castles on Rhodes. Of these, however, the ones at Lachania, Laerma, Psinthos, Apollona, Salakos, and Trianda have disappeared with time and only a few scanty remains survive of others, such as Kattavia, Apollakia, and Sianna.

The island of Kos, the largest of the archipelago after Rhodes, was also divided into a number of districts: Narangia, Pyli, Kefalos, and Andimacchia. Kefalos castle could only provide refuge against minor raids and its inhabitants had to retreat to the safety of Narangia in 1504.[28]

At the time that the Order invaded Rhodes, the Hospitallers regarded the island as a base from where military operations could be launched for the recovery of the Holy Land. However, growing Turkish power led instead to a policy of resistance and to the defence of the Latin possessions in the eastern Mediterranean.[29] The Hospitallers were drawn into anti-Turkish alliances, formed for the first time by the Venetians in 1327, and when in 1329 Umur of Aidin captured the castle at Smyrna on the coast of the Anatolian mainland from Martino Zaccaria, the Order participated fully in the Latin crusade that led to the recapture of the castle in 1344.[30] The fortress of Smyrna, however, could only be held with great difficulty not the least because the citadel on a nearby hill had remained in Turkish hands. Though Smyrna became a papal city, the Hospitallers came to be increasingly burdened with its defence until in 1374, Pope Gregory XI made them entirely responsible for its defence.[31]

As the Ottomans advanced farther into the Balkans, the Order became increasingly involved in the defence of Greece and after 1356 there were even proposals which favoured

establishing the Hospital on the mainland.[32] In 1374, there was a scheme for the Hospitallers to defend the Byzantine towns of Gallipoli and Thessalonika, but this came to nothing.[33] In 1377, however, they occupied the Latin part of Morea (Peloponessos) but were unable to defend it and withdrew in 1381.[34] Further efforts to acquire claims in the principate of Achaia were made between 1384-89.[35] From 1397 to 1404, the knights occupied the castle of Corinth and had purchased most of Latin Morea, doing much to defend the Peloponnese against Turkish occupation.[36] They apparently even invested in strengthening the defences, as a gun platform at Corinth datable to *c.*1400 seems to be Hospitaller work.[37] In 1403 the Turks attacked the Hospitallers at Corinth and in the following year, unable to sustain themselves, the knights withdrew from mainland Greece.[38]

By 1402, the Hospitallers had realistically decided that large-scale operations in Greece were beyond their resources

Drawing, after Gabriel, depicting the land front defences of Rhodes along the Post of Spain.

and instead decided to concentrate their efforts at Smyrna, but the city did not last for long and in July of that same year it was destroyed and dismantled by the Mongol ruler, Timur.[39] The Hospitallers tried to retake Smyrna and even succeeded in constructing a great tower there but this was soon pulled down by the Turks.[40] Always aware of the necessity of maintaining a Turkish front, the Hospitallers established another castle on the Anatolian mainland in 1407, at a place which later came to be known as Bodrum, opposite the island of Kos.[41]

After the initial Turkish counter-attacks of 1310-12 and 1318-19, Rhodes enjoyed periods of comparative peace and there was no major assault on the island until the unsuccessful Egyptian Mameluke campaigns of 1440 and

1444.[42] The Mamelukes had already invaded Cyprus in 1428 and, after the fall of Constantinople in 1453 to Sultan Mehmed II, Rhodes became the easternmost Christian outpost in the heart of an ever-growing Turkish empire.[43] Thereafter, the retention of the Order's position in the Aegean depended on the capacity of Rhodes to resist major assaults and the re-fortification of the city became almost unceasing. In 1480 Mehmed besieged Rhodes but the fortress held out heroically under the able leadership of Grand Master D'Aubusson and the Turks were forced to withdraw.[44] After 1480 Rhodes was relatively safe again for a while because of the death of Mehmed in 1481 which threw the Ottoman empire into chaos, diminishing the threat to Christendom.[45] One reason for this was that for much of the reign of Bayezid II (Mehmed's successor) the Hospitallers played host to his brother Jem, a pretender to the Ottoman sultanate.[46] Bayezid was thus content to pay for his brother to be kept in the West and to refrain from hostilities.[47] Work on the fortifications of Rhodes, however, continued unabated and by 1487 massive gunpowder fortifications had begun to take shape around the city's enceinte.

By the opening decades of the sixteenth century, however, Rhodes and the surrounding islands were once again subjected to an increasing pressure of raids and the Hospitallers were forced to hold the island in a perpetual state of military readiness. Their own continual aggressive preying on Muslim shipping meant that the Turks could not afford to ignore an island that commanded the sea route to Syria and Egypt and, in 1521, Suleiman the Magnificent, after capturing Belgrade, turned his attention to Rhodes.[48] This time the Turks returned with heavy artillery and some 200,000 men. Grand Master Philip Villiers de L'Isle Adam, a

Frenchman, inspired another valiant defence but after six months of fighting and bombardment, manpower, munitions, and morale had run low. With no hope of any assistance from the West, the Order was forced to surrender and accept the good terms offered to it by Suleiman. On 1 January 1523 the Hospitallers left Rhodes, taking with them all the possession and weapons they could carry away.[49]

Below, General view of the fortress of Rhodes, engraving by Breydenbach. Above, The earthquake of 1481, engraving in Caoursin's Stabilimenta.

From Medieval Castles to Gunpowder Forts
The early development of the bastion in Rhodes

The Hospitaller fortifications in the Rhodian archipelago fall basically into four categories. The first, and the most important element, was the mother fortress of Rhodes itself which represented the largest and most heavily fortified Hospitaller entity. This was the seat of the Convent and served as the Hospitaller headquarters and base for their military and naval forces. Undoubtedly, it was here that the knights invested most of their efforts in fortification. Secondly, and on a smaller scale, there were a few other fortresses and fortified towns scattered around the islands, such as Narangia and Andimacchia in Kos, Horio in Kalymnos, and so on. Thirdly, there was a considerable number of castles and strongholds, of varying sizes, and of predominantly Byzantine origin, scattered around the islands. These served both as administrative units and shelter for the population in the rural areas.[1] Few of these castles were as formidable and impregnable as those of Lindos, Pheraclos, or Philerimos since the majority were small and crudely built outposts that relied, without exception, on the strength of their naturally defensible sites for their protection. Lastly, there were a few watch towers and other lesser outposts which the knights helped expand into a system of coastal signalling-posts.

Gabriel rightly remarked that the Hospitaller fortifications in Rhodes show nothing of the essential features of the Order's earlier strongholds in Syria.[2] Indeed, the fourteenth- and fifteenth-century fortifications in the Dodecanese reflect a predominantly Byzantine influence.[3] This is attributed partly to the fact that many of the fortifications in the Greek islands were of Byzantine origin and partly because the Hospitallers, after 1310, continued to utilize indigenous labour functioning in Byzantine tradition. Nearly all of the fortifications, particularly those in the lesser islands, are undoubtedly of Byzantine construction with minimal Hospitaller additions. A few of the strongholds, particularly those built anew by the knights, however, such as those of Apolakkia, Sianna, and Lardos,

Right, top, Detached wall-towers at Santa Catalina castle in Jaén, Spain. Influence of this 'albarra' style is found at Rhodes, such as at the Tower of the Virgin Mary, right.

One of the rectangular wall-towers built by Grand Master Heredia along the harbour side of the fortress of Rhodes. These towers are equipped with cruciform arrow-slits and have sloping bases.

View of the antemural at the foot of the ramparts along the Post of Auvergne.

reflect other influences as well. The castle of Apolakkia, for instance, of which only a few sparse remains survive today, consisted of a central tower or keep surrounded by an outer enceinte similar to the donjon-and-bailey type of earlier Frankish strongholds in Syria.[4] The donjon, or strong tower, also formed the backbone of other castles, such as those found at Lardos and Sianna. However, given that many of the strongholds on Rhodes have not survived, it is difficult to draw any conclusions from so few examples. The earliest castle erected by the Hospitallers on Rhodes, that of Villanouva (1319-46), has unfortunately not survived to shed light on early architectural preferences of the Order, although it is known that this castle, too, had a large rectangular plan.

In Rhodes, the Hospitallers established a base which remained in the forefront of the struggle against the Turks, but after the initial assaults of the second decade of the fourteenth century, they were relatively untroubled by any serious threat given that the Turks did not as yet possess a sufficiently strong naval force to mount an invasion of the island. Consequently, there appeared no serious military threat to the Rhodian fortress during the first half of the fourteenth century and the Hospitaller seem to have been content with simply repairing the city's Byzantine

fortifications. Some building activity did take place during the magistracies of Villeneuve (1319-46) and De Gozon (1346-53), but most of this initial effort was directed towards the extension of the city's enceinte in both a southern and eastern direction in order to absorb the suburbs that had grown outside the city walls.[5]

The Byzantine city of Rhodes which the knights took over in 1309 occupied only a section of the ancient Hellenic city and was built on a level site where the only advantage lay in its harbours which were now vital for the Order's new naval role. The level site meant that the city's defences had to depend totally on the strength of man-made fortifications. The earliest defences built by the knights employed a system of double walls running parallel to each other, with the inner wall being higher then the outer one and stiffened at regular intervals with wall-towers. These served to provide enfilading fire along the adjoining curtain walls and to isolate whole sections of the ramparts from the rest of the enceinte.

This system of concentric defences was similar in concept to the walls of Constantinople but had only two lines of ramparts. The inner wall, the teichos (teicos), of about two metres thickness, was stiffened at regular intervals with rectangular wall-towers.[6] In front of this, but at a lower level, stood the the proteichisma (proteicisma) or *faussebraye,* with its own walkway. Percopius had laid down that the space between the two walls had to be one quarter of the height of the inner wall. This is roughly the case at Rhodes too. A good example of this early type of Rhodian system of defence has survived in the stretch of city walls east of St Athanassios gate. Only at the castle of Narangia in Kos and at Bodrum is there any evidence that the knights employed this system of double walls elsewhere besides the city of Rhodes.

The earliest type of wall-towers built on the enceinte of the city of Rhodes were squarish ones. Apart from the remains of the square towers to be found on the walls of the collachium which, however, are actually Byzantine in origin, the oldest surviving towers actually built by the knights date to the period 1377-96. These are the two towers sited on the north seaward side of the city along the trace between the towers of St Peter and St Paul. These are rectangular structures and bear the coat-of-arms of Grand Master Heredia. These are quite archaic in appearance and are armed only with cruciform arrow-slits. Rounded towers appeared relatively late in Rhodian fortifications and not until the first half of the fifteenth century when they coincide with the appearance of gunpowder-operated weapons. By this date, the design of Rhodian fortifications was being heavily influenced by Iberian ideas.[7] Thus, wall-towers were built in the Portuguese *albarra* style, i.e.

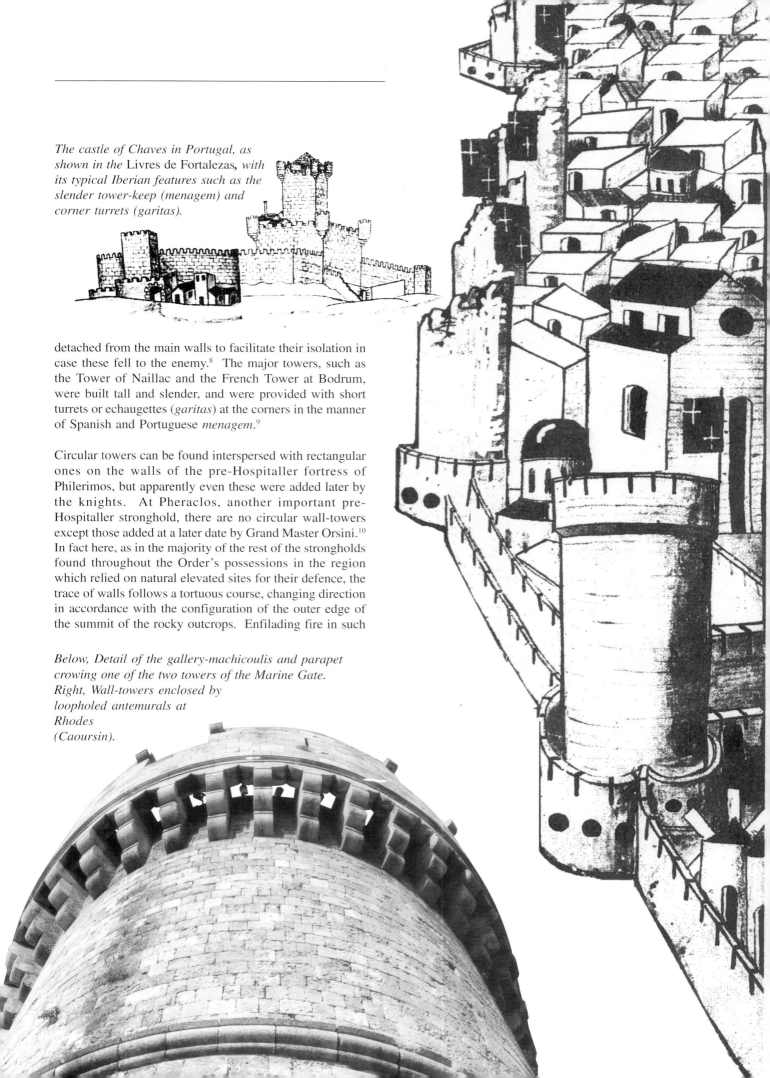

The castle of Chaves in Portugal, as shown in the Livres de Fortalezas, *with its typical Iberian features such as the slender tower-keep (menagem) and corner turrets (garitas).*

detached from the main walls to facilitate their isolation in case these fell to the enemy.[8] The major towers, such as the Tower of Naillac and the French Tower at Bodrum, were built tall and slender, and were provided with short turrets or echaugettes (*garitas*) at the corners in the manner of Spanish and Portuguese *menagem*.[9]

Circular towers can be found interspersed with rectangular ones on the walls of the pre-Hospitaller fortress of Philerimos, but apparently even these were added later by the knights. At Pheraclos, another important pre-Hospitaller stronghold, there are no circular wall-towers except those added at a later date by Grand Master Orsini.[10] In fact here, as in the majority of the rest of the strongholds found throughout the Order's possessions in the region which relied on natural elevated sites for their defence, the trace of walls follows a tortuous course, changing direction in accordance with the configuration of the outer edge of the summit of the rocky outcrops. Enfilading fire in such

Below, Detail of the gallery-machicoulis and parapet crowing one of the two towers of the Marine Gate.
Right, Wall-towers enclosed by loopholed antemurals at Rhodes (Caoursin).

places was not provided by means of wall-towers but from jogs in the indented trace. The castle of Narangia in the island of Kos is the only one which reflects Venetian influence in its rectangular *castrum* plan with circular corner wall-towers. The Venetians seem to have been responsible for erecting the inner *castrum,* since the island is known to have been in their hands at an earlier date. Indeed, this type of castle can be seen on many other Greek islands which were once Venetian outposts, such as at Kelefa in the Poleponnese, Aptera, and Francokastello in Crete.[11]

The introduction of gunpowder-operated cannon in the late fourteenth century led towards a gradual technological revolution in the art of poliorcetics and did much to assure that castles design did not ossify. The medieval castle, however, did not disappear over-night in the face of this new siege weapon, mainly because of the vast investment in existing castles and, therefore, the first reactions were minor practical alterations to the castles themselves. High walls, once proof against scaling and direct assault, became exposed targets and were either thickened or backed up with terrepleins to withstand the impact of shot; exposed walls were sometimes covered with earth or timber to absorb the shock of impact while fragile structures, such as machicolations and combustible wooden brattices, were removed from battlements. The defence of castles, however, remained a predominantly vertical one. The greatest importance of Hospitaller fortifications during the Rhodian

period is that these illustrate the important transition from medieval defences to gunpowder fortifications and ultimately to the development of the bastioned trace in its embryonic form.[12]

The gradual development of firearms in the later middle ages is first reflected in the provision of gun-loops and gun-ports to accommodate the new weapons to the advantage of the defenders. To mount cannon, castle walls required stable platforms and the most adaptable feature in castle design suited for this purpose was the wall-tower. Logically, cannon were placed on top of wall-towers and effectively, these became gun-platforms. At the Tower of St George we find one of the first provisions for defence with guns in Rhodes. This appears to date to the period 1421-37, a comparatively late appearance that is somewhat surprising since gun-ports had been in use, even in England, as early as 1380.[13]

Above, View of the salient of the first pentagonal bulwark of St John - note the arrow-slits in the merlons and the rectangular gun-loops below. Left, View of two of the irregular polygonal bulwarks situated along the walls of the Post of Provence.

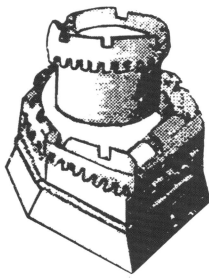

The Rhodian bulwarks bear great likeness to the bastions of Castel Sant'Angelo in Rome, built contemporaneously in the late 15th century. Historians have still to determine which structures influenced which.

The period from 1454 to 1467 saw the Hospitallers add various large but low polygonal towers liberally supplied with gun-ports along the *faussebraye* of the city's land front defences. The addition of these works performed a function not unlike the medieval barbican although here these served not only to cover gateways and entrances but also enabled enfilading fire to be directed along the faces of the adjoining curtain walls. In effect, these projections of the *faussebraye* were actually bulwarks built specifically for use with cannon.[14] Such bulwarks, as are still to be seen behind the Koskinou Gate and in front of the Tower of St George, were already approaching the solution of the bastion - only their solidity and dimensions were different.[15]

Following the siege of 1480, D'Aubusson began to reconstruct and strengthen the city's defences along quite different lines than those that had been employed till then. Evidently drawing on the lessons learnt from the siege, in which the city had experienced for the first time Turkish siege artillery fire, massive and solid polygonal bulwarks, or boulevards as these were called, were projected ahead of the earlier defences to shield them from cannon fire.[16] These boulevards, together with the large tenailles cut out in front of the long curtain walls, were all built to different shapes. One can therefore regard them as being virtually experimental works, or better still, attempts to find the optimal method of defence along different sections of the terrain.[17] A tendency towards regularity in the design of these massive structures began to manifest itself in the boulevard of Spain (1489) and then the boulevard of Auvergne which dates to 1496. The latter was the largest and most impressive of these works, pentagonal in plan in the manner of later Italian bastions and with a bomb-proof casemated battery in its flank. Actually the boulevard of Auvergne has long been disputed as being the prototype of

the first true bastion developed by the Italian military engineers. It was definitely a step in the right direction but, for reasons which will be discussed later, it was not actually conceived as a true pentagonal bastion.[18]

So much so that the Hospitallers abandoned the development of pentagonal bastions in the following decades in favour of semicircular ones. A number of these were built during the magistracy of Del Carretto, the most striking example being the bulwark at the post of Italy, but other examples can be found at the castle of Andimacchia in Kos, at Symi (but on a much smaller scale) and at Narangia, also in Kos, where the structure was actually incorporated into the main enceinte and thus can actually be called a bastion. Only on the island of Leros does the polygonal form re-appear, where one of three bastions with a sloping base has survived on the Hospitaller-added enceinte, though it is difficult to date this work.

The transformation from medieval castle to the bastioned fortress is attributed as a development which first took place in Italy in the late fifteenth and early sixteenth centuries but it is evident that at Rhodes important developments were taking place on parallel lines throughout the same period.[19] Indeed, Italian engineers were operating in Rhodes throughout this period. The first documented reference to an Italian military engineer working in Rhodes dates to 1502, when the 'Cremonese ingeniere e architecto, Bartholino de Castellione' is reported as being in the service of the Hospitallers.[20] Bartholino appears to have been in the Order's employ for a number of years ('e stato stipendiato ali servitij nostri') and was employed also at Kos and at 'castello sancti petri quanto altre nostre isole'.[21] Apparently, he was still in the employ of the Order at Bodrum in 1507.[22]

Rectangular gun-loop with accompanying vision-slit as found on the walls of Fort St Nicholas. Similar ports for early cannon are common along the Rhodian ramparts. This particular type was designed for two-men weapons mounted on low static 'cavalcature'.

Pietro Spagnesi, in his book on Castel Sant'Angelo, mentions the Hospitaller knight Frà Antonio di S. Martino as one of the persons employed by Pope Alexander VI to 'sovrintendere alla fabbrica' of the Roman stronghold. The great similarity between the bulwarks erected by D'Aubusson at Rhodes and those built by the pope at Castel Sant'Angelo tends to indicate a common author, though historians have yet to determine which influenced which.

The first mention of a military engineer in the employ of the Order is given by Giacomo Bosio. This was the German Georg Frappan, 'Mastrogiorgios', who was finally hanged by the knights for traitorously assisting the Turks during the siege of 1480, after he had actually defected from the Turkish army to join the knights.[23] Prior to 1480, however, there is no information on the military engineers working for the Order. The post of 'Provediteur des Fortifications', which was held by Pierre d'Aubusson before his election to grand master in 1476, during which time he was responsible for strengthening the city's seaward defences, however, seems to have been only a temporary one resulting from the fact that D'Aubusson was especially well versed in military engineering.[24]

The large circular bulwark of the Post of Italy, also known as Del Carretto Bastion .

During the last two decades of the Order's stay in Rhodes, the Hospitallers made increasing use of the services of Italian engineers, a practice they were to retain in Malta throughout the rest of the sixteenth and first half of the seventeenth centuries. Both Grand Masters Del Caretto and L'Isle Adam employed mostly Italian engineers like Basilio della Scuola and the Sicilian Maestro Zuenio (Geoini), the Bergamese Gabriele Tardini da Martengo, and the Florentine Gerolamo Bartolucci.[25] During this period, one can also begin to encounter the two categories of engineers employed by the Order, a practice that is well documented in Malta; that is, the distinction between a resident engineer, the 'Ingeniere della Religione', who was employed by the Hospitallers and was responsible for executing and maintaining all works of fortification like Maestro Zuenio, and the foreign expert loaned by some European monarch to design specific projects, such as 'Basilio della Scuola, Ingegniero dell'Imperatore Massimiano; il quale era il maggiore huomo di quella professione ch'in quei tempi vivesse.'[26] Gabriel refers also to a request by the Hospitallers, in 1516, for the services of the military engineer Scarpagnino which request, however, was turned down by the Venetian Republic.

The relief model in wax of the fortified city of Rhodes which 'Maestro Zuenio' prepared for Pope Leo X in 1521 must have shown the latest improvements in the art of fortification - the semicircular and polygonal bulwarks, the use of caponiers and curved parapets and gun embrasures.[27] The fortifications were soon put to the test in the course of the following year. In effect, the siege of 1522 proved to be a complete departure from contemporary medieval siege warfare and was instead fought out with powerful artillery and explosive subterranean mines. The fact that 6,000 men were able to resist 200,000 Turks for six months says much about the effectiveness of the early bulwarks of Rhodes. Had the knights received substantial reinforcements from Europe they would probably not have had to surrender the city.

Building the Rhodian Fortress
Building Methods & Techniques in the Dodecanese

The castle and medieval fortress remained the forms of fortification which were most widely utilized by the Hospitallers for the defence of Rhodes and the neighbouring islands, although very different conditions prevailed in the fourteenth and fifteenth centuries than those in the previous period. The knights who ruled over Rhodes and the nearby islands no longer had at their disposal the same resources of their brethren in the Outremer. This state of affairs is quickly reflected in the modest defences encountered throughout the Dodecanese.

To begin with, most of the castles in this region were of Byzantine origin, and some were built on the sites, and with the materials, of ancient acropolis - the castle of Lindos, for example, stands on the crest of a rocky outcrop that still retains the ruins of the Lindian acropolis and the sanctuary of Athena. Few of these strongholds possessed the solidity and magnificence of the earlier Hospitaller works in the Outremer. All derived most of their strength from the inaccessible and naturally defensible sites on which they were built. Their fragile and crudely-built walls sometimes appear insignificant and nearly superfluous in relation to the natural strength of the site on which they stand.

The vulnerability of the Greek islands to frequent corsair attacks necessitated secure refuge against such incursions and the mountainous and hilly nature of these islands lent itself adequately towards inaccessible strongholds. Invariably, these defences took advantage of natural defences, where security far outweighed convenience. Several different types of fortified sites appear in the Dodecanese. The first is the acropolis type found in the smaller villages, standing on an isolated bluff or crag; a good example is Sianna in Rhodes. For larger fortified settlements, a piece of high ground, either level or unevenly terraced, was more suitable. The fortress of Chorio in Kalymnos stands on an elevated and unevenly terraced plateau, surrounded on nearly all sides by inaccessible ravines and can only be approached up a tiring winding path. The fortified village on the nearby island of Telendos is protected by cliffs on the seaward side and mountain

heights to the rear. The fortresses of Philerimos and Pheraclos in Rhodes are two other good examples. The third type was the coastal fortified city, such as Rhodes itself and, on a smaller scale, Narangia in Kos, which were both built on level coastal sites and relied mainly on man-made defences but these were also commercial and naval centres.

A practical advantage of the elevated site was that it provided a healthier living environment; it was open to the winds, cleansed by rain water, and protected from the malarial mosquitoes of the lowlands. Refuse and human excrement was dumped over the walls or out of a window into the adjacent ravine. Sanitary consideration still held good in later centuries, as is clearly seen from Baldassare Lanci's report of 1562;[1] one of the reasons he cites in recommending the Sciberras peninsula as the site of a new fortress was that this elevated position was healthier than Birgu, open to the winds as it was.

The Hospitallers occupied and adapted the majority of the existing fortified sites when they took over Greek islands though a number of castles must have already been in ruins

The Hospitaller castle at Kastellorizo.

by the time of their occupation. The knights apparently chose to retain and adapt only the most strategic of these strongholds, especially those coastal hill-sites commanding good harbours or direct access from the sea, such as the castle at Platanos in Leros, and Livadia in Telos. The sea was the life-line linking the various islands together, on which provisions and reinforcements could be ferried by the ships and galleys of the Order's navy. Each island kept and equipped its own galley both for its own defence and also to prey on enemy shipping in the area.[2] The castle of St Peter established on the Turkish mainland in 1407 by Grand Master Naillac would not have survived for long against Turkish pressure had it not been built on the Zephyrion peninsula overlooking the Straits of Kos.

Where a suitable promontory could not be found, a ridge or plateau rising above the shore was chosen, such as at the fortified village of Telendos. Chateau Rouge on the island of Megisti (Kastellorizo) was built on the edge of the cliffs overlooking the entrance to two bays. Coastal sites, although guaranteed a direct life-line in times of acute danger, were also exposed to sudden harassment by corsair fleets. For this reason a number of castles, like Askiplion, Kritinia, Monolithos, and Archangelos in Rhodes, were located some distance inland from the coastline, sometimes hidden from direct view from the sea, such as the castle of Lardos. This rendered them slightly more secure against piracy, and enabled the inhabitants of surrounding districts to assemble within the safety of the fortified places once the alarm was sounded on the sighting of unidentified shipping.

Opposite page, View of the rampart walls of the fortress of Pheraclos along the northern part of the enceinte and, below, along the more approachable southern front. These ramparts were mainly the work of Grand Master Orsini. The site was chosen for its natural defensive qualities and inaccessibility.

The Hospitaller castle at Kastellorizo was erected on a promontory overlooking the main anchorage, thereby ensuring that its garrison could be easily assisted by sea from Rhodes in the event of siege.

A good water-supply was an indispensable element in the survival of a fortress. Where possible, a site which had its own natural spring was preferred but if there were none on or near the site, reliance was placed on cisterns. Cisterns could usually serve a garrison during an emergency but would not have been adequate for the everyday needs of the community. Thus the existence of springs somewhere in the vicinity of a fortress was doubtless often a factor governing the choice of one site rather than another. Periods of drought affected the water supply of cisterns, and at times seriously compromised the defence of a fortress; the castle of Aliminia had to be abandoned during the defence preparations of 1479 because it did not have an adequate reserve of water.[3]

The selection of sites already strong by nature reduced the need for large quantities of building materials, but what masonry was required had preferably to be found or quarried on site or in the immediate surroundings. The early fortifications of St Peter Castle in Bodrum, are said to have been built with materials specifically transported from Rhodes, but this was a rare case dictated by exceptional circumstances and a great sense of urgency.[4] Where possible, use was made of building materials which already lay at hand, in ruined or even existing buildings. Most of the building material at Bodrum after 1495, the green lava stones, white marble ashlars and fragments of the friezes and sculptures, came from the mausoleum at Halicarnassus.[5] The castle of Narangia in Kos was built largely from the materials quarried from the ruins of the Hellenistic city founded in 336 BC. Here, apart from the use of large ashlar blocks and column-drums of marble and blocks of green lava stone, one finds antique marble and granite columns bonding the thickness of the walls, and augmenting their strength against mining. The use of antique marble through-columns can be also found at many sites in the Latin East, such as at Ascalon, Giblet, Caesarea, and Arsuf.[6]

Aesthetic considerations were significantly less important in the Hospitaller strongholds throughout Rhodes and the other Dodecanese islands than had been in the Order's castles in Outremer. Here the knights had occasion of using pre-existing Byzantine structures which were built in a hurriedly and rough manner with materials which lay conveniently at hand and which could not be easily utilized to create regular courses. With the exception of the fortress of Rhodes and the castles of Lindos and part of Pheraclos, Bodrum and Narangia, the rest of the Hospitaller strongholds were built with stones found on site and used indigenous workmanship functioning in Byzantine manner. Much was made of rubble work, heavily galleted with tile, pottery, and stone pinnings and usually laid in heavy mortar. Only door and window surrounds and quoins were made of blocks, but these were usually irregular pieces. Quoins were reinforced with heavier ashlar. At Kastellorizo, the keep has quoins of re-utilized classical masonry; the lower quoins being the largest, with faces some 1.5m by 0.75m and growing progressively smaller with height.

Sometimes effort was made to bring the rubble masonry to courses. At Chorio in Kalymnos, each course of rough, undressed, and irregular blocks of hard grey rocks of roughly equal size was separated from the adjoining ones by a thin horizontal layer of red tile or stone pinnings in the manner of an *opus listatum*. A similar method of construction can be found in the small fortress at Agias Vassillios close to the harbour of Kalymnos, at Paleo Pyli in Kos, Platanos in Leros, at Alimonia, and at nearly all the existing rural strongholds in Rhodes. At Kastelli, facing the islet of Telendos, a pre-Hospitaller stronghold of Byzantine origin, every effort to produce some semblance of coursed masonry was immediately defeated by the nature of the very irregular stones used in its construction and the result was similar to an *opus incertum*. At Andimacchia, in Kos, the walls were built of coursed rubblework, but these were so heavily plastered that the final effect was one of a reasonably smooth and homogeneous surface, especially on the lower battered half of the exterior sections of the land front. Heavy plastered walls can also be found on the tower-keep at Kastellorizo. A greater tendency towards cleaner masonry, with roughly squared stonework laid in regular courses, can be found at Kefalos, in Kos, and at Kastellorizo, especially on the seaward enceinte of the castle. In the Hospitaller castle at Nisyros, one finds various types of masonry that reflect different stages in the castle's development, from heavily-plastered rubblework to *opus quadratum* of neatly-laid, quarry-faced ashlars of black volcanic rock and sandstone.

Frequently, the builders were able to re-utilize heavy classical masonry. At Aliminia and Chalki large blocks of classical masonry were used as wall socles. At Symi a short stretch of wall of pseudo-isodomic masonry from the original acropolis wall was incorporated into the medieval enceinte. At Narangia much use was made of Hellenistic masonry taken from the ruins of the old city and large marble blocks and green lava stone are intermixed with courses of quarry-faced ashlar blocks of sandstone. In Bodrum, especially on the structures built in the post-1436 period, large blocks of the rough-faced ashlar stones were laid in roughly regular courses and imparted an overall effect of solidity and impregnability to the curtain walls and bastions. In Rhodes, the crudely-built walls of the Byzantine fortified city were gradually replaced by ashlar masonry. Walls were built with the local yellowish sandstone but not all in a consistent isodomic style. Much fourteenth-century work at Rhodes used large, squared sandstone blocks with courses about 50cm in height. Works built between 1421 and 1436, have ashlar courses 40cm high with fragments of tile in their mortar, while those built between 1436 to 1454, are some 25cm in height. The use of *opus quadratum* was not confined to the city of Rhodes, and can be found in the castle of Lindos and on the section of the enceinte of Pheraclos rebuilt by the Hospitallers. Building with re-used classical masonry, and much tile and pottery pinnings is rare in the fortress of Rhodes.

Where large and carefully-fitted blocks of ashlar masonry were used, mortar was not necessary in the jointing of blocks and courses, since the sheer massiveness of the blocks themselves was enough to keep them in position. In facings made of small stones, however, mortar was indispensable

Grand Master D'Aubusson, accompanied by his retinue, instructs master masons and craftsmen on the repair of the fortifications. Note the tools of the trade, particularly the wooden scaffolding and the quantities of lime (Bibl. Nat., Paris).

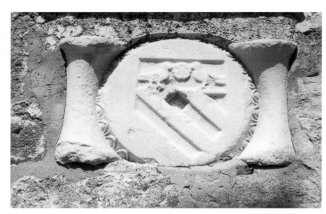

Examples of masonry styles employed in the construction of Hospitaller fortresses in the Dodecanese. Above, top left, Heavily-plastered coursed rubblework, Archangelos. Top right, re-utilized Corinthian capital at St Peter Castle, Bodrum. Middle left, Detail of galletting employed in the bonding mortar at Kastellorizo. Above, Ancient marble columns used as lintels, fortress of Narangia, Kos. Left, Large, ancient marble blocks used in the lower courses and as quoins at Kastellorizo. Below, Heavily-plastered, coursed rubble-work at Choria in Kalymnos.

in holding the wall together. In such cases, mortar was used even in the fill.

Once exposed, however, rain water quickly washes away the earth and the fill crumbles away. The normal practice was to use mortar composed of lime, sand and water. Lime was produced by burning limestone and the practice of binding masonry with lime-mortar is encountered throughout the various periods under review here. The masonry of the mausoleum at Halicarnassus, for example, was used not only in the fabric of the walls of St Peter Castle, but also in the production of lime-mortar; many precious statues were burnt in the 'fornace della calcina', to produce the required bonding material.[7]

Winter rain prevented the mortar from setting. In 1472, various 'magistri latomi' in Rhodes advised against the building of a castle there during the winter for torrential rain could seriously damage half-finished works.[8] The use of lime-mortar was indispensable in the coursed rubblework type of walls found throughout the Hospitaller strongholds in the Dodecanese. Indeed, large quantities of lime were required to bond each small irregular stone to the adjoining blocks and courses and to the rubble fill behind it. In order to economize and reduce the amount of mortar used, the joints were heavily galleted with pieces of broken pottery and stone pinnings

Works on fortifications were authorized by council decrees based on decisions reached after consultation with delegations of commissioners appointed to fulfil specific tasks.[9] Knights and military engineers were appointed commissioners in an *ad hoc* manner and for an indeterminate period, to prepare reports, examine fortifications, execute designs, or mobilize the local work force.[10] Thus, in 1475, a commission of 'due Signori della Gran Croce', one chosen by the grand master and the other by the council, was specially set up to inspect and record, every two years, the state of the towers and castles of Rhodes, 'visitar dovessero ogni due anni, tutte le Torre, Castella, e Casali dell'Isola di Rodi; E che di detta visita, un libro autentico far dovessero.'[11] A competent commissioner of fortification was the knight Frà Filippo di Guidone, 'Commendatore di Randazzo, Commissario delle Fabriche e fortificationi e le munitione necessarie ... il quale era molto pratico; per aver lungamente atteso alle fortificationi della Città di Rodi.'[12]

The commissioners themselves, however, were rarely versed in the art of building, with the major exception of D'Aubusson, and had to rely on the services of architects and engineers. It was the latter who designed the new enceintes, supervised the building contracts and repair works, and came in contact with the craftsmen and labourers. The *capomastro dell'opere*, the foreman of works, usually a local craftsman, was responsible for executing the orders of the engineer and supervising the work of the craftsmen and labourers. Below the foreman came the master masons, each of whom was in charge of a company of labourers and slaves. An inscription dated 1457, on a marble plaque inside St John Gate in Rhodes, records that a section of the wall of Rhodes was built by the Greek 'protomaistro murador' Manolis Kountis.[13] Another known Greek 'murator et protomagister' was Giorgios Singan who worked on the fortifications of Rhodes and at St Peter Castle, Bodrum, while two Greek 'muratores' from Kos who worked on the latter were freed from servitude in 1414.[14] It is not clear, however, whether the Greek master masons were simply competent craftsmen or trained engineers. In the middle ages, the office of master mason was usually akin to that of architect. Nicolò de Flavari an architect who accompanied the Order to Malta in 1530, described as 'protomaestro delli architettura nostra' i.e. official architect of the Order, referred to himself as 'muratore et capo mastro delle opere di Muraglia'.[15]

Woodcut depicting masons at work in Rhodes, after Caoursin.

Rhodes under Attack
The Sieges of Rhodes

'Nothing in the world was so well lost' - *Charles V on the fall of Rhodes*

In Rhodes, the knights acquired an island base well protected by the sea around it. To invade it, an enemy required a large fleet to transport troops and provisions and, in the days of oar-powered ships, such an attack had to be conducted and completed in the summer months. In the initial years of the fourteenth century, the Turks did not have a sufficiently strong navy with which to undertake such an endeavour. Consequently, Rhodes prospered in relative peace after the initial Turkish counter-attacks of 1310-12 and 1318-19.[1]

By the end of the first half of the fifteenth century, however, the picture had begun to change drastically. In 1440 the Egyptians attacked Rhodes but misjudged the time it would take them to overcome the defences and were obliged to withdraw. They returned in 1444 but were defeated.[2] With the loss of Cyprus in 1428, and the fall of Constantinople in 1453 to Sultan Mehmed II, Rhodes became effectively the easternmost Christian outpost in the heart of an ever-growing Turkish empire, vulnerably exposed and

Portrait of Mehmet the Conquerer by Gentile Bellini.

continually subjected to hostile Turkish attention. The Hospitallers' reaction to this growing threat was to invest huge resources in the re-fortification and strengthening of their major fortresses and the setting up a network of coastal signalling towers to warn of enemy raids. Throughout the the 1460s and 1470s the Turks continually raided and harassed Hospitaller possessions in the Dodecanese. These *razzie,* although not as serious as full-scale invasions, still had the effect of disrupting the rural settlements and the islands' economy.

From 1477 onwards, each spring the knights waited for a Turkish attack. It eventually came in 1480, when Mehmet the Conqueror launched a naval force against Rhodes with a 100,000-strong army. The size of the force may have been exaggerated by contemporary chroniclers after a fashion, and it is more probable that there were only 20,000 men, since other campaigns had a call on Mehmet's army.[3] The knights, on the other hand, did not have more than 2,500 men at their disposal. Moreover, the Turkish supply lines were comparatively shorter than those of the defenders. The site and disposition of the fortifications of Rhodes were not ideal. Situated on level ground with long lines of walls, the city had also the disadvantage of being surrounded by higher ground from where the defenders could command the ramparts with cannon. By medieval standards, however, the walls were quite strong with their double line of ramparts and flanking towers, even though the Turks had acquired an impressive array of cannon. By 1480, gunpowder-operated siege artillery was developing into an effective weapon with which to attack castle defences and the Turks were among the first to appreciate the full potential of this weapon.

The Turks began their attack with a bombardment of the tower of St Nicholas, the small harbour fort on the mole north of the city, probably because they wanted to be able to use their navy to the full in the attack on the city walls. Fort St Nicholas was defended by a handful of knights under the command of Fabrizio del Carretto. The capture of this work should have been an easy matter and, although they used every stratagem to capture it, the Turks only managed to sustain severe losses. Eventually the capture of the fort became an obsession with the Turkish command. After two major amphibious assaults which saw the loss of 3,000 men, the Turks were forced to abandon the endeavour and concentrate their attack on the land front.[4] Their attacks were directed against the posts of Italy and Provence. Within a few days Turkish bombardments had destroyed nine towers and part of the grand master's palace.[5] On 27 July the Turks unleashed a general assault. Behind the ruined walls of the post of Italy the knights had managed to build an internal crescent-shaped entrenchment but the Turks began to spill into the city propelled by the momentum of their own numbers. Grand Master D'Aubusson himself led a counter attack and managed to stem the attack but was seriously wounded in the attempt. This last battle appears to have seriously depleted the Turkish strength and morale because they soon struck camp and fled back to Constantinople.[6]

The victory over the Turks in 1480 had raised the prestige of the Order to a prominence which had largely escaped it eversince the fall of the Holy Land. Gifts and manpower came from Europe. But the city was in ruins and D'Aubusson knew too well that the Turks would come back. He, therefore, lost no time in rebuilding and improving the defences. The vulnerability of the city's high slender walls to Turkish gun-fire was well illustrated during the siege so that rebuilding on the same lines was unthinkable. Instead, the main walls were thickened and built up to provide a wide terreplein while strong bulwarks were projected forward in front of the original walls. D'Aubusson's prolific military works, slightly augmented and finalized by D'Amboise and Del Carretto, basically reshaped the city's defences. This feverish building activity continued unabated right up to the siege of 1522.

The Hospitallers' greatest shortcoming, and one they could do very little to remedy, was their limited manpower resources. The Order's failure to attract western settlers to Rhodes and the Dodecanese islands compelled the knights to rely heavily on mercenaries.[7] As early as 1340, it was proposed that the city of Rhodes itself should be defended by 50 mounted secular men-at-arms, 1,000 infantry *servientes* in addition to the 200 Hospitallers, each with a squire and two horses, and 50 mounted sergeants.[8] A later scheme proposed that the existing mercenaries be replaced by 50 Hospitaller sergeants. By 1391 the Hospitaller commander of the island of Kos, the most strategic of the Dodecanese islands after Rhodes, was supposed to maintain the garrisons of four castles with 25 *miles*, 10 *homme d'arms latins*, 100 Levantine *turcopoles* and some 150 men, together with a few mercenaries from the *squadra* of the single galley stationed there, all from the island's income.[9]

Two scenes from Caoursin's illustrations of the siege of Rhodes of 1480 (Bibl. Nat., Paris). Above, The effects of siege artillery and repeated assaults on the Rhodian ramparts. Note the defender's artillery protected by gabions. Below, The knights lead a counterattack on the Turkish lines.

The garrison of St Peter Castle in Bodrum was likewise usually composed of 100 Latin mercenaries, the *stipendiati* or *socii,* and 50 knights.[10] In 1409 these *stipendiati* cost the treasury 6,000 florins annually.[11] In 1520 there were 150 mercenaries at Bodrum and every time the castle was threatened by attack, its garrison was reinforced with more soldiers from Rhodes, such as the contingent of 300 men dispatched in 1470.[12]

Problems with mercenaries were not rare in such places where garrisons were either confined on some remote island like Kastellorizo or, worse still, within the restricted area provided by insecure strongholds such as Bodrum. At St Peter Castle in Bodrum there was some trouble with mercenaries in 1409 and 1412, and even among the knights themselves.[13] The *caravana* or term of duty at Bodrum was limited to two years but when the castle was under threat of a possible attack the 'muta dei cavalieri' was deferred until the crisis subsided, such as happened in 1475.[14] Turks and roaming corsairs were not the only danger to the small Hospitaller garrisons dispersed around the various islands. Sometimes the inhabitants themselves were a real threat; in 1319, the garrison of knights and soldiers at Leros were massacred by the Greek population, but the revolt was short-lived and most of the Greeks, some 1,900, were either killed or taken captives to Rhodes.[15]

The shortage of troops meant that some of the lesser islands were usually so poorly defended that both their small garrisons and inhabitants had frequently to be evacuated to the safety of Rhodes every time there appeared a serious threat of an attack. Even against relatively minor corsair raids, there was generally very little that these islands' garrisons could do except retreat, together with the inhabitants, within the safety of their strongholds and wait for assistance from Rhodes while they helplessly watched

Provisions for the discharge of projectiles - piombatoi, dove-tailed and cruciform arrow-slits, and circular gun-loop.

the suburbs and surrounding fields being sacked and burnt by the enemy. Such devastating raids were very common, especially during the later half of the fifteenth century. Kos, for example was attacked in 1440, 1457, 1460, 1461, 1464, 1492, 1502, and 1522;[16] Telos in 1479 and 1504;[17] Kalymnos in 1457, 1460, and 1478;[18] Nisyros was sacked in 1457and attacked again in 1478 and 1504;[19] Symi in 1457 and 1504; Leros was raided in 1457, 1460, 1477, 1502, and 1506.[20] When Leros was attacked in 1506 by the 'Corsale Turco Nichi', there were only six Hospitaller brethren within the castle, together with the women, children and old men who had taken refuge. The Hospitaller

The Hospitaller Knights of Rhodes, left, in the early 14th century, right, in the 15th century, wearing North Italian armour, and German 'Gothic' armour, far right.

The attack on Fort St Nicholas during the siege of Rhodes in 1480 after Caoursin

castellan, who was too sick to fight, entrusted the castle to Frà Pietro Simeone. The situation was so desperate that this knight had the women and old men dress in the 'sopraveste rosse con la croce bianca in mezzo' and parade themselves behind the battlements.[21] Thus the Turks, duped into thinking that reinforcements had arrived from Rhodes during the night, re-embarked their artillery pieces and sailed away.[22]

Another force used for the defence of Rhodes was made up of turcopoles, numbering between 300 and 400 men, formed into a body of light cavalry which was frequently used to patrol the coastline and the remote rural areas.[23] These were also responsible for mustering the peasant or rural militia for the defence of the various castles scattered around the island.[24] The garrison of these castles too was kept to a minimum and many of the strongholds had to be abandoned in times of danger. Lindos, one of the strongest castles on Rhodes, was defended in 1522 by a small force of twelve knights and twenty-two mercenaries together with an *ad hoc* force of peasants which had gathered from the surrounding villages to seek shelter from the invading Turks.[24] After 1490, the lesser islands were subjected to continual raids. These raids, however, were more daring than the swift *razzie* of the previous decades and on many occasions the Turkish corsairs were strong and confident enough to lay siege to some of the strongholds. In 1504 the Turkish corsair Camali attacked the castle of Symi with artillery and his guns were quick to breach the walls of the stronghold but the assaults that followed were repulsed by the defenders. Nonetheless, the island was ransacked, villages and crops were burnt so that the inhabitants were reduced to poverty.[25]

The full might of the Turkish war machine finally fell on Rhodes in 1522. Sultan Suleiman landed with a 200,000-strong army and heavy artillery batteries. Amongst the Turkish force was a veritable army of 60,000 skilled miners and their presence in such large numbers is particularly significant since it reflects the importance that mining had acquired in Turkish siege tactics. By 1522, the explosive mine, fired with gunpowder, had become the most devastating of all siege weapons and the Turks were quick to appreciate its value. The fortifications which faced the Turks in 1522 were considerably different from those which had confronted Mehmet in 1480. Massive bulwarks and terrepleined walls, equipped to mount cannon and protected with thick sloping merlons, presented a more formidable obstacle.

Facing Suleiman's forces from behind the city's ramparts were some 5,000 men, amongst which were 'da seicento dell'Habito, fra Signori della Gran Croce, Comendatori, Cavalieri, e Fra Servienti. Quattrocento Soldati Candiotti

(from Candia in Crete) & il resto erano Soldati, Marinari, & houmini delle Galere e delle Navi... e fra loro c'erano anche molti Cittadini di Rodi.'[26] The city's enceinte was divided amongst the various languages to ensure that no part of the fortifications, especially on such a long perimeter as the walls of Rhodes, remained undefended - a practice introduced in 1465 by Grand Master Zacosta.[27] It also helped to exploit the rivalry between the various nationalities within the Order to the advantage of the defenders since none of the tongues could afford to lose or abandon their posts to the enemy without some loss to the prestige and honour of their country.

Some 600 knights and sergeants, the highest number of brethren ever assembled, were deployed on the ramparts of the city. There was also a body of 400 professional soldiers from Crete, recruited by Frà Antonio Bosio.[28] These soldiers were equipped with their own 'arme bianche alcuni di quale portavano spadoni da due mani (double handed swords), alcuni archibugi e altri archi.' The bulk of the Christian fighting force was made up of sailors from the Order's ships and galleys and the city's inhabitants, all armed and equipped from the Order's armouries.[29]

The bulk of the Hospitaller force comprised the urban militia formed from amongst the civilian population. This was composed of separate legions representing various sections of the Rhodian society. The Jews, for example, were formed into a legion of 250 volunteers with their own officers and manned that section of the walls surrounding the Jewish Gate overlooking the commercial harbour, while the guild of butchers was detailed to guard St Anthony Gate leading out from the *collochium*.[29] Earlier in 1471, a company of 'trecento huomini fioriti, Cittadini e habitanti' versed in the use of arms, had been set up to help defend the city under the command of 12 captains.[30] The population of the lesser islands and secondary castles on Rhodes too were transported to the mother city to augment the number of defenders.

Armed with a huge force, Suleiman was confident that the city would be easy prey. He deployed his troops around the land front while his fleet was ordered to blockade the city from the sea. The first Turkish batteries were set up against the posts of England, Provence, and Spain but devastating return fire from the ramparts forced the Turks to change their tactics. Instead, huge earthen platforms were raised opposite the post of Aragon in order to command the interior of the city and its ramparts. The army of sappers then began digging their mines at various points along the enceinte. The knights were fortunate to have in their services the Bergamese military engineer, Gabriele Tadini da Martinengo, whose extensive countermining successfully neutralized the Turkish efforts.[31] Tadini employed listening devices in the form of stretched parchment diaphragms which caused small bells to tingle at any subterranean vibrations, and also constructed a system of vents to disperse the blasts of Turkish mines. The Hospitallers, however, were handicapped by the shortage of labour, timber, and powder, and Tadini's few trained miners could not cope with the imbalance. While the sappers dug at their mines the powerful Turkish batteries kept up their bombardment, even by night. By the middle of September, huge breaches had been blown by mines, and artillery along most of the ramparts on the land front. At dawn on 24 September, the Turks launched their first general assault but, after six hours of fierce hand-to-hand combat, they were forced to withdraw.

Gunpowder-operated weapons featured prominently during the struggle. By 1522, bombardiers and arquebusiers had come to constitute important elements in the Hospitaller's armed forces. The siege itself proved a complete departure from medieval warfare. It was fought out with heavy artillery, explosive mines, and firearms. The armoured knight, however, still had an important role to play in the defence of the fortress for, once inside the fortifications, the attackers soon had to abandon their unwieldy firearms with their slow rate of fire for the more conventional swords, maces, axes, and pikes, and in the ensuing *mêlée*, the heavily armoured knight held a marked advantage over the lightly armoured janissaries and spahis. A small number of knights, stationed in a breach and hacking away at the enemy with their heavy two-handed swords, could effectively stem the tide of an assault.

The combination of bastioned ramparts, artillery, and armoured men kept the Turks at bay for around six months. The last major assault was launched on 30 November and it cost the Turks 11,000 dead.[32] The knights had clearly decided to resist to the last man but the townspeople had heard of Suleiman's offer to spare their lives if they surrendered and threatened to rebel unless a truce was made with the Turks. The picture facing Grand Master L'Isle Adam was a bleak one: his forces had been decimated, the fortifications ruined, and powder and shot almost exhausted. Worse still, there was practically no hope that a large Christian relief force could be expected to arrive to the aid of the defenders. Most of the insignificantly small relief forces that had reached the island had been sent from the other Hospitaller strongholds in the Dodecanese, such as Bodrum, and from Candia.[33] It was only a matter of time before the city would eventually fall to the Turks. After six months of siege, the Order was faced with two alternatives: total extermination or surrender. Suleiman's terms were generous and it was decided to accept them. On 1 January 1523, L'Isle Adam and the battered remnants of the Order's force left Rhodes for Crete. The grand master also sent word to the garrisons of the other Hospitaller strongholds in the nearby islands to abandon their positions. After 200 years the Order was once again homeless.

The siege of Rhodes in 1522, as depicted in a print by the German artist Hans Sebald Beham (coutesy of Michael Losse).

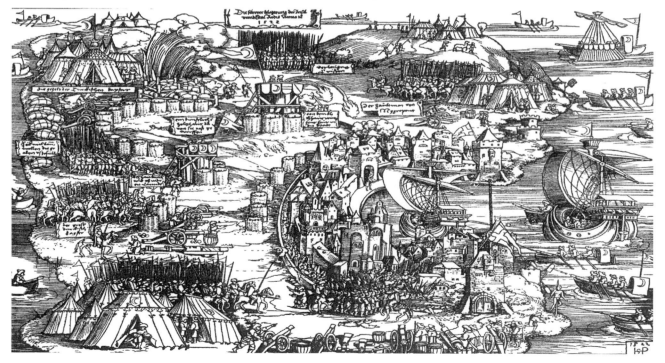

Framed escutcheon decorating the façade of the Sea gate (after Rottiers)..

A Bulwark of Christendom

The fortification of Malta and Tripoli

'Because we wish to go out to help that Order of soldiers which has always stood as a firm defender of the Christian faith, we have sent much aid as we could to the master at Malta'

Letter of Pope Pius IV - June 1565

From Crete, the remnants of the Hospitaller force made their way to Civitavecchia in the Papal States and then settled down to a temporary residence at Viterbo. The next seven years were spent casting around for a new home as Grand Master L'Isle Adam toured the courts of Europe trying to muster international support for his scheme to reconquer Rhodes. As early as 1523, the Spanish crown had offered the island of Malta to the Order for its new base but a commission of Hopitaller knights sent to inspect the island in 1524 returned unimpressed by the arid and infertile land, and its poor, run-down fortifications. The alternative options, however, were few, and as the years wore on the knights were forced to reconsider Charles V's offer.

In 1530 the Order of St John took possession of Malta, together with the burdensome fortress of Tripoli, a Spanish North African outpost that was included in the deal. When the knights arrived in Malta, they found a poorly defended group of islands whose sole refuge lay in the walls of three old medieval *castra* - Mdina, the fortified capital town of Malta, the *castello* in Gozo, and the *castrum maris* inside the Grand Harbour. None of these strongholds was considered by the knights as being capable of providing adequate defence, for the Hospitallers took possession of the Maltese islands at a time when the technological revolution and destructive force generated by gunpowder artillery called for strong bastions capable of withstanding the tremendous impact of shot and the fragile medieval walls of the Maltese castles were, like all medieval fortifications, still primarily designed to counter scaling and assault, offering little protection against cannon fire. Neither the Spanish crown nor the local population had been able or willing to invest in a rebuilding of these defence *alla moderna*. The knights, however, had no other option if they were to continue to use the islands as their military base. Still, at first they could not afford to affect but minor modifications to the existing medieval defences. The

decision to erect adequate fortifications was also hampered further by the Order's indecision as to whether it ought to settle down in what was seen as a temporary island base.

Of the three strongholds, the Hospitallers chose to establish their base inside the *castrum maris* and its suburb - a logical choice dictated by the Rhodian tradition. Being a seafaring body, the Order of St John needed a harbour-city from where its naval force could conduct its aggressive maritime activities. The fleet of galleys was the Order's chief instrument of action that perpetuated the fight against Ottoman empire in typical crusading tradition. Giacomo Bosio writes that when L'Isle Adam set foot on the island in October 1530, he took up residence in the castle and ordered that Birgu, the suburb of fishermen's and sailors' houses that had grown under the shelter of the castle, be enclosed by a fortified wall.

The new works of fortification progressed slowly and it was not until nearly a decade later that Birgu and the old castle were finally fitted out with new bastioned ramparts. The military engineers called in to advise on the new

Map of Malta, from Quintin's Insulae Melitae Descriptio, Lyon, 1536.

defensive works were quick to point out that the Order had not chosen to fortify the best position within the Grand Harbour for the ideal site for a fortress lay on the commanding heights of the Sciberras peninsula. The knights were well aware of this fact. As far back as 1524, the commission of eight knights sent to evaluate Malta by L'Isle Adam had already realized the great strategic importance of this peninsula, about one mile long and separating the two largest natural harbours on the island.[1] However desirable this might have been, the Order was then in no position to undertake such an enormous task in the years after its arrival in Malta. The knights had thus no other option but to settle down at Birgu and repair as best they could the old *castrum maris*. The hope of recapturing Rhodes was still in the hearts of many knights and so no attempt was made to commit the Order's resources to the construction of a large fortified city on what was seen as a temporary island base, even though military engineers continued to point out that the fortification of the Sciberras peninsula was the only real solution to the defensive problem. The knights were also concerned with the plausible threat of Turkish retaliatory raids which would find a new fortress in a vulnerable unfinished state.

That such fears were not unfounded was clearly revealed by the *razzia* of 1551, when a large Ottoman armada of some hundred vessels carrying 10,000 men, under the command of the admiral Sinan Pasha, and flanked by Dragut and Salih Pasha of Algiers, attacked Malta.[2] At first the Turks attempted to invest the fortress of Birgu and

the old city of Mdina but, fortunately for the Order, the Turkish force was not strong enough to take on the fortifications. The Ottoman commanders then led their men to Gozo and laid siege to its weak castle which fell after only a couple of days' bombardment and all those found within were carried off into slavery. The citadel itself is said to have been razed to the ground.[3]

The armada then set sail for Tripoli and attacked the Hospitaller outpost there, then under the command of its governor Gaspar de Vailleirs and defended by 30 knights and 600 soldiers. Tripoli was not much of a fortress: a native settlement surrounded by inferior earth-packed walls stiffened with wall-towers and enclosing roughly a pentagonal area. At one corner of the city stood the *castello*, an old-fashioned squarish fort with some added bastions partly of stone and earth. Finally a small detached fort, the *castillegio*, built on a spit of land, commanded the entrance to the harbour with its cannon. On 8 August the invaders launched a major assault and with the help of three batteries hammered the defenders into submission. The garrison soon mutinied and forced the knights to surrender. The negotiations were brief and Tripoli capitulated on 14 August 1551, after 40 years of Christian domination.[4]

The Grand Harbour as illustrated by Georg Braun and Frans Hogenberg in Civitates orbis Terrarun, *1572, possibly showing Baldassare Lanci's project of 1562.*

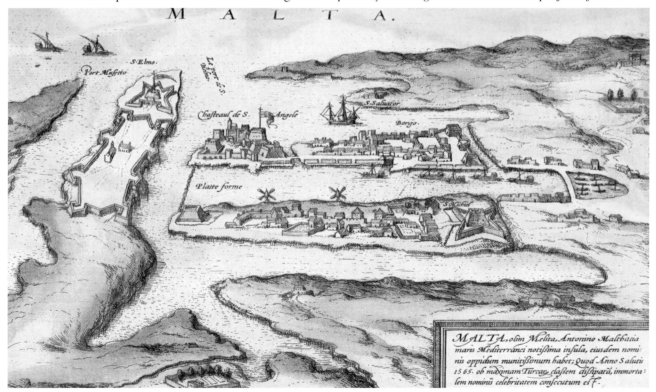

The loss of Tripoli, the sacking of Gozo, and the attack on Birgu and Mdina clearly illustrated the weakness of the Order's position in Malta and left no doubt at all as to the gravity of the Turkish threat. Even Pope Julius III advised the knights to withdraw immediately to Syracuse or Messina in Sicily, leaving only a token garrison on the island.[5] Instead, the Hospitallers chose to stiffen the island's defences. A commission of three knights assisted by the military engineer Pietro Prato was set up to review the existing defences and advise on the best possible course of action.[6] In their recommendations, the commissioners were again of the view that a new fortress should be built on the Sciberras peninsula but this project was to be carried out in stages. The first step was the construction of a small fort at the tip of Sciberras peninsula to command the entrances to the Grand Harbour and Marsamxett. This fort would, at a later stage, be incorporated within the defences of the new fortress. The commission also recommended that a second fort be built on the Isola peninsula south-west of Birgu in order to protect the latter from artillery bombardment.

The first to be built was Fort St Elmo at the mouth of harbour, but so acute was the sense of urgency induced by the fear of a renewed Turkish attack that the Order had both forts practically ready by March 1552.[7] The island's labour force was duly conscripted but, even so, Sicilian workmen had to be brought over to supplement the local workforce.[8] When the harbour defences were well under way, Prato was dispatched to repair Mdina's defences. The old city had by then only been fitted with one bastion, which was still incomplete, although two were actually planned to protect the land front and provide the old citadel with sorely-needed artillery platforms and flanking defences.[9]

During the brief reign of Grand Master Claude de La Sengle, Fort St Michael was enclosed within a bastioned enceinte and a new town, Senglea, sprang up within its walls. This was a logical and practical development on Strozzi's original idea that helped extend further urbanization in the harbour area and ease the congestion in Birgu.[10] In the post-1551 period, the Hospitallers attempted to consolidate their position inside the harbour area by periodic bursts of building activity aimed at perfecting and strengthening the existing defences, culminating in the feverish efforts in the early months of 1565 and during the early stages of the siege itself.

With the election of Jean de Valette to the magistracy, enthusiasm for a new fortress on Sciberras heights gathered momentum following the resolution taken by the council of the Order in June 1558, implying that the Hospitallers had at last committed themselves to settle down in Malta.[11] Within a short time, Bartolomeo Genga, one of the foremost European military engineers, was persuaded to visit Malta

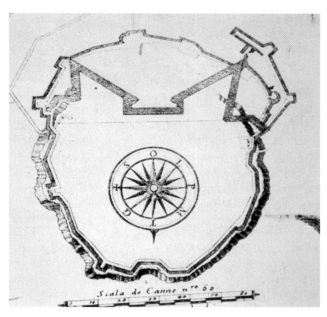

The small citadel provided the only defence for the inhabitants of Gozo against corsair incursions.

to draw up the plans for the new fortress. Genga, however, died in Malta before work could begin on the fortress he had designed.[12] The deterioration in the general military situation brought about by the Djerba crisis induced the knights to attempt to entrench themselves more securely in the island, the Order's first reaction being to petition for the services of another good engineer from the grand duke of Florence, a demand that resulted in the loan of Baldassere Lanci.[13] In 1562 Lanci was brought over to design the new fortress and, by the following year, the project had received papal approval but once again the Order did not press on with the building of the fortress.[14] It appears that the menace of a Turkish reprisal had become more apparent, and the knights probably felt sure that a major attack was imminent.

During the early 1560s reports began to filter through from the Levant of a new Ottoman armada being prepared for a thrust into the western Mediterranean. The armada did not leave port in any strength from 1561 to 1564 and during this period there was much talk of Turkish preparations and speculation as to which place was to be the principal target of the forthcoming attack: La Goletta, Sardinia, Malta, and Oran were considered the most likely candidates.[15] Amidst this scarcity of information and false rumours, the knights dispatched their galleys to seek news of Ottoman intentions. In the early months of 1565, there was no more doubt that the Ottoman armada would sail west the following spring and La Goletta and Malta, the foremost bastions of Christendom, were feared as the positions most likely to be attacked. By April the exact destination was still unknown. The Spaniards feared that La Goletta was the objective, but at Corfu it was rumoured that the fleet was heading for Malta.[16]

In early May, the fleet arrived at Navarino and on the 18th of the same month the Turkish armada anchored off Malta. The knights had not been caught unprepared, since the grand master had ordered preparations to be taken in hand from quite some time before. Adequate provisions of wheat and gunpowder were secured, troops and mercenaries recruited, the fortifications strengthened in the best possible manner, and all the defensive positions pre-assigned to the various langues and their companies of soldiers. Throughout the siege the knights held four defensive positions within the harbour area, and two to the rear. Fort St Elmo, with its cavalier and hastily-built ravelin, commanded the entrance to the two harbours. Fort St Michael commanded all the works on the Senglea peninsula, while adjacent to it lay the Birgu land front, the Order's major first line of defence, stiffened with bastions and cavaliers. These two fortified works were linked to each other by means of a wooden pontoon bridge that enabled the defenders to deploy their troops between the two cities as the tactical situation dictated. Undoubtedly, the Order's main stronghold was Fort St Angelo, acting as the keep of the southern flank defences and where, if all the rest was lost, the Hospitallers could retreat and make their last stand awaiting the relief forces.

The Turks were quick to exploit the basic weakness that threatened all these defences: the high ground that overlooked them. Turkish engineers made good use of this land feature by setting up powerful batteries with which they hammered and softened the walls in preparation for infantry assaults. The first to fall to the enemy was Fort St Elmo, after a month-long siege driven by the Turkish obsession to protect their fleet. This unforeseen delay is seen by historians as the turning point in the conflict in favour of the defenders. In the interval the knights had strengthened further their fortifications and kept communications open with Sicily by way of Mdina and Gozo.

After St Elmo, the Turks concentrated their efforts on the land fronts of Birgu and Senglea. They again subjected the defences to crushing artillery bombardment followed by massive assaults. They frequently sought to storm the defences from various directions, at one time even attempting a sea-borne assault, but on each occasion they were driven back by fire and steel. Sappers also sought to mine the bastions and managed to bring down a section of the enceinte near the Post of Castile, but the knights had set up internal retrenchments and managed to keep the Turkish forces from breaking in. At one time the Turks came

close to overrunning the defences, had it not been for the timely intervention of the small Christian cavalry. This puny mounted force, under the command of the knight Frà Melchoir d'Eguares, was stationed in the old city of Mdina from where it was used to attack the Turkish rear. In one sortie, the cavalry attacked their camp at Marsa, causing so much confusion and panic that the Turks, who were about to capture Fort St Michael, were forced to beat a retreat in order to face what they thought was a large Christian relief force attacking them from the rear. As the siege dragged on Turkish strength and morale declined rapidly but still it was the arrival of a large Christian relief force in early September which finally convinced the Turks to abandon their enterprise and sail back to Constantinople.[17]

The successful conclusion of the siege, whilst a matter of great rejoicing among the princes of Europe, had weakened the Order considerably. All the forts were ruined, huge debts had been incurred, and many knights had died. Added to these difficulties was the spectre of a second Turkish attack in the following year. The task of rebuilding the fortifications to withstand another siege induced the majority of the surviving members of the Order to express their preference for leaving the island and to set up base elsewhere. There is some reason to believe that Jean de Valette did not subscribe to these views, preferring to remain in Malta since he foresaw less difficulty in raising the funds required for the general rehabilitation of the island. However, he used the first option as leverage in his demands for financial aid from the Christian monarchs, who expressed apprehension at the possibility that the Order might decide to abandon Malta. Two months after the siege the grand master was still deliberating on what best to do. A letter dated 26 October 1565 sent from Messina, probably by Don Garcia de Toledo, urged him not to waste any more valuable time and to proceed with the construction of a new fortress on Mount Sciberras, for which a labour force and an engineer would be provided.[18]

The Order's financial problems, however, were so grave that even ordinary expenditure could not be met without difficulty. Grand Master de Valette was worried that the project, once initiated, could not be completed before the dreaded return of the Turks the following spring. Pope Pius IV himself, anxious that the Order retain Malta, offered immediate financial assistance and sent over one of his ablest military engineers, Francesco Laparelli, to design the new fortified city.[19]

Laparelli arrived in Malta at the end of December 1565 and was promptly informed by the grand master that the walls of the new fortress had to be completed within three months before the expected Turkish attack. Laparelli prepared a report on how this could be achieved indicating that an estimated labour force of 4,000 men was required for such a task and 3,000 soldiers to man its defences. Laparelli's plan consisted of a bastioned land front sited some 500 *canne* from the ditch of St Elmo, on the highest part of the peninsula. By the end of February 1566, six months after the siege, Jean de Valette had still not reached a final decision owing to the overall lack of response to his repeated requests for an adequate labour force, plentiful supplies of building material, and enough troops to provide the defensive elements. But with the arrival of Gabrio Serbelloni, prior of Hungary, on 11 March, things began to move as he promised to heal the rift that had developed between the grand master and Don Garcia. On 14 March 1566 the council, in the presence of Serbelloni, officially undertook to build the new city in accordance with the design prepared by Francesco Laparelli. The first stone was laid by Grand Master Jean de Valette on 28 March 1566 in the presence of members of the Order, the bishop of Malta, and a multitude of people.

Work on the fortifications of Valletta, as the city was called, together with its title of *Città Humillissima*, progressed steadily despite the recurrent shortages of money, labour, and building materials. By mid-1567, the fortifications on the land front had begun to take shape and work was then concentrated on finishing the ditch, which had to be dug to a depth of 40 palms, the glacis, the batteries in the flanks of bastions, the sally ports, and the platforms. Work on the lateral sides lagged behind that on the land front where most of the effort was being concentrated, but by 1568 most of the enceinte had been laid out. Laparelli's design for the fortress of Valletta incorporates most of the ingredients of the successful system advocated by the Italians, especially the land front which was the strongest sector of the defences. Owing to the restricted front across the highest point of the peninsula, Laparelli was able to trace an almost straight line of walls with obtuse-angled bastions with two-tiered flanks dominated by cavaliers and protected by a deep ditch. The whole front was anchored at each end by two strong bastions, that of St Michael restricted to a demi-bastion form by the outward projection of the San Andrea platform. Only two of Laparelli's nine proposed cavaliers were built and these were soon found to be too low and had to be later raised considerably.[20]

The new city within the Valletta fortifications was built to a grid pattern with a systematic distribution and division of streets, piazza, and *pomerium,* a Vitruvian concept, using the open space between the urban buildings and the fortress walls for troops to assemble. That part of Laparelli's design which was not executed was the construction of an arsenal and the *manderaggio,* or galley pen. Work on the construction of the *manderaggio* was actually commenced and the stone excavated from the site was used for the

Francesco Laparelli and his fortress of Valletta.

construction of houses, but at a certain depth the material was found to be unsuitable for building. This, together with the realization that the *manderaggio* would not have been safe and large enough to house the Order's galleys, eventually led to the abandonment of the scheme. Laparelli left Malta in 1569 and entrusted the continuation of the work to Gerolamo Cassar. He volunteered for service with the papal fleet and died of the plague at Candia in the following year. By 1571 the Valletta fortifications had reached an advanced stage in their construction for the Order to feel safe enough to transfer its convent there.[21]

The building of the fortified city of Valletta heralded the third and most important phase in the development of the harbour fortifications. This decision was to spark off a chain reaction of fortress-building activity that was to occupy the Order for the rest of its stay on the island. Once committed to their new home, the knights endeavoured to

Capitain Pietro Paolo Floriani.

overlooking Marsa, the low-lying marshland that had served as a Turkish camp during the Great Siege.

Floriani's plan, however, came in for much criticism from the start. Although the council of the Order sanctioned its construction on 10 December 1635, opposition to the scheme did not diminish, such that one of the commissioners of fortifications, Balì Gattinara, resigned in protest.[23] The criticism levelled against Floriani's design centred around the fact that the project was too ambitious and required too much money and men to garrison. Nonetheless, work on these fortifications commenced immediately and, by the beginning of February, Floriani had already traced the outline of the works on site. The opponents of Floriani's scheme strongly believed that the Valletta land front could have been more effectively protected had its outerworks been completed and the bastions provided with counterguards but Floriani justified his grandiose scheme by claiming that the large area enclosed by the fortifications would shelter the whole population of Malta during a siege. Floriani, who had to leave Malta on 23 October 1635, entrusted the execution of the project to his assistant Francesco Buonamici, to whom he passed on written instructions.[24]

Once he departed, however, the knights began to doubt the merits of the project.[25] On 17 January 1637, the council decided to consult other renowned experts on the project's feasibility and the knight Vertoa was despatched around Europe to consult the military experts of the time on the matter.[26] In the meantime, a Frenchman by the name of Jardin, then on a visit to the island, confirmed the general criticism raised by Floriani's opponents, mainly that the lines were too large. He proposed that the lines be abandoned and that the Valletta land front be provided with outerworks instead. His plans were approved by the council in May 1638, but by the time that the Order received approval for his scheme from other foreign military experts, interest in Jardin's project had failed and the Order opted to continue with Floriani's design.[27] In the 1640s, work began on the construction of a set of four counterguards on the Valletta land front according to a scheme proposed by the Marquis of St Angelo, who also proposed linking the new outerworks to the Floriana land front by means of two straight walls. Still, work on the Floriana lines progressed quite faithfully in keeping with the original plans.[28]

make the new city a capital and a fortress worthy of their fame, a second Rhodes. The evolution of the fortifications inside the harbour area in the following centuries, including the adjoining harbour of Marsamxett, can be seen to constitute nothing more than the incremental consolidation of the surrounding terrain in an attempt to ensure the security of the Sciberras peninsula. The Order's major preoccupation in the years following the siege right up to the late 1630s was the fortification of Valletta and the security of harbour. This would prove an obsession that would lead the Order to embark upon massive schemes of fortification that would eventually stretch its resources to the limits.

In the early years of the seventeenth century various engineers and military experts realized that, although Valletta was well designed, it lacked strong outerworks, then considered increasingly essential to keep enemy siege batteries as far as possible from the main enceinte. This shortcoming eventually led to the creation of a new enceinte ahead of the old Valletta land front. The work was designed by the Italian papal military engineer Pietro Paolo Floriani during the magistracy of Grand Master Antoine de Paule (1622-36) following growing rumours of an impending Turkish attack in the 1630s.[22] Floriani believed that Valletta, at the time lacking any outerworks whatsoever, was not adapted for contemporary warfare with its high bastions and narrow ditch. He therefore proposed that a new line of fortification be projected, instead, further south at the neck of the peninsula some 1.6 km from St Elmo, on a plateau

Serious complications really began to arise when a new project, the Sta Margherita Lines, designed by Vincenzo Maculano da Firenzuola in order to enclose the Birgu and Senglea fronts, was initiated in 1638, three years after beginning of the Floriana fortifications.[29] After the Great Siege, the towns of Birgu and Senglea, renamed Città Vittoriosa and Città Invicta respectively, were eventually

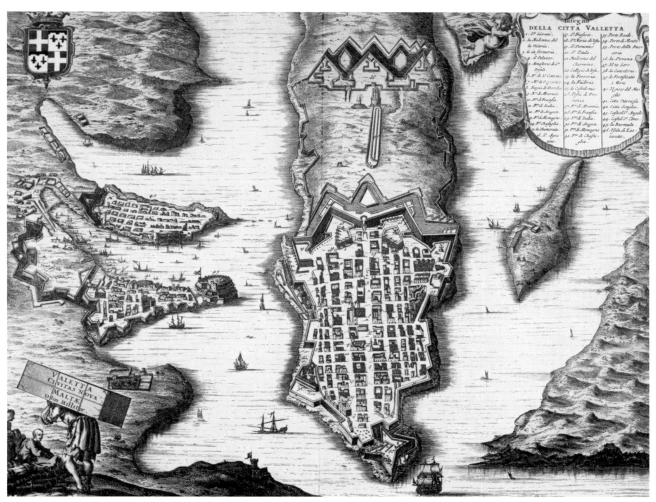

The harbour fortifications in the mid-17th century after Oliver Dapper, 1668. Note the incomplete Sta Margherita enceinte.

repaired but thereafter little was done to improve their defences for, commanded by the surrounding high ground, these remained badly situated 'in a pit like an amphitheatre.'[30] The Sta Margherita enceinte, or Firenzuola lines as this was also called, was intended to secure the enveloping heights and remove once and for all the threat posed to the two fortresses. The money set aside for the project, however, soon ran out and, as a result, work on both the Floriana and Sta Margherita enceintes dragged on interminably and neither scheme was completed before well into the 1700s, by which time both works had been subjected to a number of improvements.

It was the serious crisis brought about by the fall of the Venetian fortress of Candia in Crete to the Turks in 1669, however, that brought about a renewed interest in the Floriana defences and an urgent need to finish off and perfect the design. To review these defences and advise on the best course of action, the knights borrowed from the duke of Tuscany, his military engineer, Antonio Maurizio Valperga.[31] Valperga eventually produced what may be described today as the first masterplan for the defence of

the harbour area and Marsamxett. This envisaged the creation of a ring of fortifications around Valletta, securing all the approaches to the fortress and its habours. The most ambitious element in his scheme was the enclosure of the partially-built Sta Margherita enceinte within an even more massive ring of ramparts, the Cottonera lines. This new bastioned enceinte, named after Grand Master Nicholas Cotoner who commissioned its construction, consisted of a massive trace of eight large bastions, encircling the Sta Margherita and San Salvatore hills and joining the extremities of the old fronts of Vittoriosa and Senglea. Work began in August 1670 and continued incessantly for a decade until the death of the grand master in 1680, by which time the main body of the enceinte had already been laid down under the supervision of Mederico Blondel, the Order's resident engineer.[32] The funds allocated for the Cottonera fortifications had also run out and the new grand master ordered the cessation of the project. As a result the

Grand Master Cotoner showing off his grandiose scheme for the fortification of the southern approaches to the Grand Harbour. Below, Coronelli's map believed to illustrate Valperga's plan for the defence of Valletta and its harbours.

ravelins and cavaliers, together with the ditch and the covertway that were originally proposed by Valperga, were never constructed. The project remained virtually abandoned until well into the eighteenth century when some effort was made to bring the works to completion.

Valperga was also responsible for redesigning the land front of the Floriana lines with the addition of a *braye* (frequently referred to as the *faussebraye*) and a crowned-hornwork, and the building of a new fort at the entrance to the Grand Harbour, Fort Ricasoli, so named after the knight Giovanni Francesco Ricasoli who donated 20,000 scudi towards its construction.[33] The other forts he proposed in his wider scheme for the defence of the harbours, those on the *Isoletto* and Dragut Point, would eventually materialize in the course of the following century but, already by the late 1600s, the harbour fortifications presented a complex system of defence that was already beyond the Order's power to man and maintain. As early as 1645 the French military engineer Louis Nicholas de Clerville remarked that the defence works had to be proportionate to the number of defenders available and it was useless to construct massive works when the Order did not possess the manpower to defend them. These words seem to have gone unheeded.[34]

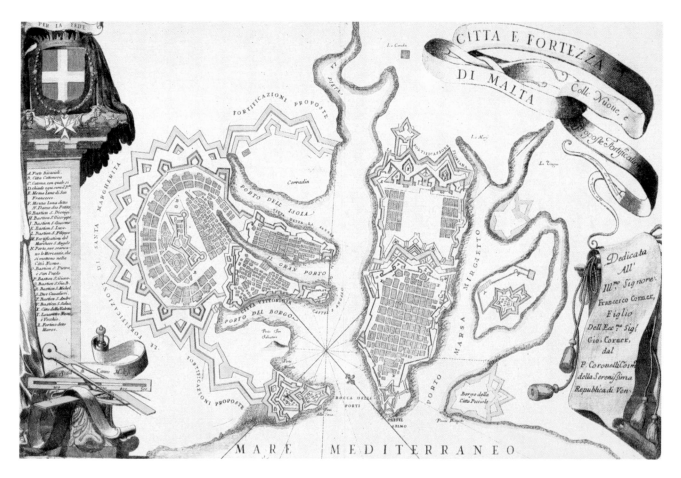

The Development of Military Architecture

The Hospitallers took possession of the Maltese islands and Tripoli at a time when the technological revolution brought about by gunpowder artillery had already conditioned the principles under lying the appearance and development of fortifications.[1] These ideas, which had mainly evolved during the course of the fifteenth century in Italy, had been moulded, by the mid-sixteenth century, into a consistent mode of military architecture that came to be known as the bastioned style of fortification, the *trace italienne,* based on the invention of the pentagonal bastion developed by Italian military engineers. The great merits of the *fronte bastionato* was its flexibility, ease of construction, and adaptability to suit varying conditions - important characteristics which quickly led to its adoption as an international style of fortification.[2]

The bastioned trace gave a fortress not only the necessary solidity to withstand artillery bombardment but also the ability to bring as much fire power as possible to bear on the attackers, combining the destructive power of cannon itself with an aggressive form of mutually flanking defences. Bastions and ramparts were built low and massive, strengthened from the rear by terrepleins made from packing of earth and rubble, and forming wide passage ways along which guns and troops could be deployed and brought to bear on any part of the enceinte, thus leaving no dead ground to be exploited by the enemy. Batteries of guns concealed in the flanks of bastions provided enfilading fire along intervening *cortine* while towering cavaliers, rising from on top of bastions, dominated the surrounding ground.

Throughout the sixteenth century, Italian military engineers were to be found all over the Mediterranean disseminating this new method of fortification. The Hospitaller knights, always ready to build the best fortifications that resources of money, manpower, and military expertise allowed, were quick to follow the current practice and employ them in their service. Indeed, Italian military engineers were already redesigning the Hospitaller fortifications of Rhodes *alla moderna* by the late fifteenth century.[3]

Having invented an effective form of defence against artillery bombardment, Italian engineers also became its leading exponents throughout the sixteenth and early part of the seventeenth centuries and their style of military architecture dominated European fortifications. The cities

Drawings and plans of ideal bastioned fortifications taken from printed treatises by Maggi and Castriotto and Scamozzi.

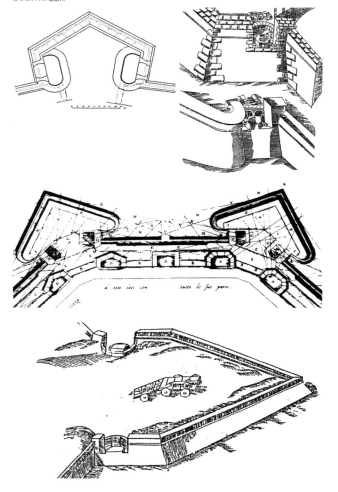

of Vienna, Antwerp, Ghent, Uthrecht, Spandau, and Gratz were all rebuilt to the conventions of the Italian 'school' of military architecture. The Order's fortifications in Malta followed suit. For 150 years leading Italian engineers such as Piccino, Ferramolino, Genga, Lanci, Serbelloni, Rinaldini, Floriani, Firenzuola, Giovanni de' Medici, and Valperga dictated the development of the shape and form of the Hospitallers' military works. The fortifications of Birgu, Senglea, Valletta, Floriana, and the Sta Margherita lines, with their obtuse-angled bastions, flanking orillion batteries, towering cavaliers, rock-hewn ditches, counterguards, and *mezzelune* (detached outerworks projected in front of curtain walls to shield the latter from frontal attacks) all illustrate the Italian principles of defence employed in the particular geographically-confined setting of the Maltese islands. The sixteenth-century fortress of Valletta in particular, is considered to be one of the earliest and finest examples of a newly-built bastioned fortified city erected on a peninsula. None of the greatest cities of Europe by the end of the sixteenth century could boast of a complete and fully-bastioned enceinte. Fortresses with star-shaped bastioned fronts such as Valletta, Palmanuova, Sabbioneta, and Vitry-le-Francois and Villefranche-sur-Meuse were not typical of sixteenth-century urbanism since most cities

existing then were still draped in their medieval enceintes and only partially fortified with additional bastions. Complete bastioned schemes were reserved for new urban foundations, such as Valletta.[4]

Having conceived the basic principles of the bastioned system, however, the Italians failed to take advantage of their lead and the initiative in development of the bastioned fortifications was eventually seized by northern engineers.[5] The Dutch, with able military engineers like Kemps, Menton, and Stevin, developed a variation of the bastioned system which placed greater emphasis on defence in depth, producing detached outerworks such as *faussebrayes,* large ravelins, hornworks, and crownworks that made their defences far more aggressive.[6] The flat nature of their country allowed the design of symmetrical multi-sided enceintes that enabled the construction of obtuse-angled bastions and shorter, more easily defendable, curtains. Significantly, Antonio Maurizio Valperga, the last Italian engineer to be employed by the Order and to have influenced the development of Maltese fortifications in the 1670s, designed his fortifications *all'Olandese* with *faussebraye,* crowned-hornworks, and large hollow bastions - the Cottonera enceinte, Fort Ricasoli and *La Galdiana*.[7]

Vying with the Dutch throughout the seventeenth century were the French. It was actually their military engineers who perfected the bastioned system of defence, successfully achieving a practical combination of the bastioned trace

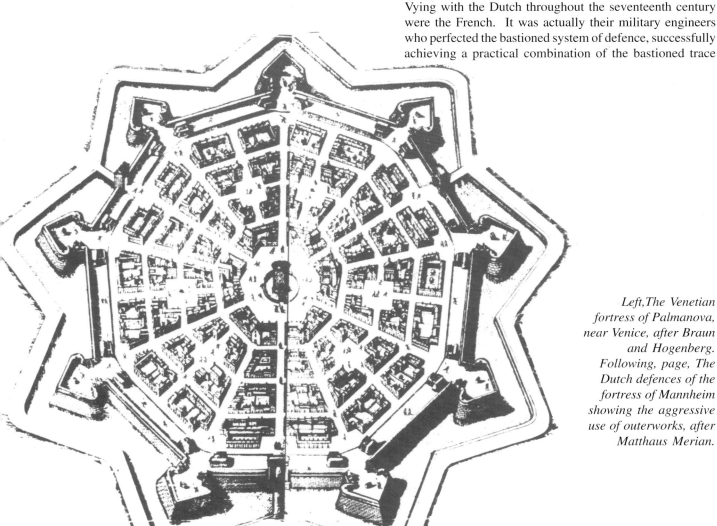

Left,The Venetian fortress of Palmanova, near Venice, after Braun and Hogenberg. Following, page, The Dutch defences of the fortress of Mannheim showing the aggressive use of outerworks, after Matthaus Merian.

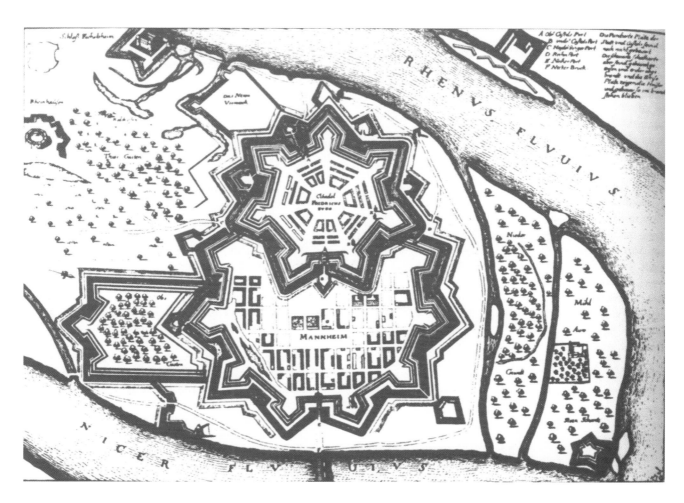

with well-developed systems of outerworks. By the mid-seventeenth century French engineers such as Louis Nicolas de Clerville and Blaise François Comte de Pagan, were already advising the Order on its fortifications. The man who established the French engineering corps as the leading exponents in the art fortification, however, was Sebastian le Prestre de Vauban, himself a practical engineer who in his long military career constructed and remodelled hundreds of fortresses.[8] Although his name is associated with three important systems of defence, he never published a treatise on military architecture. It was his pupils who deduced his methods from his works.

Vauban's first system, which was the most commonly employed, did not vary greatly from contemporary French and Italian developments. It consisted of large bastions and curtains protected by low tenailles connected by simple caponiers to ravelins farther out in the ditch. It had, by then, become the practice to break up the *braye,* or *braga,* into shorter stretches, the portion remaining in front of the curtain wall becoming the tenaille and those in front of ravelins and bastions, counterguards. Surrounding the ditch, on the counterscarp, lay the *strada coperta,* or

covertway, interspersed with traverses, and re-entrant and salient places-of-arms. In his second system, introduced after 1680 as a result of his practical experience, Vauban introduced the detached bastion, as a form of counterguard, to help prolong the defence of fortresses once their bastions had been breached. Curtain walls were fitted with corner casemated gun-towers to provide bombproof batteries. Vauban's third method, employed only once at the fortress of Neuf Briasch, was the most complex, being actually a further development of the second system and comprising fronts of greater depth, with cavaliers on the bastions, counterguards, tenailles, and large ravelins with their own counterguards.[9]

After Vauban's time, his methods were perpetuated by numerous French engineers, chief amongst them Louis de Cormontaigne, who published his *Architecture Militaire* in 1715, and by the Mezieres school of engineering established about 1750.[10] The French engineers who were invited to Malta in the course of the eighteenth century, such as Claude de Colongues, René Jacob de Tigné, Charles François de Mondion, Philippe Maigret, Jean Charles de Folard, and Pontleroy, followed the Cormontaigne school of

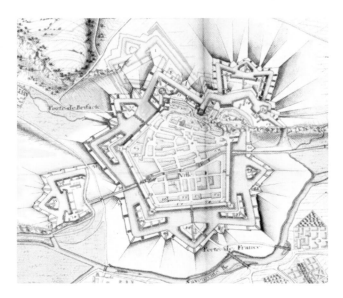

Above, The fortress of Belfort as rebuilt by Vauban. Below, Plans showing the various methods of fortification employed by Vauban.

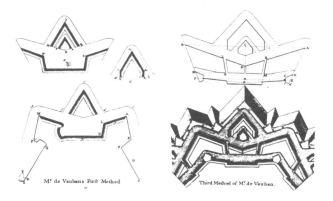

thought and two of the last major fortresses built by the knights in Malta, Fort Manoel and Fort Chambrai, reflect French military architecture at its best.

Late in the eighteenth century, the supremacy of the bastioned system came to be increasingly challenged by the growing popularity of the tenaille trace revived and developed by Marc Rene, Marquis de Montalembert, but originally proposed by Alghisi in the sixteenth century.[11] Montalembert's ideas were first accepted by the Germans, where a tradition in favour of the tenaille over the curtain had long been sought. The supremacy of the tenaille trace, consisting of a series of triangular redans forming a saw-edged front, was that it did away with curtain walls and enabled a greater concentration of guns to make full use of the increased effective range of which the latest weapons were then capable. Montalembert added counterguards beyond the tenaille trace and behind these, two-storey

circular towers. This system, known as the *perpendicular fortification*, was introduced in 1776.[12]

In 1777 Montalembert introduced his *polygonal fortification*, making use of tremendously powerful casemated caponiers, three floors high, armed with 27 guns and numerous musketry loopholes.[13] Fort Tigné, the last significant fortified work built by the knights in Malta after 1792, and designed by the Order's resident French military engineer, Tousard, does reflect a break from the traditional bastioned trace in its use of casemated tower and counterscarp galleries. Undoubtedly, this was a work inspired by the writings of Montalembert, but more particularly by the lunettes built by Jean Claude Eleonore Lemichaud D'Arçon.[14] Ironically, Montalembert's pioneering ideas found little favour in France as most French engineers clung to the traditional concepts established by Vauban, but his concepts were quickly taken up and developed by the Germans in Prussia. That his ideas were being implemented in Malta in 1793 by a French engineer proves the growing popularity of a style of fortification that eventually became the established method of fortress-building during the course of the following century. The British military, on taking over Malta in 1800, were very impressed by the design of Fort Tigné, considering it to be an excellent example of a flankless fort and went on to build similar defences in the Baltic.

Below, A triangular casemated fort designed by Montalembert in 1774 for L'Ile d'Aix.

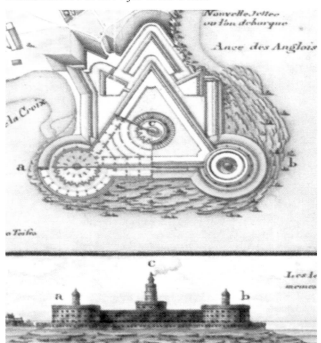

Ramparts of Stone
Building Materials and Techniques

'The rocks were not only cut into fortifications, but likewise into artillery to defend these fortifications'

P. Brydone - 1773

To construct their fortifications in Malta, the knights employed what building materials the island could offer. With wood and soil being scarce, the only building material in abundant supply was stone. In fact the Maltese islands are composed almost entirely of limestone, and one stratum, known as *tal-franka* (Globigerina limestone) provided the traditional chief building material. A pale yellowish, soft stone, known as *franka,* it provided an excellent medium for the construction of gunpowder fortifications since it was easily worked but hardened on exposure to air and weathered reasonably well.[1] Although various quarry sites existed at the time, many of the ramparts were often built with the stone excavated directly from building sites. Frequently, the rocky nature of the local terrain enabled the greater part of the ramparts to be fashioned out of solid rock. At Fort Manoel, for example, only the parapets and a few upper courses of the bastions on the land front needed actually to be constructed from blocks of masonry. Where

exposed to the sea or the southern humid wind known as the *scirocco,* however, the *franka* stone disintegrated rapidly and from the late seventeenth century onwards, coastal forts and fortifications came increasingly to be built with a tougher and more durable stone, *il-gebla taz-Zonqor,* a lower coralline limestone of greyish-white colour.[2]

Building stone was cut in small blocks, dressed with a broad axe, and almost invariably laid in regular courses of smooth-faced ashlar, although blocks of various sizes can be found on different fortifications. During the eighteenth century it became increasingly the practice to use large rusticated stonework with drafted, boldly textured, hacked or picked, faces. Field defences and entrenchments, on the other hand, were generally built of crude rubble work, *pietra a secco,* and differed little form common field walls. Rampart walls were built with an outer and an inner skin of stone, and the space between the two skins being filled in with rubble; the

Heavy blocks of drafted Franka stone such as these were used to construct many of the 18th-century coastal fortifications.

A sketch by the Order's resident military engineer, Francseco Marandon, showing a profile of the parapet at Fort Chambrai, typical of many of the ramparts of other forts in Malta (NLM).

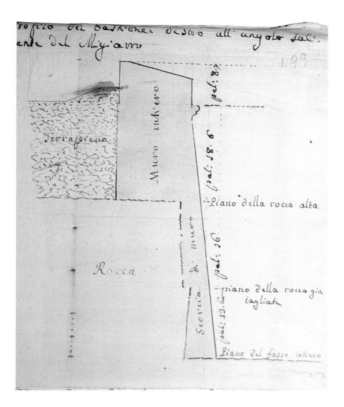

whole united by occasional bonding stones. The exterior walls were increasingly built with a batter to help deflect shot. The local scarcity of timber meant that buildings had to be roofed with stone. Most structures were thus either barrel-vaulted, or had roofs made of small stone slabs, x*orok,* resting on stone-arched ribs thrown across from wall to wall. *Xorok* slabs were covered with a layer of chippings and clay, known as *torba,* on which were laid floor stones or a layer of lime and finely-ground pottery called *deffun,* which had waterproofing properties that kept the interior well dry while at the same time it did not crack when exposed to extreme temperatures.[4]

Stone, too, had to be used to substitute earth, given its scarcity, in the construction of parapets and terrepleins even though this was liable to splinter upon the impact of missiles and aid ricochet. The body of a bastion, where not carved out of solid rock, comprised a mass of packed earth formed from rock chippings, or *mazzacani,* produced during the excavation of the ditch and the quarrying of the stone, and mixed with earth cleared off the site prior to the start of construction works. Normally this mass of earth, known as the terreplein, was packed tight but left uncovered, except where it was necessary to mount or deploy batteries of heavy guns on carriages, when it was then usually covered with flagstones of hard *zonqor* to provide stable gun-platforms. Frequently, the earth-packing near gun embrasures was given more rock chippings than normally applied to terrepleins in order to provide stronger platforms for the deployment of cannon.

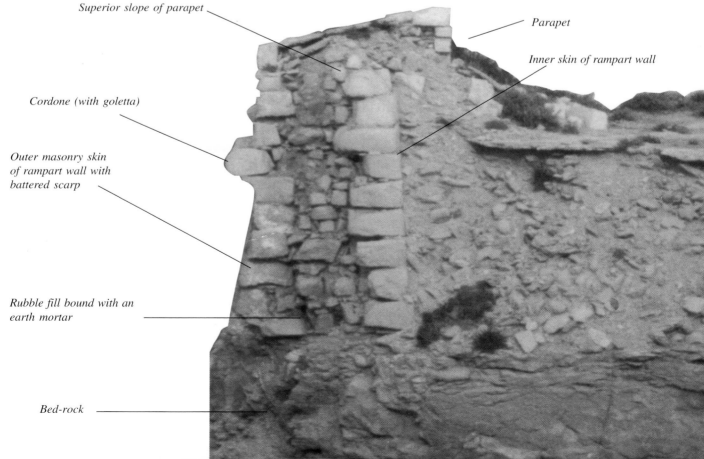

Superior slope of parapet

Parapet

Inner skin of rampart wall

Cordone (with goletta)

Outer masonry skin of rampart wall with battered scarp

Rubble fill bound with an earth mortar

Bed-rock

The soft local stone gave itself easily to ornamentation and many a Baroque gateway was decorated with elaborately carvings and escutcheons.

Besides stone, the Maltese islands were also able to provide the essential components for the production of mortar necessary to bind the masonry. Although earth was frequently employed as a binding agent, particularly for binding rubble-fill and for backing revetment walls, it was normally the practice to use a mortar made from lime, sand, and water. The lime was produced by burning local stone in kilns, known as the *fornace della calcina* or *calcara*. In 1533, for example, a *maestro di calcina* accompanied the engineer Piccino to Tripoli with instructions to erect a kiln in the ditch of the castle.[5]

The Maltese summer heat was high enough to dry out the mortar before it could be used effectively during construction. For this reason Laparelli had advised against building at all during the months of June, July, and August.[6] To prevent the mortar from drying out too quickly, walls were continually bathed with water while the supply of lime was kept moist. On the other hand, winter rain prevented the mortar from setting and it was similarly considered inadvisable to build during the rainy season. Torrential rain caused serious damage to half-finished works and it was essential that all works were rendered rainproof by October. The hydraulic qualities of Maltese lime were often improved with the addition of *pozzolana*, a siliceous volcanic earth imported from Italy.[7] The mixture of lime and *pozzolana* had cement-like properties and was also effectively used to waterproof the head of walls and parapets when flagstones and capstones were not employed.

Below, A casemated rampart constructed from a series of adjoining barrel-vaults. The piers supporting each vault, known as counterforts, served mainly to stiffen the outer wall of the rampart. The space provided by such casemates was frequently used either as covered gun emplacements, with the guns firing through embrasures, as magazines or stores, or sometimes even as living quarters for troops and poor peasants alike, despite the lack of sanitary facilities.

Terreplein composed of a packing of earth mixed with rock-chippings (mazzacani)

Platform or Piattaforma

Inner revetment of terreplein to hold earth packing from spilling out into the fort

The skill of the Maltese builders is dramatically illustrated in this arcone situated in the bastion of Provence, Floriana, attributed to the Maltese architect, Giovanni Barbara.

An Island Fortress in the Mediterranean
The Completion of a Scheme

By the end of the sixteenth century, the old medieval defences of Mdina and Gozo had improved very little from those which the knights had found when they came to Malta in 1530. The first to receive some form of artillery defence was Mdina which was fitted out with a couple of small bastions in the years prior to the siege. The Gozo citadel, on the other hand, hardly received any attention for the knights realized that they could derive very little military advantage from the possession of this puny land-locked stronghold. At best, its only merit lay in its convenience as a refuge for the local population in times of danger. Even so, in 1551, the Turks under Sinan Pasha reduced the castle to ruins in the course of a devastating *razzia* in which some 6,000 Gozitans found sheltering within were carried off into slavery.

Although the castle was rebuilt, Gozo remained practically uninhabited for many decades after. In a bid to attract settlers to the island by providing some measure of security through the building a powerful fortress, attempts were made in 1599 to seek a permanent solution for the defence of Gozo. To this end the Order secured the services of Giovanni Rinaldini, an Anconitan engineer.[1] Rinaldini sought to convince the knights not to re-fortify the *Castello* but to construct instead a new fortress on a coastal site, either at Mgarr, Marsalforn, or Della Rena. Rinaldini thought that the best suited was Marsalforn where he estimated a fort could be constructed for the moderate cost of 80,000 *scudi*. The knights, however, were only interested in making alterations to the old castle and so Rinaldini was asked limit his advice to the modification of the old stronghold. His contribution led the Order to initiate the renovation of the *castello* in 1600. Bartolomeo dal Pozzo, an official historian of the Order, states that Rinaldini's design was accepted and quickly executed. However, from his written report, it is clear that his plans was altered by the time the new fortifications were eventually completed in 1620.[2]

The new defences of the *Castello* were those which gave it its present form. Once these modifications were completed, the Order believed that the it would be defensible, an opinion, however, not shared by the majority of the engineers who were to inspect Gozo in the following years. With the exception of Valperga and Tigné, they all advised the Order to abandon the citadel and construct a new fortress at Marsalforn. Amongst those of such opinion was Giovanni de Medici, marquis of St Angelo, who visited the *Castello* in 1640 and confirmed Rinaldini's idea that the citadel should be abandoned in favour of a new fortress although he judged the timing then not opportune. The other alternative measure advocated was the enclosure of the suburb of Rabat within an outer wall at a cost of 10 to 12,000 scudi, an attempt begun prior to Rinaldini's visit and abandoned.[2]

In 1643 the Order actually decided to demolish the *Castello* and to proceed with the construction of the new fortress at Marsalforn which was to be financed by a new tax on wheat, but the Gozitans protested strongly that they were too poor to pay the toll and the Order, realizing that it was unequal to the task of financing the work, decided to postpone the project.[3] Still, two years later in 1645, under threat of a Turkish attack, the citadel was mined for destruction although the Turkish fleet never appeared. The idea was revived again in 1657 when the engineer Francesco Buonamici was

The Gozo citadel in the mid-18th century (NLM).

Grand Master Manoel de Vilhena presenting a plan of the proposed new fortifications of Mdina and its outerworks, designed by the French military engineer Charles François de Mondion, then the Order's resident engineer in charge of fortifications.

dispatched to Gozo to trace out the outline of a new fortress at Marsalforn but the project soon ground to a halt for lack of funds.

Other serious emergencies swept the island in 1670, 1708, 1714, and 1715, and every time criticism of the *Castello*'s military worth was revived. A document entitled 'Progetto per assicurare l'Isola del Gozzo contro ogni attacco del Nemico' shows that the French military mission headed by Tigné was once more evaluating the *Castello*'s defences and proposing the building of a new fortress at Mgarr. As the century progressed, increasing emphasis was laid on coastal defences and the land-locked castle came to be seen as being more and more obsolete until finally, in 1749, a new fort was built at Ras-et-tafal.[4] However, even after the construction of Fort Chambrai, the old citadel was not demolished and never actually lost its importance, mainly because of its central position and the fact that the new city failed to attract settlers.

The thorny question of the defence of the old capital of Malta was also to continue to preoccupy the Order throughout the seventeenth and eighteenth centuries. After the addition of bastions in the years prior to the siege of 1565, the citadel's appearance remained basically unaltered. Moreover, with the building of the new city of Valletta, Mdina, or Città Vecchia as it then came to be known, fell into rapid decline. By 1658, the old city was in a very bad state of repair. It also lacked an effective defence, particularly a wide

ditch and flanking works on the northern part of the enceinte, while the houses of the suburb of Rabat had crept too close to its walls. It is not surprising, therefore, that the various suggestions to abandon the old fortress seemed very attractive to the Order, but when these were made public, the Maltese strongly opposed the idea. The decision to raze the citadel to the ground was, fortunately, never implemented, though suggested many times through the course of the following years.[5]

It was the reign of Grand Master Martin de Redin that brought Mdina a new lease of life. De Redin paid for the repairs to the various bastions and curtains and also initiated the construction of a large central bastion on the land front, setting aside 4,000 *scudi* for the project. Mederico Blondel, the Order's resident engineer, designed the bastion, which was known as the De Redin bastion, and supervised its construction. However, the death of the grand master in 1660 brought the project to an abrupt halt and the fortifications remained half-completed for many a decade after. The earthquake of 1693 severely damaged many buildings in Mdina, destroying the Norman cathedral and shaking the northern enceinte spanning from St Mary bastion to the cathedral. More damage was later caused to the south-western ramparts by the Muscat family who, in the process of enlarging their house, introduced many unauthorized windows into the walls and occupied the *piazza* where the Mdina regiment of urban militia used to assemble.

The true revival of the old city, however, really came with the arrival of French military engineers to Malta in the early decades of the eighteenth century. Although little was done during the reigns of Grand Masters Ramon Perellos and Marc'Antonio Zondadari, most of the French engineers' proposals were implemented during the reign of Grand Master Manoel de Vilhena. In fact, Mdina owes its final form, its palaces, fortifications, and Baroque buildings and gateways, to the works undertaken during this period of its history by the Order's resident French military engineer Charles François de Mondion. The final addition to the defences of Mdina were made during the reign of Grand Master Ramon Despuig with the building of a bastion beneath the cathedral in 1739.[6]

Prior to the 1700s, the position of Mdina was solely that of an outpost, but the adoption of a coastal defensive strategy during the eighteenth century gave the citadel a new role in the island's overall system of defence. The construction of new inland entrenchments along the natural fault at Falca and Naxxar, accentuated further its defensive position. Still, the military engineers who were to accompany the French military expedition during the general emergency of 1761 had a very poor opinion of the old city's ability to withstand a siege and also feared that it could serve to entrench an invading force once it fell to the enemy. Fortunately, their advice to have the citadel razed to the ground was never acted upon.

Throughout most of the fifteenth, sixteenth, and seventeenth centuries, Malta and Gozo were plagued by frequent raids, for the Mediterranean sea was then infested with corsairs and pirates. Many an inhabitant was carried off into slavery during the course of a rapid *razzia*, even though every effort was made by the local militias to watch and guard the islands' shores. Then, unlike today, the remote parts of the island, particularly the northern half, were practically uninhabited for most people preferred to live within the safety, or in the vicinity, of the main fortresses. The outlying areas, with their secluded anchorages, were perilous places exposed to corsair raiding parties. When the knights came to Malta, their main preoccupation was that of securing themselves within the harbour area and for most of the sixteenth century they directed most of their resources and efforts to reaching this goal, giving little attention to the protection of the island's shores.

For the defence of the coast, they retained the same system of militia guards and watch-posts used by the Maltese before 1530. It was only in the early years of the seventeenth century the knights began to construct towers to guard the islands' shores and this was then largely made possible by the generosity of various grand masters. The system of coastal watch-towers which the Order was to set up around the shores of Malta, Gozo, and Comino during the course of the seventeenth century had already been developed in Rhodes. There the knights had built watch-towers around the island and also on neighbouring Kos, Chalki, Tilos, Nisyros, Kalmnos, Leros, and Symi, deploying carrier-pigeons by day and fire-signals by night to relay alarms from tower to tower and tower to fortress all the way up to the Order's stronghold in the city of Rhodes. In all 32 coastal towers were built in the Malta islands, 7 during Wignacourt's reign (1601-20), 9 by Lascaris-Castellar, 14 by De Redin (including one in Gozo), one during the magistracy of Cotoner, and the last in 1720. The towers and other lookout posts were initially manned by the local peasants but this system was changed by De Redin in 1661, who introduced the *Guardia Torre*, a permanent guard paid for by the *Università*, which kept watch all year round. Each tower was to have had one bombardier and three gunners.[7]

After the death of De Redin in 1660, the enthusiasm for coastal defences appears to have waned. For the next five decades the knights showed little interest in coastal defences. It was only at the start of the eighteenth century

Map of the fortifications of the two harbours of Valletta by Palmeus, entitled Plan générale de la ville capitale de Malta, *printed in Paris in 1751.*

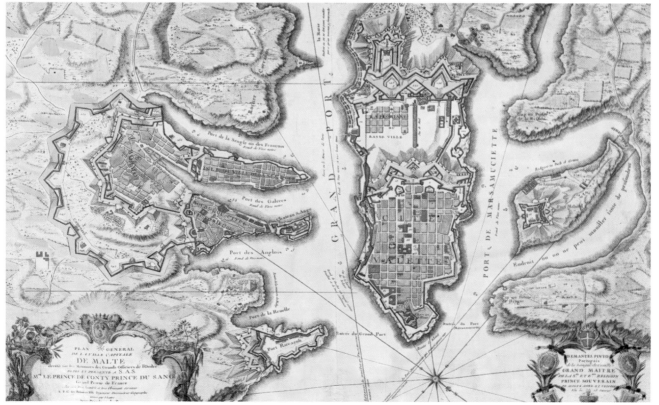

Marble plaque above the entrance to Fort Tigné, the Order's last major work of fortification, erected during the reign of Grand Master de Rohan.

veritable barriers against invasion, designed to engage and hinder an enemy's inland advance upon landing his forces ashore. The coastal entrenchments consisted of long stretches of walls and ditches, frequently rock-hewn, running along the shores of bays and inlets. These were undeniably the most ambitious element of the coastal defence scheme and proved the most costly to build and maintain. Inevitably the planned lines of entrenchments were never completed on the original scale proposed for there were at least 13 miles of coastline to defend.[8]

By attempting to fortify the coastline, the knights had unwittingly embarked on a never-ending task as each battery and redoubt built, required others to ensure that the rest would not be out-flanked. By 1722, when the island was once again faced with the threat of a Turkish attack, the fatal flaw in the ambitious scheme had already become all too clear. The Order could neither muster enough resources to build and arm the fortifications nor did it have enough troops to man even those works it had managed to erect. Consequently, it was decided that the batteries and redoubts in the north of Malta were to be abandoned in the case of an invasion and a set of new entrenchments were built instead on the natural fault dividing the island at Falca Gap and Naxxar. This was intended to reduce the area to be defended by half.[9] Ironically, the difficulties in manning the vast network of coastal batteries, towers, and entrenchments did not deter other French military engineers in 1761 from again advising the Order to endorse and perfect the coastal defence strategy.[10] New work on the construction of more entrenchments and batteries was then once again set in motion and the effort was continued as late as 1792, when the last coastal work, a mortar battery, was erected at Delimara Point.[11] Perhaps the most original tool employed by the knights for the defence of the island's

that the Order, under the influence of French military engineers, once again began to show concern for coastal defence. A vast network of coastal batteries, redoubts, and entrenchments was introduced during the emergency of 1714. These works, however, were not mere lookout posts but

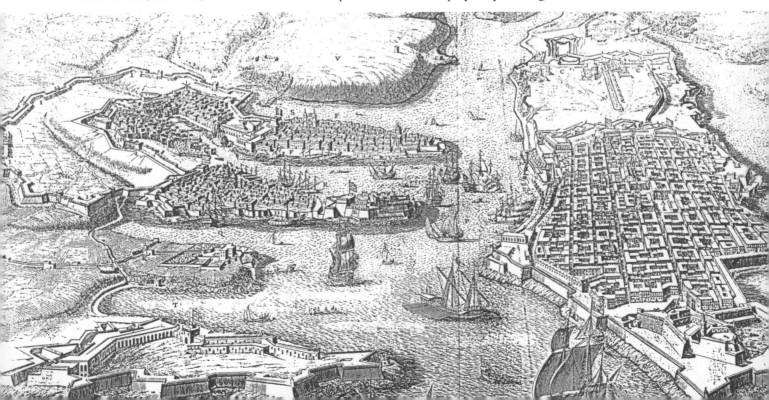

shores was the fougasse, the *fogazza*, a stone-firing mortar excavated in the natural rock. Although the invention of the fougasse is attributed to the resident engineer Francesco Marandon in 1741, the Order's records show that there were already plans for the adoption of a large number of these weapons as early as 1716.[12] The fougasse consisted of a large rock-hewn mortar in the shape of an inclined tumbler facing out to sea. It was designed to fire a large quantity of stones onto approaching enemy boats by means of a powder charge placed at the bottom of the pit. In all 50 fougasses were built in Malta and 14 in Gozo.[13]

At the end of the seventeenth century, the Grand Harbour was more or less well protected but the western side of Valletta was still susceptible to bombardment and attack for the harbour of Marsamxett was devoid of any form of fortification. The greatest threat posed to Valletta was seen to come from the *Isolotto,* a small leaf-shaped island on which was located the quarantine hospital. Many military engineers had pointed out this threat once the strategic value of this little island had begun to emerge with the construction of Valletta. The earliest scheme to fortify the *Isolotto* appears to have been first proposed in 1569, and repeated frequently throughout the course of the seventeenth century, but it was not before 1723 that work was actually commenced on a fort. Originally designed by the French engineer René Jacob de Tigné in 1715, the final design of Fort Manoel, as it was named, was produced by Charles François de Mondion, during his term as the Order's resident military engineer in charge of works of fortification and defence. Financed by the then grand master, Antonio Manoel de Vilhena, in whose honour it was named, the design of Fort Manoel, a classic square fort, with four corner bastions, a ravelin, a tenaille, a covertway, and a glacis, encountered no criticism. Its low silhouette, system of

bastioned trace making the widest use of crossfire to sweep the approaches, together with its aggressive outerworks and countermines, was then in line with the established theories in the science of fortification. So impressive was the fort that in 1761, a delegation of visiting French military engineers, called to review the island's fortifications in preparation for an impending attack, described it as a 'model du fortification fait avec soin.'[14]

With the *Isolotto* secured, the knights then turned their attention to Dragut Point at the mouth of Marsamxett. This strategic promontory commanded the entrance to Marsamxett. During the siege of 1565, the Turkish corsair Dragut had set up a battery of guns there to bombard Fort St Elmo. It was not until 1792, however, that the Order could afford to undertake the construction of a fort on the site and then only with the help of financial donations from its members. Fort Tigné, as the new fort was called, was a very small work by eighteenth century standards, actually more of a large redoubt, but its design was probably the most revolutionary and influential of all the fortifications built by the knights in Malta. Designed by the Order's chief engineer, Stephan de Tousard, its most important features were the lack of bastions and the counterscarp musketry galleries.[15] For the design of Fort Tigné was heavily influenced by the writings of Montalembert and more particularly by the lunettes built by the French general, Jean-Claude Lemichaud D'Arçon. By the end of the eighteenth century, the supremacy of the bastioned system was being challenged by the growing popularity of the tenaille trace. The new style of fortification known as the polygonal system, of which Fort Tigné is one of the earliest examples, was to dominate the art of military architecture through most of the following century. Fort Tigné, too, was the last major work of fortification built by the Order in Malta.

By 1798 the fortifications of Malta constituted a vast, complex network of Renaissance and Baroque permanent gunpowder fortifications. Two centuries of continual building activity had rendered the whole harbour area, indeed the whole island with its coastal towers, batteries and entrenchments, into one large fortress with the city of Valletta as its inner keep. The sheer concentration and volume of the defences coupled with the solidity offered by the local method of stone construction, frequently carved out in virgin rock, made these works some of the most formidable bombproof gunpowder fortifications ever to be constructed prior to the introduction of concrete and the application of iron to defensive works.

The fortifications of Valletta and its harbours in 1798.

The Last Crusaders
Hospitaller Armed Forces in Malta

'It has pleased God, this year 1565 ... that the Order should be attacked in great force by Sultan Suleiman.'

Francesco Balbi di Correggio

The arrival of the knights in Malta occurred during the time when the lightly-armoured common soldier with his arquebus was beginning to achieve supremacy over the heavily armoured nobility. It was only in siege warfare that heavy armour was to survive. Actually, the siege of 1565 limns a closing phase in chivalric warfare, since it represents the last instance where the Hospitaller knight fought out a major land battle as the armoured backbone of the Order's fighting forces in the crusading tradition of Outremer and Rhodes. Technological advances in the late fifteenth and sixteenth centuries had struck a singularly forceful blow at the military supremacy of the heavily armoured warrior and with the introduction of firearms,

Hospitaller knight of the Order of St John wearing typical European half-armour of the type worn during the Great Siege of 1565.

and the adoption of professional standing armies, efficiency in war ceased to be the attribute of the knightly class. D'Aleccio's illustrations of the Great Siege show the knights wearing half-armour and fighting from behind the ramparts, wielding sword, lance, firearms, and cannon as the tactical situation dictated. Of the army of 8,000 men which Grand Master Jean de Valette gathered in Malta in 1565 to resist the Turkish invasion, only 541 were Hospitaller knights. As ever, companies of paid foreign troops and local militia formed the bulk of the Order's forces. Amongst these were companies of Spanish and Italian mercenaries recruited from Spain and Sicily but it was the Maltese militia, mustered from around the island's towns and villages, which formed the bulk of the infantry. [1]

The Order's manpower was deployed among the island's strongholds, with the greatest part concentrated in the harbour area and only token contingents at Gozo and Mdina. The latter, however, also held the Hospitallers' small cavalry detachment and proved an ideal base for reconnoitering Turkish movements. The first to receive the brunt of the Turkish attack was Fort St Elmo. Once Turkish intentions became clear, the grand master reinforced this small fort at the tip of the Sciberras peninsula, which had an ordinary garrison of 80 men under the command of the Piedmontese knight Luigi Broglia, with a further 760 men. Supplied each night under the cover of darkness with munitions and fresh reinforcements of men from Birgu, Fort St Elmo was able to hold out for nearly a month in the face of unrelenting bombardment and assaults before it finally succumbed to the Turkish hordes. With St Elmo out of the way and a safe anchorage assured for their fleet, the Turks then turned their attention to the fortresses of Birgu and Senglea. These they similarly subjected to a relentless and systematic bombardment interspersed with massive infantry assaults.

Facing the knights was a large Turkish army of some 40,000 men, well equipped with siege artillery. The Turks were quick to exploit the high ground that overlooked the Order's fortifications and Turkish engineers made good use of this land feature by setting up powerful batteries with which they hammered and softened the walls in preparation for

Detail from D'Aleccio's frescoes showing Grand Master de Valette directing the defence of the Post of Castile.

major assaults. The unexpected tenacious resistance that they encountered, however, disrupted the Turkish scheme, sapping most of their resources of men and equipment. On many occasions, the jannisaries and sipahis came very close to breaking through the Christian lines yet, in spite of their numerical superiority, they were repeatedly repulsed by Christian defenders holding out amidst the battered and breached ramparts of their fortresses, fighting from behind improvised inner lines of defence erected with the rubble and debris from the ruined walls.[2]

Much dispute has arisen over the siege tactics employed by the Turks; the decision to ignore Mdina, the failure to concentrate all their efforts on Birgu and Senglea from the very start, and their fleets' inability to intercept the Christian reinforcements are all seen as the basic causes of the Turkish defeat. Surely, it was the timely arrival of a 10,000-strong Christian relief force that convinced the Turks to beat a retreat. News of the Hospitallers' victory spread fast but the situation which confronted the Order as the dust of war began to settle down was not encouraging. The fortifications were in ruins, many knights had been killed or wounded, the treasury was empty and heavy debts had been incurred. Worse, there was every prospect that the Turks might return

the following year. The post-siege situation developed painfully as the Order set about rebuilding its military strength, directing all its efforts towards the erection of the fortress of Valletta and equipping it with the artillery and munitions necessary for its defence. The Turkish defeat at the battle of Lepanto in 1571, a naval encounter in which the Order's fleet of galleys took an active part, helped to relieve the island from the threat of attack.[3]

A resurgence of the Turkish menace, however, began to manifest itself again towards the end of the sixteenth century. Once again, large Turkish fleets began to roam the western Mediterranean sea in search of plunder. The knights soon placed their island on a war footing, initiating a new programme of fortification, and rearmament. The reorganization of the militia set-up saw the erection of a string of watch-towers while the defence of the sister island of Gozo was taken in hand with the reconstruction of the old citadel. The sighting of Turkish vessels in the vicinity of Malta and Gozo, frequently led to the call up of the militia. That all these fears of attack were not idle was demonstrated by the Turkish incursion of 1614, when 60 vessels under the command of Khalil Pasha put ashore 5,000 men in the then still unguarded St Thomas bay, ravaging some villages in the south of the island before being compelled to withdraw by the militia force sent out to confront them.[4] In order to guard against similar raids, the knights set about erecting a number of coastal forts and towers. Up until then, the Order was still operating the local medieval militia arrangement whereby every night 'i piu poveri e i più miserabli di detta isola' stood guard at a number of watch-posts around the island's shores.[5] By the mid-seventeenth century, however, this system was no longer considered satisfactory and was replaced by a network of armed watch-towers built at the expense of various grand masters and manned instead by a permanent guard paid for by the *Università*. Plans were also made to raise a corps of 4,000 musketeers from amongst the inhabitants but the reorganized militia force never reached the high standard that had been envisaged.[6]

By 1716, the eight rural regiments of militia, totalling some 3,095 men, had been reformed into six, brigaded into the northern and southern units under the overall command of the *Senescalco*. Each regiment was made up of a number of *Bandiere*, formed from a number of companies.[7] Every village regiment was made up of about twelve companies. A number of small villages, such as Attard, Balzan, Mosta, and Siggiewi, did not have enough men to form their own separate regiment and, therefore, had to attach their respective contingents to the nearest regiment. Each urban settlement, too, had its militia regiment as did the nearby island of Gozo. Around 1700, the Gozitan militia comprised 1,063 men: a 64-strong cavalry detachment, a company of 76 musketeers, an infantry regiment of 434 soldiers and a *stuolo* of 479 men detailed for guard duty around the island.[8]

Soldiers of the Order during the 17th and 18th centuries.

By the mid-eighteenth century, the knights could count upon a total militia force of some 13,000 men.[9] Although an impressive figure, this army comprised an undisciplined and unmotivated mass of peasants, notwithstanding the repeated attempts made to train them on a more efficient basis with proper military training. The knights had no illusion as to the true military value of this body of men, and after the so-called 'Insurrection of the Priests' even their loyalty became suspect. So by 1776, the knights were anxious to raise regular units for the defence of the island. The chapter general of 1777 decreed the formation of two infantry corps, the Regiment of Malta and the Regiment of Cacciatori or Chasseurs.[10] The former was initially made up of 1,200 officers and men and its formation was based on that of a French Regiment of the line. It was composed of two battalions of 600 officers and men, each divided into twelve companies of *fusiliers* and two companies of *grenadiers*. The men were initially all enlisted from abroad, from such places as Avignon, Corsica, and Marseilles but most of these proved to be unreliable and by 1796, the total strength of the regiment had fallen to 521 all ranks, so that Maltese soldiers had to be recruited to make up for foreigners who had left.[11] The regiment of Cacciatori, on the other hand, was a militia infantry unit of volunteers placed under military discipline and was composed of six infantry companies of a hundred men each. By 1778, the total strength of the Cacciatori regiment had decreased to 522 all ranks and the unit was reorganized into five companies, although expanded again, however, to include 1,200 men by 1798.

Left, Musketeer armed with matchlock musket and bandoleer, c.1670.

Left, Grenadier trooper c. 1761 armed with French flint-lock musket. Right, Officer of the Grand Master's Guards c. 1780.

Maintaining regular regiments proved a heavy drain on the Order's resources. The annual expenditure amounted to over a hundred thousand scudi, a large part of which went to pay for salaries. Most of the expenditure was made good by the common treasury with the balance coming from the Cotoner and Manoel foundations, together with those established for Fort St Elmo and St Angelo. As a compensation for this subsidy, the regiment of Malta was bound to provide detachments to help garrison Fort Manoel (87 men), Ricasoli (111 men), St Elmo, and St Angelo.[12] Another significant regiment was that of the grand master's guards, raised in 1701 to protect the magistral palace and the main gates of Valletta. Initially, the strength of this unit was 150 men but by 1798 this had grown to 300.[13] This regiment, however, was more of the grand master's personal bodyguard and was financed directly out of magistral funds.

Undoubtedly, the spearhead of the Order's fighting forces were the marine units which fought on the galleys and warships.[14] These were the Order's front-line troops, continually involved, by their participation in the annual caravans, in numerous sea battles against the Turks and Barbary corsairs. Every year, with the opening of the shipping season, the Order's galleys would depart on naval excursions in search of Muslim shipping, frequently also raiding Turkish interests along the shores of the Mediterranean thus perpetuating their crusading tradition in the manner first evolved in Cyprus and perfected during their sojourn in Rhodes. The frescoes along the corridors in the grand master's palace commemorate many such a naval encounter between the Order's navy and Muslim ships. Inevitably, the naval troops evolved into the Order's most experienced and efficient fighting force and when not serving on the ships and galleys, they helped bolster up the island's garrison, particularly with detachments deployed to man the coastal fortifications. During the eighteenth century, the marine units consisted of two battalions with a total strength of 700 officers and men - the *'battalione delle galere'* and the battalion of the man-of-war. In times of danger, some 1,200 naval gunners were taken off the Order's ships and used to help man the guns of the numerous coastal batteries and entrenchments scattered around the islands.[15]

By the end of 1700s, the extent and magnitude of the fortifications began to pose serious problems. The disastrous loss of revenue from the Order's European commanderies, brought about by the French revolution, impoverished the Order overnight and prevented the knights from maintaining, let alone perfecting, their ponderous defensive network. Already in 1761, when the fortifications had reached more or less their full extent, it was estimated that at least 20,000 men were required for the defence of the island.[16]

Ironically, when an attack by a hostile power did finally materialize in 1798, the enemy was not the Turk but the French under the command of General Napoleon Bonaparte. The French capture of Malta, however, was no accidental affair. General Bonaparte had set his eyes on the island as early as September 1797, realizing both its strategic importance and the need to prevent the British from acquiring the place. The opportunity presented itself in 1798 when a vast French armada carrying over 40,000 men

Left, Trooper of the Regimento di Malta, *c.1777, wearing the white summer uniform. Right, officer and trooper of the* Regimento dei Cacciatori, *c. 1777.*

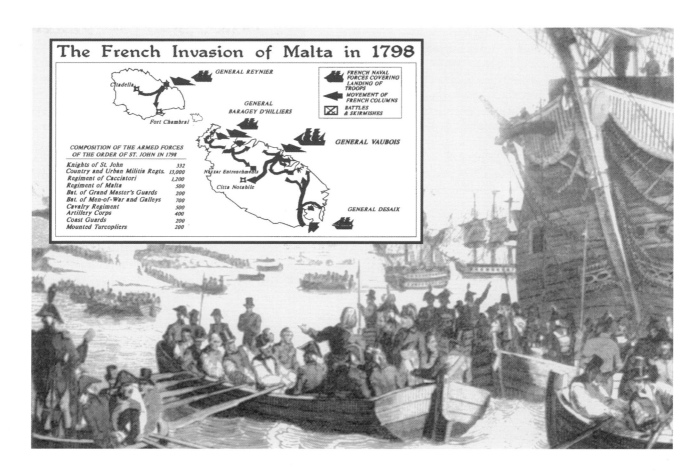

The French Invasion of Malta in 1798

GENERAL REYNIER

Citadella

GENERAL
BARAGEY D'HILLIERS

Fort Chambrai

GENERAL VAUBOIS

FRENCH NAVAL
FORCES COVERING
LANDING OF
TROOPS

MOVEMENT OF
FRENCH COLUMNS

BATTLES
& SKIRMISHES

COMPOSITION OF THE ARMED FORCES
OF THE ORDER OF ST. JOHN IN 1798

Knights of St. John	332
Country and Urban Militia Regts.	13,000
Regiment of Cacciatori	1,200
Regiment of Malta	500
Bat. of Grand Master's Guards	200
Bat. of Men-of-War and Galleys	700
Cavalry Regiment	500
Artillery Corps	400
Coast Guards	200
Mounted Turcopliers	200

Naxxar Entrenchments

Citta Notabile

GENERAL DESAIX

appeared off Malta on its way to Egypt, and attacked the island. French troops were landed at three different areas with the intention of neutralizing the coastal defences but met hardly any resistance from the columns of militia sent out to intercept them, all of whom fled back in panic to the safety of the fortifications after their brief encounters with the French troops.[17]

After securing the coastal defences and island's hinterland, the French troops then converged towards Floriana. The marshal of the Order, the knight De Loras, perceiving the French intentions, ordered a small force of 900 men from the *Regimento di Malta* and the marine battalions to intercept the French columns but this was lulled into a trap and ambushed by Colonel Marmont's troops on the San Giuseppe road. As the French troops took up their positions around the harbour, the situation inside the fortified cities, crowded with terrified civilians and refugees, deteriorated rapidly. Control of the military situation was wrenched out of the hands of the irresolute grand master and the doors of the fortresses were thrown open to Napoleon's troops. As things turned out, the fortifications were never put to the test. The Order had collapsed from within.

General Bonaparte's invasion of Malta was a swift, well-planned, multi-pronged attack that caught the defenders ill-equipped and unprepared (National Museum of Fine Arts). Inset, Diagram showing the manner of the French invasion.

Hospitaller Castles in the

Holy Land

and the Latin East

i

The tour-église on the inner ward of Crac des Chevaliers.

Bait Gibrin

The castle of Bait Gibrin (Bethgibelin) marks the beginning of the Hospitaller military role in the Outremer since it was the first castle that was held by the Order. Bait Gibrin was one of three castles built by King Fulk of Jerusalem in 1136 to confine the Muslim fortress of Ascalon.[1] Together with Tell es-Safi and Gaza, Bait Gibrin was a military post of the highest importance and King Fulk would not have donated it to the Order unless the Hospitallers already possessed some form of military establishment within their organization.[2] Together with the castle, the Hospitallers were given a large tract of surrounding territory including ten villages and these became the first great religious-military lordship in the Holy Land, locally autonomous and controlled by the Hospitallers.[3] Although the capture of the Muslim fortress of Ascalon was not achieved until 1153, the effectiveness of the Hospitallers was quickly recognized and followed up by the grant of other important fortresses.[4] Among the castellans who governed Bait Gibrin was Garnier de Naples who held the office from 1173 to 1176 and was later to become master of the Hospital.[5]

Following the disastrous battle of Hattin in 1186, the Hospitaller garrison at Bait Gibrin, depleted of most of its fighting men, surrendered to Saladin without offering any resistance on the same terms accorded to the defenders of Jerusalem.[6] In 1241 As-Salih Aiyub, the sultan of Egypt, returned Bait Gibrin, together with Belvoir, to the Christians but it is not clear whether it went back to the Hospitallers.[7] Unfortunately, little remains of Bait Gibrin to enable a sufficient reconstruction of the castle. William of Tyre states that it was a 'praessidum muro insuperabili turribus munitissumum' (a strong fortress surrounded by an impregnable wall with towers and ramparts).[8] It appears that Bait Gibrin, like the other castles erected around Ascalon, was a rectangular *castrum* with straight curtain walls and mural towers, and did not include a great tower or donjon. Excavations carried out in 1982 revealed that the castle formed a rectangular plan measuring some 56 m x 53 m with square corner towers.[9] Internally, the stronghold had a rectangular ward similar to that at Belmont.[10] Adjoining the castle was a fortified town, also rectangular in plan and surrounded by a moat. The northern section of the moat, having both scarp and counterscarp made of ashlar, has been preserved. The remains of a number of wall-towers can be distinguished along the south stretch of moat filled in with debris. Along the east side the remains are much more scanty but the line of the walls can still be traced.[11]

Within the ruins of the fortified town, south of the castle, are the remains of a church, storerooms, and other quarters datable to the Crusader period, all built in relatively hard limestone of good workmanship.[12] Only the north aisle of the tri-apsidal church survives today, built from fine ashlar, most of which was re-utilized from earlier Roman and Byzantine buildings.[13]

Belmont

The date at which the Hospitallers first acquired Belmont (Suba) is difficult to assess but this seems to have been around 1140.[1] The castle surely existed by 1169, when there are references to its Hospitaller castellan.[2] Willelmus de Belmonte, a Hospitaller knight, may have been one of its earlier castellans around 1157.[3] In 1186 the castellan was Frere Bernard de Asinaria who, from 1163 onwards, had been the master of the hospice outside Jerusalem.[4]

By 1160 the Hospitallers appear to have been in possession of a number of properties in the territories around Belmont.[5] Amongst the neighbouring castles owned by the Order were Castellum Emaus and Belveer (Qastal).[6] In August 1187, in the wake of the disastrous battle of Hattin, Belmont, most probably already abandoned by its Hospitaller garrison, was occupied by Saladin. Later, in September 1191, Saladin ordered it to be destroyed along with the castles of Toron, Castellum Ernaldi, and Belveer.[7]

Excavations carried out in 1986, have revealed that the castle of Belmont was a twelfth-century concentric stronghold with an inner and outer ward.[8] The nature of the site did not allow a regular plan. Belmont castle had no central keep or donjon.[9] Instead, the central part consisted of a rectangular inner ward crowning the summit of a hill, with vaulted structures set around three sides of an inner courtyard defended by four projecting corner-towers. The open courtyard measured about 13.5 m x 20 m and was flanked by barrel-vaulted rooms. The enceinte of the outer ward described an irregular octagon and enclosed an area of some 11,500 m^2 with the line of battered walls following the contours of the hill. The battered scarp, or talus, is inclined at an angle of around 70 degrees with the lower parts carved from the bed-rock of the hill and the upper sections revetted in fine point-dressed ashlar blocks varying in height between 0.33m and 0.42m at the lower courses and at the quoins, and between 0.21m and 0.36m higher up the scarp.[10] The blocks are set in a hard white lime mortar and are laid end on. Nowhere at Belmont do the walls of the outer ward stand higher than the inclined talus, but most probably, like at Belvoir and Caesarea, the talus would have been surmounted by vertical walls with parapets. Nor are there any traces of any projecting wall-towers and if any existed, their projection would have probably begun at the point where the talus gave way to the vertical wall. The remains of the main gateway are located on the south-east angle of the outer ward.[11]

Between the outer walls and the inner ward on the south-east flank survive the ruins of a barrel-vaulted range, some 6.5m wide, running parallel to the outer wall.[12] These appear to have formed, as at Belvoir, an extended *chemin-de-ronde*. Such vaults would have housed the mercenaries and turcopoles, stores, and stables. The storerooms would have held not only the garrison's food supplies but also the agricultural wealth that the Hospitallers reaped from their surrounding domains.[13] The discovery of a wine press within the courtyard of the inner ward helps underline the economic role played by this medieval castle.[14]

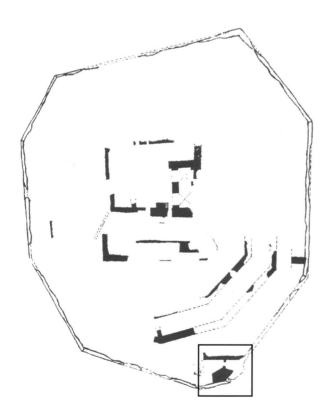

Plan of the remains of the concentric Hospitaller castle of Belmont (after D. Pringle). Note the main entrance to the castle (enclosed box), the various wards, and the inner castle-keep.

Gibelcar

The castle of Gibelcar, also known as Chateau Akkar, was given to the Order, together with Archas, by King Amery I of Jerusalem when Raymond III, count of Tripoli had fallen captive to the Saracens (1164-72) on condition, however, that the knights were to restore and strengthen the castle's defences.[1] Raymond confirmed the Hospitallers in their possession of these strongholds even when released from captivity. The Order continued to hold on to these outposts until shortly after the fall of Crac des Chevaliers in 1271.[2] Prior to the siege of Gibelcar, Baybars had great difficulty transporting the siege engines to the castle due to the rugged mountain terrain. It only took the Saracen army two days of incessant bombardment, however, to effect a breach in the ramparts.[3] They kept up the bombardment for a further seven days, at the end of which the defenders offered to surrender on the favourable term granted them by the sultan.[4]

The ruins of the castle of Gibelcar surmount a large sloping plateau. The area enclosed by the walls, once fitted with square towers and rectangular salients, was divided internally by a *fosse* into two unequal wards. The upper ward, situated to the south, contained the principal tower. This measured 13m x 13m and had a vaulted interior with a staircase leading up to the roof. Its walls were given a pronounced talus and were pierced by two arrow-slits on the south and east sides.[5]

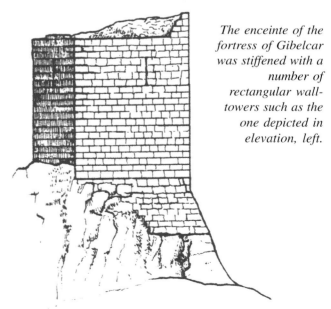

The enceinte of the fortress of Gibelcar was stiffened with a number of rectangular wall-towers such as the one depicted in elevation, left.

Touban

The castle of Touban, also known as *Hosn al-Tufan* and *Tuban*,[1] was ceded to the Hospitallers by Raymond III, count of Tripoli, in July 1180.[2] Touban served as an observation post to the east of Crac.[3] In March 1181 Raymond also gave the Hospitallers a tract of territory surrounding

The castle of Touban (after Deschamps).

The castle of Mont Ferrand (after Deschamps).

The castle of Gibelcar (after Deschamps).

Castellum Melechin.[4] Very little remains have survived from the castle at Touban except for a natural *tell* (hill), revetted with blocks of masonry that once constituted the talus of an octagonal castral ward, similar in many ways to Belmont.[5]

Mont Ferrand

This castle of Mont Ferrand, known also as *Mons Ferrandus* and *Barin*,[1] was donated by Raymond II, count of Tripoli, to the Hospitaller Order in 1142.[2] Situated north-east of the mighty fortress of Crac des Chevaliers, it served mainly as a base for raids directed against the Muslim city of Hama.[3] It was demolished sometime between 1283 and 1289 by Malek al-Mizza, prince of Hama.[4] Like Touban, Mont Ferrand exploited the site of a natural *tell* but was built on a much larger scale and consisted of two adjoining wards. The higher ward, polygonal in plan and similar to Belmont and Touban, formed the main castle, which was large enough to have had concentric defences with an inner ward, while the lower ward appears to have housed a fortified settlement. Only the lower sections of the walls survive for most of the enceinte, showing an inclined talus at the base.

Forbelet

The castle of Forbelet, known also as *Afrabala*, was acquired by the Hospitaller Order around the mid-twelfth century and was dependent on the nearby Hospitaller stronghold of Belvoir.[1] It was attacked and sacked by Saladin in 1183 but was repaired by the Hospitallers who, eventually, had to abandon it after the defeat at the battle of Hattin. It was quickly occupied by Saif-al-Din Mahmud, one of Saladin's generals who used the fort as his main military base for directing the siege of the castle of Belvoir. In 1188 Mahmud was surprised and killed there during a night sortie by the Hospitaller garrison from nearby Belvoir.[2] The surviving remains of the castle of Forbelet show it to have had a substantial donjon or tower-keep, about 26 m² in plan with walls 4 m thick. Only the southern half of the tower survives. This is located in the centre of an Arab village. Some traces of walls show that the tower-keep was enclosed by an outer ward.[3]

Castrum Rubrum

Castrum Rubrum, or *Qal'aat Yahmur,* found on the coast of modern Syria north-west of Crac des Chevaliers, and once located within the territory of the county of Tripoli, is one of the best-preserved examples of the keep-and-bailey type of castles built by the crusaders in the initial period of the Latin occupation of Outremer. The first reference to this castle reaches back to 1177, when Raymond III, count of Tripoli, gave it to the Hospital.[1] Apparently, prior to its being ceded to the Order, the stronghold was in the possession of Raymond of Montolif, to whom the Hospitallers paid 400 besants in compensation the following year.[2]

The main feature of Qal'aat Yahmur is undoubtedly its tower-keep or donjon, sited centrally within the courtyard of a rectangular outer bailey. The tower stands about 12 m high and measures 16m x 14m at the base with walls 1.8m to 2.2m thick.[3] It is divided into two storeys, each floor having four bays of groin-vaults springing from a central pier, the lower one, being square in plan and that on the upper floor, octagonal. The bays on the first floor are separated from one another by transverse arches springing from rounded corbels. The first floor was itself divided into two levels by means of a wooden floor.

The ground floor is entered through a door set in the centre of the east wall while that on the first floor, set on the west side, is approached from a vaulted terrace built between the tower and the outer wall of the bailey. A staircase leads upwards within the thickness of the north wall of the tower to the roof. At present, there is no direct internal communication between any of the floors but originally there could have been such an arrangement since this is found in other similar tower-keeps.[4] There are two types of windows to be found piercing the thickness of the tower walls: splayed arrow-slits and rectangular openings, the latter apparently later insertions. The greatest concentration of arrow-slits faces the main entrance to the castle set in the south wall.[5]

The rectangular outer enceinte enclosing the tower measures some 37m x 42m with walls about 2m thick. The main gateway into the castle, an early crusader feature similar to the north town gateway at Tarsus, is set on the south wall and slightly off-centre. Flanking it to the east is a small solid corner-tower. A similar, but slightly larger,

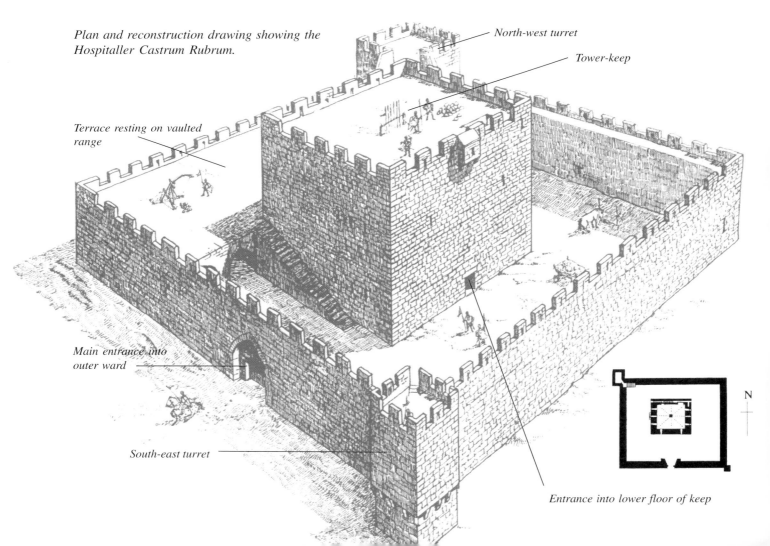

Plan and reconstruction drawing showing the Hospitaller Castrum Rubrum.

North-west turret

Tower-keep

Terrace resting on vaulted range

Main entrance into outer ward

South-east turret

Entrance into lower floor of keep

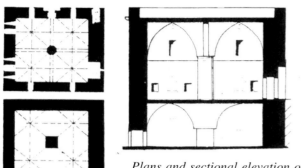

Plans and sectional elevation of f Castrum Rubrum (after Pringle). Right, Sectional elevations of Turris Rubea (after Pringle).

It appears in the list of lands captured by Baybars and most probably it was dismantled as part of the Mameluke policy of reducing the coastal plains to an inhospitable wasteland, in order to discourage further Latin attempts at colonization.[9]

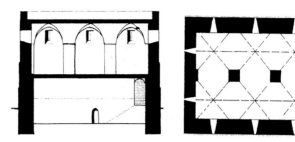

corbelled tower occupies the north-west corner of the outer wall. Both these towers seem to be the product of Hospitaller modifications.

Qula

Remains of a modest Hospitaller agricultural administrative centre, comprising a rectangular tower and a nearby barrel-vaulted building, are still to be seen south-east of Qalansuwa, once a Hospitaller village itself equipped with administrative quarters and a defensive tower.[1] Qula was acquired by the knights in 1181.[2] The tower, which measured about 13m x 17m is mostly demolished with only the north and part of the east side still left standing.[3]

Turris Rubea

Turris Rubea, known also as *Al-Burdj al-Ahmar* (the Red Tower) and *Turriclee,* represents another example of the early keep-and-bailey castles erected by the Crusaders in Outremer during the first half of the twelfth century.[1] This small castle, of which little remains today, was similar in form to *Qal'aat Yahmur* in Syria. The central tower-keep, or donjon, measured 19.7m x 15.5m at the base and had walls 2.2m thick. Internally, the donjon was divided into two floors.[2] The lower one was divided into two barrel vaults and the upper one into six bays of groin-vaults supported by two centrally-mounted masonry piers. The tower was about 13m high and would undoubtedly have been surrounded by a crenellated parapet.[3] The masonry of the tower in those sections which are still standing consists of roughly squared blocks set in courses and bonded with a reddish sandy mortar and small stone pinnings.[4]

Turris Rubea was occupied by the Templars for sometime between 1191 and 1236.[5] After 1236, Guerin, the master of the Hospital, made arrangements for the lease of Turris Rubea but it was not until August 1248 that this small castle, together with other properties in the area, came into Hospitaller possession.[6] The Order paid 800 besants annually as rent and the lease was renewable every 25 years.[7] Turris Rubea, however, disappears from the written record after 1265, when it seems to have been captured by Sultan Baybars following the fall of Caearea and Arsuf.[8]

Recordane

A defensive tower with mill and dam formed part of the Hospitaller properties in the plain of Acre, at the Spring of Kurdana, the crusader Recordane.[1] The mill was in Hospitaller hands by 1154 but the tower appears to date to the late twelfth and early thirteenth century.[2] This tower, known also as *Khirbat Kurdana*, stands on a rock-hewn crag projecting outwards into a mill-pond with three wheel-chambers flanking it to the south (the third was added during the Ottoman period) and a single one to the north.[3] Internally the tower is divided into two storeys. The ground floor is groin-vaulted with a broad pointed-arch doorway set into the west wall. This was defended by a box-machicoulis resting on a pair of large corbels at roof level. The north wall is pierced by three arrow-slits of the long splayed type with dove-tailed bases while the south wall was defended by a single arrow-slit.[4]

Bordj Arab

The tower of Bordj Arab, situated in the plain of Akkar, was one of a number of watch-posts and outposts of Crac des Chevaliers.[1] Bordj Arab is one of the best preserved of such towers and measures some 14m x 13.4m and is divided internally into two storeys. The outer masonry is of a cruder type than that at Bordj es-Sabi, empoying both rough blocks of stone and re-utilized ashlar blocks from ancient Byzantine and Roman buildings.[2] Bordj Miar, another Hospitaller tower, can be found much farther to the west of Qal'aat Yahmur.

Bordj es-Sabi

The tower of Bordj es-Sabi, situated along the route from the fortress of Marqab and the sea, was one of a number of small fortifications which were designed as watch-posts and policing stations rather than as defensive structures. Bordj es-Sabi acted also as advanced post of the fortress of Marqab and was used to warn of the approach of enemy armies with smoke and fire signals.[1] It consists of a large square tower, similar in scale and appearance to most donjons of crusader fortresses. The only difference was that, here, the tower stood isolated and unprotected by an outer enceinte. In plan, the tower measures 15m x 15m and, internally, consisted of two vaulted storeys. The main entrance was located at ground-floor level in a similar fashion to other crusader donjons. It led directly into the interior of the tower with an opening for a staircase in the right side of the passage. The staircase was set into the thickness of the wall and proceded upwards to the second floor. Both floors were fitted with arrow-slits, two on each side. Another staircase led up to the roof. This was once ringed by a parapet with box-machicoulis of which only the corbels now survive. Each box-machicoulis rested on two corbels, except for the corner ones, which had three. The tower is built of rough rectangular stones of dark grey basalt bonded with white mortar. Larger blocks were used as quoins.[2]

Left, and below, The tower of Bordj es-Sabi (Deschamps).
Above, The tower of Bordj Arab (Deschamps).

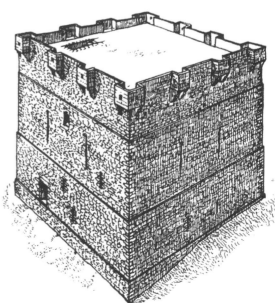

Coliath

The small crusader castle of coliath, situated in the plain of Akkar, north of Tripoli, was ceded to the Order of St John by the count of Tripoli.[1] The exact date of this donation, however, has still to be determined. The castle was confirmed in Hospitaller possession by Pope Eugene III in 1153.[2] Coliath was captured and destroyed by Malek al-Adel sometime between 1207 and 1208.[3] Willbrand of Lodenburg saw it in ruins shortly afterwards in 1212.[4]

The castle of Coliath is a typical example of the *'castrum'* type of stronghold built on a level site. It consisted of a rectangular enceinte measuring some 63m x 56 m, fitted with corner towers and rectangular projections in the centre of the north, west, and south walls. A fifth rectangular tower projected outwards from the centre of the east wall. Equipped with four arrow slits, it appears that this tower was purposely built to provide some protection to the adjoining main entrance into the stronghold.

Internally, two of the curtain walls, namely those spanning the north and south sides, were backed by long barrel-vaulted buildings, their roofs serving as fighting platforms. The castle's outer walls are more than two metres thick with the masonry being of the drafted type, typical of the early crusader-built strongholds in Outremer. A dry rock-hewn fosse surrounded the castle.[5]

Aerial view and plan of the castle of Coliath. Note the similarity in the plan of this crusader castle to that of late Roman frontier forts (Deschamps).

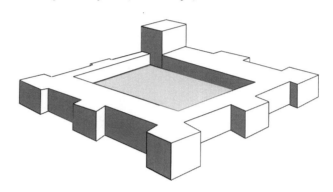

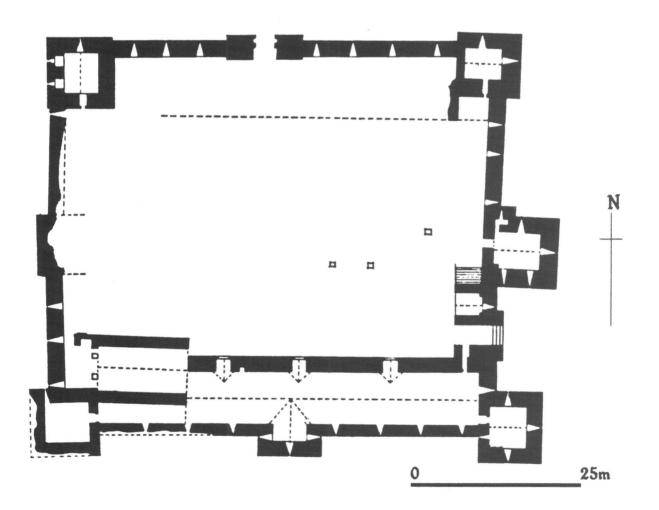

N

0   25m

Belvoir

The castle of Belvoir, the crusader *Coquetem (Kaukab al-Hawa)*, was built in the second half of the twelfth century and is considered one of the greatest crusader achievements in the field of military architecture.[1] Although smaller than the gigantic Crac des Chevaliers in Syria, it is nonetheless unique in the sense that it represents one of the earliest attempts at concentric defences.[2] The castle of Belvoir was sold to the Hospitallers by Ive Velos in 1168 for 1400 besants.[3] It is not clear if the castle had already acquired its final form before it came into Hospitaller possession. Architectural evidence, however, tends to show that the castle constituted a homogeneous entity and was all built during the same period.[4]

Even though heavily ruined, the castle of Belvoir still presents an impressive site. Originally, it consisted of three distinct units: a large fosse, an outer enceinte, and an inner castrum. The fosse, an impressive engineering feat in itself, was cut into the rock of a basaltic plateau overlooking the Jordan valley. Most of the masonry used in the construction of the castle was actually excavated from the ditch itself. The outermost enceinte, nearly rectangular in plan, has quadrangular towers at each corner and additional towers in the centre of each side. Three of the seven towers of the outer enceinte have posterns set in the flanks of their lower battered half, leading from inside the castle to the fosse via L-shaped staircases. The posterns face that part of the plateau where the enemy siege engines could have been mounted. The talus, or battered lower half of the towers, reaches up to the ground level of the outer ward. From here the curtain and towers rose perpendicularly to an unknown height since the walls from the ground-level upwards are missing. Together with the depth of the fosse (12m), the ramparts of the castle must have formed an obstacle some 20m in height. A line of long vaulted halls set behind the curtain wall provided a spacious and solid fighting platform together with a continuous walkway. Behind this lies the courtyard of the inner ward, varying between 14m and 16m wide, and forming the open space between the two enceintes.[5]

On the east side of the castle, a large rectangular tower, isolated from the main enceinte, served as a sort of barbican.[6] The remains of this structure have often been interpreted as donjon[7] but it appears instead to have been designed to command an elaborate entrance route into the castle via the east inner gateway across a bridge and up a ramp. The inner arched gate appears to have been closed by double doors and portcullis as evidenced by surviving pivot holes, bolt openings, and grooves. Another gateway was located on the west side of the castle.

The inner castrum, rectangular in plan, measures some 50m square and was defended by four solid and identical corner towers, whereas the west wall had an additional gate-tower at its centre which provided access into the inner ward. All that remains of these towers is the low talus (about 2m high) revetted with drafted masonry typical of early crusader constructions.[8] The inner courtyard had three doorways set on the north and south sides which once led into the vaulted halls that served as living quarters, stores, and service rooms. The kitchen was located in the south section near the small postern leading to outer ward. The inner ward was also fitted with its own cistern. The living quarters of the Hospitaller brethren were most probably above ground-floor level. A large structure, once supported on three arches, spanned the whole width of the courtyard. Remnants of a chapel with a bas-relief of St Matthew were found inside the castle.[9] The outer walls of the inner castrum, about 3m thick, were pierced by a number of arrow-slits.

After the disastrous battle of Hattin, the Hospitaller castles contributed much to the defence of Latin Syria in the face of Saladin's onslaught. The most heroic defence was provided by the garrison of Belvoir, reinforced by the Hospitaller survivors from Hattin and amply provisioned.[10] Saladin was too preoccupied to direct the siege of the castle himself but sent one of his generals, Saif-ad-Din Mahmud, to isolate the castle. The latter occupied the nearby, and probably abandoned, castle of Forbelet.[11] In January 1188, however, the Hospitaller garrison of Belvoir made a sortie at dawn and caught the enemy camp by surprise, inflicting heavy losses on the Muslims. Saladin sent another force of 500 cavalry under the command of Qaimaz and, after disbanding his army, he personally went to attend the siege of Belvoir but soon realized the inadequacies of his force.[12] Therefore, he withdrew in May leaving Qaimaz with his troops to blockade the castle and returned again in December 1188 with a large and well-equipped force. When the Hospitallers refused his terms for surrender, Saladin began a systematic assault on the castle. Using miners, he breached the outer walls and unleashed a series of assaults under the cover of concentrated volleys of arrows.[13] As the outer enceinte succumbed to Saladin's troops, the defenders retreated into the inner ward of the castle. Since they could hardly expect any assistance from the their hard-pressed allies, the knights offered to surrender if their lives were spared. Saladin agreed and, after six weeks of stubborn resistance, Belvoir was occupied by the Saracens on 5 January 1189.[14]

In 1241, Belvoir was ceded back to the Christians by the sultan of Egypt, As-Salih Aiyub, but it does not appear that the castle was given back to its Hospitaller owners.[15] Archaeological evidence does not indicate that the Franks actually reoccupied the castle at all after 1188.[16]

Right, Plan of the castle of Belvoir (after M. Ben-Dov). Below, Reconstruction of Belvoir castle.

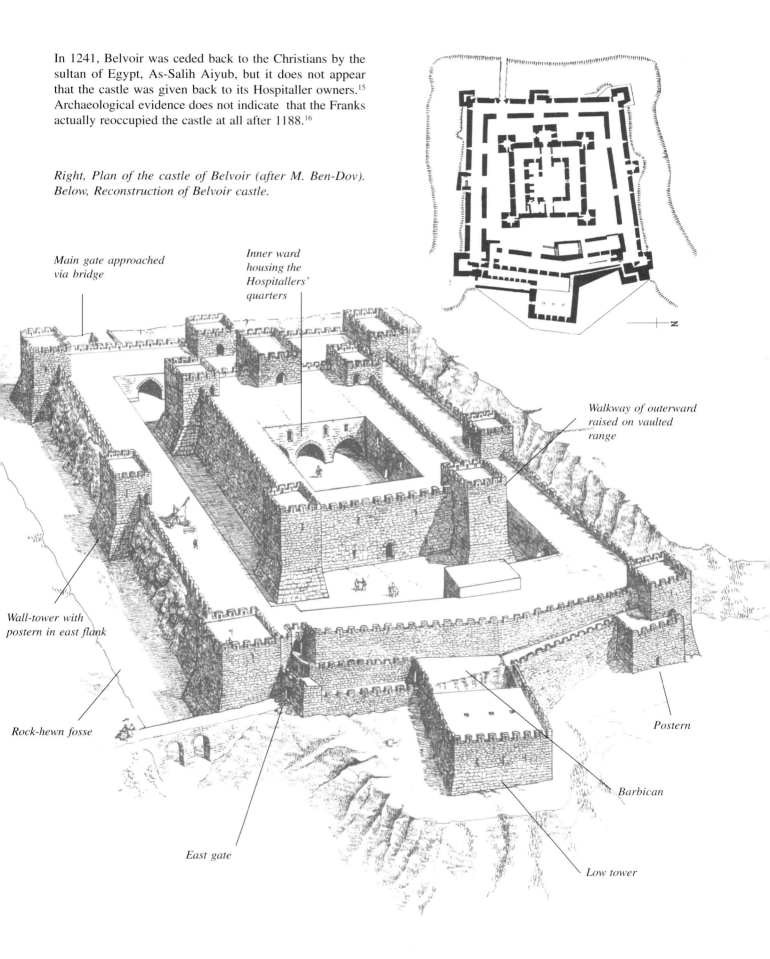

Main gate approached via bridge

Inner ward housing the Hospitallers' quarters

Walkway of outerward raised on vaulted range

Wall-tower with postern in east flank

Rock-hewn fosse

Postern

East gate

Barbican

Low tower

Crac des Chevaliers
Hosn el-Akrad

Crac des Chevaliers stands on a bare black-basalt hill above the Homs Gap, an important pass through which runs the road from Tripoli to Homs, some 35 km from the Mediterranean and about 650 m above sea-level.[1] In its day it commanded a position of great strategic importance as it looked out over a fertile plain to the east and, as a result, was occupied even before the Crusades by a Kurdish garrison, hence its earlier name Hosn al-Akrad, the stronghold of the Kurds.[2] The Franks first appeared in the vicinity of the castle in the first week of January 1099.[3] The Muslim peasants of the surrounding districts sought refuge, together with their livestock and cattle, within Hosn al-Akrad.[4] The crusaders under Raymond de Saint-Gilles immediately set about attacking the castle and scaling its walls. Fearing that all was lost, the peasants threw open the castle doors and allowed part of their herd of cattle to escape.[5] The Franks, forgetting the battle at this opportunity for plunder, hurled themselves after the cattle. Seeing the ensuing confusion, the defenders made a sortie and attacked the Christian camp and nearly captured the Frankish commander. That same night, taking advantage of the darkness, the Saracens slipped noiselessly away and in the following morning the Franks found an empty fortress. For several days in February 1099,[6] the Franks used the stronghold as their headquarters but it was only permanently occupied by the Christians in 1110 when Tancred, prince of Antioch, took it for the benefit of the Pons of Tripoli.[7] Then in 1142 Raymond I, count of Tripoli, ceded it to the Hospitallers in whose hands it remained until it was lost to Baybars in 1271.[8] The Hospitallers made Crac the centre of their network of castles and towers in Tripoli and entirely remodelled it over the years.

The present-day concentric castle is much different from the eleventh-century stronghold when it was first acquired by the Order. In all, one can distinguish four major building phases in the expansion and remodelling of the castle. The earliest phase corresponds to the pre-crusader fortress, the Kurdish Hosn al-Akard, of which very little survives. The second phase involves the early crusader reconstruction of the castle and most of this can be found incorporated into the walls of the inner ward. Deschamps was able to distinguish the oldest parts of the castle by studying the various methods employed in the dressing of masonry. At Crac, the oldest form was the drafted masonry found mostly on the walls of the inner ward which once formed part of

the eleventh-century crusader castle.[9] The main elements contained in this early enclosure were a gateway set between two rectangular towers, a chapel, a rectangular tower with buttress-machicoulis and postern, two other towers, and the adjoining curtain walls, sections of which are hidden behind the great talus.[10] The curtain walls were lined internally with a continuous ring of vaulted buildings that served also as a *chemin-de-ronde*. The chapel, consisting internally of three vaults and a semi-polygonal apse is, however, a Romanesque building of the twelfth century.

One of the most interesting structures inside the castle is undoubtedly the tower with the three large buttress-machicoulis. The type of buttress-machicolation found on this tower betrays a strong Arab influence and the tower itself, placed as it is asymmetrically onto a rectangular and well-planned enceinte, suggests that it was rebuilt on its pre-crusader foundations.

The position of the castle was a strong one protected by sloping ground on three of its sides. Only on the south side, where the ground rises in front of the fortifications, were the defences less secure but, there, a large fosse was cut to isolate the fortress from any direct access. This ditch was later incorporated into the castle's outer ward. Even in its early crusader form the castle of Hosn el-Akrad looked strong enough to have dissuaded Saladin from attacking it in 1187, then at the height of his fortunes.[11] Notwithstanding, and probably as a result of an earthquake which hit Crac in 1196, it was very thoroughly reconstructed and enlarged.[12] During these works the north and east sections of the old castle were left unaltered but the weaker south and west fronts were encased in a large pronounced talus and the original towers replaced by larger rounded ones. The talus on the south side of the inner ward rose from the fosse which was soon converted into the *berqule,* or great cistern, providing the garrison with a large water supply.[13] The castle was then enclosed within a larger outer enceinte stiffened with a number of towers. As a result, the original ramparts came to form the inner ward of the new fortress.

On the south side of the remodelled old castle, the side that faced the main approach to the stronghold, the new ramparts were projected considerably in front of the older walls. Deschamps was the first to discover a passage within the large talus and noted that the inner walls inside this passage belonged to the early crusader stronghold since these were made up of the drafted type of masonry similar to that found on other existing parts of the older castle, such as the chapel.[14] Here were built the strongest of the castles defences - three massive and solidly built towers rising majestically from the sloping talus and set very close together. The westernmost of these (tower A) is a rounded

View of the inner enceinte and the postern in the flank of the tower with the buttress-machicolation.

tower while the other two are D-shaped in plan and much larger. The upper room of tower A opens onto a large arched window with floral enrichment. This pleasant apartment appears to have been the castellan's quarters or that set aside for the master whenever he was visiting the castle.[15] The middle tower (tower B) has two upper chambers which seem to have housed the quarters of the Hospitaller brethren. There are known to have been 60 *equites* amongst the garrison of Crac in 1255 and this massive tower, together with its similarly built neighbour (tower C), would have provided adequate accommodation.[16] These quarters were isolated by a gap in the lower vaults, a *saut-de-loup*, which could only be crossed by a movable bridge thus affording the Hospitaller knights some degree of protection against an unexpected mutiny or insurrection by the mercenary contingent in the garrison. Cathcart King believed that this was the primary function of this close group of towers and not that of a true a donjon or keep, since none of the three great towers, nor the three together, were independently defensible. As a matter of fact there was no internal communication between the floors and no arrow slits were directed towards the inner courtyard, while the doors were unfortified and quite defenceless.[17]

Around the same time that the old castle was remodelled, an exterior line of defence was added, carrying the perimeter of the castle farther outwards. On the east side, this enclosed the zigzagging approach up into the castle. Later in the thirteenth century this approach was reconstructed to form the present main entrance known as the Great Ramp.[18] Beginning at an arched gate situated in the face of a rectangular tower (tower 11), the ramp rises gradually up a vaulted tunnel, with open sections at intervals, for about 100m before it turns sharply northwards along the second leg and continues for another 50m before it ends at fore-tower (E) that leads towards the old gate (H) into the inner ward. This passage, or covered way, was wide enough to allow mounted knights to ride on horseback all the way into the heart of the fortress. Although the outer gate itself in tower 11 was a relatively-weak and not an easily-defensible structure, once inside the ramp any attacker would immediately have come up against an internal double gate just behind tower 10. Beyond that point the covered way divided, one path continuing up the ramp, the other turning to the west into the open space between the outer and inner wards. Another gate (M) provided access to the south front. There was no gate in fore-tower E.

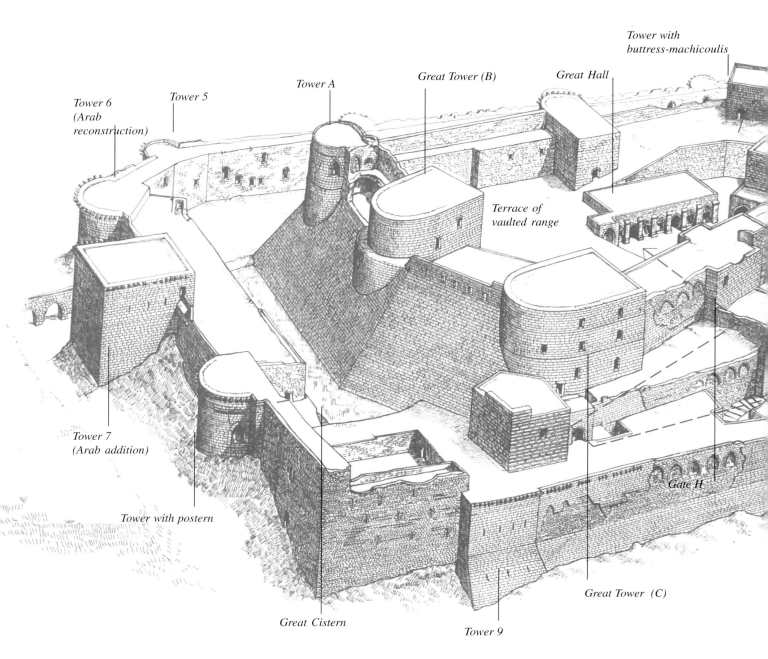

Tower 6
(Arab
reconstruction)

Tower 5

Tower A

Great Tower (B)

Great Hall

Tower with
buttress-machicoulis

Terrace of
vaulted range

Tower 7
(Arab addition)

Tower with postern

Gate H

Great Cistern

Tower 9

Great Tower (C)

Considerable effort was also invested in remodelling the courtyard of the old castle, now the inner ward, which was rebuilt with two different levels. The higher courtyard to the south, just to the rear of the three great towers, rests on top of a great vaulted hall which opens on to the level of the lower courtyard. One of the most imposing non-military buildings erected by the knights in this area was the great hall.

The outer enceinte was equipped with a long straight curtain wall stiffened at regular intervals with wall-towers. Along the western side the castle was defended by four identical semicircular towers. Both towers and adjoining curtain walls were fitted with merlons and a row of box-machicoulis, while the towers were each pierced by three arrow-slits. A fifth tower (tower 1), similar to the others, occupied part of the north front and was enfiled by an adjoining rectangular tower, later rebuilt with a rounded face. This stands adjacent to a small defended entrance known as the Barbican of Nicholas Lorne, constable of Marqab between 1250 and 1254 and datable to the mid-thirteenth century by an inscription which reads 'Au tens de Fre(re) Nicioli Lorne fu fete ceste barbacane'.[19] To the south of the barbican the curtain wall between towers 12 and 11 is very roughly built with crudely-hewn and undressed stonework, much unlike the fine ashlars employed throughout the rest of the enceinte. Deschamps suggested that, together with another similar short stretch of wall at the south-east corner of the outer enceinte, these crudely-built sections may have been erected during a period when the Order's resources were at a low ebb.[20] On the other hand, these could also represent hurried rebuilding efforts carried out to rectify damage inflicted by earthquakes, very common in the region.

On the south front the outer enceinte consisted of three rounded towers but this part of the enceinte underwent considerable alterations during the post-Hospitaller period

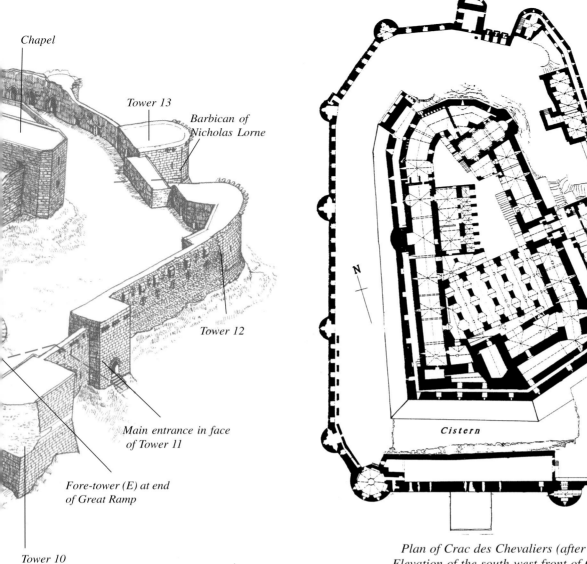

Chapel

Tower 13

Barbican of
Nicholas Lorne

Tower 12

Main entrance in face
of Tower 11

Fore-tower (E) at end
of Great Ramp

Tower 10

N

Cistern

0   15m

Plan of Crac des Chevaliers (after Deschamps). Below,
Elevation of the south-west front of Crac des Chevaliers.
Bottom, Elevation of the inner ward along the same
front, showing the massive talus.

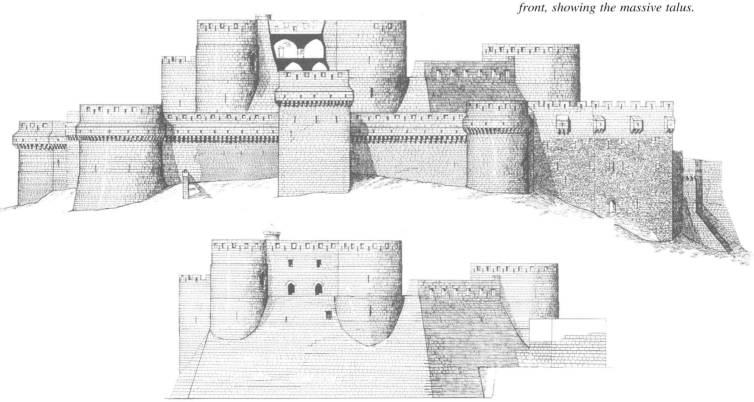

*Crac des Chevaliers as seen from the east (below) and
west (above).*

Above, left, View of Crac from the west and the main towers and talus on the inner ward (right). Bottom left, Tower with postern along the south-west front. Main picture, Crac as seen from the adjoining modern suburb.

mainly as a result of the rebuilding of the castle by Baybars to make good those sections of the walls mined and demolished during his siege of Crac in 1271.[21] The Arab works in this sector constitute the great rectangular tower (7) and the nearby round tower (6). The only original tower to be found on the south front, tower 8, has a large arched gate built into its left side. Deschamps considered this structure to have been a late Hospitaller addition because of the very presence of the large opening itself and also because the portcullis was actually situated in the gorge of tower 9, a rectangular tower with pronounced talus situated just to its rear.[22] A short distance to the east of tower 8 sits a small postern above which are two sizable openings in the wall that are thought to be groves for the chains of a drawbridge.

Undoubtedly, both gates were built to provide access to the large triangular outerwork, similar in many ways to a ravelin, that was erected on the south of the castle. Judging by the amount of black balsalt used in its construction, it is thought that this outerwork was built late in the life of the castle, prior to its surrender to the Mamelukes. Whatever

form of defences this outerwork actually possessed is difficult to ascertain at present. The silted condition of the two lateral rock-hewn ditches suggests that the masonry of its walls may have fallen down its scarp. Rey suggested that the outerwork was protected by a wooden palisade but, given the local scarcity of timber, this may not have been the case.[23] It also seems unlikely that the Hospitallers would have failed to have strengthened the walls of such an important advanced work, at least with some form of dry walling or light masonry similar to the crudely built wall found between towers 11 and 12.

Throughout the twelfth and thirteenth centuries Crac des Chevaliers served as a headquarters from where Hospitaller knights controlled their territories and strongholds and also as a base for conducting raids into enemy territories. This 'key to the Christian Lands'[24] was considered to be 'the greatest and strongest of the castles of the Hospitallers, exceedingly injurious to the Saracens' owing to its aggressive garrison which fulfilled the Hospitaller policy of unrelenting raids into neighbouring Muslim states.[25] Increasingly during the thirteenth century Crac and its sister

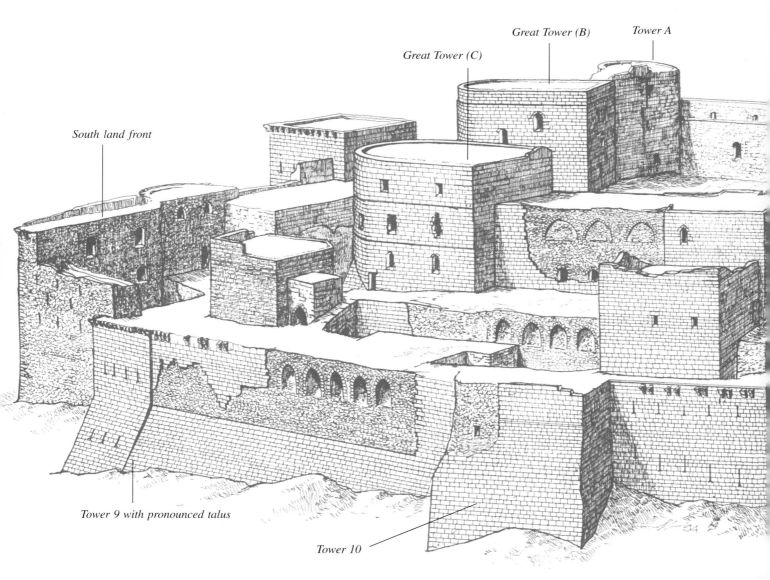

Great Tower (C)

Great Tower (B)   *Tower A*

South land front

Tower 9 with pronounced talus

Tower 10

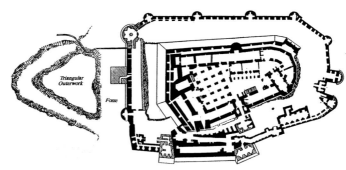

Above, Crac des Chevaliers as seen from the south-west (after Rey). The aquaduct spanning the ditch on the land front of the fortress was a post-Hospitaller addition, as was the large rectangular tower. Right, Plan of Crac des Chevaliers and its triangular outerwork. Below, General aerial view of Crac from the east.

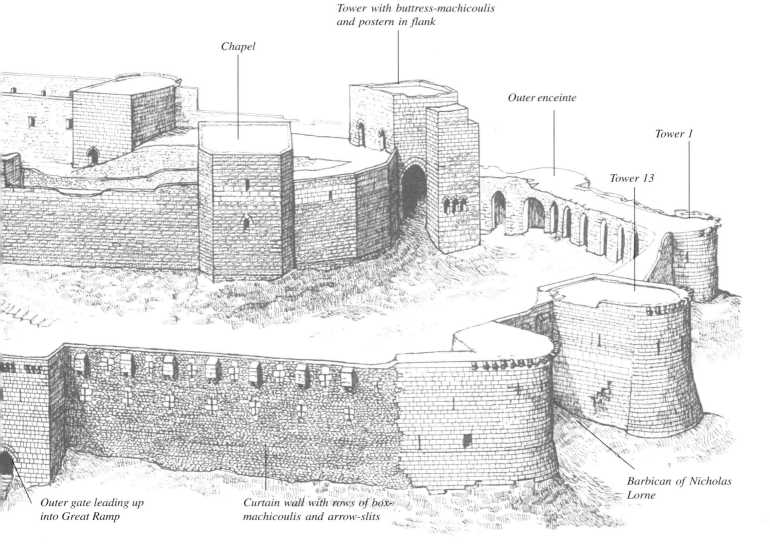

Chapel

Tower with buttress-machicoulis
and postern in flank

Outer enceinte

Tower 1

Tower 13

Barbican of Nicholas
Lorne

Outer gate leading up
into Great Ramp

Curtain wall with rows of box-
machicoulis and arrow-slits

fortress of Marqab began to seriously attract the attentions of the Muslims. As a result, Hospitaller territories were attacked and many of the Order's subjects were carried away into slavery. Crac itself was besieged by large Saracen armies in 1207, 1218, and 1265.[26] By then, the master of the Hospital, Hugh Revel, was harbouring grave doubts about the Order's ability to hold on to Crac in the face of an ever-daring and aggressive Baybars.[27] Indeed two years later the Mamelukes descended by surprise on Crac and attacked it.[28] Although the Hospitaller garrison was hard put to hold the castle, and its first sortie against the attackers was put to flight, the knights managed to survive the ordeal.

Following the failure of the second crusade of St Louis, Baybars was soon to return and on 3 March 1271 he appeared before Crac in force and quickly set up his mangonels in battery.[29] The first to fall to the Mamelukes was the *burgus*, the fortified suburb, standing in the shadow of the mighty fortress. No traces of this suburb seem to have been unearthed to date. Owing to a spell of heavy rain, the Saracen siege engines could not be brought to bear against the castle.[30] However, by 21 March, the second *bashuriya* (this apparently refers to the triangular outerwork mentioned earlier) was overrun and the sultan immediately

set his miners to work on the walls of the fortress.[31] Eight days later the south-west tower (6) collapsed and the Muslims stormed into the courtyard of the outer ward, slaughtering the peasants found sheltering there and those knights who had failed to gain the safety of the *qulla,* the inner castle.[32] The Hospitaller garrison, however, held out from behind the formidable ramparts and towers of the inner ward for more than ten days until 8 April. They only surrendered after being offered favourable terms, apparently after being presented with a forged permission to yield. The knights were allowed to retire to Tripoli.[33]

Once in Muslim hands, Sultan Baybars set about executing a number of new major works at Crac both to repair the damaged caused by his own attack on the fortress and also to add a number of improvements for the defence of the castle. Amongst these was the re-erection, but on a much larger scale, of tower 6 which had been demolished by mining and the building of a massive rectangular tower in the centre of the south front to replace tower 7.[34]

The Great Tower (C), below, overlooks the east section of the castle's enceinte and the passage leading up from the great ramp.

The Fortress of Marqab

The origins of the mighty fortress of Marqab (Margat) date back to the eleventh century. It appears to have been built by the Arabs around 1062[1] and was then captured by the Byzantines in 1104 during the course of a raiding expedition by Admiral Cantacuzene. It later fell again into Saracen hands[2] until finally captured by the Franks in 1117-18. Thereafter the fortress was to form the seat of one of the mightiest seigneurial families in the principality of Antioch, the Mazoirs.[3] Around 1181the Hospitallers began to purchase, little by little, many of the estates that belonged to the large domain of Renaud II Mazoir. On his death, his son Bertrand Mazoir, who could not afford to defend the territory, sold the fortress of Marqab to the Hospitallers for an annual payment of 2,200 Saracen besants - this was still being paid to his heirs in 1269.[4] Amongst the signatures on the deed of acquisition dated 1 February 1186, are those of the castellan of Crac des Chevaliers and *frere Henri*, the first castellan of Marqab.[5] Like at Crac des Chevaliers and Apamee, the Hospitallers acquired not only the possession of Marqab but also all the rights of lordship, including liege-lordship, over the knights in the fief. They also owed no service to the prince of Antioch and were not obliged to share their spoils of war. Moreover, the Hospitallers had the right to conduct their own treaties with neighbouring Muslims irrespective of any other agreements made by the prince.[6]

With the acquisition of the mighty fortress of Marqab the Hospitallers effectively took over the defence of the southern territory of the principality of Antioch and also of the northern reaches of the county of Tripoli against the Assassins and other Saracens in the region. Among the many properties which came with the fortress there were four other castles which were dependent on Marqab, namely Cademois, Laicas, Malaicas, and Bokeibas.[7] A year after the Hospitallers took over Marqab, the Franks in the East suffered a major defeat at Hattin and, as a consequence, northern Syria was soon invaded by Saladin. Marqab, well provisioned and almost impregnable, was one of the few fortresses which did not follow the same fate as Sahyun, Bourzey, and Shoghr-Bakas. Actually, Saladin had great difficulty moving his troops along the road in the vicinity of this mighty stronghold.[8]

After the fall of Jerusalem in 1187, the Hospitallers made Marqab the seat of the Order's government and it remained so for a number of years before this was transferred to Acre

in 1191.[9] From Marqab, the Hospitallers conducted unceasing raids into neighbouring Muslim territories. In retaliation for these incursions the sultan of Aleppo sent a large force under the command of Moubariz ad din Akdia to attack Marqab in 1205.[10] In the ensuing siege many of its wall-towers were destroyed. Fortunately for the Hospitallers, however, the Muslim general was killed by an arrow and the Saracens were forced to retreat at the moment when the Christians thought they were about to lose the place. During this period important chapter generals were held at Marqab in 1204, 1205, and 1206.[11] The raids on the nearby Muslim territories did not cease and in the following decades the Hospitallers continued to utilize Crac and Marqab as bases for raids on Homs, Hama, and Ba'rin. Such attacks were motivated by the desire to maintain payments of tribute. Willbrand of Oldenburg noted in 1212 that the Arabs around Marqab were obliged to pay the Hospitallers 2,000 marks a year in tribute.[12] In 1242 Grand Master Pierre de Vieille-Bride went personally to Marqab in order to direct operations against Aleppo.[13]

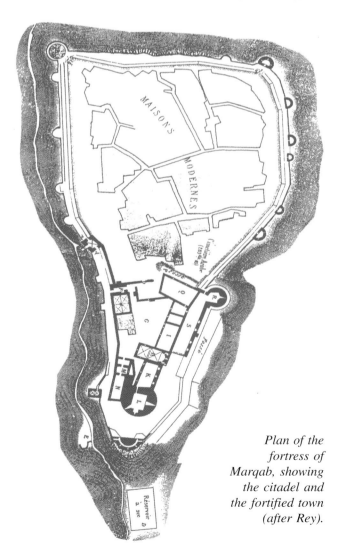

Plan of the fortress of Marqab, showing the citadel and the fortified town (after Rey).

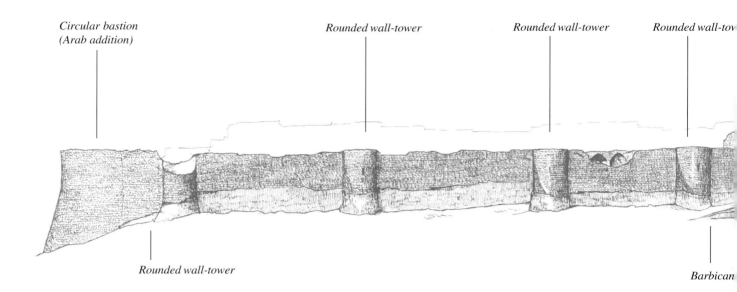

Circular bastion
(Arab addition)

Rounded wall-tower

Rounded wall-tower

Rounded wall-tov

Rounded wall-tower

Barbican

After 1261 Sultan Baybars subjected the Christian territories to annual raids and in 1269-70, he twice advanced towards Marqab but on each occasion was forced to return to Hama owing to bad weather.[14] Following the fall of Crac des Chevaliers in 1271, the Hospitaller position was reduced to the area around Marqab. This, however, the Hospitallers continued to hold quite strongly. Even though the Hospitallers in Marqab were still able, occasionally, to take the initiative in performing aggressive raids, these were isolated instances compared to the level of influence they enjoyed in the region earlier in the century. In 1279 the fortress was subjected to yet another siege, this time by an army under the command of Balban al-Tabbakhi, the governor of Crac.[15] The garrison of Marqab comprised of some 200 Hospitaller brethren and an equal number of infantry, heroically held out, losing only one knight and 12 sergeants.[16] Wilbrand of Oldenburg reported that the fortress was garrisoned by a 1,000 men in 1212, including the Hospitallers. Each night, 4 knights and 28 soldiers guarded the castle.[17]

On 17 April 1285 a large Mamluke army, well-provisioned and supplied with siege engines, appeared off Marqab.[18] During the fiercely fought siege that followed, the Muslims made considerable use of siege-engines although some of those which were placed too close to the walls of the fortress were destroyed by the defenders' own weapons. The Saracens also made extensive use of mining and one mine which was set on fire penetrated so deep into the fortress that the *Tour de l'Esperance*, a main tower, was believed to be about to collapse and the Hospitallers were obliged to surrender.[19] Twenty-five Hospitallers, the full complement of knights engaged in garrisoning Marqab, were allowed to leave the castle with their arms.[20]

The present day fortress of Marqab, which represents one of the best preserved crusader fortresses in the east, is still basically the same castle, except for a few post-1285 Saracen alterations, that the Hospitallers surrendered to the Mamelukes in 1285. The fortress comprises of a large triangular enceinte enclosing within both it the fortified village and a citadel at the southern salient. The citadel, which incorporated the buildings of the Hospitallers - the church, refectory, main hall and so on, into a sort of *collachium,* was more of a fortified complex of buildings rather than a castle. Its main defences were those of the outer enceinte where one still finds three rectangular wall-towers dating to the pre-1186 Mazoirite period. One of these, tower 2, contains the remains of a gateway.

The main defensive feature of the citadel, or castle, was the large circular donjon (R) which was constructed by the Hospitallers sometime between 1186 and 1203. This massive tower, 20.8m in diameter, dominates the southern salient of the fortress. Together with the rectangular keep at Sahyun (Saone), the donjon at Marqab is considered by many to represent one of the most important works of Latin military architecture in Syria.[21] Internally, the donjon is divided into two storeys each with a square vaulted room, the lower one having a single arrow-slit while the upper one, two arrow-slits and a two windows, and all about 2.5m high. The roof of the donjon was enclosed by a parapet ,now mostly demolished, which was also equipped with arrow slits and a number of box-machicoulis of which only a few corbels survive.

Above, Elevation of the west front of the fortress of Marqab. Right, the fortress of Marqab from the east.

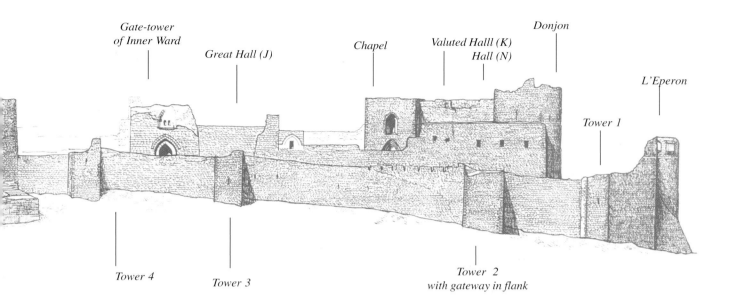

Gate-tower
of Inner Ward

Great Hall (J)

Chapel

Valuted Halll (K)
Hall (N)

Donjon

L'Eperon

Tower 1

Tower 4

Tower 3

Tower 2
with gateway in flank

Adjoining the donjon, to the west, is a large rectangular vaulted building (N) of a later construction than the tower itself. Next to this building is another vaulted structure and beneath both works lie two large, partially-underground vaults which were built in the Mazoirite period. The southernmost of these rests below building N and the other, about 60m long, is pierced by seven arrow-slits which overlook the passage up the ramp rising from within tower 2. This vaulted hall spans directly towards the great hall (J), now mostly ruined but still retaining enough of its decorated rib arches to show the heavy late thirteenth-century French influence in its design.[22] Adjoining the great hall, is a rectangular gate-tower or barbican leading into the inner ward of the castle. The passage from the main entrance leads directly into a large room and from there the passage turns sharply to the right before opening out into the inner courtyard. Above the entrance gate there once was another chamber which Deschamps believed to have served as the personal quarters of the castellan.[23]

North of the donjon, and adjoining it, is a large rectangular vaulted building (K) which appears to have been erected during the same phase of construction as the donjon itself. This consists of two storeys with a platform at roof-level, once enclosed by a crenellated parapet. The wall linking the donjon to building K contains the staircase that leads to the upper floors, all of which are inter-linked. Inside the ground floor hall lies a cistern, while the east wall is

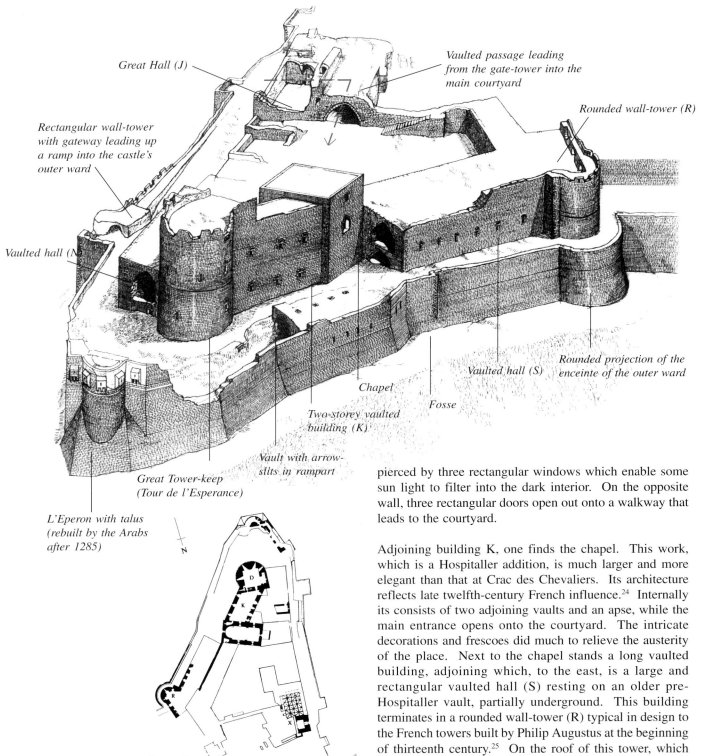

Great Hall (J)

Vaulted passage leading
from the gate-tower into the
main courtyard

Rounded wall-tower (R)

Rectangular wall-tower
with gateway leading up
a ramp into the castle's
outer ward

Vaulted hall (N

Rounded projection of the
enceinte of the outer ward

Vaulted hall (S)

Chapel

Fosse

Two-storey vaulted
building (K)

Vault with arrow-
slits in rampart

Great Tower-keep
(Tour de l'Esperance)

L'Eperon with talus
(rebuilt by the Arabs
after 1285)

N

0   20m

Plans of the castle
of Marqab
showing, above,
the keep and main
buildings and,
below, the
underground
vaults
(Deschamps).

pierced by three rectangular windows which enable some
sun light to filter into the dark interior. On the opposite
wall, three rectangular doors open out onto a walkway that
leads to the courtyard.

Adjoining building K, one finds the chapel. This work,
which is a Hospitaller addition, is much larger and more
elegant than that at Crac des Chevaliers. Its architecture
reflects late twelfth-century French influence.[24] Internally
its consists of two adjoining vaults and an apse, while the
main entrance opens onto the courtyard. The intricate
decorations and frescoes did much to relieve the austerity
of the place. Next to the chapel stands a long vaulted
building, adjoining which, to the east, is a large and
rectangular vaulted hall (S) resting on an older pre-
Hospitaller vault, partially underground. This building
terminates in a rounded wall-tower (R) typical in design to
the French towers built by Philip Augustus at the beginning
of thirteenth century.[25] On the roof of this tower, which
measures some 11.4 m in diameter, lies an elevated *chemin-
de-ronde* with two levels of defences and a crenellated
parapet resting on a line of four vaulted arrow-slits - an
arrangement similar to that found at Sahyun. To the east,
the tower is preceded by a semicircular projection of the
outer ward. Tower R projects northwards and links to a
short stretch of curtain wall that gives it a similar
appearance to the D-shaped towers at Crac. The north wall
which once separated the castle from the rest of the town is
partially demolished and in ruins and, consequently, difficult
to define.

The outer enceinte of the fortress can be divided into two
sections. The first, and oldest, part is that section which

envelopes the trace of the castle at the south salient and the second is the large trace of two concentric walls enclosing the adjoining town. The section which encloses the south salient forms roughly a triangular plan. The west side still retains three rectangular wall-towers (together with the remains of a fourth) which date to the pre-Hospitaller period. Tower 2 has a gateway set into its south flank. North of this tower lies a long stretch of curtain wall fitted with five arrow-slits. This is linked to a smaller rectangular wall-tower which has a single arrow-slit on each of its three faces and a small postern set in its north flank. A short distance farther north is yet another small rectangular wall-tower, linked to which is a large gate-tower, or barbican, built after 1200.[26] The barbican itself is approached by a stepped L-shaped ramp, with the second leg of the ramp traversing an arched bridge. The immediate approaches to the gateway were once shielded between two traverse-like walls, fitted with arrow-slits. The gateway itself was flanked by two arrow-slits and defended by a box-machicoulis of which there still survive four corbels.

The entrance passage opens onto a vaulted square room while another arched opening in the centre of the south wall ensured a bent entrance into the fortress. The upper vaulted storey, reached by a staircase set into the thickness of the east wall, has collapsed leaving only the walls to the west and south, the latter pierced by a large arched window

The wall-tower (R) that guards the eastern extremity of the citadel of Marqab. Above, right, One of the rounded wall-towers along the perimeter of the fortress.

with two stone benches. To the east, the outer enceinte enveloping the inner ward of the castle is largely Hospitaller work, but a large underground vault (D), dates back to the Mazoirite period.[27]

The enceinte enclosing the village consists of two concentric walls. The inner enclosure, devoid of wall towers and defended only by arrow-slits, is for the most part ruined and some traces show it to have had a battered lower half. The outer enceinte is fitted with 12 semicircular wall-towers (one of which was replaced by a massive circular bastion during the later Arab period) nearly all identical in plan and resembling similar towers found on the outerward of Crac des Chevaliers. Four of these towers are in a ruinous state and all seem to have had, internally, a single vaulted room provided with arrow-slits. The remains of a rectangular wall-tower can be seen roughly half-way along the long stretch of walls to the north.

The fortress of Marqab was undoubtedly one of the greatest Hospitaller strongholds in Outremer. The great vaulted magazines which the knights added to this castle could absorb an annual harvest of 500 cartloads of crops.[28] According to Willbrand of Oldenburg, the Hospitallers at Marqab held enough stocks of supplies to sustain themselves for five years. Ironically, the castle only held out for six weeks before the knights surrendered it to the Mamelukes in 1285.[29]

Silifke

The castle of Silifke, which in the twelfth century frequently changed hands in the border wars between Armenia and Byzantium, was ceded to the Hospitallers sometime after 1210.[1] It was attacked by Kai-Kaus in 1216-17, but the knights repulsed the attack and held onto this remotest of all their outposts until 1224 when they sold it back to the Armenian kingdom.[2]

The castle of Silifke is sited on the top of a steep-sided ridge overlooking the river Saleph. In plan it is approximately oval in shape with eight rounded towers preceded by an antemurale. Several parts of the circuit were lined internally with long vaulted buildings attached to the walls. Externally, the castle is protected by a ditch around most of the enceinte though not towards the east and north-east where the grounds falls steeply and where a ramp ascends towards the main entrance instead. There is also a postern on the opposite west extremity of the castle.[3]

The barbican, below, commands the main entrance into the fortress of Marqab. Previous page, The Hospitaller chapel at Marqab.

Ascalon

In 1243 Emperor Frederick II entrusted the fortified coastal city of Ascalon, situated on the shores of the Mediterranean north of Gaza and Jaffa, to the Hospitallers.[1] Earlier in 1241the fortress had been refortified by Richard of Cornwall.[2] The Hospitallers began to strengthen its defences in 1244, the cost of which works Frederick II promised to refund to the Order.[3] In April 1247 Ascalon was besieged by an Egyptian army but the fortress held out until the following October.[4]

The defences of Ascalon consisted of a semicircular trace of walls stiffened by a citadel which once stood on an artificial *tell* located at the northern end of the fortress.[5] According to Richard of Cornwall the citadel, now no longer in existence, had a double wall encircling it and high towers and ramparts, square-hewn stones, and cut columns of marble.[6] Veritably, marble through-columns can still be seen today protruding from the remains of the fortress walls.[7] These old columns, removed from nearby ancient sites, were used to provide added mural strength since they helped bond the masonry walls together.

A long straight wall, devoid of towers, protected the city on its seaward side. The walls on the land front were defended by a large number of rectangular towers and a fosse. There were three gates set opening onto roads leading to Jaffa, Jerusalem, and Gaza respectively. The destruction of Ascalon in 1247, and again in 1270, has left very little of the original crusader structures intact.[8]

The sea-walls of the fortress of Ascalon, shown in plan below, were bonded with marble through-columns removed from nearby ancient sites. Above, Crusader siege artillery.

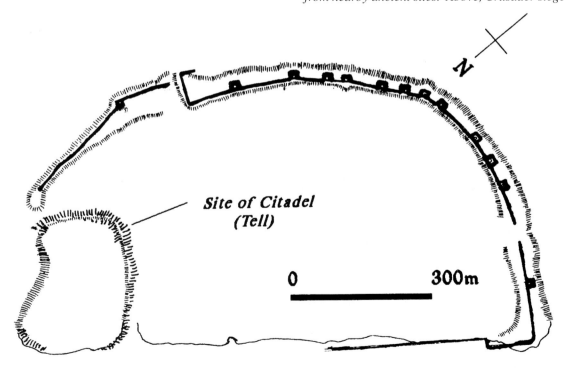

Site of Citadel
(Tell)

0   300m

Acre

The coastal fortress of Acre, situated on the coast of Palestine north of Haifa, constituted one of the most important centres of Christian colonization in Outremer. The city first succumbed to the Franks in 1099 but fell to Saladin in 1187.[1] When the fortress was recaptured in the course of the Third Crusade, the Hospitallers were temporarily placed in charge of its defence.[2] Then in 1191 the Order transferred the seat of its convent there from Marqab, given that the knights had acquired extensive quarters inside the city.[3]

Willbrand of Oldenburg, who visited Acre in the early thirteenth century, described the fortress as being quadrangular in plan and separated by a wall from its suburb to the north while two of its sides, bound by the sea, were undefended by ramparts.[4] The land front was defended by a double line of turretted walls. The outer of these was lower than, and overlooked by, the inner rampart and the whole protected by a rock-cut ditch. The Hospitaller quarters were located on the wall that separated the city from the suburb of Montmursad.[5] There the knights held two towers, the so-called Tower of the Hospital and the Tower of Our Lady. To the rear of these *turri* stood a complex of Hospitaller buildings, a hospital, recfectory, church, crypt, stables, magazines and halls. Another tower-like building projected

outwards from the main complex into the town and seems to have served as the master's private quarters.[6]

On 5 April 1291 the Mamlukes attacked Acre with a large army but the fortress held out until 18 April when the Saracens finally managed to breach the outer walls of the city and assaulted the inner line of defence.[7] The Hospitaller and Templar knights led furious counter attacks but they were greatly outnumbered and were driven back. The master of the Templars was killed in action while John of Villiers, master of the Hospital, was badly wounded in the attempt and had to be carried away to a boat which took him to Cyprus.[8]

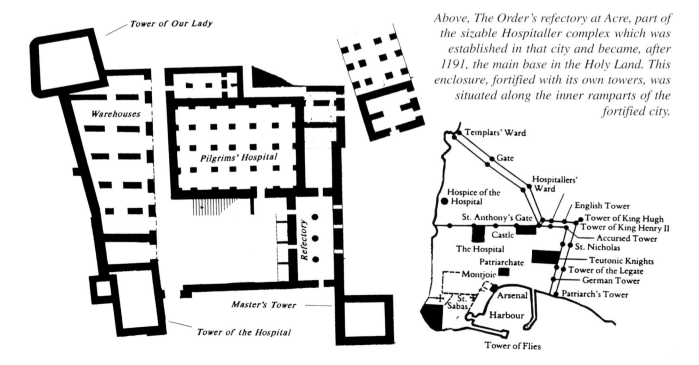

Above, The Order's refectory at Acre, part of the sizable Hospitaller complex which was established in that city and became, after 1191, the main base in the Holy Land. This enclosure, fortified with its own towers, was situated along the inner ramparts of the fortified city.

Kolossi   *(Cyprus)*

Among the many properties which the Order held on the island of Cyprus after the loss of Acre in 1281 was the 'casale quod dictur Colos', granted to the Hospitallers by King Ugo I in 1210.[1] A castle existed there during the thirteenth century and in 1301, the chapter general made it a special base.[2] Today it is practically the sole surviving evidence of Hospitaller fortifications on the island.

The castle of Kolossi, located west of Limassol, comprises a massive square tower, or keep, surrounded on two sides by the remains of an outerward. To the south, the rectangular ward, measuring some 30m x 40m, was flanked by rounded towers only one of which, however, survives and can still be found at the south-west corner. The existing tower-keep dates from the fifteenth century for it was rebuilt in 1454 by Louis de Magnac, grand commander of Cyprus.[3]

Internally, the donjon is divided into three storeys. The ground floor consists of three vaulted magazines. Beneath the stairs which lead to the middle floor lies the castle's well. The second storey is divided into two vaulted rooms. The one to the south served as the main hall. This also contained the main entrance which was protected by a drawbridge. The present drawbridge is a modern replica except for the small wheels on which the chains were run during the lifting and lowering of the bridge. Internally, to the right of the entrance, is a large mural painting of the crucifixion accompanied by the coat-of-arms of Louis de Magnac. The second room seems to have served as the kitchen, as it contains a large open fireplace. A spiral mural staircase set in the south-east corner of the building leads to the uppermost storey. This also consists of two vaulted rooms each measuring 14m x 6m, and lit by four windows. The windows have small seats built in the thickness of the walls, similar to the ones found in the barbican at Marqab, Syria.

In the northern room, built in the thickness of the north wall, is a latrine. Each of the two rooms has a fireplace decorated with the coat-of-arms of Louis de Magnac. A continuation of the spiral staircase leads to an open platform on the roof of the tower. A crenellated parapet, with merlons provided with arrow-slits, crowns the roof while a single box-machicoulis, resting on six gothic trilobe corbels, sits just above the main entrance on the south wall. High on the east wall are the coat-of-arms of Grand Masters Milly and Lastic, King John II de Lusignan of Cyprus (1432-58), the royal arms of Cyprus, and those of Louis de Magnac.

In the vicinity of the castle are to be found a large vaulted magazine which once housed a sugar refining installation, a mill-house, and a large medieval aqueduct which conveyed water from the Kouris river.[4] These formed part of the sugar factory established by the Hospitallers for the large-scale production of sugar.

Below, plan and general view of Kolossi castle.

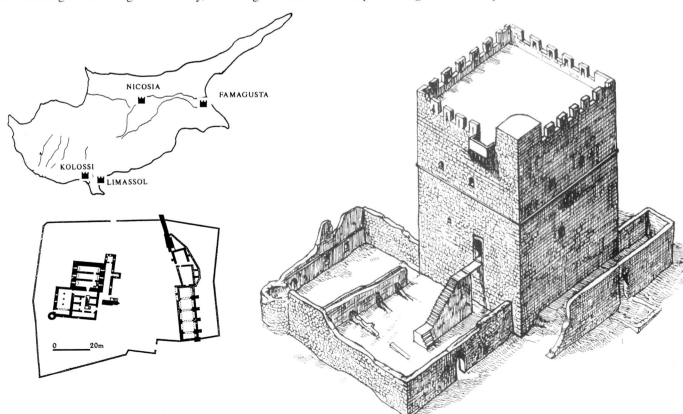

Hospitaller Fortifications
in
Rhodes
and the Dodecanese

The Fortress of Rhodes

The origins of the city of Rhodes date back to Hellenic times when the island flourished from the wealth generated by the nautical and commercial activities of its citizens. The city was founded jointly, in 408/7 BC by the three main Rhodian states of Lindos, Ialyssos and Kamiros - the *synoecismos.*[1] The geographical position of the newly established city, sited on the northern tip of the island opposite Asia Minor, together with its fine harbours, placed it directly onto the major east-west trading routes and thus further enhanced its commercial worth. The city was built according to the Hippodamian system, a grid pattern of long straight streets which covered an area of some 700 hectares of flat land, in which, at the zenith of its glory, lived between 80,000 and 100,000 people.[2] The city of Rodos was also famous for its strong fortifications which, in 305/4 BC, withstood a year-long siege by a 40,000-strong army under Demetrius Poliorketes.[3] To commemorate their brave defence, the people of Rhodes built the famous Colossus, one of the seven wonders of the ancient world, a large metal statue of the God Helios which, according to popular tradition, was erected across the entrance to the main harbour.

According to Aelios Aristides, the Hellenic city was surrounded by round walls and tall towers but these were severely damaged by an earthquake in 227/6 BC.[4] The city and its ramparts, however, were rebuilt with the financial and technical assistance of many other Greek city-states.[5] This help was not available when the city of Rhodes was again destroyed by a powerful earthquake in AD 155 as a result of which the inhabitants were obliged to re-use the masonry of the old walls and houses to build a new trace of ramparts within which a smaller city later developed during the middle ages.[6]

The decline of Rhodes continued up to the end of the Roman period, while during Byzantine times the island was devastated by earthquakes and successive corsair raids. Its strategic value, however, began to increase once again with the appearance of the Arab powers in the Mediterranean. From the seventh to the ninth century, Rhodes was at the centre of the struggle between the Byzantine empire and the Arabs. The latter repeatedly raided the island with the aim of establishing a permanent military base from where to launch their conquest of Asia Minor and Constantinople. Byzantines troops strengthened and refortified the city and used it as a naval base from where their fleet undertook naval forays against Arab-occupied north Africa. From Arab historical sources it is known that at least by the last quarter of the seventh century Rhodes already had a fortress.[7] In 807 corsairs under the command of Haun-al-Rashid sacked the city but were unable to capture its garrison.[8] In 1233 the army of the Nicaean emperor, John Vatatzes, had to besiege a strongly fortified city defended by the rebel ruler of Rhodes, Leon Gavalas and, in 1248 the Genoese seized the city when it had been left unguarded but the Byzantines recaptured it with difficulty in 1249-50.[9] The knights of St John themselves, 50 years later in 1306, found a strongly fortified city which took a three-year siege before it finally succumbed to them.[10]

Left, Plan of Rhodes (after E. Kollias) showing the layout of the medieval walls with its towers, some of which can still be seen incorporated into present-day houses, as shown in the picture below. These walls once enclosed the area of the city known as the collachium.

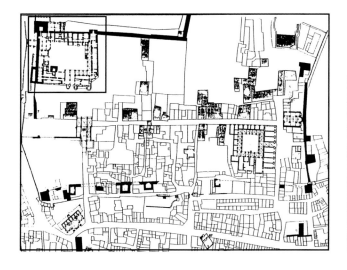

The majestic south-gate of the grand masters' palace, as partially reconstructed by the Italian governor of the Dodecanese, Cesare Matia de Vecchi, in 1937. The work was completed in 1940 under the direction of the Italian architect Vittorio Mesturino. Below, interior of the palace.

The enceinte of the Byzantine city of Rhodes which confronted the knights of St John in 1306 has today been established with relative accuracy. Its walls formed an irregular rectangular perimeter approximately 520m by 600m with walls varying in thickness from 3.2m to 6m. Internally, a strong wall stiffened with square towers divided the city into two unequal parts. The northern half corresponded with the area later used as the *collachium* by the knights. Remains of the *collachium* wall that divided the city in two can still be seen today spanning the length of Theophiliskou Street from the left of the clock-tower

right across to the section of walls facing the commercial harbour. A section of the walls on the east side, following the line of the harbour wall has remained exactly as it was. Fewer remains of the southern half of the city walls have survived but there are sufficient remains to enable historians to delineate with relative certainty the perimeter of the old enceinte. This followed the lines of the present day Ippodamou, Omirou, and Pythagora streets. A castle occupied the highest part of the fortified city, placed at the north-west corner of the enceinte, on the site where the palace of the grand masters stands today. This castle, a typical Byzantine *castrum*, was solidly joined to the enceinte of the city. It had a rectangular plan with four corner towers, three of which formed part of the outer wall.[11]

Judging from a surviving coat-of-arms of Grand Master Villeneuve (1319-46), the knights began at least as early as the first half of the fourteenth century to repair and strengthen the walls of the city. However, the early grand masters, from Villaret to Juilly, do not seem to have done much more than just maintain and repair the then existing Byzantine fortifications. The absence of any serious external threat did not warrant any major works of fortification. From the second half of the fourteenth century onwards, however, the picture began to change as the knights, increasingly asserting themselves as a major military force in the Mediterranean, began to attract the attention of the Turks. In response to this growing threat the city was incrementally strengthened and enlarged by each successive grand master. It withstood two Egyptian attacks in 1440 and 1444 but, with the fall of Constantinople to the Turks in 1453, the threat to the Order became more acute and the works of fortification received a greater impetus. This feverish building activity was only interrupted by the siege of 1480 but, thereafter, Grand Master d'Aubusson's prolific military works, slightly augmented and finalized by D'Amboise and Del Carretto, basically reshaped the city's defences.

One can distinguish four successive phases of development in the fortification of the city of Rhodes during the 200 years of the Order's stay in the island. The first period, extending from Grand Master Villaret (1309-19) to Grand Master Jilly (1374-77), seems to have involved the maintenance and perfunctory repair of the existing Byzantine walls. The earliest evidence of Hospitaller intervention is an account by Ludolf de Suchen, who visited Rhodes during the magistracy of Villeneuve (1319-46) and observed great building activity on the city walls.[12] Grand Master Dieudonne de Gozon repaired the then-existing Hellenic harbour mole and seems to have extended the enceinte so that it took in all the harbour, '...fece egli edificare nelle città di Rodi, il Molo; acciò le Galere, e le Navi, in ogni tempo, commodamente forgere, e stare si

Above, Rectangular wall-towers dating to the early 14th century. These were built by Grand Master Heredia and are situated along the harbour front of the fortress.

potessero; e fece cingere di muraglie, il Borgo di Rodi; chiudendolo dalla banda del Mare.'[13] The only testimony to works carried out during this first phase is a single escutcheon bearing the coat-of-arms of Grand Master Villeneuve which survives on the south face of the south-east gate of the *collachium*. Of the work of Villeneuve's successor until the time of Grand Master Heredia, however, no evidence has survived.

The second phase ran from the reign of Grand Master Heredia (1371-96) to that of Jean de Lastic (1437-54). Heredia repaired and strengthened the walls and towers of the harbour; his coat-of-arms are still visible on the two square towers west of St Paul gate. Grand Master Naillac, his successor, continued to strengthen the harbour works and built a large turretted tower, the famous Tower of Naillac.[14] Also known as St Michael tower, this was a lofty and elegant structure which stood at the end of a pier jutting out into the commercial port. It stood 46m high and consisted of three basic parts; a base of $25m^2$ with a heavy talus, a square tower with walls 3.7m thick at the base which rose about 37m high with four cylindrical echauguettes corbelled out from the corners of the roof, and an octagonal turret which rose about 10m from the centre of the roof of the tower.[15] The turret was reached by an external staircase winding around an octagonal plan. Unfortunately, this tower was destroyed by an earthquake in 1863 and only the base is still visible today. The Naillac tower must have had several rooms inside it, the lower one of which housed the winding mechanism of a large chain which was stretched out in times of greater danger to close off the commercial harbour. The chain was connected to the Tower of the Mills on the opposite side of the harbour. This boom was introduced during the magistracy of De Lastic and, in 1462, a chain tax, or *gabella,* was imposed on all merchandise shipped into the harbour through the chain, which was lowered in times of peace.[16] The Tower of Naillac was linked to the main enceinte by a long curtain wall which was built by Grand Master Fluvian and later terrepleined by Grand Master d'Aubusson.[17]

The Naillac tower, with its corner-echaugettes, marked a departure from the Byzantine and eastern styles of fortification till then employed in the fortification of the city and introduced instead Spanish and Provencal elements into Rhodian military architecture.[18] That the Byzantine influence was not abandoned altogether at this stage, however, can be witnessed by the walls on the land front built by Grand Masters Fluvian and De Lastic in the following decades, the best surviving example of which is that section west of the Post of Provence and east of the Kaskinou gate. The method of defence adopted here consisted of a high wall, teicos, in front of which was a lower thinner wall, the Byzantine proteicisma, with its own *chemin-de-ronde* and square towers which provided the first line of defence strengthened by a wide continuous ditch along the whole of the enceinte.[19] The main walls were strengthened at intervals, mainly where the curtain walls changed direction, by large flanking towers. Originally these towers were detached from the main curtain wall, the only link to the *chemin-de-ronde* being supplied by small bridges which could be easily demolished to isolate the towers once the latter were overrun by the enemy. These

The Tower of Trebuc. Inset, Detail of crenellation showing projecting pivot holders for a wooden shutter or mantlet.

detached towers, built in the *albarra* style, were also another peculiarity of Spanish military architecture introduced into the Rhodian fortifications.[20] With the increase in the destructive power of cannon, however, the isolated towers were later reinforced and linked to the main curtain walls.

Grand Master de Lastic was responsible for strengthening the west flank of the palace with the construction of a long and narrow bulwark that terminated in the polygonal Battery of the Olives. Both works were isolated from the main walls by a ditch. This new bulwark was also designed to defend St Anthony gate, which had previously provided a direct outlet from the city into the countryside. Consequently, another gate was erected on the west outer face of the bulwark to provide for a new exit into the countryside. After 1480 Grand Master d'Aubusson shielded this bulwark with an even larger one which he connected to the main enceinte north of the tower of St George. Finally, in 1512 Grand Master d'Amboise built an imposing gate in its outer face. In all, a system of four gates formed a tortuous passage into the city across three ditches.

Another important feature in the defence of the Rhodian harbour was the Tower of the Mills which was erected at the end of the quay of the windmills around 1440/54.[21] As its name implies, the quay was occupied by a number of windmills (15 in 1394) but, given that it was then still practically devoid of defences, was directly exposed to sea-borne attacks.[22] The Tower of the Mills was designed to protect this quay and, in conjunction with the opposite Naillac tower, secure the entrance to the harbour by means of the iron chain. Initially the design of the Tower of the Mills consisted of a cylindrical drum, 12m in diameter, topped by a hexagonal turret, identical to that on the Naillac tower. Two metres away from the tower stood a smaller staircase-tower which provided access from ground-level to both the lower and upper parts of the main tower. The structure's higher part consisted of two levels, a flat gun-platform and a higher parapet and walkway. In 1475, when

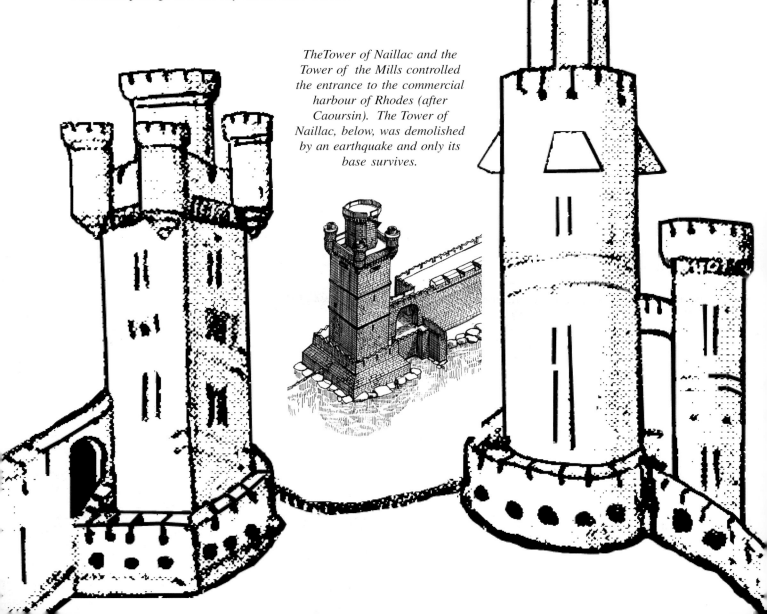

TheTower of Naillac and the Tower of the Mills controlled the entrance to the commercial harbour of Rhodes (after Caoursin). The Tower of Naillac, below, was demolished by an earthquake and only its base survives.

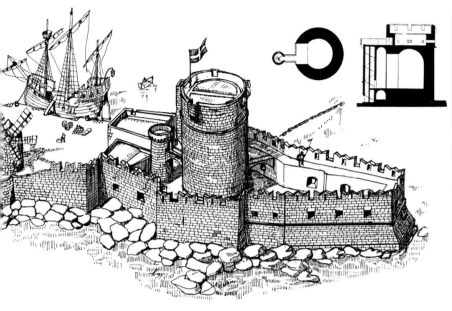

the threat of an invasion appeared imminent, the prior of Toulouse was given command of the Tower of the Mills as he personally offered to meet the cost of its defence.[23] The feared invasion failed to materialize then, but only five years later the tower was subjected to fierce bombardment during the siege of 1480 when its was heavily damaged.

After 1480 the Tower of the Mills was repaired and slightly modified by Grand Master d'Aubusson with the financial help from the king of France, Louis XI (1423-83).[24] The existence of the escutcheons of D'Aubusson and the *fleur-de-lys* coat-of-arms of France on the north and west faces of the tower bear witness to these changes and explain the alternative name given to the post as the Tower of France. It was also during this period that the hexagonal turret was removed from the top of the structure, probably to help stabilize the building. It was given further protection when it was enclosed within a low battery and practically turned into a veritable fort.[25]

The third distinct period in the fortification of the fortress of Rhodes was initiated by Grand Master de Milly (1454-61) and saw the addition of polygonal bulwarks in front of the city's old wall-towers. The land front was further strengthened during the reign of the next grand master, Raymond Zacosta, who also added to the strengthening of the harbour defences with the building of a new strong *Torre di San Nicolo*, '... la quale torre fu poi dall'istesso Gran Maestro, condotta a fine; con l'aiuto di costa, di dodici mila scudi d'oro, in oro, che Filippo Duca di Borgogna, di sua vera cortesia, e liberalità; a sollecitatione, e ricordo del Cavalier Frà Giovanni di Sailli, Commendator di Fiesses, e di Beauuois, Procuratore della Religione in Fiandra; dono al Gran Maestro.'[26]

Above, and below, The Tower of the Mills. The drawing, above left, shows a reconstruction of the tower and the battery which was added to it in the late 15th century.

Initially, this tower, built in 1464-67, consisted of a cylindrical drum surrounded by a lower roofed polygonal apron with guns at two levels. Here, too, access to the tower was through another smaller detached staircase-tower. The form of St Nicholas tower during this early phase in its history is clearly shown in Caoursin's original illustrations of the 1480 siege, when the *Torre di S. Nicolo* played a vital role in the defeat of the Turks. Its capture

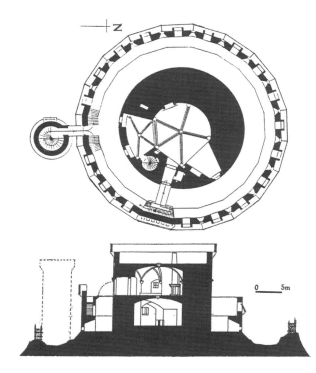

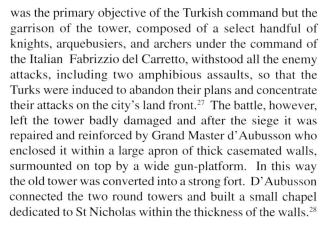

Left, Plan and sectional elevation of Fort St Nicholas circa 1480 (after Gabriel). Above, View of the partly vaulted courtyard separating the battery from the original tower.

was the primary objective of the Turkish command but the garrison of the tower, composed of a select handful of knights, arquebusiers, and archers under the command of the Italian Fabrizzio del Carretto, withstood all the enemy attacks, including two amphibious assaults, so that the Turks were induced to abandon their plans and concentrate their attacks on the city's land front.[27] The battle, however, left the tower badly damaged and after the siege it was repaired and reinforced by Grand Master d'Aubusson who enclosed it within a large apron of thick casemated walls, surmounted on top by a wide gun-platform. In this way the old tower was converted into a strong fort. D'Aubusson connected the two round towers and built a small chapel dedicated to St Nicholas within the thickness of the walls.[28]

During the siege of 1522 Fort St. Nicholas was placed under the command of Frà Guiotto de Castellana, 'detto Ragusa, Cavaliero della Lingua di Provanza.'[29] The Turks set up a battery facing the fort but were met with a fierce return fire from the German gunners such that after firing some 500 rounds against it, they were forced to abandon the enterprise.[30] By then, however, the Order had reinforced the garrison of Fort St. Nicholas with a further 20 knights and 50 soldiers under the command of the Frà Gasparo Glior.[31]

The last important additions to the fortifications during this period was the renovation of the crescent-shaped curtain walls overlooking the commercial port. That part of the wall corresponding to the city was entirely rebuilt by Grand Master Orsini.[32]

Left, Sectional elevation of Fort St Nicholas c.1522 (after Gabriel), and below, elevation of the east front.

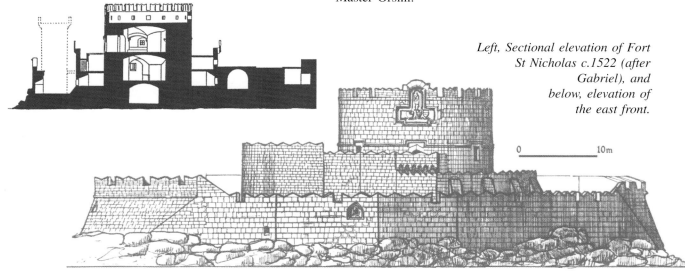

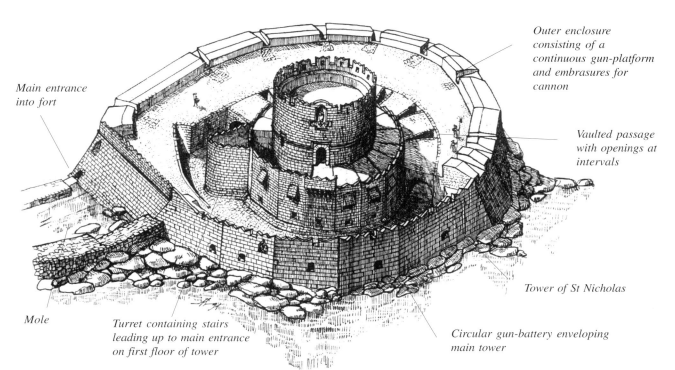

Main entrance into fort

Outer enclosure consisting of a continuous gun-platform and embrasures for cannon

Vaulted passage with openings at intervals

Tower of St Nicholas

Mole

Turret containing stairs leading up to main entrance on first floor of tower

Circular gun-battery enveloping main tower

The fourth and most eventful phase in the fortification of Rhodes began with the accession of Grand Master d'Aubusson in 1476. The years leading up to the siege of 1480 were marked by feverish preparations. All the trees and houses on the outskirts of the city were cut down and demolished to deny the Turks any form of cover. Two churches which were situated outside the city walls, those of Sant'Antonio and of Santa Maria Lemonitia, were demolished as these were considered 'di non poco impedimento alla difesa.'[33] The destruction brought about by the Turkish siege of 1480 and by a devastating earthquake in the following year, however, stimulated a fresh spasm of building activity which basically reshaped the city's defences. Grand Master d'Aubusson embarked upon an unprecedented building programme, the magnitude of which is revealed by the fact that his coat-of-arms appear more than fifty times on the city walls.

Indeed, D'Aubusson was altogether an extraordinary and energetic man, well-versed in many subjects, especially in military engineering. His previous position as Superintendent of Fortifications had prepared him well for this task such that he was able to conceive and supervise personally many of the various works.[35]

The vulnerability of the city's high and slender walls to Turkish fire had been well-illustrated during the siege so that rebuilding on the same lines was unthinkable. Instead, the main walls were thickened and built up to provide a wide terreplein which enabled a wider walkway for a faster deployment of troops along the whole length of the walls.

Fort St Nicholas.

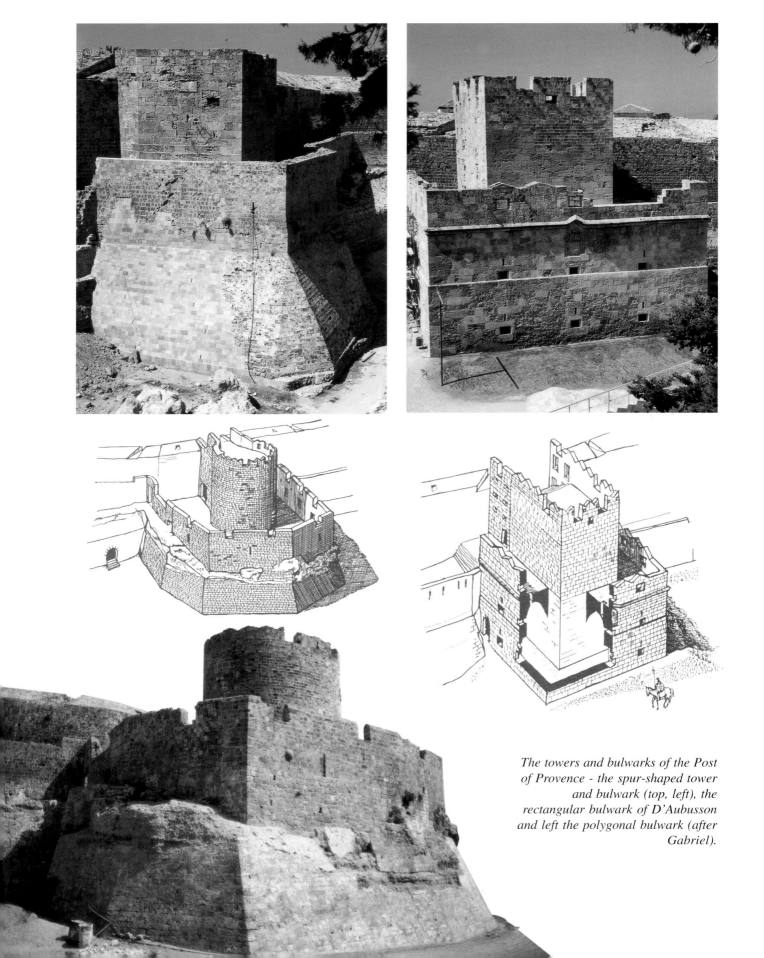

The towers and bulwarks of the Post of Provence - the spur-shaped tower and bulwark (top, left), the rectangular bulwark of D'Aubusson and left the polygonal bulwark (after Gabriel).

The wide terreplein also enabled guns to be mounted behind parapets, themselves also thickened, sloped back, and fitted with embrasures. The other important innovation was the excavation of a second outer ditch leaving tenailles of rock to protect the curtain walls at the Posts of England, Spain, and Italy.

Only a few years after 1481, new works sprang up outside the western and southern part of the enceinte. Four of the main towers, including those of Spain, St Mary, and St John, were reinforced with polygonal bulwarks isolated from the main curtain. The bulwark of England was completed in 1487, that of Koskinou before 1489, that between the Koskinou bulwark and the tower of Italy before 1489, and the bulwark of Spain in 1489.[36]

The bulwark of England was built as a huge crescent-shaped and solid polygonal gun-platform isolated from the rest of the enceinte and the tower of the Virgin by an inner ditch. This bulwark has a battered outer face with no string course below the parapet, but this was probably removed when the present solid parapet was rebuilt in the early sixteenth century. The east flank of the bastion was enclosed by a curtain wall designed to protect the entrance into the city via St Athanasios gate. This protected passage rested on top of a long and narrow-vaulted gallery, which, fitted with embrasures, was designed to provide flanking fire along the inner ditch enclosed by the tenaille and the faussebraye. According to a Turkish inscription on the south face of the bulwark, this section of the fortification was rebuilt by the governor of Rhodes, Abdul Djelil, in 1530-31.[37] A Latin inscription on St Athanasios gate states that in 1487 Grand

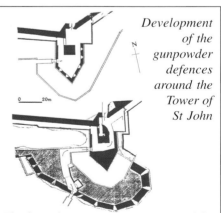

The bulwark of the Post of Spain.

Master d'Aubusson, victor over the Turks, built the bulwark in front of the tower of the Virgin and gave the St Athanasios gate its final form; AD FIDEI CATHOLICE: HOSTES ARCENDOS: DIVVUS E. PETRVS DAVBVSSON: RHODIOP V M MAGNVS MAGISTER BETVRCIS: IN CLITVS VICTOR. RHODIAM VRBEM MVNIENS: HOC ANTE MVRALE EM XIT MCDLXXXVII. During the siege of 1522 this bulwark was assigned to the knights of the langue of England.[38]

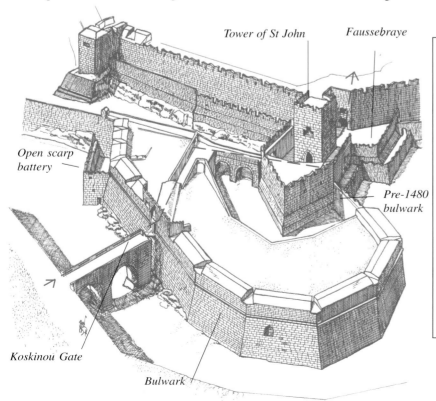

Tower of St John

Faussebraye

Open scarp battery

Pre-1480 bulwark

Koskinou Gate

Bulwark

Development of the gunpowder defences around the Tower of St John

The first phase saw the projection of the old faussebraye into a pentagonal barbican fitted with gun-loops. The second (post-1480) saw the enclosure of the old works within a huge polygonal bulwark (after Gabriel).

Above, View of the flank and gorge of the pre-1480 pentagonal bulwark of the Tower of St John. Below, The polygonal bulwark of the Post of Spain, as seen from within the ditch. The continuous gallery runs parallel to the outerwalls of the bulwark, opening up in a number of rectangular gun-loops.

West of the bulwark of the post of England, approximately 350 m away, lies another important bastion not dissimilar from the former but covering a larger area of ground. The bulwark of St John was added by Grand Master d'Aubusson to reinforce the earlier fortifications in the area and seems to date from before 1489 because the coat-of-arms of D'Aubusson which grace it does not include the cardinal's hat which he had received in that year. Unlike the other bulwarks, this new work was added in front of the earlier antemural which, as a result, remained intact. Next to the lofty rectangular tower of St John the Baptist stood the original entrance into the city. Above this doorway one can still see the coat-of-arms of Grand Master Jacques de Milly (1454-61) and inscribed on a marble plaque to the west of the gate is the bilingual inscription which mentions the Greek mastermason, or *muratora*, Manolis Kountis, who worked on this section of the wall in 1457.[39] The tower itself is very similar to that of St George and incorporated into its south face is a relief of St John the Baptist and an escuthcheon of Grand Master Fluvian. The tower's ground floor was initially used as a church but the knights later filled it in with rubble in order to give it added strength.[40] A quadrilateral spur-shaped bulwark, very similar to the one which stood in front of the tower of St George, was later built around the outer faces of the tower.

This hollow bulwark was in effect an outward projection of the faussebraye fitted with gun-ports and designed to provide flanking fire along the adjacent enceinte. A doorway in the flank bearing the coat-of-arms of Grand Master Zacosta (14611467) indicates the period in which this work was

completed. The road leading outwards from this gate then passed over a wooden drawbridge across the ditch and into the countryside. After 1481, a large, solid and irregularly shaped polygonal bulwark encased the older works and projected aggressively outwards across a wide ditch. D'Aubusson's coat-of-arms appear in four places on these ramparts and also embellished the new outer gate fitted into the southern face of the bulwark. The bastion's outer faces were designed with a slightly steeper batter than that of the bulwark of England and have a string course with double moulding which seems to have been the mark of D'Aubusson. No gunports were built at ditch level but as the existing parapet is due to a heightening rather than a complete rebuilding in the early sixteenth century, there are still traces of gunports at parapet level.[41]

From this point the enceinte followed a zigzagging course in a north-easternly direction right up to the tower of Italy. Three towers defended this part of the enceinte. The first, spur-shaped, bears the coat-of-arms of Grand Master Jacques de Milly; the second is rounded and has a hollow polygonal outwork around its base formed from an outward projection of the faussebraye and reinforced by a masonry talus, and the third is square with a rectangular casemated bulwark at its base bearing the coat-of-arms of Grand Master d'Aubusson without the cardinal's hat (pre-1489). This last is the weakest and the most primitive in appearance of all the bulwarks built during this period. It consists of a low vertical wall clasping three sides of the rectangular tower behind it. It is connected to the faussebraye and has three tiers of rectangular gun-ports with vision-slits. In all its purposes it resembles the bulwarks built by Grand Master Zacosta except that it has no salient angle and does not cover an entrance into the city.

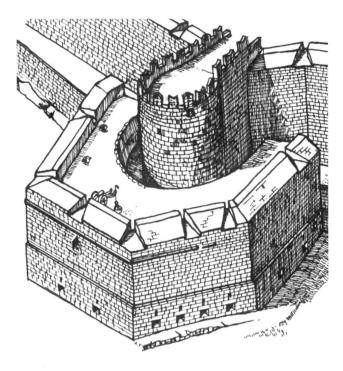

This page, The polygonal bulwark of the Post of Spain. Below, Detail of one of its gun-loops with vision-slit.

A tendency to regularity in Grand Master d'Aubusson's bulwarks, when this is compared to its three predecessors, first shows itself in the bulwark of Spain. This work has four sides, two faces and two flanks, the northern flank, however, being slightly bent backward to form another very short ineffective flank where the bulwark meets the

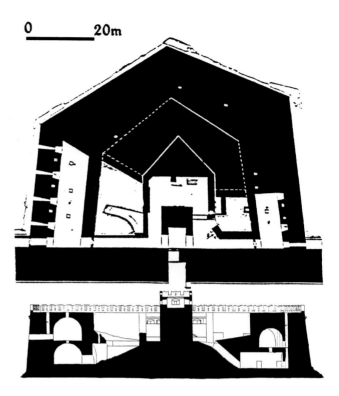

Above, Left flank of the boulevard of St George. Right, Plan and section through gorge of bastion (after Gabriel).

faussebraye. The outer walls are vertical and pierced with rectangular gun-ports of the divided keyhole type, with vision-slits above small rectangular muzzle openings. These gun-ports were designed for two-men weapons on low static mounts; the gunner laid the gun on its simple wooden mount according to the instructions of the *collineator* or gun aimer, who, watching through the upper smaller slit, would then fire the weapon at the right moment by putting his slow-burning match to the priming powder of the gun. The upper gun-platform of this bastion is enclosed by a solid sloping parapet of thick merlons interspersed by seven embrasures which are the product of the early sixteenth century. A large niche bearing the coat-of-arms of Grand Master D'Aubusson decorates one of the faces of the work.

The largest and most important of the city's polygonal bulwarks is that of St George. Before the siege of 1480 the tower of St George was protected by a hollow pointed bulwark attached to the faussebraye, similar to that which has survives today behind the Koskinou gate. This antemural protected the tower and a gateway leading into the city through a stone bridge which spanned the dry ditch. In 1496 D'Aubusson closed off the old gate and threw up a huge pentagonal gun-platform round the whole work.[42] The flanks of the bastion enclosed two levels of casemates designed to enable the defenders to enfilade the ditch while an underground countermine gallery was excavated beneath the ditch.[43]

Many historians have suggested that the boulevard of Auvergne, as this bastion was then known, was in fact the first example of the true Italian pentagonal bastion, having two outer faces designed to be flanked from adjacent works, and two straight flanks connected to the curtain.[44] It appears, however, that this bulwark was originally isolated from the main curtain wall with the flanks reaching back

General view of the bastion of Auvergne. The bastion enclosed the old bulwark and tower of St George within its gorge. The casemated flank sheltered the crews working the guns.

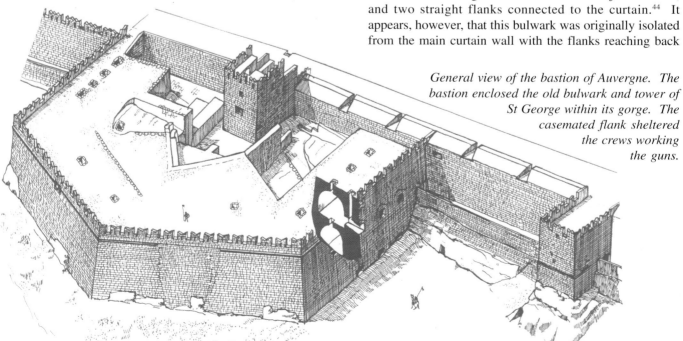

only to the line of the faussebraye. This can be judged from the fact that the string course below the parapet ends at the line of the faussebraye while the parapet on the curtain wall south of St George tower isolates the bastion's platform from the terreplein of the curtain thus defeating the idea of having the bastion connected to the enceinte in the first place. This can only mean that when the sloped parapet and embrasures were built, possibly by Grand Master Fabrizio del Carretto in 1513-21, the curtain wall was then still isolated from the flanks and gorge of the bulwark. The flanks seem to have been only extended backward to abut the curtain wall in 1522 by Grand Master Villiers de L'Isle Adam.[45] Furthermore, the two faces of the bastion could not be easily flanked from the adjacent works, especially from the northern section of the city walls, while none of the embrasures on the adjacent ramparts on either side of the work were designed to provide enfilading fire along the faces of the bastion. Although the boulevard of Auvergne was not conceived as a true bastion in the later sense of the word, its design is considered to have certainly been a step in the right direction of the later Italian solutions.

Above, Front view of the Marine Gate, and below, detail of left turret, showing the circular gun-loops and gallery-machicoulis.

As stated earlier, Grand Master d'Aubusson also strengthened the Tower of the Mills and the Tower of St Nicholas by enclosing them within an outer apron of thick walls. D'Aubusson likewise rebuilt the harbour walls corresponding to the *collachium,* the residential quarters of the knights, behind which were the arsenal and the magazines. The most striking feature of the harbour walls was the Porta Marina, built by D'Aubusson in 1478.[46] This gate, with its two elliptical towers and elaborate machicolation round their top and decorated with statues of the Virgin flanked by St John the Baptist and St Peter, was mainly designed to impress rather defend against cannon. The importance of its symbolism is clearly illustrated by Caoursin in one of his drawings depicting the Turkish Prince Djem being heralded from his ship into the city through the Porta Marina.[47]

Grand Master Emmery d'Amboise succeeded D'Aubusson in 1503. During his nine-year reign the only significant addition to the city's fortifications was the construction of the fortified gate built on the face of the rampart erected earlier by D'Aubusson north of St Michael tower. D'Amboise gate, as it is known, was built in 1512.[48] The defence of this entrance was entrusted to two massive semicircular drum-towers fitted with embrasures for cannon on three levels. Above the arched entrance is a marble plaque bearing in relief an angel clasping the coats-of-arms of the Order and Grand Master d'Amboise with the inscription, DAMBOYSE MDXII.

Fabrizio del Carretto (1513-21) was the last grand master to affect significant additions and alterations to the city of

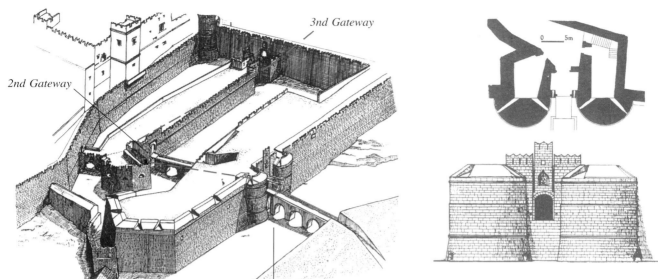

2nd Gateway

3nd Gateway

Caponier

D'Amboise Gate

Left, General layout of the fortifications on the west side of the grand master's palace, a series of successive walls and gates terminating in the heavily fortified entrance known as D'Amboise gate, shown above in plan (after Gabriel) and elevation. The most innovative feature in the defence of the ramparts in this area is the caponier projecting into the ditch. This structure, shown in plan, bottom left, was designed to provide low-level enfilade fire along the floor of the ditch.

Rhodes. Most definitely the most important and revolutionary defensive works erected during this period were the large caponiers placed inside the ditch and designed to provide low-level. One of these, built at the north-west corner of the city defences, bears the date 1514 inscribed beneath the arms of the Del Carretto. This casemated caponier, with its solid spur-shaped northern face and pitched roof, was designed to provide enfilading fire along its two flanks through eight gun-ports. Internally the caponier was divided into four interconnected chambers. The gun-ports, or embrasures, of the caponier have their openings drawn back to increase the gunners' arcs of fire.

Some historians have doubted the antiquity of the caponiers and suggested that these may have been later Turkish additions. The date on the coat-of-arms affixed to the caponier shows otherwise, and moreover, one can see a very similar design in a contemporary casemated battery built by the knights at Bodrum in 1513, similarly to provide enfilading fire within the ditch along the land front of the castle of St Peter.[49] It is not difficult to imagine that the

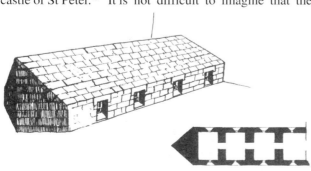

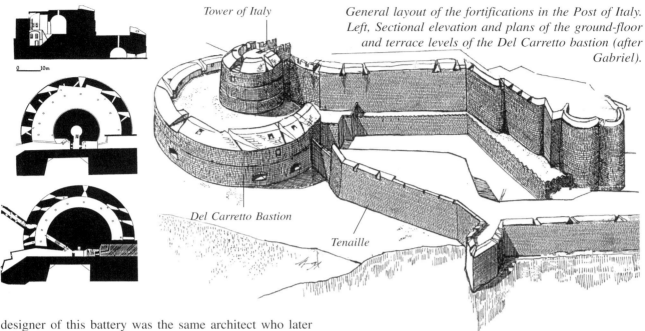

Tower of Italy

General layout of the fortifications in the Post of Italy. Left, Sectional elevation and plans of the ground-floor and terrace levels of the Del Carretto bastion (after Gabriel).

Del Carretto Bastion

Tenaille

designer of this battery was the same architect who later perfected the concept in Rhodes.

The next impressive work of fortification was the large semicircular casemated bastion built in 1515-17, around the tower of Italy.[50] Del Carretto's bastion, nearly 50m in diameter, was attached to the faussebraye and its casemated interior, forming one large curved vaulted tunnel, opened out into six embrasures and two sally-ports. Another opening led into a caponier that connected the bastion to the adjacent tenaille built by D'Aubusson. Carretto's bulwark was attached to the faussebraye while the cannon embrasures on its thick, sloped parapet were arranged in an irregular manner that took the best advantage of enfilading adjacent works. The old tower of Italy was also

reinforced and fitted with a thick parapet and embrasures and in this manner the combined works formed three tiers of gun emplacements.

Like D'Aubusson, Del Carretto continued to reinforce the main curtain walls by augmenting the thickness of their terreplein especially in the sector of the Posts of Italy and Provence, 'cominciando da' Mulini, e dalla casa di Gianatis Mastrorisas, fin alla Porta di Cosquino'.[51] In an attempt to cause minimal destruction to the existing walls, the terreplein was reinforced internally and, consequently, some houses within the city had to be demolished to make room for the new ramparts, 'era perche stato necessario, per questa fortificatione, a gettare a terra alcune case di Cittadini.'[52] A sum of 4,104 *fiorini* was paid in September 1520 in compensation to various citizens whose houses were demolished in the process of the new works.[53] Del Carretto was also responsible for replacing many of the older parapets

View from the counterscarp of the circular Del Carretto Bastion.

*Vaulted interior of the caponier which links the
Del Carretto Bastion with the tenaille of the Post of Italy.*

with the much-improved sloped type of his time.[54] An interesting detail used by the engineers during this period was the curved parapet merlons erected on a section of the curtain wall east of St Athanasios gate and similar to those at the Sangallo bastion in Rome and to the parapets that were later built on the coastal forts in England.[55]

To design the city's new fortifications Del Carretto employed mostly Italian engineers like the Sicilian Matteo Gioeni (Zuenio), *Ingeniere della Religione* who, in 1521, prepared a relief model of Rhodes that was presented to Pope Leo X de Medici in Rome.[56] Another engineer was Basilio della Scuola di Vicenza, military engineer to Emperor Maximilian who was loaned to the Order in 1520.[57] The Order also sought to obtain the services of the military engineer Scarpagnino in 1516, but the request was refused by the Venetian Republic.[58]

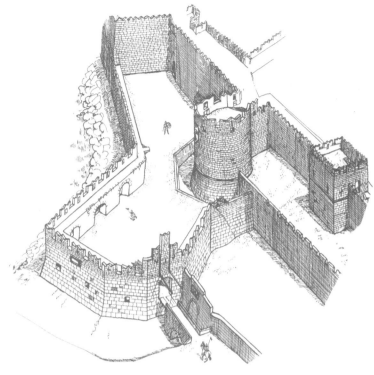

Right, General layout of the fortifications in the area around the Tower of Trebuc. Below, One of the vaulted gun-ports in the bulwark enveloping the tower.

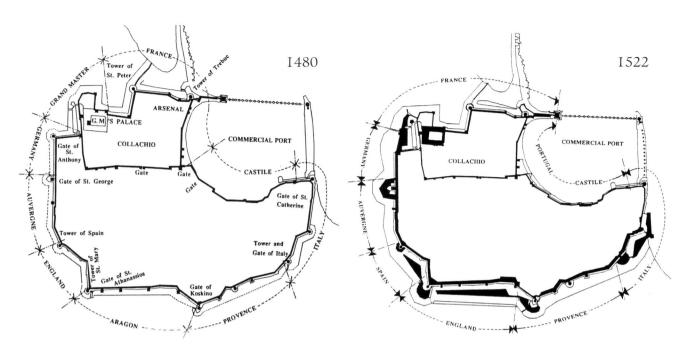

1480

1522

Below, Aerial perspective of the fortified city of Rhodes (taken from Gabriel) showing the fortress as it would have appeared in 1522 just prior to the Turkish Siege. The annotations have been added by the author.

Above, Plans of the fortress of Rhodes showing the distribution of the various sections of the city's ramparts, or Posts, among the different langues of the Order during the sieges of 1480 (left) and 1522 (right). Note the changes in the allocation of the Posts.

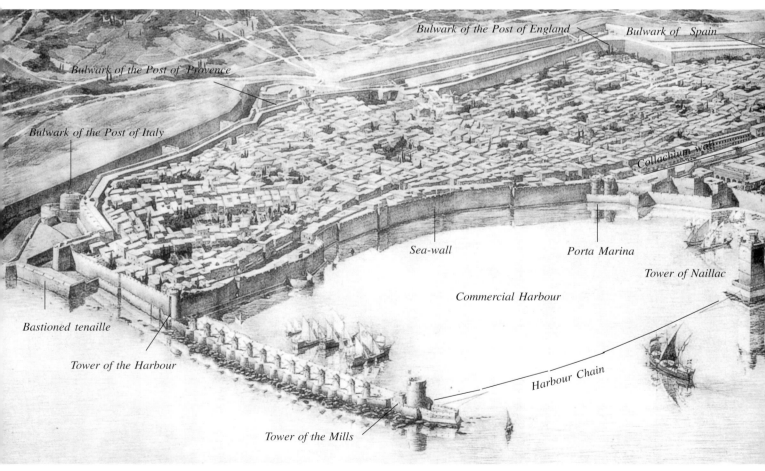

Plan of the fortress of Rhodes (Gabriel).

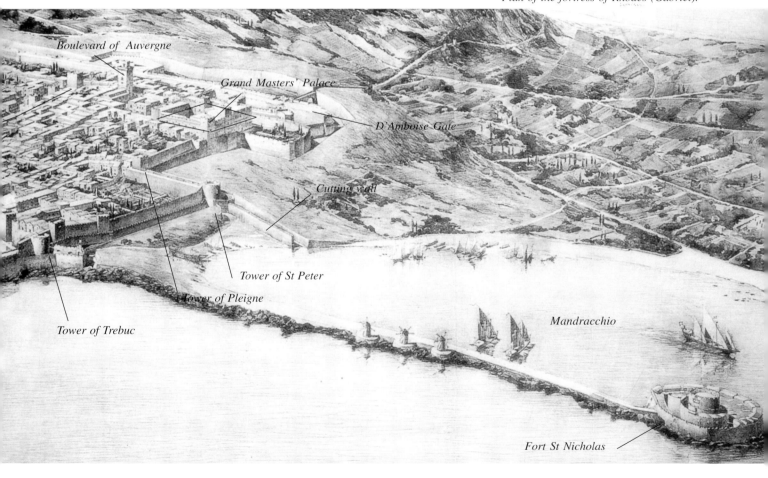

Boulevard of Auvergne

Grand Masters' Palace

D'Amboise Gate

Cutting wall

Tower of St Peter

Tower of Pleigne

Tower of Trebuc

Mandracchio

Fort St Nicholas

Pheraclos   *(Rhodes)*

The mighty fortress of Pheraclos (Faraklos) was the first Rhodian stronghold captured by the knights of St John when they set out to conquer the island.[1] At Pheraclos the Hospitallers established a foothold from where they directed their operations for the capture of the other important castles on Rhodes. The origins of this fortress reach back to ancient Greek times when the site served as an acropolis. The Byzantine stronghold which confronted the knights in 1307 occupied the highest part of the ancient fortified settlement and was basically, though with some later alterations, that which can still be seen today. The flat plateau on which the fortress is situated separates two large bays, those of Haraki to the south and Aghia Agathi to the north. The fortress also commanded an unobstructed view of the coastline right up to the large bay of Malona to the north.

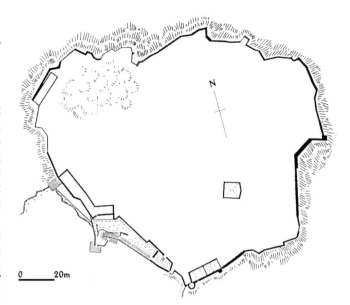

Plan of the fortress of Pheraclos (after Poutiers).

The Byzantine walls of Pheraclos crown the edge of the precipitous summit of a large oval plateau enclosing a site some 170m by 100m in area. This is approached by a rock-hewn flight of steps which leads towards the castle's outer gate, initially sited within the walls of a barbican. A series of four successive gates then led up a winding passage and into the main enclosure. Although most of the castle's walls have collapsed, sufficient remains survive to enable a reconstruction of its layout. The main enceinte consists of an irregular perimeter of vertical walls which follow the outline of the summit. In most places the walls lack towers and provision for flanking defences was only provided by re-entrant angles in the trace. The knights were mostly

responsible for adding wall-towers and strengthening the ramparts. The oldest parts of the castle are found along the north-east, north, and west sections of the enceinte. There the walls are crowned with the simple rectangular type of merlons attributed to the Byzantine period. These rudimentary merlons have neither arrow-slits nor gun-loops. A later stage in the development of the fortress occurred during the magistracy of Gian Battista Orsini (1467-76). This is deduced from the presence of an escutcheon bearing the coat-of-arms of the same grand master which has survived on the outer face of the ramparts on the east front

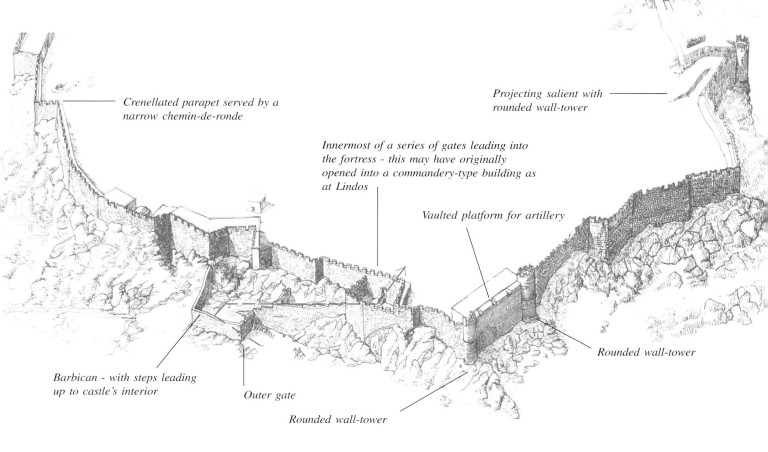

Projecting salient with rounded wall-tower

Innermost of a series of gates leading into the fortress - this may have originally opened into a commandery-type building as at Lindos

Vaulted platform for artillery

Rounded wall-tower

Barbican - with steps leading up to castle's interior

Outer gate

Rounded wall-tower

of the fortress where the walls follow a tenaille trace.[2] From the present remains it appears that these works involved the reconstruction, with ashlar masonry, of a considerable section of the enceinte to the south-east and south. Two rounded wall-towers of very fine construction and similar to circular wall-towers built on the ramparts of the city of Rhodes during the first half of the fifteenth century occupy the south-west part of the enceinte. The final stage in the development of the fortress seems to have involved the construction of a large vaulted platform behind the curtain wall adjoining the two circular towers on the south stretch of ramparts, undoubtedly a work for mounting artillery.[3]

Above, For most of their length, the ramparts of the fortress are girded by a crenellated wall with rectangular merlons and served by a narrow walkway. Below, Elevation of the land front of the fortress of Pheraclos to the south, lying mostly in ruins except for the two rounded wall-towers and adjoining curtain.

Apart from being a fortified settlement, the fortress of Pheraclos was also, from 1479 onwards, the seat of an administrative centre responsible for the government of a large region consisting of the villages and castles of Archangelos, the tower of Massari, and the villages of Malona, Salia, Katanagro, Kamiro, and Platania.[4] The building housing the administrative headquarters seems to have been situated on the west part of the fortress, directly above the main inner entrance into the castle in a manner similar to the layout of the commandery at Lindos.[5] This is borne out from the fact that this area of the fortress still retains a number of foundation walls that seem to indicate the remains of a large building. Inside the castle's vast enclosure the space was occupied by many buildings and dwellings as evidenced by the many scattered traces of walls littering the site. Roughly in the centre of the fortress lies a large well-preserved vaulted cistern. At one point in time, the castle of Pheraclos was used to detain errant knights, like the Catalan Pere de Castellsent, who was deprived of his habit in 1382. The chapter general of 1383, held at Valence, stipulated that the castles in which knights and other brethren of the Order were to be held prisoners were to be the fortress of Philerimos, Kastellorizo in the island of Megisti, and the fortress of Andimacchia on the island of Kos.

Above, Detail of the rectangular merlons along the crenellated ramparts of the fortress of Pheraclos. These seem to predate the Hospitaller occupation of the fortress. Below, Elevation (after Poutiers) and reconstruction of the tenaille trace on the eastern part of the enceinte.

Ramparts made of heavily-plastered courses of stone crown the summit of the naturally-fortified and largely inaccessible site of the fortress of Pheraclos (Photograph by courtesy of E. Kanataki).

Lindos   *(Rhodes)*

The impregnable castle of Lindos was built on the site of an ancient acropolis of the sacred sanctuary of Athena, dating back to the Hellenistic period.[1] Actually, the city-state of Lindos was one of the three powerful city-states that ruled the island of Rhodes during classical times. Its prosperity began in the Geometric period when, as a large naval power, Lindos was renowned for its fleet and maritime exploits and the foundation of colonies in southern Italy and Sicily.[2] The city grew rich through trade with Cyprus, Egypt, and the Phoenicians, and its population bloomed. By the time of the arrival of the knights of St John, however, Lindos had passed into obscurity after centuries of insecurity and successive corsair raids, although it was never completely abandoned.[3] From the sixth century AD onwards the inhabitants abandoned the lower town and settled inside the acropolis. During the Byzantine period the acropolis was fortified and acquired the form of a medieval castle.

With the coming of the knights the island began to prosper again owing to the Order's policy of colonization and settlement. The town was once again transferred outside the acropolis on the ruins of the ancient city. The knights also reinforced the castle and made Lindos the seat of an administrative centre responsible for the control of the villages and castle of Lardos and Asklipion and the villages of Kalathos and Pilona.[4] The coastal towers at Pefka and Aghios Yorgos also came under the control of Lindos.[5]

The castle of Lindos was built on two levels. The upper part, which was the site of the ancient acropolis, constituted the main enceinte and its ramparts were built on the very foundations of the old acropolis walls. The lower level consisted of an outer bailey and a barbican. Entrance to the castle was through two gates. The first entrance, set in the barbican, was surmounted by an escutcheon bearing the coat-of-arms of the knight Antoine Aimer, grand prior of Aquitaine, which dates the work to the end of the fourteenth century.[6] The second gateway was placed in the north-east wall of a large building that served as the administrative headquarters of the knights. This was only accessible by means of a steep flight of steps. The present staircase, protected by a thick stepped traverse, was built on the remains of the original Hellenic flight of steps. The remains of another earlier medieval staircase can also be seen to the left of the main entrance. The ground floor of the vaulted administrative building which was reconstructed by Grand Master Pierre d'Aubusson, whose coat-of-arms

decorate the façade of the building, consists of a long corridor leading into the interior of the fortress. Internally, the entrance was protected by a small guardroom fitted with a singular arrow-slit. The walls of the main enceinte consisted of a crenellated parapet and were served, along most of their length, by a *chemin-de-ronde*. Three types of

Above, The main entrance into the castle, through the commandery building. Note the old staircase of an earlier entrance. Below, Detail of rectangular merlons.

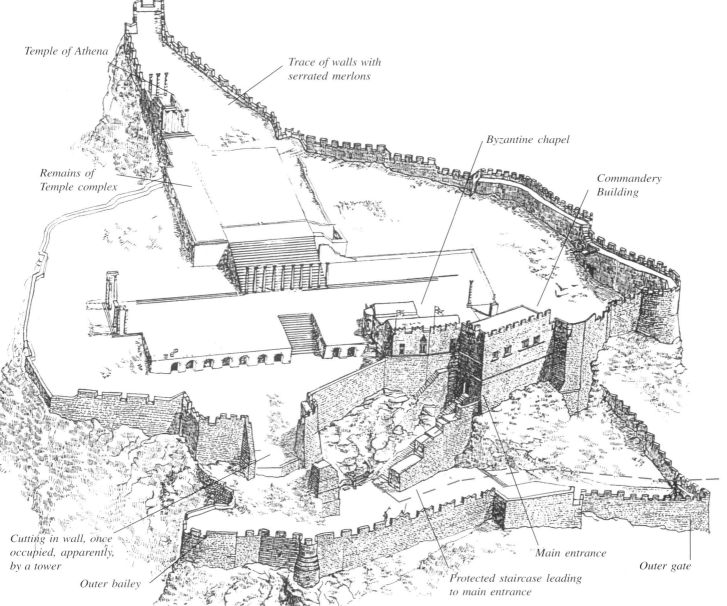

Temple of Athena

Trace of walls with serrated merlons

Byzantine chapel

Commandery Building

Remains of Temple complex

Cutting in wall, once occupied, apparently, by a tower

Outer bailey

Main entrance

Outer gate

Protected staircase leading to main entrance

crenellations crown the walls. The earliest are rectangular merlons with rounded tops, then come much wider ones with triangular indentations on top, and finally thick merlons with splayed ends designed for cannon. The enclosure on the plateau was occupied largely by the remains of the old acropolis, consisting of a Doric stoa, a broad stairway, a propylaea, and a temple once dedicated to Athena Lindia.[7] A small Byzantine church was erected on the stoa and this was later used by the knights. The castle's water supply was stored inside a series of three ancient cisterns, the largest, some 28 m x 6 m, was placed inside the platform surrounded by the portico of the stoa. In all a total of 80 wells were found on the acropolis. Lindos served as a refuge for Grand Master de Villaret when he was removed from his office by the Order's council and replaced by De Pagnac. He remained trapped there until called to Avignon by the pope and forced to resign.[8]

Above, Interior of the castle showing the commandery building. Below, The castle of Lindos as seen from the west.

Philerimos   (Rhodes)

Plan of the the fortress of Philerimos showing the citadel and the various wards (after Gabriel).

The remains of the fortress of Philerimos are situated on the crest of Mount Philerimos, some 8 km south of the city of Rhodes and occupy the site of the ancient Greek acropolis of Ialyssos, one of the three main cities of Rhodes in antiquity.[1] After the establishment of the city of Rhodes, Ialyssos declined in importance but the fortress remained an important stronghold during the middle ages.[2] It was in this fortress that John Cantacuzene resisted the Genoese when they attacked the island in 1248.[3] During the Hospitaller invasion of Rhodes, the fortress at Philerimos was strongly garrisoned with the assistance of 300 Turkish soldiers sent over from the neighbouring mainland to assist the inhabitants.[4] Still, on 9 November 1306, the knights managed to capture the castle by emulating the ruse, according to tradition, that Ulysses played upon Polyphemus, that is by slipping into the fortress under sheepskins as the Greeks were driving in their flocks back inside at sunset.[5] Another account speaks of the treachery of one of the Greeks inside the castle who helped the Hospitallers through a postern gate.[6] The Turks within the fortress were all massacred.[7]

With its capture the Hospitallers acquired an important base from where they conducted their siege operations against the fortress of Rhodes. The importance of the castle of Philerimos to the safety of the fortress of Rhodes manifested itself again prior to the siege of 1480 when the Hospitallers were forced to strengthen it because of the threat it was seen to constitute were it to fall to the enemy,[8] 'il Sito, e la Qualità del luogo, che per esser'eminente, e molto vicino alla Città di Rodi; haverebbe potuto fare molti danni alla detta Città; se da' Nemico occupato, e fortificato fosse, fu determinato ... nel miglior modo, che per all'hora far si poteva, fortificare si dovesse, e ch'alcun Homini valorosi, non Greci, ma Franchi, in Presidio mandare vi si dovessero.'[9] Indeed, such was its fate during the last siege of Rhodes in 1522.[10]

Little remains today of the vast fortified enceinte that once surmounted the summit of Mount Philerimos. From the surviving ruins it is possible to distinguished three main distinct features forming this fortress: a large irregular enceinte occupying most of the summit and forming the main fortified enceinte, an outer ward to the north-west, and a citadel sited at the eastern salient of the main enceinte, in all, some 700m of perimeter walls.[11] The plan of the fortress has no particular shape, being of an elongated form with very irregular sides that follow the configuration of the summit. The walls were stiffened with numerous towers of both curvilinear and rectilinear plan of which only a few examples have been preserved to a considerable height. Those parts of the enceinte which can be definitely attributed to the medieval period, apart from the citadel, are two rounded towers looking seaward in the direction of Trianda, built with fairly regular masonry and much use of mortar. The citadel, built in a roughly rectangular plan with polygonal corner-towers, was rebuilt by Grand Master d'Aubusson. A large building on the east flank of the castle, restored by the Italians before the war, seems to have served as the residence of the castellan of Philerimos.[12] The polygonal tower to the south-east of the citadel is built of varying blocks of stone brought to courses and incorporates, especially in the lower levels, numerous large blocks of ancient sandstone and marble ashlar, together with marble drums of Hellenic columns that were probably re-utilized from the remains of the ancient city itself.

There are very few structures which have remained standing within the site. Amongst these the most important are the Byzantine monastery and the church dedicated to the Virgin Mary. In 1480, prior to the siege, the Holy Image of the Virgin Mary[13] was transferred to the city of Rhodes for safety and later, after Rhodes fell to the Turks in 1523, the Hospitallers carried the icon with them to Malta.[14]

Opposite page, View of the wall-tower situated on the east salient of the citadel of Philerimos. Inset, Detail of the wall of the same tower showing the utilization of ancient through-columns (left) and the remains of a rectangular wall-tower on the main enceinte (right).

Lardos   *(Rhodes)*

Though the *casale* of Lardos had been granted by the Order in fiefdom to the VignoloVignoli shortly after the capture of Rhodes, the nearby castle of Lardos was never included in this donation and remained in the hands of the knights.[1] This *kastro* was in effect a small fortified work built on a low hill and its sole role seems to have been to afford refuge to the local inhabitants.[2]

The castle's enceinte consisted mainly of a simple elongated ward stiffened by two square towers linked together by a curtain wall. The southern flank of the castle was made up of a straight wall some 30m long, 1.65m thick at the base, and crowned by a parapet 0.5m thick. This wall joined the two square towers together. The eastern tower has disappeared altogether except for a small section of its outer face, but the west tower, which also served as the keep, has survived in better shape. The walls of the tower-keep are 2.2m thick and enclose a single vaulted room. The rest of the trace of curtain walls followed the line of the escarpment of the hill and little provision was made for flanking fire except on the north flank of the castle where there seems to have been a short stretch of faussebraye.

Today there are hardly any structures inside the castle walls except for a small vaulted cistern minus its vault. The inner face of the south curtain wall, that joining the two towers, however, appears to have had dwellings adjoining it. The castle of Lardos was overlooked by a high hill to the west. This land feature would have posed serious defence problems had the castle been called to withstand an enemy force armed with siege artillery. Such was the unsuitability of the site that the knights never attempted to strengthen the stronghold with bastions or terrepleins *alla moderna*. This would seem to indicate that, throughout

Above, Exterior and interior views of the tower-keep of the castle of Lardos. Below, Reconstruction of the castle of Lardos. Below left, Plan of the castle (after Poutiers).

most of the fifteenth and the early sixteenth century, the role of Lardos castle had been relegated to that of a policing and observation post guarding the southern route towards Gennadion.[3]

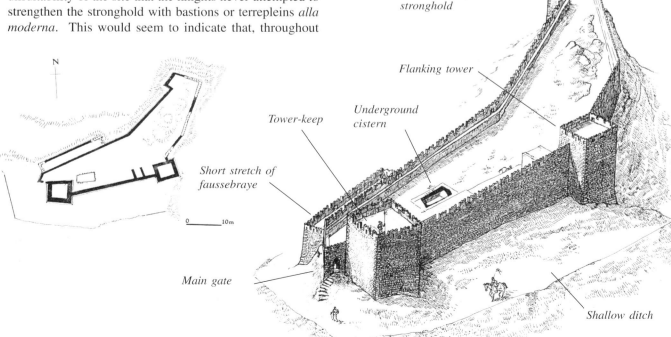

East salient of stronghold

Flanking tower

Tower-keep

Underground cistern

Short stretch of faussebraye

Main gate

Shallow ditch

N

0   10m

Sianna   (*Rhodes*)

The castle of Sianna is located on the slopes of Mount Akramitis and once served to control an important inland route across the island. The Hospitallers made Sianna the seat of a powerful administrative centre which controlled the region extending from Kritinia to Apolakkia.[1] The castle, now in ruins, was erected high on the edge of a cliff, towering over the present-day village. It consisted of two distinct parts, a *castrum* occupying the highest point on the rocky outcrop and an outer bailey which enclosed an adjoining plateau perched on the descended slopes along the south-west side of the castle. Very little remains today of this settlement.

The upper part of the castle, on the other hand, can be intuited with relative confidence. The best preserved part of the enceinte is the northern section of the walls where a large rectangular wall-tower with a heavily-battered lower half still occupies a commanding position along the north-east corner of the enceinte. Adjoining this tower, to the east, there stands a short but thick curtain wall crowned by three merlons. This curtain wall, with its wide *chemin-de-ronde* and crenellations fitted with gun-loops, was certainly a late addition to the defences as it was designed to upgrade the fortress into the cannon era. The north-west part of the enceinte consisted of a small roughly semicircular tower of which only the base survives. This was linked to another wall from which projected a bastion with heavily battered faces. These works covered the principal approach to the castle. The south walls, on the other hand, were perched along the edge of the cliff and were much weaker in build. The enceinte here consisted of a chapel-tower and a circular corner-tower of which only a few remains survive. No buildings have survived within the fortified enclosure except for what was once a large oval cistern.

Above, The remains of the lower half of the tower-keep and adjoining crenellated curtain wall. Below, General layout and left, plan of the castle of Sianna .

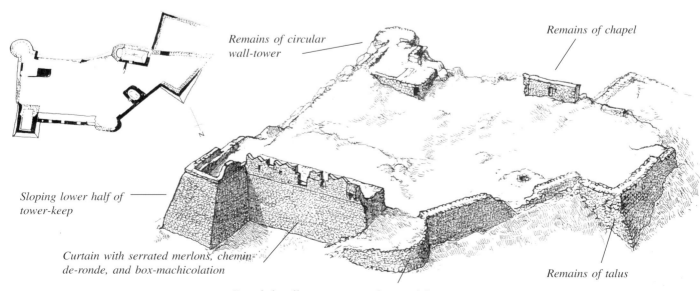

Remains of circular wall-tower

Remains of chapel

Sloping lower half of tower-keep

Curtain with serrated merlons, chemin-de-ronde, and box-machicolation

Remains of talus

Rounded wall-tower apparently containing gateway

Archangelos   *(Rhodes)*

The village and castle of Archangelos are situated about 27 km south of the city of Rhodes, some distance inland from the coast on the island's east littoral plains and north of the fortress of Pheraclos. The origins of this castle appear to go far back to the pre-Hospitaller area. In 1457 the stronghold did not prove strong enough to withstand a Turkish *razzia*. Most of the inhabitants of the *casale*, then the 'più popolato di tutta l'Isola di Rodi', were carried off into slavery and the small castle itself was sacked and ruined.[1] Subsequently, Grand Master Jacques de Milly had the stronghold rebuilt and enlarged, the effort being completed by Grand Master Zacosta in 1467, 'nel istesso Consiglio fu determinato, che si finisse, e si conducesse a perfettione, il Castello, che'l Gran Maestro defunto, faceva edificare al Casale Archangelo; per guardia, e sicurezza dell'istesso Casale; acciò gli Infedeli, non potessero più saccheggiarlo, ne rubbarlo; come per l'addietro fatto havevano.'[2]

These works, which were undertaken between 1457 and 1466, involved mainly the addition of a larger quadrangular enceinte onto the older structure. The latter, as a result, then became the donjon of the new fortified work.[3] The new enceinte also enclosed a bailey and chapel. The north-west face of the castle, next to the entrance, bears escutcheons with the coat-of-arms of Grand Masters Zacosta (together with the date MCCCCLXVII) and Orsini who later enlarged the bailey of the castle to give it its present elliptical plan.[4] The arms of Orsini also appear on the long wall along the castle's west front. Remains of a third frame, similar to the one bearing the arms of Zacosta, lie above the arms of Orsini which seem to have replaced it. The enceinte on the north-west front, overlooking the

village, was designed to command the passage up into the entrance of the castle. Only a few flagstones and the foundations of walls, together with two pivot holes, show where the main entrance was located. This approach was protected further by an outer wall serving as a barbican while the south salient projected outwards to form a wall-tower fitted with a well-preserved gun-loop. A small circular tower, sited within the enclosure just behind the gate marks one of the corner-turrets of the original pre-1457 stronghold.[5] Flanking defence along the castle's enceinte, devoid as it was of any towers, was provided instead by small dents and jogs along the irregular trace of the walls. The walls do not have a *chemin-de-ronde*, but

Below, View of the north front of Archangelos castle. The framed escutcheons (above) are of Grand Masters Orsini and Zacosta. The right extremity of this front terminates in a rectangular salient designed to provide enfilading fire along the castle's western enceinte (top).

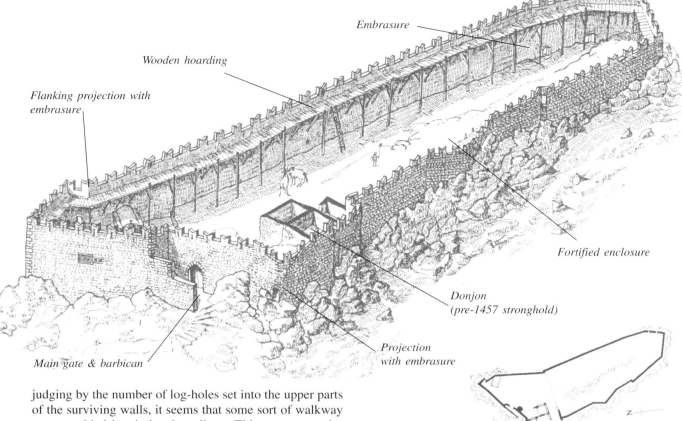

Embrasure

Wooden hoarding

Flanking projection with
embrasure

Fortified enclosure

Donjon
(pre-1457 stronghold)

Main gate & barbican

Projection
with embrasure

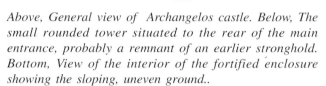

judging by the number of log-holes set into the upper parts of the surviving walls, it seems that some sort of walkway was provided by timber hoarding. This was a popular practice in Rhodian fortifications due to the local abundance of wood.[6] No merlons or parapets have survived. The walls themselves are built in similar fashion to other fortifications in Rhodes and the Dodecanese, that is, with rough and unequal blocks of stone, brought to courses with the heavy use of stone pinnings and lime mortar. In some places the covering of mortar was so thickly applied over the masonry that it is difficult to distinguish between the separate courses of stone. A number of gun-loops, some of which are thought to be of later Turkish construction, can be found set within the walls and opening outwards at the ground-level.[7] The foundations of a number of rooms occupy the north-west salient of the keep. In the fifteenth century the castle of Archangelos featured increasingly amongst those castles that were considered strong enough to shelter the rural population in times of impending danger.[8] In 1479, however, the inhabitants of this *casale* were ordered to retreat to the safety of the nearby fortress of Pheraclos.[9] In 1503 Archangelos was once again sacked by Turkish corsairs.[10]

Above, General view of Archangelos castle. Below, The small rounded tower situated to the rear of the main entrance, probably a remnant of an earlier stronghold. Bottom, View of the interior of the fortified enclosure showing the sloping, uneven ground..

Monolithos   *(Rhodes)*

The castle of Monolithos was built on the summit of a steep rocky outcrop about 200m in height, a short distance inland away from the sea. From its strategic position, the castle commanded an unobstructed view of the southern seaward approaches to the island. When enemy ships were sighted in the strait of the island of Chalki, messages were signalled from Monolithos to the other observation posts on the surrounding hills and the warning was relayed to the neighbouring castle of Kritinia until it eventually reached the city of Rhodes farther north.

Like an eagle's nest crowning the crest of a hill, Monolithos was virtually unassailable as the castle could only be reached by a narrow winding footpath. The inaccessibility of the precipitous site contributed much to the defence of this stronghold and made up for its fragile walls which follow a very irregular trace along the contours of the rocky outcrop. Only on the southern and south-eastern part of the enceinte was any effort made to provide stout walls equipped with a *chemin-de-ronde* and well-defined defences. There, a squarish tower commanded the path leading to the small entrance situated in the flank of the tower. Behind and to the west of the tower, stood a series of buildings built so close to the parapet wall that they only allowed for a very narrow walkway. The parapet along this section of the ramparts was fitted with a single box-machicolation

Above, top, The castle of Monolithos perched inaccessibly on the summit of a precipitous rocky crag. Above, Detail of a vaulted embrasure.

supported on two stone corbels. A single vaulted embrasure for cannon, built inside and beneath the *chemin-de-ronde* of a short stretch of projecting curtain wall provided the sole means for enfilading fire along the castle's southern enceinte. The stronghold's western enceinte, facing seaward and consisting mainly of a low parapet minus crenellations, followed an irregular outline. Still visible are many remains of stone walls placed at right angles to the parapet. These seem to indicate that a system of traverses was used to afford better protection to the defenders. On the northern extremity of the castle, on a partially detached outcrop of rock, the knights built a large vaulted building which seems to have been used as a magazine for the storage of gunpowder.

The rectangular tower that confronts visitors to the castle on climbing to the top of the summit.

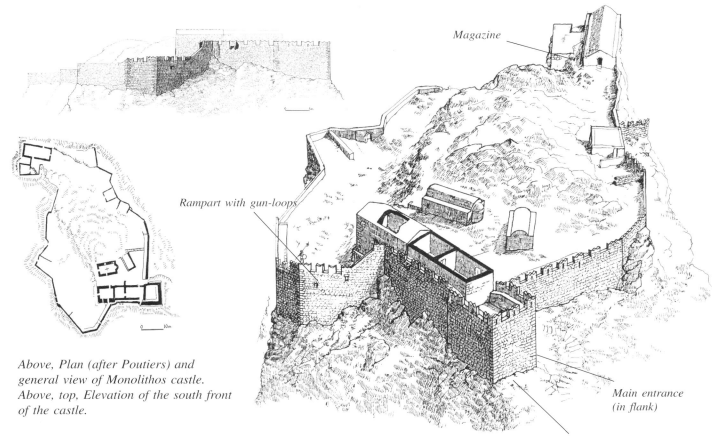

Magazine

Rampart with gun-loops

Main entrance
(in flank)

Rectangular wall-tower

*Above, Plan (after Poutiers) and
general view of Monolithos castle.
Above, top, Elevation of the south front
of the castle.*

Internally, the remains of a large number of walls seem to
indicate that the castle was once crowded with small
dwellings. The present chapel found within the castle is a
modern construction. It was built, however, next to the
foundations of a church which was still in existence in the
nineteenth century.[1]

Little is known about the history of this stronghold, though
it seems that the use of the site as a place of refuge predates the arrival of the Order. Bosio states that the castle
of Monolithos was rebuilt in 1476 to make it a safer refuge
place for the inhabitants of the locality; 'che facesse
riedificare il castello di Monolito in modo, che da contadini
habitare si potesse.'[2] These works may have included, apart
from the construction of small dwellings to accommodate
the local inhabitants, the remains of which are still to be
encountered on site, also the erection of the small tower
keep and the provision of gun-embrasures and walkways.
The latter features would seem to date to around that period.

*Below, Rampart and chemin-de-ronde link up to one of the
buildings on the south front of the castle. Below left,
A vaulted magazine placed out of reach on the northern
salient of the stronghold.*

Asklipion   *(Rhodes)*

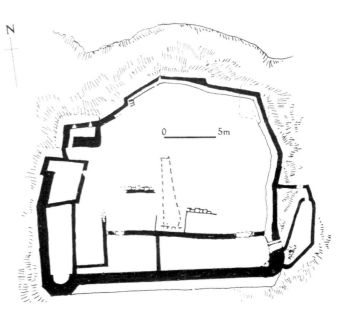

The castle of Asklipion is situated in the south-east part of the island of Rhodes. Its strategic position enabled the surveillance of a large part of the coastline and overlooked the inland routes that traversed the island, including the approaches leading from Gennadion in the southern part of Rhodes. This gave the stronghold an important role in the defence of the rural areas. Built atop a rocky spur of land a considerable distance inland from the shore, it was screened from view by a number of hills situated between the shore and castle, rendering it practically invisible from the sea. The village of Asklipion does not appear to have been fortified by any tower or castle before the arrival of the knights.[1] The surviving remains of the castle seem to date from the Hospitaller period and the stronghold itself bears witness to at least two major phases of construction. The first saw the building of a quadrilateral castle flanked by four corner towers. The thickness of the tower and curtain walls varied between 1.30m and 1.50m. The south-east tower, formed from a pronounced rounding of the corner of the walls, contained the main entrance to the castle. This was surmounted by a box-machocoulis of which only the three corbel stones survive to this day, and a moulded box frame which contained an escutcheon bearing a magistral coat-of-arms. The north-west tower was square in plan, having rounded corners and battered wall. It was built on the highest part of the rocky outcrop and the thickness of its southern wall (1.55m) suggests that originally the tower was larger than that which survives today, having been modified in the second phase of construction when its other walls were rebuilt to a thickness of 0.70m.[2] The northern wall was fitted with a few loopholes.

Although no remains have survived, a north-east corner tower must have existed to provide enfilading fire along the exposed north and east curtain walls. It is possible that this tower was removed when the northern enceinte of the castle was rebuilt during the second phase of construction. The south-west tower, of which only the foundation walls remain, appears to have been of the chapel-tower type, similar to the well-preserved example at Kastellos. This provided flanking fire along the face of the south curtain wall.[3] The first phase of the castle's construction, mirrored in the thick walls and total absence of any provision for the deployment of cannon, clearly indicates that the castle was constructed well before the latter half of the fifteenth century. Internally, the castle was divided into two unequal

Above, Plan of Asklipion castle (after Poutiers). Below, View of the surviving walls on the southern part of the stronghold, and bottom, the small tower with sloping walls which occupies the north-west corner of the enceinte.

The remains of the barbican and main gate, once protected by a box-machicoulis resting on three corbels.

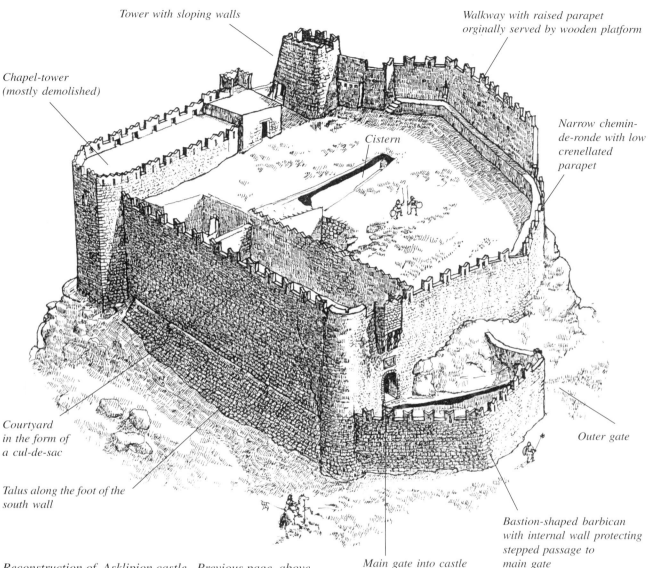

Tower with sloping walls

Walkway with raised parapet orginally served by wooden platform

Chapel-tower (mostly demolished)

Cistern

Narrow chemin-de-ronde with low crenellated parapet

Courtyard in the form of a cul-de-sac

Outer gate

Talus along the foot of the south wall

Bastion-shaped barbican with internal wall protecting stepped passage to main gate

Main gate into castle

Reconstruction of Asklipion castle. Previous page, above, View of the inner wall separating the lower courtyard from the main enclosure. Below, The narrow walkway on the east side of the enceinte.

areas. The main entrance opened onto the narrower and lower part, which was flanked on one side by what seems to have been a crenellated wall that provided an inner, second line of defence against an enemy breaking through the main gateway, a sort of *cul-de-sac*. The main enclosure contained some dwellings and a long and narrow underground cistern.

The second phase of construction, dating to the early years of the sixteenth century, reflects the response to the growing threat of gunpowder-operated weapons. The new works, however, were very limited in scope and would not have radically effected its defence. These consisted of a complete restoration of the castle's northern enceinte and the construction of a barbican in front of the castle's gate. The foot of the south curtain wall was also reinforced with a masonry buttress or talus. The new northern enceinte, which did away with the north-east tower, was built to a slightly bastioned trace that permitted a limited flanking defence of the curtain wall. As a result of these alterations, the *chemin-de-ronde* was also modified. The barbican was a work in the form of a small fragile bastion, with very short flanks and orillions. Its walls, however, were too thin to offer any effective form of protection against cannon. The efforts to modernize the castle of Asklipion were cut short by the Turkish invasion of 1522, and the stronghold remained intrinsically medieval in character.[4]

Kastellos   *(Rhodes)*

The north-west coast of Rhodes was protected by a number of strong castles, the southernmost of which was Kastellos. From its strategic position, Kastellos, today also known as Kritinia castle, controlled a vast section of coast line and the routes leading southwards from the mountains to Sianna and Embonas. Kastellos also commanded a clear view of the island of Alimonia and its adjoining islets of Makri, Strongili, and Tragoussia, together with the straits that separated these islands from Rhodes.

Interior view of the tower-keep of Kastellos.

The origins of Kastellos date back to the magistracy of Orsini who fortified the site, then known as Telemonias, in 1472.[1] The original fortification consisted of a simple squarish tower which was built on the crest of an outcrop of rock. This tower, which still bears an escutcheon with the coat-of-arms of Grand Master Orsini, was later on incorporated as a keep into the enceinte of a larger fortress. Today, much of the tower has collapsed but originally it consisted of a single large room topped by a roof supported on wooden beams and enclosed by a crenellated parapet. Apparently, the tower was erected to provide some measure of protection against corsair raids to a small rural habitat situated in the area, as was the case at Lardos, Askiplion, and Archangelos.[2] At a later stage, the small village was enveloped within a fortified enclosure which incorporated the tower itself. A fortified chapel, built on heavily-sloping ground and rising majestically in the form of a tower, was

added to the enceinte, enabling the defenders to provide enfilading fire along two faces of the perimeter wall. The lower part of the chapel-tower was fitted with embrasures for cannon. The roof of this gun-chamber, now missing, formed the floor of the nave. Externally, a marble escutcheon bearing the coat-of-arms of Grand Master Pierre d'Aubusson (1476-1503), bears witness to the period when the erection or, most probably, reconstruction of this structure took place.

A third stage in the development of Kastellos was the erection of a strong second enceinte, primarily designed to mount cannon. A large rectangular battery, fitted with two tiers of embrasures, was added to the west flank of the castle. The upper embrasures were set in a thick parapet that crowned the high vertical walls but no provisions were made to provide this enceinte with a strong permanent gun

The tower-keep of Kastellos as seen when approached up the rocky crag on which it was founded. This tower was the earliest part of the stronghold. It was erected, in 1472, by Grand Master Orsini on the site then known as Telemonias.

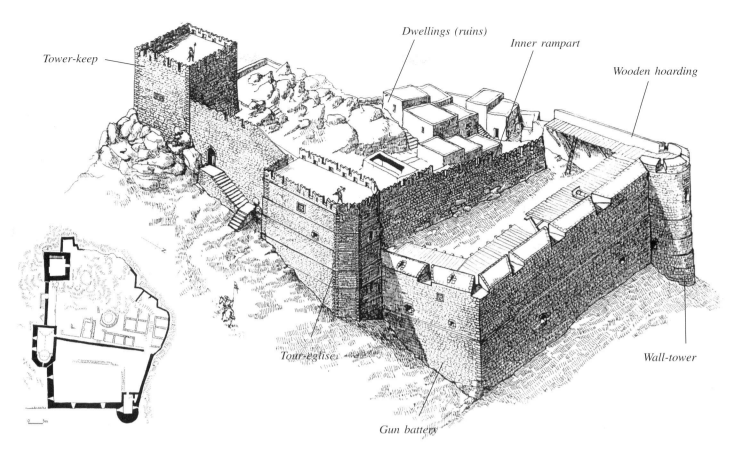

Tower-keep

Dwellings (ruins)

Inner rampart

Wooden hoarding

Tour-eglise

Gun battery

Wall-tower

platform. Instead an overhanging, wooden *chemin-de-ronde*, once supported on logs, provided the only means from which the guns could be fired from behind the parapet. Definitely, this was a very poor arrangement that must have provided a weak and unstable platform for discharging the guns. It is, however, an interesting example of the transitional stage in the development of gunpowder fortifications as it clearly illustrates how old medieval techniques were fused with the then still-developing concepts of gunpowder defences. It also reflects the knights' apprehensions as they hastily sought to improve the island's defences against the ever-increasing threat of Ottoman power.[3] This battery bears the coat-of-arms of two grand masters and clearly indicates that work on the later development of Kastellos was initiated by Grand Master Emery d'Amboise (1503-12) but was only completed by Grand Master Fabrizzio del Caretto in 1515 as the date beneath the escutcheons suggests.[4] Enfilading fire along the new enceinte was provided from the roof of the chapel-tower along the southern face and from a new round corner-

tower erected on the north-east corner of the new walls. Internally, this tower consisted of a vaulted room at ground floor level. This was fitted with two embrasures and was connected to a smaller annexe that seems to have been used as a powder-magazine.

Above, left, Plan of Kastellos (after Poutiers) and reconstruction. Above, The tour-eglise as seen from the lower inner courtyard. Below, Elevation of the main land front of the castle.

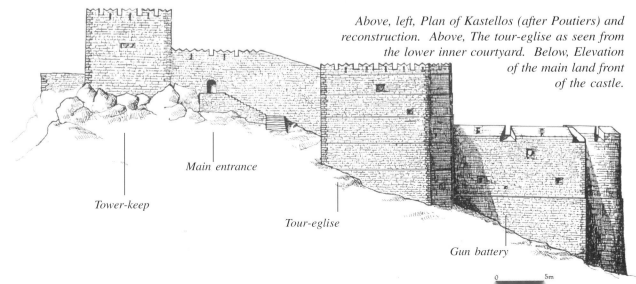

Tower-keep

Main entrance

Tour-eglise

Gun battery

0   5m

The Tour-eglise, or chapel-tower. The
chapel is situated high up in the tower.
Inset, view of the interior of the chapel
showing the apse and partly-ruined
vaulted roof.

The last stage in the development of this fortress, however, corresponds to the re-deployment of the native rural population as a result of the increasing Turkish threat. Consequently, the neighbouring medieval villages of Kamiros, Skala, and Kritinias were abandoned and their inhabitants transferred to the safety of Kastellos.[5] But since the space inside this fortress was very limited, the additional population was settled outside the southern walls of the castle, where a new quadrangular wall was hastily built to surround and protect the quickly erected huts.[6] Little evidence of these external works has survived.

Above, flank of the rectangular gun battery. The escutcheon bears the arms of Grand Master del Carretto. Below, the rounded wall-tower which occupies the north-east corner of the battery enclosure. Below, left elevation of the east front of the castle.

Kremasti   *(Rhodes)*

The castle of Kremasti stands on the west coast of the island, some 13 km south-west from the city of Rhodes. It commanded the southern route leading to the strong fortress of Paradissi and was itself preceded by the castle of Trianda. The latter was demolished in the sixteenth century on the advice of the Order's military engineers. The stronghold at Kremasti, also known as the *Kastro*, was itself under the direct surveillance of the mighty nearby fortress of Philerimos.[1]

Kremasti castle was more of a tower-keep rather than a veritable castle and consisted of a large rectangular box-shaped structure raised on two adjacent vaulted chambers, its walls pierced with embrasures for cannon and its roof crowned with a crenellated parapet. Internally, two vaulted chambers, one of which as a pointed arch, divided the *Kastro* in two unequal parts along its length. The sole entrance to the fortress, situated in the north wall, led to the narrower chamber which was fitted with two loopholes on both of its flanks. The wider south chamber was fitted with four embrasures each piercing a wall three metres thick. The roof does not seem to have been provided with ventilation shafts that would have allowed the escape of noxious fumes generated by burnt gunpowder. Instead two windows, placed one in each side of the large vaulted chamber, enabled the circulation of fresh air. At a later stage during its history, the *Kastro* seems to have been fitted with an external open battery, rectangular in plan, of which a few remains survive.[2] This work seems to have been added to cover the immediate approaches to the fort.

The *Kastro* was designed more as a policing and surveillance post rather than as a feudal castle. Still, the chapter general of 1479 stipulated that in the event of a Turkish landing, the inhabitants of the villages of Kremasti and Trianda were to seek refuge within their respective strongholds.[3] This clearly shows that these small fortresses

were expected to bar the road to the city of Rhodes. As a matter of fact, the gun embrasures of the *Kastro* were trained southwards onto the route coming up from Paradissi.[4] The stronghold at Kremasti was relatively very close to the city of Rhodes and would have been quickly reinforced with troops and munitions both from the city and from the nearby fortress of Philerimos.

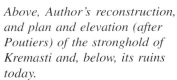

Above, Author's reconstruction, and plan and elevation (after Poutiers) of the stronghold of Kremasti and, below, its ruins today.

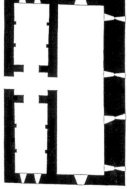

Above, The few scanty remains of the tower-keep at Apollakia. Left, One of the gun embrasures of Kremasti castle.

Villanova   *(Rhodes)*

The castle of Villanova, of which no traces remain, was situated south of the village of Paradissi on the west coast of the island of Rhodes. At the time of its demolition during the middle of the nineteenth century, the site still retained important remnants of the castle's towers, curtain walls, and vaulted buildings.[1] Described as 'bellissimo e forte',[2] it was considered capable of resisting an attack by the 'gente che quaranta Galere sbarcare potessero; ma anche a maggior numero.'[3] The castle of Villanova had a rectangular plan with sides some 50m long.[4]

Villanova was established by Grand Master Villeneuve around 1338 together with an accompanying suburb.[5] In the middle of the fourteenth century, the castle formed the seat of one of the island's smallest commanderies, having the administrative responsibility over the villages of Lorio, Damatria, Altoluogo, Niocorio, Dioscoro, and Chimides.[6] In 1364 Villanova was sacked by a Venetian fleet but after 1470, and right up to the siege of 1480, it was to form one of the principal strongholds on Rhodes. Still, prior to the siege of 1480, the council decided to abandon the castle and withdraw its garrison to the fortress of Rhodes,[7] but the decision was altered because 'considrato il Sito, e la qualita del Castello...ch'era di importanza grandissima, perche i Nemici ivi haverebbono potuto fortificarsi, e fare gli apparecchi, e le provisioni loro... fu mandato il Cavaliero Frà Antonio del Mas, per Capitano; con altri Cavalieri religiosi, e Soldati, in Presidio; con le munitioni a quella difesa necessarie.'[8] The siege of 1480, in fact, marks the decline of the castle and village of Villanova as a direct result of the destruction suffered at the hands of the Turks.[9]

Apolakkia   *(Rhodes)*

The castle of Apollakia was situated on the south-west side of the island of Rhodes, halfway between the castles of Monolithos to the north, and Kattavia to the south. It was built on a small hill overlooking the present day village about 2.5 km from the sea. Very few remains of Apollakia castle have survived to this day but still enough to show that it was a small medieval work, rectangular in plan and with two concentric enceintes. The inner enceinte consisted of a square tower connected to one corner of a rectangular ward, the walls of which were 1.75m thick. The outer enceinte, evidence of which is much more sparse, consisted of straight curtain walls some 0.75m thick. The north and north-east corners of the outer wall were stiffened by small towers three metres square in area. Poutiers suggested that these were external counterforts supporting bartizans.[1] The remains of the castle's southern walls are very fragmentary and do not allow for the reconstruction of a plan.

Plan of the castle of Apolakkia showing the tower-keep and various wards, arranged in a concentric manner typical of crusader castles in Outremer (after Poutiers).

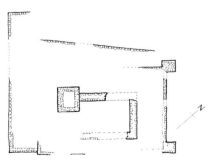

Kattavia   *(Rhodes)*

The castle of Kattavia was the southernmost defensive outpost on the island of Rhodes. This stronghold, probably dating to pre-Hospitaller times, was considered to be an important element in the defence of the island. Even so, it was not a formidable work of fortification by contemporary standards and became ever more inadequate with the introduction of gunpowder-operated artillery. By 1470, the castle at Kattavia was considered as 'non tanto sicuro'[1] although it was thought that with the implementation of 'certi ripari, e con mandarvi alcuni Cavalieri, e Soldati di più si poteva tenere benissimo.'[2] These recommendations seem to have been carried out for four years later, in 1474, in the course of defence preparations set in motion by the fear of an impending Turkish invasion, the garrison and inhabitants of the nearby 'Castellania di Messinagro' were ordered to seek refuge in the castle at Kattavia.[3]

In 1477, Grand Master d'Aubusson, following a tour of inspection of all the island's defences, advised the council of the necessity of renovating and fortifying *alla moderna*[4] (with bastions and terrepleined ramparts) the castle of Kattavia, 'il quale per l'antichità sua minacciava rovina.'[5] Earlier in 1474, a wide *fosse*[6] had been excavated around the castle and the new works proposed in 1477 were intended to render its fortifications at least as strong as those of Lindos and Pheraclos.[7] Still it does not appear that the improvements were adequate enough for, during the course of the next emergency in 1479, the people of Kattavia were ordered to retreat to the safety of Rhodes in case of attack.[8] This suggests that works on the castle were still uncompleted and vulnerable to attack. In the following

year, however, when there appeared again the danger of attack, no such order was issued. Instead, the castle was detailed to provide refuge to the inhabitants of many villages in the southern part of the island, suggesting that the new works were eventually completed and the castle considered defensible. Indeed, a slab with the arms of the Order and of D'Aubusson inscribed with the date 1481 (which Gerola saw affixed to the police barracks inside the village of Kattavia in the early years of this century)[9] seems to suggest that this was the case. The village of Kattavia was sacked by corsairs in 1503.[10] Little survives today of the castle of Kattavia apart from some sparse mural remains and the foundations of a circular wall-tower. From these it can be seen that the castle's ramparts were built of rubble work brought to courses with much use of plaster and stone pinnings, a form of construction typical of most strongholds in the Dodecanese.

Fanes   *(Rhodes)*

The stronghold of Fanes, or Fiando, was situated on the west coast of the island of Rhodes and occupied a hilltop site some distance inland from the shore. This stronghold appears to have been a weak defensive work and may owe its origin more to a place of refuge rather than a veritable castle. Nonetheless, it had its own garrison which, however, in times serious danger, was often recalled to the safety of Rhodes together with the inhabitants of the nearby villages. The Turkish armada anchored in the vicinity of Fanes in December 1479. Only some scanty remains survive of the stronghold of Fanes today, suggesting a squarish fort similar to that at Kremasti.[1] The sides of this stronghold were not larger than the length of thirty paces.[2] Of the other Hospitaller castles which were once found on Rhodes, such as as Lachania, Laerma, Psinthos, Apolona, Salakos, and Trianda, there are no longer any significant traces of their fortifications to be seen.

Remains of circular tower at Kattavia (Courtesy of the Archaeological Institute of the Dodecanese). Above, right, old map showing the location of Kattavia.

The Coastal Towers of Rhodes

The Hospitaller knights do not appear to have built watch-towers around the shores of Rhodes and the other islands before the fifteenth century. This is explained by the fact that, under the Order's rule, Rhodes only began to experience repeated raids and incursions with the rise of Turkish power in the fifteenth century. The frequency of corsair attacks throughout the late fifteenth century did much to disrupt the rural settlements and resulted in serious economic setbacks as much of the island's agricultural produce was devastated. In the course of these attacks, the rural habitats were pillaged and set afire, and many of the peasants themselves carried off into slavery,[1] 'nonostante le diligenze, e le guardie vigilantissime, ch'intorno all'Isola di Rodi, per Ordine del Gran Maestro si facevano.'[2] One of the most serious of these episodes was the Turkish *razzia* on the village of Archangelos in 1457.[3]

An *incursum* near Sianna in 1474 was instrumental in the formation of a fifty-strong cavalry force intended to patrol the coast and repel any landing wherever this occurred, but this unit proved ineffective as there was no established method by which alarms and warning signals could be relayed along the length of the island.[4] The Hospitallers thus sought to render the island more secure with the erection of a chain of coastal towers which were sited around the whole coast, a policy later reintroduced in Malta in the seventeenth century. These towers were intended to warn of any suspicious vessels with carrier pigeons by day and fire signal by night, relaying the alarm from tower to tower and castle to castle, way back to the main fortress of Rhodes. The first reference to the construction of a watch tower dates back to 1366, when the Hospitallers had bound Borrello Assanti of Ischia to build a strong tower on the nearby island of Alimonia in return for the grant of the islands of Tilos and Chalki.[5] However, this tower does not appear to have been built because a ship loaded with materials for the construction of a tower was only sent to Alimonia in 1476.[6]

It was in 1474 that the council of the Order decreed that a large number of towers were to be set up around the whole coast of Rhodes, 'ch'intorno alla detta Isola di Rodi, molte Torri fabricare si dovessero. E con tal deliberatione, fu nell'istesso giorno, mandato il Comendatore Frà Battista Grimauld Provenzale, Cavaliero molto giuditioso, intendente, e pratico; accompagnato da'venticinque altri

Above, Two views of the Hospitaller coastal watch-tower of Paliochora near Monolithos (courtesy of the Archaeological Institute of the Dodecanese).

Cavalieri ben'a cavallo, e ben'in ordine; per visitare i Luoghi, dove dette Torri fabricare so dovessero; accioche i poveri Rodioti, le possessioni loro sicuramente, e quietamente coltivare potessero.'[7] It was only two years later, however, that any tangible action was taken to implement the decision to build coastal watch-towers when the council ordered the construction of two 'Torri di guardia, ne'Lidi, e nelle Marine dell'Isola di Rodi', one facing the island of Alimonia (Kamiros Skala) and 'un'altra grossa Torre co'suoi Barbacani, verso Santa Marta.'[8]

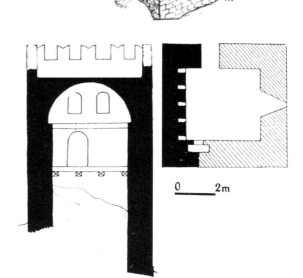

Above, Remains of the tower at Glifada and right, reconstruction and plan and sectional elevation (after Poutiers). Below, left, Plan of the remains of the tower of Stegna, east of Archangelos (after Poutiers).

With the death of Grand Master Orsini in 1476, it was realized that the financial situation confronting the Order would not even allow the completion of the two towers already initiated.[9] Grand Master d'Aubusson, however, conscious of both the urgent need to erect some castles and many towers and the Order's many debts, ordered that a new tax be paid on the Order's properties and commanderies to finance these new fortifications.[10] As a result, work on the coastal towers began in 1477, and when completed, these were 'ben provedute di gente, d'Artglieria, e di munitioni; accio guardare e difendere si potessero i Luoghi, onde facile adito, e discesa a Nemici si dava.'[11]

The towers built under Grand Master d'Aubusson all appear to have had a rectangular plan. In all, 14 such rectangular towers have been identified but nearly all are in ruins. One of the best preserved today is the tower at PalioChoria, near the castle of Monolithos on the west coast of Rhodes. Another, though partially ruined one, is found at Glyfada

Below, The Pyrgos at Trianda (courtesy of M. Losse).

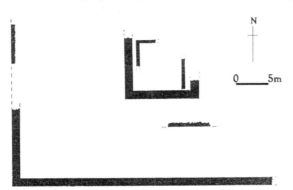

Map of Rhodes showing the distribution of coastal watch-towers.

(known as Pirgho pi Pirati), in the vicinity of Sianna.[12] Its best preserved part is the rear section to the east facing inland. In plan, both towers are roughly square, the latter measuring 6.7m on each side. The walls of the Glyfada tower measure 1.5m thick and rise about 9m on the landward side.

Below, the Pyrgos on the island of Telos (after Gerola).

On the seaward side, the walls, now demolished, fell further downwards since the structure was built on sloping ground. Internally the tower consisted of a single, high barrel-vault divided into three storeys by means of two wooden floors which were each supported along five beams judging by the log-holes cut into the inner faces of the walls. The main entrance was situated at the level of the first floor, in the centre of the south wall. Opposite the entrance, stood a small fire-place set in the thickness of the wall. The higher floor was lit by two windows set in the south and north walls. Two stone corbels show that a box-machicoulis projected from the parapet above the entrance. The roof of the tower was undoubtedly enclosed by a crenellated parapet. At Lahania, in the vicinity of the church of St Irene, lie the remains of another squarish tower built in 1477, but now robbed of most of the ashlar blocks that faced its outer walls.[13] The tower was decorated with a cordon and the lower half seems to have had battered walls. Internally this tower consisted of a large barrel-vault.

Remains of other towers built at an unknown dates can be found in other parts of Rhodes. At Dimilia, in the mountainous centre of the island, are the scattered ruins of a massive rectangular tower, internally vaulted, and located some distance away from the adjoining village.[14] Gerola also mentioned another two rectangular tower-like buildings sited in a locality known as Lelos, near the village of Apollona.[15]

Kastellorizo

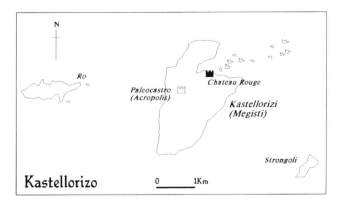

Kastellorizo, a small mountainous island lying a a few miles off the Turkish coast, was the first of the Greek islands to be occupied by the Hospitallers. Their small naval fleet had stopped there to regroup whilst on its way from Cyprus towards the invasion of Rhodes.[1] The date when the Order actually occupied Kastellorizo, however, has still to be determined. By 1381, there was a *castellenus* of *Castrum Rubeum*[2] while in 1383 the island was being used to incarcerate unruly knights.[3]

Lying some 115 km south-east of Rhodes and only 2.5 km south of the Anatolian mainland, opposite Lycia and towards the sea of Cyprus, Kastellorizo is the easternmost of the Greek islands. It is barely 10 km[2] in area but very mountainous. In antiquity, the island was known as Megiste and was occupied since Neolithic times, as can be seen from a number of Cyclopean walls on the island.[4] Dorian settlers later built fortresses at the site of the present village and at Palaekastro. That at Palaekastro was built at a considerable altitude on one of the island's two highest summits, nearly 300m above sea-level. This was the acropolis of Megiste, Kisthene, the ruins of which can still be seen crowning the summit.[5] At that time there was also a fort dominating the harbour which was built by the Rhodiot Sosicles of Nikagros on the site of the later medieval fort.[6] During the Byzantine occupation, both fortifications were retained in use right up to the coming of the Hospitallers in 1306.[7]

The island of Kastellorizo was too small to have any strategic value and served mainly as a lookout post for the monitoring of Turkish shipping in the area. Smoke and mirror signals from the summit of the Vighla heights were used to warn the island of Rhodes of any Turkish movements in the area.[8] The Hospitallers did not invest much energy in the fortification of the island. They concentrated their efforts only in strengthening the defences of the harbour fort. This castle, which later came to be known as Chateau Rouge, because of the reddish earth that surrounds it, was a very small structure. It consisted of two main parts, a stout tower-keep and a small outer bailey. Although ruined, much of the castle has survived and these ruins, together with a few scanty historical references, provide a reasonably clear picture of its development.

The oldest part of the stronghold is definitely the tower, a sturdy squarish structure with a base of about 35m x 32m,

having a heavily battered lower half. The sloping talus, however, is not present on the seaward side of the castle where the vertical face of the tower, the only section to survive that is higher than the first floor, is punctuated by a blocked-up doorway topped by a moulded box-frame (once containing an inscription) of the type found at Rhodes during the time of Grand Master Lastic. On its northern face, one finds a narrow berm instead of the talus and the wall has a number of log-holes which show where there could have been some form of wooden walkway linking the tower to the lower bailey below. Large ashlar blocks of re-utilized classical masonry form the quoins of the talus. It is known that this castle was demolished by the Egyptians in 1444 and reconstruction works were initiated in 1451.[9] The tower's heavy talus could probably be buttressing added during this period as a form of reinforcement, as was done

Below, Detail of the framed recess which once supported escutcheons, situated high on the north face of the tower-keep.

Detail of the blocks of re-utilized Hellenic marble serving as quoins in the talus of the tower-keep at Kastellorizo. Inset, View of the north façade of the tower-keep.

on the walls of Antimacchia after the earthquake of 1496. The box-frame moulding mentioned above is datable to the period 1437-54 and therefore corraborates the fact that the tower was rebuilt in 1451. The walls of the tower were built of roughly-hewn blocks of stone of unequal sizes and shapes, brought to courses with the use of much mortar and stone and clay pinnings. The tower had a small ground floor doorway set in the south face wall which has now been blocked up. This must have led into a vaulted room. Another small doorway was placed centrally in the south face of the upper floor. This was once roofed and surmounted by a crenellated parapet, traces of which, however, have not survived. Another entrance to the first floor is situated on the east side where a small circular wall-tower, once connected to the rest of the walkway of the outer bailey, provided some limited form of enfilading capability along the keep's east face. The vertical walls of the upper part of the tower average about 1.7m thick and inside these are the remains of a staircase that ran up to the roof.

The walls of the outer bailey, especially the corner towers, are built with slightly more regular masonry that indicates a later phase in the castles development but there is little to indicate if this was built before or after 1451. The outer

enclosure probably already existed before this date, but the round towers seem to date to the post-1451 period. The outer bailey was built on a lower shelf at the foot of the tower and its walls trace the edge of the cliff. From this position the stronghold held a commanding view of the entrance to the harbour. Two flanking walls stretched outwards from the tower to link up with the two rounded towers. A small postern, set in the face of the intervening curtain wall, opened on to the precipitous cliffs. Inside the bailey, there was a cistern and a couple of buildings set against the outer wall. The whole complex was quite small and would definitely have not been able to absorb the inhabitants of the island in times of attack. There could have been, therefore, another outer wall, or ward, to the south of the castle which would have served as a refuge but no such traces are visible.

It is much more probable that the old acropolis would have served as the islanders' sanctuary in times of danger. This was definitely in use throughout the Byzantine period as can be seen from the number of medieval ruins lying within its ancient walls. Moreover, the height on which the acropolis stands faces towards Rhodes and would definitely have been the best place from where to communicate with the larger island by means of smoke and mirror signals. Such signals could not have been made from the castle down by the harbour since this was overlooked by higher ground.

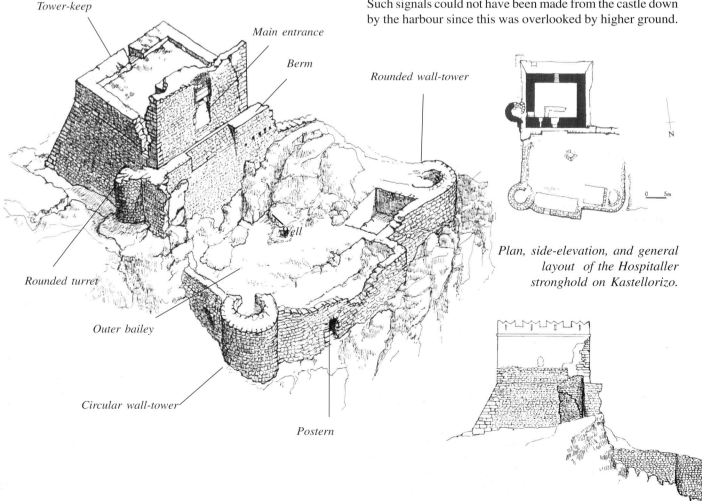

Tower-keep

Main entrance

Berm

Rounded wall-tower

Well

Rounded turret

Outer bailey

Circular wall-tower

Postern

Plan, side-elevation, and general layout of the Hospitaller stronghold on Kastellorizo.

It would have been also necessary for the Hospitaller garrison to retain some form of presence on the acropolis height since this undoubtedly provided an excellent lookout to monitor Turkish shipping.

Given that it was situated closer to the Turkish mainland than to Rhodes, the island of Kastellorizo was consequently much more exposed to Turkish pressure. So much so that in 1395, the Hospitallers at Kastellorizo were rumoured to be in truce with the Turks[10] from the nearby mainland. The Order's precarious hold was shattered in 1440 when a fleet of 18 Mameluke vessels attacked and sacked the island and its castle before proceeding to Rhodes.[11] The island was sacked again in 1444 and the castle apparently demolished because in 1451 Bernardo di Villamarino, general of the king of Aragon, occupied the island and set about 'riedificare il Castello, ch'ivi era stato dall'Armata del Soldano, gia sett'anni prima rovinato, quando andò all'assedio di Rodi.'[12] The grand master and his council reacted quickly to this violation of their sovereignty by dispatching the knight Frà Pietro Cariol to Kastellorizo to order Villamarino to abandon his enterprise. The inhabitants of the island were also warned not to help Villamarino in the reconstruction of the castle on pain of confiscation of all their property. Once Villarino left the island, however, Frà Cariol was ordered to continue with the reconstruction of the castle.[13]

It seems, however, that these new works were undertaken instead by King Ferdinand of Naples, to whom the Order apparently ceded the island: 'teneva a quei tempi, il Re Ferdinando di Napoli, l'Isola di castel Rosso, che la Religione ceduta gli haveva; e egli con molta spesa haveva fortificato il castello di quella.'[14] In 1471 a revolt broke out amongst the garrison of the castle of Kastellorizo in the course of which the governor and captain were put in chains. The Hospitallers, on behalf of the king, dispatched a galley under the command of Frà Cencio Orsino to subdue the revolt.[15] Thereafter, little is heard of the castle until during the early sixteenth century when it was once again

Above, Two views of the wall-tower on the east side of the outer bailey.

subjected to the growing fury of the Ottoman power.[16] It was attacked in 1512 and with the fall of Rhodes in 1522, it was lost to the Turks. The Venetians occupied the castle in 1570 and again in 1659, during the Turko-Venetian war over Crete.[17]

The tower-keep at Kastellorizo as seen from the south-east. Note the small circular turret flanking the tower.

Chalki & Alimonia

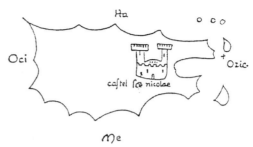

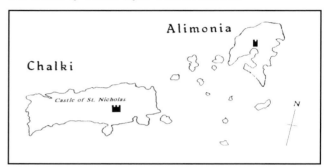

The island of Chalki (after Buondelmonte).

Just off the west coast of Rhodes, facing Kritinia, lies a group of small islands, the largest and most important of which are Chalki and Alimonia. Both islands are mentioned by Bosio as being amongst the first occupied by the Hospitallers after their conquest of Rhodes, 'i nomi delle quali, sono Nissaro, Episcopia, Calchi, Limonia, Simie, Tilo, e San Nicolo di Cardo.'[1] This entry, however, makes some strange reading because *Episcopia* and *Tilo* (Tilos) are the same island; so are *Calchi* and *San Nicolo di Cardo*. In antiquity Chalki was famous for its copper mines but by the middle ages it had sunk into oblivion. In Hospitaller times, both Chalki and Limonia were administered directly from Rhodes. In 1366 the Order granted Chalki, together with Tilos, *in feudo* to Borrello Assanti of Ischia, a *borghese* of Rhodes on condition that he was to construct a tower on Alimonia and that he was to pay 'dugento fiorini d'oro di tributo ogni anno ... ordinandogli di non riscuotere da quei Vassalli, Schiavi e Villani più di quello, ch'alla Religione pagar solevano.'[2]

Although quite small, just 28 km² in area, Chalki is a mountainous island and its former capital, Chora, was situated inland on the site of an ancient acropolis. The old castle of the knights, albeit much ruined, still crowns the crest of that hill. The old castle walls trace the configuration of the summit, as a consequence of which the plan of the stronghold forms an elongated rectangle. Flanking defences were very limited. On the main north and south flanks there were two wall-towers, one polygonal and the other rectangular. The walls on the south side of the castle have in most parts collapsed but do not seem to have stood very high because on that side the summit fell steeply downwards into a deep ravine.

The castle's walls were constructed with fairly regular pieces of stone, brought to courses and held together with much use of mortar, heavily galletted with stone and pottery pinnings. The best-preserved section of the ramparts is found on the northern side overlooking the deserted *borgo*. At the extreme east end of this front lies the main entrance into the stronghold, next to which, affixed high on the adjoining wall in a square moulded frame, is a marble escutcheon bearing the arms of Grand Master d'Aubusson. For their larger part, the walls rest on Hellenic foundations of coursed trapezoidal masonry. Provision for flanking defences along this long stretch of ramparts was achieved mainly through re-entrant angles in the trace of walls but there were also two small rectangular towers, one placed halfway along the front and the other at the extreme end of the enceinte. The centrally-placed tower was provided with small gunloops. No further effort was ever made to render the castle *alla moderna*.

The fortress of Chalki relied for its defence mainly on the inaccessibility of the site and its medieval walls were served by a narrow *chemin-de-ronde*. Large merlons, with serrated tops, typical of other contemporary Hospitaller works,

Elevation of the main front of the castle of St Nicholas.

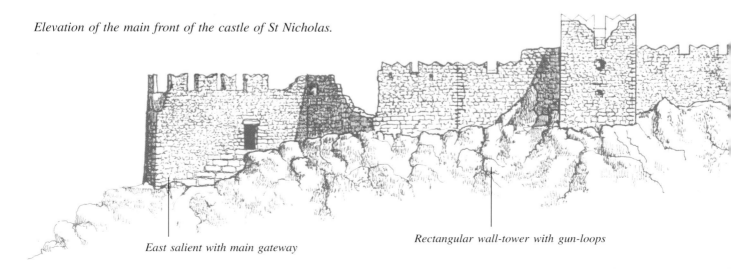

East salient with main gateway

Rectangular wall-tower with gun-loops

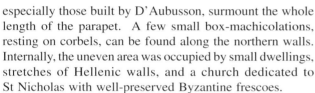

especially those built by D'Aubusson, surmount the whole length of the parapet. A few small box-machicolations, resting on corbels, can be found along the northern walls. Internally, the uneven area was occupied by small dwellings, stretches of Hellenic walls, and a church dedicated to St Nicholas with well-preserved Byzantine frescoes.

Notwithstanding the fact that the stronghold was difficult to attack, the inhabitants of Chalki were frequently compelled to abandon their island for the safety of Rhodes. Such episodes occurred in 1475 and 1480.[3] Again in 1493, the inhabitants received permission to retreat to Rhodes on condition that they contributed towards the construction of the Tower of Sta Marta.[4] The lack of artillery defences at Chalki would seems to imply that the island had lost much of its importance to the Hospitallers from the later half of the fifteenth century onwards.

Above, left, View of the east salient of St Nicholas castle (after Gerola). The path up the steep mountain was rendered more difficult by the uneven surface and rocky bolders. Right, Detail of the merlons and arrow-slits along the same section of ramparts.

On the nearby island of Alimonia, the Hospitallers' concern was to provide a look-out post with which to monitor shipping movements along the west coast of Rhodes. In 1366, Borrello Assanti was to construct a tower of stipulated dimensions in return for the grant of Chalki and Tilos from the Order: 'edificare una Torre nell'Isola di Limonia, gagliarda, e forte; conformo al disegno, che dato gli sarebbe da due Cavalieri.'[5] Borrello was also to provide three of the stipulated six-men garrison[6] but it does not appear that this tower was actually erected for, in 1475,[7] the Hospitallers again ordered the construction of a strong tower on

Alimonia, and early in the following year 'fu mandato una gran Nave Genovese caricata di tutti gli apparecchi necessarji, per fabricar la torre all'Isola di Limonia.'[8]

In actual fact, the Hospitallers built more than a tower, but a small fort. They constructed their fortification on top of a hill overlooking the main bay, using the ruins of an ancient Hellenic fort as a foundation. The knights only utilized a small section of the Hellenic fort, the eastern part, thus creating a work in the form of a squattish rectangular tower. The eastern side of the fort, containing a small main entrance, was constructed mainly from re-utilized ancient blocks of masonry, with the wall having a slight batter and topped by a number of merlons. The north flank, retains the best-preserved parts of the original Hellenic walls, including a projecting rectangular tower. The west wall, which separated the Hospitaller work from the rest of the remains of the Hellenistic fort, had two large *speroni*, while that to the south, has disappeared. Internally, the fort was divided into two by a wall laid out along an east-west axis, the northern half of which was covered by a vaulted roof.[9]

The small fort on Alimonia was not designed to withstand determined attacks and could only house a small garrison. Its water supply was particularly insufficient and, for this reason, the tower was abandoned in 1479 prior to the Great Siege of Rhodes: 'l'Castello di Limonia haveva gran mancamento d'Aqua; e che per questo difendere non si poteva; ordino che s'abbandonasse, e che gli Habitatori di quello, ad altri luoghi forti passar.'[10]

Above, Ancient masonry blocks form part of the foundation of the northern side of the Hospitaller stronghold of Alimonia (after Gerola).
Below, View of the castle from the south west (Archaeological Institute of the Dodecanese).
Right, Elevation of the east side, showing the main entrance into the stronghold.

Symi

Lying some 36 km north-west of Rhodes, Symi was the island nearest to the Hospitaller base. Its strategic location close to the Anatolian mainland meant that the knights could control the shipping traffic sailing through the straits along the Turkish coastline. Not surprisingly, Symi is recorded by Bosio amongst the first five islands occupied by the Order soon after the fall of Rhodes and, together with those of Chalki and Tilos, constituted the 'Isole Magistrali ... le quali erano del Gran Maestro.'[1] These were administered personaly by the grand master directly from Rhodes.[2] In 1352, for example, Grand Master de Gozon released the inhabitants of Symi 'dall'obligo di certo Diritto, che pagar solevano, chiamato il Mortuario, trasmutandolo in cinquecento aspri, di moneta di Rodi, da pagare ogni anno.'[3]

Symi is one of the smaller islands of the Dodecanese with an area of some 58 km[2]. In antiquity it was also known as Aigle and Metapontis; right up to the last century it was an important shipbuilding centre.[4] It was also heavily wooded though today it lies largely barren as a consequence of its former industrial activity. The main settlement in Symi is the small town of Yialos in the north of the island, built like an amphitheatre around a cresent-shaped harbour. The main commercial main harbour, however, was at Emborion, north-east of the town of Symi, but now deserted. In the

Above, 17th century map of the island of Symi and neighbouring Turkish coastline.

middle ages, the island had one major stronghold and this was situated on a hill overlooking the main town and harbour. It was built on the site of a Hellenic acropolis and incorporated stretches of the ancient ramparts into its enceinte. The site did not hold any major strategic significance other than that it overlooked the harbour, since it was easily approachable, especially from the south were the ground was less steep. Inevitably, it was here that the castle's strongest defences were built.

Of the castle's medieval enceinte only the walls on the south and east sides have survived. These consist in part of Hellenic foundations, Byzantine walls and Hospitaller additions. The walls followed the configuration of the summit and relied mostly on re-entrant angles for flanking devices. A single, rounded, and sloping wall-tower, of probable Byzantine origin, survives on the north-east side of the castle attached to a stretch of curtain wall built of similar neat rubble-wall construction with flat, slate-like stones brought to irregular and inconsistent courses.

Watch-tower (reconstructed - only the base survives today)

Lower bailey

Chapel

Modern church

Semicircular bulwark with arms of Grand Master d'Amboise

Blocked-up gate in side of bulwark

Remains of ancient wall of Hellenic acropolis

Modern ramp into fortress

Rounded wall-tower with battered walls

The rounded wall-tower with pronounced sloping walls facing the upward approch towards the castle through the narrow streets of the adjoining suburb. Above, inset, The masonry remains of the base of the watch-tower that crowns the summit of the rocky crag dominating the interior of the castle of Symi.

Adjoining this wall is a section of the old acropolis rampart consisting of massive, coursed trapezoidal blocks of stone.

That section of ramparts today replaced by a large ramp was originally occupied by serrated line with flanks that covered the entrance into the castle through the machicolated gateway in the side of the D'Amboise bulwark. This embryonic semicircular bastion is the only surviving part of the castle which can be definitely attributed to the Hospitallers although various coat-of-arms of different grand masters (though not *in situ*) can still be seen at the castle. These escutcheons bear the arms of De Milly and Antonio Virieu with the inscription 10 April 1456 (this

was once affixed above an inner gateway into the castle known as the Sidhereni),[5] Zacosata, and the English knight, De Gorges.[6]

A marble escutcheon with the coat-of-arms of Grand Master d'Amboise, inscribed with the year 1507 is affixed on the semicircular bulwark. This structure is definitely an artillery platform and was designed to provide enfilading fire along the weakest part of the castle's enceinte. It is a very small work, which although once fitted with the medieval trappings of crenellations and machicoulis, still looks more *alla moderna* than the gun towers of nearby Venetian outposts such as Famagusta. Internally, the bulwark was partially hollow to allow for an open passage into the castle. There was also a vaulted gun emplacement trained on the main approaches to the castle. The farther end of the bulwark tapered slightly outwards for the work was not a perfect semi-circle. It was also heavily terrepleined and provided a good artillery platform. Its merlons were of the medieval type and had not been replaced by thick sloping ones built during the time of Del Carretto. It is probable that this bastion was designed by Bartholino de Castellion, the military engineer who was at that time in the employ of the Order. Around that time Bartholino was definitely inspecting the Order's various outposts and is found in Bodrum in 1507.[7] If this is the case, than on stylistic grounds alone, it is also possible to attribute to him the design of the bulwark at Andimacchia in Kos, similarly built to a semi-circular plan with a hollow interior.[8]

Within the castle the space was occupied by a number of buildings of which little remains: a monastery (now a heavily-restored church dedicated to the Virgin Mary) and, for the larger part, by a steep rocky crag on top of which stood a watch-tower.[9] Given its proximity to the Turkish mainland, the island received its fair share of piratical incursions and *razzie*. Prior to the Turkish attack of 1444, the knights Frà Guido de Domaugne and Frà Ettore d'Alemagna commissioned to inspect the defences of the lesser islands, visited Symi but it is not clear whether as a result of their recommendations the inhabitants of the islands were evacuated to the safety of Rhodes.[10] The castle was definitely not considered to be a weak one, for in 1457 it was able to hold out against a 7,000-strong Turkish force which had just sacked Archangelos in Rhodes. The defenders of Symi managed to repulse repeated assaults and 'vedendo, che con gli assalti pigliare no potevano; posciache sempre con mortalita, e strage di molti di loro..erano valorosamente risospinti; cominciarono a cavare segretamente molte mine.'[11] The defenders were quick to discover these mines and when they realised that these were full of Turks ready to assault the castle, 'si

sforzavano; gettando sopra di loro copia grandissima d'olio bollente e di pece liquefatta (che di cio era quell'Isola molto abbondante).'[12] Disheartened by their losses, the Turks abandoned the island a few days later.

In 1485 the island was attacked by the Turks but the Symians once again proved their mettle and held out.[13] Another furious siege occurred in 1504 when the Turkish corsair Camali invaded the island. With the use of some artillery pieces, he inflicted 'una buona breccia' which his soldiers attempted to assault but were repulsed with heavy losses. Repeated assaults failed to overcome the Symians and Turks were compelled to abandon the island in search of easier prey, not, however, before having sacked and set fire to the crops and buildings in the countryside.[14] Symi surrendered to the Turks only after the fall of Rhodes in 1522.

The semicircular bulwark at Symi. On the side are a stretch of ancient Hellenic rampart and a blocked-up gateway, once surmounted by a box-machicoulis and the coat-of-arms of G.M. D'Amboise.

Tilos

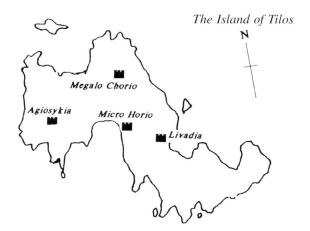

The Island of Tilos

The island of Tilos, known also as Episkopia in medieval times, lies roughly halfway between the islands of Rhodes and Kos. Although a small island, with a surface area of around 63 km², Tilos is a very mountainous place. This feature enabled its inhabitants to rely mostly on the inaccessibility of mountainous heights for their own safety in times of danger. It has often been suggested that the medieval name given to the island, Episkopia, which can be taken to mean vedette or look-out post, implied that the island performed an important role in keeping watch on the surrounding seas and, according to Coronelli, there was a Byzantine tower on there from which guards could observe (*episkopo*) shipping movements.[1] In reality, however, this was a role played by many of the islands and it is much more realistic to assume that Tilos may have been the seat of an important bishopric.[2] Tilos was one of the islands which fell into the Hospitallers' possession with the conquest of Rhodes and, together with Chalki, it was given *in feudo* to Borrello Assanti in May 1366.[3]

In medieval times, Tilos was quite heavily fortified. There exist today the remains of at least four castles at Megalo Chorio, Mikro Horio, Agiosykia, and Livadia respectively. Megalo Chorio, the island's capital, is located inland in the northern part of the country, with most of the old houses built like an amphitheatre around the slopes of the hill of Aghios Stefanos, on the summit of which stands the castle of the knights. In antiquity, this was the site of a Hellenic acropolis and the medieval fortress incorporates many features of the original defences, particularly the foundations and considerable sections of the walls and the main gate. The castle has a roughly triangular plan with very irregular sides. The eastern salient is occupied by the remains of a massive rectangular tower, at the foot of which, internally, there was a large cistern. The western salient is occupied by a massive semicircular projection of the enceinte that has the rudimentary feel of a bastion as it protects the passage leading upwards along its flanks towards the castle's

main entrance. The main gate is an original Hellenic work, but the doorway was partially blocked up in medieval times to provide a narrower entrance. Above the doorway, the Hospitallers added a parapet with merlons and a small *machicoulis*. The walkway rested on the arched ceiling of the entrance passage.

For flanking devices, the castle relied almost totally on dents in the trace, or re-entrant angles, and, apart from the large tower to the east which, however, was basically a continuation of the curtain wall, there were no projecting towers to enable enfilading fire. The whole trace of the enceinte was surmounted with merlons of which only a few examples remain. The castle of Megalo Chorio relied mostly on the strength of the natural features of the site as its main means of defence. Actually, the medieval stronghold was very crudely built with much use of rubble walls made up from irregular stones that could be found lying around the site and other regular pieces quarried from the remains of the old acropolis, the whole held together with little use of mortar. In places, considerable stretches of coursed rusticated ashlar blocks of the original acropolis walls form the foundations of the ramparts. Inside the castle are the remains of many dwellings and cisterns, and a church dedicated to St Michael built on the site of the ancient temple.

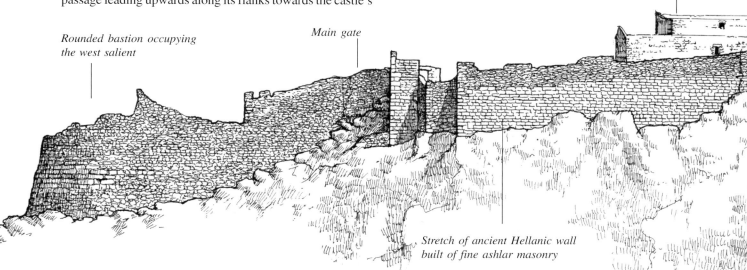

Church of St Michael

Rounded bastion occupying the west salient

Main gate

Stretch of ancient Hellanic wall built of fine ashlar masonry

Above, top, Front view of the main gate and bastion, (Archaeological Institute of the Dodecanese), also shown in elevation, left. Above, left, Detail of ancient masonry. Above, the remains of the castle of Micro Chorio (courtesy of M. Losse).

Large tower on east salient of castle

In the centre of the island lies the abandoned village of Mikro Chorio, surmounted by the remains of a small castle, the best preserved part of which is a semicircular tower, the *Pyrgos*, standing on the highest part of the summit. Until the beginning of the century, the tower still retained a few typically Hospitaller merlons with protruding sockets for wooden shutters that protected the rectangular crenels and parapet. It was relatively well built with small stones, brought to courses and held together with mortar and with much stone and pottery pinnings, in similar fashion to other strongholds throughout the Dodecanese.[4] The fortified enceinte was originally quite extensive but only a few rudimentary traces survive. South-east of Mikro Chorio lies the port of Lividia. This was protected by a small medieval fort, now also a ruin. Other sparse traces of medieval strongholds exist at Agiosykia and Mesaria.[5]

Plans of the castles of Mesaria and Agiosykia (after H.M. Koutelis)

Above, The stronghold of Agiosykia (courtesy of M. Losse) and below, close-up of its rounded salient (courtesy of A. Martegani). Left, The remains of the castle of Mesaria (courtesy of M. Losse).

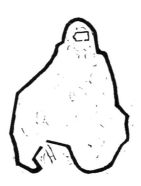

Lacroix mentioned that Tilos was protected by two *kastra,* that of St Etienne and the castle of Zuchalora (Caucalora).[6]

Notwithstanding the presence of many strongholds, the island of Tilos proved vulnerable to Turkish raids and on many occasions its defences were not considered sufficiently powerful to resist attack such that its inhabitants had to be evacuated to the safety of Rhodes. Episodes as these are

recorded in 1475 and 1480, [7] yet when forced to fight, the inhabitants of Tilos were able to repulse Turkish attacks. In 1479, for instance, the knights and men garrisoning the castle of Tilos sallied out and captured many of the corsairs then raiding the island.[8] Again in 1479, the Turks laid siege to the castle of Tilos, although Bosio does not indicate which of the strongholds they actually assaulted, although presumably this was the main castle of the knights at Megalo Chorio. After eight days of siege, the Turks were compelled to withdraw from the island, 'havendo posto l'Assedio intorno al Castello di Tilo; & havendo furiosamente battuto; e per otto giorni continoui cambattuto, & assalito; fu finalmente con danno, e vergogna sua grandissima (L'Armata Turchesca), costretto a partirsene.'[9] Other attacks were also successfully repulsed in 1485 and in 1504, when the island was ravaged by the Turkish corsair Camali. Tilos was only surrendered to the Ottomans after Rhodes had fallen to the Turks.[10]

Nisyros

A 16th century map of the island of Nysiros.

The small volcanic island of Nisyros lies north of Tilos and south of Kos. In antiquity, the island was known as Porphyris and its destiny throughout the ages was linked to that of its larger neighbours. During the thirteenth century, the Dodecanese islands were contested by the Venetians and Genoese who eagerly sought to establish staging posts along the lucrative Levantine trade route. In 1306 the Venetian Jacopo Barozzi led an unsuccessful attack on Nisyros, but with the conquest of Rhodes, the island was one of the first to fall in the hands of the Hospitallers. In 1316 the knights granted it *in perpetuo feudo* to Giovanni and Buonavita Assanti of Ischia, 'famigliari della Religione, per lungo tempo servita l'avevano, con la robba, e con le Persone Loro nelle guerre.' In exchange the Assanti were to maintain an armed galley 'ben armata.., pronta, & apparecchiata al servigio della Religione; la quale Galera fosse di cento, e venti remi, armata come volgarmente, si diceva, a Fernello, e proveduta di tutte le cose, ch'a buona Galera armata si convengono.'[1] By 1341 Ligorio Assanti, the son of Buonavita, was using the island as base from where to conduct piratical raids. In retaliation for his incursions, the king of Cyprus confiscated some Hospitaller properties within his domains, claiming the Ligorio was a vassal of the Order.[2] The Hospitallers immediately deprived Ligorio of his share of Nisyros, which he had held in fief. Ligorio's cousin, however, quickly sought to buy it back from the Order.

In 1374, through the intercession of the queen of Naples, the Hospitallers commuted Assanti's obligation to keep a galley for a payment of 200 florins a year, less than half the cost of a galley.[3] The Assanti lords of Nisyros seem to have ruthlessly exploited the islanders, forcing them to work the sulphur mines or till the fertile soil for, in 1352, they rose up in rebellion. As a result, the Hospitallers were forced to dispatch the commander of Kos, the knight Frà Bertrando di Cantesio, with a force of men to silence the disturbances, which he did, quickly reducing the 'vassalli alla solita ubbidienza.'[4]

The last male descendant of the Assanti family died in 1386 and the island reverted to the Order. The Hospitallers then granted it *ad vitam* to the knight Frà Domenico d'Alemania. In 1392 Frà Domenico renounced his right and the island was granted to Buffillo Brancaccio. Thereafter there followed a succession of feudal lords; Draginetto Clavelli in 1402 and Rinaldo Breissolles in 1422.[5] In 1433 the island was granted to Fantino Querini, prior of Rome and commander of Kos, in return for the annual payment of 600 *fiorini d'oro* and on condition that the island's strongholds were kept 'ben guardati, ben muniti, e riparati.' He was also expected to support, at his expense, two knights and a chaplain.[6] Other subsequent lords were Lodovico Serra, marshal of the Order (1453), Giovanni Delfino (1454), Nicolo da Corogna, admiral of the Order (1468), and Galcerano da Lugo (1471).[7] Little is known about the island in the remaining decades of Hospitaller rule.

The island of Nisyros, albeit only 41km[2] in area, was apparently healthily populated during the fourteenth century. Niccolo de Martoni, who visited Nisyros in 1394,

Below, The uppermost gate leading into the castle of Nisyros. Its is surmounted by the arms of Grand Master Milly and was once fitted with machicolation.

Left, The flank of the Torre Superior showing how it interrupts the chemin-de-ronde. It is surmounted by the framed arms of the Order, Grand Master Orsini and an unidentified knight-commander of the castle (above).

noted that there were three castles on the island, one of them quite strong, and several *casalia*. The inhabitants worked the sulphur mines and the fertile soil produced a great quantity of fruit.[8] A later description spoke of five strong towns.[9] Throughout the fifteenth century, however, Nisyros began increasingly to experience Turkish *razzie*. In 1457 the dwellings, vines, and crops on the island were burnt and sacked with tremendous ferocity by the Turks who, however, did not assault the 'Castelli, e...Terre forti' within which the islanders had sought refuge.[10] In 1471 the inhabitants of the castle of Mandracchi, the strongest fortress on the island, were evacuated to the safety of Rhodes when it was feared that the Turks were about to launch an attack on Hospitaller possessions in the Aegean. When the threat eventually subsided, the inhabitants of Nisyros refused to return to their island and had to be ordered to do so. Frequent raids had ruined the island's economy and reduced the inhabitants to poverty 'per non potuto coltivare i terreni loro.'[11]

The grand master tried to ease their plight by freeing the inhabitants from their annual obligation to pay 300 gold florins. Such was the situation that the Order could not find anyone 'chi la volesse accettare', although finally it was granted to the knight Frà Galzerano de Luge.[12] Again in 1478 Nisyros was raided by corsairs and in 1480, prior to the siege of Rhodes, the inhabitants were evacuated to the safety of the Rhodian fortress although a small garrison was retained in the castle. In 1504, it was unsuccessfully

attacked by the corsair Camali. Like the other Hospitaller strongholds in the Dodecanese. Nisyros was abandoned with the fall of Rhodes in 1523.

As a refuge against corsair raids and Turkish attacks the inhabitants of Nisyros had three strongholds, 'In qua insula sunt tria castra, unum prope litus maris et alia in altitudine montium.'[13] These were sited, at Mandraki, Nikia, and Emborios. In 1453 there is mentioned the need to construct a fourth in the centre of the island, at a place called Perva where there already existed the ruins of ancient fortifications.[14] This was probably the site of the ancient Hellenic fortress of Argos. The remains of another ancient Hellenic fort, the Paleocastro, can be found on the hill above the castle at Mandraki. The strongest of the island's fortifications was the Hospitaller castle at Mandraki, sited on a small and narrow, clayish promontory, on the eastern side of the island. The present castle is actually the result of various phases of construction which reach backwards in time much earlier than that indicated by the coat-of-arms of Grand Master de Milly affixed above the second gateway along the tortuous uphill path into the castle.

The oldest part of this castle, found on the summit of the promontory, is a stretch of Hellenic wall which must either have been the foundations of an ancient tower or else formed part of the larger circuit of the ancient fortress of Paleocastro situated farther inland on the same promontory. The original medieval stronghold seems to have been formed from just a simple trace of walls which followed the configuration of the summit of the promontory. Up to the late fourteenth century, when the island was enfeoffed to the Assanti family, the Hospitallers would have had little reason to re-fortify the works. The earliest datable part of the fortress is the gateway surmounted by the coat-of-arms

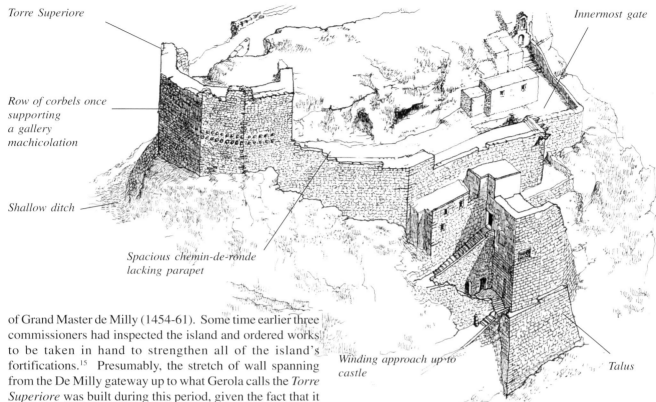

Torre Superiore

Row of corbels once supporting a gallery machicolation

Shallow ditch

Spacious chemin-de-ronde lacking parapet

Innermost gate

Winding approach up to castle

Talus

of Grand Master de Milly (1454-61). Some time earlier three commissioners had inspected the island and ordered works to be taken in hand to strengthen all of the island's fortifications.[15] Presumably, the stretch of wall spanning from the De Milly gateway up to what Gerola calls the *Torre Superiore* was built during this period, given the fact that it is all constructed in the same manner.

The *Torre Superiore* was not originally a tower but simply a continuation of the rising curtain wall. A line of corbels, once supporting a gallery machicolation, reveals the original height of this wall. Here, the trace of the curtain wall turns back to form a polygonal front facing the inland heights of the promontory. The Hospitallers had to cut a *fosse* across the neck of the promontory in order to separate the castle from the rising ground to the rear. With the increase in range of gunpowder artillery, these heights began to constitute a serious threat to the castle. The knights then realized that they needed not only to heighten this front but also to increase the thickness of its walls. The work was executed

during the magistracy of Grand Master Orsini (1467-76) as is implied by the set of three coats-of-arms. Amongst these arms are those of Nicolo da Corogna, lord of the island after 1468. The new work took the form of a massive tower that was isolated from the rest of the enceinte. The *chemin-de-ronde* was cut short abruptly with the imposition of one of the lateral walls erected within castle. Its not clear whether or not this tower, which seems to have acted also as a sort of donjon or keep, was roofed. The weight of the restructured work, however, seems to have placed a considerable stress

Mandraki castle as seen from the commanding higher ground overlooking the Hospitaller stronghold.

*The Torre Superior resting on its talus
by a shallow ditch. Inset: White-washed interior of
one of the castle's gates.*

on the friable ground below for the knights were forced to buttress the scarp with a sloping talus of masonry.

Along the rest of the enceinte on the west and north part of the promontory, the castle was adequately protected by cliffs and here the walls were relatively low. The east flank of the castle also received considerable reinforcement with the addition of a flanking tower overlooking the winding path up from the village below. On the wall adjoining the castle's first gateway are the filled-in traces of a crenellated parapet and two blocked-up gun-loops of the square type. Apparently, as the coat-of-arms of Grand Master d'Aubusson seems to imply, this work was restored during his magistracy, when the flanking tower was rebuilt to an increased height and buttressed with a large sloping talus. To the north, a considerable section of the wall has collapsed. The medieval ramparts are built with a mixture of various types of masonry, ranging from irregular rubble work, to coursed rubble work, heavily plastered and galletted, finely-dressed courses of yellow sandstone ashlar of varying sizes, and large rusticated ashlar blocks of black volcanic rock. The mixture of yellow and black stones gives the castle a rich and bold rustic texture.

The stronghold of Emborios, 8 km south-east of Mandraki, is not actually a castle but a compact formation of houses built on an outcrop of rock at the summit of the village, forming a communal stronghold similar to that at Astypalaia. Internally, the group of houses is traversed by a single street with a doorway at either end. The outer walls of the houses which formed the exterior defensive arrangement were pierced by a few narrow windows which served also as embrasures. Internally there was no communication between adjacent buildings, but along their roofs, the houses formed one continuous terrace, an adequate fighting platform and walkway. Internally, there was also a small chapel dedicated to St Michael. Although, the stronghold at Emborios would have provided the villagers with adequate protection against corsair raids, it would have been extremely vulnerable to artillery fire or determined attacks by large armies and one can therefore appreciate the islanders' anxiety and their need to flee to the safety of Rhodes every time the terrible prospect of a Turkish attack presented itself. South of Emborios, further inland towards the centre of the island, on the slopes of the extinct volcano, lie the remains of a small medieval fort located on the old road near the village of Nikia.

Right, The solid talus of the castle where its walls meet the village houses. Above right, Detail of the chemin-de-ronde along the village side of the stronghold. The parapet is missing.

Narangia   (*Kos*)

The island of Kos, the third largest in the Dodecanese and situated about 128km north-west of Rhodes, was the most important Hospitaller possession after Rhodes. In 1306 Vignolo dei Vignoli ceded his claim to the island in favour of the Hospitallers. Early during the Order's expedition against Rhodes, Grand Master Villaret sent a small force to try and seize Kos. Two knights and 50 men managed to capture a castle from the Greeks who held it for the Byzantine emperor but were unable to keep it for long.[1] In 1314 the island became part of the Hospitallers' domains but, sometime before 1319, it was lost to the Turks and was not recovered until around 1336.[2] Thereafter, Kos became the most important Hospitaller commandery in the east, from where the adjoining islands of Kalymnos, Leros, Pserimos, and, later, Nisyros, were administered.[3] In antiquity, the island's capital was Astypalaea on the south-west part of the island. This was destroyed by the Spartans during the Pelponnesian War and so the new city of Kos was founded, around 366 BC, and this remained the main settlement until it was destroyed by an earthquake in the sixth century AD.[4] During the middle ages, when it was also known as Lango, the island was organized into four major districts, each of which possessed a stronghold and village. These were the coastal settlement of Narangia, built on the ruins of the ancient city, and the villages of Paleo Pyli, Andimacchia, and Kefalos. Narangia, which was situated on the north-east coast of Kos, facing the Anatolian mainland, was served with a good harbour and there the Hospitallers chose to establish their base.

Apparently, the pre-Hospitaller *borgo* of Narangia was not enclosed within a defensive wall but there definitely existed a castle on the small peninsula north of the town. The

Above, Maps of Kos, also known as Lango, showing the various strongholds which guarded the Hospitaller island. Bottom, left, Detail of one of the circular corner-towers of the original Hospitaller fortress, later incorporated as the inner castrum.

present castle, however, is the product of numerous additions and alterations affected by the Hospitallers. The original castle corresponds to the inner rectangular enceinte. This was probably a Venetian fort, of the *quadriburgum* type, rectangular in plan and stiffened with four corner towers, although it could also have been a late Byzantine work. The Venetians were established on Kos by 1302, and the castle is similar to other forts scattered among Venetian settlements, such as at Frankocastello and Aptera in Crete and Karystos in Euboia. The *castrum* form of castle, as shown earlier, was well suited for a level site, and at Kos the site chosen for the castle was a level one. The earliest specific reference to the Hospitaller castle dates to 1391, when it is known to have been garrisoned by 15 knights, four sergeants and two chaplains, a doctor, an apothecary, 'dieci Huomini d'armi', and a hundred levantine troops, while the commander of Kos was obliged to arm a ship 'di venti banchi, per guardia di quell'Isola.'[5]

The inner *castrum*, with its rectangular plan and rounded corner towers of which only three survive, was fitted with *antemurali* of which considerable remains can be seen on the north and west sides. On the south side, the antemural defences were heavily refortified during the 1454-78 period and form impressive outerworks. These consist of a small semicircular tower, bearing the arms of Grand Masters Lastic and de Milly, in the flank of which is a bent entrance that led to the main gate of the inner *castrum* situated in a

rectangular tower, surmounted by the arms of Grand Master d'Aubusson and those of Carmadino, balì of Kos.[6] Above the gateway stood a box-machicoulis on three corbels while the roof of the entrance passage into the castle rested on ten granite columns taken from the nearby classical ruins. Today this wall-tower stands slightly detached from the adjacent curtain wall but originally it formed a continuous part of the enceinte. Attached to it, on the west side, is a rounded corner-tower also adorned with the same three coats-of-arms. The merlons on top of this tower were later removed as the top of the structure was converted into a magazine.

In front of the south curtain wall stands an isolated rectangular rampart, a sort of tenaille, with a large tower projecting from its east end. The circular south-east tower of the inner castle, which later on was partly hidden by a rectangular battery, was slightly larger than the other two corner towers and was decorated with the heraldic arms of France, surmounting those of the Order and of Commander Dupuy, accompanied by the date 1465, and flanked by two marble lions, one of which is missing. The west curtain wall bears the arms of Grand Master Orsini and Carmadino with the date 1472, while the north-west tower has three sets of arms identical to those above the gateway. The north curtain wall has the same set of escutcheons and halfway along its length there is another wall-tower with the arms

Above, Rectangular wall-tower, built neatly with ancient masonry from the nearby Hellenic city, guarding the entrance into the inner core of the inner Hospitaller castle. This passage into the castle was protected by a line of outerworks in the form of a low turreted barbican with rectangular gun-loops, shown below, adorned with the arms of Grand Masters Fluviono, Lastic, and De Milly.

of Grand Master Orsini and the knight Geltru, dated 1471. The east half of the north curtain wall is missing because it was demolished in a violent explosion during the nineteenth century. Of the fourth rounded corner-tower there is no trace, since this was replaced by a rectangular battery incorporated into the outer enceinte. Here again the walls bear the arms of d'Aubusson and the knight Dupuy.

The inner castle was restored and refortified during the period 1454-78, as can be inferred from the coat-of-arms of Castelnouvo, Dupuy, De la Geltru, and Cardamino; during this time it was also fitted with numerous gun embrasures and thick merlons. Most of the walls were rebuilt with large blocks of re-utilized Hellenic masonry taken from the ruins of the nearby ancient city. Some works must have also been undertaken by Fantino Querini after 1436, and maybe even before by the other commanders of the castle, but no evidence has survived, not even in the form of coat-of-arms. In 1451, however, Querini sought to enlarge the castle's enceinte southwards towards the *borgo*, for which he had to demolish a number of houses, 'volendo il Bagliuo di Lango ... far rovinare alcune Case della Terra di Narangia; per fortificare quel Castello.'[7] This caused a serious uprising among the inhabitants of the town and assistance had to be dispatched from Rhodes to crush the rebellion.[8] The enceinte was also extended northwards towards the edge of the peninsula. Two escutcheons with the coat-of-arms of Querini point to some of these early additions. One of these is located near the entrance into the castle and the other on a merlon of the north-east tower. A large, rectangular casemated battery, or *mŷne,* was built by sometime after 1489, possibly in 1494, and bears the arms of D'Aubusson on its inner wall, showing the cardinal's hat, and set within a frame of the type found at Rhodes on the Koskinou gate and on the commandery at Lindos.[9]

Around 1495, new works were initiated to envelope the inner castle within a larger terrepleined outer enceinte. The

Left, top, Interior of the ramparts of the inner castrum. Left, View of the outer works added to the first castle before it was eventually enclosed within a larger terrepleined trace of walls. Below, The French tower and adjoining ramparts. The walls were pierced with gun-loops for artillery in the course of the 15th century. Originally the sea came very close to the foot of the castle's walls but today a tarmacked road encircles the fortress.

first part of this perimeter to be completed was that on the north side of the castle. There, a hollow polygonal bastion bears the arms of Grand Master d'Aubusson and the date 1503. The adjoining curtain wall is datable to 1505 but a third escutcheon bears the arms of Del Carretto. The north-east tower displays the arms of D'Amboise with the date 1506. On the west side, the enceinte consists mainly of a long stretch of wall with a pronounced batter, except for a small re-entrant angle fitted with a box machicoulis, and dated between 1505-10 by the arms of D'Amboise. The long east wall forms a dented line and is of varied construction and height, a considerable part of which formed part of the inner castle. The northern section bears the arms of D'Amboise and the date 1505, while the southern rounded end is dated to 1510 and here the enceinte turns westward along a straight line to end at the Del Carretto bastion. Roughly half-way along this wall, which was protected by a fosse, stands the main entrance into the castle surmounted by the quartered arms of D'Amboise and the date 1511. The gate is also decorated with a re-utilized Hellenic frieze of masks and festoons. Large serrated merlons, of the type which also appear at Andimacchia but which could easily be later Turkish additions, crown the rampart along this land front.

At the south-west end lies a massive circular bastion, dated 1514 and bearing the arms of Grand Master del Carretto, surmounted by a sloping parapet and large gun embrasures. The bastion has a vaulted interior and two levels of gun-ports, one at ground-level and the other halfway up the wall, the embrasures designed to enable the cannon to enfilade the adjoining curtain walls. Internally the walls of the outer enceinte were backed by a thick terreplein, including that section of the inner castle incorporated into the outer east wall. The overall result of the new works was a formidable castle rebuilt *alla moderna*.

The fortification of the *suburbium* of Narangia began around 1381, an endeavour in which the inhabitants of Kos were obliged to participate. Little remains of the fortified enceinte that once enveloped the town. Among the surviving remains are short stretches of the curtain walls and a rectangular tower. This has arrow-slits and is topped by three rectangular windows, probably as a result of the building having been used as part of a house during the Turkish period. Some distance away is a short stretch of curtain wall containing one of the town gates, a plain

Right, top, Inner view of the turreted barbican. Middle, One of the wall-towers which once stiffened the line of ramparts enclosing the adjoining town of Narangia. Bottom, Marble slab embedded in a section of the town walls possibly bearing evidence of the works undertaken during the reign of Grand Master Heredia.

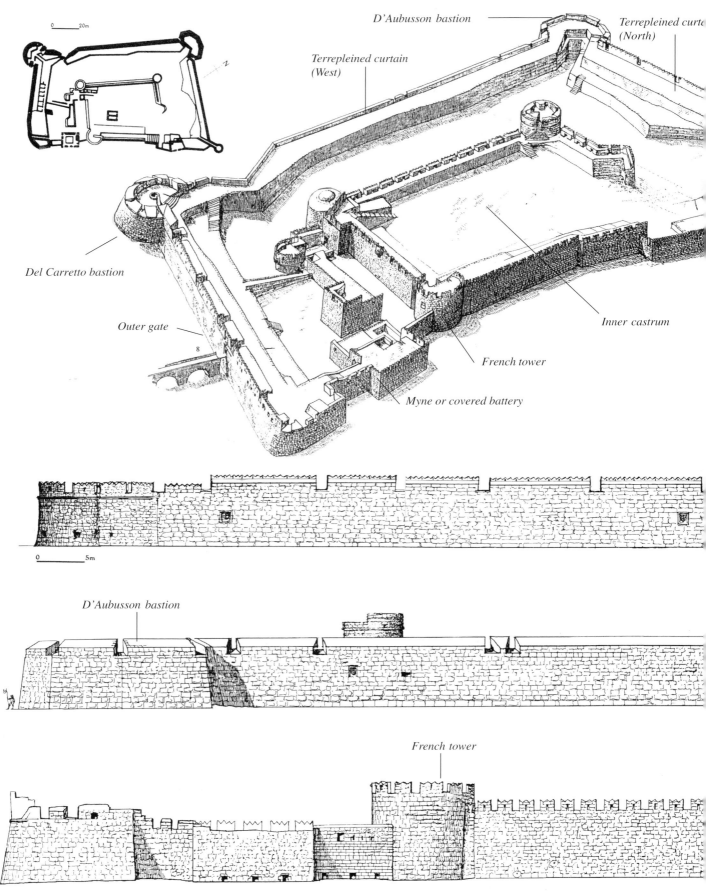

D'Aubusson bastion

Terrepleined curtain
(North)

Terrepleined curtain
(West)

Del Carretto bastion

Inner castrum

Outer gate

8

French tower

Myne or covered battery

D'Aubusson bastion

French tower

Elevation of the east front

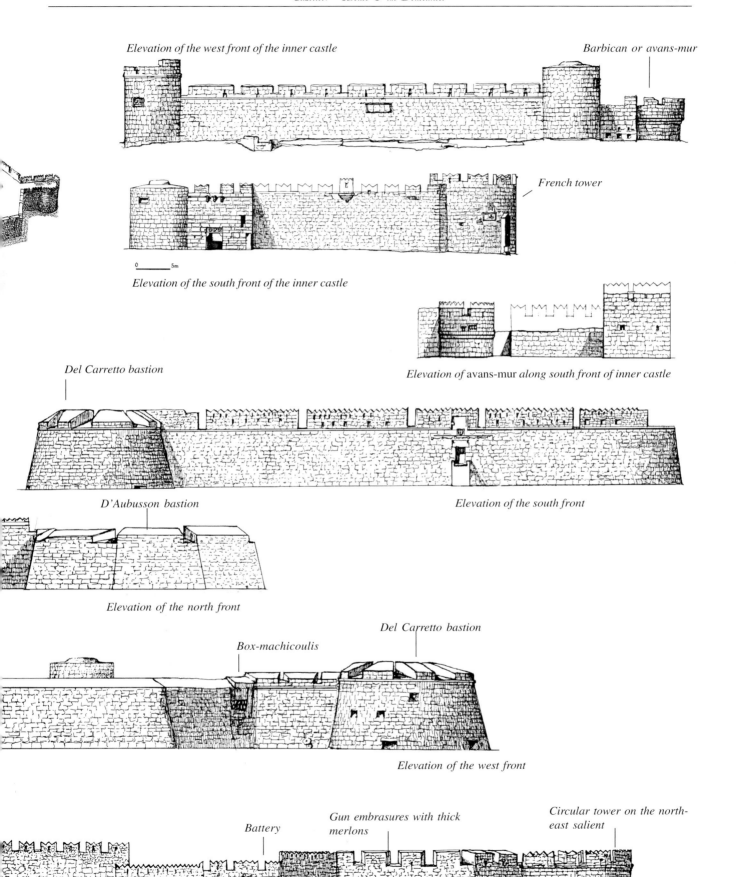

Elevation of the west front of the inner castle

Barbican or avans-mur

French tower

Elevation of the south front of the inner castle

0 ___ 5m

Del Carretto bastion

Elevation of avans-mur *along south front of inner castle*

D'Aubusson bastion

Elevation of the south front

Elevation of the north front

Box-machicoulis

Del Carretto bastion

Elevation of the west front

Battery

Gun embrasures with thick merlons

Circular tower on the north-east salient

rectangular opening surmounted by a lintel formed from a large, re-utilized ancient block of stone, and surmounted by the coat-of-arms of Grand Master Heredia and the knight Schlegelholt, commander of Kos from 1386 to 1412. A finer gateway, surmounted by a large box-machicoulis can be found north of a small circular bastion fitted with a vedette and large embrasures which occupied the south-west corner of the town's perimeter.

During the fifteenth century, the island began to find itself increasingly the target of corsair attacks and Turkish raids. It was invaded by the Mamelukes in 1440, and by the Turks in 1457, by which time it was reduced to such a ruinous state that Balì Castelnouvo was constrained to renounce his commandery. As a result, the island, together with Kalymnos, Leros, and Nisyros, was given to the grand master.[10] In 1461 the council ordered that the inhabitants of Kos abandon the island altogether and seek shelter in Rhodes.[11] Again in 1464, Kos was raided by a corsair fleet, but when, in 1471, it was feared that the Turks were about to raid Bodrum and Kos, the Hospitallers dispatched 'un buon soccorso di Cavalieri, e di soldati' to stiffen the island's defences.[12] Again in 1488, strong reinforcements were dispatched from Rhodes to help defend Kos and Bodrum.[13] In 1493 a strong earthquake severely damaged the fortifications of Kos and immediately repair works were taken in hand and a new enceinte was designed to enclose the old castle.[14]

In 1495 Grand Master d'Aubusson accepted the commandery of Kos and decided to restore the castle at his own expense.[15] He inspected Narangia in 1501 to see for himself the progress of these works. In the following year, Turkish corsairs attacked the island and reinforcements

Top, Circular bastion on the enceinte of the fortified town. Above, Detail of the thick merlons on the inner castrum, pierced with gun-loops.

were sent to its aid under the command of the knight Frà Galcerano Sans.[16] Again in 1504, the council ordered that more soldiers be sent to Kos under the command of Frà Raimondo de Balaguer, 'acciochè in compagnia di Frà Bernardo d'Airasaca, luogotenente di Lango, attendesse con vigilanza alla difesa di quell'Isola.'[17] Whilst the Turks were

The rounded wall-tower projecting from the north-east corner of the outer enceinte. It would seem that, originally, this tower stood isolated from the main castle.

investing Rhodes in 1522, another force descending upon Kos. The attack was repulsed by the garrison of the castle of Narangia under the command of Frà Preainni de Bidoux, *Prior di Lango* who, 'montando subito a cavallo, insieme coi cavalieri, ch'ivi in presidio se ne stavano; co' soldati, e con gli Huomini dell'Isola; diede sopra quelli ... con tanto impeto, che ben tosto si posero in fuga.' Still, there was little that the Hospitaller garrison could do and, after the surrender of Rhodes to the Turks, Kos followed suit.[18]

Above, top, Del Carretto bastion and detail of one of its gun embrasures. Above, left, Marble escutcheon with arms of Grand Master del Carretto, and right, view of the D'Aubusson bastion.

Right, Left flank of the polygonal D'Aubusson bastion, showing its two tiers of rectangular gun-loops and sloping parapet with embrasures. This bastion, together with other parts of the castle, were built and reinforced at the expense of Grand Master D'Aubusson who took over the commandery of Kos in 1501. The bastion, like the adjoining terrepleined curtain, was built of ashlar blocks quarried from the nearby ruins of the ancient Hellenic city.

Paleo Pyli (Kos)

South of Narangia, about 14 km inland, stand the ruins of the castle and abandoned village of Paleo Pyli. Located beneath the slopes of the mountainous range that spans the south part of the island, the castle of Pyli provided a safe refuge against corsair raids and attacks, hidden from view as it is by the mountainous terrain. Indeed, one has to get very close to the stronghold, perched as it is amidst a number of rocky crags, to be able to actually make out its silhouette. Even today, albeit in ruins, the castle still manages to impart an aura of impregnability. There was actually a time when this castle was considered to be the island's strongest fortified place.[1] In 1461, for example, the Hospitaller council ordered that all the island's strongholds, including Narangia, be abandoned except for the 'Castello di Pilli, quale s'era risoluto, che si tenessero, e difendessero; con mandarvi alcun soccorso.'[2]

In 1493 the castle of Pyli, together with the other fortresses on Kos, suffered considerable damage as a result of a terrible earthquake which hit that part of the Aegean.[3] The fortress of Narangia alone required 'due mila cinquecento fiorini d'oro' to restore.[4] A special commission of two knights, Frà Rinaldo di San Simone and Frà Giovanni D'Avalon, and the balì of Kos, Caramandino, was set up to report on the extent of the damage. Among the places they visited were the 'Castelli di Pilli, di Cognino(?), d'Entoemo (?), e di Chefalo ... nel quale dimostrarono essere necessario di riedificar quasi di nuovo tutte le Fortezze, e Castelli di quell'Isola.'[5]

The origins of Paleo Pyli seem to go back to the Byzantine times, as is evidenced by the type of construction of certain sections of the castle's walls, particularly the main gate.[6] The enceinte of the stronghold is not well defined as it descends down the slopes of the rocky crag and into the valley below, overlapping with the walls of the old dwellings of the adjoining settlement. The core of the stronghold is the upper ward, crowning the summit. This has a lozenge-shaped plan with the strongest defences located on the north part of the enceinte. The east end is occupied by a rounded tower, beneath the floor of which is a vaulted cistern. This is also linked by a stretch of crenellated curtain wall to another cistern located in the west corner south of which stood a high building, now partially demolished, into which opens the stepped passage rising from the lower bailey. Halfway along the north curtain wall there projects a small, roughly semicircular tower-like bulwark. This vaulted

Above, Marble block with the arms of the Order and the knight Fantino Querini, commander of Kos. Top, Interior view of the remains of the vaulted gate into the castle.

structure has an embrasure on each flank from which small cannon could provide enfilading fire. The roof of the bulwark forms a small gun-platform and was ringed by a number of merlons, a few examples of which survive.

The curtain adjoining the bulwark was fitted with a narrow *chemin-de-ronde* and a few loopholes pierced the wall at random. On the south front of the upper ward, overlooking the flight of steps, there was a long building resting against an enclosure wall, possibly the commandery or castellan's quarters, judging by the hierarchy of the structure. Below the north wall, where the ground slopes downwards into small plateau, are the scanty remains of yet another outer ward or bailey. This stretches westward along the summit of a ravine. A flight of steps leads from the upper ward down to an irregular stepped ward which hugs the south side of the of hill. The present remains show that a number of dwellings rested against the fragile ramparts and the line of walls eventually came to rest at a small rectangular gate-tower. A flight of step continues the descent towards the main entrance set in the flank of this tower, the rear part of which forms a polygonal spur.

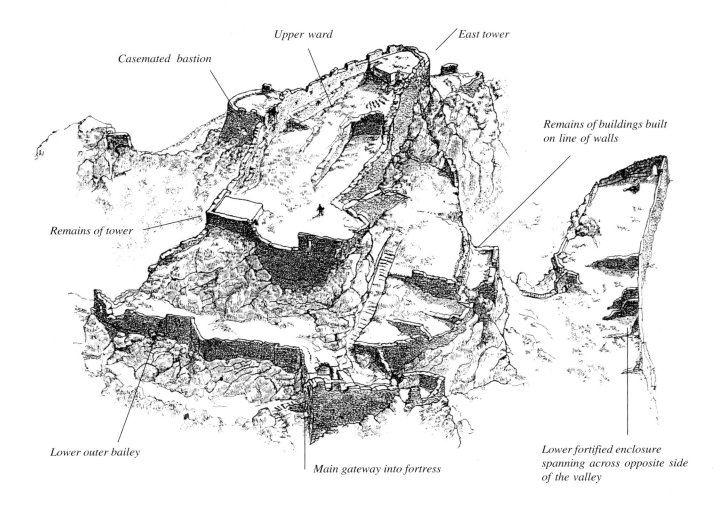

Casemated bastion

Upper ward

East tower

Remains of buildings built on line of walls

Remains of tower

Lower outer bailey

Main gateway into fortress

Lower fortified enclosure spanning across opposite side of the valley

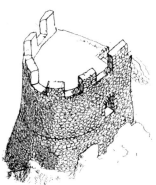

Polygonal bastion-like projection along the ramparts of the outer ward of the castle of Paleo Pyli.

Projecting spur found to the rear of the main entrance (inset).

The main entrance is definitely a Byzantine work and is quite an interesting structure, the only one of its kind to survive among all the Hospitaller strongholds in the Dodecanese. The façade consists of an arched doorway formed of brickwork, flanked on each side by a niche, each composed of a triple arch of bricks. The façade, part of which has collapsed, was topped by a parapet fitted with loopholes. The passage into the castle, again fitted with niches, was once vaulted over and flanked by two small vaulted guardrooms, also made of brickwork. Strewn on the ground along the passage is a heavy marble block bearing the arms of the Order and those of Balì Fantino Querini who held the commandery of Kos from 1436 to 1453.[7] The walls of the castle are built in the normal fashion with rubble work, heavily mortared and held in place with stone and pottery pinnings, and displaying very little effort at coursing except in the later Hospitaller additions.

Farther down the valley, another wall expands outwards to enclose a number of dwellings. Many of these were actually set into the wall of this outer ward itself. The enclosure spans onto the opposite side of the valley. A small chapel, dedicated to the 'Presentation of Christ'and built with re-utilized ancient masonry, is one of the few buildings outside the castle which are still in a good state of repair.[8]

Right, The casemated bastion as seen from in front and the left side. Possibly, the large gaping hole in the flank of the work was once a gun embrasure or postern leading down to a lower outer bailey situated below the castle to the north. Above, Section of crenellated parapet adjoining the bastion.

Andimacchia   *(Kos)*

A section of the medieval enceinte along the southern enceinte of the fortress of Andimacchia. Below, Elevation and cross-section of the main gate.

South of Paleo Pyli, approximately 25 km from Narangia, stands the fortress of Andimacchia, a stronghold of possibly pre-Hospitaller origin but one which begins to appear only during the time of the knights.[1] The modern village of Andimacchia is located some distance away from the fortified medieval settlement and the fortress occupies a site of no special strategic significance, sited as it is at the edge of level plane with little defensive qualities. Only on the south part of the enceinte, where the ground slopes rapidly downwards towards the littoral plains, is it difficult to approach the walls. On the rest of the enceinte, to the north and west, the walls are built on level ground and were extremely vulnerable to direct assault since these lacked even a simple fosse.

Initially, the fortress of Andimacchia served no military role, since it was simply a fortified refuge for the inhabitants of the central plains of Kos. The Hospitallers, too, found little use for it other than as a place where to incarcerate unruly knights.[2] In 1457, however, an 18,000-strong Turkish force invaded Kos and ignoring all the other castles 'ch'erano in sito più difficile, se n'ando ... ad assediare il Castello di Lindimacchio.'[3] After having 'con fieri, e terribili assalti' kept up the attack for 20 days, the Turks were forced to beat a retreat 'vedendo, che i nostri valorosamente si difendevano; perdendo la speranza di poter ivi far effetto alcun; dopo havere sfogata l'ira sua sopra bestiami, che'alle Campagne si trovarono, che alle Campagne si trovarono.' Four years later, when the Hospitallers were once again faced with the threat of a Turkish attack on the island, the council ordered that the castle of Andimacchia be abandoned and its inhabitants withdrawn to the safety of the castle at Pyli or Rhodes.[4]

The terrible earthquake which struck the island of Kos one hour after sunset on 18 October 1493 wrought great havoc amongst the fortifications of the island,[5] 'rovinò la maggior parte delle Case, e parte delle Muraglie delle Fortezze; uccidendo alcuni Cavalieri' and many civilians.[6] The commission of three knights which was sent from Rhodes to inspect the castles hit by the earthquake reported that it was necessary to rebuild anew nearly all the forts and castles on those islands.[7] One of the strongholds which was worst hit by the earthquake was the fortress of Andimacchia. So ruined were its walls that its was decided to demolish the place and build a new fortress on another site, ' E perche il Castello dell'Antimacchia, o sia di Landimacchia era

rovinato affatto; fu determinato, che di nuovo riedificare si dovesse ivi vicino, in Sito più forte è più comodo, chiamato Cochinocremo. E perche i Procuratori del Tesoro protestarono, che tutte quelle spese, dal Baglivo di Lango fare si dovessero; decretò il Consiglio, che per publico beneficio, quelle Fabriche tirar' inanzi con diligenza si dovessero; e che quella differenza, al Capitolo Generale, rimessa fosse.'[8] Instead, the walls of the fortress of Andimacchia appear to have been rebuilt and reinforced with a line of buttressing. This buttressing reveals that the greatest damage inflicted by the earthquake was mostly confined to the north-west part of the enceinte.[9]

The main gateway of the fortress is situated on the north walls and was surmounted by a *piombatoi* and an escutcheon bearing the coat-of-arms of Grand Master d'Aubusson and the date 1495, a testimonial commemorating the rehabilitation of the fortress in the years following the earthquake. The reconstructed walls, which were also fitted

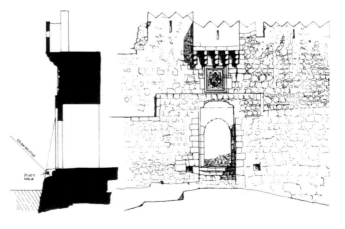

Plan of the fortressof Andimacchia

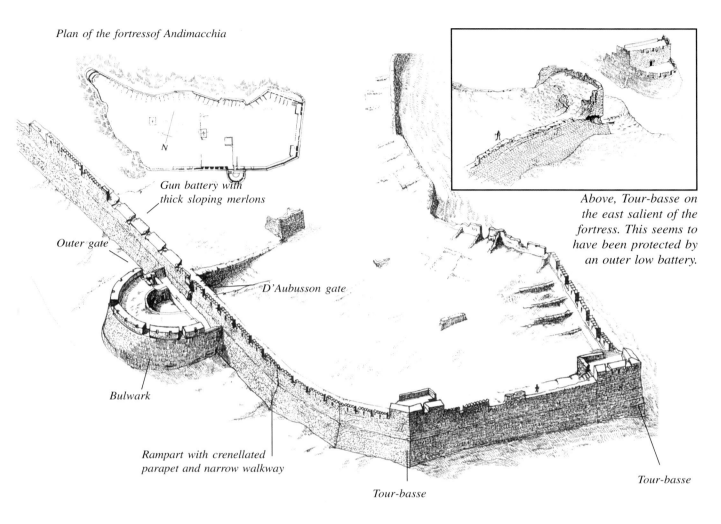

Gun battery with
thick sloping merlons

Outer gate

D'Aubusson gate

*Above, Tour-basse on
the east salient of the
fortress. This seems to
have been protected by
an outer low battery.*

Bulwark

Rampart with crenellated
parapet and narrow walkway

Tour-basse

Tour-basse

with a new parapet, walkway, and merlons of the serrated type are conspicuous for their lack of flanking defences or towers. A desperate attempt was made to remedy this defect some time early in the sixteenth century with the construction of a singular semicircular bulwark, placed roughly in the centre of the land front. This impressive artillery platform, surmounted by a sloping parapet fitted with three cannon embrasures and horizontal gun-ports at ground level, was intended to cover the vulnerable northern approaches to the fortress. The new bulwark also protected the main gate, serving as a kind of *couvre porte* and, to this end, a new large gateway, once served by a bascule drawbridge, had to be cut into the right flank of the work.

It is difficult to ascertain when this bulwark was actually built as there are no magistral escutcheons affixed to its walls. Its design, however, seems to be influenced by the Del Carretto bastion built in Rhodes and it does bear a considerable similarity to a smaller semicircular bulwark built on the island of Symi in 1506.[10] Both may possibly be the work of the Cremonese military engineer Bartholino

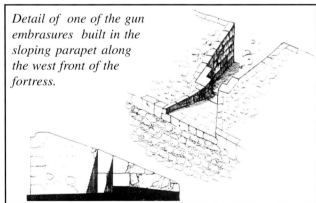

*Detail of one of the gun
embrasures built in the
sloping parapet along
the west front of the
fortress.*

de Castilleon who is documented as working on the Hospitaller islands throughout this period. To the left of the entrance, a stretch of medieval crenellation was replaced by five gun embrasures set in a thick sloping parapet typical of the early sixteenth century. The earlier type of gun-ports built in the D'Aubusson parapet consisted of small vaulted gun emplacements set into the thickness of the wall.

The main gateway into the medieval fortress of Andimacchia, surmounted by the arms of Grand Master D'Aubusson (inset) and the corbels of a box-machicolation.

The enceinte of Andimacchia covers a very large area of ground and is roughly triangular in plan. The south-west stretch of wall, which was also rebuilt after the earthquake, was fitted with a *tour-basse* at each salient corner. The merlons on these small towers were later replaced by sloping parapets and the crenels turned into embrasures. From the *tour-basse* to the south, the enceinte turns eastwards and follows a straight line for a short stretch of wall before giving way to the older walls of the fortress as these follow an indented trace westwards towards the east salient. For most of its length, this part of the enceinte, which was built in the form of a number of adjoining tenailles,[11] is characterized by the way in which dwellings were set into the walls. Only a few isolated parts of the ramparts were higher than the walkway. The old ramparts

Above, Crenellated parapet and, right, view from the interior of the outer gate situated in the flank of the semicircular bulwark, shown as seen from the adjoining ramparts. The gate was served by a bascule type of drawbridge, fitted with two wooden baulks.
The main body of the bulwark, that is the terrepleined platform, is detached from the main ramparts. The thick sloping parapets are pierced with small rectangular vision holes, large enough to allow the discharging of small firearms. Horizontal gun embrasures pierce the base of the bulwark. The embrasures are approached through long low tunnels entered from the courtyard in the centre of the bulwark.

Right, View of the open hollow gorge of the semicircular bulwark showing the spacious gun-platform and one of the shafts that end in the horizontal embrasures at the base of the bulwark.

were built with hardly any mortar, the masonry laid in courses of rough blocks of stone, held together with a large number of stone pinnings, the courses of stone growing gradually smaller with height. Incorporated into this section of wall is an example of a rectangular gun-port surmounted by two corbels that seem to have belonged to a box-machicoulis. Another *tour-basse* with a slightly curved face, and topped by the remains of merlons and gun-ports, occupies the north-east salient.[12] The remains of a small semicircular antemural, or battery, once occupied the foot of this tower.

The fortified enclosure at Andimacchia enveloped a large area. Today, this is littered with the ruins of numerous dwellings, cisterns, and pathways. There are also two chapels, one dedicated to St Parasceve and the other to St Nicholas. The former bears the arms of Grand Master d'Aubusson while the other has a marble slab with three coat-of-arms, one of which is that of Grand Master del Carretto, and the date 1520.[13]

Above, The gorge of the semicircular bulwark and, below, graphic reconstruction.

Below, Side view of the semicircular bulwark protecting the main entrance into the fortress of Andimacchia. This was served by a bascule drawbridge. Note the mouth of the horizontal gun-port at the foot of the bastion. Right, Diagram showing the general layout of the semicircular bulwark and its relationship to the medieval enceinte.

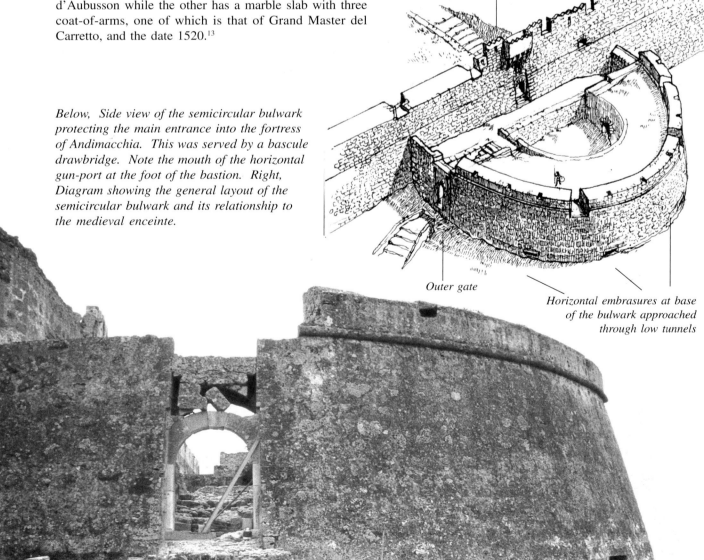

D'Aubusson gate surmounted by box-machicoulis

Outer gate

Horizontal embrasures at base of the bulwark approached through low tunnels

Kefalos   (Kos)

The fourth medieval district of Kos corresponded with the south-west extremity of the island and had as its centre the small castle and village of Kefalos: This was located around 43 km south-west of Narangia. Today, the castle of Kefalos, known as *Kastro,* lies in ruins.[1] Its remains occupy a little hillock to the south of the present village, overlooking the large bay at Kamares. Perched around the summit of a small, cavernous rocky crag are the remains of a few stretches of wall that once formed the castle enclosure. On the north side of the enceinte once stood a wall-tower, of which only the rocky base remains, and, to the south-west, a section of the wall proceeds gradually down the slope of the hill. Adjoining it is the best-preserved stretch of rampart, about eight metres in height and having a slight batter. Incorporated into this is a small arched and walled-up postern. The wall also retains the remains of a parapet and a narrow *chemin-de-ronde.* To the south-east, the summit is enclosed by a long stretch of straight wall, outside which are the scanty remains of a secondary ward. None of the walls rise higher than the level of the internal area enclosed by the walls. Here the ground is levelled, rising slightly to the west, and contains a buried cistern.[2] The remains of the foundations of an internal wall suggest that this area was divided in two. The main entrance appears to have been located on the north wall, protected by the flanking tower mentioned earlier. The castle walls were built of roughly-rectangular stones, laid in neat courses and held together with mortar and small stone pinnings.

The castle at Kefalos was a small stronghold by contemporary standards, sufficient only as a refuge against the type of swift corsair raids so endemic to this part of the Aegean during this period. It was too weak to resist large-scale attacks and on many occasions had to be abandoned by its garrison.[3] The castellan of Kefalos in 1513 was the knight Frà Honorato de Torretes.[4] Other fortifications in the area consist of the scanty remains of a small coastal fort built on ruins of the basilica of St John at Kamares and a small fortified monastery situated on an islet some distance offshore in the centre of the bay. [5]

Right, Sketch showing the layout of the ruins of the stronghold of Kefalos. Above, right, View of the scarped wall along the south-east front of the castle and, below, the castle ruins as seen from the outer bailey.

Choria   *(Kalymnos)*

The history of the island of Kalymnos was always linked to that of its larger sister island of Kos. Scarcely mentioned by the classical authors, the island remained in Byzantine hands even after the Fourth Crusade of 1204. Later it was contested by the Venetians and Genoese until it fell into Hospitaller possession in the early decades of the fourteenth century.[1] Under the knights, the island of Kalymnos, together with that of Leros, formed part of the *bagliaggio* of Kos.[2] The commander of Kos was thus responsible for the fortifications on Kalymnos. In the middle ages these amounted to some five strongholds scattered around a mountainous island roughly the size of Malta. These forts were located at Choria, Pothia, Kastelli, Vathy, and Metohi.[3] Another stronghold was located on the nearby islet of Telendos, once a promontory connected to Kalymnos until severed in the sixth century BC.

The capital of the Kalymnos was the land-locked fortress of Choria set in the centre of the island on a high, sloping rocky plateau. The fortress, whose origin dates back to

Byzantine times, consists of a vast fortified plateau. The walls of the fortress form a tortuous enceinte along the edges of an inaccessible summit.[4] The main front of the fortress stands on the south-west side of the plateau, covering the more approachable part of the terrain. Here the walls form roughly a straight line stiffened with three low projecting towers. The tower to the left, which is the largest, contains a gateway in its flank. A good part of this rampart has collapsed but it is still evident that the gateway had a drawbridge which pivoted on two sockets set in the sides of protruding marble slabs. Above the doorway, according to Ross, there was once an escutcheon bearing the arms of Grand Master d'Aubusson.[5] The other two narrow wall-towers are situated on the far right end of the front. The one in the centre retains a small rectangular gun-loop in the flank facing towards the gateway. Since this tower was filled-in with rubble, the gun-loop is blocked up, implying that either the present ground level behind the walkway was originally much lower, or else the structure was terrepleined to increase its resistance to cannon shot. The tower at the extreme south corner of the front, topped by a vaulted ceiling, has a narrower face but slightly longer flanks devoid of any kind of loopholes.

All along the trace of the main front, the ramparts were served by a narrow *chemin-de-ronde*. This walkway, however, did not travel around the whole length of the enceinte with the same width of passage. Frequently it

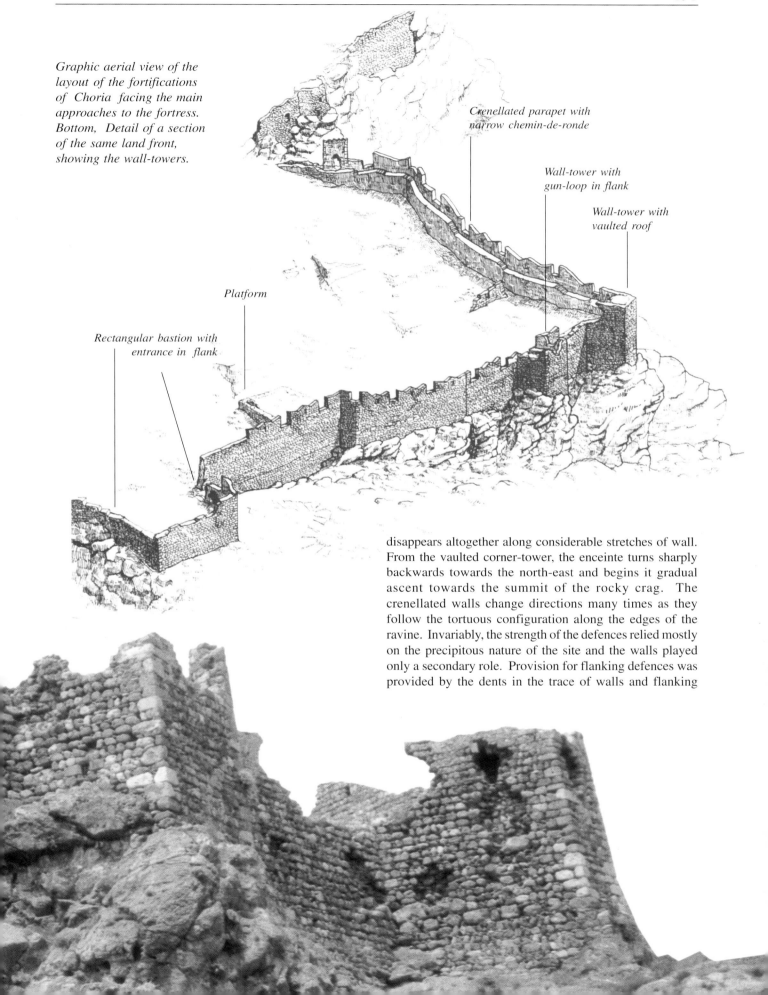

Graphic aerial view of the layout of the fortifications of Choria facing the main approaches to the fortress. Bottom, Detail of a section of the same land front, showing the wall-towers.

Crenellated parapet with narrow chemin-de-ronde

Wall-tower with gun-loop in flank

Wall-tower with vaulted roof

Platform

Rectangular bastion with entrance in flank

disappears altogether along considerable stretches of wall. From the vaulted corner-tower, the enceinte turns sharply backwards towards the north-east and begins it gradual ascent towards the summit of the rocky crag. The crenellated walls change directions many times as they follow the tortuous configuration along the edges of the ravine. Invariably, the strength of the defences relied mostly on the precipitous nature of the site and the walls played only a secondary role. Provision for flanking defences was provided by the dents in the trace of walls and flanking

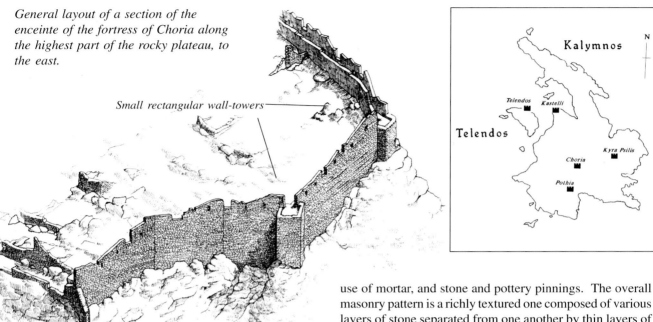

General layout of a section of the enceinte of the fortress of Choria along the highest part of the rocky plateau, to the east.

Small rectangular wall-towers

Buttress

towers only appear twice and, even then, these have severely restricted projections and short flanks only capable of accommodating singular bow-men. The line of walls changes direction again at the summit and proceed northwards for a while before taking a long and stepped descent towards the northernmost corner of the jagged enceinte. From there the wall turns westward and runs in a roughly curved line to join up with the gate-tower on the land front. Along this last stretch of wall are found a number of dwellings built onto the ramparts.

The walls of Choria employ a homogeneous form of construction throughout. These are made up of small irregular blocks of stones, brought to courses with much

use of mortar, and stone and pottery pinnings. The overall masonry pattern is a richly textured one composed of various layers of stone separated from one another by thin layers of flat stones or reddish-brown pieces of broken pottery. The merlons are generally large with serrated tops and pierced by small arrow slits, of the type found throughout most Hospitaller-built strongholds in the Dodecanese. The overall appearance of the walls is nearly identical to that of the castle of St Nicholas on Chalki.[6] Gunpowder defences, except for the single gun-loop mentioned above, are missing at Choria. Although works were taken in hand to strengthen the castle's defences during 1492-95, these did not result in the addition of any works *alla moderna* of the type which were then being erected on the nearby islands of Kos and Leros.[7] Only along the south-east side of the enceinte are there two gun embrasures separated by sloping merlons of an undoubtedly sixteenth-century type. This small isolated battery bears the coat-of-arms of Grand Master del Carretto, accompanied by the date 1519, together with that of an unknown knight. The position of this battery, however, is rather puzzling as it is sited along a section of the enceinte that is practically unassailable.

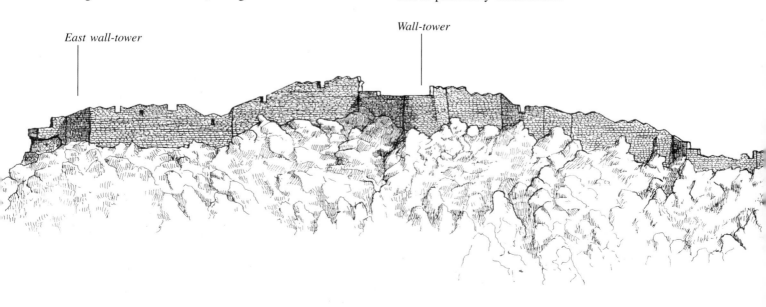

East wall-tower

Wall-tower

Being the island's principal fortified settlement, the enclosure at Choria was occupied by numerous dwellings and cisterns, all of which are now in ruins. There were also many chapels, amongst which those dedicated to St George, San Croce, the Virgin Mary, St Nicholas, St John the Baptist, Sta Niceta, St Parasceve, and Christ.[8] Two surviving cisterns are decorated with the coat-of arms of Grand Master del Carretto with dates 1514 and 1519.[9] Judging by the number of houses, and the fact that the fortress had an equally large outer *borgo,* the population of Kalymnos must have been quite considerable, at least up to the end of the fourteenth century. Thereafter, the island was rendered mostly inhabitable by incessant corsair raids and Turkish attacks, especially after its sack in 1457.[11] Many serious incursions are recorded throughout the duration of the Hospitaller occupation of the island[12] and at least once, in 1461, the inhabitants were forced to abandon Kalymnos and seek refuge elsewhere until the Turkish threat subsided.[13]

Top, The irregular trace of walls along the northern part of the fortress, also shown in elevation left. Above, Detail of the gun embrasure and merlons, below which are the arms of Grand Master del Carretto.

———— Remains of tower on western extremity

0 ———— 5m

Pothia *(Kalymnos)*

The land-locked location of the fortress of Choria, deep within the interior of the island of Kalymnos, meant that this stronghold was difficult of relieve in time of siege. An enemy force could easily isolate the fortress and intercept reinforcements landed at Pothia, some 4 km to the south. To guard against this eventuality, the Hospitallers erected a small stronghold on a hillock situated a little distance inland from the harbour at Pothia, the modern capital of the island. This was a little stronghold purposely built to guard the inland route towards the main fortress, but given its coastal position, the castle doubled also as a watch-post from where the channel between Kalymnos and Kos could be kept under constant surveillance for signs of enemy vessels. Nowadays, this castle is known as Pera Kastro, owing to the small chapel dedicated to the Virgin Mary which was built inside it.[1]

The castle at Pothia was a small outpost. In plan, it consisted of a narrow and elongated rhomboid crowning the summit of a rocky crag which rose from the summit of small hillock north of the harbour. Although in ruins, much of the structure has survived. The castle's main front was situated on the south side, where the terrain was much more approachable. Here, the walls consisted for most of their length of a dented line, stiffened by a singular semicircular projection, nowadays serving as the apse of a chapel. The walls of this wall-tower, together with the adjoining stretch of ramparts, bear the arms of Fantino Querini, commander of Kos, and of Grand Master Lastic. These walls employ a coarser and older type of construction than the rest of the south wall.[2] The remainder of the south wall, built of coursed rubble work and with the use of much mortar and stone and pottery pinnings, has a slight batter and is surmounted by the remains of a few merlons. Affixed half-way up the face of the rampart are two marble escutcheons bearing the arms of the Order and that of the knight

Above, Detail of the rounded turret and rockhewn stairway leading up to the main entrance of the castle. Below, View of the castle from the east showing the main front facing the approaches from the harbour.

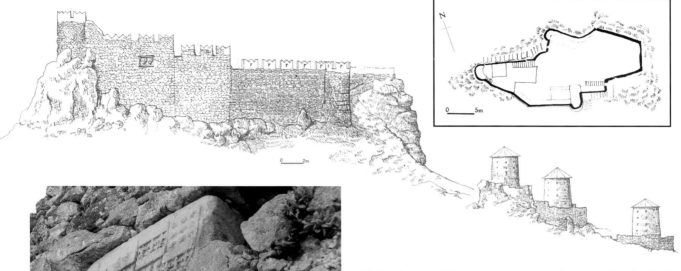

Adimaro Dupuy, who was also commander of Kos some time after 1466.[3] The west salient rose into a small rounded turret perched on the highest part of the rocky crag. This little turret was too small for defensive purposes and appears to have been intended more as a sort of vedette and signalling platform from where smoke and mirror signals could be transmitted to Kos across the channel.

The main entrance into the castle at Pothia is located on the north side of the stronghold and is approached by a

flight of steps. The gateway was set between the flank of the salient and a small rounded wall-tower. The rest of the enceinte, which is adequately protected by the precipitous nature of the site, was surmounted only by a low parapet wall, parts of which seem to have had a narrow walkway. Another entrance into the castle is set in the south wall, near the Querini coat-of-arms, but this looks like a modern addition, made to enable a direct access to the chapel. Inside the castle, the space was occupied by a few buildings and some cisterns. Further down the hill, within range of the castle's defensive weapons, stand three fortified windmills. Each conical windmill-tower, is enclosed within an outer circular wall, fitted with loopholes.

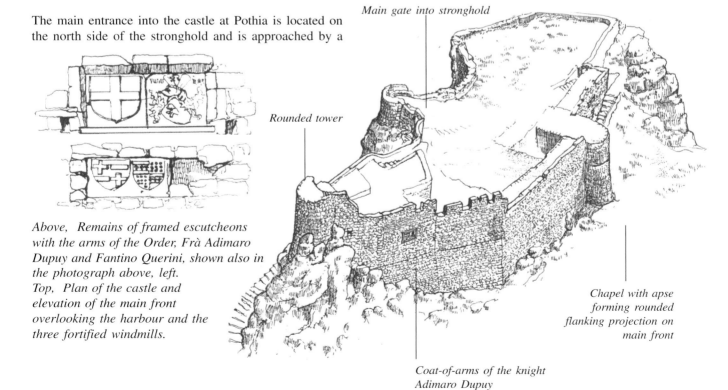

Above, Remains of framed escutcheons with the arms of the Order, Frà Adimaro Dupuy and Fantino Querini, shown also in the photograph above, left.
Top, Plan of the castle and elevation of the main front overlooking the harbour and the three fortified windmills.

Main gate into stronghold

Rounded tower

Chapel with apse forming rounded flanking projection on main front

Coat-of-arms of the knight Adimaro Dupuy

Kastelli   *(Kalymnos)*

At Cape Aspropounti, on the north-west side of Kalymnos, are the scattered remains of a Byzantine stronghold known today as Kastelli or Paleocastro.[1] This castle occupied a small conical hill at the tip of a rocky promontory, opposite the islet of Telendos, overlooking nearly all the north-west coast of the island and its littoral plains. The few surviving remains only suffice to provide an understanding of the plan of the fortress, since in most places only the foundation walls of the ramparts have survived. The Kastelli fort consisted basically of a line of fragile and coarsely-built walls laid across the neck of the promontory so as to isolate the site from the mainland. To the south seaward side of the hill, the line of walls descends steeply to enclose an outer bailey. Here lies the best-preserved part of the fortress, consisting of a stretch of stepped crenellated wall built low and very crudely with coarse, uncoursed rubblework, heavily mortared and galleted. The merlons are of the plain rectangular type, indicating a possible pre-Hospitaller origin. Along the west side of the castle stand the remains of a number of cisterns and a couple of wall-towers together with a short stretch of low crenellated wall fitted with merlons of the same type.

Detail of merlons and ramparts at Kastelli.

A steep rocky crag rises from the top of the hill to form a natural inner keep. This was fortified further with a low ring of walls. A small flight of rock-hewn steps lead up to the inner ward from the west side of the promontory. Few structures survive on the site, littered as it is with mounds of stone. There is, however, a small partially-ruined, vaulted chapel situated up within the inner ward. By the late fifteenth century, Kastelli had little defensive value as a stronghold other than as a refuge for local inhabitants against corsair raids.

On the eastern side of Kalymnos are the remains of two ruined medieval fortifications of Byzantine origin. One is situated north of the village of Vathy, and the other at Kyra Psilis (the Fortress of the Tall Lady) farther east, within which is a monastery.[2] Other remnants of ancient fortifications survive at Xirokampos, Vyrokastro, Anginaries, and Kastri.[3]

Graphic representation of the layout of Kastelli (partly reconstructed for ease of legibility)

Outerward on seaward side

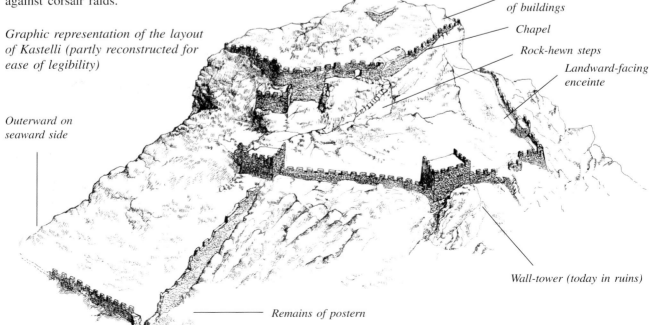

Upperward with remains of buildings

Chapel

Rock-hewn steps

Landward-facing enceinte

Wall-tower (today in ruins)

Remains of postern

Telendos

Some 700 metres off the west coast of Kalymnos, opposite Kastelli, lies the small islet of Telendos. This small but very mountainous rocky crag was still joined to its larger sister island until the sixth century BC. It only became an island after the earthquake of 535 BC.[1] On the slopes of Mount Aghios Konstatinos, on the north side of the islet, stand the remains of a large but heavily-ruined medieval fortified village. Its enceinte consisted of a simple thin line of crenellated walls which once enclosed a sloping plateau situated half-way up the side of the mountain. The fragile ramparts only protected the northern front because, to the south, the settlement was shielded by the summit of Mount Aghios Konstatinos and, therefore, no defensive walls were necessary.

For most of their length, the surviving walls have no provisions for flanking defences, devoid as they are of any wall-towers or bastions. The walls appear to have been topped with rectangular merlons of the pre-Hospitaller type, a few examples of which have survived. There also seem to have been no artillery defences. The strength of the position lay mostly in its inaccessibility and the villagers, most of whom probably lived off fishing, must have had a difficult time climbing up and down the tenuous paths to reach their abodes.

Entrance to the fortified settlement appears to have been through a small gateway situated along the surviving stretch of ramparts in the centre of the northern part of the trace of walls. On the east side of the rocky shelf, the cliffs rise slightly higher and on that point there stand the remains of a sort of keep or small *castrum* of irregular plan. This, unfortunately, is too ruined to enable a clear understanding of its form. The few remaining walls suggest a long and narrow structure with a rounded salient, a vaulted interior and a cistern. The northern end formed a rounded projection which could have been a tower.

The settlement within the fortified enceinte was quite extensive and numerous ruins of dwellings and cisterns litter the site, together with a chapel dedicated to St Constantine. To the south, on the shores of the western side of the island, stands the medieval monastery of Agios Vasileios.[2]

Right, A section of the main wall allong the fortified trace (top); the remains of the keep or 'castrum' (middle); and parapet with rectangular merlons (bottom).

Leros

The island of Leros, situated north of Kalymnos, marked the northernmost outpost occupied by the Hospitallers in the Aegean, some 200 km away from Rhodes. Although Vignolo had renounced his claims on the island in favour of the Hospitallers in 1306, Leros is not mentioned by Bosio as one of the first islands to fall into the Order's possession.[1] It is recorded as being in the hands of the knights prior to 1319, when the Greek inhabitants revolted and massacred the Hospitaller garrison stationed there.[2] The knights, however, had little trouble retaking the island, killing more than 1,900 inhabitants and carrying all the survivors captives to Rhodes.

In the middle ages, Leros was well fortified. Its inhabitants could find refuge in two castles, 'Toreo, che e nelle sue estreme sponde orientali' and Leros (lero) verso settentrione che sostiene tutta via il vanto di città risiedendosi il suo vescovo soggetto all'arcivescovo greco di Rhodi.' There were also other lesser strongholds at 'Missio fra Scirocco e levante, Syco verso ponente, Mensa, Silene, Tilo tutti diroccati danno pero contrassegni della loro antica

grandezza con avanzi spezzati di grosse colonne ed fini marmi come pure vestigia di mura e fabbriche maestre.'[3] Toreo became the large Hospitaller castle above the village of Platanos, while that of Lero refers to the present remains of the Byzantine castle on Mt Kastelli. The rest have not been located or identified, although at Xirokambos, in the southern part of the island, are the remains of an ancient Hellenistic fortress, and at Castello, below Mt Patelia, there appear to be the remains of another ancient stronghold.[4]

Toreo was the most strategically sited of all the strongholds, since it command the two most important harbours on the island, the bays at Alinda and Aghia Marina. The castle of the knights crowns the summit of a high promontory and

The front of the second ward showing the castle gateway.

The buttressed projection, a sort of wall-tower, commands the vaulted entrance (inset) into the castle's second ward.

Below, Two elevations of the castle of Platanos, showing the various wards.

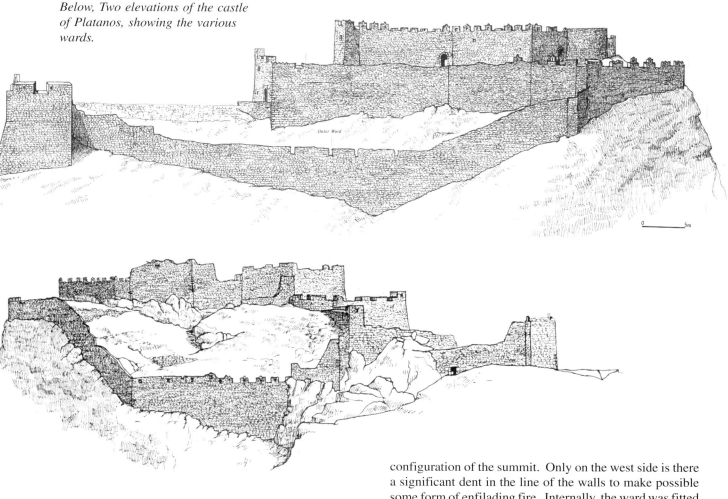

consists of three concentric enceintes. The innermost of these, surmounting the highest part of the summit, is the oldest section and predates the Hospitaller occupation. This inner *castrum* has a rudimentary plan, with roughly-rectangular, irregular sides, the walls tracing the configuration of the summit. Only on the west side is there a significant dent in the line of the walls to make possible some form of enfilading fire. Internally, the ward was fitted with a number of buildings, resting against the ramparts, some of which were vaulted. Here one could find escutcheons bearing the coat-of-arms of Fantino Querini, the commander of Kos during the 1430s.[5] There was also an escutcheon bearing the arms of either Lastic or Fluviano.[6] A small gateway opens onto the south curtain wall, while a blocked-up postern is situated on the north face of the enceinte. Another escutcheon bearing the arms of Querini was affixed to the outer face of the north wall of the inner

Detail of the low battlemented walls on the north side of the inner-most castle ward showing a rounded projection.

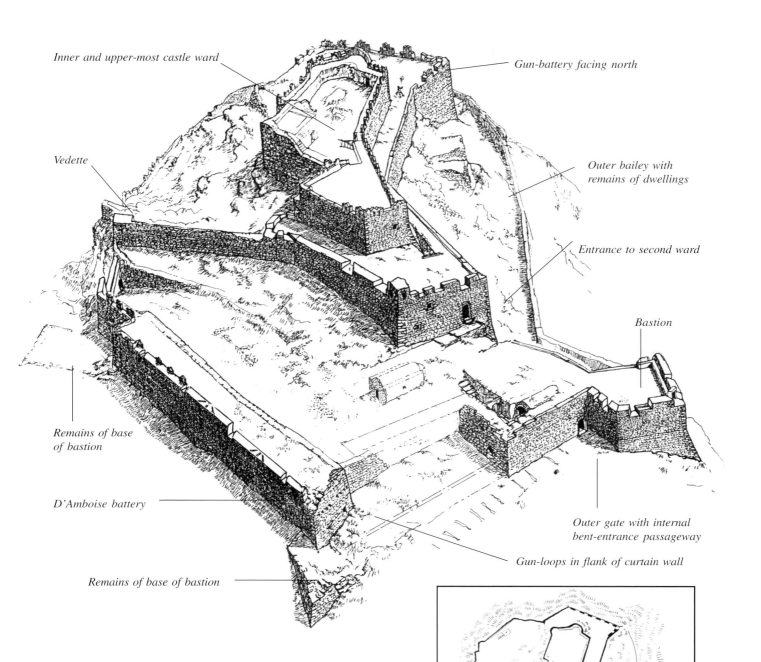

Inner and upper-most castle ward

Gun-battery facing north

Vedette

Outer bailey with remains of dwellings

Entrance to second ward

Bastion

Remains of base of bastion

D'Amboise battery

Remains of base of bastion

Outer gate with internal bent-entrance passageway

Gun-loops in flank of curtain wall

castrum. The ramparts are built of irregular masonry and employ the occasional block of ancient marble. Other parts of the enceinte reveal courses of large ashlar blocks of Hellenic origin although these do not appear to be *in situ*.

The second enceinte envelops the inner *castrum* and copies its plan except along the north side, where it follows instead the configuration of the summit. This section of the wall descends considerably downwards along the edge of the cliff. The main entrance into the second ward is located on the west salient. The opening retains two protruding slabs fitted with pivoting sockets for a drawbridge. The entrance passage into the castle is covered by a narrow barrel-vault. A small door set on the left side of the passage leads to a second vaulted room served by two windows. Both the inner and outer wards have parapets with rectangular merlons, topped with triangular forms, which Gerola believed are a later Turkish addition.

The third and outer enceinte reflects the last phase in the development of the castle a development undoubtedly necessitated by the growing use of gunpowder artillery. Here, the walls cover only three-fourths of the site, since to the north, the cliffs were considered sufficiently inaccessible. On the west and north-west fronts, however, the ground fell in a gradual slope and could easily be assaulted. Unfortunately, this part of the castle has suffered considerably with time and important parts of the enceinte are missing. The best-preserved section is the long stretch of curtain wall bearing the arms of Grand Master d'Amboise, inscribed with the date 1509, and surmounting that of an unidentified knight dated 1511. It is known that considerable works of fortification were begun in 1492, under the direction of 'Frà Filippo di Guidone, Commendatore di Randazzo, Commissario delle fabriche, e fortificationi ... il quale era in ciò molto pratico.' [7] Possibly these works were finally completed by 1511. Sufficiently well terrepleined, and fitted with sloping parapets, this artillery platform is an interesting defensive device, well built with regular courses of heavily mortared masonry. The short west flank of this curtain wall has two gun-ports but, since a large section of the walls to south is missing, it is difficult see how the work was connected to the rest of the enceinte.

The D'Amboise curtain, or battery, was flanked by two polygonal bulwarks of which only the foundations survive. The ruins on the western end reveal the battered lower courses of a solid triangular spur which must have formed

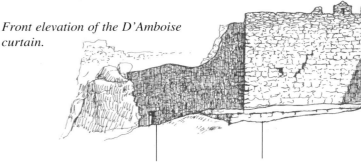

Front elevation of the D'Amboise curtain.

Postern   Remains of base of bastion

the base of a ravelin or a bastion similar to the one that has survived on the south-west corner, flanking the main entrance into the castle. This work, which must date to the post-1511 period, is surely one of the first true bastions which the Hospitallers must be credited with. Although slightly small, and at first glance looking like a rectangular gun-tower with a battered lower half, the bulwark has all the properties of an Italian pentagonal bastion - two faces projecting outwards towards a salient, two flanks, and an open gorge connected with, and level to, the rest of the enceinte. Its parapet is fitted with a number of embrasures and sloping merlons. No coat-of-arms can be found affixed to any part of the structure. It must be said, however, that

Left, The bastion on the south-east corner of outer ward. Above, Remains of the sloped base of a bastion, once situated near the D'Amboise curtain and, below, detail of the escutcheons of Grand Master D'Amboise and unidentified knight.

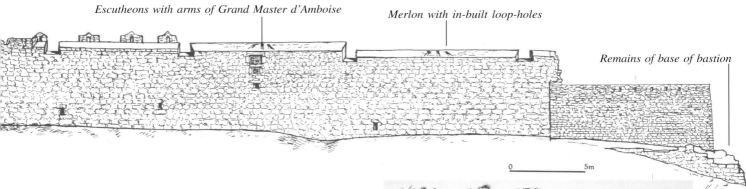

Escutheons with arms of Grand Master d'Amboise   *Merlon with in-built loop-holes*

Remains of base of bastion

0   5m

this bastion shows signs of having been partially reconstructed at some later date and its present details, as such, may not relate to its true Hospitaller form.

As an outlying Hospitaller station, Leros received its fair share of Turkish incursions. It was sacked in 1457, together with Kos and Kalymnos, and reduced to such a ruinous state that the knight commander Frà Giovanni di Castelnuovo was 'costretto a rinunciare liberamente il Bagliaggio, ... in mano al Convento; il quale dubitando, che l'entrate di esso Bagliaggio adassero dal tutto in rovina; ne vedendo, chi meglio a cio, del Gran Maestro istesso, rimediar potesse; glie lo conferi in vita sua, acciò lo ristaurasse, e lo megliorasse; con autorità di poterlo anco conferire ad alcun Religioso di quest'Ordine.' [8] The island was threatened with attack in 1460 and invaded in 1477 and 1502.[9] Early in 1506 the notorious corsair Nichi laid siege to the castle, but owing to the ingenuity of the Hospitaller knight in command of the fortress (he had the inhabitants wear surcoats with the Order's insignia and parade themselves on the ramparts) the Turks lost heart and sailed away.[10] Leros surrendered to the Turks with the fall of Rhodes.

Top, Detail of embrasure on D'Amboise curtain. Above, one of the merlons found along the second ward.

Below, Sloping merlons on the D'Amboise curtain.

Smyrna and Bodrum

When the Hospitallers invaded and captured Rhodes, it was officially considered that the island would serve as a Christian base for military operations aimed at the recovery of Latin Syria, given the island's proximity to the Turkish mainland. In the early years Grand Master Foulques de Villaret was astute enough to carry the war to the Turks and secure, and temporarily hold, various castles on the mainland.[1] These hostilities against the Turks of Menteshe and Ephesus were presented as necessary for the maintenance of open and secure sea-routes to Cyprus and the Holy Land.[2] The Hospitallers' policies in the region guaranteed a degree of stability and quite probably the knights even received tribute from some of the Turks.[3] By the 1340s, however, it had become more important to resist the Turks and perceive the defence of the Latin East rather than continue the abortive schemes aimed at Jerusalem or Constantinople. The major enemy then was Umur of Aidin who, earlier in 1329, had captured the castle of Smyrna from Martino Zaccaria.[4] Rhodes was one of the outposts being troubled by Umur's *razzie* in 1341, and these provoked Pope Clement VI's demand for a more aggressive policy in the Aegean.[5] The knights participated fully in the Latin crusade that followed, which led to the capture of the sea-castle of Smyrna in a surprise attack in October 1344.[6] The Order had also provided a naval base at Rhodes for the crusading fleet and sent its galleys on the expedition.

Below, The city of Smyrna c.1865 showing a section of the sea-castle and the citadel on the hill (Paris Bibliotheque Nationale).

Smyrna became a papal city but the Christians only held on to it with great difficulty, not least because of the fact that the citadel on the hill remained in the hands of the Turks. The Hospitallers played a leading role in the fortification of the sea-castle with the knight Giovanni de Biandrate being nominated captain-general of the papal fleet.[7] Retaining Smyrna meant depriving the Turks of a major naval base. It also followed, however, that Smyrna dramatically lost most of its commercial value, especially after the Genoese had seized the nearby island of Chios. Consequently, the Venetians and Genoese lost interest in the venture and were reluctant to pay for its defence and soon they were quarrelling with the Hospitallers.[8]

In April 1347 Grand Master de Gozon forbade the captain of the Hospitaller galleys from assuming any responsibility for the defence of Smyrna, lest the Order should be burdened with the task.[9] But by then the situation had deteriorated so precariously that the pope had sanctioned secret negotiations with the Turks for a ten-year truce.[10] Umur's demands, and that of his brother Khizir of Ephesus, involved the demolition of the sea-castle. Eventually, given the multiple crises in the west, Pope Clement agreed to a truce which would allow the Turks half of the *commercium* at Smyrna but he could not approve the demolition of the castle, despite its 'pochissima utilità', since it had been captured by a crusade and any such move would undoubtedly provoke the 'disriputatione dei Christiani'.[11] The death of Umur in April 1348 changed the situation dramatically and the treaty was never ratified.

By 1350 the maintenance of Smyrna castle was costing the pope 12,000 *fiorini d'oro* annually and, to offset the expenses, he dispatched the apostolic legate 'Raimondo Vescovo di Bologna' to Greece to impose a levy, the *Decima*, on all ecclesiastical property in those nearby places for a

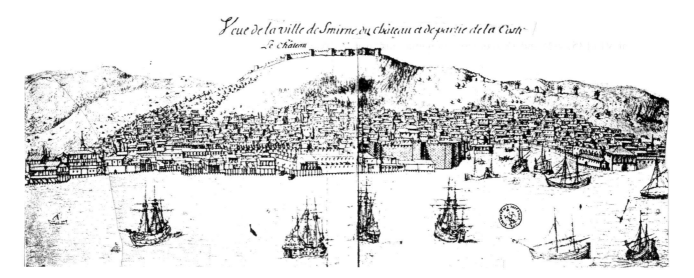

*Vue de la ville de Smirne du chateau et departie de la Cush
Le chateau*

period of ten years.[12]   He also ordered that the king of Cyprus, the doge of Venice, and the grand master each contribute towards a third of the cost of maintaining the castle for the first year. In 1371 the Genoese governor of Smyrna, Pietro Racanelli, resigned his post.[13] Pope Gregory XI ordered Grand Master Raymond Beranger to nominate another Genoese, Ottobuono Cataneo in his stead for a period of ten years and a salary of 600 *fiorini* a year.[14] However, Cataneo proved to be a poor governor who did not even bother to reside in the castle, 'e che i soldati, e gli altri Stipendati di quel presidio, stavano tutti sotsopra, e molto malsodisfatti per non esser gia molti mesi fa pagati de gli stipendij loro, maggior alterationi e disordini; in modo che in quella città ... correva gran pericolo di perdersi.'[15]

Not surprisingly, Beranger was not very enthusiastic about the idea and tried to extract the Order from the complications of such a commitment.[16] But the pope remained adamant and issued a bull to this effect, granting the castle of Smyrna and all its dependencies to the Order for a period of five years.[17] The Holy See was to defray the sum of 3,000 golf florins annually towards the upkeep of the castle over and above the *decime* collected from the king of Cyprus.[18] To ensure haste, the pope also ordered that the grand master, under pain of excommunication, take control of Smyrna within three months and settle all Cataneo's outstanding debts.[19] On its part, the Order had to pay about 3,000 florins a year for the defence of the castle.[20]

Little is known about this castle, then called St Peter, other than that it was 'una Piazza cosi grande' stiffened with rectangular and round towers, for unfortunately it was razed to the ground by the Mongul Tamerlane in December 1402.[21] Although restored in 1424, it only remained standing until 1877 and today a Turkish mosque, Hisar Cami, stands on the site of the castle.[22] Fortifications were built at Smyrna by the papal captain in Innocent VI's time Slabs at Smyrna castle combined the arms of the Papacy, Innocent VI (1352-62) and Domenico Alamania, and also those of Grand Master Heredia (1377-96), the Order, and the papacy. [23] A drawing of the city of Smyrna dated c.1658 shows the remains of the sea-castles hemmed in by the buildings and clearly dominated by the formidable citadel on the hill.[24]

On 20 March 1389 a strong earthquake badly damaged the walls of Smyrna and many of the ramparts had to be rebuilt. In 1391 a plague broke out and decimated the garrison so that in the following year it was agreed at Avignon that the perimeter of the *civitas* be reduced so that it could be defended more effectively.[25] The grand master himself donated the sum of 4,000 florins for the refortification of Smyrna while a relief force of *Commendatori, Cavalieri e*

Detail from Cristoforo Buondelmonti's Liber Insularum Archipelagi *showing St Peter castle and a Turkish tower overlooking it.*

Frati under the command of Ammiraglio Frà Domenico d'Alemagna was assembled at Avignon and dispatched, via Rhodes, to reinforce the garrison.[26]

The situation deteriorated further when the Hospitallers rejected an Ottoman peace proposal because they were unable to accept that all escaped slaves who reached Smyrna or Rhodes should be returned.[27] The garrison successfully resisted Bayazid's attack on the fortress but the situation was only partly saved in mid-1394 when the Hospitaller captain captured two sons of a leading Turkish official and secured a seven-year truce with the neighbouring Turks in return for their release.[28] However, in 1402 Bayazid was defeated by the Mongul Khan Timur who then marched on the Christian fortress of Smyrna.[29] After a fierce two-week siege which saw the blocking of the harbour and the mining of the walls, the castle was overrun and destroyed.[30] The Hospitaller captain, Frà Inigo de Alfaro and survivors from the garrison, on realizing the hopelessness of the situation, are said to have sailed away leaving more than a 1,000 Greek Christians behind them to be slaughtered by Timur's army, which then proceeded to dismantle the castle before moving away from western Anatolia.[31]

The loss of Smyrna left the Hospitallers with no outpost on the Turkish mainland. More significantly, its loss meant also the disappearance of significant income from the sale of the papal indulgences granted in 1390 for its defence.[32] Although the Hospitallers were engaged elsewhere in the defence of Corinth and the despotate of Morea, they still needed a presence on the Turkish front. So in 1405, as an alternative, the knights proposed to fortify at their own expense the Venetian island of Tenedos in the Dardanelles but the Venetians rejected the Order's suggestion.[33] The withdrawal of Timur from Western Anatolia had left the Ottomans in disorder and the Hospitallers quickly sought to reoccupy and refortify Smyrna. The opportunity seems to have presented itself in 1407, when Grand Master Frà Philibert de Naillac, playing on Turkish rivalries, went to Smyrna to assist Mehmet, ruler of northeast Anatolia against Suleiman, son of Bayezid, and once there began to construct a great tower at his own expense in the hope of re-establishing control over the port.[34] Mehmet, however, had the unfinished tower pulled down, saying that the destruction of the sea-castle was Timur's one good deed, but at the same time buying out the Hospitallers from Smyrna by granting them land on the borders of Caria and Lycia.[35]

The knights began to build a new *castrum sancti Petri* as a replacement for that at Smyrna in a region which the Turks called *Mandacchia*.[36] The location of the new castle seems to have been strategically less significant than its earlier namesake. The only gain lay in the fact that, together with the castle of Narangia in Kos, the new outpost could provide better control over the strait of Kos. Some early Hospitaller documents called it 'castrum sanctorum petrj et paulj' but this form was dropped after 1428.[37] The place itself came to be known as *petruni* or *petronion,* and in time this was corrupted to Bodrum. The exact date of the founding of the castle is not known although this appears to have been around 1407, that is, two years before the Hospital petitioned the papacy for the faculty to sell indulgences, in order to make good the 70,000 florins expended for the 'captionem, constructionem, et edificationem castri sancti Petri, ... a duobus anni citra.'[38] The founding of the castle is also

mentioned in royal French documents exempting the Order from the payment of various taxes in 1408, in order to 'ediffer un chastel appelle saint pierre.'[39]

Some accounts of the founding of the castle state that the site was taken from the Turks by force; Emir Ilyas of Menteshe arrived there with a force to prevent them from establishing a bridgehead.[40] Still, according to the Greek chronicler Doukas and to Felix Faber, the fighting only occurred after the building of the castle.[41] It is possible that the peninsula of *Zephyrion* on which the castle was built already hosted another fortress of either Turkish or Byzantine origin.[42] Indeed, the peninsula was itself a natural defensive site and written sources show that a fortified acropolis was built there by Mausolus. This was later defended for some time by the Persians against Alexander in 334 BC.[43] The Hospitallers, however, must have found only piles of ancient stone on the site since they would definitely have incorporated any surviving Hellenistic walls into the building of their new castle, if not for economic reasons then surely for ones of urgency. Such a practice is encountered in many a Hospitaller stronghold in the Dodecanese. On the other hand, the Hospitallers may have found and modified structures from a pre-1407 Turkish or Byzantine *castrum,* as some sections of the castle, especially the French tower and tower D, seem to suggest.[44]

Doukas' account of the building of Bodrum castle shows that haste was the determining factor throughout its construction since the knights transported a quantity of building material to hurry the works.[45] Whether or not the Hospitallers built the early fortified structure whilst under attack, it would still have been a matter of time before they attracted Turkish attention and any uncompleted fortress would have been difficult to defend. The fact that the knights imported building materials into Bodrum betrays

The inner core of the castle of Bodrum, showing the tower of France (left) and the tower of Italy (right).

The tower of France.

Tower of the Snakes

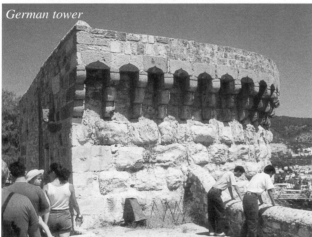

German tower

Maritime tower

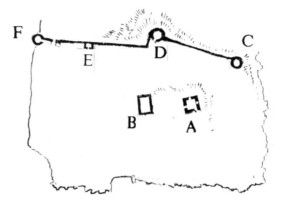

Bodrum castle - plan of initial phase

both a sense of urgency and an unfamiliarity with the nature of the site and its abundant supply of material from the old acropolis. It also suggests that the chosen promontory was an unfortified site.

Historical records contain no information concerning the initial construction of the castle and the picture of its development must be drawn up on architectural evidence and the dating provided by the armorial shields found on the buildings. Such an assessment reveals six early buildings namely, the French tower (A), the Naillac building (B), the north-east tower (C), the Snakes tower (D), the rectangular tower (E), the Maritime tower (F), and gate 3. The French tower stands on the highest part of the peninsula and is square in plan. Approximately half-way up its eastern face is a group of escutcheons bearing the coats-of-arms of Grand Master Philibert de Naillac (1398-1421) and Frà Hesso Schlegelholtz, preceptor of the nearby island of Kos from 1386 to 1412.[46] Below these are the arms of Drogonetto Clavelli, a financier from Rhodes and receiver of the grand master from 1382 to 1415. Clavelli, who was a very rich man, may have financed the building of the tower himself.[47] Two other arms, dating to 1421-51, probably record later additions and the reconstruction of the tower's upper section.

West of the French tower is a low rectangular and crenellated building, partly reconstructed, bearing the arms of Grand Master de Naillac and Frà Schlegelholtz on one

of the merlons. The Naillac building, as it is known, was presumably strengthened sometime during 1510-12 when Frà Antoni de San Marti was captain of the castle.[48] The works included the opening of a new doorway in the north wall and the buttressing of the west wall with a new talus. Internally the building was barrel-vaulted and had a slightly pointed arch built with small grey stone blocks. This building may have been used as the castle's earliest chapel.

To the north of the French tower and the Naillac building, stood a line of outer defences consisting of four towers presumably linked by a curtain wall. Tower C was a tall round tower that was later encased within the east curtain wall. A shield of Grand Master Naillac, however not *in situ*, rests at the top of this tower. Half-way along the neck of the peninsula stands a circular tower D, known as the Snake tower, also datable to 1407-12 by the escutcheons affixed onto it, which include those of Naillac and Schlegelholtz.[49] Alteration works were undertaken on it in 1462.[50] The tower of the Snakes was crudely built with irregular pieces of masonry and much use of tile. Internally, it has a domed roof and two rooms, the upper one approached by an external ramp

West of the tower of the Snakes stands the small rectangular tower E, its lower courses crudely built of heavily galleted, coursed rubble work. Its top part was rebuilt and can only be entered at that level. The tower's west wall has gunports that suggest a post-1421 date for its construction. Farther west of tower E is the round Maritime tower (F) and gate 3. This tower is solid and its platform is approached along the *chemin-de-ronde* of the adjoining wall. It is built of large squared stone laid in roughly regular courses. This tower was repaired in 1469. This tower is itself bonded into a short stretch of wall in which gate 3 is located. This opening is datable to the period 1407-21 by an escutcheon bearing the arms of Grand Master Naillac[51] but was reconstructed at a later date and fitted with a new façade. The arms of Naillac were brought forward and placed on the renovated section, together with the unidentified arms from the later period. During these alteration works the gate itself was also provided with a portcullis. Both tower C and the Maritime tower were built of large and heavy ashlar masonry which, when compared to the crudely-executed French and Snake towers, appear to belong to a secondary phase in the building of the main land front.

Dr Anthony Luttrell has shown that when the structures dated to the pre-1421 period are superimposed on a plan

Right, Tower of France and adjoining wall of the inner 'castrum'. Top right, The tower of Italy. Note the arms of Grand Master Orsini carved on a Corinthian capital.

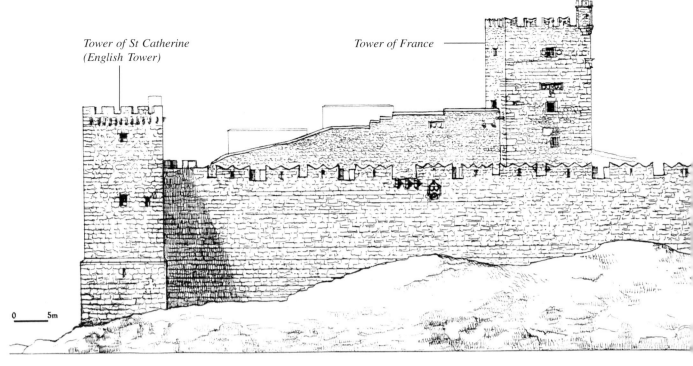

Tower of St Catherine (English Tower)

Tower of France

0   5m

and linked by curtain walls, the result is a defensive line cutting across the neck of the peninsula from towers C to F, overlooked by the French tower and the Naillac building on the summit of the hill and acting as the keep of the defensive position.[52] In Rhodes, the pre-1421 wall-towers were built into the main curtain walls and were mainly square in plan. Between 1421 and 1436, a number of tall circular towers were also built along the main enceinte of Rhodes. These projected outwards and were detached from the main walls in the contemporary Spanish style.[53] Possibly, the original wall towers at Bodrum were built in a similar fashion but any such evidence has been obscured by subsequent works. The Hospitallers seem to have exploited the natural minor scarp at the neck of the plateau and built their towers on the solid rock above the natural drop. Initially the towers may have been linked together by a wooden palisade.[54] Indeed, according to Felix Faber's account of the founding of Bodrum castle, the Hospitallers

cut a ditch and erected a wooden fortress under the cover of which they began to erect strong masonry walls.[55] As a matter of fact, considerable quantities of wood are recorded to have been used at Bodrum castle. In 1418 the Venetian senate authorized the Hospitallers to import 500 beams and an equal number of planks from Crete to be used in this castle[56] but these, especially the planks, could also have been employed in the construction of hoarding, raised walkways, and for secondary dwellings within the stronghold itself.

With the exception of towers C and F, all the early defensive structures were built with small, rough, and irregular stones gathered from around the site. The use of small stones, easily gathered and manhandled at the building site, eliminated the need for specialized labour, heavy hoists, and other tools that would have been necessary if larger worked ashlar blocks were employed, all of which would not have been available in adequate quantities to the Hospitallers at Bodrum. It also allowed the soldiers to participate in the construction and thus speed up the work. Subsequent ramparts erected at Bodrum by the Hospitallers became more elaborate and employed heavier masonry, evidently a result of the knights' increased control over the surrounding countryside and the importation of specialized labour and building equipment.

The initial years at Bodrum seem to have been very unstable ones. The fragility of the early defences is reflected in the written instructions sent to the captain of the castle on 14 December 1409 ordering him to refrain from engaging or

Bodrum castle - plan c. 1470.

Myne or closed battery (1495)

Opertis Revellino

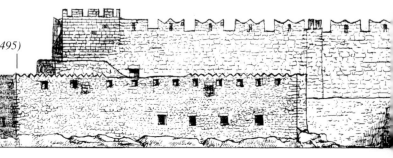

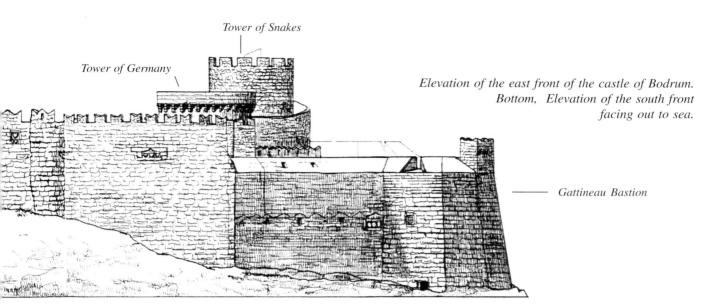

Tower of Snakes

Tower of Germany

Elevation of the east front of the castle of Bodrum.
Bottom, Elevation of the south front
facing out to sea.

Gattineau Bastion

provoking the Turks, the purpose being to avert any reprisals on the vulnerable and unfinished defences.[57] That the Hospitallers were constrained to the confines of their castle and not dare to leave it to stock wood was also reported by Corianlanus Cippico in 1472.[58] The situation was similar to that at Smyrna were the Hospitallers controlled the sea-castle but not the surrounding areas. It is not surprising, therefore, that there were problems with the *stipendarii*, or mercenaries, in the garrison in 1409 and 1412, and even among the Hospitaller knights themselves.[59] As a result, the *caravana*, or term of duty, which the brethren were expected to carry out at Bodrum was reduced to two years even though at times, as occurred in 1475, the *muta dei cavalieri* was deferred until such time as the crisis subsided.[60]

The complement of soldiers at Bodrum was usually 50 knights and 100 Latin mercenaries, the *stipendiati* or *socii*.[61] In 1409 these mercenaries cost the treasury 6,000 ducats annually, while in 1504 they required 7,200 florins to maintain. Another 550 florins were needed to feed the

knights.[62] In 1470 the castle was garrisoned by 50 knights and 100 mercenaries and, in 1520, by 50 knights and 150 soldiers. When the castle of St Peter was threatened with attack, its garrison was usually reinforced with more men sent from Rhodes.[63] On 26 October 1470, the captain of Bodrum, Frà Francesco Boxolles, went personally to Rhodes to report on the castle's condition and seek reinforcements following rumours of renewed preparations for an attack on Rhodes and other Hospitaller possessions by the Turks who were known to be arming 40 galleys.[64] Eleven days later a contingent of 300 soldiers was dispatched to Bodrum to reinforce its garrison together with 'due mila moggi di formento; gran quantità di tavole Venetiane; di fartie per legare i ripari; chiodi, pece, pale, zappe, polvere, salnitro, zolfo, e altri materiali da far fuochi artifitiati; Piombo, palle, meccio, e molte altre provisioni da guerra.'[65] Other reinforcements were sent in 1471 (25 knights 'oltre l'ordinaria caravana'), in 1475 (70 knights under the command of Frà Christosano de'Corradi di Lignana), in 1488 and in 1502, the latter being a large relief force under the command of Frà Francesco di Monserat.[66]

Tower of Italy

Tower of France

Tower of St Catherine (English Tower)

Naillac building

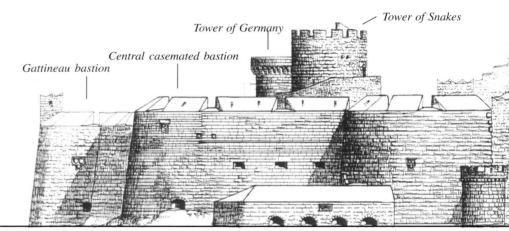

Right, Elevation of the west front of Bodrum castle facing the approaches to the harbour. Bottom, Elevation of the main land front where most the late 15th- and early 16th-century efforts in the re-fortification of the castle were invested. This front is further protected by a ditch, counterscarp, and glacis.

Tower of Germany

Tower of Snakes

Central casemated bastion

Gattineau bastion

Covered battery

Maritime tower (F)

The castle at Bodrum was governed by a captain, appointed in Rhodes, for a period of two years, who in turn nominated a lieutenant to exercise command at St Peter castle. The pilier of the language of Germany, the grand bailiff, had the prerogative of inspecting the castle of St. Peter. This duty was assigned to him at the chapter general of 1428.[67] Apart from its garrison of soldiers, the castle had a chaplain and a surgeon, together with small Christian and Greek communities living within the compound. Two churches, *Sancta Maria* and *Sanctus Gregorius,* served both the Greek and Latin rites.[68] The 'consocii et mainarii' in the castle kept an armed 'galiotta' with which they preyed on Turkish shipping in the area.[69] The garrison was quartered in a number of houses built inside the castle. In 1416, the treasury was licensed to sell a 'domus' there.[70] The castle also kennelled a number of specially-bred dogs which were trained by the garrison to guide Christian slaves, escaping from the Turks, back to the castle.[71] In 1513 the Hospitallers were worried that these dogs were not breeding enough

puppies and, by 1520, their number had fallen to around 50.[72] Every evening a trumpet was sounded from the castle to call the dogs to their food.

The first phase in the development of the castle at Bodrum came to an end with the death of Grand Master Philibert de Naillac in 1421. The second phase involved the consolidation of the site and saw the enclosure of the summit within an inner *castrum,* followed by the gradual enclosure of the rest of the peninsula within massive walls. This period lasted right up to the beginning of the 1470s. Work in the years following 1421 witnessed the erection of an inner *castrum* enclosing the summit of the peninsula with the French tower being utilized as a corner tower. Another strong tower, the tower of Italy, was built east of it behind the Naillac building. Both the wall south of the French and the Italian towers display the arms of Angelino de Muscettola who was captain of the castle by 11 May 1433, and served in this capacity until 7 March 1435. Muscettola's

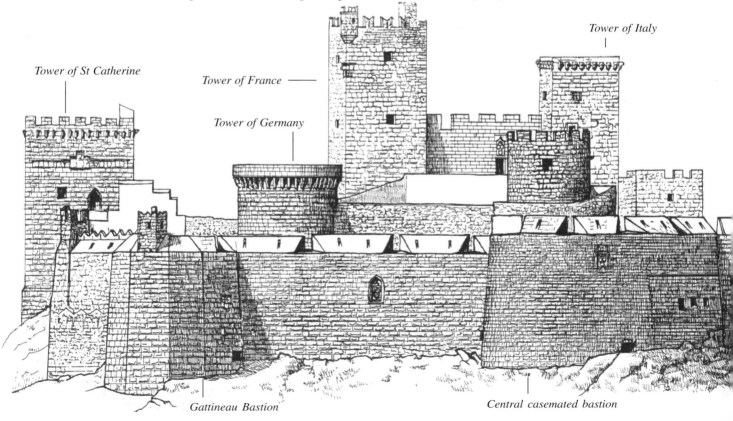

Tower of St Catherine

Tower of France

Tower of Germany

Tower of Italy

Gattineau Bastion

Central casemated bastion

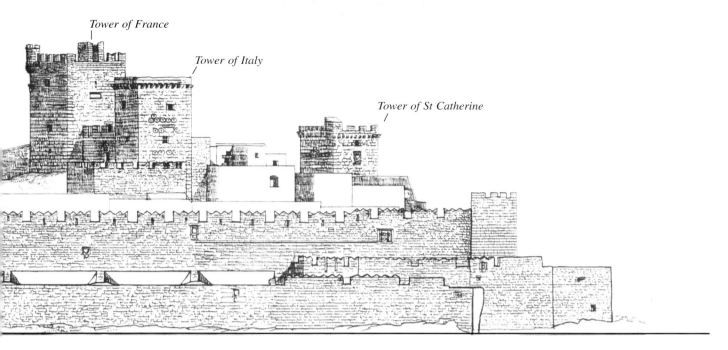

Tower of France

Tower of Italy

Tower of St Catherine

arms can be seen inscribed on the drum and capital of a Corinthian column affixed to the walls of the tower of Italy. The coat-of-arms of Grand Master Fluviano appear next to those of Muscettola on the enclosure wall south of the French tower. This wall, however, is built of rubble and is relatively quite weak. Rather than being a line of defence it seems to have been conceived more as *collachium* wall, designed to separate the knights' quarters from the rest of the garrison, especially the rather unreliable mercenary contingent which was often susceptible to insubordination, mutiny, and even treachery. Both in 1471 and 1474, the Hospitallers suspected that there were some Turkish spies within the garrison and in 1474 even ordered that all the castle's sea-facing windows be blocked up.[73] The remains of a pair of corbels protruding outwards next to the French tower, however, suggests that the enclosure wall was machicolated and thus also intended for defence. Of the walls enclosing the upper *castrum*, if it ever existed as a separate entity, only the northern section survives but then only in its rebuilt form and bearing the arms of Grand Master del Carretto. The walls of this *castrum* appear to have been replaced by various buildings along the west and south sides.

The third phase in the development of the castle involved the enclosure of the remaining unfortified areas on the peninsula within three groups of walls, together with the erection of a number of towers to provide enfilading fire. The oldest coat-of-arms that appears on these works are

Bodrum castle - plan c.1522

found on the east curtain wall, on tower E (Fluvian or Lastic) and the adjoining wall (dated 1444) and on the German tower (Lastic) which seems to have been built in the 1437-57 period. This tower, D-shaped in plan, projected outwards from the original curtain wall. It was fitted with two gun-ports to enable the defenders to enfilade the adjoining rampart. In the period 1454-61, the German tower was re-located onto the rebuilt curtain wall, itself brought forward from towers C and D. These new walls seem to have had gun ports.[74] Most of the outer enclosure was completed during the times of grand masters Jacques de Milly (1454-61), Zacosta (1461-67), and Orsini (1467-

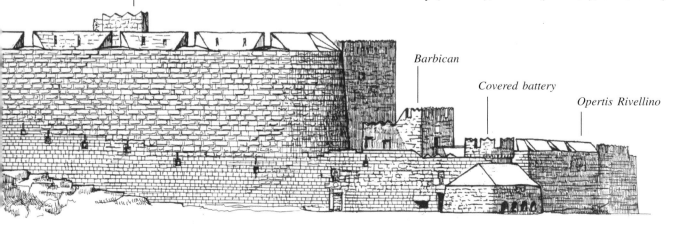

Tower (E)

Barbican

Covered battery

Opertis Rivellino

76). De Milly's arms appear, together with those of Giacomo Gialtru, captain of Bodrum from 1454 to1455, on the gate leading out into the barbican in front of the west curtain wall and on the south wall of the refectory in the English tower. Also known as the tower of *saincte katherine,* this was constructed sometime before 1437.[75] Its interior consisted of a high barrel vault divided into three floors. The main room was approached through a doorway fitted with a drawbridge. Half-way up the face of the north wall of the English tower is an impressive array of coats-of-arms which were erected in honour of the chief contributors who had financed its construction. The focal point in this display of English heraldry is the escutcheon bearing the arms of King Henry IV, flanked by 22 others, six of which belonged to members of the royal family.

The arms of Grand Master Zacosta appear on the south sea-wall and date the completion of this section of the enceinte to the period 1461-67. Grand Master Orsini's coat-of-arms appears high on the lower half of the west

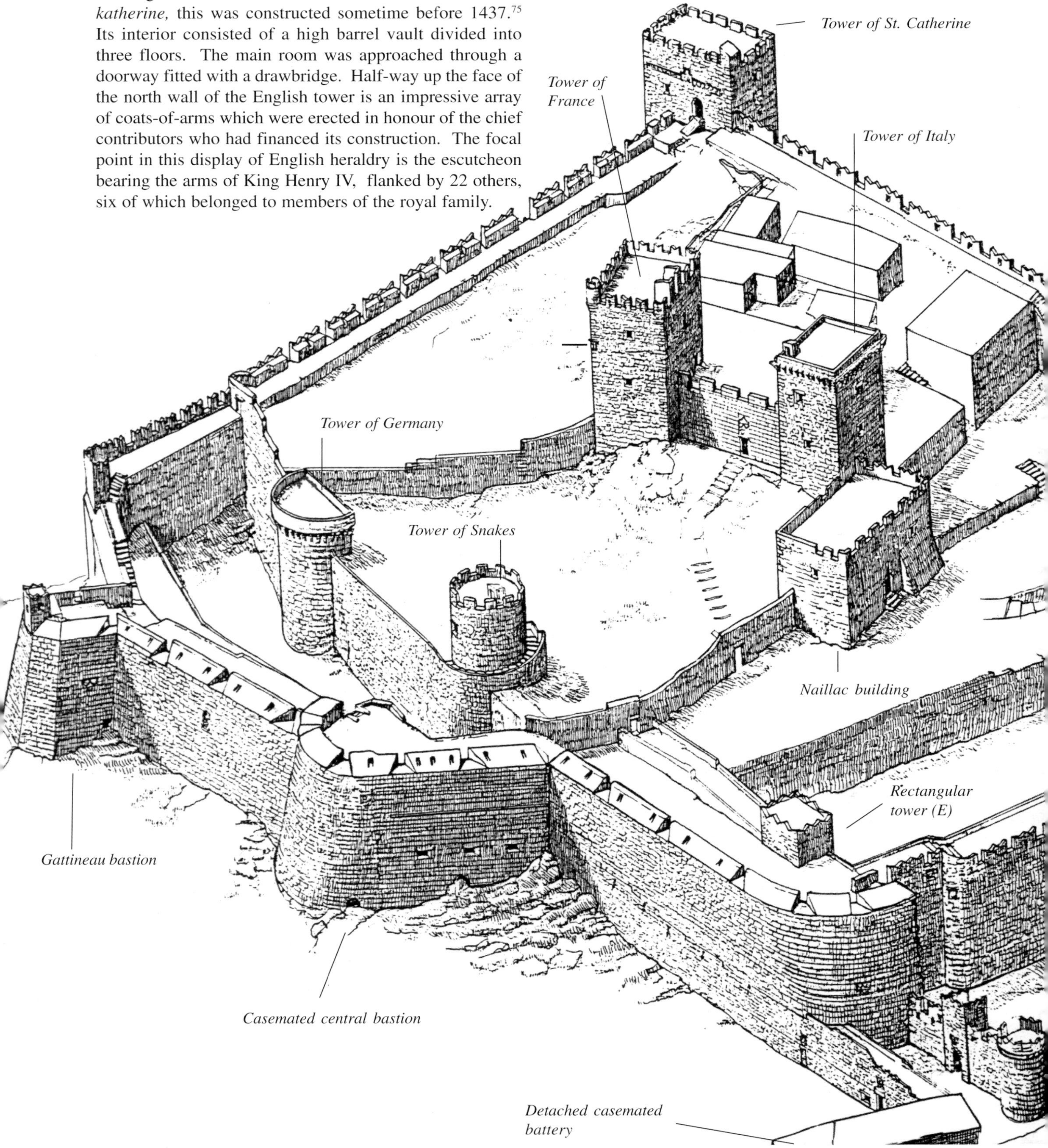

Tower of St. Catherine

Tower of France

Tower of Italy

Tower of Germany

Tower of Snakes

Naillac building

Rectangular tower (E)

Gattineau bastion

Casemated central bastion

Detached casemated battery

wall together with that of the then captain of the castle Francesco Boxolles (1470-72). The inscribed year 1472 dates the termination of the west curtain wall. Orsini's arms also appear above the doorway into the castle's outer bailey, along the south wall. The coat-of-arms of Grand Master d'Aubusson farther up the west wall imply that this rampart was later altered, heightened, or repaired, following the terrible earthquake which shook the Dodecanese in 1481.[76] Shortly after that earthquake, Grand Master d'Aubusson personally visited Bodrum and inspected its defences 'per consolare, e fortificar gli animi de' Sudditi, e Vassalli della Religione; come per dar ordine alle fortificationi, e provisioni, che per assicuramento, e difesa di quelle piazze erano necessario.' [77]

The walls of the outer enclosure developed slowly over a period of nearly 70 years, during which time almost continual repairs, alterations, and additions were carried out. That the work progressed slowly can be judged from the amount of money expended on the fortifications. In 1466 only a total of 300 florins were spent on repairs while

Above, North face of the tower of St Catherine. Affixed high on the tower are the arms of English knights and King Henry IV of England, below. Left, General layout of the castle of Bodrum.

from 1480 to 1486 an average of 380 florins were devoted annually to 'beluardi, fossati,' and other types of works.[78] By 1494, however, the nature of these works had increased to the tune of 650 florins annually and, in 1495, to 700 florins.[79] Throughout the early sixteenth century these figures would undoubtedly have risen still more dramatically considering the extent of the fortifications erected in the first two decades. Most of the alterations, especially those undertaken along the land front were in response to the growing use of gunpowder artillery.

The Venetian attack on the Turkish-held town of Bodrum in 1472, outside the castle walls, may have had a very important effect on the subsequent development and appearance of the castle itself.[80] Following this *razzia,* the Hospitallers were able to acquire greater access to the ruins of the ancient town of Halicarnassus and, after 1494, the famous mausoleum itself (one of the seven wonders of the ancient world) was discovered and systematically

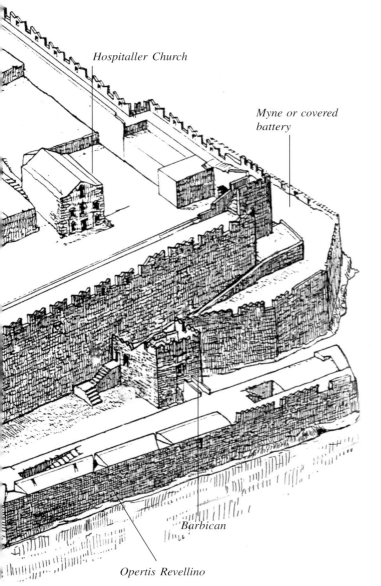

Hospitaller Church

Myne or covered battery

Barbican

Opertis Revellino

The polygonal bastion of Gattineau crowned by a rectangular vedette and heavily-sloped merlons.

dismantled to provide building material, especially green lava stones, marble ashlar and bluish limestone ashlar, for new fortification works at Bodrum.[81] Ancient carvings and friezes from the mausoleum were also used to decorate the new defensive works such as the *Opertis revellino*.[82] The rich abundance of stone provided by the mausoleum remains allowed the defence works to proceed at a steadier pace.

The heavy earthquake of 1493 seems to have caused less harm to Bodrum than Kos. No explicit record of the damage has so far been brought to light, but, in the following year, the Hospitallers began to refortify the castle at Bodrum even more drastically than ever before and these works may have been a direct result of the earthquake of the previous year.[83] Thus, in 1494-96, the knights built a vaulted battery, the *Myne*,[84] on the south-west corner of the castle; in 1148-99 the western end of the north antemural was newly built as an outer curtain.[85] In 1505-6 a powerful *revellino* was erected along the west part of the enceinte by the knight commander Frà Constanzo Opertis.[86] This solid outerwork is similar to another battery built at Leros. In 1512-13 the Gattineau casemated battery was erected at the mouth of the ditch with one side facing the harbour, and the other designed to fire into the ditch and enfilade the land front.[87] To all intents and purposes, this battery was really an embryonic form of caponier, attached to but not incorporated into, the main wall. A similar but improved version of a caponier, this time directly incorporated into the main enceinte through internal passages, was built in Rhodes the following year. In 1512 the Hospital sent a galley from Rhodes under the command of the knight Frà Ugo Coponea to Bodrum to help clear the *fossa* of the castle, initially enlarged in 1476, 'per votare i fossi di quella fortezza, i quali erano pieni, dalla banda di Turchi, per la rovina di certa muraglia.'[88] The arms of Gattineau, placed on the counterscarp, show that the works undertaken in 1512 included also the heightening of the counterscarp and glacis.

The land front was fitted with heavy artillery defences *alla moderna* in the years 1512-22. The pentagonal bastion on the east end of the front seems to have been the first of the new works to have been completed since it bears the arms of Frà Jacques Gattineau (1512-13). On the opposite end of the front, the new ramparts were grafted onto the low *avans mur* which can still be seen incorporated into the

Right, The heavy casemated bastion situated in the centre of the land front of the castle. Above, right, Close-up of the wooden drawbridge (reconstruction) of the tower of St Catherine.

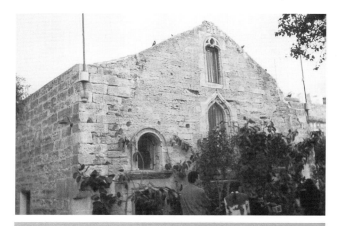

base of the ramparts. The strengthening of the *avans mur* was still in progress in the last decade of the fifteenth century as attested by the arms of Frà Tomas Provan (1490). The new rampart, completed by 1514, also necessitated the blocking-up of an old gateway in the *avans mur* bearing the arms of Grand Master d'Aubusson and this had to be replaced by another opening, built in 1518, and situated nearer to the Gattineau battery. It was flanked by two gun-ports opening at ground level. Other stretches of the *avans mur* can be found east of the pentagonal bastion, at the foot of the south sea-wall and behind the west barbican. The large central bulwark with its casemated gun battery bears the coats-of-arms of Frà Thomas Sheffield, captain of the castle in 1514-19 and Frà Cornelius Hambroeck (1517-18). The curtain wall between the bulwarks is adorned with the arms of Grand Master del Carretto and Frà Hambroeck and is dated 1517.

Most of the land front was completely remodelled by 1518. The last works on the defences were undertaken by Grand Master L'Isle Adam and his arms appear, together with those of Frà Bernardino Piossasco Di Airasca (the last captain of the castle), on the north end of the east curtain wall. These, however, only seem to attest to minor alterations. Notwithstanding the heavy investment in the massive shield of bulwarks, the land front continued to provide a high profile, exposed to artillery fire, mainly because of the fact that the castle was sited on rising ground. An attempt to remedy this situation involved the erection of a steep glacis but this did not really solve the problem. In 1521 the Italian engineer Basilio della Scuola was sent to Bodrum to inspect its defences but it does not seem that he could have executed any major works.[90] Little is known of the engineers who modelled the Hospitaller fortifications in the early sixteenth century. Bartholino de Castellione del cremonese 'ingeniere e architecto' is known to have been working at Bodrum in 1507.[91]

The last captain of castle of St Peter castle was Frà Piossasco Di Airasca. During the siege of Rhodes, Bodrum was heavily defended but it was by-passed by the Turks. Airasca, therefore, sent most of his men and munitions to Rhodes to assist in its defence. When L'Isle Adam surrendered to the Turks he sent instructions to Airasca to abandon Bodrum and proceed with the garrison to Crete, where they eventually arrived in mid-January.

Left, from top to bottom: The Hospitaller church at Bodrum, later used by the Turks as a gunpowder magazine; View of the barbican situated to the rear of the seaward Opertis Revellino; The casemated battery frequently referred to as a caponier.

Hospitaller Fortifications
in
Malta
Gozo & Tripoli

Tripoli Castle

In 1530 the fortress of Tripoli was one of a few isolated Spanish outposts situated on Muslim territory along the North African coast. It had been captured by assault in 1510 but was held only with great difficulty surrounded as it was by hostile tribes. When the knights took over its defence, they found a dilapidated fortress surrounded by ruinous ramparts and protected by a small quadrangular castle, the origins of which dated to the Byzantine occuptation of Tripoli. This little stronghold had walls 5 *canne* high and was protected by a ditch 44 *passi* wide and 24 *canne* deep. The castle was 'fondato sopra pietra marmorea' and had been given two bastions by the Spaniards. The remainder of its enceinte, however, was still *all'antica*. The city itself was enclosed by a wall 2.5m high and protected by weak barbicans 'poco resistenti alle artiglierie, senza baluardi, con fossati stretti e poco profondi.' A stretch of wall some 200 hundred paces in length had been demolished by the Spaniards and the masonry used to strengthen the castle.[2] The Spaniards had also erected a small coastal fort, the 'Castellegio', with which to command the entrance to the harbour, and a 'batteria di San Pietro' near the tower of St Peter at the north end of the sea-wall.[3]

The Hospitallers' initial concern was to strengthen the fortifications, especially the ancient and ruinous town walls. The knights believed that the town could only be made defensible if rebuilt anew with artillery bastions and terrepleined curtain walls, an undertaking estimated to cost 25,000 scudi and one which the Order was in no position to finance.[4] Various petitions were made to the Spanish crown for financial help. In 1539 the Order even sent the knight Frà Giovanni Bosmedinol 'co' disegni, e co' modelli in mano' to inform the emperor of the actual state of the fortress of Tripoli and elicit his support.[5] The knights saw little advantage in retaining the castle if the adjoining town could be easily overrun. The emperor, however, was in no way disposed to consider abandoning Tripoli and pressed the knights to fortify and defend it as best they could. Still, throughout their twenty-year stay in Tripoli, the Order could do little more than repair and maintain the old ramparts, failing even to reinforce the existing walls with terrepleins.[6]

The knights did, nonetheless, introduce minor adaptations to improve the town's defences. In 1536, for example, the captain of Tripoli, Frà Georg Schilling, pierced a number of walls with musketry loopholes to provide flanking fire for the landward gates. These helped the garrison repel and

The castle and town of Tripoli around 1559. The pentagonal earthworks were added by the Muslims (Bib. Naz. Centrale di Firenze).

defeat an assault on the city.[7] Jean de Valette, when he was captain, did his utmost to improve the defences but never failed to warn the Order 'che più tardare non si dovesse in fortificarla con Beluardi reali alla moderna.'[8] By the time of Dragut's siege in 1551, the town still lacked bastions. The existing bastions were the work of the Turks in the post-1551 period.

Instead, the Hospitallers invested their efforts in the refortification of the castle and the small harbour fort, the 'Castellegio'. In 1533 the Florentine engineer Piccino was sent over from Malta to inspect the defences and prior to his return, prepared designs and written instructions for the construction of a tower within the fort.[9] The new works in the 'Castellegio' were taken in hand immediately and continued throughout 1534 under the direction of Frà Schilling. The quality of these works, however, left much to be desired so that in 1543 it was necessary to reinforce the tower with timber beams removed from a wrecked galley.[10]

The castle's walls were terrepleined and new gunpowder defences added. A new bastion, the 'bastione di San Iacomo' and a 'piattaforma di Santa Barbara' were added on the south flank of the castle.[11] St James bastion was built very solidly, forming 'la più forte parte di quella fortezza.'[12] It was terrepleined with thick earth mixed with fascines to provide a compact fill. So strongly was it built that when the outer retaining face wall collapsed under the weight of Turkish bombardment during the brief siege of 1551, the exposed terreplein effortlessly absorbed the artillery shot without crumbling away.[13] Bosio tells us that the two Spanish bastions were poorly built, 'terrapienati di terra labile e flussible.'[14] A kiln was specially set up inside the ditch to supply the necessary lime for the re-plastering of the castle walls but these interventions did little to solve the inherent structural shortcomings and most of the plaster, we are told, crumbled away under the vibrations of the Turkish artillery bombardment.

Internally, the old castle accommodated a number of buildings. There was a chapel dedicated to St Lawrence, attended by four chaplains of the Order, a powder magazine, the captain's residence, and a few barrack blocks housing the garrison.[15] Both the captain's house and the magazine were built with their backs to the inner walls of St James bastion and adjacent curtain. During the 1551 siege, these buildings were quickly packed with earth to reinforce the ramparts behind them. Bosio also mentions a cavalier, the 'Ribas altas', which was on the south side of the castle.[16]

The authority of the knights and that of the Spaniards before them did not proceed far outside the confines of the city, except for some villages situated on the west coast. Initially, a few of these, such as Zanzur, Lmaia, and Zuaga, paid a yearly tribute.[17] Tagiura, only seven miles away, was in Muslim hands and formed the seat of Muslim resistance.[18] Khair ud-Din, its governor and one of the lieutenants of Barbarossa, kept up a constant pressure on Tripoli with the help of neighbouring corsairs and even managed to erect a tower, the tower of Alcaide, less than a mile away from the castle.[19] This was eventually captured in 1536 by Frà George Schilling von Cannstatt, with the help of a force sent over from Malta under the command of the knight Bottigella.

In 1542 the corsair Morataga (Murad Agha) entrenched his forces within three miles of the city. Jean de Valette, who held the governorship of Tripoli from 1536 to 1549, conducted many expeditions and raids against Morataga and in so doing released the pressure on Tripoli. In one attack, Valette and his squadron of arquebusiers managed to set fire to one of Mortaga's galeottes.[20]

Dragut's attack on Tripoli in 1551 found the fortress defended by 50 knights and a few hundred men. The Turkish force landed east of the town and immediately began setting up three large batteries of 12 guns each with which to bombard the defences. The *Castellejo,* under the command of the knight Frà Iacomo de Rosher and defended by a garrison of 30 soldiers, was ignored by the Turks who immediately concentrated their efforts on the castle. Initially, they were over-confident, given their recent successes in the island of Gozo, and the Christian guns took a heavy toll of the attackers. Notably effective was the gun battery placed

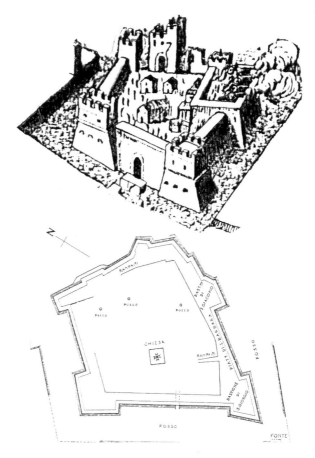

Above, The castle of Tripoli in 1559 and a plan of the same drawn by L. Turba in 1913 and published in a book by Aurigemma.

on the 'Ribas altas' under the command of Giovanni Caccialepre Rodiotto, 'Capo Maestro de' Bombardieri.'[21]

The Turks concentrated their bombardment on the bastion of St James, but the structure was solidly built and absorbed the punishment inflicted by the cannon. The Turks then shifted their efforts on the adjoining curtain wall, the 'piattaforma di Santa Barbara', and soon began to breach its walls. Behind the curtain wall stood part of the captain's house and powder magazine. The defenders transferred the munitions to the church and packed the buildings with earth to give the walls some added strength. Villiers, the captain, ordered the garrison to construct an internal entrenchment with 'gabbioni di tavole terrapienate' but the Calabrese soldiers, sensing the hopelessness of their predicament, mutinied and forced the governor to negotiate a surrender with the Turks. The negotiations were brief and Tripoli capitulated on 14 August 1551, after 40 years of Christian domination. The unfortunate Villiers, on his arrival in Malta, was tried and imprisoned for having failed to crush the mutiny and for losing Tripoli.[22]

Fort St Angelo

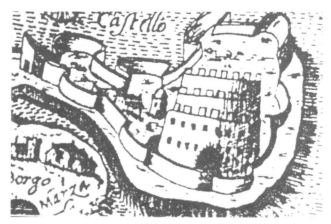

The history of Fort St Angelo begins in obscurity, its origins popularly credited to the Arabs who occupied Malta in the ninth century AD; however, no mention is made of the castle in the terms of surrender of the island to Count Roger in 1091.[1] There is no shred of documentary evidence to support the tradition that Count Roger repaired and garrisoned the harbour castle. The first documented evidence to its existence only appears in thirteenth-century royal mandates during the Angevin domination (1266-84) of the island where the castle was referred to as the *castrum maris*.[2]

Little has survived of the original medieval fortress since most of the structure was replaced by later additions and alterations carried out by the knights, particularly during the closing decades of the seventeenth century. Most of what we know has been culled from the medieval documents and a stone model commissioned in 1687 to illustrate the layout of Grunenberg's proposed new works of fortification.[3]

It would appear that the pre-1530 castle consisted basically of an inner and outer ward. The inner *castrum,* and possibly the oldest part of the stronghold, the 'castro interiore, retro ecclesia Sancti Maria',[4] formed a triangular enclosure in which stood the castellan's residence. This corresponded roughly to the perimeter now enveloping the highest part of the promontory including the magisterial palace and the chapel of St Anne. This inner enceinte was stiffened with a number of wall-towers of which at least two were rounded and were sited on the front facing Senglea. One of these towers has survived and reveals the use of large ashlar masonry blocks, probably re-utilized classical masonry, in its lower courses. The second rounded wall-tower was located close to the chapel and appears to have been that which the Sicilian documents refer to as the 'Tower of St Angelo'.[5] This wall-tower is known to have been rebuilt and repaired in 1517 with the use of some 130 *cantuni* (stone blocks), 30 capstones, and 900 *salme* of rubble.[6]

Above, top, The castrum maris as depicted in a 16th-century map of Malta. Above, The castle of St Angelo in the 16th century, after Schelling. Bottom, left, Fort St Angelo during the Great Siege as depicted by Perez d'Aleccio, showing D'Homedes bastion and the cavalier.

The main residence of the *castellan* appears to have survived as the inner core of the magisterial palace. Architectural evidence shows that the knights enveloped the original building within a stronger outer shell fitted with corner buttresses and the whole structure was given the form of a compound keep. The upper ward was itself served by a gateway, the foundations of which were unearthed during the course of restoration works undertaken in the 1990s. The enceinte of the outer ward is more difficult to discern. Medieval documents refer to the 'castro exteriore ante ecclesiam Sancti Angeli,'[7] which would place it on the north part of the peninsula. Some evidence shows that the walls of the outer ward also stretched as far south as the cavalier. Here the antemurale would have absorbed the shock of a direct attack from the mainland. Another rounded wall-tower is known to have stood just to the rear of the cavalier. Grunenberg's stone model clearly shows this part of the medievel enceinte as having had a heavily sloping talus. This feature is attested by the historical documents which speak of the rebuilding of a pronounced 'scarpa di lu Castellu' facing Birgu in 1477.[8]

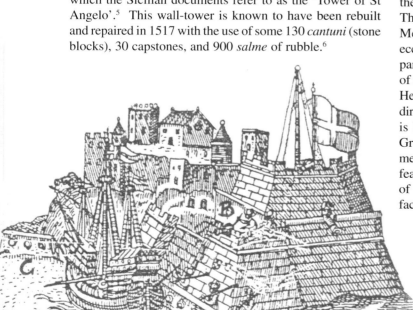

The area within the outer ward seems to have been occupied by a number of buildings, including a tavern. One block was actually built onto the east flank of the bailey, facing Kalkara. These dwellings survived well into the seventeenth century and were only replaced after the earthquake of 1693, when the commission of war ordered their demolition.[9]

The medieval documents speak also of a barbican which was in need of repair in 1477.[10] The word *barbican,* of Arabic etymology, is explained as deriving from *bab khank,* meaning gatehouse or a kind of fortification defending a particular point like a gate. In this sense, the barbican of the *castrum maris* would be the L-shaped structure which can be seen covering the route up to the castle through the gate near the chapel of St Mary. This was designed to ensure an anti-clockwise turn into the castle, thus exposing the attacker's unprotected right flank (shields were carried on the left arm), a common medieval practice. This structure was retained by the knights and has survived, albeit partly rebuilt and refaced.

Above, from left to right: Entrance to the magisterial palace; Remains of one of the rounded wall-towers of the castrum maris: Façade of the chapel of St Anne. Below, D'Homedes bastion as seen from across the moat.

However, in Italian or Latin medieval texts, the word barbican meant also the *antemurale (murus minor)* or *faussebraye.* This would then explain the appearance, in a number of plans and also in D'Aleccio's drawings, of a wall with towers and gates situated down by the shore, cut short by the D'Homedes bastion built in 1536. This bastion was actually built 'davanti la porta del castello in questo Borgo.'[11] In 1523 a tower was erected over a gate of the castle under the superintendence of Antonio Fantino. The antemural would have also stretched along the length of the castle's land front for, in 1478, a section of the walls facing the ditch was in ruins. The ditch itself, which some historians believe to be the 'Tagliata' mentioned in the medieval documents as far back as 1438, appears to have originally been just a rock-

The cavalier of Fort St Angelo, designed by the Italian engineer Antonio Ferramolino and erected after 1541. The cavalier is raised on three vaulted casemates.

hewn dry fosse cutting across the narrowest part of the peninsula in order to restrict the front to defensible proportions. The 'Tagliata' also demarcated the jurisdictional boundary of the castellan.[12]

For more than 200 years, the *castrum maris* served its feudal lords adequately enough but, by 1530, its was an obsolete stronghold, easily mined and stormed from its landward approaches. Only because it was the sole available fortification within the harbour was it taken over by the Order. The 'Ingegniere e Soprastante dell'Opere', Frà Diego Perez de Malfreire, was sent over with an advance party of workmen to carry out the necessary repair works, both to improve its fortifications and to enable the grand master take up his abode inside the castle.[13]

The first significant alteration to the sea-castle's defences was the conversion of 'la Tagliata' into a moat. This effectively isolated the castle from the rest of the mainland and reduced the threat of a direct landward assault. By 1536, Bosio states, the ditch between the *borgu* and the *castrum* had been excavated to just below sea-level. Simultaneously, the knights undertook the construction of the ramparts flanking the moat and facing Birgu. On these the knight Jaconio Pellequin placed the coats-of-arms of Grand Masters

L'Isle Adam, Del Ponte, and Saint Jaille.[14] Four such escutcheons can be seen on the left face of D'Homedes bastion. Two of these bear the dates 1535 and 1537. Curiously, D'Aleccio, in his illustrations, shows three escutcheons but on the other face of the bastion.

The acute-angled D' Homedes bastion was built in front of the castle's outer gate.[15] It was raised on two casemates, the lower one opened up into two sea-level embrasures designed to enfilade the face of the short stretch of curtain flanking the moat and facing Birgu. This bastion has rounded orillions, while a similar contemporary bastion in Mdina, also known as D'Homedes bastion, has squarish ones. Rounded orillions were a later development and it is quite possible that originally, D'Homedes bastion at Fort St Angelo had square orillions too, and these could have been altered when the bastion was rebuilt after the siege. The left flank of the bastion, too, shows signs of later alterations, particularly the grafting of a new solid wall that obstructed the two sea-level embrasures.

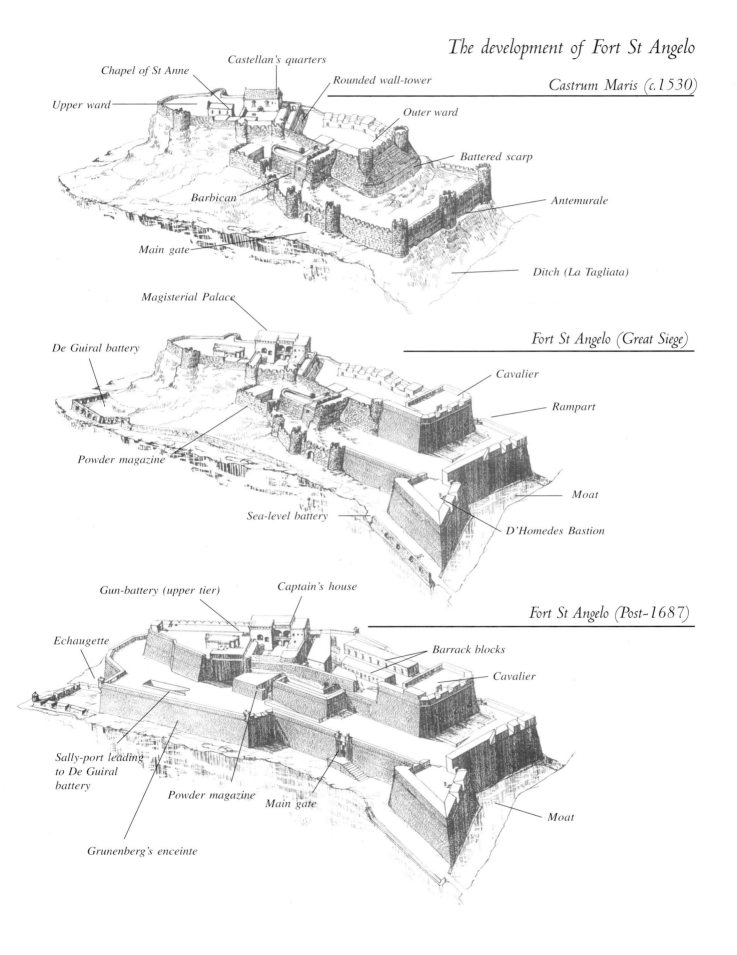

The development of Fort St Angelo

Castrum Maris (c.1530)

Chapel of St Anne

Castellan's quarters

Upper ward

Rounded wall-tower

Outer ward

Battered scarp

Barbican

Antemurale

Main gate

Ditch (La Tagliata)

Fort St Angelo (Great Siege)

Magisterial Palace

De Guiral battery

Cavalier

Rampart

Powder magazine

Moat

Sea-level battery

D'Homedes Bastion

Fort St Angelo (Post-1687)

Gun-battery (upper tier)

Captain's house

Echaugette

Barrack blocks

Cavalier

Sally-port leading
to De Guiral
battery

Powder magazine

Main gate

Moat

Grunenberg's enceinte

By 1540 the land front had been well defined and consisted of a single bastion and rampart. The new front, however, was soon to be criticized by the Italian military engineer, Antonio Ferramolino who was called to Malta in 1541 to advise the Order on its defences.[16] Ferramolino must have quickly realized that the 'Tagliata' was not only too narrow to enable a fully-developed *fronte bastionato,* which only allowed enough room a single bastion, but that the overlooking heights of Sta Margherita and the Sciberras peninsula provided ideal siege artillery positions. Countering this threat called for the erection of defensive batteries raised to equally commanding heights. Ferramolino's solution was to design a large cavalier overlooking the moat.[17] This was begun in 1542 and placed on the gorge of the land front but progress on the new work was slow. It was not until January 1547 that the council entrusted the completion of the cavalier into the hands of the knights Gondisalvo Guiral and Carlo Durre.[18] The threat of a Turkish invasion in 1541 forced the knights to block the mouth of the creek between the castle and Isola Point with a barrier of boats tied together and placed at the mouth of the creek. This operation involved a great deal of preparation and so, in 1546, an iron chain was ordered from the arsenal of Venice and brought over to Malta on the timber transport vessel, the *Contarina.* This chain was replaced in 1564 prior to the siege.[19]

It is not known exactly at what point in time that the *castrum maris* came to be called Fort St Angelo. It had a chapel dedicated to this saint as far back as 1274 but this name is not met with until 19 July 1540, when the knight Claudius de Humblieres is documented as having been confined in the 'Carcere Sti. Angeli.'[20]

The Great Siege of 1565 found Fort St Angelo a partially-developed stronghold. D'Aleccio's prints depict effectively the crude amalgamation of its two different styles of

Above, View of Fort St Angelo from across the Grand Harbour showing the fort around 1870, with, as yet, very few British alterations. The fleur d'eau *battery was heavily demolished by a storm and only partially rebuilt. Opposite page, Early 18th-century plan of Fort St Angelo (NML) and below, graphic aerial view of the fort.*

fortifications, the obsolete medieval and the contemporary bastioned trace. His illustrations clearly identify the cavalier and D'Homedes bastion as the focal point of the fortress. D'Aleccio also depicts De Guiral's battery. This *fleur d'eau* battery was a hastily improvised work thrown up just prior to the start of the siege. It was sited at the mouth of the creek and armed with five cannon. These were mounted there to thwart any sea-borne assault against the castle itself, the chain, and the 'spur' of the Senglea fortifications. Early in May 1565 the battery was entrusted to commander Francesco de Guiral, his lieutenant Barrientos, and the men of his galley, the *San Giovanni,* who soon earned their distinction during a Turkish sea-borne assault on the spur by firing a well-directed salvo against Turkish boats, sinking nine of ten large troop-laden vessels. Thereafter it came to be known as De Guiral's battery.

Throughout the course of the siege, the other batteries on Fort St Angelo, one of which was sited on top of the cavalier, were used to provide supporting fire to the nearby harbour defences. The castle's garrison, under the command of the Catalan knight Galceran Ros, served as the main reserve, running to the aid of the threatened posts. When the siege was over, Jean de Vallette, assured by the pope of forthcoming financial assistance, set about repairing the battered fortifications. The fear of a second invasion in the following year led the council to appoint a commission responsible for ensuring Fort St Angelo's readiness to withstand another long siege.

Thereafter, the shape of Fort St Angelo remained practically unchanged until late in the seventeenth century. It was Colonel Don Carlos de Grunenberg, engineer to the king of Spain, who was responsible for the replacement of the remaining medieval walls with a new bastioned enceinte designed primarily to provided powerful gun batteries trained against the mouth of the Grand Harbour. In his report of 26 February 1687, this Flemish engineer recommended the raising of four new batteries.[21] Still, the council, while approving his proposals, was in no position to finance the project since the Order was already heavily committed to the construction of the Floriana lines.

So on his return to Malta in 1689, Grunenberg offered to construct the batteries at his own expense. His memorial to the grand master, read to the grand council on 17 December 1689, stated that as the castle of St Angelo was the most advantageous and adequate for the defence of the entrance to the port, it was important that it should be put in a much better state of defence. In order not to delay the completion of the Galdiana and Floriana, Grunenberg offered the council to build at his own expense the batteries designed to command the entrance to the harbour. The first of these being at the water's edge, was to be 'entirely constructed of hard stone, with a length of 70 *cannes*' and 'capable of mounting 17 pieces, covered by their merlons and parapets 12 palms in thickness, with a platform of over 6 cannes in breadth.' The other two were to be higher and rise one above another, and were to be constructed 'in part from the site ... most suitable and time resisting.' The fourth was to be added at a later stage.[22]

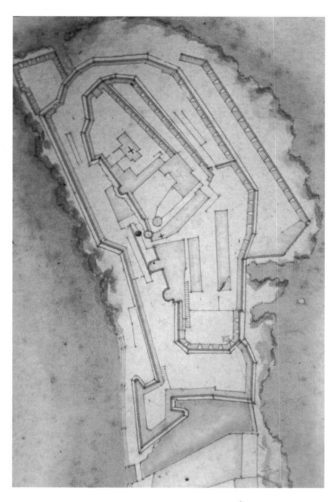

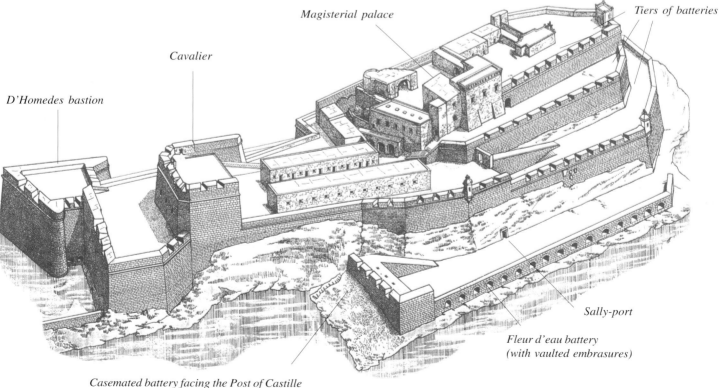

D'Homedes bastion

Cavalier

Magisterial palace

Tiers of batteries

Sally-port

Fleur d'eau battery (with vaulted embrasures)

Casemated battery facing the Post of Castille

Above, An echaugette, or guardiola, at Fort St Angelo. Such vedettes usually projected outwards from the parapet on corbels. Below, Fort St Angelo as seen from Senglea.

Grunenberg originally intended to have the upper batteries fitted with low parapets so the guns could fire *en barbette*, thus allowing a greater number of guns to be deployed. The rest of the enceinte, too, was remodelled, 'l'altro con fortificazione irregolare, accomodata al luogo, secondo le varie disposizioni e risguardande propii siti, contorni, ed eminenze convicine alle diverse parti della fronte.'[23] So was the main gate, which now provided better access to the new batteries. A marble plaque, bearing Grunenberg's coat-of-arms, was placed over the entrance to commemorate the improvements to the castle.

Actually Fort St Angelo owes its present form to these works since no other interventions were carried out thereafter. The many French engineers who were to inspect the fort during the course of the eighteenth century only recommended that it be kept in a good state of repair.

At the time of the arrival of Napoleon in 1798, Fort St Angelo was one of the most powerful fortresses on the island, armed with some 80 guns and four mortars, and garrisoned by a detachment from the Regiment of Malta (1777-98) under the command of the knight de Hourney, major of the grand master's guards. The four tiers of batteries, mounting a total of 48 guns, provided an effective deterrent to any enemy fleet attempting to force its way into the harbour. It was only the Order's pliancy which deprived the fort's gunners from demonstrating its awesome firepower against French ships in 1798.

Città Notabile *(Mdina)*

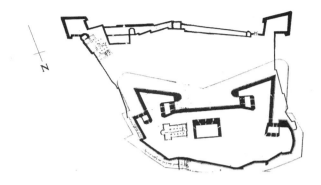

Città Notabile, or Città Vecchia as it was later called when the new city of Valletta was built, prides itself on being Malta's oldest fortified settlement. Ever since its inception, it has been occupied with astonishing continuity. The first town on the plateau most probably dates back to the Bronze Age and Punic periods but it was later enlarged during Roman times. Traces of the walls of the Roman city of *Melita* have been dug up in many places along the Rabat-Mdina plateau. The area occupied by the Roman city seems to have been roughly three times the size of the present fortress but sometime during the troubled Byzantine and Muslim occupations of the island, its was was reduced in size. The Arabs are traditionally credited with having provided the town with a new land front and a ditch. Mdina, as it was called by the Arabs, fell to Count Roger in 1091. After the Normans came the Hohenstaufens in 1194, the Angevins in 1266, the Aragonese in 1282, the Castellans in 1479, and finally in 1530, the Hospitaller Order.

Little has survived of Mdina's medieval enceinte since much of the old walls were enveloped within bastioned ramparts. Some idea of the general layout of the medieval fortress can nonetheless be gained from two sixteenth-century prints by Matteo Perez d'Aleccio and Gabrio Serbelloni respectively.[1] These show a roughly-triangular enceinte stiffened very sparsely by wall-towers, the majority of which occupied the land front. The left extremity of the medieval front was occupied by a small castle but this was dismantled by popular demand around the mid-1400s. A glimpse of the medieval defences of the city can be had at Greeks gate and its adjoining wall, constructed of rough and unequal blocks of masonry laid in irregular courses and growing progressively smaller in the upper courses. Some of the stones in the lower courses reach the size of huge boulders.

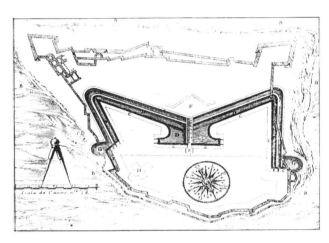

Above, Plans of Mdina by Serbelloni (top) and Perez d'Aleccio showing both the medieval trace of walls and a proposed retrenchment cutting the town in half. Bottom left, Mdina as depicted by d'Aleccio.

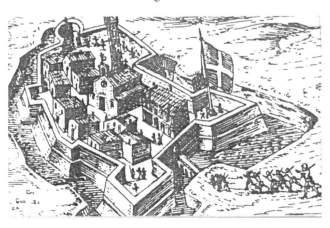

When the knights took over Mdina in 1530, they found a fortress that was totally unsuited for artillery warfare. Its thin vertical walls lacked suitable artillery platforms and were incapable of providing adequate defence against cannon. Worse, its landlocked position, right in the heart of the island, though providing a secure refuge for the inhabitants against corsair raids, meant that the town could easily be cut off from any outside help by a large enemy force intent on besieging the place. Notwithstanding its many shortcomings, the knights, who had settled down at Birgu, still chose to take over its defence. Even though they were quick to realize its potential as an outpost - a role it played so well during the siege - they were less hurried to invest in its refortification.

It would seem that the first significant intervention was that of providing terrepleined ramparts capable of mounting cannon, mainly along the land front. Little attention was paid to the rest of the enceinte along the precipitous crags and cliffs. Bosio states that these were neither defended by towers nor observation posts other than a single clay wall which was crumbling with age. The real conversion of the citadel into a gunpowder fortress, however, only came with the erection of two new bastions. These were built on the corners of the land front. The first of the two bastions to be erected was that known as D'Homedes bastion, situated on the left side of the front overlooking Saqqajja. This was already under construction in 1547 and may have been designed by Antonio Ferramolino.[2] The bastion adjoining Greeks gate came later and seems to have been just about completed prior to the Great Siege. Another bastion, known as St Mary's or *Ta' Bachar*, was added along the north west part of the enceinte but it is not clear if this structure was added before or after the siege, although it does seem to be depicted in d'Aleccio's fresco.

Dragut's *razzia* of 1551 obviously found the new fortifications of the Mdina relatively much weaker than those of Birgu for the Turks preferred to lay siege to the old town rather than the Hospitaller fortress. Even so, the siege was lifted after only three days possibly because Mdina's defences and the resoluteness of its defenders proved a more formidable obstacle than was initially apparent to the Turkish commanders. Fourteen years later, the island was once again invested by a Turkish force, but this time the huge invading army totally ignored the old citadel, much to the detriment of the success of the Turkish campaign. It was only towards the end of the siege that a last desperate effort was made in an attempt to produce a victory and secure a winter refuge on the island, that the Turks sought to capture Mdina. A spirited display by the garrison, however, soon caused the attackers to lose heart and run back to the safety of their ships.

Thus, Mdina survive the conflict of 1565 practically unscathed. Still, the knights were far from happy with the state of its defences. In 1566 the Italian papal engineer Francesco Laparelli was asked to visit the old citadel and draw up plans for its improvement.[3] He recommended that the ditch be deepened and the rest of the enceinte provided with spacious artillery platforms. A contemporary proposal involving the shortening of the city's enceinte is depicted in D'Aleccio's illustrations, but it is not possible to attribute this scheme to any engineer. Thereafter, for the next century or so, the citadel's appearance remained basically unaltered. Moreover, with the establishment of the new fortress-city of

Below, Reconstruction of the medieval layout of the land front defences of the fortress of Mdina.

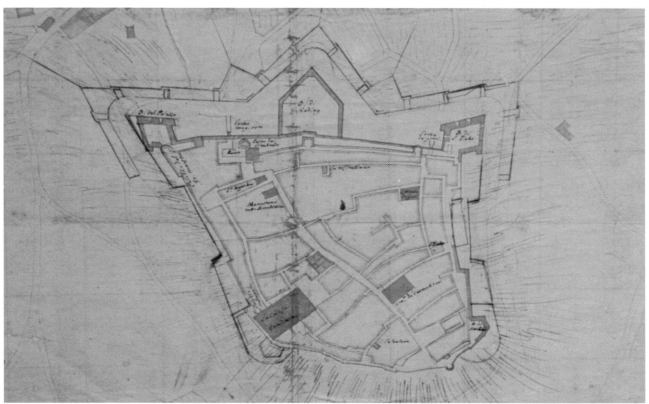

This page, 18th-century plans showing proposals for improvements to the defences of Mdina by French military engineers (NML).

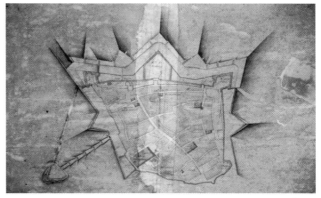

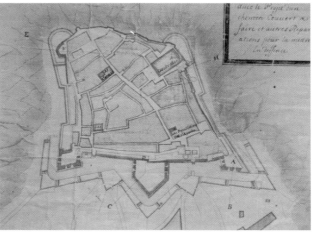

Valletta on the heights of the Sciberras peninsula in 1566, the old capital city quickly fell into rapid decline. By 1658 the fortifications of Mdina were in a terrible state of repair. The citadel still lacked an effective ditch and flanking defences along the major part of its enceinte while the houses of the adjoining suburb had crept too close to its walls. Unsurprisingly, various suggestions were made to abandon and demolish the old fortress, but when these plans were made public, the Maltese strongly opposed the idea and the project was discarded. Decisions to raze the citadel to the ground, however, continued to appear throughout the course of the century although, fortunately, these were never implemented.[4]

A second important phase in the development of Mdina's defences was initiated by Grand Master de Redin in 1658. De Redin paid for various repairs to the bastions and curtain walls and also initiated the construction of a large central bastion on the city's land front, setting aside 4,000 scudi for the work which was designed by the Order's resident engineer Mederico Blondel.[5] As a result, this large artillery platform came to be known as the De Redin bastion. The death of the grand master in 1660, however, brought all works on the bastion to a halt. The knight Tarascone, then in charge of

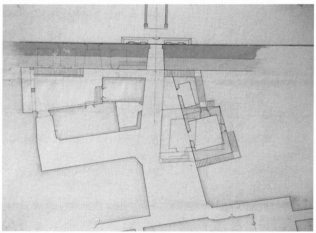

Above, Greeks gate as rebuilt in the 1700s. Right, Sectional elevation of the main gate as designed by Mondion. Note the drawbridge, its drop-pit and sally-port. Bottom, Plan showing the alterations to the old entrance undertaken by Mondion (NML). Opposite page, The main gate into Mdina and the coat-of-arms of Grand Master Manoel de Vilhena set above the entrance (inset).

the construction works while Blondel was away from the island, hastily improvised the conversion of the uncompleted bastion into a shallow redoubt.[6]

The earthquake of 1693 severely damage the ramparts of Mdina, particularly the older works spanning from St Mary bastion to the walls beneath the cathedral. The Norman cathedral was badly damaged and had to be rebuilt.[7] The ever-increasing abandonment of the old city and the decline of its military role enabled the encroachment of civilian houses onto the city's ramparts. The Muscat family, in particular, introduced many unauthorized windows into the enceinte overlooking Saqqajja in the process of enlarging their house, occupying even the piazza where the Mdina regiment of urban militia used to assemble.[8]

The next important phase in the reconstruction of Mdina began with the arrival of the French military mission headed by the engineer René Jacob de Tigné. The recommendations put forward by the French engineers centred around the perfection of the citadel's outerworks, namely the construction of a covered way and flanking batteries inside the ditch. Although, in effect, little was done to implement these proposals during the reign of Grand Master Perellos and his successor Zondadari, most of Tigné's suggestions were implemented by his assistant Mondion during the reign of Grand Master Manoel de Vilhena (1722-36). Within month

of his election, Vilhena ordered the excavation of trenches within the ditch in order to meet a feared Turkish attack.[9] During Vilhena's magistracy, a large effort was invested in the rehabilitation of the city and its defences. A vast building programme saw the construction of many a baroque palace and public building and the re-fortification of the town's defences. The gates were repositioned and rebuilt as imposing architectural monuments, while the outerworks - the covertway, ditch, batteries and glacis - were brought to completion. The main gate, bearing the date 1724, was designed by Mondion and was constructed, together with

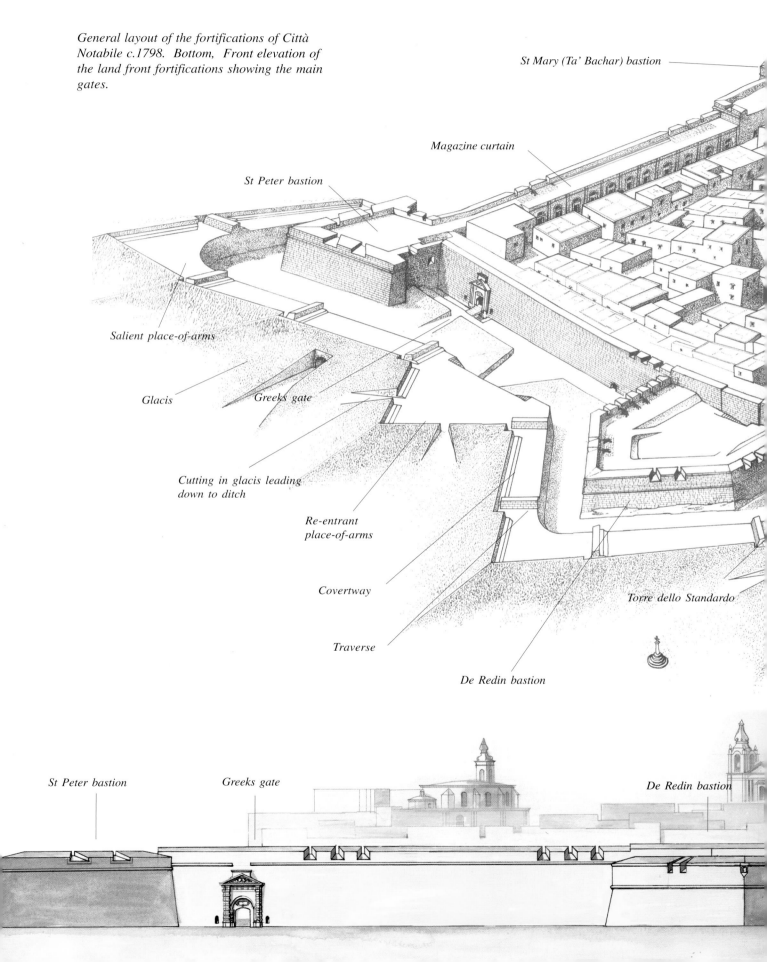

General layout of the fortifications of Città Notabile c.1798. Bottom, Front elevation of the land front fortifications showing the main gates.

St Mary (Ta' Bachar) bastion

Magazine curtain

St Peter bastion

Salient place-of-arms

Glacis

Greeks gate

Cutting in glacis leading down to ditch

Re-entrant place-of-arms

Covertway

Traverse

De Redin bastion

Torre dello Standardo

St Peter bastion

Greeks gate

De Redin bastion

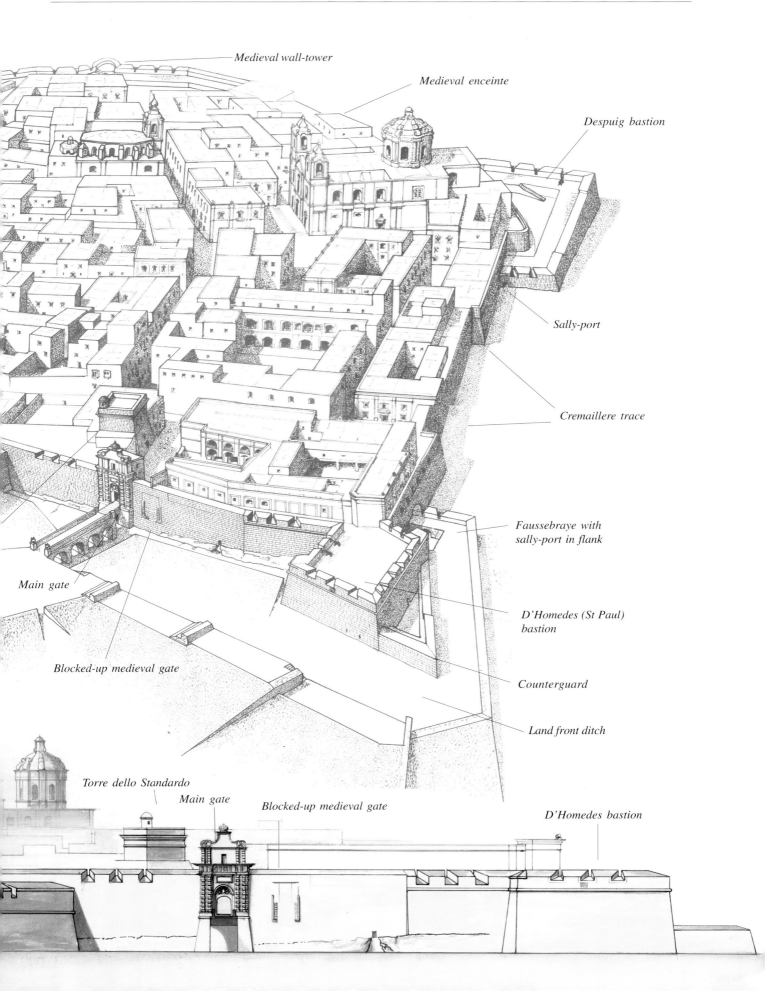

Medieval wall-tower

Medieval enceinte

Despuig bastion

Sally-port

Cremaillere trace

Faussebraye with
sally-port in flank

D'Homedes (St Paul)
bastion

Counterguard

Land front ditch

Main gate

Blocked-up medieval gate

Torre dello Standardo

Main gate

Blocked-up medieval gate

D'Homedes bastion

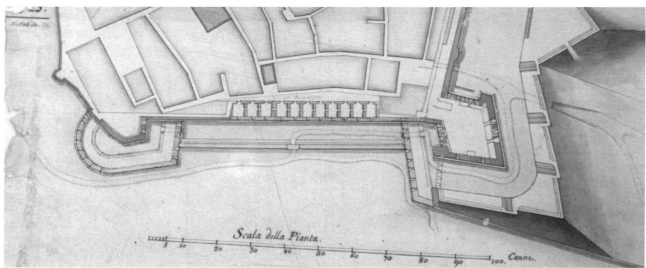

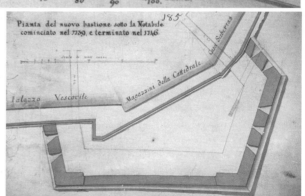

Above, Early 18th-century plan showing proposed low batteries at Mdina. The one at the mouth of the ditch near St Peter bastion was actually built but was demolished in the course of the 19th century. Right, Plan of Despuig bastion (NML) and below, the Torre dello Standardo.

the bridge which had already been completely rebuilt in 1703, some 13m to the left of the old gate. The repositioning of the gate was accompanied by the demolition of the medieval bent-entrance arrangement leading into the city through the *interavllum,* and the old *Torre Mastra,* which was replaced by the *Torre dello Standardo.*[10]

The final addition to the fortifications of Mdina was begun during the reign of Grand Master Ramon Despuig and involved the construction of a hollow bastion beneath the cathedral in 1739. The engineer Marandon claimed that this bastion had already been projected in 1715 but it does not appear in Tigné's reports.[11] Work on Despuig bastion, as it came to be called, commenced on 5 June 1739 and was completed in 1746, although finishing touches were still being added in 1748.[12]

Prior to the 1700s, Mdina's position was solely that of an outpost but the adoption of a coastal defensive strategy during the eighteenth century gave the old city a new role as an inland redoubt. The construction of entrenchments at Ta' Falca and Naxxar accentuated further this new role. Still, all military engineers who were to inspect its defences in the closing decades of the eighteenth century held very poor opinions on the city's ability to withstand a siege and also feared that it could serve to entrench an invading force if it ever fell in enemy hands. Indeed, Mdina proved to be the first of the Order's fortifications in Malta to surrender to the French in 1798.

Cittadella　*(Gozo)*

When the knights took possession of Gozo in 1530, they found an exposed and largely defenceless place. The sole refuge afforded to the inhabitants was a small, old castle straddled on a fragile rocky hill in the centre of the island. This medieval stronghold seems to have occupied the site of the citadel of the former larger Roman town of *Glauconis Civitas*, the lower part of which was believed, according to Agius de Soldanis writing in 1746, to have been enclosed by a fortified wall and ditch equipped with four towered gates.[1] It seems that during the troubled times associated with the Byzantine, Muslim, and post-Norman domination of the Maltese islands, the Roman town was gradually abandoned in favour of a more defensible position higher up on the site of the present citadel itself. There was definitely a *castrum* in existence there by the year 1241, and this offered shelter to the population of Gozo, some 366 families in all.[2]

The commission of knights of St John that inspected the castle in 1524 found it to be very small, 'molto picciola', and round in shape, 'di forma rotonda'. A plan drawn by Perez d'Aleccio, shows the castle as having had a typical medieval enceinte with a continuous perimeter of vertical walls stiffened at intervals by a number of rectangular wall-towers open at the gorge. The *castrum* also contained a church, a barbican, a south-facing entrance (*beb il medina*), and a ditch, the latter apparently used also as a place for the internment of criminals, or as in 1475-76, Jews.[3] The *castrum* had at least one postern which has survived on the northern section of the medieval enceinte.

According to Bosio, there were also houses which had windows cut into the citadel's walls. Through these, we are told, many Gozitans escaped during the fateful *razzia* of 1551. By 1599 the citadel's ramparts were still encumbered with a number of houses. This implies that either a considerable number of dwellings had in time encroahed upon the walls to rest directly onto the ramparts or, more interestingly, that the ramparts themselves were made up of a compact formation of houses linked together to form a communal stronghold in a manner similar to a number of strongholds still to be found in some of the Greek islands, such as Emborios on the island of Nisyros, one of the Hospitaller possessions in the Dodecanese, and the citadel of the island of Astypalia.

D'Aleccio's plan of the medieval castle of Gozo also shows three artillery platforms sited along the more vulnerable

Above, interior view of the main gate into the citadel. This was served by a bascule drawbridge (a fleccie).

southern part of the enceinte. These may represent the first intervention by the knights in their attempt to stiffen the weak walls with a backing of packed earth and so produce stable platforms for artillery. The existence of only three small gun platforms explains why the *Castello* only required the services of one master gunner. It is small wander that, in 1551, the Turkish raiders out-gunned the defenders and that the latter's hapless resistance was overwhelmed within days by the superior strength of the Turkish bombardment. It only took the death of the sole English gunner to convince the small garrison into surrendering. These and the large number of terrified inhabitants sheltering within its walls, around 6,000 souls in all, were all carried away into slavery and the *Castello* sacked and ruined.

It is difficult to understand why, following the disastrous raid of 1551, the ruined *Castello* was resurrected as a medieval fortress, especially if the degree of devastion wrought by the Turkish corsairs was as extensive as stated by many early historians. It is more likely that the *Castello* only required repairs, albeit extensive, to make good the damage inflicted by the Turks. This would explain why it still lacked bastions by 1565 when the island was awaiting another Turkish attack. Indeed, in 1565, we again find the *Castello* featuring as a liability with suggestions being made

St Martin cavalier as seen from the gorge of the adjoining bastion.

for its demolition and the evacuation of its population. The advice was not heeded and in the event the castle was manned by a token garrison of 80 soldiers under the command of the knight Juanoto Torella, the governor of Gozo. It was only the fact that the Turks chose to ignore Gozo that allowed the *Castello* to survive the siege unscathed.

Late in September 1567, Grand Master de Valette visited the *Castello* in the company of Francesco Laparelli. Laparelli was asked to advise the Order on the best possible way of modernizing the old stronghold and although he may have actually come up with a new plan, nothing came out of his brief involvement as the Order was then too heavily committed to the construction of the new city of Valletta and the repair of the battered harbour fortifications. So, for the next thirty years, the knights could do little more than maintain the castle's old walls.

In 1583, when a *razzia* by the galleys of Bizerta was feared, the Order obtained a papal brief permitting the collection of 5,000 scudi by means of a tax on foodstuffs over a period of five years, for use in the *Castello*.[4] By 1590, however, disquiet

over the stronghold had grown considerably to force the Order to seek a solution to the problem of the defence of Gozo. The knights first sought to secure the support of Philip II of Spain in order that he might provide the Order with both the necessary finances and a military engineer. Philip reacted by releasing the 40,000 scudi of accumulated revenue from the vacant priory of Leon but died soon after. For a military engineer the Order had to look elsewhere and finally, in 1599, it secured the services of an Italian from Ancona, Giovanni Rinaldini, who had studied the art of fortification under the renowned Germanico Savorgnano and was then working in Rome.[5]

Rinaldini came over in March 1599 and was quickly detailed to the task. He wasted no time in preparing a critical appraisal of the situation in a bid to find a permanent solution to Gozo's problems. Rinaldini found little to recommend in the *Castello's* defences save its central position which enabled an easily-accessible refuge. He found the rock on which the castle was built was soft and could be easily mined, especially by the Turks for whom 'la mine e la zappa', were 'offeza naturale' while the walls were weak and ruined, and still lacked terrepleins, ' non ci sono terrapieni di alcune sorte...e dalla venuta del Mugiarro vi se buonissimo posto per attaccarlo allogiando le genti nel Borgo, che loro chiamano Rabato luogo aperto e libero da entrarsi et impadronisene ... con comodità di farvi approccio e piantarvi batteria e con quattro canoni in due giorni l'innemico potrebbe conseguir l'intenta suo.'[6] Everything considered, Rinaldini advised the Order not to fortify the *Castello* as this was an unduly expensive undertaking. He recommended instead that the Order concentrate its efforts on the construction of a new Valletta-type fortified city at Mgarr, Marsalforn, or at Della Rena, preferably Marsalforn, where a fort could be constructed for 80,000 scudi.[7]

The knights rejected Rinaldini's recommendations and he was asked to prepare a second report indicating only modifications to the *Castello*. Accepting these instructions, and convinced that such an effort would be unjustifiably expensive and never completely adequate, Rinaldini set out preparing a new scheme of defences for the old castle. He proposed a land front of two demi-bastions linked by a short curtain wall containing the main gate, 'duoi mezzi beluardi per difesa di quella faccia, in mezzo della quale farei la porta del Castello,..a non essere veduta dal Monte.'[8] The curtain wall was to be protected by a detached ravelin with faces 31 *canne* long and 'donde doverebbe esser l'angolo, per la congionzione di essa sara interrotto a guisa di forbice come nel disegno.' Elsewhere around the citadel 'per la parte di dietro quante circonda tutto il rimanente ad una spalla all'altra', he suggested that all the debris be removed, 'e lasciar la rocca nuda, et a perpendicolo e questo per assicurarsi qual sino assalto o altra offesa ... non occorrerebbe far altra fortificazione da questo lato perciò che l'altezza del dirupo sarebbi si grande che tutto assicurerebbe.'

Rinaldini recommended that all the existing walls were to be terrepleined with the material cleared from the outside circumference. The new parapets were to be 4 *canne* wide while the ditch was to be 8 to 13.6 *canne* deep and 20 *canne* wide. He was convinced that the main threat came from the Gelmus hill and, to counter this, he proposed that the enceinte facing it be strenghtened by a 'spalla', or shoulder, 30 *canne* long.[9] A similar shoulder, he believed, could be constructed on the opposite side of the citadel. Rinaldini also proposed that a small fort be built on the 'Monte detto il Padrastro'. This was to be armed with eight guns and garrisoned with 300 soldiers in times of war. The houses of Rabat, together with a partially-built wall intended to enclose the suburb, were to be demolished while the inhabitants, 'in tutto...40 famiglie', were to be rehoused within the citadel.[10]

Dal Pozzo, the official historian of the Order, states that Rinaldini's design was accepted and quickly executed although Rinaldini was criticized for exceeding his brief and creating a new front with a longer enceinte.[11] The works began in 1600 and the new fortifications were eventually completed in 1620s. The castle's main land front with its main central bastion was built in the first decade of the 1600s, St John cavalier by 1614, and the ravelin and St Martin cavalier by 1622.[12] Unfortunately, Rinaldini's reports have survived without his series of plans and sections and it is consequently difficult to attribute with certainty any of the works to him since the enceinte as actually built does not conform to all the details mentioned in his report. The reason for these alterations is not clear. Architectural evidence reveals the grafting of two different styles of fortification on the same enceinte.

St Michael bastion. Above right, View showing the rounded salient and the sperone, *the spur at the foot of the work. Below, View from within the main ditch of the rounded orillion, or* orecchino, *which stiffens the shoulder of the large pointed bastion with its very short and restricted flank. A small sally-port, protected by the large orillion, is located in the flank.*

Above, The cavalier of St John. Left, Kink in the cremaillere line of walls along the north flank of the demi-bastion of St John. Below, Elevation of the east side of the Castello.

than the southern one - implying that the left demi-bastion in Rinaldini's design was converted into a full bastion to allow the construction of a new front adjoining the main church. Curiously, too, St John demi-bastion has a squarish orillion while the other bastions have rounded ones. Moreover, St John's demi-bastion seems to have been hurriedly designed and built as not much thought was given to the defence of its main northern flank with little provision in the way for enfilading fire. As an afterthought, a small low battery was affixed to the main enceinte to make up for this deficiency.

The new defences of the *Castello* were those which gave it its present form and these consisted of two demi-bastions joined at right angles to an 'arrow-head' corner bastion by short curtain walls, 'tre bastioni piccoli li quali formano due fronti con un piccolo fosso al piede, e una strada coperta

Rinaldini's design, comprised a main front of two demi-bastions linked by a curtain wall and supported by a ravelin - similar to that shown in D'Aleccio's plan, but the new fortress was built with two fronts. It is possible that Vittorio Cassar, 'architector Sacrae Religionis Hierosolimitane', who was in charge of the actual construction of the new works on the *Castello* found it necessary to erect a new curtain on the eastern side, the latter forming one of the weakest sectors of the enceinte having been bombarded by Dragut in 1551.[13] A study of St Michael bastion reveals it to be curiously asymmetrical, with its eastern face being considerably longer

St Michael bastion

Ravelin

St Joh

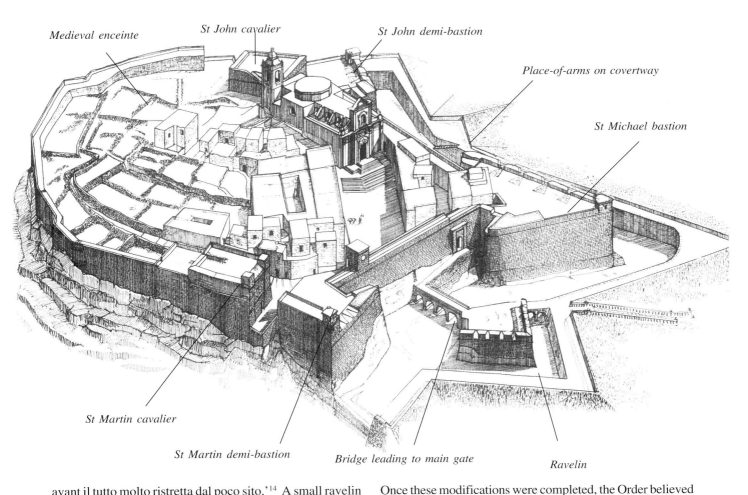

Medieval enceinte   St John cavalier   St John demi-bastion

Place-of-arms on covertway

St Michael bastion

St Martin cavalier

St Martin demi-bastion   Bridge leading to main gate   Ravelin

avant il tutto molto ristretta dal poco sito.'[14] A small ravelin defended the southern curtain between St Martin demi-bastion and St Michael (St Philip) bastion while the main enceinte was strengthened further by two cavaliers. An L-shaped raised walkway connected the ravelin to the main gate, the latter being partly sheltered behind the orillion of St Michael bastion. The northern enceinte was left practically untouched since it occupied the highest ground on the cliff face.

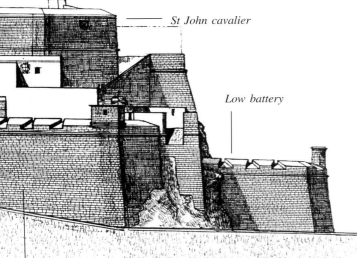

St John cavalier

Low battery

stion

Once these modifications were completed, the Order believed that the *Castello* was rendered defensible, an opinion, however, not shared by the majority of the engineers who were to inspect Gozo's defences in the following years. With the exception of Valperga and Tigné, they all advised the Order to abandon the citadel and construct a new fortress at Marsalforn. Amongst these, Giovanni de Medici, the marquis of St Angelo, visited the *Castello* in 1640 and confirmed Rinaldini's idea that the citadel should be abandoned in favour of a new fortress at Marsalforn, although he did not judge the time as opportune. The other alternative measure which he advocated was to enclose Rabat within an outer wall at a cost of between 10 and 12,000 scudi, an attempt begun prior to Rinaldini's visit and abandoned.[15]

In 1643 the Order did actually agree to demolish the *Castello* and to proceed with the construction of the new fortress at Marsalforn which was to be financed by a new tax on wheat. The Gozitans protested strongly that they were too poor to pay the tax and the Order, realizing that it was unequal to the tax of financing the project directly from its own resources, decided to postpone the work.[16] The alarm of 1645, however, revived the criticism of the *Castello*. Giovanni Bendinelli Pallavicino and Louis Viscount d'Arpajon recommended that

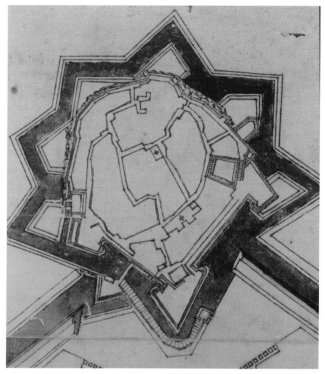

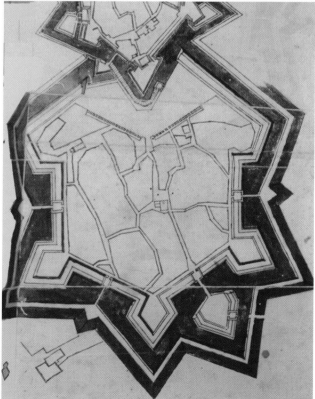

Top, Detail from Valperga's plan showing his proposal for the fortification of the Castello with counterguards and low batteries, and the enclosure of the suburb of Rabat within a bastioned enceinte all'Olandese.*(N.M.L.)*

the citadel be evacuated because the state of 'quella piazza, qual si suppone che a pena in quindici giorni debbi per forza restar espugnata anche da moderato nemico.'[17] A small garrison with two-weeks' supplies was left there while all the heavy equipment was withdrawn to Malta. On their advice, the citadel was actually mined for destruction but the Turkish fleet never appeared since it was destined for Crete and not Malta.

The need for a new fortress was rekindled in 1654. In 1657 the layout of the new fort was traced out on site at Marsalforn by Francesco Buonamici, though, for some unknown reason, the works were soon abandoned.[18] The next military engineer to visit Gozo in 1670, Antonio Maurizio Valperga, was against fortifying Marsalforn. He was actually one of the few who advocated the strengthening of the *Castello,* or *Cittadella* as it also came to be known, and the fortification of its suburb. Valperga proposed to enclose the latter within a bastioned enceinte *all'Olandese* while the citadel itself was to be fitted with counterguards and low batteries. The Order opted to implement Valperga's advice but in the end, owing to other important commitments, the scheme to fortify Rabat had to be put off.[19]

Like many experts before him, the next foreign military engineer to inspect the citadel's fortification, the Frenchmen Claude de Colongues - who arrived in Gozo in 1703 - criticized its antiquated design, particularly the short bastion flanks and the presence of 'quelques angles morts.'[20] Colongues found that the covertway lacked a banquette and so recommended that one be built. Colongues rejected Valperga's proposal to enclose Rabat within a bastioned enceinte not because he disagreed with 'il disegno de S. Ing. Valperga fatto nelle buone regole che è con bastioni capaci' but because the nature of the terrain would have rendered the ramparts and bastions vulnerable to mining.[21] Colongues preferred to transform the citadel into a purely military establishment but out of 'charite Chrestienne' he proposed to enclose Rabat within 'deux lignes de communication a droit e a guache des dehors du chateau.'[22] Since a Turkish attack was expected to materialize that same summer before the two lines of trenches could be built, Colongues proposed that the streets around Rabat be barricaded with stones and rubble while advanced posts were to be set up at the *convent Augustins, St François* (square), *Ste Sabine* (square). and *a la croix;* St George square was to serve as a place-of-arms. Colongues' scheme to surround Rabat with trenches was in effect implemented during the emergency of 1708, under the supervision of the Order's German engineer Johannes Person. Although the Turks did raid Gozo then, Person's trenches were not attacked.[23]

Other serious emergencies swept the island in 1714 and 1715 and these inevitably revived the criticism of the Castello.

From a document entitled 'Progetto per assicurare l'Isola del Gozzo contro ogni attacco del Nemici' it is known that the French military mission headed by René Jacob de Tigné proposed to erect a new fortress at Mgarr.[24] This, however, was not intended to replace the citadel but to compel the enemy to attack two strongholds and thus relieve it of some of the pressure, 'che possa obligare il nemico, di fare due assedij al luogo di uno, onde consumarebbe maggior tempo e maggior quantità di munizioni.'[25] Again the French engineers also proposed to enclose Rabat within a bastioned enceinte some 3km long and a partially rock-hewn ditch 3 *canne* high costing over 15,000 *doppie*.[26] To help secure the proposed fortress, Tigné proposed that the surrounding heights were to be occupied 'con qualchè piccoli Fortini, almeno sopra d'una che si trova più vicina, e più pericolosa.'[27] Such an ambitious scheme, however, was difficult to implement and, as the century progressed and increasing

emphasis was laid on coastal defences, the landlocked citadel remained isolated. Still, even after the construction of a new fortress at Ras-et-Tafal, the old castle never lost its importance, mainly because of its central position and the fact that the new city failed to attract settlers. Its continued significance was reflected in its ordnance, a total of 39 cannon compared to the 18 guns of Fort Chambrai. The arrival of the French in 1798, however, caught the Gozitan inhabitants unprepared and the governor, Chevalier de Mesgrigny, instead of rallying the defenders, escaped to Malta leaving the Gozitans with no option but to surrender.

Graphic aerial view showing the layout of the fortifications adjoining the demi-bastion of St John.

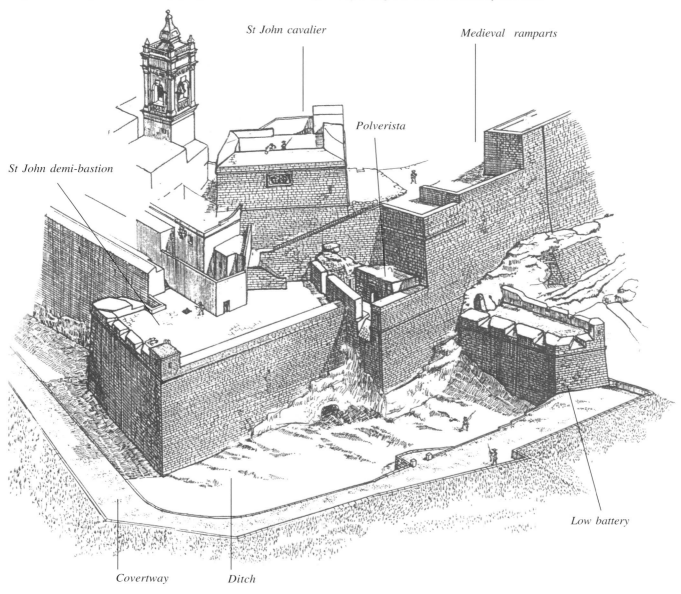

St John cavalier

Medieval ramparts

Polverista

St John demi-bastion

Low battery

Covertway   Ditch

Città Vittoriosa   *(Birgu)*

The right extremity of the Birgu land front during the Great Siege and, bottom, the Kalkara front, as depicted by D'Aleccio.

Birgu is a name derived from the Arab word *borg*, meaning castle, and originally referred to the suburb of fishermen's houses that had grown up on the landward side of the *castrum maris*, the old medieval harbour fort which the Order took over from the De Nava family upon its arrival in Malta in 1530. In the wake of the Hospitallers came the refugees from Rhodes, merchants, tradesmen, and craftsmen. Inevitably, the little village soon grew overcrowded and new houses and inns had to be built. L'Isle Adam set about repeating the pattern of the Order's old home in Rhodes. He strengthened the defences, established a hospital while each langue of the Order set up its own auberge or inn. The town quickly assumed the prerogatives of a new municipality distinct from that of Città Notabile. The grand master also set up a commission of four Jurats to carry out its administration.[1] The Order itself had to adapt to the restricted space within the Birgu, so that the *collachium,* the enclosed space reserved for the members of the Order, had to be replaced by the establishments of zones within which different parties could dwell. Balbi states that Birgu was renamed Città Nuova.[2]

The first fortifications undertaken by the knights on the Birgu peninsula were those added to the *castrum maris*. A moat was excavated to separate the castle from Birgu under the supervision of the Florentine engineer Piccino.[3] In 1541 Antonio Ferramolino designed the massive cavalier on Fort St Angelo which faced Birgu and the high ground of the Salvatore hill. Bosio states that L'Isle Adam, immediately

upon the Order's arrival in Malta, ordered that the town of Birgu be enclosed within a wall but it is not clear at exactly when and by whom these fortifications were designed. By 1536 Antonio Ferramolino was advising the Order on the fortifications of Birgu and St Angelo. Work on these fortifications was still being carried out in 1552, 1553, 1555, and 1560, particularly to enlarge the bastions and deepen the ditch.[3] By then, the land front had evolved into an almost straight line with two bastions, spanning across the neck of the Birgu peninsula. There was a cavalier on St James bastion, beyond which the curtain terminated into a demi-bastion which dropped down in stages to a hornwork, known as the Post of Castile. From there, lateral walls connected the work to the ditch of Fort St Angelo.

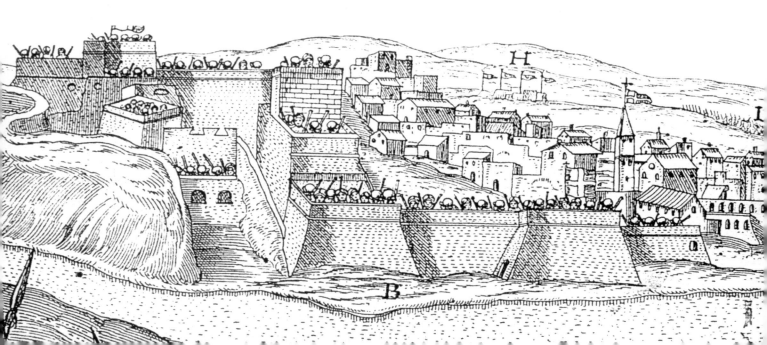

In 1562 Baldassare Lanci, engineer to the duke of Florence, advocated the construction of retrenchments and traverses within the Birgu fortifications so as to shelter the defenders from enfilading fire from enemy batteries which could easily be sited on top of San Salvatore hill.[4] He also proposed that, in the case of a siege, various houses could be demolished and interior retrenchments be constructed with their masonry. His advice was well taken because during the siege of 1565, Balbi records how the grand master ordered the demolition of many houses and their masonry was used to barricade whole streets and erect *ritirate*. A retrenchment some 200 paces long was built between the Posts of Castile and Germany.[5] Balbi also records how the Post of Castile was fitted with many traverses designed to protect the men fighting on the ramparts while others supported the cavalier.[6] Lanci also recommended the reconstruction and resiting of many of the embrasures, while some were even to be casemated. He then went on to propose a new cavalier on St John bastion.[7]

Matteo Perez d'Aleccio, in his prints depicting the Great Siege, shows the Birgu fortifications as having two cavaliers, thus suggesting that Lanci's proposal for the construction of the cavalier on St John bastion was acted upon immediately and completed within three years. To the right of this bastion, the curtain wall dropped in stages

Above, left, Plan of the bastion of St John at Birgu c.1645, after Clerville. Above, Two late 19th-century views of the bastions of St John and St James.

to terminate in a small hornwork known as the Post of Castile. The main entrance to Birgu was situated in the left flank of St John bastion. This was approached from a ramp rising from within the ditch.

During the Great Siege, Birgu was the Order's strongest defensive position within the harbour area. The Turks wrongly decided to concentrate their efforts on Fort St Elmo first, hoping to reduce it within a week. But St Elmo held

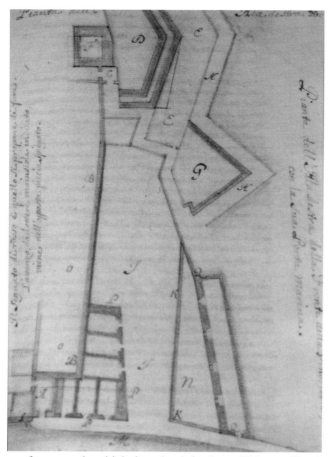

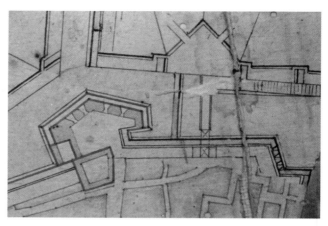

Left, Detail from a sketch by Blondel showing the layout of the bastion and cavalier of St John around the end of the 17th century, and the faussebraye. Above, Detail from plan of Birgu by Tigné showing the same feature and the large orillions. (NML)

out for a month, which time the defenders of Birgu utilized to strengthen the enceinte with retrenchments and other secondary lines of defence within the bastions. The posts were pre-assigned to the different languages and were supplied with the 'munitions and all the necessities of war.'[8] The bastion of Provence (St John) was under the command of Jean de Montagut while that of Auvergne (St James) was under the command of the pilier of that particular langue. The Post of France (the curtain between the two bastions) was under the command of François de la Bucera. The Post of Castile was under the knight Luis de Pac, while Konrad von Schwalbach was in charge of the Post of Germany. Oliver Starkey held the Post of England facing the Bighi peninsula. The knights of Aragon occupied some form of outerwork beyond the ditch which, according to Balbi, extended as far as Bormola, the suburb of Birgu.[9]

During the course of the siege, it was realized that the houses of Bormola were too close to the Birgu land front and so the grand master sent out strong detachments of men to have them demolished in order to deny the Turks of their cover. The timber beams of most of these houses were carried back to Birgu and used in the construction of barricades. Notwithstanding all these important preparations, Birgu suffered from one serious defect - it

was overlooked by surrounding heights and the Turkish engineers wasted no time in exploiting this weakness to their full advantage. With the batteries of siege artillery which they set up on these commanding positions, the Turks pounded the Birgu fortifications incessantly, stopping only to allow their troops to assault the battered and ruined walls; only to be repelled time and again by the cannon, swords, arquebuses, boiling pitch, and other incendiary missiles of the Christian defenders. The most critical moment came on 18 August when the Turks set off a mine under the bastion of the Post of Castile. A tremendous explosion brought down a great section of the wall. As the Turks poured into the breach panic ensued among the defenders and for a moment all seemed lost. It was only the grand master's cool and timely appearance on the scene that gave new heart to his men and the advancing tide was stemmed.[10]

After the siege the city was renamed Vittoriosa to commemorate the victory over the Turks. Its defences were so ruined that there hardly remained a stone upon stone. Such was the degree of devastation that Laparelli advised the Order to abandon Birgu and Senglea and move to Mount Sciberras. Rebuilding these defences was estimated to require 345,000 men/ days, a little less than that required to build the much desired new city on Mount Sciberras[11] and, in any case, the rebuilt defences would still remain exposed to enemy fire from the surrounding higher ground.[12] As things turned out, both the new city and the repair of the existing fortifications were taken in hand.

The reconstruction works were entrusted into the hands of Gerolamo Cassar but thereafter little was done to improve

its defences. The construction of the fortress of Valletta placed a great strain on the Order's resources so that the upkeep of the old fortress was neglected until rumours of a possible Turkish attack in 1633 forced a re-appraisal of its state of repair. It was then proposed that a retrenchment be constructed in the rear of the Post of Castile together with a covertway on the land front but it does not seem that these works were taken in hand because, in 1645, Louis Nicholas de Clerville was still stressing the importance of erecting such a work,[13] 'Supposto che la posta di Castiglia sia come se già detto la più debole e la più pericolosa di tutte, sarei anche di parere, che se mai dal tempo e dalle facoltà della Religione fosse conceduto che detta posta

Above, The three gates into Vittoriosa, as rebuilt by Mondion in the early 1720s, from right to left, Couvre Porte, the first gate, and the second gate.

General layout of the Birgu land front c.1798.

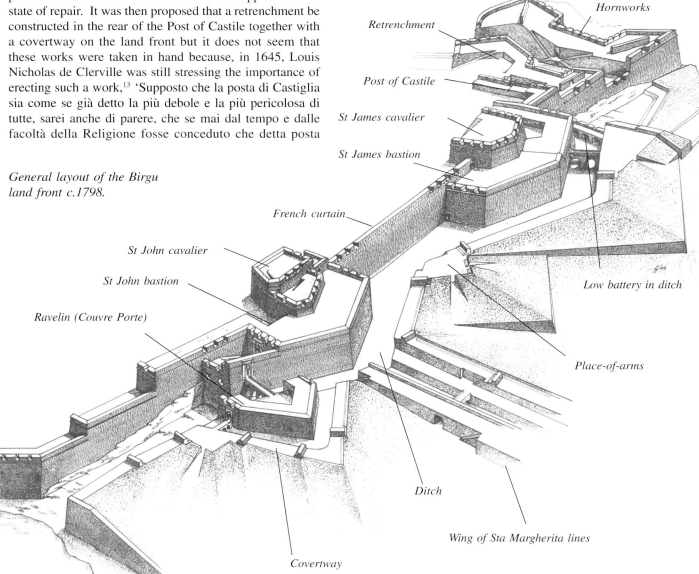

Hornworks

Retrenchment

Post of Castile

St James cavalier

St James bastion

French curtain

St John cavalier

St John bastion

Ravelin (Couvre Porte)

Low battery in ditch

Place-of-arms

Ditch

Wing of Sta Margherita lines

Covertway

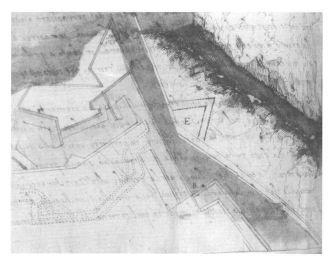

A 17th-century plan showing the Post of Castile and the internal retrenchment proposed by the French military engineer Clerville (NLM). Bottom, Graphic reconstruction of the Post of Castile c.1798.

heartedly so that the defensive problem facing the old fortress remained unsettled. During the magistracy of Grand Master Antoine de Paule (1623-36) a *mezzaluna* was built on the glacis 'per coprire l'avvenuta della Porta Superiore', as the main gate leading into the Birgu was called. In 1640 the marquis of St Angelo proposed to strengthen the Birgu land front with the addition of two ravelins and to fortify the Post of Castile with a retrenchment, 'una ritirata, che sara molto più forte della prima muraglia. Che avanti la front del Borgo si faccino due Rivellini ... alla ritirata si farà la muraglia e parapetto a prova di cannone secondo il solito e la sua altezza deve venir quattro filate più basso del Posto di Genova.'[16] Again, Birgu featured low on the Order's list of priorities and the new works proposed by the marquis were not built.

maggiormente s'assicurasse et a dentro si facesse la ritirata gia in altri tempi proposta.'[14] Clerville also proposed that the foot of the hornworks be strengthened by the construction of a *falsa braga* and that a ravelin be built on the re-entrant angle of the lip of the glacis on the land front near the post of Castile (qualche rivellino assicurato tanto per scrutinare il vallone ... che per fiancheggiare le parti steriori della contrascarpa). His proposals, however, were never followed through.[15]

The commencement of the Sta Margherita enceinte in 1638 promised to release the front-line pressures off Birgu but work on the former progressed very slowly and half-

The *Porta Superiore*, situated in the right flank of St John bastion was 'priva di fianco e difesa.'[17] By 1665, the *mezzaluna* was still unfinished and the excavation of its ditch and counterscarp had hardly begun. The layout of this section of the Birgu fortifications is described and illustrated in detail by Blondel in his report of 14 July 1695 entitled 'Discorso della riparatione necessaria delle rouvine dell' Ala destra della fronte della Citta Vittoriosa e della sua Porta Marina.'[18] His annotated plan shows that the land front was then quite different from that which exists today. St John bastion had *orecchini*, or orillions, on both

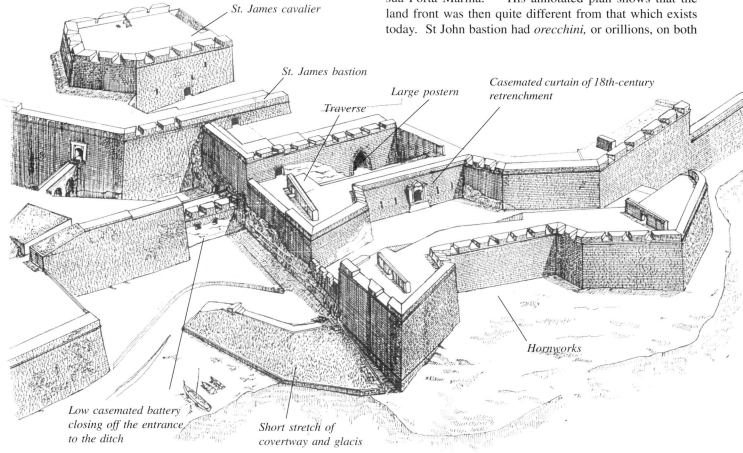

St. James cavalier

St. James bastion

Large postern

Casemated curtain of 18th-century retrenchment

Traverse

Hornworks

Low casemated battery closing off the entrance to the ditch

Short stretch of covertway and glacis

Above, A 19th-century photograph showing a virtually intact system of fortifications along the eastern extremity of the Birgu front, known as the Post of Castile. Right, One of the large and high traverses placed on the ramparts along the same post, considered necessary owing to the surrounding high ground. Bottom, right, View of the gorge of the hornwork of the Post of Castile.

flanks. These are also clearly depicted by D'Aleccio. The entrance to the gate was inside the flank of the bastion and the whole bastion seems to have been protected by a *faussebraye* (Baluardo principale di Fronte con Falsabraga, nel cui fianco destro e l'avvenuta della porta).[19] The faussebraye may have been a form of buttressing that was added to the face of the bastion when it was reconstructed after the siege. After Tigné's visits in 1715-16, the land front of Birgu was renovated so that St John bastion was practically rebuilt; the recessed flanks enhanced by the orillions were filled in to form one solid platform, while the cavalier was fitted with a battery.

There was another gate leading into Birgu, known as the *Porta Marina*. This was situated in the flank of the bastion facing Senglea. By the 1660s it was 'tutta rovinata eccetto la facciata esterna, più volte rinovata da G.M. Wignacourt e Lascaris.'[20] But the most urgent task then was the rebuilding of the curtain wall between the two gates of Birgu and the addition of a casemated demi-bastion. Within the demi-bastion, Blondel proposed the construction of six magazines to provide storage space for the galley stores. The council sanctioned Blondel's design on 28 July 1695. By the time of the next general review of the fortifications in 1715, the Marine gate and its fortifications were no longer criticized.[21] Still Tigné's plan of Birgu, together with that shown in Palmeus' *Plan generale de la ville capitale de Malte* (1751), omit Blondel's demi-bastion altogether, replacing it with a flank facing Senglea.

The flank of Birgu facing Senglea was the only part of the peninsula which was left unfortified. Similarly, Senglea was undefended along the creek since the two towns were intended to shield one another. The neck of the narrow creek between the two peninsulas was sealed off in times of danger by a large iron chain. Some time in the late seventeenth century, a French engineer by the name of Busser designed a rampart that would have linked the Birgu land front to that of Senglea and seal off the landward aproaches to the creek. This wall, illustrated in a report entitled 'Dissen en general pour faire une Muraille qui joigne le front du Bourg avec L'isle', was also intended to shelter the ships and naval facilities inside the creek but the project was never implemented.[22]

The arrival of French military engineers in Malta in the spring of 1715 found the unfinished fortifications of Ricasoli, Floriana, Cottonera, and Sta Margherita competing for the same limited funds. The completion of the Sta Margherita lines was seen to be the first priority, particularly the provision of strong lines of communications between the new enceinte and the fronts of Birgu and Senglea which were now secured within an outer ring of defences. Tigné also proposed various alterations to the Birgu land front istelf.

These works were estimated to cost around 24,800 scudi and included the construction of a retrenchment in the gorge of the hornworks at the post of Castile, similar to that recommended by Clerville in 1645, the completion of the 'chemin couvert devant la courtine de la fronte' and its connection to the Sta Margherita lines (5,000 scudi), the reconstruction of 'les parapets de la petite piece' along the front (200 scudi*)*, the fitting of 'a petite tenaille au piede du dit front' (200 scudi), and the repair of the 'Bastionement de la tête du Bourg d'une mer a l'autre' (10,000 scudi).[23]

On his return to Malta in 1716, Tigné found that the work on the retrenchment, which consisted of a wide ditch cut in the gorge of the hornworks and covered by two demi-bastions and a casemated curtain fitted with musketry loopholes, a gate, and a drawbridge, had progressed rapidly under the direction of his assistant Mondion but an estimated further 3,000 scudi were required before it could be completed. Most of the work was carried out throughout the 1720s under the supervision of Mondion.

During the following decades right up to 1798, there were various other proposals to try and improve the Birgu fortifications, the most notable being by Bourlamaque and his team of military advisors in 1761 though none of these seem to have been implemented. In any case the Cottonera and Sta Margherita lines had rendered the Birgu land front defences, together with those of Senglea, practically obsolete and, as a matter of fact, both these fortresses played no part in the events of 1798.

Right, top, An early 18th-century plan of the Birgu fortifications and Fort St Angelo showing various proposals put forward by visiting French military engineers (National Museum of Archaeology). Right, An interesting 18th-century proposal, entitled Dissen en general pour faire une Muraille qui joigne le front du Bourg avec L'isle, *for the linking of the Birgu and Senglea fronts as put forward by the French engineer Busser (NLM). Opposite page, The postern situated in the rear of the retrenchment of the Post of Castile.*

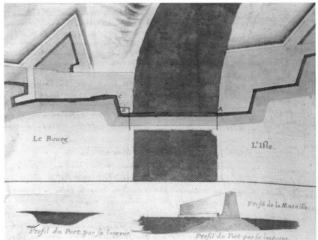

Fort St Elmo

Dragut's raid and the unopposed landing at Marsamxett harbour in 1551 exposed the weakness of the Order's defensive system in Malta, for it revealed how easily an enemy force could land practically unhindered on the doorstep of the Order's stronghold. The raid also emphasized the strategic value of the Sciberras peninsula and confirmed the need for a strong fortress with which to command the entrance to the anchorages of Marsamxett and the Grand Harbour. Among the exponents of this course of action was Frà Leone Strozzi, prior of Capua, who had returned to Malta in 1551.[1] His impassioned appeal to the council that Malta, being the principal and most important frontier of Christendom, should not be abandoned but fortified and prepared for an impending Turkish attack, convinced the grand master and the council of the Order to embark on the fortification of the harbour. On 8 January 1552 it was decreed that a fort should be built at the tip of the Sciberras peninsula. The knights Frà Georg Bombast, grand bailiff of Germany, Frà Leone Strozzi, prior of Capua, and Frà Louis Lastic, lieutenant to the marshal and knight of the langue of Auvergne, were given the task of supervising the construction of the new fort.[2]

The idea of building some sort of fortification on the tip of the Sciberras peninsula was not a new idea and had been conceived earlier in the fifteenth century. Following the Turkish raid of 1488, the Università representatives appealed to the viceroy of Sicily for improved harbour defences.[3] The viceroy, on the advice of his royal council and with the approval of King Ferdinand II, ordered the building of a large tower and bastion armed with heavy artillery at the entrance to the harbour, near the chapel of St Elmo. These defences, however, were never constructed, a fact confirmed by the commissioners' report of 1524 in which the *castrum maris* features as the only harbour fortification. Nonetheless, there is some evidence to suggest that at the extreme end of the Sciberras peninsula, known as Tarf il-Ghases, there once stood a watch-post or vedette dating from the late thirteenth century.[4] This was one of the 24 coastal look-out posts that existed in 1417, and was manned by the *Mahares*, a maritime watch. Geronimo Zurita y Castro, a Spanish writer, in his *Libro XX de los Annales do Rey don Hernando II il Catolico,* refers to this structure sited on the living rock on the long promontory called St Elmo and goes on to state that it was badly constructed and incorrectly positioned.[5]

*Above, The medieval tower at Tarf il-Ghases (Czapaki map).
Below, Plan of Fort St Elmo found at the Simancas archives
(after De Giorgio).*

Some three years after the Order's arrival in Malta, the Florentine engineer Piccino was asked by the Order to prepare plans for a bastion on St Elmo point.[6] His early departure from the island in 1535, however, seems to have led to the abandonment of this project. Later, in 1541, the military engineer Antonio Ferramolino de Bergamo recommended the building of a fortress that would enclose all the Sciberras peninsula but, given the financial and military situation then facing the Order, this ambitious project had to be shelved.[7] The raid of of 1551 provided the necessary impetus. Early in January 1552 Grand Master

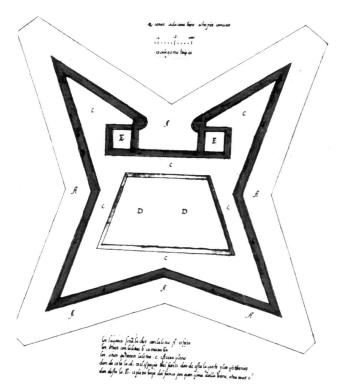

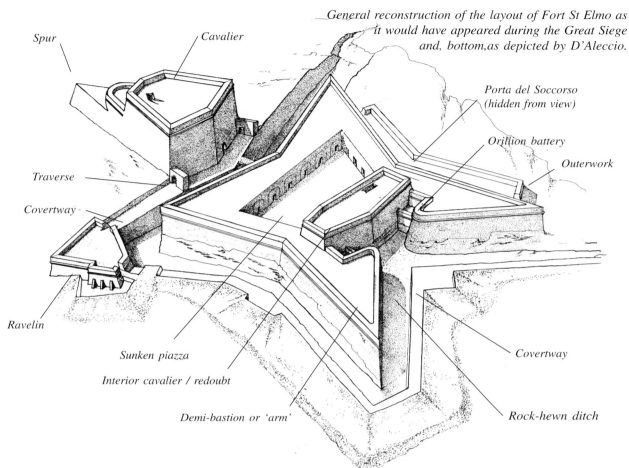

General reconstruction of the layout of Fort St Elmo as it would have appeared during the Great Siege and, bottom, as depicted by D'Aleccio.

Spur

Cavalier

Porta del Soccorso (hidden from view)

Orillion battery

Outerwork

Traverse

Covertway

Ravelin

Sunken piazza

Interior cavalier / redoubt

Demi-bastion or 'arm'

Covertway

Rock-hewn ditch

Juan de Homedes asked the viceroy of Sicily for the services of a military engineer to help design a new fortress. Don Juan de Vega agreed to send Pietro Prato who arrived in Malta on 6 January 1552.[8] Prato wasted no time to carry out his commission and in less than six days drew up the plans of the new fort.

The commission appointed to oversee the completion of the project had set up a time limit of six months within which the work was to be completed. Bosio states that it was this constraint that fundamentally dictated the small size of the fort since the grand master, afraid of another Turkish reprisal, would not risk embarking upon a project that could not be completed in a short period of time, 'ciò fu cagione che l'ingegnere fece il desegno, e la pianta del Forte S. Elmo ... troppo piccola, in forma di stella, di quattro piccioli beluardette; con intenzione che dovesse poi servire per uno de' grandi baluardi della nuova città, che disegnavano di fabricarsi appresso.'[9]

The first stone of the new fort, called St Elmo, was laid down with great solemnity on Thursday, 14 January 1552 in the presence of the grand master and other dignitaries of the Order.[10] From the very start work on the new fort

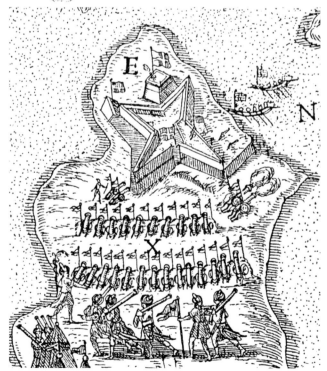

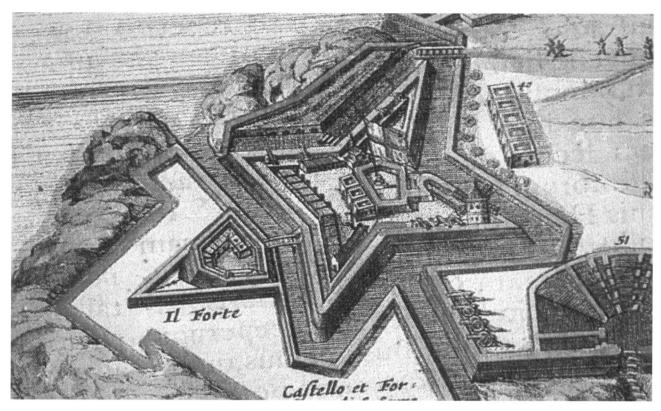

Above, top, Detail from a late 16th-century plan of Valletta showing Fort St Elmo as rebuilt after the Great Siege. Above, View of the remains of the sloping wall of what was once the internal cavalier, or redoubt, of the original fort built in 1552.

proceeded with military discipline and precision. The three commissioners, Strozzi, Lastic, and Bombast, took it in turns to supervise the work in three four-hour shifts. Within six months, most of the structure was ready and Fort St Elmo was in a state of 'ragionevole difesa'.[11] The cost of skilled labour was met by various donations from the members of the Order. The enceinte of the new fort enclosed within in it the old chapel dedicated to St Elmo whilst the old vedette or watch-tower at *Tarf-il-Ghases* was left standing to the north of the fort.

A drawing forwarded to Charles V by Don Juan de Vega on 22 May 1552, believed to be that of Fort St Elmo, shows a symmetrical star-shaped hollow fort with very narrow arms or bastions and a large internal piazza. On the southern front the bastions were rounded off to provide orillion batteries. The fort was surrounded by a ditch 7 *canne* (14.6m) wide. The land front of the fort faced southwords towards the rising heights of Mount Sciberras, 'hoggi occupata dalla Città Valletta, ma allora semplice scoglio peninsulare, e nudo terreno, ... per questa ragione separata, e contra di esso trincierato e riparato d'un buono fosso intagliato nella rocca viva.'[12] The original plan, however, does not show the small inner pentagonal keep or redoubt on the landward side of the fort - this is depicted both in D'Aleccio's illustrations and on Laparelli's plan made in 1566. This internal redoubt seems to have been an after-thought but must have been built before the large

Right, The cavalier of Fort St Elmo as depicted by Blondel when he was undertaking its partial reconstruction to enable the building of the Carafa bastions. Below, Detail of the cavalier's vaulted interior (NLM).

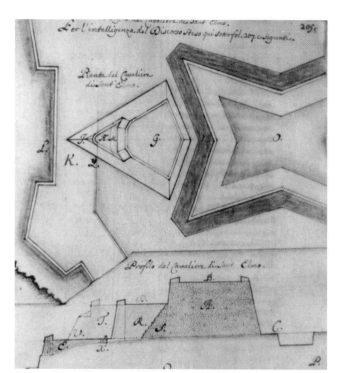

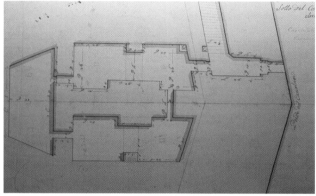

cavalier was added in 1554. Today, it survives behind the façade of eighteenth-century barracks, with a small portion clearly visible near the chapel.

It was quickly realized that one serious shortcoming of Prato's star-shaped fort was the fact that it did not rise high enough to counter the commanding high ground of the Sciberras peninsula immediately behind it. An attempt to correct this threat was initiated in 1554 with the construction of a large triangular cavalier, probably designed by Nicolò Bellavanti.[13] This was brought to completion in 1556 under the direction of Commander Orla and Frà Pietro de Juniente, the latter, captain of the fort, following a renewed threat of a Turkish attack.[14] The cavalier, a triangular structure built on two levels and terminating in a large spur, 'a guista di Sprone verso il Mare' and 'Fuera del del fuerte ... un torreon.'[5] In one document it is decribed as 'di fabrica ben intesa e fortissima disegno pentagona, occostante alla triangole-equilibrate: consistente in un ampia fronte, da due facie giunte in un angolo saliente assai ottuso ... (ma con) eccessiva altezza della plataforma primaria e superiore.'[16] It was an isolated work, however, separated from the fort by the perimeter ditch so that a drawbridge was necessary to link it to the body of the fort.

Bosio mentions that an outerwork (which he terms a ravelin) was completed in 1556 under the supervision of Commanders Orla and Juniente. This was sited on the Grand Harbour side, protecting what later came to be known as the *Porta del Soccorso,* the sea gate, through which reinforcements and supplies reached the fort during the siege. This outerwork, in the form of a tenaille is first shown in an anonymous map of the harbour dated 1563 entitled 'Li porti dell'Isole di Malta colla pianta della nuova città dove abiteranno quelli che stanno hora nel Borgo qui disegnato' and later in Francesco Laparelli's plan of Valletta in 1566, but much more clearly in Antoine Lefrary & du Perac's *Disegno vero della nuova città di Malta*, which is, however, based on Laparelli's plan.

Fort St Elmo's west front, facing Marsamxett harbour remained relatively exposed as it was devoid of any outerworks. Worse still, an enemy could attack the fort's west front with relative impunity from the guns of Fort St Angelo, hidden as this was from view behind the high ground of the Sciberras peninsula. Attempts to rectify this defect were underway in the early months of 1565, just

prior to the arrival of the Turkish armada. The military engineer Giovanni de Fayes was sent over from Sicily by Don Garcia de Toledo to design a new 'ravelino sia bastione'.[17] This ravelin, however, was built in great haste in order to have it finished and armed in time for the impending attack. Balbi di Correggio records that it was fitted with embrasures and connected to the fort by a narrow fixed bridge. It was also a low structure, so low that the janissaries found little difficulty in overcoming its defences. The exact position of the ravelin is not known since the contemporary maps and plans of the harbour fortifications are inconsistent with regards to this detail. However, Bosio states that this was sited 'in quel luogo, dove il fosso girando verso il Cavaliere, forma l'ultimo angolo, nel fine di essa contrascarpa.'[18] So sited, the ravelin would have been able, but with some difficulty, to provide enfilading fire along the ditch between the cavalier and the fort.

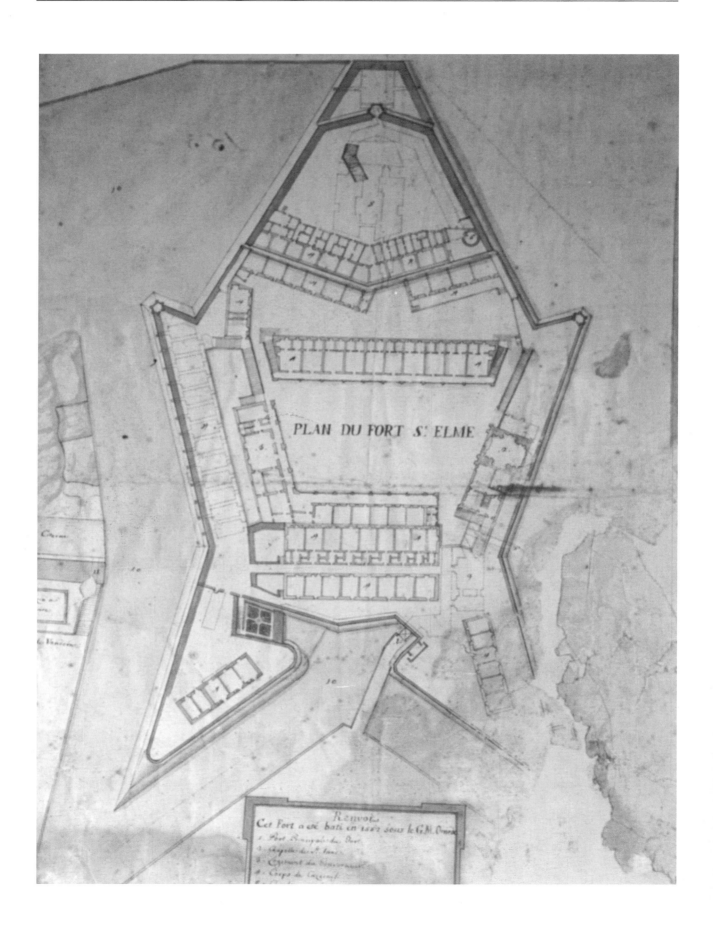

To the 28,500-strong Turkish force that invested the island in May 1565, the siege of Fort St Elmo must have seemed an insignificant affair to be done with in a couple of days so that the main force might concentrate all its attacks on the Order's stronghold at Birgu. From the outset, however, the Turks were to be proved wrong as the men of Fort St Elmo sallied out on a lightning counter-attack designed to show the besiegers that the fort held men capable of defending it. At the beginning of the siege, the garrison of Fort St Elmo under Commander Frà Brolla (Broglia) with the knight Giovanni Parpalla as his lieutenant, consisted of 80 soldiers, mostly from the company of Juan de la Cerda. Grand Master de Valette dispatched a further 50 men under the command of Juan de Guaras.[19] The knight Hieronymo Sagra was in command of the cavalier with 50 men.

Once the intentions of the Turks were made clear, De Valette hastily reinforced Fort St Elmo with 100 knights, Mass and La Motte with their companies, and 60 criminals sentenced to the galleys' together with all the supplies and munitions that could be spared. The garrison of the fort prior to the commencement of the artillery bombardment thus consisted of 946 men. The Turks opened a heavy artillery bombardment on 28 May 1565, from a large battery of ten 80-pdr guns and a large 160-pdr bombard. By 31 May, there were 24 pieces of artillery aligned against the front of the fort. The defenders were kept busy improvising repairs to the flaking walls and sniping on the attackers. A culverine proved too powerful to be discharged from the cavalier and had to be dismantled. On 3 June the Turks were joined by the corsair Dragut, who set up his guns on the promontory known as the hermitage of St Mary and with these he set about bombarding both the ravelin and the cavalier.

It took the Turks nearly a month to gain control of the fort, first capturing the ravelin and then the cavalier. Once the latter was overcome, the Turkish engineers immediately turned it to their advantage by mounting on it some pieces of artillery which they trained towards the interior of the fort. Having no traverses behind which to shelter, but only low parapets a *mezza rota*, the Christian defenders began

Above, The sea gate of Fort St Elmo, later known as Porta del Soccorso (Italian for sally-port). Below, View of the land front of Fort St Elmo. Opposite page, An 18th-century plan of Fort St Elmo, showing the various alterations made to link the fort to the cavalier (NLM).

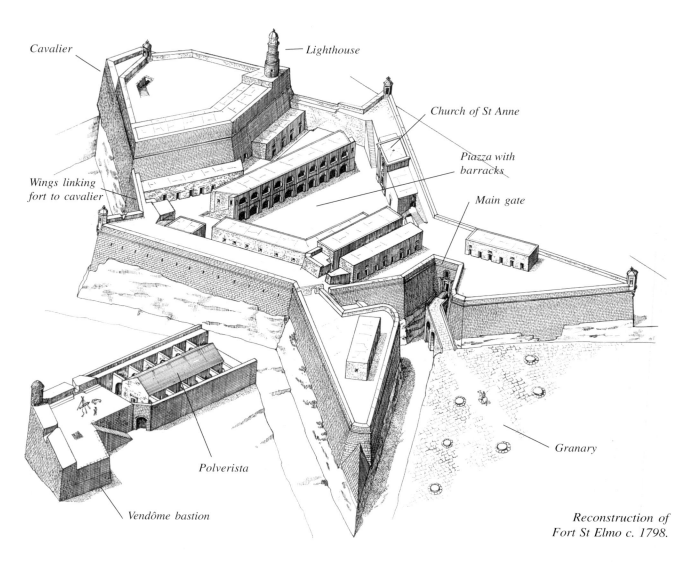

Cavalier — Lighthouse

Church of St Anne

Piazza with barracks

Wings linking fort to cavalier

Main gate

Polverista

Granary

Vendôme bastion

Reconstruction of Fort St Elmo c. 1798.

to suffer heavy casualties. The fact that no reinforcements were reaching the fort, owing to a newly-erected Turkish battery at Gallows Point, rendered the situation more desperate. Realizing that the end had finally come, the few surviving defenders retired to the church in the hope of making a conditional surrender, but seeing that they were being cut down mercilessly, they rushed to the *piazza* of the fort and there they sold their lives at a high price.[20]

The dust of war having settled, the Order set about rebuilding the demolished harbour fortifications. Fort St Elmo was the first to be completed. On the advice of Don Garcia de Toledo, it was enlarged, fitted with barracks, ovens, and cisterns. In 1566 Laparelli ordered the excavation of a deep ditch on the fort's west front to replace the demolished ravelin.[21] Later, in the second half of the sixteenth century, the ditch separating the fort from the cavalier was enclosed within two walls. In 1727 the northern ramparts of the fort were demolished and two strong walls, or wings, finally secured the cavalier to the

body of fort. The intervening ditch was filled in, resulting in a larger *piazza* which enabled the construction of a large barrack block (1727-30) designed by the French engineer Mondion.[22]

As early as 1600, the cavalier was already fitted with a beacon tower to aid the increasing volume of traffic that accompanied the development of a prosperous maritime city. It should be remembered that Fort St Elmo was left standing free of the new enceinte of the fortress of Valletta. As a result, there remained a wide area of foreshore on which an enemy could gain a foothold. Furthermore, the fort was also exposed to the threat posed by the promontory known as Dragut's Point, on which an enemy could easily set up a large battery, a lesson bitterly learnt during the siege of 1565. A proposal for the construction of a new gun platform overlooking this promontory was first put forward by Laparelli but it was only in 1614, that a gun platform, called Vendôme Bastion, was eventually constructed there.[23] Up to the end of the seventeenth century,

The right bastion of Fort St Elmo's land front. The musketry parapet is a British 19th-century addition.

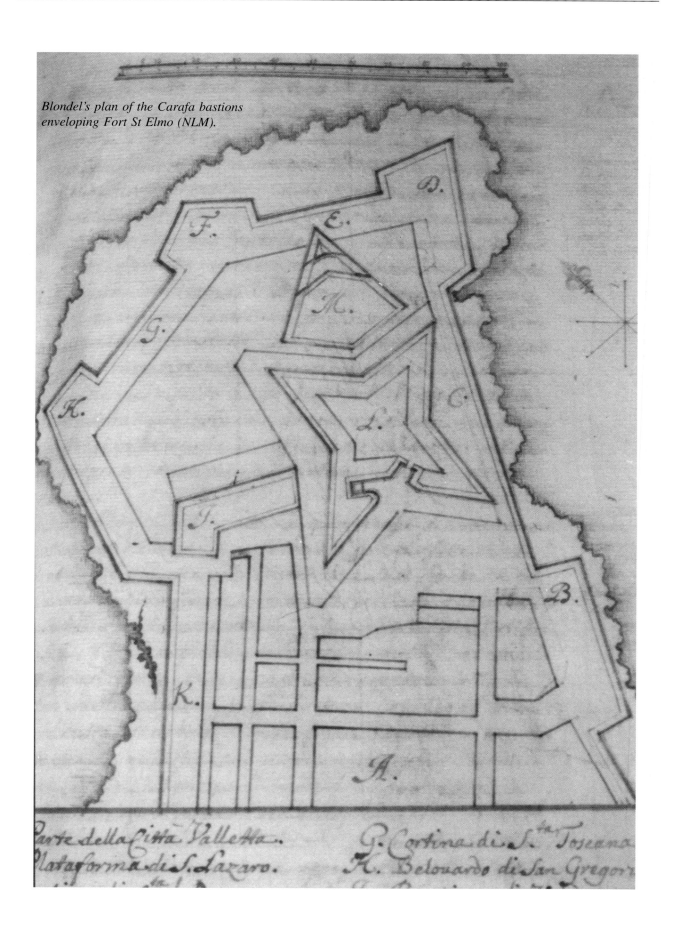

Blondel's plan of the Carafa bastions enveloping Fort St Elmo (NLM).

Parte della Citta Valletta.   G. Cortina di S.ta Toscana
Plataforma di S. Lazaro.   H. Belouardo di San Gregor

before it was rendered obsolete by the construction of the Carafa bastions, this work was a favourite position for artillery practice on targets set up on Dragut Point.

The construction of the Carafa Bastions secured the foreshore around St Elmo and enclosed the fort within a new enceinte. This ring of ramparts was designed by Don Carlos de Grunenberg and built under the supervision of Blondel, then the Order's resident engineer, in 1687. In order to accommodate one of the bastions along the new enceinte, the spur of the old cavalier had to be demolished and rebuilt.[24] The new works were completed in less than two years.

In 1761 French military engineers found 'le chateau St Elme' in a 'bon etat' and proposed no further alterations to its defences. The tragic episode of the 'Rising of the Priests' in 1775 revealed how inadequately Fort St Elmo was garrisoned. Twenty men, mostly priests, managed to seize control of the fort and raise the Maltese red-and-white flag on its ramparts. During the following night, the garrison of the fort, however, managed to free themselves and real fighting began in the restricted interior of the fort before the insurgents were finally brought to their knees. Though heavily armed, Fort St Elmo played no part in the events of 1798 and its guns remained silent as the French ships sailed beneath its ramparts into the Grand Harbour.

Above, top, View of the barracks from the cavalier. Above, The cavalier and, below, Fort St Elmo and the Carafa bastions.

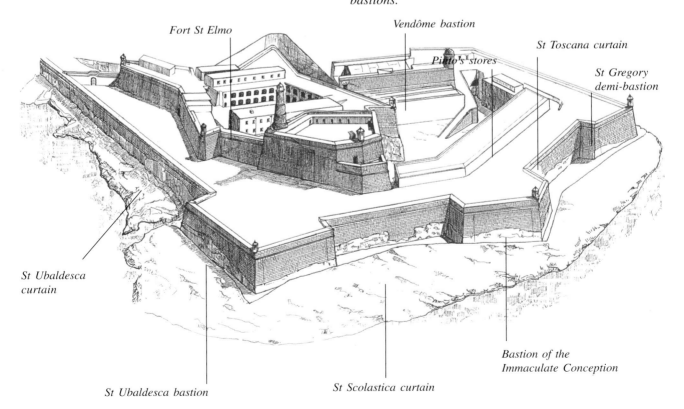

Fort St Elmo

Vendôme bastion

Pinto's stores

St Toscana curtain

St Gregory demi-bastion

St Ubaldesca curtain

St Ubaldesca bastion

St Scolastica curtain

Bastion of the Immaculate Conception

Senglea

Above, Detail from Georg Braun and Frans Hogen's map of Malta, showing Fort St Michael. Below, Senglea under Turkish attack during the Great Siege, after D'Aleccio.

Francesco Balbi di Correggio best illustrates the topography of the Grand Harbour area in one of the opening paragraphs of his book describing the events of the Great Siege and which goes as follows: 'Seven tongues of land, large and small, divide the Grand Harbour and form small harbours. On the extremity of one of these tongues of land, which is near the mouth of the harbour, stands the ancient Castle of St Angelo and behind it is the Birgu, called the New City, where the Grand Master and the Order reside. On the tongue of land next removed from the mouth of the harbour is Fort Saint Michael, a modern fort built after the plans of the ablest engineers of the time.'[1] That tongue of land next removed from the mouth of the harbour was practically barren when the knights arrived in Malta in 1530 and settled down at Birgu. But as Birgu became more and more overcrowded and accommodation more scarce, small settlements took root on the Isola, as the peninsula was known, encouraged by the measure of safety afforded by the nearby defences of Birgu and St Angelo. In the early 1550s the site was referred to as the *Monte del Mulino* and the windmills are clearly depicted in D'Aleccio's paintings.[2] The peninsula was also known as St Julian's hill, after a chapel erected there in the fourteenth century.[3] Whatever the state of the Isola peninsula at the time, it was nonetheless strategically very important for the security of Birgu and Fort St Angelo for it exposed these two strongholds to direct lateral bombardment.

The Turkish *razzia* of 1551 must have made the Order realize the importance of fortifying the Isola, for, in the following year, the council commissioned Frà Leone Strozzi, together with two other knights and the engineer Prato, to draw up a review of the fortifications. In his recommendations, Strozzi accepted that to fortify the whole of the Sciberras peninsula was then unfeasible and he proposed instead to build two new small forts, strategically sited so as to render the most cost-effective defence.[4] The first fort was built at St Elmo to command the harbour mouth, while the second was built on the Monte del Molino. The latter was commenced in 1552 and, by the end of the year, Fort St Michael, as it was called, was completed. As originally built, Fort St Michael was a large squarish and squattish tower supporting a battery on its roof. A map of the harbour by Georg Braun and Frans Hogen (1572) shows this tower surrounded by a star-shaped wall fitted with loopholes. In 1553 Grand Master de la Sengle decided to enclose Fort St Michael and part of the peninsula within a

bastioned enceinte. The work seems to have been undertaken by the Italian engineer Niccolò Bellavanti.[5] Within three years the land front had progressed rapidly and it was decided to name the new city Città Senglea in honour of the grand master. The rest of the enceinte facing Corradino heights was still unfinished by 1565. Balbi records that most of the works facing Corradino were very low, lacking parapets and traverses.[6] The work known as 'the Spur', sited at the tip of the peninsula which was designed by Evangelista da Menga, was very weak, lacking a parapet and fighting platform. During the Siege, the command of the Spur was entrusted to Francesco de Sanoguera, a knight from Valencia, who, together with the men of his galley, refortified the work by constructing a parapet and fighting platform and placing 'four caissons full of earth'.[7] With the construction of the new bastioned

land front, Fort St Michael was incorporated into the new enceinte as a cavalier. The land front itself consisted of a large casemated central bastion flanked by casemated ramparts. A small outerwork in the shape of a ravelin was hastily built to the right of the centre-bastion facing Corradino heights. The main gate opened directly into the ditch and was sited on the curtain closest to the creek. Another gateway, probably a postern, was situated facing Corradino heights. The flank facing the Birgu was without any fortification since the two towns were intended to provide mutual protection.

Senglea was the second Turkish objective after the capture of Fort St Elmo. The unexpected month-long Turkish effort to subdue the small fort at the entrance to the harbour had earned the garrison of Senglea more time in which to

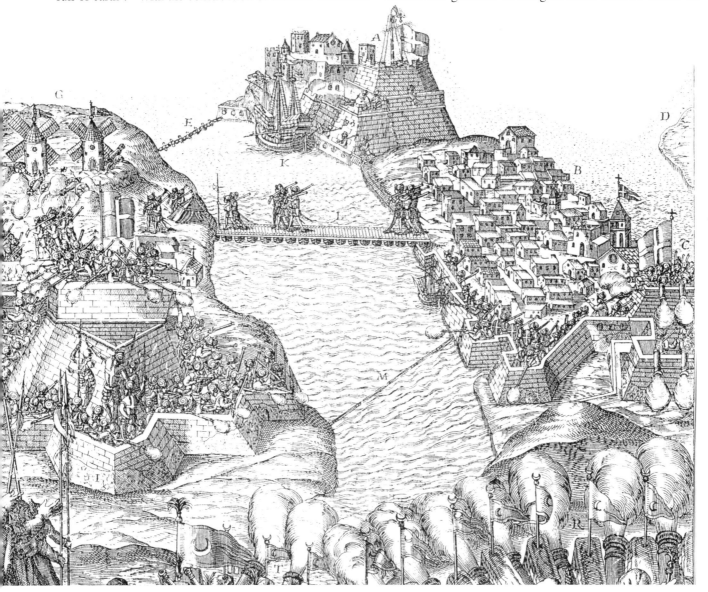

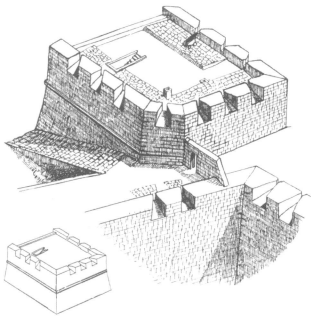

Above, top: The cavalier of St Michal, formerly the fort built in 1552, prior to its destruction in the 1920s. Below: The 18th-century gate of Senglea and its adjoining casemated ramparts.

strengthen the defences. On Saturday 30 June, Turkish engineers began setting up four heavy siege batteries on the Corradino and Mandra heights, aiming them at the walls of Senglea, while another battery sited on Mount Sciberras was directed at the Spur. During the siege, Senglea was entrusted to the command of the admiral of the Order's fleet who, together with all the Italian knights, were stationed at Fort St Michael. The rest of the enceinte was entrusted to various knights commanding motley groups of Spanish, Italian, Sicilian, and Maltese troops.

As the siege progressed, various defects in the design of the Senglea fortifications became apparent. The counterscarp of the main ditch on the land front, for example, was very low and the Turkish sappers found no great difficulty in entering the fosse. Various mines were dug beneath the ramparts by the Turks but all of these were discovered in time by the defenders who never failed to capture them before these were set off. The most critical moment during the attack on Senglea came on 7 August, when around 8,000 Turks assaulted the battered land front. Simultaneously, another 4,000 troops attacked the Post of Castile in Birgu. The assault lasted nine hours but when the Turks seemed finally to be gaining ground, their attack wavered and their troops retreated in panic back to their lines, wrongly believing that the much-awaited Christian reinforcements had finally reached the island and were attacking their rear.

So great was the destruction wrought by the Turks that, after the siege, Francesco Laparelli recommended that Senglea should be razed to the ground.[8] Although his proposal was then ignored, the defences of Senglea were still in a ruined state in 1568. The Maltese engineer Gerolamo Cassar was entrusted with their repair and these seem to have been brought to a reasonable state of defence by 1581.[9] Thereafter little was done to maintain and improve its defences since all the Order's efforts were directed towards the erection of its new fortress on Mount Sciberras. By the beginning of the seventeenth century the fortifications of Senglea were once again largely in need of repair. The general alarm of 1633 necessitated that these be quickly repaired and placed in a state of defence in order to withstand the feared onslaught but little seems to have been actually achieved.[10] A commission of knights was again appointed to examine the defences in 1635 when yet another Turkish incursion was expected. The knights were then advised to deepen and widen the main ditch outside Bormola and to 'serrar la porta verso il Corradino'.[11] The parapets, too, demanded attention, especially those facing Corradino heights, and it was found necessary to 'terrapienare et alzare li parapetti nelli luoghi più necessarij aggrandire la piattaforma'.[12] All the works were estimated to cost 6,000 scudi.[13]

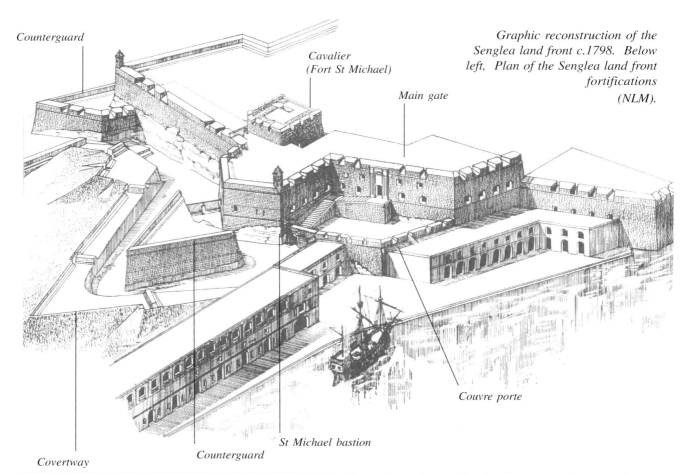

Counterguard

Cavalier
(Fort St Michael)

Main gate

Graphic reconstruction of the Senglea land front c.1798. Below left, Plan of the Senglea land front fortifications (NLM).

Couvre porte

St Michael bastion

Counterguard

Covertway

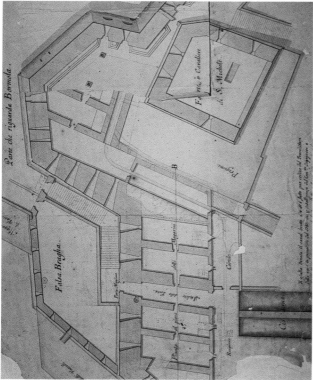

Throughout the 1660s the Order's resident engineer, Blondel, repeatedly urged the Order to repair the Senglea fortifications. In his attempts to strengthen its defences, he laid down various proposals, amongst which were the erection of artillery platforms facing Birgu and the fashioning of the rocky shore beneath the Spur into a *faussebraye*. This last proposal was re-advocated by Grunenberg in 1690, and through his financial help the Order was able to construct a large sea-level battery capable of mounting ten guns at the mouth of the creek, facing De Guiral battery beneath Fort St Angelo. By 1785 this battery was armed with seven guns, six 18-pdrs and one 3-pdr. On 3 December 1792, the congregation of war ordered that the 'batteria bassa della punta dell'Isola' be armed with the extra 24-pdr guns then found in Fort St Angelo.[14]

The Senglea land front defences had by then evolved to include a large ravelin, or counterguard, sited ahead of the salient angle of the centre-bastion. This work was built during the reign of Grand Master Antoine de Paule (1623-36).[15] Other significant additions were the *couvre port* or tenaille which controlled the approach towards the main entrance and a counterguard protecting the demi-bastion facing Corradino hill. This work seems to have replaced the small detached outerwork which was built just before the Great Siege and is so clearly depicted in D'Aleccio's frescoes. There was then the ditch and a covertway with two re-entrant place-of-arms which seems to have been added in the early eighteenth century, though this seems to have been partly later redesigned to allow for the construction of large magazines on the wharf.

The French engineers who inspected the harbour defences in the early eighteenth century found little to recommend in the Senglea defences. By then the old fortress had lost its front-line value once it had been enclosed within the double enceintes of the Sta Margherita and Cottonera lines. In 1716 Tigné laid down a list of various works which he considered as necessary for strengthening the Senglea defences. The cost of these works was estimated at 6,900 scudi, of which 5,000 scudi were to go towards the construction of a new bastioned retrenchment projected ahead of the old land front, just behind the flank of St Raphael demi-bastion, 'a la tête des magazines de la marine'.[16] This retrenchment, in the shape of a crownwork, would have afforded some protection to the large magazines on the wharf but it was never constructed. Tigné also proposed to 'vouter en flanc bas de petit Bastion de la droite de L'Isle expose au Coradin' but it seems that only the

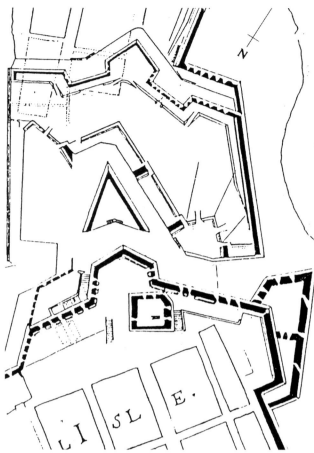

Right, Plan of Tigné's proposed retrenchment in the form of a crownwork placed ahead of the Senglea land front (NLM). Below, Aerial view of Senglea (DOI).

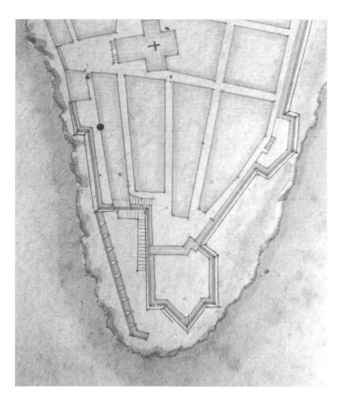

'chemin couvert a la tête de cette fort' was actually constructed from all of his detailed scheme.

The greatest defect of the Senglea fortifications, as clearly illustrated during the siege of 1565, remained the Corradino heights. There were various proposals to solve this problem by fortifying Corradino. The earliest of these was put forward by Count Vernada, who proposed to defend the site by sealing it off within a defensive line consisting of two bastions and two demi-bastions. More realistic schemes appeared in the early eighteenth century when French engineers proposed that Corradino heights be defended by a large casemated redoubt but none of their schemes were ever carried out. The military value of Senglea diminished rapidly during the eighteenth century so that what was once one of the bulwarks of Christendom in 1565 was, in 1788, armed solely with nine guns. Not surprisingly, the fortress of Senglea played no part in the events of 1798.

Above, The Spur of the Senglea fortifications as shown in an 18th-century plan (National Museum of Fine Arts). Right and below, 19th-century views of the Spur. Note also the fleur d'eau battery added by Grunenberg. This faced the mouth of the Grand Harbour.

Valletta

From a military engineers's point of view, Malta in the age of gunpowder fortifications offered few naturally-endowed sites that gave themselves so readily to the founding of a *piazzaforte*. The nature of the local landscape rarely combined the requisites of command and defensibility inherent in elevated sites with the vicinage of a safe anchorage, the presence of an adequate water supply and a topography congenial to the urban and social functions of a city. Perhaps one of the few exceptions to this geographical reality was Mount Sciberras, a mile long peninsula separating the Grand Harbour from Marsamxett. Its potential as a veritable *sito reale* was immediately recognized by the Hospitaller knights long before the actual arrival of the Order in Malta. A commission of eight knights sent over to inspect the island in 1524 lost no time to point it out as the ideal site for the Order's new convent - a second Rhodes.

This opinion was reiterated many times by the Order's military engineers in the course of the early half of the sixteenth century. Antonio Ferramolino was the first to strongly prescribe the Sciberras heights as the solution to the Order's defensive problems but on each occasion the financial, political, or military situation did not favour the implementation of any of the proposed schemes.[1] A real commitment towards the fortification of the Sciberras peninsula only began to materialize with election of Grand Master de Valette in 1557. In June 1558 the Order's council took a decision to build a new city on Mount Sciberras on a design drawn up by the Italian engineer Bartolomeo Genga.[2]

Genga's scheme envisaged the enclosure of the entire peninsula within a bastioned enceinte, the land front of which was to be sited at the neck of the tongue of land at the site now occupied by the Floriana lines. The landward defences were to consist of a large central flat-faced bastion flanked by two corner bastions. Genga, however, died shortly afterwards in the summer of 1558 and the project ground to a halt. His place was taken up, in 1562, by another Italian engineer by the name of Baldassare Lanci who proposed to fortify a smaller area instead, one with a land front situated much closer to St Elmo than that proposed by Genga.[3]

Once again the whole project failed to proceed further than the drawing board, plagued as it was by official indecision and the ever-looming threat of a Turkish attack which forced

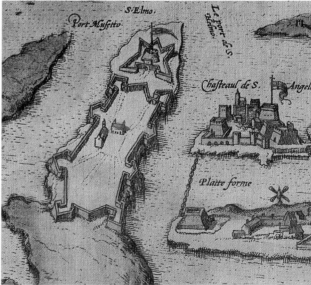

Above, Two mid-16th century designs for a fortress on Mount Sciberras, possibly illustrating Baldassare Lanci's project of 1562.

the knights to divert all their energies and attention to the strengthening of their existing defences. The Great Siege, however, proved once and for all that if the Order was to be securely settled on the island, it needed a new fortified city on the commanding heights of the Sciberras peninsula. The destruction wrought by four months of Turkish bombardment presented a good opportunity for building the new fortress although fears of a return of the Turkish armada and an impoverished treasury made the implementation of such a task seem an impossible venture. Two months after the lifting of the siege, Grand Master de Valette was still deliberating on what best to do. A letter dated 26 Ocober 1565 from Messina and probably written by Don Garcia De Toledo, the viceroy of Sicily, urged the grand master not to waste any more valuable time and to proceed with the construction of the new fortress, for which a labour force and an engineer would be provided. Jean de Valette, however, was also worried that the project, once initiated, could not be completed before the feared arrival of a new Turkish force in the following spring. Pope Pius IV, anxious that the Order retain Malta, also offered immediate financial assistance and sent over his military engineer Francesco Laparelli to help design the new fortified city.[4]

Laparelli arrived in Malta at the end of December 1565 and was promptly informed by the grand master that the walls of the new city had to be completed within the short span of three months, before the expected Turkish attack. Laparelli prepared a report on how this could be achieved indicating that an estimated labour force of 4,000 men was required for such a task while 3,000 soldiers were needed to men the defences. His design for the new fortress comprised a bastioned land front of two central bastions flanked by two demi-bastions sited on the highest part of the peninsula some 500 *canne* from the ditch of Fort St Elmo and connected to the latter by lateral walls. The enceinte was to be strengthened further by means of nine cavaliers.

Despite Laparelli's arrival and the promise of financial aid, the Order's decision to build the new city was not formally taken until 14 March 1566, after many months of indecision and political manoeuvring in which the grand master sought to ensure the assistance of foreign powers given the Hospitaller's dependence upon outside help. The first stone of the new fortress was laid by Grand Master de Valette on 28 March 1566 in the presence of members of the Order, the bishop of Malta, and a multitude of people.[5] Work on the fortifications of Valletta, as the city was called, together with its title of *Città Humillissima,* progressed steadily in spite of the recurrent shortage of money, labour, and building materials.[6] By mid-1567 the fortifications on the land front had begun to take shape and work was then concentrated on finishing the ditch (which had to be dug to a depth of 40 palms), the glacis, batteries in the flanks of bastions, the sally-ports and the platforms. Work on the lateral sides lagged behind that of the land front but by 1568 most of the enceinte had been laid out. That part of Laparelli's design which was not executed was the construction of an arsenal and the *manderaggio* or galley pen.[7] Work on the construction of the latter was actually

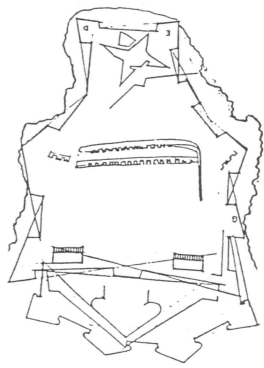

Above, Copy of the Uffizi plan showing various proposals for a fortress on the Sciberras promontory (after De Giorgio). Below, Plan of Valletta by Lafrery and du Perac, showing Laparelli's nine proposed cavaliers.

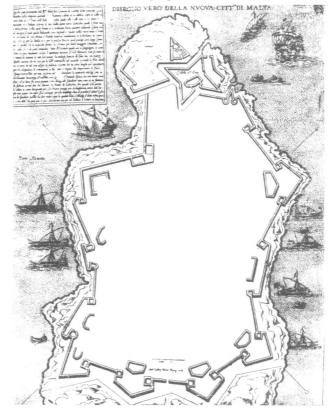

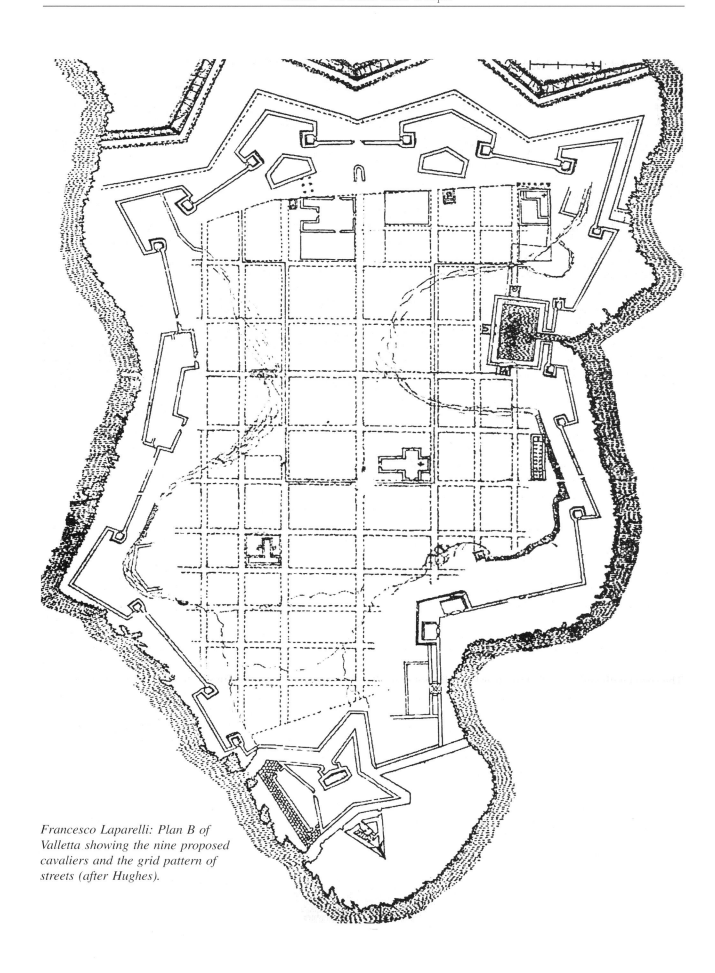

Francesco Laparelli: Plan B of Valletta showing the nine proposed cavaliers and the grid pattern of streets (after Hughes).

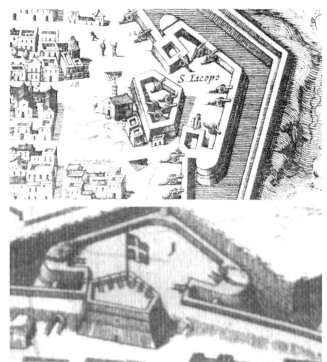

Above, top, St James cavalier and bastion, detail taken from engraving by Pierre Mortier (after De Giorgio). Above, St John cavalier. Above, left, The rock-hewn parapet of the original covertway along the Laparelli front.

commenced and the stone excavated from the site was used for the construction of houses, but, after a certain depth, the rock was found to be unsuitable for building. This, together with the realization that the *manderaggio* would not have been safe and large enough to house the Order's galley's, led to the abandonment of the scheme.

Laparelli left Malta in 1569, having entrusted the continuation of the work to his assistant, the Maltese military engineer Gerolamo Cassar.[8] Eager to gain military glory, he volunteered for service with the papal fleet but whilst in the service of the Venetions, died of the plague at the fortress of Candia, in Crete, in the following year.[9] By that time, however, the Valletta fortifications had reached an advanced stage in their construction. The shape and form of the new fortress had been settled and most of the outline of the enceinte fashioned out of living rock. Apart from the failure to complete the *manderaggio*, the fortfications of the new fortress were very much as Laparelli had intended them to be. His design quickly achieved international renown as a classic of the engineer's art and was eulogized in Daniel Speckle's treatise *Architectura von Festungen* published in 1589.[10] The Order transferred its convent from Birgu to the new city of Valletta in 1571.

The speed with which the fortress was built did not in itself give rise to those faults which were later to arouse criticism. The smallness of the bastions, the excessive depth and narrowness of the ditch, and the vulnerability of the lateral walls, perched as these were on the precipitous slopes overlooking both harbours, were seen to constitute the main defects inherent in Laparelli's design. But once the construction of the new fortress had reached a certain stage it was no longer feasible to effect but minor improvements. Among the improvements suggested and implemented were those of Scipione Campi in 1577.[11] These involved the addition of rounded orillions to the shoulders of the bastions in order to protect the *piazze basse* in the flanks and the raising of the height of the two cavaliers. Although Laparelli

had originally designed nine cavaliers to be erected on the bastions around Valletta, only two were actually built, sited along the land front on St John and St James bastions respectively.

Another weak point in the enceinte of the new fortress was found to be its northern extremity where a large section of the foreshore close to Fort St Elmo had been left unfortified. Laparelli's plans reveal that he had considered various proposals for enclosing the tip of the peninsula with an irregular bastioned front though none of these ideas were incorporated into the final scheme. Eventually, a large artillery platform was built on that part of the enceinte adjoining the fort which was closest to Dragut Point. This was erected around 1614 and was known as the Vendôme bastion, named after Alexandre of Vendôme, grand prior of France, who probably financed its construction.[12]

In 1632 Grand Master Antoine de Paule commissioned the Maltese architect Tommaso Dingli to design a new baroque gate to replace the older Porta San Giorgio built earlier on by Laparelli and above which had been placed the arms of the Pope Pius V and Grand Master Jean de Valette.[13] Dingli's gateway was replaced in the mid-nineteenth century by a British-built structure. Only the masonry

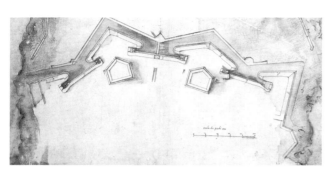

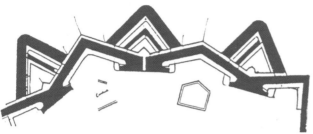

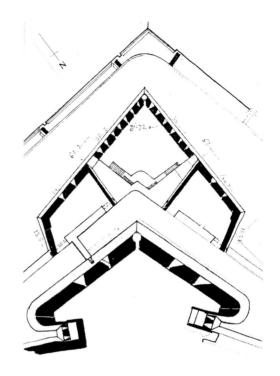

bridge which once served the main gateway has survived, albeit sandwiched between later additions. A more popular gateway into the city was that which Grand Master Del Monte, de Valette's successor, had directed to be built on the Grand Harbour side of the new fortress. The Marina or Del Monte gate was intended to facilitate communication between Birgu and the new fortress. Unfortunately, this gate, too, was demolished in the nineteenth century (1884) and replaced by another gateway known as the Victoria gate. A third gateway was eventually opened on the Marsamxett side of the enceinte, though even this was demolished in the nineteenth century. A number of sally-ports were cut at the base of the rocky scarps in various places around the enceinte.

The development of the Valletta land front: above, left, c.1645 (Bar. Lat. 9905/5); left, Firenzuola's proposal for the addition of three ravelins, and bottom, the Marquis of St Angelo's four counterguards and lunette (NLM). Above, Detail of one of the Valletta bastions with its ditch, counterguard, advanced ditch, and covered way (NLM).

Those qualities of the fortress which had been much debated in the late sixteenth century continued to form the basis of the criticism levelled at it by the many military engineers who were called to Malta in the course of the early decades of the seventeenth century. By the 1630s, it was widely accepted that it was no longer possible to reconcile

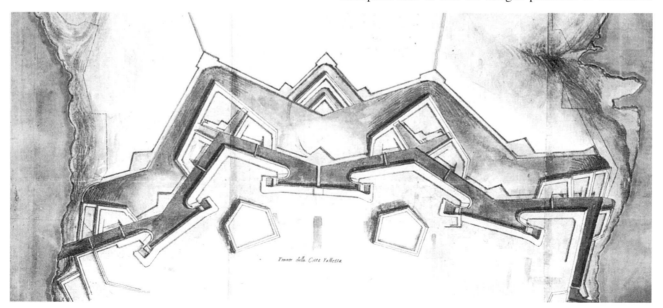

The piazza bassa *and* place haute *in the right flank of St John bastion.*

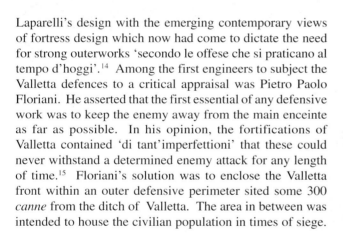

The three principal gates of Valletta - above, Porta Reale, right, Porta del Monte, and bottom right, Marsamxett gate. All these gates were either demolished or replaced by later structures (National Museum of Archaeology).

Laparelli's design with the emerging contemporary views of fortress design which now had come to dictate the need for strong outerworks 'secondo le offese che si praticano al tempo d'hoggi'.[14] Among the first engineers to subject the Valletta defences to a critical appraisal was Pietro Paolo Floriani. He asserted that the first essential of any defensive work was to keep the enemy away from the main enceinte as far as possible. In his opinion, the fortifications of Valletta contained 'di tant'imperfettioni' that these could never withstand a determined enemy attack for any length of time.[15] Floriani's solution was to enclose the Valletta front within an outer defensive perimeter sited some 300 *canne* from the ditch of Valletta. The area in between was intended to house the civilian population in times of siege.

The Floriana project, although eventually built, encountered much criticism. Indeed, even as the works unfolded, the flanks of the new enceinte proved to be relatively very weak and so the danger to the Valletta land front remained. In 1638 the military engineer Maculano Firenzuola, when asked to evaluate possible ways of improving the old land front, recommended that this be strengthened by 'tre ravellini, li quali l'un l'altro si difendessero, poiche quelli con il calore della fronte, e delli due gran Cavalieri, e con poco numero di soldati i quali haverebbono generosamente combattuto, sicuri.'[16] Initially no attempt was made to have the three ravelins built but, in the following year, the marquis of St Angelo proposed to strengthen the land front by means of four counterguards and a lunette, 'formare alcuni baluardi avanti la fronte del Vecchia, co li quali si rimedia all'inconveniente seco un fosso così stretto e profondo, le piazze cosi sparse de vecchi baluardi, & le difese troppo imperfette.'[17] The two central counterguards were designed in the form of large pentagonal bastions with retrenched interiors open at the gorge. The counterguards at both extremities of the front were to be much smaller, consisting of stepped platforms. Work on the construction of these outerworks began in 1640 and these were completed in less than five years. The lunette, on the other hand, seems not to have been completed until well into the eighteenth century.

Above, The orillion and face of St John Bastion. All of Valletta's land front bastions were originally designed with square orillions. Below, view of Abercrombie's bastion situated along the enceinte enveloping Fort St Elmo. Most of the structures on the bastion are actually late 19th century and early 20th century British additions.

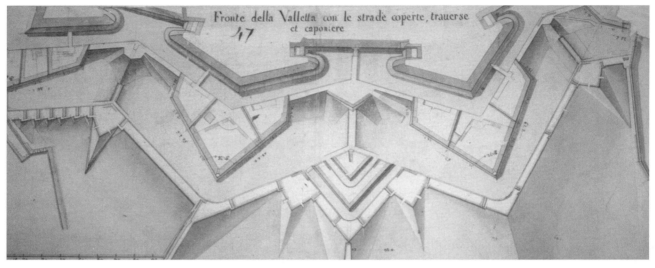

The Valletta land front - above, 18th-century plan (NLM) and below, graphic view of the general layout.

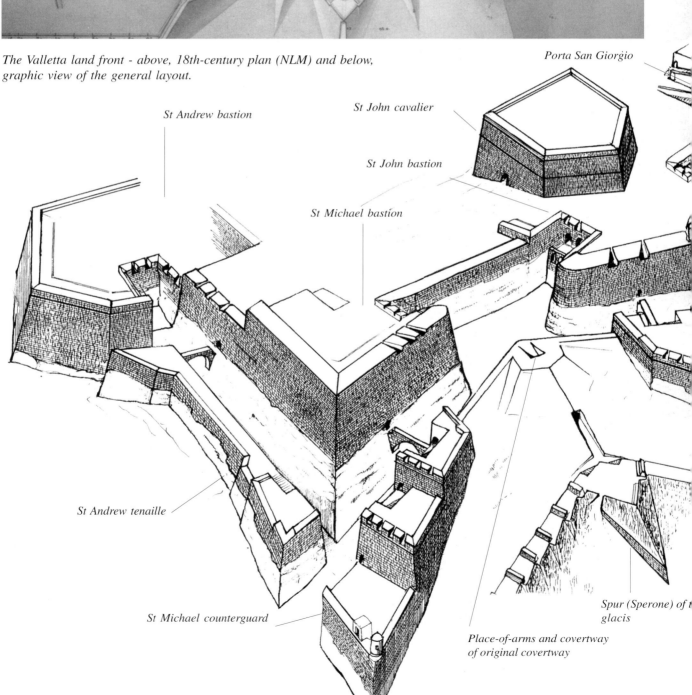

St Andrew bastion

St John cavalier

Porta San Giorgio

St John bastion

St Michael bastion

St Andrew tenaille

St Michael counterguard

Place-of-arms and covertway
of original covertway

Spur (Sperone) of
glacis

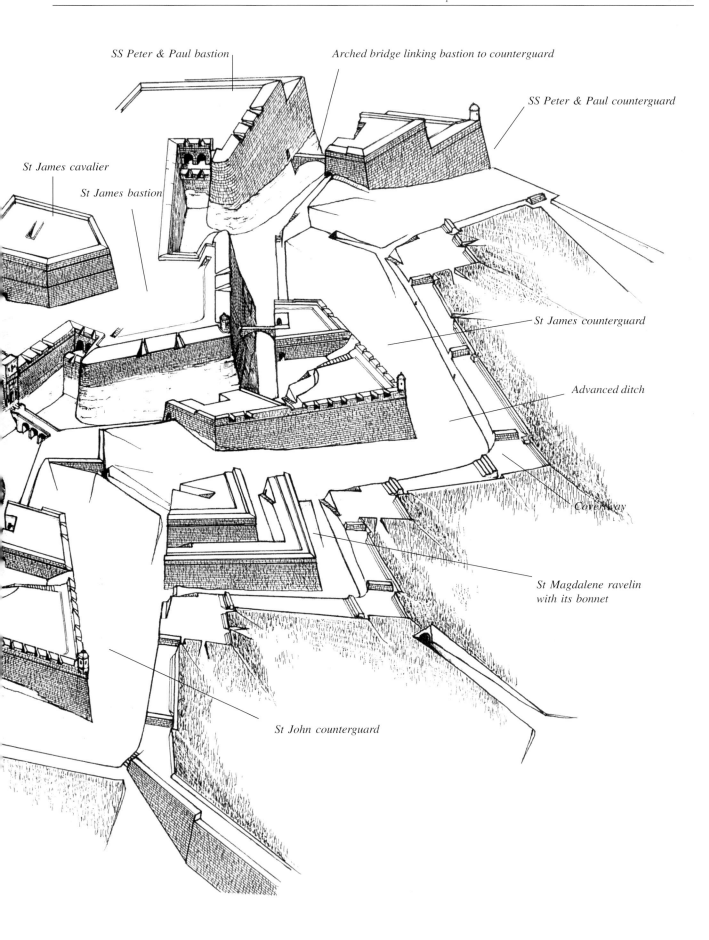

SS Peter & Paul bastion

Arched bridge linking bastion to counterguard

SS Peter & Paul counterguard

St James cavalier

St James bastion

St James counterguard

Advanced ditch

Coveredway

St Magdalene ravelin
with its bonnet

St John counterguard

Towards the end of the seventeenth century, the question of the exposed rocky shore at the tip of the peninsula was brought once again to the fore for it was always considered to provided an easily accessible foothold to any attacking enemy force. The idea for enclosing the area with a new bastioned enceinte was put forward in 1687 by Carl Grunenberg, a Flemish engineer in charge of the fortifications of the Sicilian kingdom, who was loaned to the Order by the viceroy.[18] Grunenberg did not remain long enough in Malta to supervise the execution of his scheme and the task was entrusted in to the hands of the resident engineer Blondel.[19] Work on the new enceinte, designed in the form of a crownwork was begun without delay. The first stone was laid with due ceremony by the grand master on 28 May 1687 and the works were speedily completed within a short span of two years.[20]

According to his 'Discorso intorno al suplimento del recinto della Città Valletta', Blondel believed that the new enceinte, apart from fulfilling important military functions, would also be useful in confronting visitors to the island with a sight worthy of the island's reputation as an invincible fortress and bastion of Christendom, 'dare anche all'occhio la dovuta parte, col fare, per mezzo di questo suplimento di fortificazione nel recinto della Città Valletta, che a tutti, ma principalmente ai forestieri, nell'approdare a Malta, ed a chiunque ne passa vicino, o in vista nel canale, ella comparisca si fattamente fortificata, che vegni a sostenere la propria riputazione, e correspondere a quello nobile e grande idea di cui ritrovansi per lo più prevenuti e piene dalla publica fama, d'inespugnabile fortezza, di Antemurale d'Italia, di Belouardo della Christianità.'[21]

The building of the new enceinte entailed the reconstruction of the spur of the cavalier of Fort St Elmo. It also enclosed within it the old Vendôme bastion. There were many who believed that this structure was rendered obsolete by the new works. One of these was Blondel's temporary replacement, the knight Vauvilliers who was appointed to supervise the completion of the project in the absence of the resident military engineer. Vauvilliers believed that the Vendôme bastion had to be dismantled but this proposal

was strongly objected to by Blondel on his return.[22] Still Vauvilliers' idea caught on, for, sometime during the mid-eighteenth century, the structure was hollowed out and converted into a Vauban-style powder magazine. One of Grunenberg's proposal was to open part of the ditch of St Elmo in order to allow some degree of protection, in case of a siege, to small sea-craft bringing supplies to the fortress from Birgu but the scheme was not given any consideration.

Blondel's final years as the Order's engineer saw no new major defensive works being undertaken in Valletta and the next engineer to forward serious proposals for the perfection of the city's defences was the Frenchmen Louis François d'Aubigné de Tigné who headed a French military mission to the island during the emergency of 1715. Tigné believed that the Valletta land front constituted the best defensive work in Malta but the parapets and orillions of the bastions were in a neglected state while trees had encroached on the *piazze* of the bastions.[23] In his many reports, Tigné expressed his preference for a three- rather than four-bastioned front and also criticized the high arched bridges linking the main enceinte to the counterguards and the narrow covertway with its lack of traverses. He also suggested that *Porta Reale* be defended by a lunette, similar to that which was proposed by the marquis of St Angelo in

Below, A 19th century photograph of St James counterguard from the rear. Bottom, St Magdalene ravelin and its bonnet in the 18th century, just prior to their demolition in order to make way for the electric tram (National Museum of Archaeology).

1645 but never built. In order to improve communications with Floriana, Tigné proposed underground communication passages beneath the covertway and glacis, and along the flanks of Floriana.[24]

On his second visit to the island in 1716, Tigné set about preparing a detailed scheme for the improvement of the city's fortifications. Tigné estimated that some 13,300 scudi were required to bring the Valletta fortification to completion. Of these, 9,300 scudi were thought necessary to ensure the restoration of the parapets and banquettes. Another 4,000 scudi were believed necessary 'pour reformer le chemin couvert de la Place y faire des Place d'Armes et traverses'.[25] Other vital works involved repairs to the flanks of the bastions, the refashioning of the glacis, the building of 'caponieres et traverses de retraite dans les fossé des dites contregardes quis communiquente au chemin couvert' and the construction of 'magazines à preuve de bombe ... sour les Cavaliers et la Porte Reale'.[26] A futher threat to the Valletta fortifications was perceived to come from the small undefended island inside Marsamxett harbour, which Tigné hoped one day the Order's resources permitting, could be fortified in order to deny the invader the possibility of setting up a battery there aimed against the flank of the city, 'un fort à faire sur l'Isle du Lazaret pour ... (non) offrir à l'eniemi la facilité de s'etablir, d'on ne pourroit fer in commoder la Cité Vallette et attaquer la Religion dans son centre.'[27] He estimated that this fort would cost 25,000 scudi. It was eventually built in the 1720s and named Fort Manoel. The last significant addition to the Valletta fortifications was the construction of a retrenched ravelin in front of *Porta Reale*, named St Magadalene ravelin.

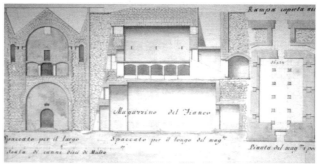

Top, View of San Salvatore bastion in the third quarter of the 19th century. The two expense magazines date to the British period. Above, Plan of a gunpowder magazine built into St John cavalier, dated 1742. Below, Vendôme bastion today, as seen from Fort St Elmo. This was converted into an armoury by the British in the 1850s and linked directly to St Gregory bastion.

Above, St Peter and St Paul counterguard. Below, view of the Valletta enceinte along the Grand Harbour, showing St Barabara bastion and Lascaris battery, a 19th century British addition.

Floriana Lines

The Floriana lines were conceived in order to provide further protection to the Valletta land front. These defences were designed by the Italian engineer Pietro Paolo Floriani during the magistracy of Antoine de Paule (1622-36) following growing rumours of an impending Turkish attack in the 1630s.[1] Floriani believed that Valletta, at the time lacking any outerworks whatsoever, was not adapted for modern warfare with its high bastions and narrow ditch. He proposed instead that a new line of fortification be projected farther south at the neck of the peninsula some 1,600m from St Elmo, on a plateau overlooking Marsa, the low-lying marshland that had once served as a Turkish camp during the Great Siege.[2] Floriani's design consisted of a large retrenched centre bastion flanked by two demi-bastions with the adjoining curtain walls protected by a tenaille. In front of the curtains, Floriani projected two large ravelins and, beyond these, a covertway with two salient crown-shaped place-of-arms.

Floriani's plan came in for much criticism from the start. The commissioners appointed to review his 'due modelli' were of the opinion that these would entail 'una spesa eccessiva, e da finirsi se non con tempo longhissimo.' Floriani, however, reiterated by pointing out that no

Two proposals showing the Floriana land front (Vat. Lib. Barb Lat. 9905/3 I and II). The plan on the right shows a shorter, and slightly convex, front with the two ravelins placed very near to each other.

fortifications could ever be strong enough against 'una potenza come quella del Turco' and it was for this reason that his design was not conditioned 'ne' a spese, ne a fatiga'.[3] Although the council sanctioned its construction on 10 December 1635, opposition to the scheme did not diminish, so that one of the commissioners of the fortifications, Balì Gattinara, resigned in protest.[4]

The unending criticism levelled against Floriani's design centred around the fact that the project was too ambitious, requiring too much money and men to garrison it. It was also seen as being exposed and susceptible to flanking fire from the Corradino heights. Nonetheless, work on these fortifications commenced immediately and, by the beginning of February 1636, Floriani had already traced the outline of the works on site.[5] The opponents of Floriani's scheme strongly believed that the Valletta land front could have been more effectively protected if its outerworks were completed and the bastions provided with counterguards. Floriani, however, justified his enormous design by claiming that the large area enclosed by the fortifications would shelter the whole population of Malta during a siege, 'non

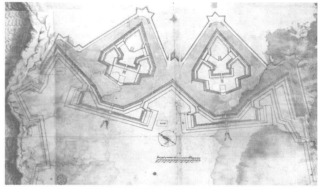

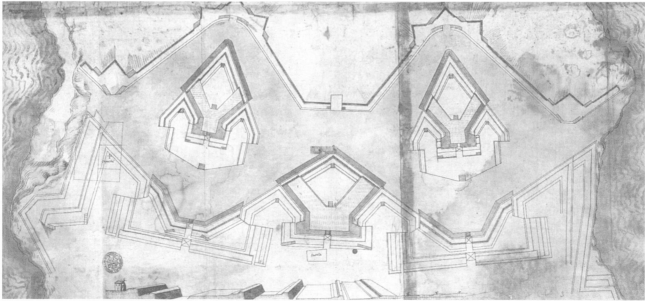

Plan of the Floriana lines, c.1637-40, showing works in progress. Note that the tenailles and piazze basse are not featured, indicating that these had then not as yet been cut out of the rock, nor had the counterscarp and most of the lateral walls (Vat. Lib. Barb. Lat. 9905/4). Below, inset, Plan possibly showing the marquis of St Angelo's proposal to turn the Floriana lines into a crownwork (Vat. Lib. Barb. Lat. 9905/5).

ad altro fine che a poter salvare tutti il Popolo dell'Isola in occasione d'assedio'.[6]

Floriani left Malta on 23 October 1636, having entrusted the execution of the project in the hands of his assistant Francesco Buonamici, to whom he passed on written instructions.[7] Once Floriani departed, however, the knights began to doubt the merits of the project and, on 17 January 1637, the council decided to consult the opinion of other renowned experts.[8] A Frenchman named Jardin, then on a visit to the island, confirmed the general criticism raised by the opponents of Floriani's scheme, mainly that the lines were too large.[9] He proposed that the new works be abandoned and that the Valletta land front be provided with outerworks instead. His plans were approved by the council in May 1638 but by the time that the Order received the approval of his scheme from other foreign military experts, interest in Jardin's project had failed and the Order opted to continue with the original design.[10]

Still, in the 1640s, work began on the construction of the outerworks of Valletta according to a scheme put forward by the marquis of St Angelo, who also proposed linking the new works to the Valletta land front by means of two straight walls.[11] Another visiting engineer, Louis Nicolas de Clerville, proposed a 'tenaglia a corni', or hornwork, in front of *Porta Reale* of Valletta, projecting into the open space behind the Floriana lines so as to deny an enemy the use of the Floriana works were these to be overwhelmed and thus enable the defenders to retreat safely into Valletta.[12] As a cheaper alternative, Clerville suggested the construction of a series of small, mutually-covering palisaded redoubts placed along the esplanade. Although none of these proposals were ever implemented, Clerville did in fact influence the final design of the two large ravelins when he recommended that their internal retrenchments, 'le ritirate nelle mezzelune', should not be built, because unlike those inside the large central bastion, the former

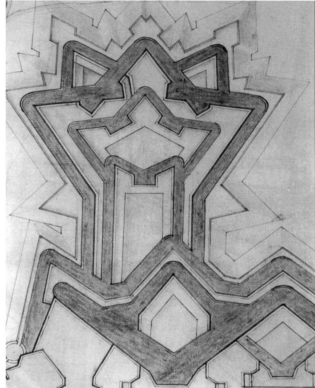

Above, top, Coronelli's depiction of the crowned-hornwork, showing it without the ailes. Above, Blondel's unexecuted proposal to enclose 'la Galdiana' within an extension of the so-called faussebraye, also formed into a crownwork supported by two ravelins. Bottom left, A rectangular, palisaded redoubt designed by Clerville to cover the retreat of the garrison of Floriana into Valletta (NLM).

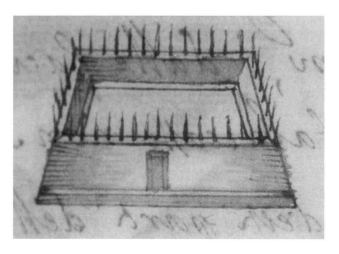

were useless, 'dette ritirate cosi difetuose ... si troveranno le fianchi tanto vicini l'uno dell'altro che non si possano una reciproca difesa comunicare'.[13] His other advice to remove the *orecchini* and have instead a 'mezzaluna schietta' was likewise heeded.

The second important stage in the construction of the Floriana lines began with the arrival, in 1670, of Count Antonio Maurizio Valperga, chief military architect to the house of Savoy. Valperga overhauled Floriani's design, ironing out its inherent defects and stiffening the whole

Above, Grunenberg's stone model of the bastion of Provence and adjoining ramparts added by Valperga (National Museum of Fine Arts). Below, Quarantine gate, situated in the Floriana rtrenchment, to the rear of Msida bastion cemetery.

trace with new aggressive outerworks. This he did by pushing forward a *faussebraye* and a crowned-hornwork, the latter projecting onto the high ground overlooking the Marsa which was not visible from the main enceinte. He was also responsible for re-designing the bastion of Provence overlooking the Pietà.[15] Valperga also proposed a round tower behind the Capuchin convent but this was never built.

Valperga designed a retrenchment in the San Salvatore bastion and a sallyport in the *faussebraye* near the bastion. Another sallyport was constructed in the re-entrant angle of St Francis bastion, providing access to the crowned-hornwork across an open walkway hugging the face of the bastion hundreds of feet above the ground. The main gate was to be sited on the faussebraye exactly in line with Porta San Giorgio. Valperga's visit was a short and hectic one but, before departing from Malta, he had time to trace the outline of the crowned-hornwork and San Salvatore retrenchment on site. Work on the crowned-hornwork commenced in 1671 and was made possible by the generosity of the knight Juan Galdiano, prior of Navarre, who financed the project. The work was named *La Galdiana* in his honour.[16] Work on the *faussebraye* was also begun before the end of that year and was eventually finished by the early1680s.

Valperga's improvements, despite doing much to remove the weaknesses inherent in the old design, did not pass uncritized. Among those to find fault with his work was Count Vernada, who had served in Crete against the Turks for nearly two-and-a-half years as chief engineer. Vernada criticized the crown-hornwork as being too small to accommodate the troops required for its defence. Blondel,

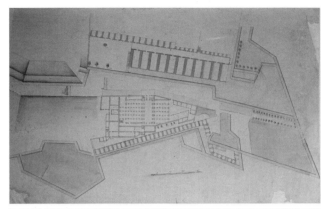

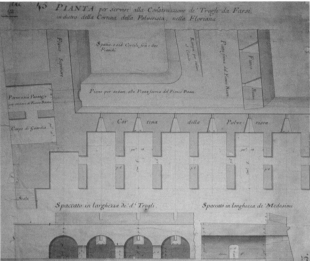

then the Order's resident engineer, was also very critical of the crowned-hornwork and the *faussebraye*. He proposed that the latter be extended around the *Galdiana* and strengthened further with two ravelins.[18] His proposals were never implemented.

In his report of 15 March 1681, the next visiting engineer, Grunenberg, recommended the completion of the ditch, *faussebraye*, and glacis of the Floriana lines and also proposed the excavation of caponiers within the ditch, but it does not seem that his intervention contributed much towards the completion of the project.[19] In 1715, Tigné found Floriana in an advanced state of completion and did not suggest any major alterations but advised the Order to 'donner à ce front toute la perfectione qu'il peut avoir'.[20] In July the congregation of war instructed Tigné to draw up, once and for all, a general plan outlining all that was necessary for the termination and perfection of the many half-finished fortifications. In September, Tigné presented his report and, in discussing the Floriana lines, he reiterated the widespread notion that the flanks were too weak compared to the over-protected land front. To remedy these defects he proposed the construction of retrenchments in

Above, left, Plan of the fortifications in the area of Polverista curtain showing the Casa di Carità *which was built on the esplanade between the two sets of walls. Left, Detail of the casemated Polverista curtain which was completed in 1723. Below, Plan of Capuchin bastion on the Grand Harbour side of the Floriana enceinte (NLM).*

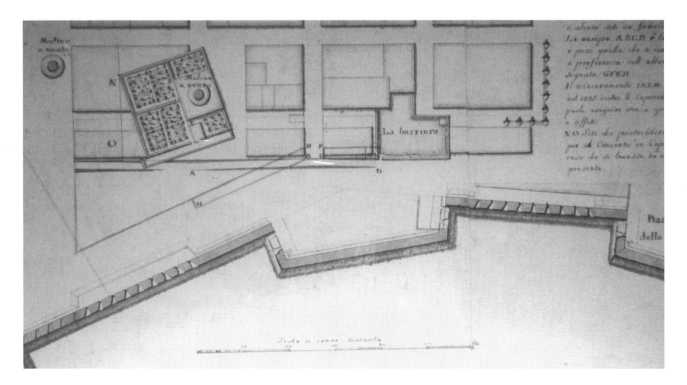

Graphic reconstruction showing the general layout of the Floriana land front fortifications c.1798.

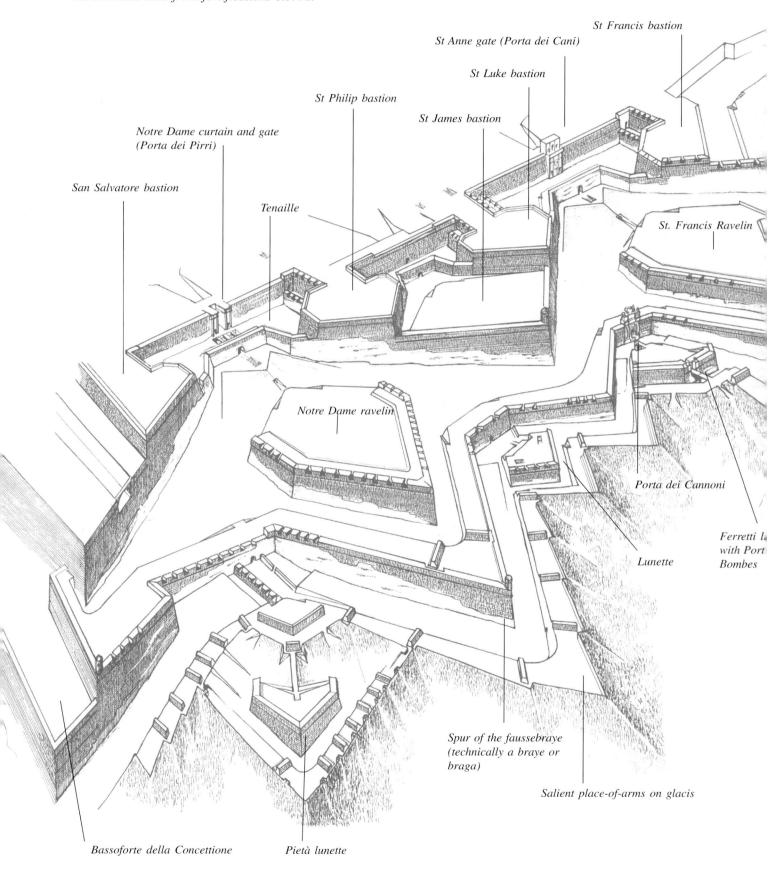

St Francis bastion

St Anne gate (Porta dei Cani)

St Luke bastion

St Philip bastion

St James bastion

Notre Dame curtain and gate
(Porta dei Pirri)

San Salvatore bastion

Tenaille

St. Francis Ravelin

Notre Dame ravelin

Porta dei Cannoni

Ferretti l
with Port
Bombes

Lunette

Spur of the faussebraye
(technically a braye or
braga)

Salient place-of-arms on glacis

Bassoforte della Concettione

Pietà lunette

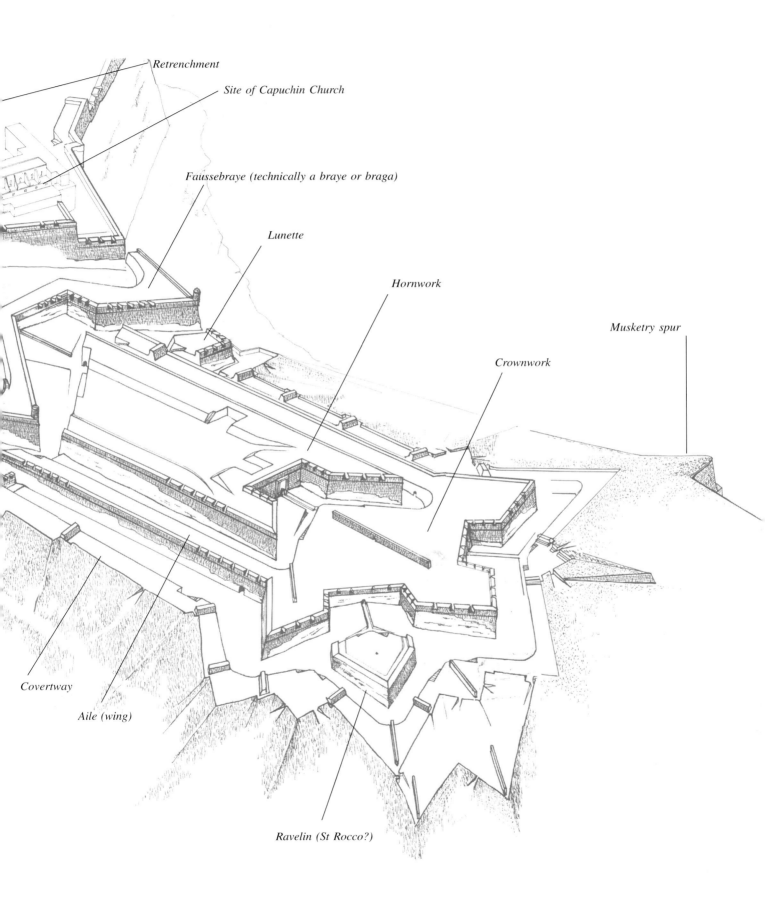

Retrenchment

Site of Capuchin Church

Faussebraye (technically a braye or braga)

Lunette

Hornwork

Musketry spur

Crownwork

Covertway

Aile (wing)

Ravelin (St Rocco?)

Some of the main gates of the Floriana lines. Left, *Porta dei Cannoni (frequently referred to as* Porte des Bombes*), middle left, the true* Porte des Bombes, *situated in the lunette outside the main gate. Bottom left, Notre Dame gate or* Porta dei Pirri, *so called because it had escutcheons bearing the arms of Grand Master Perellos. Above, St Anne gate or* Porta dei Cani, *as rebuilt by the British.*

the rear of San Salvatore bastion, since the salient angle of this bastion was too acute, and also in the gorge of the Capuchin bastion.[21]

The other faults which Tigné listed were the lack of caponiers connecting the main front to the two large ravelins, the lack of traverses and enough sally-ports in the *faussebraye*, the re-siting of the main gate in the re-entrant angle of the *faussebraye,* and the completion of the covertway and glacis. Tigné criticized the *Galdiana* as being too small but, since work on the latter was in an advanced stage, he realized that there was no other option but to complete it. The congregation of war recommended that the *Gran Consiglio* implement Tigné's proposals but, since Tigné was recalled back to France, his assistant Mondion was to remain and supervise the work. [22]

Tigné returned to Malta in early September 1716 and found that work on the Floriana fortifications had progressed further although most of his proposals had not been carried out. In his report of 15 September, Tigné allocated a total of 37,300 scudi for the completion of Floriana, and of these only 13,300 scudi for the most urgent works. Priority was to be given construction of the main gate 'et la lunette au devant la porte (300 scudi), ... des magazine à preuve de Bombe, ... quelques traverses et caponiers à faire dans le fossé' (1,000 scudi), the completion of the 'chemin couvert, ... la branche gauche de l'ouvrage a corne, le parapet su la courtine de la porte de Poires' (500 scudi), and the completion of the centre bastion of the front. As less urgent works, Tigné proposed three lunettes in front of the *faussebraye* as well as the completion of the covertway with its countermines.[24]

One of the last major works at Floriana was the construction of a 'secondo recinto alla sinistra della Floriana dalla parte di Marsamxetto per supplire alla debolezza di quello già fatto in quella parte vicino al mare per altro troppo basso', begun in 1731. This retrenchment spanned all the way from the salient angle of the covertway in front of St John counterguard right up to the bastion of Provence. It was also considered advisable to secure the gorge of Quarantine and Msida bastions with *trincieramenti*. By 1761 visiting French engineers complained these were still unfinished. For their size and strategic importance, the Floriana fortifications were surprisingly very lightly armed. In 1785 there were only ten guns on the crowned-hornwork, two on the Pietà ravelin, three at the Floriana chain post, and four on Polverista curtain.

On 13th June 1798, the Floriana land front underwent its baptism of fire when, at three o'clock in the morning, Napoleon's troops attacked Porte des Bombes. The Floriana lines were then under the command of the French knight D'Adelart who unwisely ordered the Maltese troops to place lighted lanterns on the ramparts. The Maltese, suspecting ulterior motives behind his orders, turned against him and cut him down. Taking over command, they managed to repulse the French attack. The fate of the Floriana lines, however, was not in the hands of its defenders and, on the following day, the gate at Porte des Bombes was thrown open to the French.[25]

Below, Plan of Polverista bastion and its Vauban-style magazine (NLM). Top, right, Plan of the spur of the musketry gallery facing Marsa (N L M). Right, 18th-century plan of the Floriana lines.

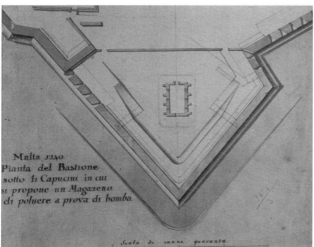

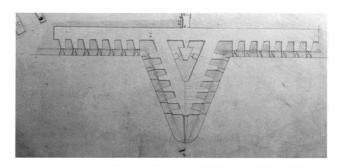

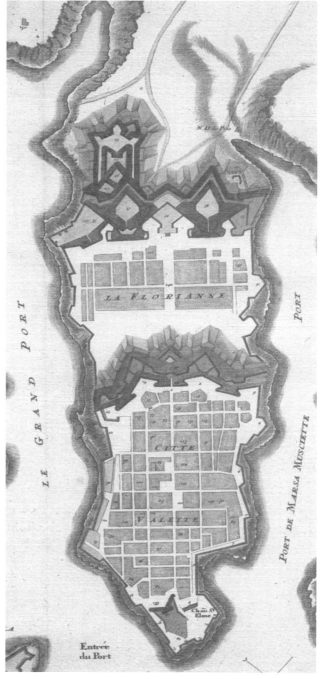

Sta Margherita Lines

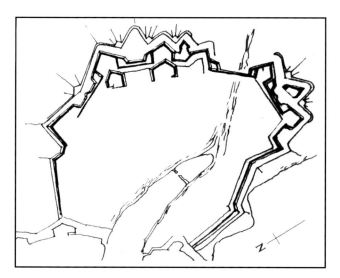

The vulnerability of Birgu and Senglea to enemy bombardment from the surrounding heights of San Salvatore and Sta Margherita was well illustrated during the Great Siege of 1565. Laparelli's recommendations to abandon these fortifications after the siege, however, could not be easily adopted by the knights since both towns, together with the creek which they enclosed, provided the safest accommodation for the Order's galleys and naval installations within the Grand Harbour area. The first tentative attempts by the Order's engineers to counteract the threat posed by these heights was the construction of cavaliers on Fort St Angelo and the Birgu land front. These, however, did little to remedy the situation for the only solution entailed the denial of these hills to the enemy by enclosing them within a defensive line.

The first to suggest this course of action was the military engineer Pietro Paolo Floriani in 1635. Floriani considered it necessary to fortify the Sta Margherita heights both in order to protect against 'Vascelli et a quelli che venissero di soccorso' and to defend Bormola, 'luogo incasar fuori dell'Isola di più d' 800 case'.[1] The Order was not convinced of Floriani's design and dispatched Giovanni Battista Vertoa round the courts of Italy to seek the expert opinion of foreign military engineers but before he returned in 1639, Vincenzo Maculano da Firenzuola was called to Malta to advise the Order on a new scheme of fortifications. In November of 1638, Firenzuola presented the Order with his own recommendations for the fortification of the Sta Margheirta heights. He judge these works of utmost importance 'per assicurare il porto, senza la cui sicurezza ne è da sperarsi soccorso in tempo d'assedio ne di potersi difendere dal nemico ... il Borgo e S. Michele'.

Firenzuola's proposals were accepted by the council and although a commission was appointed to examine his scheme in detail, the first stone was quickly laid down with due ceremony on 30 December 1638. Firenzuola's design comprised a fortified front of five bastions and a demi-bastion, linked by long lateral curtain walls to the fronts of Senglea and Vittoriosa, enveloping in the process the Sta Margherita heights and the hill in front of Senglea.[3] The enceinte was to be stiffened further with two large cavaliers, a ditch, tenailles, two ravelins, and a covertway. The whole set of fortifications was to be open at the rear thus enabling the defenders of Vittoriosa, Senglea, and Valletta to direct

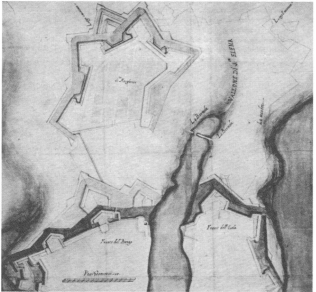

Above, top, Floriani's unexecuted proposal for the fortification of the Sta Margherita heights (after Hughes). Middle, Proposal to convert Firenzuola's unfinished enceinte into a closed fort. Bottom, Firenzuola's proposal to convert the enceinte into a detached fort (after Collignon). Following page, top left, Plan of the Sta Margherita lines showing Firenzuola's original scheme.

their fire onto the interior of the new fortified enceinte, 'non sara un forte chiuso che habbia bisogno d'esser guardato in ogni tempo, sara aperta al Borgo e a S. Michele anzi all stessa Città Valletta'.[4] Firenzuola estimated that these lines would cost the Order between '60 in 70 mila scudi che è niente rispetto al beneficio'.[5]

The design, however, encountered much criticism from many other contemporary military engineers, something which Firenzuola himself anticipated. In his report he pointed these out as being ' la spesa grande che andera in fabricarle' and the threat that the new works would pose were they ever to fall into the hands of an invading force. These fears he dismissed by stating that the new eneciente would be 'in tanta distanza dal Borgo e da S. Michele che da essi non potranno ricevere offese maggiore di quella che potra venirgli da quel posto emminente non fortificandosi' while their actual cost would not prove excessive.[6] Still, the general criticism that continued to be levelled against Firenzuola's fortifications was that these were too large to build and man.[7]

The desire to replace Firenzuola's scheme by a closed work was repeated frequently. Claudio Riccardo, engineer to the king of Spain, for example, when presented with the plans of the project for his appraisal, commented that Birgu and Senglea fronts could have been more effectively protected instead by two forts. One anonymous author proposed that Firenzuola's original enceinte be restricted from 914 to 520

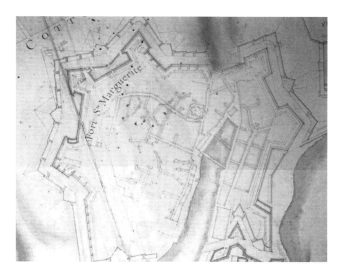

canne in order to enclose a smaller area for half the cost.[8] Unlike Firenzuola's design, which was calculated to require a garrison of about 1,800 soldiers, this restricted front required only 700 'soldati di guardia ordinaria si può ben mantenere, mettendosi 300 per giorno alla guardia della contrascarpa, 100 alla piazza d'armi, 100 al baluardo che verso la chiesa di S. Theresa conviene fabricarsi e 50 a

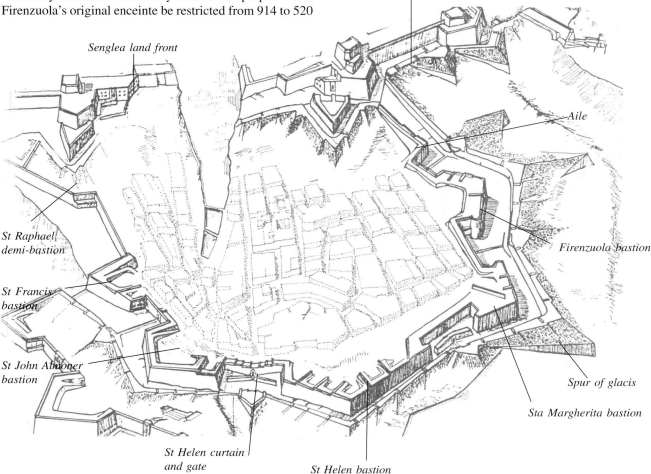

Senglea land front

Birgu land front

Aile

St Raphael demi-bastion

Firenzuola bastion

St Francis bastion

St John Almoner bastion

Spur of glacis

Sta Margherita bastion

St Helen curtain and gate

St Helen bastion

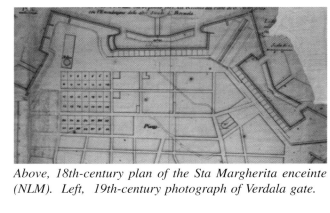

Above, 18th-century plan of the Sta Margherita enceinte (NLM). Left, 19th-century photograph of Verdala gate.

chiascuno delli altri baluardi.'[9]   A similar proposal, but this time for a singular fort, was put forward in 1645 by Capitano Domenico del Guazzo. The marquis of St Angelo, on the other hand, recommended that the part of the enceinte which had already been constructed by then be converted into a five bastioned fort, open at the rear, thereby enclosing solely the Sta Margherita hill.[10] Only Blaise François, Count

de Pagan, advocated the fortification of the two hills adjoining St Helen's valley. [11]

Yet, notwithstanding the conflicting advice and criticism, work on the Firenzuola lines went ahead. By 1645 the three central bastions on Sta Margherita hill were more or less completed but the rest of the enceinte had only been traced on site by means of trenches. The simultaneous construction of the Floriana and Firenzuola enceintes, however, placed enormous burdens on the Order's financial resources. As early 1639, Balì Valencay had estimated that the Sta Margherita project required a further 100,000 scudi before it could be completed.[12] Consequently the knights were forced to choose and it was decided to complete the Floriana lines first and postpone the construction of the Sta Margherita enceinte until such time when resources permitted.

For the next two decades the half-finished Sta Margherita lines remained practically abandoned. The construction of the Cottonera lines in 1670 by Grand Master Nicholas Cotoner contributed further towards the lack of interest in the Sta Margherita enceinte since the former enclosed the latter, robbing it of much of its front-line importance. Firenzuola himself, in a letter to the Order, proposed that if the lines could not be completed, then the three finished bastions be converted into a detached fort whose rear,

Original trace of St Helen curtain demolished in the 1700s

Verdala gate

St Helen's curtain

Tenaille

Sta Margherita bastion

Tenaille

Gate

Firenzuola bastion

Sally-port

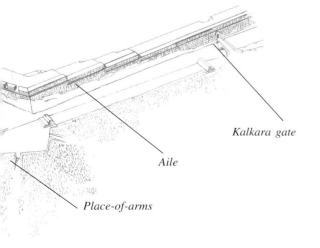

View from St John Cavalier, Birgu, showing the Sta Margherita fortifcations. Left, Small gate facing Kalkara, now demolished (National Museum of Archaeology).

overlooking Senglea, was to be defended by a tenaille flanked with two round towers.[13]

For decades nothing much was done on these fortiifications until the arrival of French military engineers in 1715. Tigné and his team of engineers believed that the Sta Margherita lines were more important than the Cottonera lines and estimated that these could be respectibly completed for some 81,000 scudi, of which 76,000 were to finance the most urgent works such as the completion of the 'glacis et chemin couvert devant les trois Bastions de la tête de ce fort', the forming of 'les ramparts dans l'interieur', and the construction of the vital lines of communication linking the Sta Margherita fortifications to Birgu, and Senglea land front.[14]

Tigné's assistant, Mondion, was entrusted with the supervision of the work. In 1719 he advised the Order to develop the unfinished bastion of St John Almoner in such a way that it could easily be converted into a redoubt. The congregation of fortification resolved to allocate '4,000 scudi che si incominci il Bastion di s. Gio. d'Auscia per farne una ridotta, che cuopra l'Isola e il porto'.[15] St Helen bastion and curtain were enlarged and re-positioned to enable a better defence of the valley. By 1761 the Sta Margherita lines were more-or-less completed, presenting

Kalkara gate

Aile

Place-of-arms

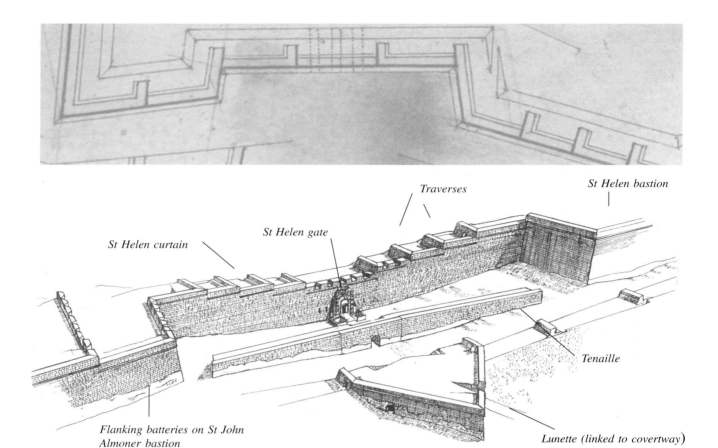

St Helen curtain

St Helen gate

Traverses

St Helen bastion

Flanking batteries on St John Almoner bastion

Tenaille

Lunette (linked to covertway)

Above,top, Plan of the proposed layout of St Helen curtain (NLM) and general view as actually built. Bottom, right, St Helen gate during the mid-19th century (National Museum of Archaeology).

an unbroken trace of bastions. Even so, François Bourlamaque considered them to be far from perfect and believed that these could only be held for a few days against a determined attack.[16] He recommended that Tigné's earlier proposal for a hornwork projecting from Sta Margherita into the unoccupied space between the two sets of lines be built so as to deny an enemy the possibility of roaming around freely were the outer Cottonera lines to fall to the enemy.[17]

The Order continued to struggle with the completion of Sta Margherita fortifications up to the end of its rule in 1798. Although, in some respects, this vast enceinte was never actually finished and perfected according to eighteenth-century standards, it did, however, offer a further intact and substantial obstacle which would have delayed attackers for a considerable time once bravely and diligently defended. Eve so, the Sta Margherita played no part in the events of 1798.

Cottonera Lines

The fall of Candia to the Turks in 1670, rekindled the fear of a Turkish invasion and Grand Master Nicholas Cotoner decided to settle once and for all the question of the harbour's security. The fortifications designed by Firenzuola to enclose the Sta Margherita hill in 1638 were then still far from completed and had been practically abandoned for nearly a decade. The Italian engineer Antonio Maurizio Valperga was summoned to the island to inspect its defences and submit his proposals.[1] Valperga presented a scheme for a new trace of eight bastions, encircling the Sta Margherita and San Salvatore hills and joining the extremities of the old fronts of Vittoriosa and Senglea. The new enceinte was to be strengthened further with cavaliers and large ravelins. Further protection to the harbour was to be afforded by a new fort on Gallows point opposite St Elmo.

To finance this ambitious project, the common treasury was instructed to pay out 8,000 scudi a month (96,000 scudi a year), to which 100 scudi a month were added from the grand master's own pocket, some 100,000 scudi from taxation, and 300,000 livres from the sale of wood from the Order's property in France.[2] The scheme was approved by the council on 2 April 1670 and work on the new enceinte was initiated in the following August with a stone-laying ceremony on the site of St Nicholas bastion together with a procession and solemn religious ceremonies as befitted such a monumental endeavour.[3] Work on these new fortifications continued incessantly and when Grand Master Cotoner died in 1680, the main body of the enceinte had already been laid down under the supervision of Mederico Blondel, the resident engineer.[4]

Valperga's scheme received much criticism from the outset. It was considered too ambitious and costly. The Milanese engineer Gaspare Beretta believed that the bastions and curtains were too small and recommended instead a trace of six bastions with faces of 60 paces (240 feet) and curtains of 100 paces (400 feet) to enclose the same area.[5] Since the bastions were constructed so close to each other, Beretta believed that it was impossible to construct *mezzealune buone* in front of these.[6] Count Vernada, on the other hand, favoured retaining the original eight bastions but preferred to extend the enceinte in both directions to enclose the Corradino hills, Bighi, and the Rinella peninsula.[7] Writing in 1681, Blondel, voicing Beretta, believed that Valperga's scheme followed the Dutch school, *all' Olandese,* in trying to impose a geometrically regular trace on an irregular

Above, Pianta Generale delle Fortificationi di Malta, Relativa al discorso fatto del Conte Verneda Ingegnere della Republic. *Count Verneda, chief engineer of the Venetian Republic, proposed to extend Valperga's design to enclose Salvatore and Orsi points (NLM). Below, Francesco Collignon's map of the Grand Harbour, showing Vaperga's scheme.*

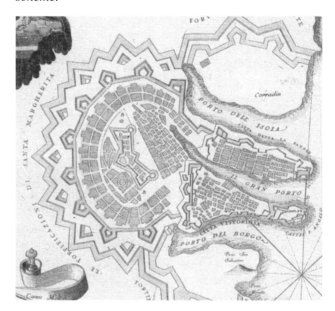

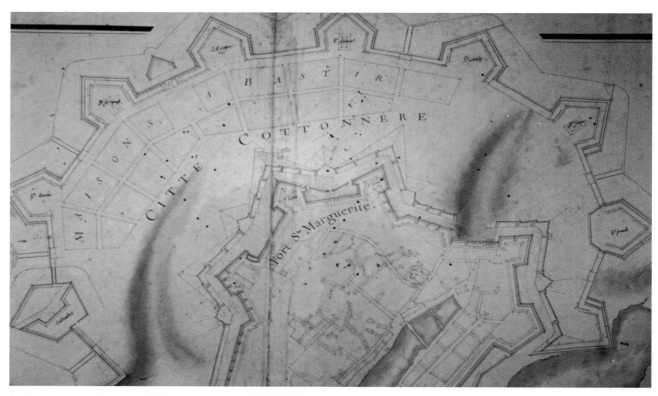

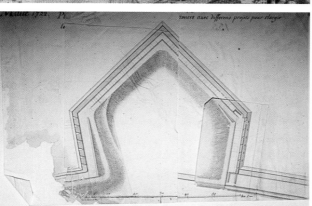

Above, Plan of the Cottonera and Sta Margherita lines drawn by the French military mission in 1714 (National Museum of Archaeology). Left, The Cottonera lines in the 18th century. Bottom, plan of St John bastion and adjoining enceinte (NLM).

terrain.[8] But such ideas were by then becoming obsolete in the light of the new system that was being propagated by Vauban, which Blondel preferred. However, as major alterations were by then impossible to effect, Blondel limited his suggestions to recommend the widening of the ditch, the construction of *piazze basse* or low flanking batteries, the re-siting of the still-unbuilt cavaliers, the extension of the terreplein to allow for the later construction of internal retrenchments, and the erection of two new counterguards in front of the bastions of St Louis and St John in order to impede enemy attacks from the north-east and south respectively. Grunenberg too, in 1681, was not convinced with the layout of the land front with its resultant restricted potential for enfilading fire provided from the flanks of the bastions and advised the Order to complete Valperga's design by building the projected *mezzelune*.[9] Valperga himself, after his departure from Malta in October 1670, retained an interest in the development of the project and, in 1680, urged the Order to ensure the completion of the fortified lines by constructing the ravelins which featured in his original plan.[10]

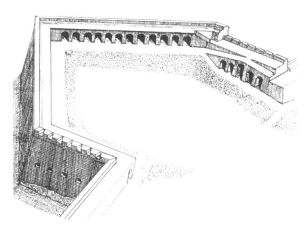

Graphic view of St John bastion showing its casemates and vaulted batteries in the flank. Valperga's intention was to arm each bastion with a cavalier.

Within a decade of their initiation, however, the Cottonera lines had consumed most of the funds allocated for their construction such that Grand Master Gregorio Carafa (1680-90) ordered the cessation of the project and as a result the ravelins were never built while the project was virtually abandoned.[11] By 1715 the Cottonera fortifications had consumed the sum of 1,400,000 scudi and were still far from complete. The French engineers then called to the island gave priority to the completion of other half-finished

works such as Fort Ricasoli and Floriana. As a result work on the Cottonera lines had to be temporarily abandoned except for San Salvatore bastion which they recommended be converted into a detached fort. Philippe de Vendôme, grand prior of France, and the French engineer Philippe Maigret, on the contrary, believed that priority had to be given to the urgent completion of the Cottonera lines after the Floriana fortifications were finished.[12] They believed that the Cottonera lines were better suited to provide shelter for the Maltese population than the Sta Margherita lines, which were preferred by Tigné and his team. It was then estimated that some 40,000 inhabitants could be sheltered within the walls of the Cottonera lines in the event of an invasion.[13] Tigné considered that some 128,000 scudi were required before both the Cottonera and Sta Margherita lines could be completed.[14] The Cotoner foundation, which had been set up by Grand Master Nicholas Cotoner to finance the construction of these works was, however, being drained in order to finance the construction of Fort Ricasoli leaving little for the completion of the massive enceinte. The French engineers were much more in favour of completing the Sta Margherita enceinte but in any case eventually agreed to retrench the San Salvatore bastion overlooking the Post of Castile in Birgu, 'une nécessité pour la plus grande protection de cette partie de faire le retraunchement proposé dans la gorge du Bastione du Salvador', which was estimated

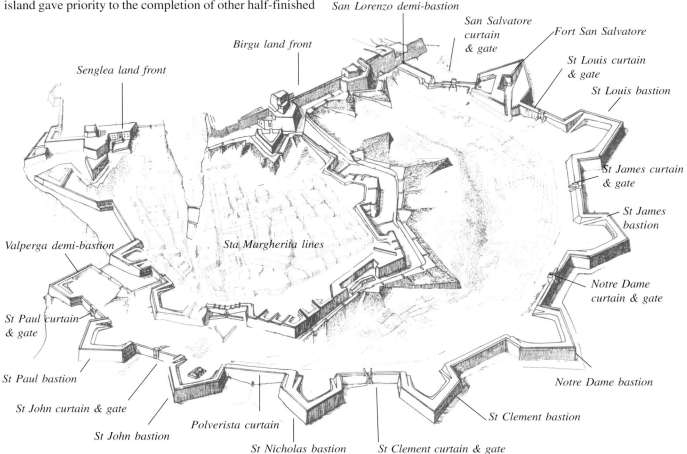

San Lorenzo demi-bastion

San Salvatore curtain & gate

Fort San Salvatore

St Louis curtain & gate

St Louis bastion

Birgu land front

Senglea land front

St James curtain & gate

St James bastion

Valperga demi-bastion

Sta Margherita lines

Notre Dame curtain & gate

St Paul curtain & gate

St Paul bastion

Notre Dame bastion

St John curtain & gate

St Clement bastion

St John bastion

Polverista curtain

St Nicholas bastion

St Clement curtain & gate

The gates of the Cottonera lines, below, Notre Dame or Zabbar gate, above, left to right, San Salvatore, St Louis, St James and St John.

to cost only 4,000 scudi.[15] Work on the retrenchment in San Salvatore bastion was supervised by Mondion and Fort San Salvatore, as it came to be called, was completed in 1724. The retrenchment consisted of a short casemated curtain flanked by two small casemated demi-bastions built into the bastion in such a way that it divided it into two. By 1788 Fort Salvatore was armed with four 4-pdr iron guns. In 1761 French engineers recommended that this fort be mined to prevent it from falling to the enemy and being turned against the Birgu.[15]

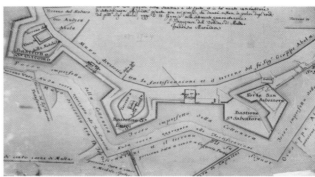

Tigné's programme for the Cottonera lines in the early eighteenth century, while setting aside the costly construction of the mezzalunas, allocated a sum of 47,500 scudi for works such as the construction of 'trois magazines a poudre en forme de retrenchments dans le gorge des bastion' at a cost of 9000 scudi, 10,000 scudi 'pour former une contrescarpe de 10 a 12 pau', and 15,000 scudi for the levelling of the ditch.[16] Works of a more urgent nature comprised the finishing of parapets (6,000 scudi), the construction of three 'ordinarij magazines, une communicatione au pied des ramparts pour le mouvement de troupes et de cannon', and the construction of a tenaille in front of Notre Dame gate, which was re-designed by the Italian architect Romano Carapecchia.[17]

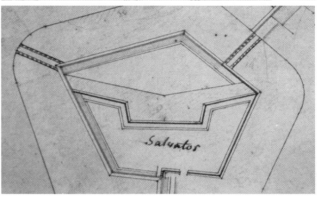

Fort San Salvatore is actually a retrenched bastion, above, right (NLM). One French proposal, right, involved the conversion of the bastion into a detached polygonal fort, surrounded by its own ditch and caponiers (National Museum of Archaeology). Below, Fort San Salvatore.

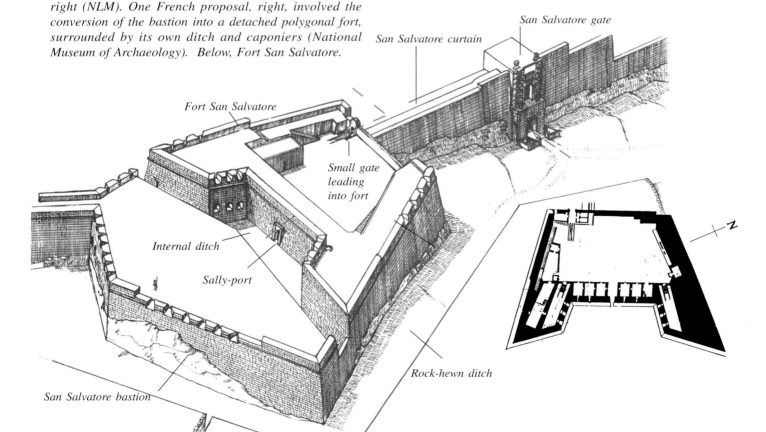

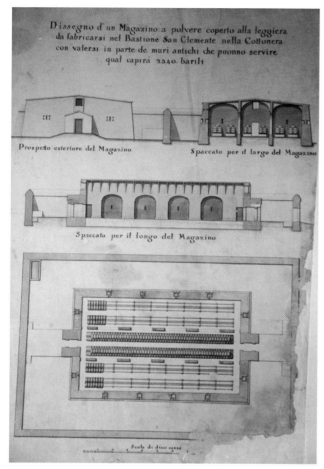

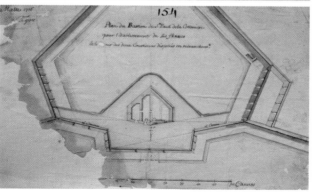

The Birgu land front was strengthened further by the construction of St Lawrence demi-bastion and St Ursula platform which were connected to Fort San Salvatore. In 1715 Tigné had recommended that the esplanade, the unoccupied area between the Cottonera and Sta Margherita lines, be defended by a hornwork projecting from the latter.[18] This would have assured against the threatening possibility of having an enemy roaming around between the two lines. Further still, the large bastions of the Cottonera lines were open at the gorge and this rendered their defenders vulnerable to attack from the rear. In 1719 the congregation of war allocated 3,500 scudi for the construction of 'tutte le piatteforme dei fianchi della Cottonera nella maniera più solida che si potra', 500 scudi for the completion of St Nicholas bastion, 600 scudi for the levelling of the ditch in front of St Clement bastion, and 3,000 scudi to finish 'di tutto punto il fortino nel bastione del Salvatore con i suoi magazini.'[19]

The French military mission which arrived in Malta in 1761 formed a poor opinion of the defensive potential of the Cottonera lines and believed that these would only be able to hold out a few days in the event of a determined siege. They thus urged the Order to carry out Tigné's recommendations made nearly half-a-century earlier.[20] The French engineers under Pontleroy also suggested a number of retrenchments as a partial remedy to rectifying the inherent weaknesses of the Cottonera works. They proposed to retrench the bastions at the gorge with tenailles beyond which were to be casemated redoubts. These interesting works, however, were never constructed though the idea was eventually taken up by the British in the nineteenth century and implemented in at least two of the bastions.

Like the Sta Margherita lines, the Cottonera enceinte was more-or-less completed between 1723 and 1761, that is, it formed at least an unbroken trace of bastions enclosing Birgu and Senglea. Still, it was never finished since the ravelins and cavaliers, together with the ditch and the covertway as originally proposed by Valperga, were never constructed. Moreover, the massive enceinte required a garrison of more than 5,000 men to be defended properly. The few regiments of country militia which had managed to retreat behind its walls during the French invasion in 1798 had little hope of conducting an adequate defence. Even so, these massive walls presented the French troops with a large obstacle and their task was made much easier by fifth columnists who threw open the gates.

Left, top, Plan of a large powder magazine for St Clement bastion. Left, middle, St Paul gate, demolished in the late nineteenth century. Left, bottom, A proposed retrenchment in St Paul bastion (NLM).

Fort Ricasoli

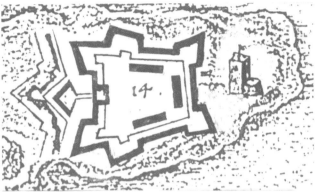

The Grand Harbour is flanked by two mandibles of rock, the tip of the Sciberras peninsula and the promontory known as the Gallows point or Rinella. The earliest fortifications built on Gallows point date back to 1602, when the council decreed that a sea-level battery be built there to prevent slaves from escaping by boat.[1] A small semicircular battery was erected on the site in 1629, together with a tower, at the expense of the knight Alessandro Orsi, after whom it was named, although it was also known as the San Petronio battery.[2] It was only in the late 1630s that serious suggestions were made expressing concern for the threat posed by this stretch of land to the security of Valletta and its harbour. There were then many military engineers who believed that it was necessary to fortify the promontory. Amongst these were Count Ferrente Bolognino, Giovanni de Garay, and the Marquis of St Angelo, Giovanni de Medici.[3] The latter proposed a fort *alla Punta dell'Orso* with a land front of two bastions and a ravelin separated from the mainland by a dry ditch.[4] His proposed fort was intended to occupy half the area of the present fort and incorporate the San Petronio battery into its enceinte.[5] Athough the council approved the marquis' recommendations, nothing was done to implement the scheme for such a work came well down the list of the Order's priorities.

In 1645 another visiting military expert, Giovanni Bendinelli Pallavicino, again urged the Order to fortify Orsi Point as a fortified work erected there would ensure the safety of the Grand Harbour, 'pare che convenga applicar l'animo principalmente alla conservatione di quello porto, quale totalmente consiste nell'entrata della Ponta degl'Ursi.'[6] Blaise François, Count de Pagan, similarly urged the Order to fortify the Rinella peninsula and to execute the 'disegno del Marchese di S. Angelo' without, however, fortifying the side facing the 'Salvatore, gia che la rocca di quella parte è da se stessa tanto scarpata, e cosi alta che alli nemici resta inacessibile e abbasta fare un parapetto.'[7] Pagan preferred to surround the rocky shore outside the proposed fort with a parapet *a fior d'acqua* in order to deny the enemy the possibility of gaining a foothold

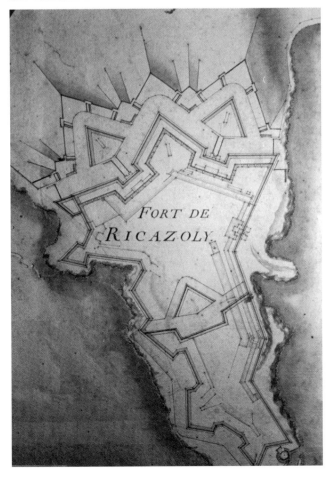

Right, from top to bottom: Orsi tower, 17th-century proposal for a fort on Gallows point, and plan of Fort Ricasoli showing Tigné's proposed internal retrenchment (NLM).

on 'quel gran spatio che restera nella parte d'abasso'.[8] He even suggested that the new fort should be strengthened by a tower *(una torre superiore)* or cavalier so as to reduce the need for a large garrison.

It was not before 1670, however, that a decision was actually taken to build a new fort 'nell'entrata della Ponta degl'Ursi'. This occurred when Count Antonio Maurizio Valperga was invited to Malta to help prepare an overall scheme for the defence of the southern approaches to the harbour.[9] The construction of the new fort commenced in June 1670 and was made possible by the generosity of the knight Giovanni Francesco Ricasoli who donated 20,000 scudi to help finance the project. Twenty-three years later, in 1693, the fort was still under construction and by then some 100,000 scudi had already been spent on it. It was finally completed and fitted with artillery in 1698.[10]

Valperga's fort was designed with its major defences facing southwards. Its land front occupied the neck of the peninsula and consisted basically of a crownwork connected by short curtain walls to two demi-bastions. The gorge of the bastions and the connecting curtains were fitted with a large number of bomb-proof casemated barracks. Internal passages enabled the safe movement of troops from one section to another along the land front. The main front was protected further by a *faussebraye*, two ravelins, and a ditch. The rest of the enceinte comprised two fronts, a seaward facing bastioned enceinte fitted with powerful batteries and a tenaille trace overlooking the harbour.

This page, top, 18th-century engraving showing Fort Ricasoli as seen from the sea. Above, The main gate and the governor's house to the rear, also shown from the interior, above. This building, which also housed an armoury, was hit by bombs during the Second World War. Only the gate itself was rebuilt. Above, right, The church of St Nicholas (National Museum of Archaeology).

Although Fort Ricasoli was designed as a closed fort, its interior was commanded by the batteries and bastions of Valletta. Most of the internal area was occupied by a large barren *piazza* in which were sited a chapel, two large barrack blocks, a few small buildings, and a powder magazine. Six sally-ports enabled the defenders to reach every part of the outerworks; two on the land front, one behind St Domenic demi-bastion, two leading to the ditch on the rocky shore facing the sea, and one leading to the San Petronio battery which was left outside the new enceinte. The main gate faced the harbour and was protected by a ditch and fitted with a drawbridge.

The design of Fort Ricasoli attracted its fair share of criticism. Both Blondel, in July 1671, and then Grunenberg in March 1681, considered it to be a mere 'figura di un obra coronada'.[11] The curtain walls on the land front were seen to be too short and the bastions too small to enable adequate enfilading fire. Those bastions facing the sea, on the other hand, were preceded by a large stretch of rocky shore on which an enemy could easily gain a foothold. Blondel modified the design of the flanks of the fort to decrease the amount of dead ground in front of the ramparts and also proposed the construction of low outerworks on the rocky shore facing the sea. These, however, were not built.[12] In 1681, and again in 1687, Grunenberg suggested a large semicircular battery be built at the tip of the promontory 'a la entrada del puerto, al pie del Ricasoli sopra la rocca a flor d'acqua', near the San Petronio battery

so as to command the entrance to the harbour.[13] The Milanese engineer Gaspare Beretta, while confirming the advantages gained by the fortification of the site, criticized Fort Ricasoli as being too small and its ravelins as being too close to the bastions on the land front. He also thought it necessary to enclose 'più sito, che si facessero corpi maggiori per la parte di terra, e li rivelini più staccati da baloardi, et difesi dalle cortine'.[14]

By the end of the 1680s, Fort Ricasoli was in an advanced stage of completion. Work on the barrack blocks and the powder magazines began in the 1685, that on the governor's house in 1686 and on the chapel of St Nicholas in 1696.[15] An inscription on the gateway states that Fort Ricasoli was completed in 1698, the same year that the council appointed a governor to command the fort. Fort Ricasoli was manned, garrisoned, and equipped with artillery and munitions out of the Cottonera foundation, a fund set up by Grand Master Nicholas Cotoner on 12 June 1674. Around 1785, the fort

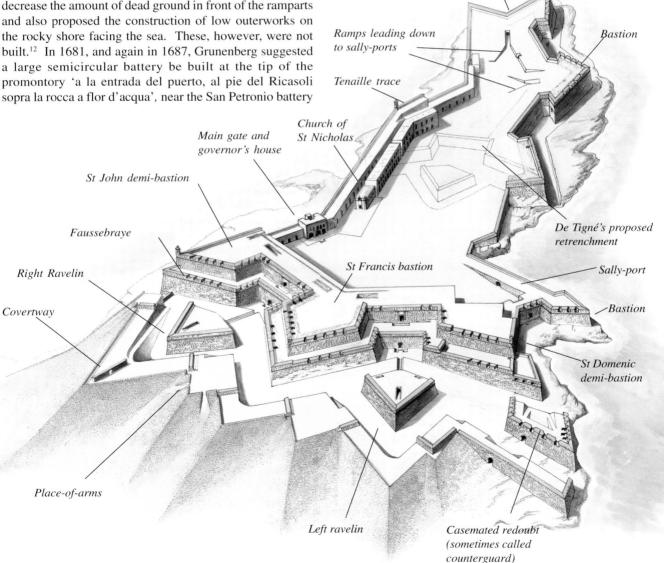

Orsi Tower & Battery (hidden from view)

Bastione delle forbici

Ramps leading down to sally-ports

Bastion

Tenaille trace

Church of St Nicholas

Main gate and governor's house

St John demi-bastion

Faussebraye

De Tigné's proposed retrenchment

Right Ravelin

St Francis bastion

Sally-port

Covertway

Bastion

St Domenic demi-bastion

Place-of-arms

Left ravelin

Casemated redoubt (sometimes called counterguard)

was armed with a total of 80 cannon and 20 mortars and *petreros*, the calibre of the guns ranging from as low as six ounces up to 24-pdr.

The arrival of the French military mission in Malta in 1715, under Tigné, found Fort Ricasoli armed and garrisoned, and fulfilling its intended role in the defence of the entrance to the Grand Harbour. Still, the French engineers were not much impressed by its ability to withstand a siege. Tigné, like many engineers before him, was convinced that the bastions on the land front were too small and too close together to enable a good defence. He found that the ditch, covertway, and glacis were still unfinished and recommended that these be completed. He also proposed that a large semicircular battery be constructed at Orsi point to cover the entrance to the Harbour but both these proposals were never carried out.[16] Tigné's principal solution for the defence of the work was to recommend the excavation of an internal retrenchment half-way down the fort.[17] The grand prior of France, Philippe de Vendôme, in his turn suggested that Fort Ricasoli could be considerably strengthened if isolated from the rest of the mainland by means of a sea-filled moat. So did Maigret, although he considered the scheme as being too costly.[18] As things turned out, none of these major projects were ever implemented.

Above, 18th-century plan of the land front defences of Fort Ricasoli showing the network of countermines, or 'mine', excavated beneath the covertway and glacis (NLM).

The construction of the outerworks, mainly the covertway and the glacis, were the only part of Valperga's design that had still not been attended to by 1716, the year of Tigné's second visit to Malta. Consequently work on the *opere avvanzate* was given prominence and Tigné estimated that some 10,950 scudi were required before the fort could be considered satisfactorily defended. Of these, 3,950 scudi were to be directed towards the reforming of the covertway and the construction of 'le place d'armes et traverses ordinaires' (100 scudi).[19] Two hundred scudi were thought necessary for the construction of the *pas-de-souris* leading from the ditch to the re-entrant place-of-arms and 400 scudi for the construction of 'deux caponiers de communicatione du fort dans les demi-lunes et six traverses de retraite, dans le fossés.' He also thought pressing the repairs to the parapet and banquettes and the construction of a large 'traverse sous le bastion de la droite, ...decouvre dans le fond de la Rinela'. Tigné also proposed a small redoubt or 'demi-contragarde sur la côté gauche de ce fort, trop decouvert, de la mer et de la terre' in order to protect the salient angle of St Domenic demi-bastion.

No progress had as yet been made on these works by 1719. The alarm of 1722, however, ensured that most of Tigné's recommendations were executed and that the covertway, traverses, parapets, and caponiers were brought to completion. The glacis was heavily mined but the internal retrenchment, the sea-level and battery and the demi-counterguard were not built. In 1761 Bourlamaque and his group of French engineers had little to add to Tigné's remarks. They stressed that his recommendations be implemented, paticularly the construction of 'le retrenchements interieur proposé par M. de Tigné ... nécessaire de conserver et reparer incessamment les revetements et parapets.' [20]

In 1789 the redoubt or demi-counterguard proposed by Tigné was added to the left flank of the land front under the supervision of the Balì Rene Jacques de Tigné.[21] Under his directions, repairs were made on the covertway and the seaward enceinte but the Cottonera foundation was soon exhausted and the works were suspended.[22] The fort's exposure to the heavy seas led to the rapid deterioration of its walls, so that by 1752 it was already reported that Fort Ricasoli was in a very bad state of repair.[23] The latter half of the eighteenth century, thus, saw the intermittent repair and renovation of its walls. On 25 August 1792 the congregation of war approved a scheme for repairs to the fort which works were undertaken under the supervision of 'Il Sig. Ingegnere' Tousard.[23] Later that year, on 5 November, the congregation ordered that the fort be armed with a total of 64 guns, of which 31 were 24-pounders, 22 were 12-pounders. There were also two 18-pounders, seven 8-pounders and two 4-pounders.[24]

In the closing years of the eighteenth century Fort Ricasoli was absorbing a fair share of the Order's expenditure but, by 1798, the repairs to Fort Ricasoli had eventually come to a halt. Napoleon's troops found the fort very well prepared and adequately provisioned to withstand repeated assaults. It was then under the command of Balì de Tillet who, together with some companies from the Regiment of Cacciatori, repulsed three French attacks. Its gates were only thrown open to the French troops after the Order's capitulation.

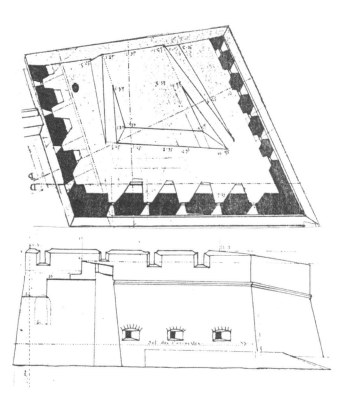

Above, right, One of the two sally-ports which open into the main ditch of Fort Ricasoli. The original opening was reduced in size by the British. Originally, the sally-port was served by an open caponier of communication, linking it to the ravelin. This, however, was later replaced by the British with a vaulted and loopholed caponier (National Museum of Archaeology). Below, Plan and elevation of the casemated redoubt, or demi-counterguard as it is sometimes referred to, which was built in the last quarter of the 18th century in order to secure the left extremity of the ditch, where it meets the sea (NLM).

Fort Manoel

Inside Marsamxett harbour lies a small leaf-shaped island once known as the *Isoletto*. Its strategic value emerged with the construction of Valletta on Mount Sciberras, when the threat it posed to the western flanks of the new city began to feature prominently in the engineers' reports. The earliest scheme to fortify this little island appears to have been proposed in 1569, in a report 'Discorso sopra le fortificatione' signed 'Cavagliere di Malta', written by an anonymous foreign member of the Order who realized that the enemy would attack Valletta from Marsamxett Harbour and bombard St Michael's bastion from the *Isoletto*.[1] To deny the enemy this possibility, the 'Cavagliere di Malta' proposed the construction of a 'piatta forma' with 'due teste dipendente, affine che nella batteria che vi si facesse sempre vi restasse piazza di buona forma.'[2] This small fort, consisting of a cavalier surrounded by a detached low battery, was to be surrounded by a glacis but this work was never taken in hand even though the threat posed by the 'Isoletto assai eminente' was again demonstrated by Scipione Campi in 1577 and by Giovanni Battista in 1582.[3]

In 1643 the land on the *Isoletto*, which then belonged to cathedral chapter of Mdina, was acquired by the Order in exchange for an area of land known as Tal-Fiddien, in the vicinity of Rabat, in order to enable the knights to build the *Lazzareto,* a quarantine hospital.[4] It was only in the late seventeenth century, however, that the Order seriously began contemplating the fortification of the *Isoletto*. In 1760 Maurizio Valperga produced a scheme for the defence of the harbour in which he included a design for a fort to defend the *Isoletto*.[5] Francesco Collignon's plan of the harbour, dated 1688, probably shows Valperga's fort.[6] This depicts an irregular hexagonal work with four bastions and one demi-bastion facing Valletta. A small hornwork protected the fort's land front while a small tenaille, connected to the covertway by a small caponier, was so designed to command the harbour.[7]

Valperga's proposed fort was criticized both by Count Vernada and Blondel in 1671, as being too small. This prompted Grunenberg in 1682, to design a larger fort with a 'falsabraga, assi a los dos flances, como a la cortina, su fosso abierto, ravelin, estrada en cubierta, y explanada, y la demas obra que la revine'.[8] At that time, however, the Order was already heavily committed to the construction of the Cottonera lines and Fort Ricasoli and, consequently, the erection of yet a new fort fell well down the list of its priorities.

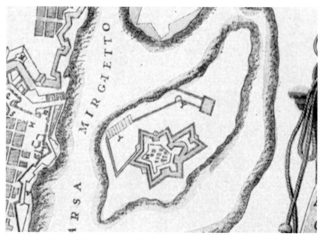

Above, Detail from Collignon's map of Valletta and its harbours, possibly showing Valperga's proposal for a fort on the Isoletto. Bottom, Plan and section of Tigné's fort proposed in 1715 (National Museum of Archaeology).

The next recommendations came in 1715 when the French engneer Tigné designed a small square fort with four corner bastions and a ravelin on its land front with which the knights could deny an enemy 'la facilité des'establir, d'on ne parroit por in commander la Cité Vallette et attaquer la Religion dans son centre.'[9] He estimated that this would cost 25,000 scudi. Philippe Maigret, on the other hand, proposed a small casemated redoubt with covertway and *polverista*, to be situated in the middle of the *Isoletto* and connected by a long caponier to a large battery covering

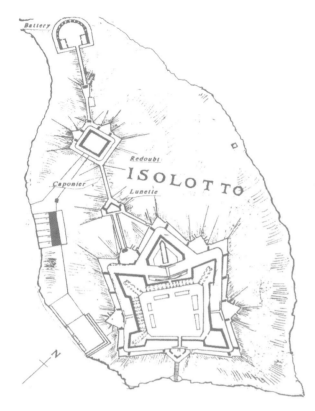

a dry ditch and a covertway with two places-of-arms. The centre of the redoubt was to be occupied by a conical *polverista* similar to the one later built inside Fort Chambrai. The stretches of caponier linking the various works were reinforced at intervals by short traverses with crochets, i.e. short and narrow passages made round the head of the traverse to enable troops to bypass the traverse when moving along the caponier or covertway.

The fort designed by Tigné was a star-shaped work with four corner bastions, a large ravelin, and tenaille in the ditch. One version of his design shows an asymmetrical fort contorted to one side. Both engineers, however, classified this project as being non-urgent and were ready to postpone the building of the fort until the Order's financial position rendered itself more favourable. The opportunity presented itself during the reign of Grand Master Antonio Manoel de Vilhena. The decision to fortify the *Isoletto* was finally taken in 1723, and this was only made possible by the grand master's generosity. Charles François de Mondion, the Order's resident engineer, was commissioned to design the new work, but in effect Mondion only modified and elaborated Tigné's original design ('le Forte Manoel execute par MM. le Chev. Mondion d'apres les projets de M. le Chev. de Tigné').[12]

the narrow strip of water separating the island from the mainland for the cost of 2,600 scudi.[10] Contemporary plans reveal that both these proposals were incorporated in another elaborate scheme, whereby troops inside the battery could retreat safely in stages through the long caponier to the separate outerworks, i.e. to the redoubt, through the lunette, and up to the place-of-arms, and into the fort. The large casemated redoubt, roughly in the centre of the island was a perfect square in design and was to be surrounded by

The first stone was laid with due ceremony by the grand master on 14 September 1723, in the presence of 'molte Gran Croce e da una grande comitiva di Cavaglieri, affinchè

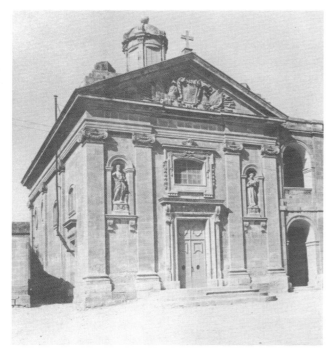

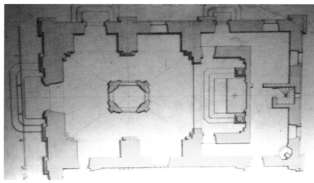

Above, The main gate of Fort Manoel. Left, Façade and plan of the chapel of St Anthony of Padua. (NLM - Museum of Archaeology).

ben fosse in sua presenza collocata la prima pietra in detta fabbrica, come seguito dopo aver l'Emin. Sua lasciato a futura memoria diverse monite.'[13] Vilhena offered to pay for the fort and established a fund of 6,000 scudi to provide for its garrison and maintenance 'con intenzione altresi di stabilire una rendita annoale e sicura che basta a mantenere un competente presidio.'[14] Work on the fort progressed rapidly and, by 1732, the ditch had already been excavated.[15] The date on the main gate reads 1726.

The design of Fort Manoel, as it was called, encountered no criticism. Its low silhouette and system of bastioned trace, making the widest use of crossfire to sweep the approaches, was then in line with the latest developments in the art of fortification. In 1761 Bourlamaque described Fort Manoel as 'un model de fortification fait avec soin, et fini dans toutte ses parties.'[16] In plan, the fort was a square with four corner bastions, a tenaille, and a ravelin in the ditch facing the land front and a small demi-lune *(couvre porte)* facing the sea. The bastions on the land front were strengthened by two low cavaliers joined together by a long curtain wall fitted with eleven embrasures and containing large bomb-proof barrel-vaulted casemates. These were designed to accommodate the garrison in times of siege. The outer bastions facing the harbour were each provided with a large gunpowder magazine or *polverista*.

Inside the fort, the space was occupied by a large piazza, or parade ground. This was flanked on three of its sides by barrack blocks and a chapel dedicated to St Anthony of Padua. A marble slab in the chapel has the date 1755 inscribed on it. The design of the chapel is popularly attributed to the Italian architect Romano Carapecchia who was also responsible for designing the Notre Dame gate on the Cottonera lines but may have actually been designed by Mondion himself.[17] Two of the four barrack blocks were built on either side of the chapel. The one adjoining the chapel housed the chaplain and the fort's second-in-command. The other block, to the left, housed the commander of the fort together with a large armoury. Beneath the *piazza*, two huge underground cisterns provided the fort with its own water supply. A life-size bronze statue of Grand Master Manoel de Vilhena, commissioned by Chevalier Savasse, was erected in the middle of the *piazza*. This may have been the work of the Maltese sculptor Pietro Paolo Troisi.[18]

The main entrance to the fort was through a baroque gateway in the centre of the east curtain between the bastions of St Anthony and St Helen. Internally, the gateway was flanked by two guardrooms, each fitted with two musketry loopholes facing the approaches to the gate. In front of the gate, was a small drop-ditch defended by a wooden palisade. The fort was flanked on three of its sides by a deep rock-hewn ditch. On top of the counterscarp ran a wide covertway fitted with traverses, places-of-arms, and cuttings that enabled the defenders to sally forth onto the glacis. Three sally-ports and caponiers connected the fort to its outerworks. The glacis was elaborately countermined. The ravelin in the ditch contained a large vaulted chamber which was intended to serve as an assembly point for a company of about 100 troops.

In 1757 it was decided to build a coastal battery at Qala Lembi on the promontory opposite Fort Manoel, some distance away from Dragut point.[19] This was intended both to prevent an invading army from bombarding the northern flank of the fort and also to command the entrance to Marsamxett Harbour. During the military exercises of 1760, the garrison of Fort Manoel was augmented with soldiers from the *Battaglione delle Galere* and the Qala Lembi battery was garrisoned and provided with the necessary munitions at the expense of the *Fondazione Manoel*.[20] In 1761 French military engineers proposed that this battery be connected by 'une communicatione pour faciliter a la garrison de retirer au Fort Manoel, quan elle ne pourroit plus tenir.' [21]

Perfect in design as it might have been, the security of the fort was jeopardized by its proximity to two large buildings already existent when the fort was built. The first was a large abandoned magazine situated roughly in the centre of the *Isoletto*, and the second, the one which posed the greatest danger, was the Lazzareto, a quarantine hospital. The latter was difficult to remove and replace, and it is easy to understand the Order's reluctance to demolish this building, despite the engineers' many persistent recommendations, 'demolizione progettata come indispensabile sià dal tempo che si fabrica il Forte Manoel

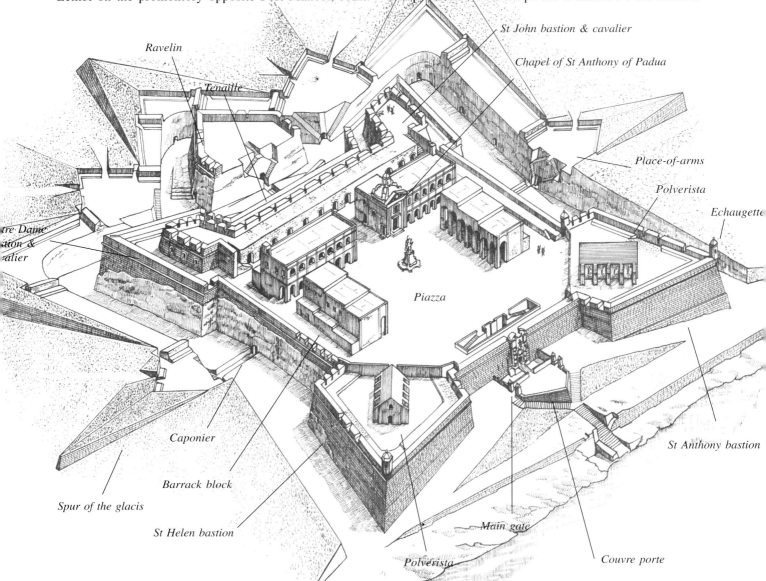

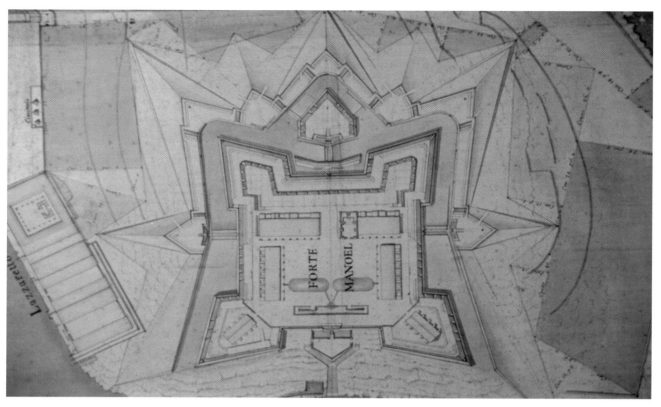

Above, Plan of Fort Manoel (NLM). Below and right,
Elevations and sections of Fort Manoel, showing the fronts
facing Valletta (bottom), Ta' Xbiex, and Gzira.

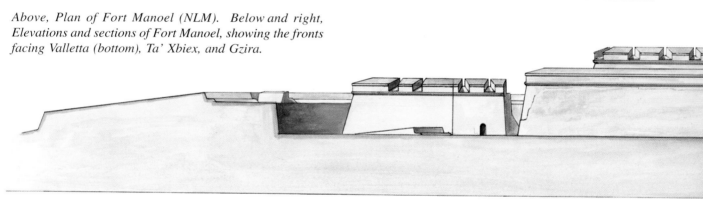

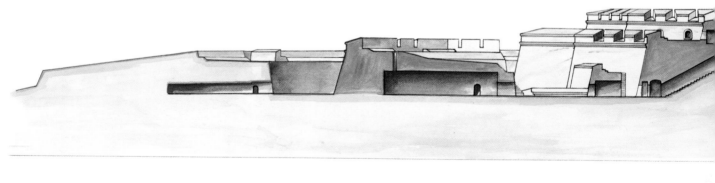

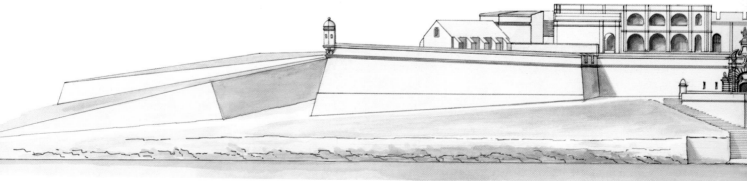

al quale il magazino sudetto darebbe comodo al nemico di avvicinarsi.' [22]

The maintenance of Fort Manoel was provided for out of a special fund, the Manoel Foundation, which was set up by Grand Master Manoel de Vilhena out of his *Quint,* that part (1/5) of his property which he was permitted to dispose of by will. This had an annual income of some 10,000 scudi and enabled, apart from many other things, the purchase of a new gun every three years.[23] Normally the garrison of the fort was composed of 19 officers and men, together with two boatmen. In an emergency the fort was designed to accommodate up to 500 troops in bomb-proof barracks.

During the invasion of Malta by Napoleon on 10 June 1798, the fort was garrisoned by 200 men from the Regiment of Cacciatori (1777-98) under the command of the knights Gourgeau and La Tour de Saint Quentin. The garrison of the fort was then joined by the Birchircara militia which had just retreated in disorder from its encounter with the French troops at St Julians Bay. Shortly afterwards, the French columns under Marmont surrounded the fort and thrice attempted to seize it by assault, but each attack was repulsed by the loyal Maltese troops. The garrison only surrendered after the capitulation was signed on board the French flagship.

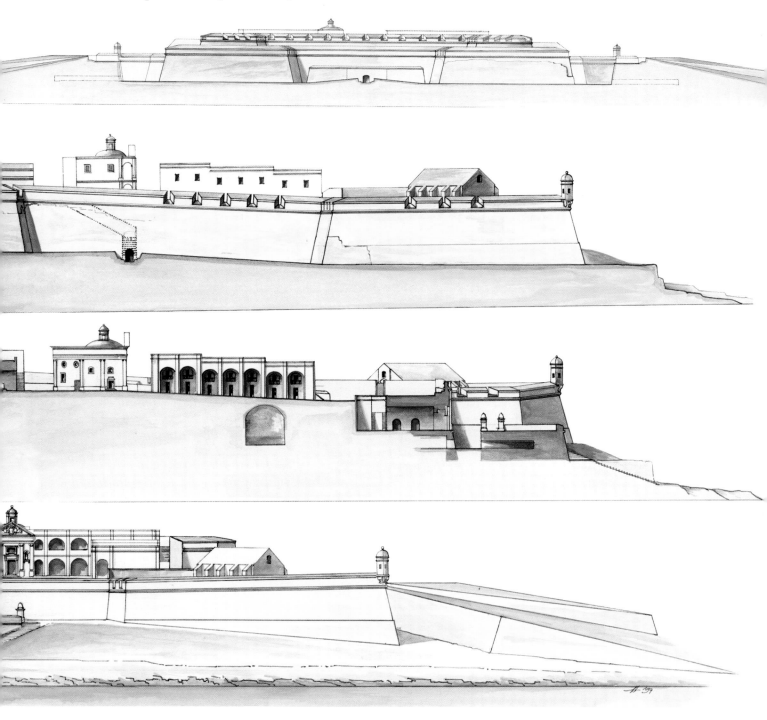

Fort Chambrai

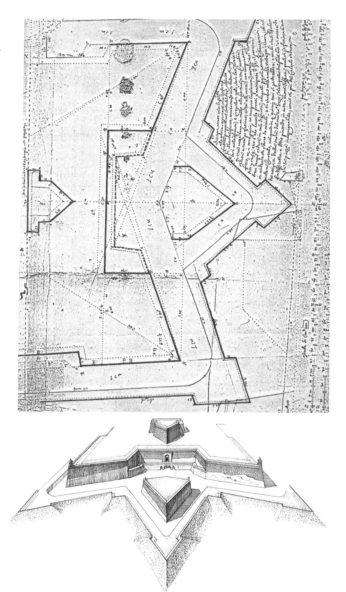

Until late in the first half of the eighteenth century, the Castello remained Gozo's sole refuge available to its inhabitants when subjected to swift Turkish raids. Many of the Order's engineers put forward alternative sites for the construction of a new fortress. Giovanni Rinaldini, in his first report of 1599, suggested three possible locations, Mgarr, Marsalforn, and Ramla Bay, but he considered the site at Marsalforn as being the best suited for a new city with a three-bastioned land front some 200 *canne* wide, that would cost around 80,000 scudi to build.[1]

Nothing came of Rinaldini's proposal as the knights preferred to fortify the Castello instead, but the marquis of St Angelo, who visited the island 40 years later in 1640, reiterated Rinaldini's proposal to fortify Marsalforn 'particolarmente per esser il sito più capace di buona fortificazione riducendosi ad una fronte sola la quale repartirei in un Baluardo ed due mezzi cingendo il restante con un parapetto fiancheggiato.'[2] The threat of a Turkish attack in 1645 again brought a number of new engineers to Malta and nearly all of these advised the Order to build a new strong fortress at Marsalforn.

In May 1654 Grand Master Lascaris visited Gozo and confirmed the need for a new fortified city. The project was taken in hand immediately but the failure to finance the works by means of a tax imposed on the Gozitans brought it to an abrupt halt.[3] The idea was revived again in 1657 and on 9 May of that year, the engineer Francesco Buonamici and Balì Frà Baldazan were dispatched to Gozo to initiate the construction of the new fortress at Għajn Damma, overlooking Marsalforn bay.[5] Buonamici traced out the outline of the fortress on the site itself and calculated that the work would cost some 62,799 scudi.[6] The design of the new city, based on the marquis of St Angelo's original plan, consisted of a land front of 158 *canne* having two bastions, a cavalier, ditch, tenaille, and ravelin. The rest of the enceinte was to rely on the precipitous cliffs for its defence.

Once again, however, the new fortress did not progress beyond its initial stages and for some unknown reason the site at Marsalforn was abandoned. In 1670 it was the turn of Valperga to review the defences of Gozo. Among the engineers, he was the first to oppose the fortification of Marsalforn, although he confirmed that the new site was 'veramente propio e capace di Real fortificatione'.[7] Valperga pointed out that the fortification of Marsalforn

Above, Plan and graphic reconstruction of the land front fortifications of the proposed fortress of Marsalforn drawn up by the engineer Buonamici.

involved the incursion of heavy expenses especially if 'l'acqua assai vicina' at the foot of the hill had to be enclosed.[8]

The proposal for the building of a new fortified city was not revived again until 1715, during the reign of Grand Master Perellos, when the French military mission headed by Tigné suggested that a new city be sited at Mgarr rather than at Marsalforn where it was easier to establish 'commando, e la sicurezza'.[9] The site at Ras-et-Tafal, overlooking Mgarr harbour had its own 'buona fontana abbondante' and, better still, it had 'il solo porto pratticabile in tutta l'isola' in which all the 'commercio fra le due isole' was conducted.[10] Moreover, Mgarr was already defended by a large tower armed with eight 'pezzi d'artiglieria e da una batteria che diffende la Spiagga', while the site could be easily re-supplied and relieved by sea.[11]

On 25 September 1722, the council approved the project and the engineer François de Mondion was asked to prepare a scheme for the new fortress based on Tigné's designs.[12] The new fortified city, which was to be called *Cité Vilhena*, was however, postponed until Fort Manoel, begun in 1723, could be completed.[13] The construction of Fort Manoel was only made possible through the generosity of Grand Master Vilhena himself and it took the generosity of another member of the Order, Balì Jacques François de Chambrai, to make possible the building of a new fortified city at Ras-et-Tafal.[14] In 1749, Chambrai offered to finance the project himself and on 2 September the congregation of war, with the consent of the grand master, ordered that the fort be built. The citation in the Order's records states that the fortress with all its 'opere esteriori, con sua gebbia, e Magazzeni a prova di Bombe' was to be built 'secondo la pianta lasciata dal su Ingegnere Cav. de Tigné Brigadiere nell'Armata di sua Maestà Christianissima, la quale serve di ritiro, et asilo a tutto quel popolo con suoi effetti e vettovoglie. The fortress was designed to deny 'lo sbarco, e l'acquata al Migiarro da una parte all'altra costa accessibili di Ras el hops dall'altra' and impede 'il stanziamento ai vasselli nemici tra l'Isola del Gozo e Comino', facilitate 'il ricervimento di Soccorsi, et a gl'Isolani al ritiro a Malta' and communicate 'con segnali col medesimo e colle Torri di Comino e Rossa.'[15]

Marandon, the Order's resident engineer, was dispatched to Gozo to supervise the work and examine the site which was already found to be made of friable rock and thus rejected by Rinaldini earlier in 1599. But the advantages of the site (it had its own source of water) seemed to outweigh its shortcomings. By 1753 the work had progressed slowly as the Order was attempting to seek the best advice on Tigné's plans, drawn up some 30 years earlier, from Europe's then prominent engineers like Giuseppe Bertola, Juan Zermano, and Charles Louis Auguste Fouguet Bellisle.[16] Still, these engineers were not unanimous in their opinions and the Order had to make the best of their conflicting advice.[17]

The fort that was eventually built had a large land front facing northwards. This consisted of a central bastion flanked by two bastions, two ravelins, and protected by a counterguard placed inside the wide ditch which was enclosed at both ends by two small batteries. A covertway was well provided with traverses and places-of-arms. To

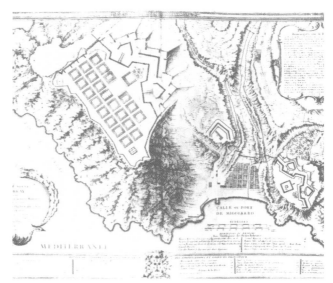

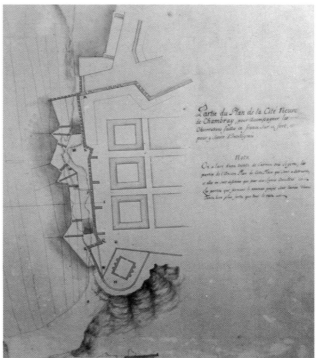

Top, Plan of Fort Chambrai, after Palmeus. Above, Proposed plan of the west flank of the fortress of Ras-et-tafal showing a Vauban-style 'polverista' on a rounded bastion (NLM).

the north-west the enceinte consisted of a long curtain that terminated in a large bastion fitted with a conical *polverista*. The rest of the enceinte to the south, facing the Fliegu, was protected by the cliff face and thus was not fortified. By 1760, work on the fort had progressed considerably so that the two ravelins and counterguard within the ditch had been completed. The fort's western flank, terminating in Guardian

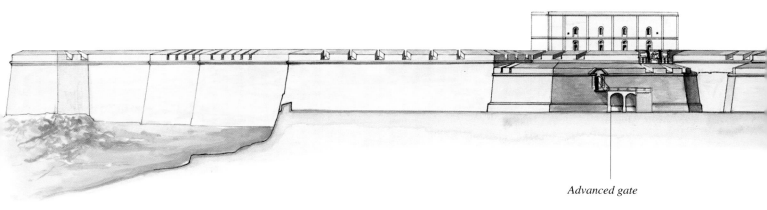

Advanced gate

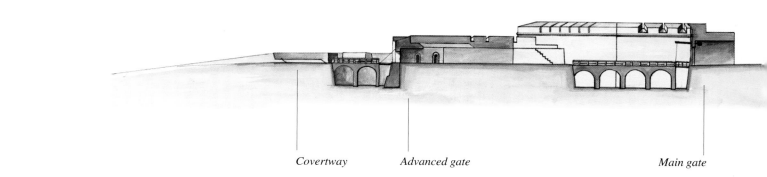

Covertway   *Advanced gate*   *Main gate*

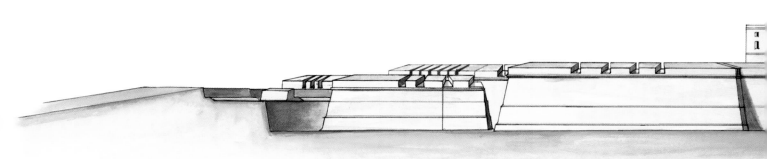

Elevations and sections of Fort Chambrai.

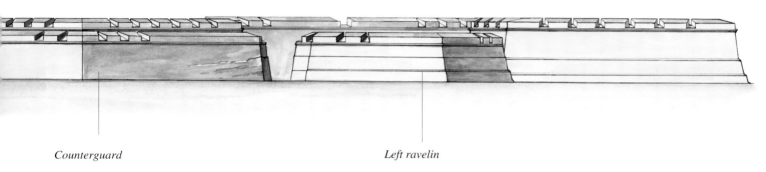

Counterguard   Left ravelin

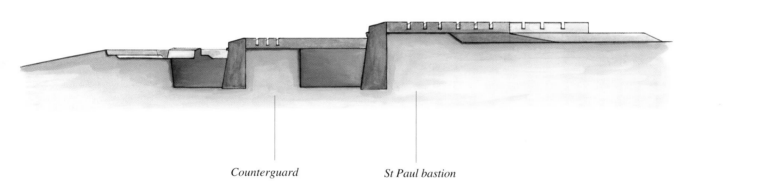

Counterguard   St Paul bastion

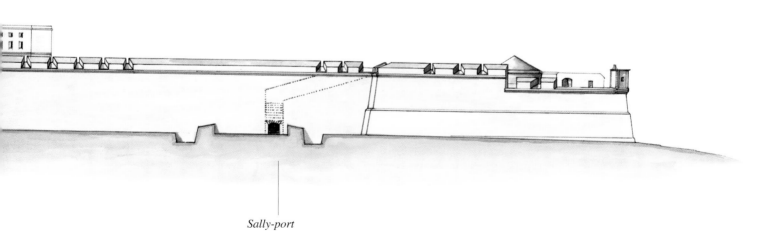

Sally-port

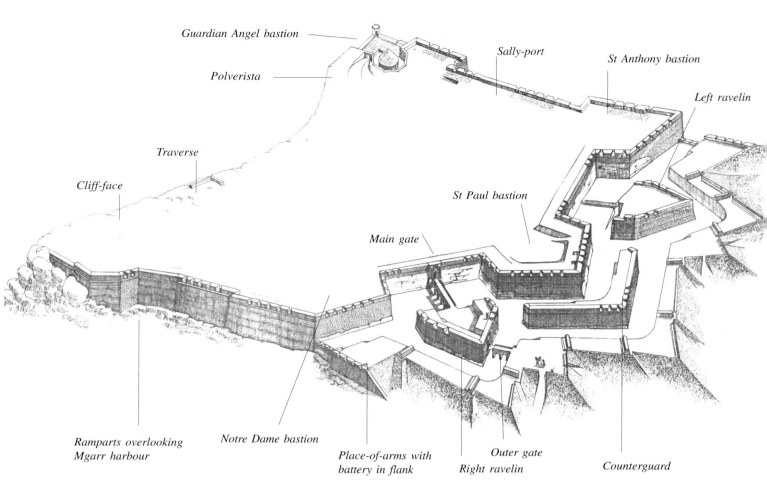

Guardian Angel bastion

Polverista

Sally-port

St Anthony bastion

Left ravelin

Traverse

Cliff-face

St Paul bastion

Main gate

Ramparts overlooking
Mgarr harbour

Notre Dame bastion

Place-of-arms with
battery in flank

Outer gate

Right ravelin

Counterguard

Angel bastion, was the only part of the original plan that was significantly altered. Fort Chambrai was originally designed as a fortified city for the protection of the Gozitan inhabitants. A town was planned out on a grid pattern of square blocks, avenues, and streets but the only buildings to rise within its walls were a large barrack block and a chapel dedicated to the *Madonna della Grazia* in 1758.[18]

In 1761 Bourlamaque and his company of French engineers did not question the need for a fort overlooking Mgarr nor did they criticize the design of the fort's land front. However, they regarded the flanks of Fort Chambrai as weak and threatened from the nearby hills. To strengthen the flanks of the fort, Bourlamaque proposed the construction of 'retrenchemens intereurs sur les deux branches de la droite, e de la gauche', while the right flank was to be strengthened by the construction of 'un lunette au redoute' on a small plateau rising from the valley between the fort and Garzes tower.[19] He also proposed to envelope 'la Tour Garzes d'un fossé'.[20] Fort Chambrai itself was to be provided with more magazines and casemates. Bourlamaque realized that the construction of interior retrenchments and magazines would reduce the inner area

A 19th-century photograph showing bridge and main gateway Fort Chambrai. The gate was fitted with a drawbridge 'a fleccie'.

of the fort and deny shelter to the inhabitants and, in order to provide alternative shelter, he proposed to enclose the area between the fort and the sea. Athough his recommendations were accepted by the council, none of the works were actually carried out.[21]

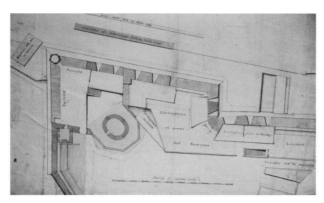

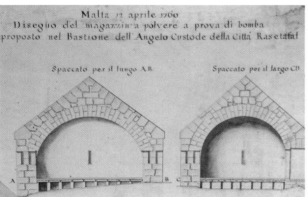

The fear of corsair raids on Gozo had long since diminished and it seems that the Gozitans felt sufficiently secure in their farmhouses not to be attracted by the security of the new fortress. The new city failed to take root. The friable nature of the rock on which the fort had been built soon began to pose serious structural problems. By 1789 some of the ramparts had deteriorated seriously enough to require major reconstruction. At the time of Napoleon's invasion in 1798, Fort Chambrai was armed with 18 cannon, mostly 8-pdrs, but it was surprisingly very lightly manned by a only few soldiers. Most of the inhabitants, together with their possessions and animals, sought refuge inside Fort Chambrai, but they soon surrendered after only a token show of resistance.

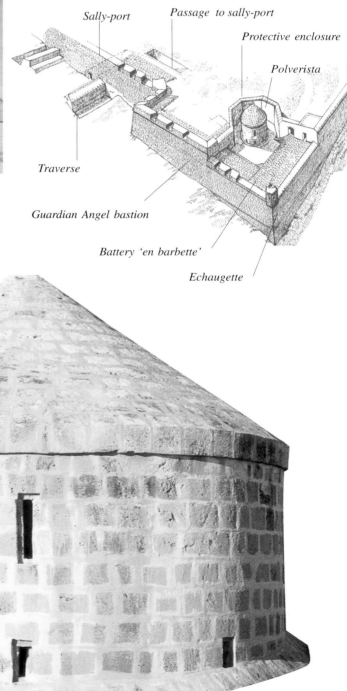

Above, Plan of the 'Bastione del Angelo Custode' and sectional elevation of the gunpowder magazine, or polverista, built into the bastion (NLM). Note the raised floor, an attemptt at damp-proofing. Below, View of the Polverista after restoration. Note the apertures for ventilation.

Fort Tigné

The fall of Fort St Elmo during the siege of 1565 is mainly attributed to Dragut. By setting up his siege batteries on the two promontories facing the small fort, he effectively isolated it from its reinforcements and eventually brought about its systematic destruction. The Turkish siege guns placed on the promontory known as St Mary hermitage were particularly effective in subduing the cavalier of Fort St Elmo and, consequently, this was the first part of the fort to fall to the besiegers. Legend has it that while aiming one of the guns in the battery, Dragut was fatally wounded by a cannon ball fired from the cavalier of Fort St Elmo.

Dragut point, as the place came to be known after the siege, continued to pose a constant threat not only to the flanks of Fort St Elmo but also to the new city of Valletta. Notwithstanding its strategic value, it was only during the late seventeenth century that proposals for the building of a fort on the site began to feature in the military engineers' reports. The earliest of these can be traced back to 1662, when Count Vernada proposed a large fort, possibly shown in Vincenzo Maria Coronelli's map of the harbour, similar in plan to Fort Ricasoli built later in 1670. Count Vernada also proposed to fortify other important areas inside Marsamxett harbour, mainly Ta' Xbiex, Pietà, and the *Isoletto.*

Although major works of fortification were undertaken to protect most of the approaches on the landward side of the Grand Harbour, the beginning of the eighteenth century still found the Marsamxett side totally unprotected and vulnerable to attack. While the construction of Fort Manoel in 1723 on the *Isoletto* secured the inner reaches of Marsamxett, the entrance to the harbour remained undefended. A decade earlier, French military engineers sought to secure Dragut point with small works of fortification. Tigné, in 1716, proposed defending the site with a large triangular battery, open at the gorge and

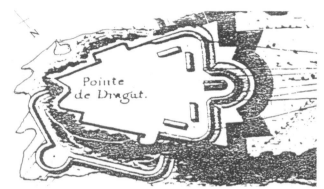

A proposal for a fort on Dragut point after the system of Montalembert (after Hughes).

protected with its own ditch and covertway at a cost of 3,000 scudi.[1] Maigret proposed instead a large casemated redoubt similar to the one he planned for Fort Manoel which he estimated would cost 2,600 scudi.[2] But the French engineers, and the Order, gave little priority to these works, so that nothing was actually done to fortify the place. In 1575, however, a coastal battery was erected at Qala Lembi, close to Dragut point. This was intended mainly to prevent an enemy force from landing along the stretch of shoreline to the north of Dragut Point but the battery was badly sited and too small to be of any effective use.

In 1763 an anonymous author proposed to enclose the peninsula within a line of fortifications, the main front of which was to be sited in the area then known as the 'Madonna della Sliema ... dove e la maggiore altezza, che dal livello del mare sorge, e si alza di canne 9: e questo sito di canne 180 largo, 140 lungo, e 9 alto, che va in declino dall'uno e l'altro lato fin al canale che tocca il mare.' The work was to have its bastions, curtains and outerworks hewn out of rock to render them bombproof. This scheme, which is strikingly similar to that shown depicted in the plan of the proposed fortress on page 321, however, found no support from the contemporary 'Intendenti e Professori dell'Architettura militare'.[3]

The late eighteenth century witnessed another proposal for a casemated fortress on Dragut's Point following the system of Montalembert.[9] This proposal consisted of a large

Fort Tigné in the mid-19th century.

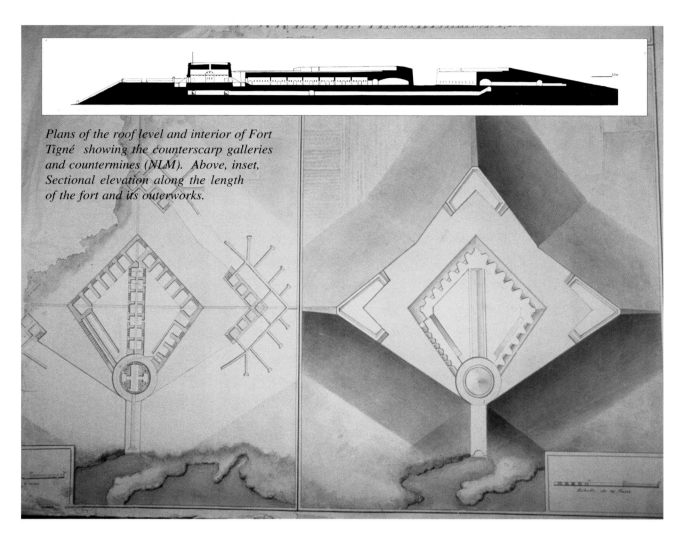

Plans of the roof level and interior of Fort Tigné showing the counterscarp galleries and countermines (NLM). Above, inset, Sectional elevation along the length of the fort and its outerworks.

fortified work having a semicircular casemated bastion facing the landward approaches and, on a lower level, a waterfront battery facing the mouth of the harbour. Again, this scheme did not proceed beyond the drawing board stage.

Finally, in 1792, the congregation of war and fortification decided to build a fortified work on Dragut's Point. The decision 'che si facesi una ridotta a Dragut' was taken on 11 December 1792 and Balì Renè Jacques de Tigné donated 1,000 scudi towards its construction. The work was built 'secondo il piano e disegno fatto dall' Ingegniere Comm. de Tousard.' In consideration of the fact that it was Balì Tigné who paid 'i primi mille scudi col quali si è incomminciato la fabbrica', the Grand Master, on the suggestion of the congregataion of war, named the fort in his honour, 'volendo cosi di mostrare ... gratitudine'.[5] It was the reigning grand master, Emanuel de Rohan, however, who eventually paid the remaining balance of 6,000 scudi 'per le costruzione di quel forte' and promised

to make good any outstanding expenses.[6] Balì di Tillet also donated 'cinque cento scudi per la sudetta fabbrica.'[7]

Fort Tigné, as it was named, was designed by the Order's chief engineer, Stefano de Tousard, who seems to have been influenced by the writings of Marc-Rene de Montalembert in the 1770s and most particularly by the *lunettes d'Arçon* built earlier in 1792 by the French general Lemichaud d'Arçon, to which it bears a very close resemblance.[8] Fort Tigné, in effect, can be described as a refinement of the *lunette d'Arçon,* the main difference being that the former had lost its umbilical link to the parent fortress, in this case Valletta, and became a veritable fort in its own right, self sufficient and capable of providing all-round defence. The supervision of the construction of the fort was entrusted to the Maltese engineer Antonio Cachia.[9]

Fort Tigné was built as a strong casemated redoubt, diamond-shaped in plan with a circular tower, or keep, at its rear facing the mouth of the harbour. Notwithstanding

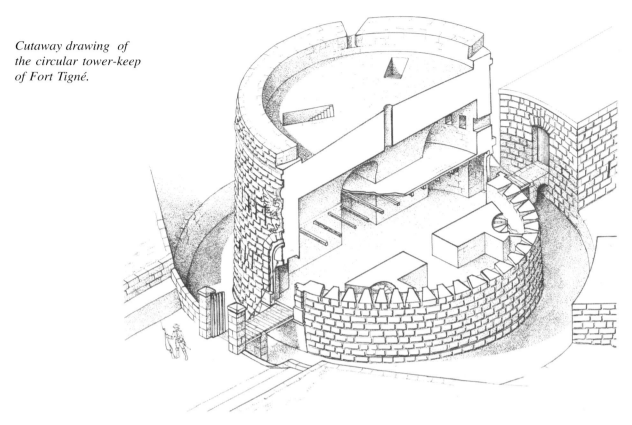

Cutaway drawing of the circular tower-keep of Fort Tigné.

its small size, the work could accommodate a large number of guns. It was surrounded by a dry ditch, itself commanded by three protruding counterscarp galleries fitted with musketry loopholes. Access to these galleries was through an underground tunnel leading from the interior of the fort. The roof of each counterscarp gallery was designed as an isolated place-of-arms, access to which must have been through the roof of the gallery. All the works were enclosed within a heavily-mined glacis. The circular tower, or keep, about 11m high, was itself fitted with two tiers of musketry loopholes and a roof-mounted battery for four guns to command both the interior of the work and the entrance to the harbour. The original parapet of the keep, demolished and replaced by a thicker one in the nineteenth century, was fitted with four embrasures. A shallow ditch separated the keep from the rest of the fort.

The entrance to the fort was protected by a drawbridge, in front of which stood a large caponier with two cuttings in the parapet and a stairway leading down to the rocky shore. Another drawbridge connected the keep to the body of the fort. Three of the four sides of the fort had a thick parapet with high 'embrasures for cannon placed at rather more than the usual intervals apart, covered over at the top, interiorly, with large stones, and having intermediate banquettes formed with steps of masonry', while the side faces were pierced with a continuous row of musketry loopholes.[10] Internally, the *piazza* of Fort Tigné was divided into two by a large central barrack block fitted with musketry

loopholes to enable the defenders to command the interior of the fort. In February 1795, the fort was ready to be garrisoned and 'in stato di ricevere l'artiglieria'. The guns needed to arm the fort were ordered to be sent 'da dove stimeranno più vantaggioso.' The equipment comprised 12 guns of 24-pdr, six of 18-pdr, six of 12-pdr, four of 4-pdrs, six mortars and six *lemiere*.[11]

Subsequent to the construction of Fort Tigné, it was proposed to build a new fortified city on the Tigné promontory. Fort Tigné itself was to be incorporated into this ambitious scheme as the keep of the new city. It is doubtful if this project would ever have been realized but the French invasion of 1798 soon brought to a sudden halt all the projects planned by the Order. Being a small work, Fort Tigné was not designed to withstand a long siege, although it could be easily re-supplied from Valletta. But, under the command of the Bavarian Balì Reichberg and garrisoned by detachments from the Regiment of Malta and the Regiment of Cacciatori, Fort Tigné resisted repeated French assaults and bombardments. It engaged the French fleet with its guns and provided covering fire to Chevalier de Soubiras who rallied out in a galley to attack the French landing boats disembarking their troops at St Julians bay. De Soubiras was forced back after sinking one boat and Vaubois, the French general, seeing the damage being caused by the guns of the fort, landed some artillery and set them up against the fort. Fort Tigné only threw open its gate to the French after the surrender of the Order.

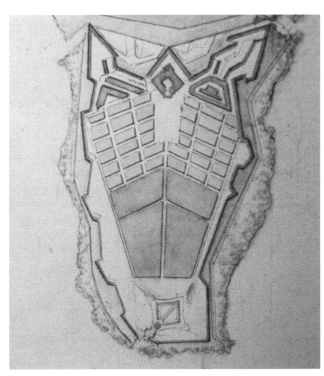

Above, A mid-19th century photograph of the circular tower-keep of Fort Tigné. The picture shows the drawbridge, the palsided gate, the covertway, and part of the parapet of the glacis. The sloping parapet crowning the tower, devoid of embrasures, is a British alteration. Right, A proposal for a fortified city on the Tigné peninsula with Fort Tigné itself incorporated as a keep (NLM).

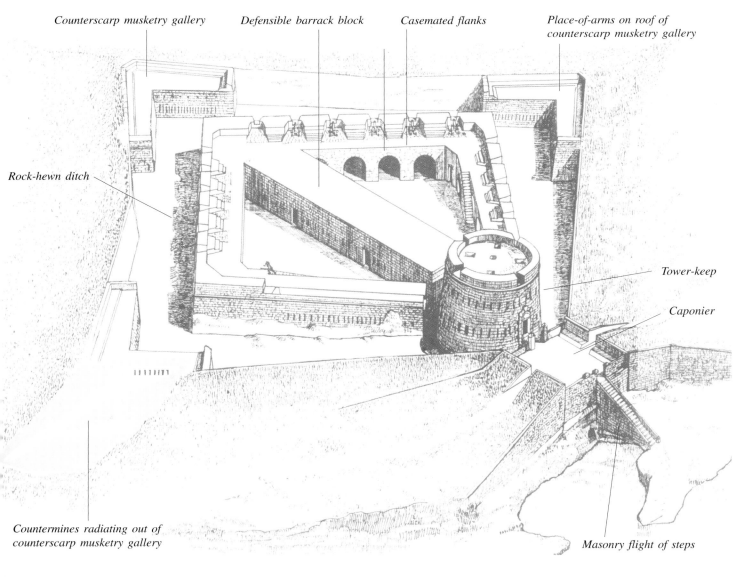

Counterscarp musketry gallery

Defensible barrack block

Casemated flanks

Place-of-arms on roof of counterscarp musketry gallery

Rock-hewn ditch

Tower-keep

Caponier

Countermines radiating out of counterscarp musketry gallery

Masonry flight of steps

Coastal Towers

When the knights assumed possession of the Maltese islands in 1530, they were unwilling to construct any but the most essential defensive works and, right up to the end of that century, the Order confined its attention primarily to the fortification of the harbour area. As far as the defence of the coastline was concerned, the knights retained the same system of militia watch-posts employed by the Maltese.[1] A determined effort to defend the island's shores with permanent defensive structures only began to manifest itself in the early years of the seventeenth century. The first of these fortified structures to materialize was St Martin Tower, erected on the island of Gozo in 1605, at Mgarr overlooking the channel between Gozo and Comino.[2] The construction of this tower was made possible by the generosity of Grand Master Martin Garzes (1595-1601) who had left provisions in his will for the financing of such a work. The idea had been conceived some years earlier as part of Rinaldini's original concept for the defence of Gozo.[3] Unfortunately Garzes Tower, as it was also called, was demolished in the mid-nineteenth century.

It was the generosity of yet another grand master that enabled the construction of the first set of towers in what was quickly to develop into a chain of coastal strongpoints. The seven towers buit by Alof de Wignacourt were erected at St Paul Bay (1609), Marsaxlokk (St Lucian Tower - 1610), St Thomas Bay (1614), Marsalforn (Gozo - 1616) Comino (St Mary Tower - 1618), and Sta Maria Delle Grazie (1620).

These towers were large squarish structures. With their bastioned turrets they were more of forts in form and use rather than simple vedettes. These massive structures were built to dominate the coastline, mounting batteries of heavy artillery on their roofs and garrisoned by sizable detachments in times of war. At times the contingents of troops sent out to reinforce some of these strongpoints would include as much as 200 men. The troops were generally expected to oppose landing parties and to reconnoitre enemy movements.

Grand Master Jean de Valette built the Torre del Capitano (above) to house the captain of the Naxxar militia, after the Order failed to take over a nearby tower built in 1548 by Francesco Gauci to safeguard his family against corsair raids (below). Gauci pleaded with the Order's council and was allowed to keep his tower. Both towers relied heavily on box-machicolations for their defence.

St Paul Bay Tower
1609

St Lucian Tower
1610

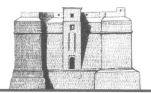

St Thomas Bay Tower
1614

Marsalforn Tower
Gozo
1616

St Mary Tower
Comino
1620

Ghajn Tuffieha
Tower
1637

The characteristic feature of these earlier towers, or 'fortini' as they were also called, apart from their massive size, were the corner turrets. These were rudimentary forms of bastions designed to allow some form of close-in defence to the tower by enabling a limited degree of enfilading fire along its faces. The system was best developed at St Thomas tower which was also provided with a ditch and a bascule-type of drawbridge approached by a flight of steps. In one tower, that at Comino, a further form of defence was provided by a kind of continuous scarp musketry gallery at the base of the walls along the top of the plinth on which the whole structure was built. Internally, all towers contained large barrel-vaulted rooms, built a 'prova di bomba' and designed to withstand the weight of a sizable number of cannon mounted on their roof batteries. All but the Marsalforn and the Sta Maria Delle Grazie are still standing. The former fell into ruin during the early eighteenth century and was replaced by a second tower built in 1720.

These heavy towers were generally well-equipped with artillery. The heaviest armed was Garzes tower which mounted four 12-pdrs, three 10-pdrs, one 4-pdr, and two 3-pdrs. St Thomas tower had four 10-pdr iron guns and St Lucian five 10-pdrs and two 6-pdrs. St Paul's Bay tower

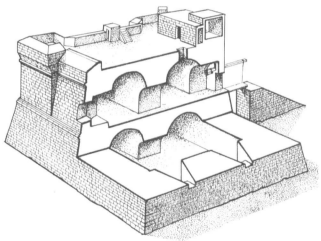

Left, Garzes tower in Mgarr, Gozo, as depicted by Salvatore Busuttil in the early 19th century prior to its demolition. Above, top, late 19th-century photograph showing Wignacourt tower in St Paul Bay. Note the wooden palisade and drawbridge, and the masonry flight of steps, now missing. In 1715/16 a small artillery platform was added at the foot of the tower on its seaward side. Above, diagram showing the interior layout of St Lucian tower in Marsaxlokk Bay. In 1715/16 this tower was fitted with a seaward-facing battery and in 1792 it was surrounded by a ditch and renamed Fort Rohan.

| *Nadur Tower* *1637* | *Mellieha Tower* *1649* | *Xlendi Tower* *Gozo* *1650* | *Dwejra Tower* *Gozo* *1652* | *Ghallis Tower* *1658* | *Mgarr-ix-Xini* *Tower - Gozo* *1652* | *San Blas Tower* *Gozo* *1661* | *Marsalforn Tower* *Gozo* *1720* |

General layout of St Thomas Bay tower and battery. The battery was added in 1715/16 and is shown here with a parapet and embrasures but it may equally have been built 'en barbette' for there are no detailed records showing how it was actually constructed. Bottom, view of the landward front of St Thomas Bay tower showing the main entrance and the wooden arms of the bascule drawbridge.

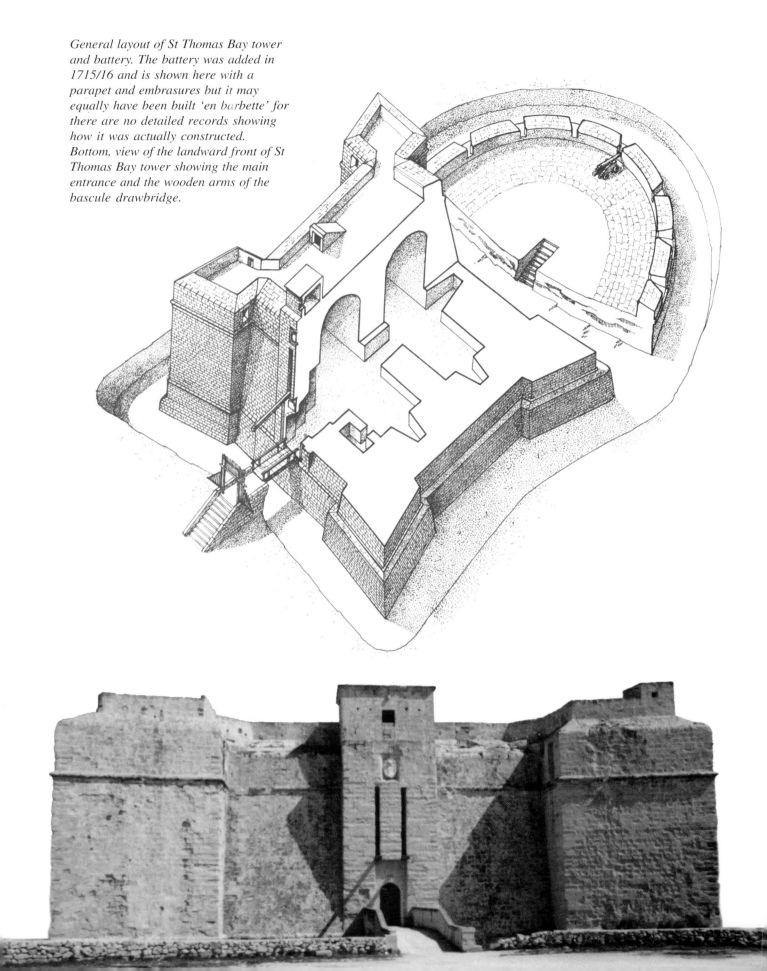

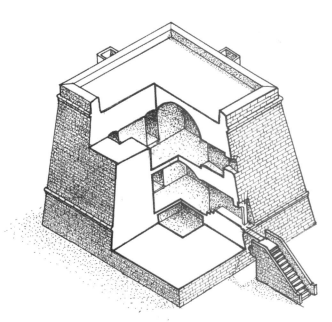

was equipped with two 8-pdr iron guns while Delle Grazie tower was armed with two 6-pdr iron guns. Each tower held a good supply of both round shot and grapeshot canisters. The Delle Grazie tower, for example, stored140 round shot and 30 grapeshot sacks in 1770.[4] It also held 13 muskets, 13 spontoons and halberds, and a box with 500 paper cartridges for muskets. No gunpowder was kept inside this tower, although other towers such as St Thomas tower stored as much as a quantity of 26 barrels (1785).

St Mary tower in Comino, below, and above, as depicted in a 17th-century manuscript, shown enclosed by a loopholed wall (no longer standing), a ditch, and glacis constructed from stone chippings (NLM). Left, Cutaway drawing showing the Marsalform tower built in 1616.

From the mid-seventeenth century onwards, the preference for large garrisoned outposts was discarded in favour of smaller structures which were designed to serve solely as watch-posts. Six such towers were built by Grand Master Lascaris in the years between 1636 to 1657 at Ghajn Tuffieha, Lippija, St George's Bay, Nadur, and Wied iz-Zurrieq. The design of these watch-towers reflected a marked departure from the massive structures built earlier. These were intended specifically as watch-out posts in order to keep the coastline under surveillance and to warn of approaching vessels. Such watch-towers were about 11m high and about 6 x 6 m in plan. Internally, each consisted of two single-roomed floors with external access provided solely to the upper floor, generally reached either by a wooden ladder or a 'scala di corda'.

A reversion to the use of large towers was made in 1649 when St Agatha, or *Torre Rossa*, was erected in Mellieha but this was a large and important bay that had to be defended. This tower followed the same pattern as that prescribed for the towers built during the reign of Wignacourt nearly half-a-century earlier. The Lascaris watch-towers were augmented by another 13 towers erected in Malta in 1658/59 at the expense of Grand Master de Redin, '... il Sig. G. Mro. mosso dall'ardentissimo zelo ... ha proposto di voler mandar fabricare a sue spese dodici, o quattordici Torri nelle marine di essa.'[5] The towers, which were to be manned by the *Guardia Torre,* a kind of permanent guard that was paid by the Università and kept watch all year round, were designed to replace the system of 60 lookout posts manned each night

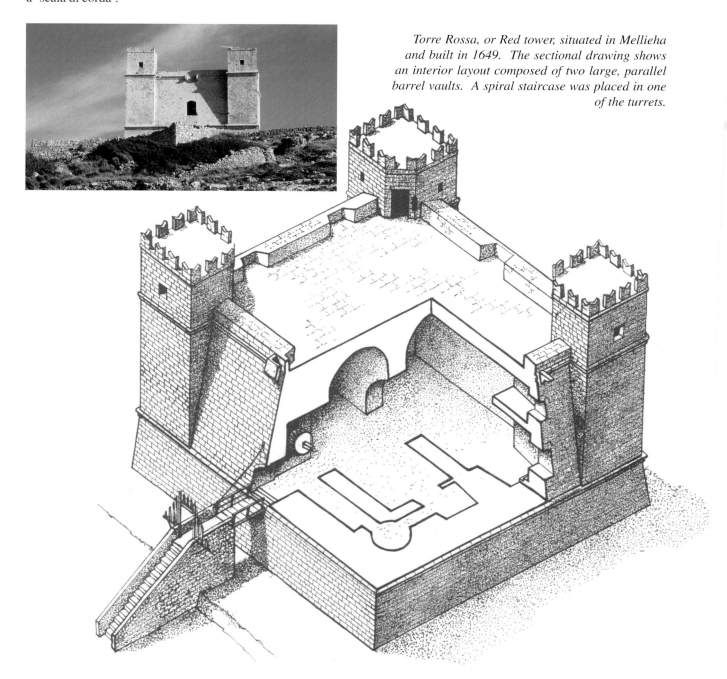

Torre Rossa, or Red tower, situated in Mellieha and built in 1649. The sectional drawing shows an interior layout composed of two large, parallel barrel vaults. A spiral staircase was placed in one of the turrets.

The Lascaris watch-towers. Main picture; Ghajn Tuffieha tower; inset, top to bottom, Nadur tower (limits of Bingemma), Lippija tower, Qawra Point tower, and Wied iz-Zurrieq tower.

by four peasants, '... il caso é che tutta questa isola tiene nella circonferenza delle sue Marine sessanta Guardie in circa più e in ciascheduna delle quali fanno la guardia quattro uomini, che ogni notte sono due cento quaranta; questi sono i più poveri e i più miserabli di detta Isola.'[6] Each tower was given a resident bombardier and three gunners, paid monthly at the rate of some 3 and 2 scudi respectively, '... quattro uomini in ogni torre ... con salario di due scudi al mese et un Bombardiere con due e mezzo, e questi soldi non pretendiamo che li pagi da nostro comun tesoro.'[7] The Order undertook to supply 'un piccolo pezzo d'artiglieria ad ogni torre quando saranno fatte' and later in the century it was decided to mount two *muschettoni da posta* in each of the towers.[8]

The coastal watch-towers were sited within visual distance of one another in order to enable signals to be relayed from one post to the next all the way down the coast to Valletta, '... queste Torri hanno da corrispondere l'una con l'altra, hanno da guardar qualsivoglia cala, che si sia nella nell'Isola, e l'acquata, che nella parte della Mellecha ... in quale si fara' la prima torre.'[9] Work on the De Redin towers proceeded at a very fast pace so that the first tower to be built at Ghajn Hadid, near Mellieha, was completed within two months, '... la torre fabricata alla Mellieha si ritrovava per finirsi, ... il dover provederla, e munirla dell'artiglieria necessaria

Above, right, Delimara watch-tower. A small 'piombatoi' hangs out from the parapet. Below, right, Cutaway drawing showing the interior layout of a typical De Redin watch-tower. Access to the door on the first floor was by means of a rope or wooden ladder. Bottom, The tower at Mgarr-ix-Xini in Gozo.

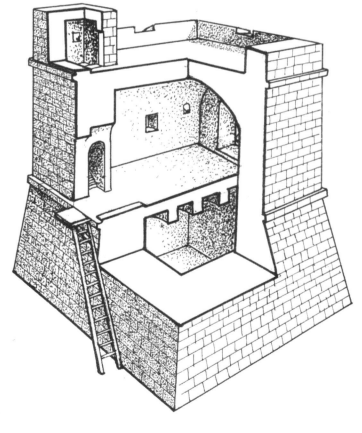

Triq il-Wiesgha Tower.

Wardija

Hamrija

St Julians

Qalet Marku

Ghallis

Madliena

Benghisa

L'Ahrax

The Dwejra and Xlendi (inset) towers in Gozo.

pigliando di quella della religione ... quelle pezze che giudicara, a proposito.[10]

A parallel investment in coastal defences was undertaken in Gozo. The towers built at Mgarr and Marsalforn at the start of the seventeenth century were augmented by two others constructed during the reign of Grand Master Lascaris at Xlendi (1650) and Dwejra (1652) respectively. A fifth was erected at Mgarr-ix-Xini during the magistracy of De Redin in 1661. Six years later yet another tower, known as ta' Isopu, was erected at Nadur on the northern coast of the island. Its construction was financed by the Università of Gozo.

The larger part of the coastal towers in Malta were fitted with seaward-facing gun batteries in 1715-16. These platforms were designed to take heavy artillery pieces and give the towers the ability to hit ships at the waterline. The towers at L-Ahrax, Qawra, St Julians, St Thomas and St Lucian were each given large semicircular gun-platforms while a few, such as those at Qawra and St Julians, were actually enveloped within new fortified structures consisting of embrasures parapets, loopholed redans, and rock-hewn ditches. The large towers were all provided with a bell to sound the alarm. Most of the gunpowder complement of the coastal redoubts and batteries was generally also stored inside the large towers, together with vast quantities of muskets and paper cartridges, spontoons, and halberds. So were the entrenchment tools of the country militia regiments.[11] In 1792, there were 20 towers which were being manned by the Università and each supported a resident Bombardier. When invasion threatened, as happened on 30 October of that same year, the congregation of war and fortification would order that the towers to be garrisoned by a further 148 gunners and guncrews taken from the Order's fleet.[12]

The last tower to be built by the Order was erected at Marsalforn in 1720. This replaced an earlier ruined structure built in 1616. The new Marsalforn tower, however, was

Above, The second tower erected on the Marsalforn plateau known as Ghajn Damma. This one was built in 1720 by Mondion and resembled more of a blockhouse or tour-reduit rather than a watch-tower. It was actually the last tower-like structure to be built for the defence of the coastline by the knights in the Maltese islands. Above, left, The San Blas tower at Nadur, built by the Gozo Università during the reign of Grand Master Cotoner.

designed more in the form of a French *tour-reduit* rather than a veritable watch-post. Large loopholes in its walls and embrasures for cannon on its roof allowed it to defend itself from all directions, while a high turret rising from the centre of the roof served as an excellent vedette.

Torre Cavalieri, a heavily-fortified private tower situated in the village of Qrendi.

The remains of Xrop l-Ghagin tower.

Coastal Batteries

The brief outburst of enthusiasm shown by the Order for the fortification of the coastal areas of Malta with the building of some 30 towers during the first half of the seventeenth century appears to have waned considerably after 1667. The concept of opposing the enemy on the beaches only began to find adherents again amongst the knights around the turn of the century, particularly through the influence of the Order's French military engineers.

In September 1714, two Frenchmen in the employ of the Order as commissioners of fortifications, Bernard Fontet and Jacques de Camus d'Arginy, sought to expose the vulnerability of the bays of Marsaxlokk and Marsascala to enemy landings and hence underline the need for the construction of a number of coastal batteries so as to enable the defence of these places.[1] At the request of the congregation of war, they later extended their inspection to the whole of the island and Gozo. The two commissioners presented their report on 10 January 1715 and recommended therein that those bays where a large fleet could disembark troops needed to be fortified with batteries and entrenchments. Amongst these were Marsaxlokk,

Below, Drawing showing the main elements of a typical 18th-century coastal gun-battery; (1) Gun-platform (2) Parapet with embrasures (3) Blockhouse (4) Redan with musketry loopholes.

RIASSUNTO DELLE SPESE DI FORTIFICAT DI MARSA SIROCCO & MARSA SCALA

Nella

Batteria di Beneissa	F 1.2	1855. L. 18.3
Ridotto di Calafrana	2	1193.5.16.-
Batteria di Amminech	3	1451.8.18.4
Ridotto di Desuebuggia	4	969.11.4.1
Batteria di Ghsira	5	1109.3.8.1
Ridotto di S. Georgio	6	354.4.6.-
Batteria della Cayenza	7	917.6.14.4
Batteria di S. Luciano	8	948.2.12.4
Ridotto di Craite	9	1051.7.5.-
Ridotto del fango	10	1078.7.6.5
Batteria di S. Giacomo	11	1117.8.11.2
Batteria di Richama	12	1179.11.19.2
Batteria di Mahsel	13	988.0.12.-
Batteria di S. Tomaso	14	382.8.11.1
Ridotto di Marsascala	15	868.0.12.1

RIASSUNTO DELLE SPESE DI FORT DA S. GIULIANO AL FREO

Batteria di S. Giuliano	AP 19	587.5.12.3
Ridotto di S. Georgio	20	288.10.19.5
Ridotto della Maddalena	21	913.5.0.1
Batteria della Punta di Cala di marco	22	1165.10.1.-
Ridotto di Cala di Marco	23	1243.3.19.5
Batteria di Sallis	24	871.6.16.5
Ridotto a Dritta delle Saline		316.9.10.2
Ridotto a Sinistra delle Saline	25	659.11.15.2
Batteria della Caura	26	787.3.10.2
Batteria della Bugibba	27	1189.9.13.5
Batteria sotto La torre di S. Paolo	28	231.3.6.3
Batteria a Dritta di S. Paolo	29	1105.1.11.4
Batteria a Sinistra di S. Paolo	30	1073.9.12.-
Batteria a Dritta della Melleha	31	737.5.15.2
Ridotto d'etta Melleha	32	1644.3.10.1
Batteria a Sinistra della Melleha	33	899.4.17.5
Batteria della Harrach	34	544.11.10.3
Ridotto della Ramla tal Sdiz	35	1213.8.4.3
Ridotto della Barriera	36	955.10.11.1
Batteria in Mezzo del Cumale	37	1059.1.9.-
Ridotto della Ramla tal fussilier	38	1239.3.19.5
Ridotto della Ramla ta Wied Musa	39	1147.11.7.-
Batteria di Wied Musa	40	938.1.8.-

Above, Copies of original lists taken from the Order's documents showing the expenditure incurred in 1715-16 on the construction of coastal batteries and redoubts in Malta, Gozo, and Comino.

Qawra Point tower and battery

St Mary battery - Comino

St Lucian tower and battery

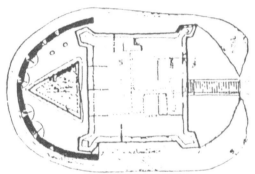

Vendôme battery - Pwales (demolished)

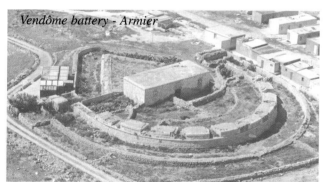

Vendôme battery - Armier

Bugibba battery (ruin)

Ferretti battery - Birzebbugia

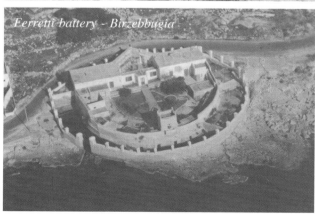

Qbajjar battery, Gozo

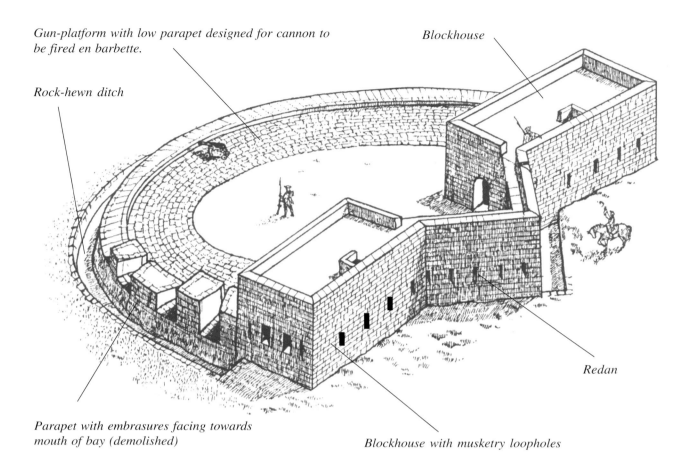

Gun-platform with low parapet designed for cannon to be fired en barbette.

Rock-hewn ditch

Blockhouse

Redan

Parapet with embrasures facing towards mouth of bay (demolished)

Blockhouse with musketry loopholes

Marsacala, St Thomas bay, St Julians, Madliena, Salina, St Paul bay and Mellieha bay, together with the whole coastline facing the Fliegu.[2] Their recommendations were taken seriously and as a result work quickly commenced on the construction of a series of artillery platforms at Marsaxlokk and St Thomas bay. By mid-1715, these works had consumed the sum of 8,057 scudi. In the meantime work also undertaken on the construction of an additional ten batteries along the northern shores of the island spanning from St Julian tower to the *Fliegu*. Commander Mongontier donated a sum of 2,455 scudi towards these works. This money was divided between the batteries of the *Fliegu* (five batteries - 1,323 scudi), Mellieha (Kassisu - 432 scudi), St Paul (103 scudi), Mistra (133 scudi), Qalet Marku (307 scudi), and St Julian

tower (166 scudi).[3] In Gozo, Arginy and Fontet proposed the construction of similar batteries at Mgarr, Marsalforn, and Ramla. The first two artillery platforms were erected at Mgarr and Il-Qolla s-Safra at Marsalforn with the help of a financial donation by Balì Gironda to the tune of 875 scudi.[4]

The scheme of coastal batteries found a stout adherent in the prior of France, Philippe de Vendôme. It was particularly his financial support which persuaded the Order to undertake a vast building programme and effectively

Above, Mistra battery c.1798. Below, View of the parapet, embrasures, and scarp of the Wied Mousa battery, situated at Marfa.

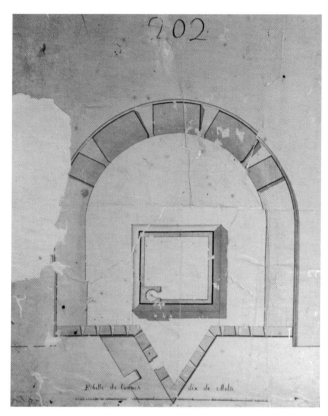

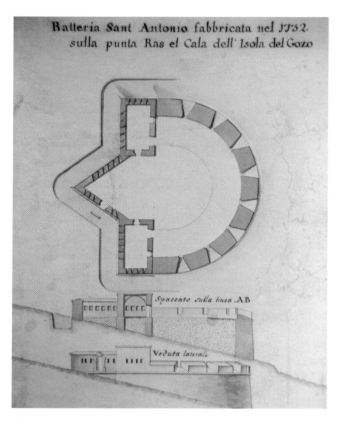

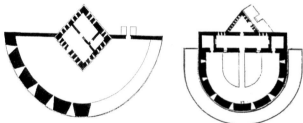

Above, Various approaches to the design of the landward defences of a coastal battery. Top left, Plans of free-standing redans at St Julian battery, and at Qala (St Anthony) battery built in 1732 (proposed plan). Left, Diagonally-placed blockhouse (Westreme battery, Mellieha) and large blockhouse with central redan (Pinto battery - Birzebbuga). Bottom, Front view of St Julian battery showing the parapet with embrasures and the rear of the redan.

Above, Interior view of the right block house of Mistra battery, built during the reign of Grand Master Pinto. Note the musktery loopholes and the arched roof. Access to the roof of the blockhouse, which was fitted with a parapet, was by means of a wooden ladder through a porthole in the centre of the roof.

assured the future of the coastal works as a permanent component in the Order's defensive strategy.[5] Vendôme sought to perfect the nascent network of coastal fortifications with the construction of additional batteries and redoubts for which he offered to advance a loan of 40,000 scudi.[6] The Order acted quickly upon Vendôme's recommendations such that between 1715 and 1716, work on the coastal fortifications consumed a total of 41,561 scudi. The list shown in the tables on page 333 give the cost of each work.[7]

The coastal batteries built by the knights of St John followed a pattern evolved by the French at the end of the seventeenth century. Basically, these comprised of prepared gun-platforms, sometimes ringed by embrasured parapets. Frequently these were fiited out with one or two small blockhouses at the gorge to accommodate the garrison and munitions and provide protection from landward atttack. To this end the walls of the blockhouses were fitted with musketry loopholes and the gorge itself was sealed off by a loopholed redan and rock-hewn ditch. At times there was a combination of both blockhouse and redans depending on the tactical requirements of the site. In one instance, at

Above, 19th-century photograph showing the redan of St Julian battery. Below, Qala battery as actually built.

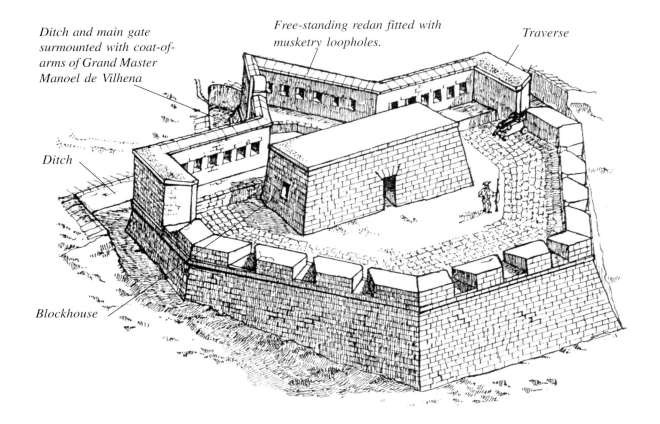

Ditch and main gate surmounted with coat-of-arms of Grand Master Manoel de Vilhena

Free-standing redan fitted with musketry loopholes.

Traverse

Ditch

Blockhouse

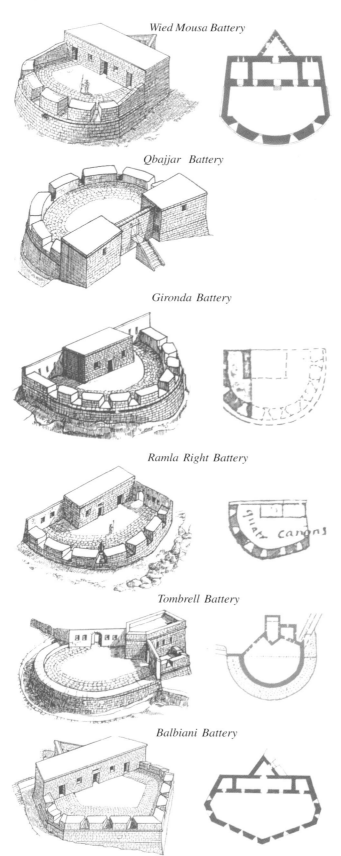

Wied Mousa Battery

Qbajjar Battery

Gironda Battery

Ramla Right Battery

Tombrell Battery

Balbiani Battery

Orsi battery was the first coastal battery built by the knights in Malta. It was built in 1627, at the tip of the Rinella Peninsula to guard the mouth of the Grand Harbour.

Mellieha (Westreme battery), the blockhouse was placed diagonally across the gorge so that two of its outer faces served as a redan. Some were protected by rock-hewn ditches either on the landward or seaward side, or both. Those batteries built very close to the seashore, like Orsi, Qajjenza, and Bugibba had moats filled with seawater.

The entrance to the batteries was from the landward side. A drawbridge was usually fitted to the gate but it seems that not all the batteries and redoubts were actually fitted with one since, in 1792, the congregation of war and fortification had ordered that those batteries still lacking a drawbridge were to be supplied instead with two wooden planks.[8]

All the batteries differed in some detail from one another, either in size, shape of the artillery platform, number of embrasures on the parapet, or the layout of the barrack blocks and landward defences. Later in the century the series of batteries built in 1715-16 were complemented by another three works at Ras il-Qala (1732), Tombrell, Mistra, and Qala Lembi (1757). The last to be built was re erected in 1792 as a simple gun-platform sited on the tip of the Delimara peninsula at 'Wied Ahsri' (Ghasri) in Gozo.

It is interesting to note that nearly all the batteries were left unguarded for most of the year. These were only manned during a threat of an invasion, such as during the general alarms of 1722 and 1761. For most of the time they were simply locked up and their keys deposited with the commander of artillery. The batteries' complement of

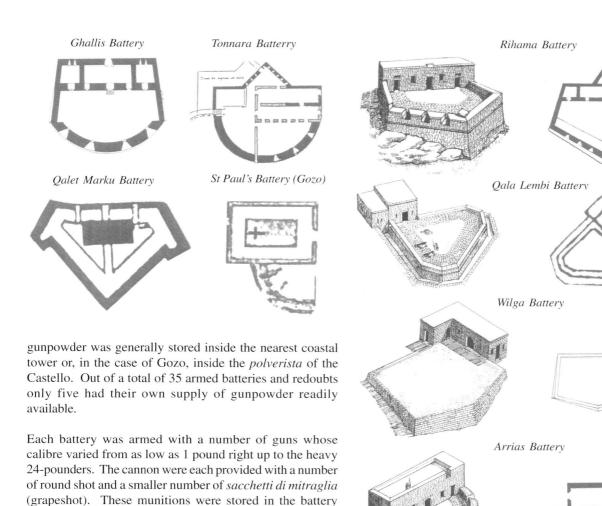

Ghallis Battery   Tonnara Batterry   Rihama Battery

Qalet Marku Battery   St Paul's Battery (Gozo)   Qala Lembi Battery

Wilga Battery

Arrias Battery

gunpowder was generally stored inside the nearest coastal tower or, in the case of Gozo, inside the *polverista* of the Castello. Out of a total of 35 armed batteries and redoubts only five had their own supply of gunpowder readily available.

Each battery was armed with a number of guns whose calibre varied from as low as 1 pound right up to the heavy 24-pounders. The cannon were each provided with a number of round shot and a smaller number of *sacchetti di mitraglia* (grapeshot). These munitions were stored in the battery itself. From time to time the congregation of war regulated the number of rounds that each gun was to receive. In 1761, for example, the guns were to have at least 20 round shot (*palle di ferro*) each together with half that number of grapeshot. The iron guns were mounted on four-wheeled 'truck' carriages similar to those found on the decks of ships, but having iron instead of wooden wheels. These could be handled and adjusted with relative ease inside the restricted space of the artillery platforms.

The coastal batteries were only fully-manned in times of danger. In November 1792, for example, it was decreed that in the event of an invasion, 'per difesa delle Marine', the batteries were to receive soldiers from the galleys to help man their artillery. The regiment of Gozo militia was to provide the men to serve the batteries of Gozo and Comino. In 1792, a thousand men were detailed to defend the coast while the rest were to act as a reserve. The Order's two marine battalions, whose men were drawn from the galleys and the men-of-war, were also frequently detailed to provide the coastal batteries with additional guncrew.[9]

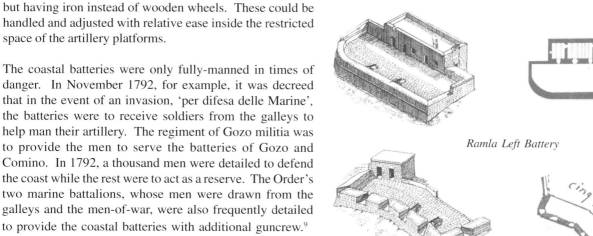

Pwales Right Battery

Ramla Left Battery

The Artillery of the Coastal Gun Batteries in 1785

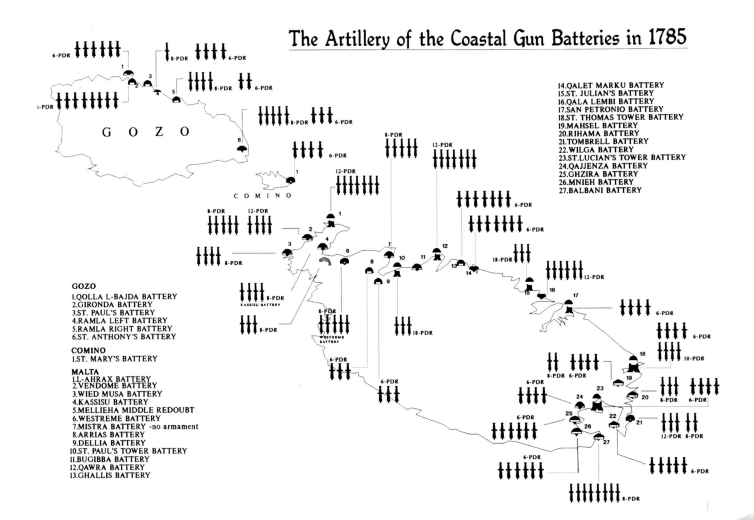

14.QALET MARKU BATTERY
15.ST. JULIAN'S BATTERY
16.QALA LEMBI BATTERY
17.SAN PETRONIO BATTERY
18.ST. THOMAS TOWER BATTERY
19.MAHSEL BATTERY
20.RIHAMA BATTERY
21.TOMBRELL BATTERY
22.WILGA BATTERY
23.ST.LUCIAN'S TOWER BATTERY
24.QAJJENZA BATTERY
25.GHZIRA BATTERY
26.MNIEH BATTERY
27.BALBANI BATTERY

GOZO
1.QOLLA L-BAJDA BATTERY
2.GIRONDA BATTERY
3.ST. PAUL'S BATTERY
4.RAMLA LEFT BATTERY
5.RAMLA RIGHT BATTERY
6.ST. ANTHONY'S BATTERY

COMINO
1.ST. MARY'S BATTERY

MALTA
1.L-AHRAX BATTERY
2.VENDOME BATTERY
3.WIED MUSA BATTERY
4.KASSISU BATTERY
5.MELLIEHA MIDDLE REDOUBT
6.WESTREME BATTERY
7.MISTRA BATTERY -no armament
8.ARRIAS BATTERY
9.DELLIA BATTERY
10.ST. PAUL'S TOWER BATTERY
11.BUGIBBA BATTERY
12.QAWRA BATTERY
13.GHALLIS BATTERY

Below, interior view of the redan of Mistra battery,
fitted with musketry loopholes, a corbelled sentry
walk, and gateway.

Coastal Redoubts

Apart from the coastal batteries, the system of coastal defence adopted by the knights in the eighteenth century relied on another important component, the redoubt. Unlike the batteries, which were usually sited at the mouth of the bays and designed to engage enemy ships and boats with their cannon, the redoubts were intended to serve as infantry strongpoints against landed troops and prevent them from setting up beachheads.

Infantry redoubts were a form of military fortification widely used by the French in the eighteenth century. The defensive roles played by redoubts varied considerably, making it difficult to give a precise definition and any particular configuration to this form of fortification. Etymologically, the word redoubt comes from the French *reduit*, which in turn comes from the Italian *ridotta* and Latin *reductus,* meaning 'a shelter or refuge'; this explains the more common French meaning of a small place or small fortification. In shape and form, there was little to distinguish a Hospitaller coastal redoubt from a coastal battery other than that these usually lacked embrasures for cannon, for both were equipped with blockhouses and ditches. The majority of redoubts erected by the knights in Malta and Gozo were built to a more or less pentagonal plan. These were enclosed by shallow parapets, fitted with a single blockhouse at the gorge, and surrounded by shallow

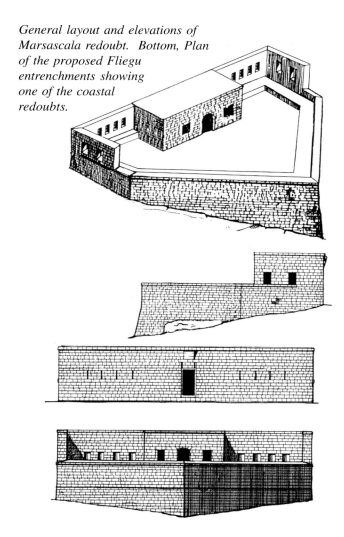

General layout and elevations of Marsascala redoubt. Bottom, Plan of the proposed Fliegu entrenchments showing one of the coastal redoubts.

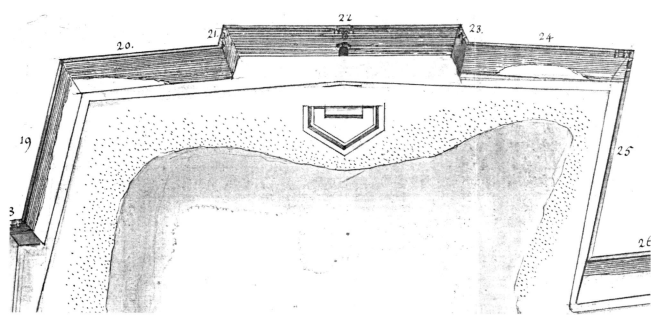

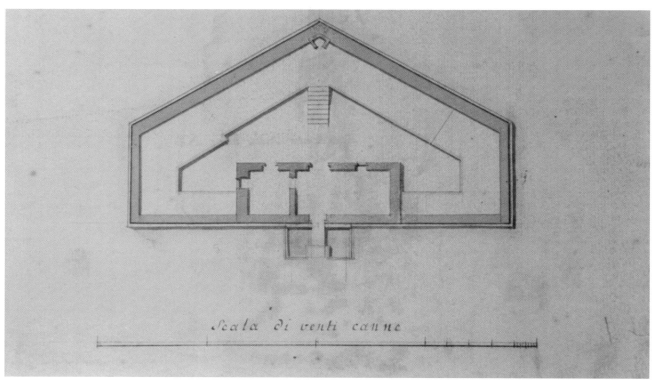

Scala di venti canne

Above, Plan of Ramla bay redoubt, typical of the many pentagonal redoubts built in 1715-16 (NLM). Most of these were named after Vendôme and had a single blockhouse to the rear. These were enveloped by shallow ditches and had low parapets as can be seen in the aerial view of the Armier redoubt, left. The Ramla redoubt also had a sentry post or echaugette at the salient of the work but this seems to have been added later in the century to serve as a watch-post during an outbreak of plague. Below, The salient of the redoubt at Armier.

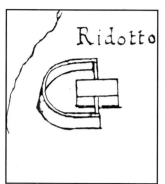

ditches. Eleven redoubts were built following this standard pattern. The majority of these were erected along the northern coast of Malta from Bahar-ic-Caghaq to Marfa, (Tal Bir, Eskalar, Armier, Louvier, Mellieha, Qalet Marku, and Bahar-ic-Caghaq) together with two in Gozo (Marsalforn and Ramla). Two were built in the south of Malta at Marsascala and Marsaxlokk (Del Fango) redoubt.

Above, left, Plans of Xwejni and St George bay redoubts, both demolished. Above, right, Aerial view of St George redoubt at Birzebbuga. Below, Ximenes redoubt, Salina.

Although designed primarily for use by the infantry, the sizable platform of the open pentagonal redoubts enabled the deployment of a small number of light cannon. However, only a few of these works actually mounted any guns. In 1792, the congregation of war ordered that the redoubts at Ramla bay in Gozo and at Mellieha be armed with two 6-pdr and four 6-pdr guns respectively. These redoubts were to receive a complement of 6 gunners and 22 guncrew.

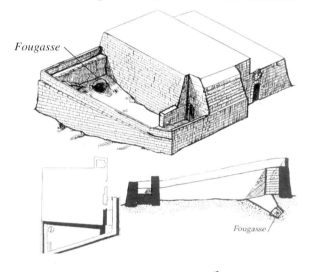

A few coastal redoubts were also built with semicircular or rectangular platforms such as St George bay redoubt, Xwejni redoubt in Gozo, St George redoubt (Birzebbuga), and the

Right, Graphic reconstruction and plan of the Salina left redoubt, or Perellos redoubt as it was also known. This work is particular in that it had a hollow polygonal enclosure ending in bastioned spur and no blockhouse. One plan, however, does actually indicate a blockhouse. A fougasse was later also excavated in the rock inside the fortified enclosure.

The Kalafrana redoubt, shown above and left , was of the closed blockhouse type with a semicircular plan.

two Salina bay redoubts. That known as the Perellos redoubt, at Salina (now demolished) was particular in that one corner of its perimeter wall was fitted with a small bastion. The Ximenes redoubt, on the opposite side of the bay, on the other hand, had its two blockhouses later replaced by a large magazine designed to house the salt from the nearby *Saline Nuove*. Both the Salina redoubts were unique in that they were fitted with an internally-placed fougasse.

The most interesting of the local redoubts, undoubtedly, were the tower-like works with walls pierced with numerous musketry loopholes. These were designed along the lines of blockhouses, a type of fortification much favoured by the French throughout their colonies and in New France, an understandable influence given the local presence of French military engineers. The redoubts erected in Malta, however, were obviously built in stone and not wood. Three

examples of such *tour-reduits* were built and all three confined to the Marsaxlokk bay: Fresnoy redoubt, Spinola redoubt, and Vendôme redoubt. The Spinola and Vendôme ones were squarish in plan but that at Kalafrana, i.e, Fresnoy redoubt, had a semicircular front and a redan to the rear facing the landward approaches. Only the Vendôme example survives to this day. Interestingly, the last coastal tower erected in 1720, at Marsalforn in Gozo, was also built along the lines of a *tour-reduit*.

An important function given to the redoubts, according to the tactical standing orders issued by the congregation of war in 1716, was their use as storage depots for militia entrenchment tools and equipment.

Below, Vendôme redoubt, Marsaxlokk, built in the form of a masonry blockhouse.

Coastal & Inland Entrenchments

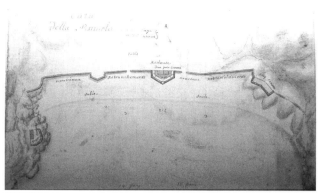

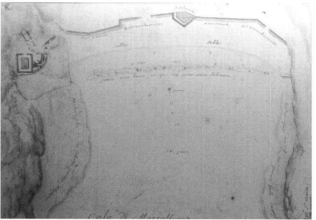

Plans of the 18th-century entrenchments at Ramla bay, top, and Marsalforn (NLM).

Perhaps the most ambitious element in the coastal defence strategy adopted by the knights were the entrenchments. Although it seems that the idea for this mode of defence was introduced by the commissioners Fontet and Arginy and the military engineer Bachelieu in 1714-15, the Order appears to have experimented with coastal entrenchments at an much earlier date.[1] Indeed the Order's historian Vertot records that in 1530 Grand Master Philippe de L'Isle Adam had ordered the construction of entrenchments in Gozo. That such works were actually built then is hard to prove since none of the many seventeenth-century reports draw attention to the existence of these structures. Still, one report, dated 1714, does refer to the 'antiche Trinciere' at Ramla bay, but even these could just date to the seventeenth century.[2] In fact, the German engineer Johannes Person is known to have supervised the construction of trenches around the Cittadella in 1708 and may have similarly been responsible for the construction of coastal ones.[3]

The strategy of Fontet and Arginy for preventing an invading force from landing troops on the island involved the construction of a network of coastal fortifications, of which the entrenchments or infantry lines were an important element intended to serve as a physical barrier against invasion.[4] In their report the two commissioners proposed the construction of entrenchments at Marsaxlokk, '...essendo la più pericolosa' and along the 'marine dell'Isola di Gozzo' followed by others at Marsascala, St Paul bay, Mellieha, and the coast overlooking the *Fliegu*.[5] The scheme was approved and work began in 1715. The idea found an enthusiastic supporter in the prior of France, Philippe de Vendôme, who went on to recommend more entrenchments at Salina, Qalet Marku, Madliena, and Birzebbuga.

Few areas, however, seem to have actually received entrenchment walls during this early period. It appears that only the ones in Gozo were built and these were erected at Marsalforn, Ramla, and Naghag-il-Bahar. Even so, these works were, according to Vendôme, very weak structures with walls 'tanto bassi, e debboli che il mare, et il vento li possono ruinare in pochi mesi'.[6] Consequently, it was soon considered necessary to rebuild them 'migliori e più solidi.'

The emergency of 1722 served to expose the Order's inability to maintain the vast coastal defensive network it had created in 1715 and, as a result, it was decided to abandon all those works in the northern half of Malta in the event of an invasion. Instead a new defensive front was adopted along the line of the Great Fault running from Madliena to Bingemma, '...prevalersi de trinceramento naturale del Vallone chiamato Wiet el assel, serrando i luoghi accessibili, con muraglie a secco, per ragione che detto Vallone e detti trinceramenti, tagliando l'Isola per il mezzo, ne lascieremo solamente una meta da difendere, onde viene minor bisogno di truppe e di batterie oltre che nella parte rinserrata si ritrovino ancor rinchiusi tutti i Casali, per il qual'effetto bisognera quanto prima mettere mano al travaglio di detti trinceramenti, impiegandovi tutta la gente, che si potrà radumare de Casali vicini.'[7] Troops were to be concentrated behind two newly-erected entrenchments at the most vulnerable spots along the ridge, at Ta' Falca and Naxxar and along a coastal passage near the Madliena tower. On 3 July 1722, the congregation of war also ordered the construction of an entrenchment beneath Città Notabile 'simile a quello del Nasciaro.'[8] The inland entrenchments at Ta' Falca, however, were not completed before 1732.

Above, Aerial view of the Naxxar entrenchment, later incorporated into the trace of British 19th-century fortifications known as the Victoria Lines (DOI). Below, Detail of one of the triangular spurs, or redans, which form the Hospitaller entrenchment at Naxxar. This work of fortification was built a secco, that is, of dry-stone walling, similar in a way to the many field walls found in the Maltese countryside.

The Naxxar entrenchment was built to a redan trace, consisting of triangular spurs linked to straight curtain walls, and this set the pattern for a number of other entrenchments built in the following years. It was a 'trinciera di pietra a secco', that is, of dry rubble-wall construction, terrepleined to provide regular banquettes and platforms for the deployment of field guns. Its four redans projected at regular intervals from along a straight line of curtain walls. These enabled enfilading fire along the intermediate curtains. The salient angles of the redans were reinforced with ashlar quoins. Similar types of entrenchments were erected around Mdina in 1722, at Xrop L-Ghagin near Delimara, and at Benghisa in 1723.[9]

In that same year the congregation of war also ordered the construction of a continuous line of entrenchments along the coast from Ricasoli to Marsaxlokk and between Dragut point and Qalet Marku though work on these was only initiated long afterwards. Under Marandon's directions 'alcuni nuovi trincieramenti' were erected in 'luoghi vicini a

Above, Site plan showing the remains of Xrop L-Ghagin entrenchment, built as a redan trace.

Above, Aerial view of Benghisa Point entrenchment (DOI). Below, right, 18th-century map of Benghisa point showing the coastal entrenchments in the area (NLM).

Marsascirocco chiamati Binisa, Tombarel e Scirop L'agin', all of which had been initated but 'non eseguiti nel tempo dell'ultima citazione'.[10] The Falca entrenchment combined the bastioned trace with the redan trace, the ramparts being built of rough-faced ashlar laid in regular courses and backed up with a terrepleined banquette.

By 1761, the time of the next serious invasion scare, the chain of entrenchments was still far short from that envisaged by the military planners in 1716. Moreover, the coastal defences built by the knights were concentrated inside the bays and no account had been taken of the many vulnerable headlands around the coast where an enemy could easily land in the calm summer months. Thereupon, the French military mission under the command of Bourlamaque drew up an ambitious scheme to augment the system of coastal defences with the addition of some 30 batteries and artillery platforms, and the encirclement of both islands within a quasi-continuous line of entrenchments and the artificial escarpment of the rocky coastline ('escarper toutes les parties de la côte qui en sont susceptible').[11] The result of these recommendations saw entrenchments springing up during the course of the next decade at Armier, Mellieha (Kassisu), Qawra, Spinola, St Julians (1767-1770), Birzebbuga, Marsascala, and on the coast between Fort Ricasoli and Zonqor tower.[12]

On 17 October 1762 the knights contracted 'Capo Mastro Geronimo Micallef ... assieme col numero sufficente d'altri Maestri picconieri da lui portati' to construct entrenchments

and scarp the coastline from Dragut point to St Julians bay, '... essendosi per difesa di quest'Isola di Malta, e Gozo pensato di fossare e trincare nella rocca viva tutte quelle spiagge della medesima nelle quali puo dall'Inemico con facilità farsi di sbarco, e per impedir cio è stata fatta una pianta, o sia un disegno, nel quale si vedono detti fossati, e tincere con chiarezza delineate; onde per dar principio all'Opera sudetta, e per mettere in chiaro la maggior parte della spesa necessaria di dett'opera, si conviene con Geronimo Micallef del fu Pietro della Terra Zebbug, come

Maestro Picconiere, il quale avendo fatta la prova esperimentale della rocca esistente nella spiaggia del mare di tutta la contrada dalla Punta di Dragut sin a S. Giuliano, e da Ricasoli sin alla Torre di Limara si è obligato, e si obliga nel modo e forma, come siegue, e sotto i patti, e condizioni gia convenuti con S. E. il Ven. Sign. Balì Frà Domenico Antonio Chisurlia.[13]

By 1763 a total of 1,872.7 *canne* of entrenchments had been constructed along the coast spanning from Ricasoli to Zonqor point; 1,312 *canne* at Marsaxlokk, 663.5 *canne* 'dalla batteria Benghisa sino al scarpato sotto la Torre S. Luciano', and 943.5 *canne* from Wied Hammiech 'sino la punta sinistra della Cala Wiet il Hain'.[14] In April 1763 300 workmen were employed on the construction of coastal entrenchments between Ricasoli and Marsascala under the direction of Balì de Tigné. The knight Chisurlia inspected these works by boat ('ho voluto...portarmi di persona per mare a goderne di vedere i siti') and expressed his doubts to Balì de Tigné about some defects in the design of entrenchments.[15] The latter, however, questioned Chisurlia's credentials and expertise in the art of fortification. Consequently, Chisurlia presented a report to Grand Master

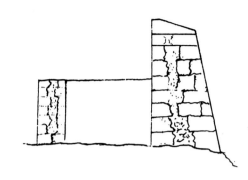

Profilo del Trincieram.to nelle Parti a.b. c d. ef.

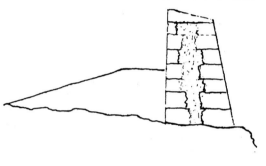

Demi-bastion

Cutting

Redan

Cutting in curtain wall to serve as a sally-port

Bastioned salient

Below, Graphic reconstruction of the Ta' Falca inland entrenchment. This entrenchment was built in the formal manner as a permanent work of fortification rather than as a true fieldwork. The two profiles shown above provide a good idea of the manner of construction of the ramparts, in parts served by an earthen banquette and a terrepleined platform (NLM).
Following page, top, Plan of the Falca entrenchment (NLM).
Far right, View of the surviving wall of the demi-bastion, practically the only remaining stretch of the ramparts of the Falca entrenchment still clearly visible.
Redan

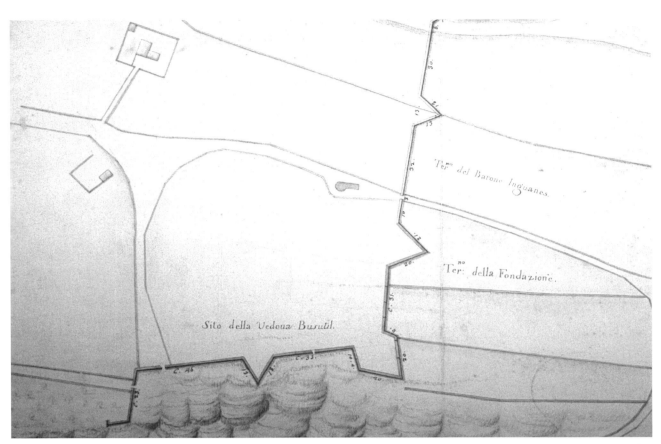

Pinto outlining his observations and recommendations. In this report, dated 25 April 1763, Chisurlia warned the grand master that in embarking on the scheme espoused by Borlamaque, the Order had not taken into consideration the costs involved in the excavation and erection of the works and the length of time required to complete the scheme and, moreover, failed to take account of the 'costo dell'artiglieria, polvere ed altre provizioni e il numero della gente per guarnirle e diffenderle.'

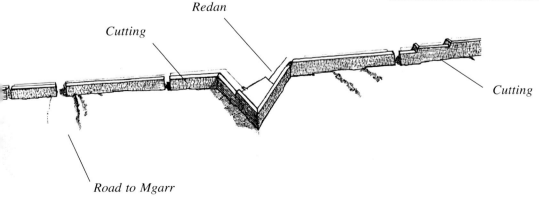

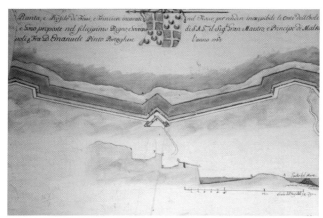

Above, Proposal for an unbuilt tenaille-trace type of redan, put forward by the knight Chisurlia. Below, Plan of the entrenchment designed for Qawra point. Only a small section of these defences was actually constructed. Above, right, Cross-section of a proposed entrenchment showing a ditch with a berm (NLM).

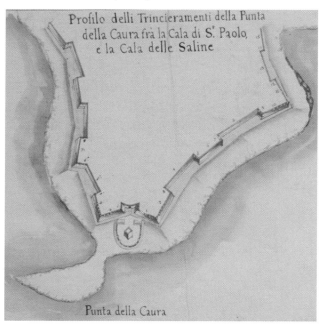

Out of the 30 miles of coastline between Marsaxlokk and the *Fliegu*, 10 miles were taken up by precipitous and inaccessible shoreline, another 10 miles comprised bays and another 'circa dieci miglia di Coste' were 'accessibili da trincierarsi.' According to Chirsulia's calculations, 10 miles were equivalent to a line of entrenchments of 50 bastions connected by curtains 200 paces long. This implied a line of fortications requiring 5,000 troops to man with a similar number to act as a reserve. Chisurlia did not believe that the rules employed in the design of fortresses held for coastal rock-hewn entrenchments for although 'nelle piazze si prescrivono i beluardi più grandi che si puo per contenere maggior numero di difensori per opporsi agli assalti delle breccie e per far delle tagliate e ritirate', coastal entrenchments were not intended to withstand the battering of 'migliaja di Cannonate di grosso calibro' and could therefore be much smaller.[15]

Chirsulia proposed, instead, a new design composed of longer curtains to reduce the number of bastions and, also, smaller bastions. The interiors of the bastions were not to be levelled except for a narrow strip equal in width to that behind the curtain walls. Only in the flanks was there to be 'spazio maggiore e piazza d'armi per maneggiare bene l'artiglieria'.[16] However, long curtain walls were defective in that they did not allow proper enfilading fire along their length due to the limitations in the range of the guns and secondly, once overrun by the enemy, a sizable stretch of ground would consequently fall into enemy hands.

To overcome these difficulties and avoid the addition of other bastions, he designed bastions with obtuse angles of flanks and, in the re-entrant angle of the curtain walls, small redans with internal ravelins, fitted with gun emplacements to provide enfilading fire along both faces of the curtain walls. Chisurlia borrowed this idea from the design of the 'Tenaglia della Cortina di questa Porta Reale'(Valletta). The coastal entrenchment bastions were to be 'lontani 200 Tese un dall'altro' and thus 'venivano ad aver la difesa della moschettaria del redan, e parte di cortina

il Comino, e nella Punta frà la Cala di Osseliet, e la Cala della Barriera

Aerial view and plan of the bastioned entrenchment at Armier bay (NLM).

nella distanza di soli 100 passi, o sieno 93 canne, e li fuochi de piccoli cannoni de fianchi de baluardi, ... ad incrocicchiare mirabilmente.' The fire of the 'piccolo Rivellino superiore che domina a cavaliere' would in turn enable the adjoining works to be enfiladed adequately.[17]

Balì de Tigné and Chisurlia held opposite views as to what constituted the best design for coastal entrenchments. Where Chisurlia considered 50 bastions to be adequate,

Tigné preferred 200 bastions connected by very short curtain walls and armed with heavy guns of at least 24-pounder calibre. Two hundred bastions implied 400 flanks requiring at least 1,600 soldiers and a total of 9,600 men to handle the guns. Evidently, Chisurlia was justified in believing this to be an unrealistic proposal given the Order's resources. Work on the entrenchments leading to Zonqor point, however, progressed according to Tigné's designs and 19 bastions linked by curtain walls were erected over

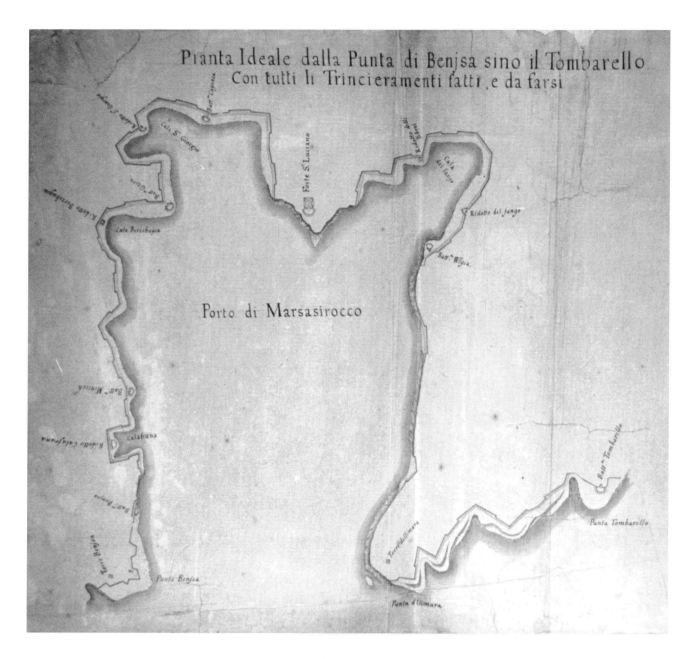

some four miles of coastline. The design involved obtuse-angled and flat-faced bastions with short flanks attached to curtain walls approximately 50 *canne* long, the walls being built of crude rubble-stone in the *pietra a secco* style.

The entrenchments erected at Armier, Mellieha, St Julians, Birzebbuga, and Zewwieqa (Gozo), however, were built in the form of solid bastioned enceintes and as permanent works of fortification rather than mere field works. The Birzebbuga entrenchments were the most extensive and spanned all the way from the Ferretti battery right up to the Kalafrana redoubt. The walls were fitted with large obtuse-angled bastions with short flanks, were some 20 feet high,

Above, Plan showing the proposed network of coastal entrenchments at Marsxlokk and Delimara (NLM).

and were crowned with a thick parapet pierced with embrasures. The whole front was strengthened by a rock-hewn ditch. Other extensive stretches were erected at Spinola, St Julians bay, and Armier. At Ta' Kassisu, in Mellieha, the works were left in an unfinished state, with a large part of the trace of walls still to be fashioned out of the bedrock. An attempt to dig a fosse along the whole length of the entrenchment wall was also abandoned when the project ground to a halt due to a lack of funds. Those at Qawra point and along the coast at Madliena were built

Profilo de Trinceramenti nella Costa trà la punta destra della Cala di S.ᵗ Giuliano, e la punta deſtra della Cala di S.ᵗ Giorgio

with flat-faced platforms of which only a few sparse traces survive.

There were other variations on the theme of coastal entrenchments. One of these involved the construction of underwater walls designed to obstruct the entrance of vessels into the bays. One such wall or artificial reef, which still survives today, is that which was built in the middle of Ramla bay in Gozo while another was built in Marsalforn bay. These are the 'gettate di pietra' and the 'catena di pietra' mentioned in the documents. A second variation involved a proposal for the construction of line of 'Abatis, che altro non sono che Alberi d'ogni specie, e qualità con tutti i rami e radici se si possono avere, sopremesse l'uno appogiato all'altro, con ... fango per sostenerli e legati insieme con corde.'[18] These wooden stakes, trunks, and branches were to be driven into the sand in a wide band across the width of the bay to prevent 'barche piatte e caicchi galeotte' from proceeding further towards the shoreline, '....basta per tratenere le barche a non poter avanzare, restando cosi bersaglio delle Batterie della spiaggia, e di fronte in mezzo a tre fuochi'. The line of abattis was to be situated just within range of musket-fire from the shore but in the case of larger and deeper bays, it was proposed to erect 'due linee una dietro all'altra in proporzionata distanza, acciò riuscendo all'inemico dopo molta perdita di barche e di uomini superare la prima linea, ritrovi l'impedimento della seconda.'[19] In order for this scheme to be effective, it was necessary that the whole circumferance of the bay, from one

Aerial view, top, and 20th-century photograph, above, of the entrenchment at Spinola. (NLM).

extreme end to the other, was to be fortified with simple *trinciere di pietre a secco*, built within 4 days from the stone and rubble scattered around the surrounding countryside by the troops detailed to defend the coasts. From behind these makeshift trenches the defenders were to engage the enemy with muskets and 'piccola artiglieria a metraglia'. The construction of an abattis, however, required large amounts of wood and trees which were impossible to find on the island.

Large bays like Mellieha and Marsaxlokk allowed enemy ships to deploy in a straight line, thus enabling those on

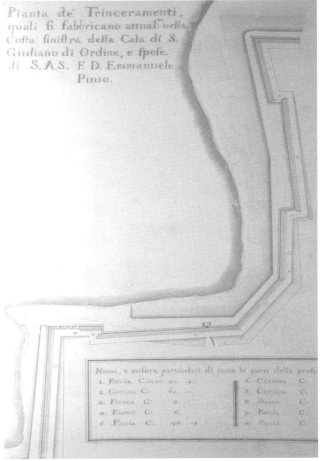

Pianta de' Trinceramenti, quali si fabbricano attual:e nella Cofta finiftra della Cala di S. Giuliano di Ordine, e fpefe di S.A.S. F.D. Emmanuele Pinto.

Nomi, e mifure particolari di tutte le parti della pref..
1. Faccia Canne 40, 4.
2. Cortina C: 42, –
3. Fianco C: 4
4. Fianco C: 6
5. Faccia C: 40 4

Above, top, Aerial view of the entrenchment at Birzebbuga and, above, as surviving in the 19th century. Left, Plan of the entrenchment at St Julians, Sliema, built by Grand Master Pinto (NLM).

the flanks to shield the intermediate boats from enfilading fire. One proposal designed to counteract this threat was to decrease the width of the bay by scuttling large old ships 'all'imboccatura di dette cale, e si affondino in proporzionata distanza in linea; nella Meleha cinque bastimenti sono sufficenti se non se ne possono avere di maggior numero.' Two floating pontoons in the middle of the bay, camouflaged with alga and within the range of the 18-pdr guns of the coastal batteries, were to mount four guns each. Another proposed method was to form an abbatis of 'pietre puntate e larga una canna ... distante del lido della Cala circa 40 canne.'

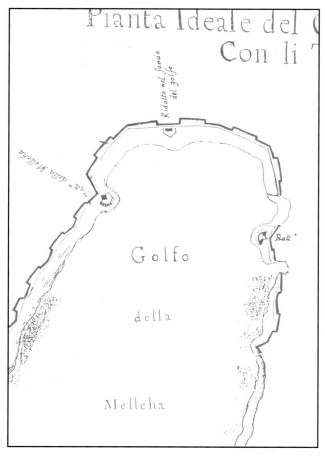

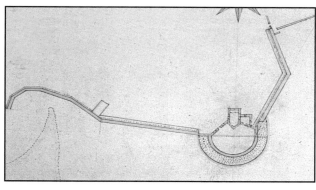

Left, Plan of the entrenchments at Mellieha bay, and above, those built near Tombrell battery, Delimara (NLM).

Surely the most impractical and far-fetched scheme for the defence of the bays was that proposing the planting of a large number of olive and carob trees along the whole length of the beaches hoping that some twenty years later these would present a natural impenetrable wall, '...di far piantare la maggior quantità d'alberi che si può lungho le spiagie delle Cale, e d'Olivi e Carrube, che fossono essere utili co'loro frutti, e tra lo spazio di 20 anni atti all' uso sudetto.'

The post-1761 effort aimed at the construction of coastal entrenchments did not progress very far and, after a decade or so, the whole undertaking ground to a halt with the death of Grand Master Pinto in 1773. Pinto had proved to be an enthusiastic supporter for the scheme of coastal fortifications and had financed the construction of the St Julians and Spinola entrenchments at his own expense. The partially excavated ditches of various works, such as those at Armier, Mellieha (Kassisu), and Spinola, bear witness to a sudden

Above, One of the flanks along the length of the Ta' Kassisu entrenchment. Below, Ta' Kassisu entrenchment at Mellieha.

Ducts for run-off rainwater

Flank with battery en barbette

Obtuse-angled bastion protected by narrow ditch

Uncompleted curtain with partly-hewn scarp and platform

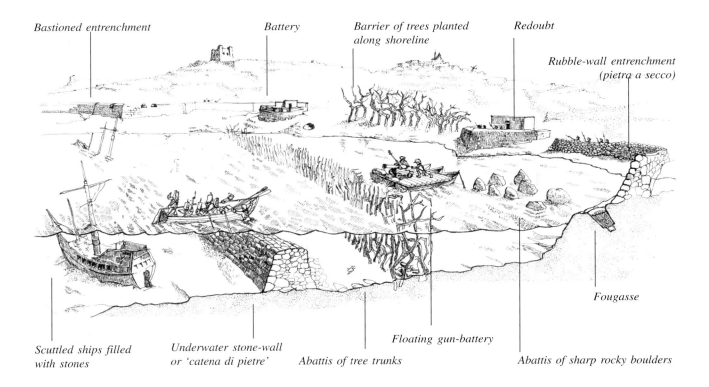

Bastioned entrenchment Battery Barrier of trees planted along shoreline Redoubt

Rubble-wall entrenchment (pietra a secco)

Fougasse

Scuttled ships filled with stones Underwater stone-wall or 'catena di pietre' Abattis of tree trunks Floating gun-battery Abattis of sharp rocky boulders

A representation of the various coastal defence schemes proposed in the 18th century. Below, Entrenchments at Ghajn Tuffieha (left) and Bahar-ic-Caghaq.

and abrupt termination of the various works. Many of the entrenchments appear to have been allowed to fall into decay, particularly the less solidly-built *pietra a secco* type. Occasionally, efforts were made to remedy the situation, such as happened in 1792, for example, when the Falca entrenchment, which had then fallen into a state of disrepair, was ordered to be repaired and maintained. Still, very little remains today of most of these defensive walls.

The Fougasses

One of the most interesting adjuncts of coastal defence employed by the knights for the coastal defence of the island was the fougasse, a kind of rock-hewn mortar designed to fire large quantities of stone onto approaching enemy ships. Although not an altogether Maltese invention as claimed by many authors, this weapon was, nonetheless, a unique adaptation of the fougasse, particularly in its method of construction and unorthodox application in a coastal defence role. Various sources have claimed that the fougasses of Malta are not fougasses at all, the word being a misnomer, but simply singular mortars cut in rock. This statement, however, is not entirely correct since the Maltese type of weapon has features which belong both to the fougasse and mortar. In actual fact, it is a combination of three kinds of weapons, the fougasse, the explosive mine, and the mortar. The best word used to describe it is *fougasse-pierrier*, the *pierrier* being a stone-firing cannon. In contemporary documents it is more popularly referred to as the *fougasse a cailloux, fogazza,* or *fornello a selci.*[1] Pontleroy , in 1761, referred to them simply as 'les puits'.

The fundamental uniqueness of the Maltese fougasse stems primarily from the nature of the Maltese terrain which dictated that the fougasse had to be cut into solid rock. The local method of construction gave the weapon a permanence, solidity, and form not enjoyed elsewhere, especially since most fougasses were generally employed in field defences and earthworks thus earning in the process an ephemeral quality. In Malta, the fougasse was a product of the eighteenth century. It is known that in the first decades of the 1700s, when the Order, under the influence of French engineers, decided to implement a coast defence scheme, the fougasse was proposed to complement the coastal defences. In 1715 the council ordered 60 stone mortars to be cut at vulnerable points around the coasts of the island but no action appears to have been taken. Of these, 48 were to have been excavated in Malta.[2]

The early attempts to introduce the weapon under the direction of the military engineer Mondion seem to have failed and it was not until 1741, under the direction of Marandon, that the weapon was adopted successfully. Marandon fired his first experimental *foggazza a selci* on 28 September 1740.[3] This was cut into the rocky foreshore below the 'bastione delle forbici' at the foot of the Valletta bastions facing Dragut point. On the day of its baptism of

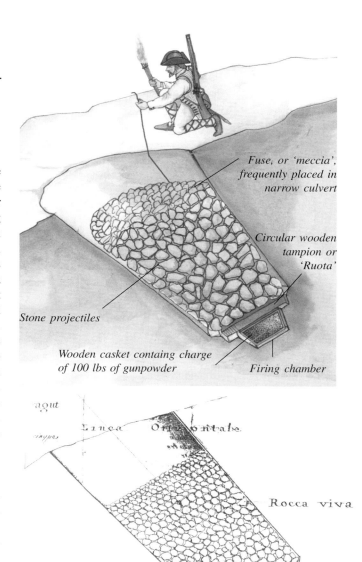

Top, Cutaway diagram of a typical fougasse of Malta and, above, Marandon's experimental fougasse fired in September 1740 (NLM).

fire, Marandon filled the fougasse with 306 stone boulders of various sizes, totalling in weight to 3,575 *cantara*. A charge of 83 *rotuli* of ordinary gunpowder was placed in the chamber and when fired this proved powerful enough to propel the said mass of stone over a distance of some 300m (160 *canne*), raising it, in the process, to a maximum height of 60 to 80m. The effect, in Marandon's own words, was that 'la pioggia

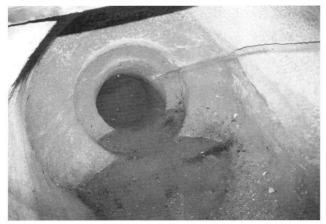

Above, from top to bottom, Detail of the firing chamber of one of the two fougasses at Birzebbuga, Ramla Bay fougasse, and Madliena fougasse (near the De Redin tower).

he was ordered by the congregation of war to excavate a network of fougasses first in Malta and then in Gozo. In all around 50 were built in Malta and 14 in Gozo.[4]

In shape the Maltese fougasse resembled a large inclined tumbler with the lower side prolonged to meet the horizontal line from the top of the brim. As a result, the mouth of the fougasse was elliptical. The bore was circular but the shaft of the pit was conical, tapering from 2.13m at the mouth to 1.52m at the bottom where it curved towards the powder chamber. This measured around 0.76m in diameter and was 4.5m deep. Arming a fougasse was a lengthy task that took about an hour. The procedure involved first the placing of the gunpowder charge of '100 au 120 livres de poudre' inside its flat barrel within the powder chamber at the bottom of the pit. A long cord-like fuse was then secured to the powder casket and passed through a narrow channel cut in the side of the fougasse.

The gunpowder chamber was then covered with a circular wooden lid, or *Ruota,* and the pit then filled in with a large number of stones, or *selci,* with the larger stones placed at the bottom. It appears that the stone projectiles for use with the fougasse were collected beforehand and stockpiled in the vicinity of the fougasse, if not within the pit itself, ready for use. Various custodians were also employed to ensure that these *selci* were not carried away. The cone-shaped pit was so designed to allow the projectiles, once fired, to spread out and cover as wide an area of ground, or sea, as possible. The stones, to quote Louis de Boisgelin, had the effect of hail and were not only capable of killing men but of sinking boats.

To ensure the greatest tactical effect, the fougasses were employed in pairs in order that a large area of sea or foreshore in each bay could be covered by their crossfire. Initially all the fougasses were made to cover the entrances to the bays but, in 1761, the French engineers advised the knights to add others for flanking fire too.

The first record of the fougasse being armed and readied for war is during the emergency of 1761. The suspicious appearance of the French Fleet in the vicinity of Malta in 1792 provided a second opportunity and indeed the congregation of war then ordered that the fougasses be armed and kept ready for eventual use, '...si rettano le fugacce, e si tengono pronte'.[5] The feared invasion did not materialize but in 1798 things turned out differently and it appears that a few of fougasses were actually fired against Bonaparte's troops as they set about invading the island. Major Ritchie quotes De la Jonquiere's reproduction of an extract from a letter written by a knight of the Order asserting that fougasses were fired against the Città Vecchia division as it was attempting a descent at Marsaxlokk bay.

delle selci si stese sin alla ponta Dragut lontana cento sessanta canne, e che salirono a 30 in 40 canne, e non ne resto' ne pur una ne dentro la Fogazza ne inanti.' Marandon was quite pleased with the result and in the following years

References & Notes

Glossary of Terms used in Military Architecture

ACROPOLIS, an elevated stronghold of a Greek city, usually containing the temple of the patron divinity within its walls.

ABATTIS, ABATIS, a continuous thick line of felled trees and shrubs driven into the ground with bows pointing outwards to form an impenetrable obstacle. It was also constructed in shallow water to impede the movements of boats towards the shore.

ABUTMENT, an end wall supporting a row of casemates.

ADVANCED WORKS, *ouvrages avancée* - F., defensive works placed beyond the glacis but still near enough to be covered from the main defences.

AIR-HOLE, a ventilating hole, usually above a musketry loophole or embrasure, to extract smoke, especially from inside casemates or musketry galleries.

ALBARRA, detached wall-tower designed to allow for better flanking fire and also to be easily isolated from the main defences if taken by the enemy; a peculiarity of Iberian castles.

ALCAZAR, a Moorish or Spanish castle or fortress.

ALURE, a gallery or passage along the parapet of a castle.

ANTEMURAL, a wall or outerwork surrounding and protecting a castle; in some late medieval documents the word barbican was used to denote an antemural.

ARCH, a curved construction spanning an opening.

ARRIS, the sharp edge produced when two surfaces meet together as at the salients of bastions or spurs.

ASHLAR, squared building masonry used in the construction of walls and other structures.

AVANCÉE, a place-of-arms situated where the road leaves the covertway after passing through the gate.

AVANS MUR, an antemural.

BAILEY, the open area or courtyard within a medieval castle. (see motte-and-bailey).

BALISTRARIA, a loophole or aperture in medieval battlements through which crossbowmen.

BANQUETTE, a raised walkway, sometimes stepped, behind a high parapet to enable troops to fire their weapons over the parapet.

BARREL VAULT, a continuous arched roof of stone, of semicircular section, supported by parallel walls.

BARBETTE, *a barba* - I., *en barbette* - F:, a platform on which guns are mounted to fire over a parapet.

BARBICAN, BARBACAN, an outer work defending the gate of a castle or citadel, frequently a fortified gate house.

BARRACK BLOCK, building, sometimes bombproof and fortified, designed to house the garrison of a fort.

BARTIZAN, a battlemented turret projecting outwards from the corner of a tower or wall.

BASCULE, a counterbalanced drawbridge of which there are two main types, the drawbridge levered by pole-arms and the counter-balanced gangway.

BASTION, *bastione, beluardo* - I., a work projecting outwards from the main walls of a defensive enceinte, designed to enable the garrison to see and defend the adjacent perimeter together with the area in front of the ramparts. In its embryonic form, the bastion can be found in both cylindrical and polygonal form. The polygonal form was perfected by the Italian engineers of the late 15th century and early 16th century into a pentagonal work composed of two faces, two flanks and a gorge. [A]

BASTIONETTE, a small bastion added to the salient of a bastion to provide enfilading fire along the two faces of the latter.

BATARDEAU, a dam or wall across a moat or ditch, built with a sharp ridge to prevent enemy troops from crossing the place; sometimes fitted with a turret as an additional barrier. [B]

BAULKS, the beams on which the planks of a bridge spanning a ditch rest.

BATTER, the inward inclination of the face of a wall from the vertical; a battered wall recedes as it rises.

BATTERY, a platform, usually protected by a parapet, for cannon and mortars; *orillion battery,* a battery placed in the flank of a bastion and sheltered by the orillion; *coastal battery,* a work, sometimes fortified against direct assault, designed to engage enemy ships close to the shore.

BATTLEMENT, a fortified parapet with merlons and crenels, or embrasures.

BAYOU, a trench in the rear of a battery designed to allow communication with a magazine; a branch of a trench.

BERM, a ridge below a parapet.

BLOCKHOUSE, a small fortified work consisting of one or more rooms fitted with loopholes in its sides to permit defensive fire in various directions.

BONNET, a small counterguard in front of the salient angle of a ravelin.

BONNETTE, an increase in height given to a parapet due to the upward prolongation of its exterior and interior slope.

BONNET DE PRETRE, a defensive work resembling a tenaille.

BOULEVARD, *Boulevart* - F., a substantial defensive work, usually polygonal in plan, projecting outwards from the main enceinte; an early bastion-like structure.

BRATTICE, a temporary breastwork, parapet, or gallery of wood used during a siege.

BRAYE, *Braga* - I., a continuous outerwork protecting the main enceinte, placed inside the ditch and separated from both the scarp and counterscarp walls.

BREACH, *breccia* - I., a gap blown open in the walls of a fortress by a mine or artillery fire.

BREASTWORK, a fieldwork thrown up breast-high for defence; a parapet.

BRISURE, a break in the line of a curtain wall in order to increase the area for guns in the flank of a bastion and to allow for a wider view and field of fire from the same.

BULWARK, *bollwerk* - G., *bolverk* - S, meaning a log-work, a substantial defensive work of earth; referring also to early bastion-like works of polygonal or semicircular plan (*boulevard* - F., *beluardo* - I.), usually detached from the main enceinte.

BUTTRESS, a mass of masonry built against a wall to give additional lateral strength, usually to counteract the lateral thrust of a roof, vault or arch.

CAPANATTO, a masonry loopholed room for defenders, usually with a triangular front and opened towards the interior of the fort.

CAPITAL OF THE BASTION, an imaginary line bisecting the salient angle

CAPONIER, a sheltered defensible passage across the ditch of a fort or cut through the glacis, linking the outerworks to the main enceinte; sometimes used to provide additional flanking fire along the ditch. [C]

CASEMATE, *cassamatta* - I., a vaulted chamber built in the thickness of the ramparts and used as a barrack or gun position (firing through embrasures).

CASEMATED RETRENCHMENT, a retrenchment fitted with guns firing through embrasures from within vaulted casemates and placed behind the main line of fortification.

CASTLE, a stronghold or fortified post; more specifically the fortified residence of a prince or feudal lord.

CASTRUM, a term originally used to refer to a Roman military camp but later also used to refer to early medieval castles,

CAVALIER, a raised earth platform, built on a bastion or curtain wall, designed to mount artillery and to command the surrounding ground.

CHEMIN DE RONDE, a continuous passage or walkway on a rampart, protected by a parapet, designed to allow the defenders access to the various parts of a fort.

CITADEL, *cittadella* - I., a fortress or castle built to dominate or protect a town.

COPING, a sloped or bevelled stone cap placed on top of a parapet or wall so as to protect the masonry and infill below from the penetration of water from above.

CORBEL, a small projecting stone designed to support a beam or other horizontal member, such as a machicolation.

CORDON, a rounded stone moulding or string-course, below the parapet of the revetment of a rampart, usually going all round the walls of a fort.

CORNICE MOULDING, a moulded projection forming the exterior trim of a wall.

COUNTERFORT, a buttress built behind a scarp wall for the purpose of strengthening the latter.

COUNTERGUARD, large outwerworks, open at the gorge, designed to protect the faces of bastions and ravelins.

COUNTERMINE, a tunnel excavated beneath the glacis through the counterscarp wall, terminating in a small shallow pit designed to house an explosive charge which was fired by the defenders when the enemy occupied by the ground directly above the mine.

COUNTERMURE, a wall raised behind another to take its place when a breach is made; a form of retrenchment.

COUNTERSCARP, *contrascarpa* - I., the outer wall of the ditch facing the ramparts.

COUNTERSCARP GALLERY, a casemate within the counterscarp fitted with musketry loopholes to defend the ditch and scarp wall.

COUPURE, a cut in the parapet and walkway of a rampart designed to prevent an enemy from turning the salient of the work.

COUVRE PORTE, a work designed to cover the immediate approaches to the main fortress.

COVERED WAY, COVERTWAY, *chemin couvert* - F., *strada coperta* - I., a path on top of the counterscarp, protected by a parapet formed from the crest of the glacis. [D]

CRENELLATION, the gap in a parapet; an embrasure.

CROCHET, a narrow passage between the head of a traverse and the parapet of the covertway to allow for movement of troops along the latter. [E]

CROWNWORK, *opera coronata* - I., a powerful outerwork, projecting ahead of the main enceinte to cover a vulnerable area, consisting of a central bastion supported by two demi-bastions.

CROWNED-HORNWORK, a hornwork protected further by a crownwork.

CURTAIN, *cortina* - I., the main wall of a defensive work, usually the length of a rampart between two bastions. [F]

CUTTING, a narrow opening in the parapet of the covered way, cut through the crest of the glacis, to allow for the passage of troops onto the glacis designed to facilitate counterattacks and are therefore usually found on the parapets of places-of-arms.

DEAD GROUND, an area of ground in the vicinity of a fortified work not covered by the defenders' guns and thus creating a vulnerable spot in the defences.

DEMI-BASTION, a half-bastion with one face and one or two flanks.

DEMI-CAPONIER, a caponier having only one protected flank. [G]

DEMI-LUNE, *mezzaluna* - I, a small detached outerwork, similar to a ravelin but smaller, placed before a curtain.

DETACHED LUNETTE, an advanced work in the form of a lunette connected to the covered way by a caponier.

DISCHARGING ARCH, an arch built to relieve the weight of the wall above a weak area.

A general schematic layout of an 18th-century bastioned front showing the various fortified elements and the terms used to describe them in French, reproduced from N. Dupain's Les Amusemens Militaires *(Paris, 1767).*

DITCH, *fossa* - I., *fossé* - F., a dry trench outside a fortified work, usually rock-hewn, to obstruct direct assault on the main walls. [H]

DONJON, the keep or strongest part of a castle.

DRAWBRIDGE, a bridge spanning a moat or a ditch, hinged and provided with a raising and lowering mechanism so as to hinder or enable passage into a castle or a fortress.

DRUM, one of the cylinders of stone which form a column, sometimes used in the walls of a fortress, especially if the latter was built in the vicinity of the ruins of a classical site, from where such material was eagerly quarried as building material.

EGLISE-DONJON, a church-keep or fortified chapel.

EMBRASURE, an opening cut in the parapet through which a gun could be fired without exposing the guncrew, normally wider at the front than at the rear; in casemates an enlargement of a window opening by means of splayed sides.

ENFILADING FIRE, fire from the flank of a bastion along the faces of the adjacent works.

ENCEINTE, the fortified perimeter of a defensive work, and the area enclosed by it.

ENTRENCHMENT, *trincieramento* - I., an inner, second line of defence sometimes accompanied by a trench; *coastal entrenchment*, a entrenchment built along the shoreline to impede an enemy disembarkation.

ENTRENCHED BASTION, a large bastion with an entrenchment built into its gorge.

ESCARPE, scarp, the wall of a fortified work which forms the side of the ditch facing outwards towards the counterscarp.

ESCARPMENT, a steep slope in front of a fortification to impede an enemy's approach.

ESCUTCHEON, a shield, usually of stone or marble, fixed to a fortress wall or above a gateway on which are depicted coat-of-arms and other heraldic insignias.

ESPLANADE, an open, levelled space between a citadel and the buildings of a town, to ensure a clear view of the immediate approaches to the fortress.

FACE WALL, the front, exposed retaining wall of a bastion or other defensive work; the wall of a bastion between the salient angle and the shoulder of a flank. [I]

FAUSSEBRAYE, *falsa braga* - I., an outer rampart, or *avans mur*, added to the walls of a fortress, but lower in height than the main walls and preceded by a ditch.

FLAT-ARCH, an arch with a horizontal intrados, having little or no convexity.

FLANK, that section of a fortified work designed to defend an adjoining work and to provide enfilading fire. [J]

FLEUR-DE-LYS, French royal lily, conventionalized as an ornament and frequently found decorating the roof of echaugettes.

FRONT OF FORTIFICATION, the distance between the salient points of two adjacent bastions.

FOOT OF GLACIS, the line were the sloping glacis meets the level ground of open country. [K]

FOUGASSE, a rock-hewn mortar.

FURROW OF GLACIS, the line where two stretches of glacis meet together at the re-entrant angle of the place-of-arms and covertway. [L]

FORT, a fortified military establishment; a fortress without a city.

FORTRESS, a fortified city or town, or other major defensive work.

FLECHE, an arrow-shaped work, similar to a redan; a lunette attached to the main works by a long caponier.

GABION, a cylindrical earth-filled wicker basket used as a temporary parapet to shield both guns and men in filed positions or in makeshift countermures.

GATE, MAIN, *Porta Reale* - I., the principal entrance into a fortress, protected by a drawbridge and a ditch, internally containing one or more guardrooms which may be fitted with loopholes to cover the approaches to the doorway; the exterior façade usually of Neoclassical design, embellished, especially in the 17th century and 18th century, with Baroque and Rococo decorations.

GATE COURT, the courtyard between two successive gates of a castle.

GATEHOUSE, a building accompanying a gateway of a castle or a fortress.

GATE-TOWER, a tower, sometimes two tower joined together, containing the gate of a fortress or castle and usually housing the mechanism for the drawbridge.

GLACIS, *spalto* - I., the sloping ground in front of a fortress spanning from the top of the parapet of the covertway down until it reaches the open country, cleared of all obstacles to bring an advancing enemy into the direct line of fire. [M]

GIBBS SURROUND, the surround of a doorway consisting of alternating large and small blocks of stone.

GORGE, the interior side, or neck, of a bastion, outerwork or other defensive work not protected by a parapet.

GUN-LOOP, GUN-PORT, a circular loophole with accompanying vision-slit through which early medieval guns and cannon could be fired from behind a wall.

GUN-TOWER, a hollow or casemated tower fitted with embrasures for cannon.

HOARD, HOARDING, a covered wooden gallery projecting from the top or a wall or parapet of a castle to enable the defenders to shower missiles on attackers at the foot of the wall.

HORNWORK, *opera a corna* - I., an outerwork consisting of a front of two demi-bastions joined by a short curtain wall.

KASR, an Islamic castle in North Africa.

KEEP, the last defensible stronghold of a fortress or castle.

LINE OF DEFENCE, the line of fire from the flank of a bastion along the face of the adjacent bastion.

LINTEL, a horizontal stone placed over an opening to carry the weight of the wall above it.

LODGEMENT, a temporary defensive work erected by the enemy on a captured section of a besieged fortress.

LOOPHOLE, a long and narrow opening in a wall to provide for vision and small arms fire; loop window or arrow slit, a loophole for crossbows; gun loop, a loophole for small early cannon.

LUNETTE, a large outerwork in the shape of a detached bastion, similar to a ravelin.

MAGAZINE, a storage place for gunpowder and other munitions. [N]

MAGISTRAL LINE, the highest point of the scarp of a rampart or any other fortification which, when shown on a plan, is drawn thicker than the other lines.

MAIDEN TOWER, the keep, donjon, or principal tower of a castle.

MARBLE THROUGH-COLUMN, antique marble columns used in the building of ramparts to strengthen the walls.

MASONRY, the stonework or brickwork of a building or wall.

MASTIO, a keep or donjon; a stronghold.

MERLON, the solid part of a parapet between two embrasures or crenels.

MEURTRIERES, holes in the ceiling or vault through which offensive materials could be dropped on attackers inside the passage of a gateway; also known as murder holes.

MEZZALUNA, a demi-lune.

MOAT, a wide and deep trench surrounding the walls of a fortress or castle, usually filled with water. [O]

MOTTE, the mound of earth on which the keep or donjon of an 11th- or 12th-century castle was built.

MOTTE-AND-BAILEY, an early form of castle which appeared in France and Normandy in the 11th and 12th centuries, consisting of a motte, a mound of earth on which stood a tall wooden tower overlooking the bailey, a larger palisaded courtyard.

MUD BRICK FORTS, fortified works built of any type of sun-dried clay brick.

MURUS, a defensive wall of stone or brick built around a Roman town.

MUSHRABIYA, in Muslim fortifications, a machicolated balcony, sometimes with embattled parapet, projecting over a gate or entrance.

NECK OF BASTION, the gorge of the bastion.

OPENWORK, any work not protected by a parapet at the gorge.

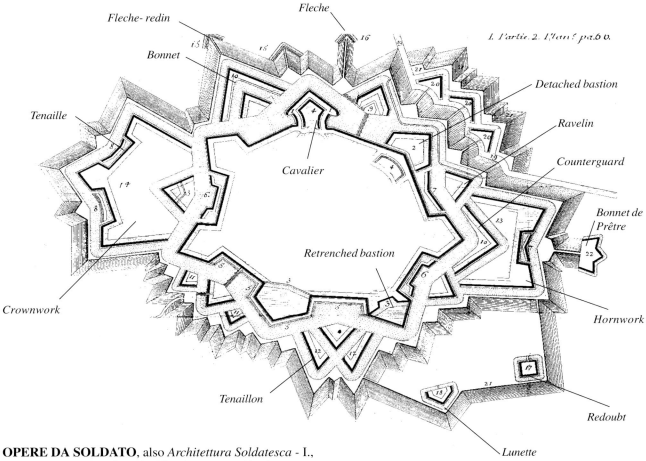

Fleche- redin

Fleche

Bonnet

Tenaille

Detached bastion

Ravelin

Counterguard

Cavalier

Bonnet de Prêtre

Retrenched bastion

Crownwork

Hornwork

Tenaillon

Redoubt

Lunette

OPERE DA SOLDATO, also *Architettura Soldatesca* - I., earthworks and other field fortifications erected by the troops themselves, such as redoubts, palisades, breastworks, and trenches.

ORILLION, *orecchino, guardanaso* - I., a projecting shoulder of a bastion designed to cover the flank.

OUTWORK, OUTERWORK, a defensive structure placed outside the main enceinte of a fortified work.

PALISADE, a series of wooden poles with pointed tips, sometimes fortified with iron tips (*punte di ferro*), driven into the earth and used as a fence or fortification; wooden palisaded gates were placed in front of the drawbridges.

PARAPET, *parapetto* - I., a breastwork on top of a rampart intended to provide shelter for troops behind it.

PAS-DE-SOURIS, a staircase giving access from the ditch to the covertway and place-of-arms. [P]

PIAZZA, a large open space or courtyard inside a fortress, a parade ground.

PIAZZA BASSA, a low platform in the flank of a bastion; a casemated battery in the flank of a bastion.

PLACE-OF-ARMS, *piazza d'armi* - I, an area on the covered way for troops to assemble. [Q]

PLINTH, a square or rectangular base so designed to give the appearance of a platform.

POLVERISTA, a specially-built magazine used for the storage of gunpowder.

POMERIO, the open areas between the walls of a fortress and the urban fabric, to allow space for troops to assemble.

PORTCULLIS, a large iron or wooden grating, used to block a passage when released vertically in retaining grooves cut in the jambs of a fortified gateway.

POSTERN, a sally-port; a vaulted stone tunnel under the ramparts leading to an inconspicuous rear gate used for sorties in war; a small door near a larger one.

QUOIN, a hard stone used to reinforce an external corner or edge of wall.

RAMPART, a thick wall of earth or masonry forming the main defence of a fortress, usually reinforced from the rear with terreplein.

RAVELIN, a triangular outerwork placed in front of a curtain to defend it. [R]

REDAN TRACE, a fortification consisting of a series of redans forming a system of serrated lines.

REDOUBT, *ridotto* - I., a small fortified work designed as an infantry stronghold; sometimes built inside a bastion or ravelin as a retrenchment, or in the field as a defence against cavalry attack; coastal redoubt, an infantry stronghold placed on the shoreline against a sea-borne invasion.

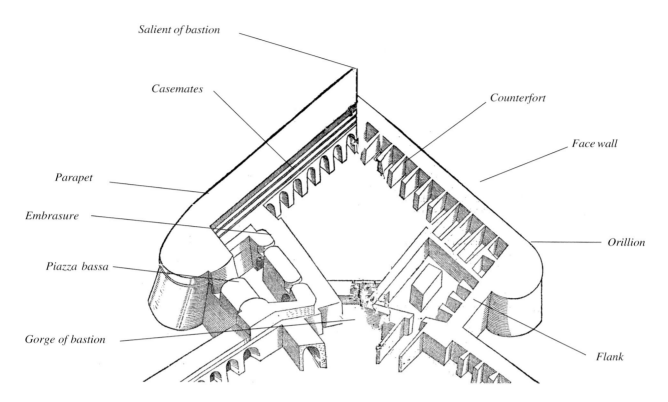

Salient of bastion

Casemates

Counterfort

Face wall

Parapet

Embrasure

Orillion

Piazza bassa

Gorge of bastion

Flank

REVETMENT, a retaining wall of a fortress.

RUBBLE WALL, a wall of uncoursed stones of irregular shapes and sizes.

SALLY-PORT, *porta falsa* - I., a concealed gate or underground passage leading from inside the fortress into the ditch; a postern.

SALIENT OF BASTION, the projecting front angle of a bastion.

SHELL-KEEP, a stone keep with an internal courtyard and dwellings placed against its inner side. Later to develop into the inner ward of a castle.

SHOULDER OF BASTION, the angle between the face and the flank of a bastion.

SPUR, an arrow-shaped work; spur of a bastion, sharp-edged buttress placed at foot of a rounded salient of bastion.

TALUS, an outward sloping wall, commonly used in medieval defences.

TENAILLON, an outerwork designed to protect a ravelin.

TERRA, term used in medieval times to denote a walled town or city.

TERRAPLEIN, the packing of earth forming the body of a rampart; the gently-sloping ground behind a parapet, formed from packed earth.

TRACE, the perimeter or ground plan of a fortified work.

TRAVERSE, a defensive barrier, consisting of a parapet or simple wall placed at right-angles to the main line of defence and in order to protect the defenders from flanking fire; commonly found on covertways (18th century) but also on the main ramparts themselves. [S]

TENAILLE, *tenaglia* - I., a small outerwork placed inside the ditch, between two adjoining bastions, and designed to protect the curtain wall; usually detached but sometimes linked to the flanks or shoulders of adjoining bastions.

TROPHIES, in Baroque fortifications, carved or sculptured features representing the trophies of war - cannon, shields, flags, etc., - used for decorative purposes.

TURRET, a small and slender tower, projecting from the main rampart.

VOUSSOIR, wedge-shaped stones used in an arch or vault.

VENTILATION SHAFT, openings in the ceilings of casemates used as cannon or musketry galleries which are designed to channel the escape of toxic fumes generated by burnt gunpowder.

WALL-TOWER, a tower built as part of a rampart of a castle, usually projecting outwards from the main curtain wall.

WARD, an outerwork of a castle.

WATCH-TOWER, a small tower, lightly fortified and used as a lookout post.

WICKET, a small door forming part of a larger one.

WING, a long and narrow rampart protecting the exposed sides of a horned or crowned work.

Abbreviations

F.	*French*
I.	*Italian*
G.	*German*
S.	*Swedish*

Grand Masters and Lieutenants of the Order of St John

The Blessed Gerard	(Founder of the Hospital - c.1180)	Philibert de Naillac	1396-1421
Raymond du Puy	1120- 1158/60	Antonio Fluviano	1421-1437
Auger de Balben	1158/60-1162/3	Jean de Lastic	1437-1454
Arnaud de Comps	1162/3	Jacques de Milly	1454-1461
Gilbert d'Assailly	1163 - 1169/70	Raimundo Zacosta	1464-1467
Cast de Murols	c.1170-1172'	Giovan Battista Orsini	1467-1476
Joubert	c.1172-1177	Pierre d'Aubusson	1476-1503
Roger des Moulins	1177-1187	Emery d'Amboise	1503-1512
Lt. Borrell & Ermengard d'Asp		Guy de Blanchefort	1512-1513
(ruled the Order after the death		Fabrizio del Carretto	1513-1521
of Roger des Moulins)	1188-1189	Philippe Villiers de l'Isle Adam	1521-1534
Garnier de Naplous	1189/90-1192	Pietrino del Ponte	1534-1535
Geoffroy de Donjon	1192/3-1202	Didier de Tholon Sainte Jalle	1535-1536
Afonso de Portugal	1202-1206	Juan de Homedes y Coscon	1536-1553
Geoffroy le Rat	1206-1207	Claude de la Sengle	1553-1557
Garin de Montaigu	1207-1227/8	Jean Parisot de la Valette	1557-1568
Bertrand de Thessy	1228-c.1231	Pietro Ciocchi del Monte San Savin	1568-1572
Guerlri Lebrun4	c.1231 - 1236	Jean l'Evesque de la Cassiere	1572-1581
Bertrand de Comps	1236-129/40	Hugues Loubenx de Verdale	1581-1595
Pierre de Vieille-Brioude	1239/40-1242	Martin Garzes	1595-1601
Guillaume de Chateauneuf	1242- 1258	Alof de Wignacourt	1601-1622
Hugues de Revel	1258-1277	Luis Mendes de Vasconcellos	1622-1623
Nicolas Lorgne	1277/8-1284	Antoine de Paule	1623-1636
Jean de Villiers	c.1285- 1293/4	Jean-Baptiste Lascaris de Castellar	1636-1657
Odon de Pins	1294-1296	Martin de Redin y Cruzat	1657-1660
Guillaume de Villaret	1296-1305	Annet de Clermont de Chattes Gessan	1660
Foulques de Villaret	1305-1317	Rafael Cotoner y de Oleza	1660-1663
Lt Gerard de Pins	1317-1319	Nicolas Cotoner y de Oleza	1663-1680
Helion de Villeneuve	1319-1346	Gregorio Carafa della Roccella	1680-1690
Dieudonne de Gozon	1346-1353	Adrien de Wignacourt	1690-1697
Pierre de Corneillan	1353-1355	Ramon Perellos y Rocafull	1697-1720
Roger de Pins	1355-1365	Marcantonio Zondadari	1720-1722
Raymond Berenger	1365-1374	Antonio Manoel de Vilhena	1722-1736
Robert de Juilly	1374-1376	Ramon Despuig y Martinez de Marcilla	1736-1741
Juan Fernandez de Heredia	1376-1396	Manuel Pinto da Fonseca	1741-1773
Riccardo Caracciolo		Francisco Ximenez de Texada	1773-1775
(Anti-Master not acknowledged		Emmanuel de Rohan de Polduc	1775-1797
at Rhodes)	1383-1398	Ferdinand von Hompesch	1797-1799

The Order's European Priories

Tongue of Italy

Priory of Lombardy	(36 commanderies)
Priory of Venice	(29 commanderies)
Priory of Pisa	(12 commanderies)
Priory of Rome	(19 commanderies)
Priory of Capua	(17 commanderies)
Priory of Barletta	(11 commanderies)
Priory of Messina	(11 commanderies)

Tongue of Aragon

Castellany of Amposta	(30 commanderies)
Priory of Navarre	(18 commanderies)
Priory of Catalonia	(29 commanderies)
Priory of Castile and Leon	(37 commanderies)
Portugal	(21 commanderies)

Tongue of France

Priory of France	(67 commanderies)
Priory of Aquitaine	(31 commanderies)
Priory of Champaigne	(24 commanderies)

Tongue of Provence

Priory of Sainte-Gilles	(53 commanderies)
Priory of Toulouse	(28 commanderies)

Tongue of Auvergne

Priory of Auvergne	(51 commanderies)

Tongue of England

Priory of England	(59 commanderies reduced to 19 by 16C)
Priory of Ireland	(18 commanderies)

Tongue of Germany

Priory of Germany (Heitersheim)	(31 commanderies)
Priory of Bohemia	(24 commanderies)
Priory of Dacia	(9 commanderies)
Priory of Hungary	(5 commanderies)
Grand Bailiwick of Brandenburg	(13 commanderies)

Anglo-Bavarian Tongue

Priory of Poland (1776)
Priory of bavaria or Ebersberg (1780)

Coats-of-arms of the Grand Masters of the Order

Many of the Order's fortifications are adorned with marble or stone escutcheons bearing the coats-of-arms of the Grand Masters responsible for their construction or repair. These help date the various works. Generally, the arms appear quartered with the emblem of the Order, a white cross on a field gules. Heraldic tinctures and metal colours are not indicated here.

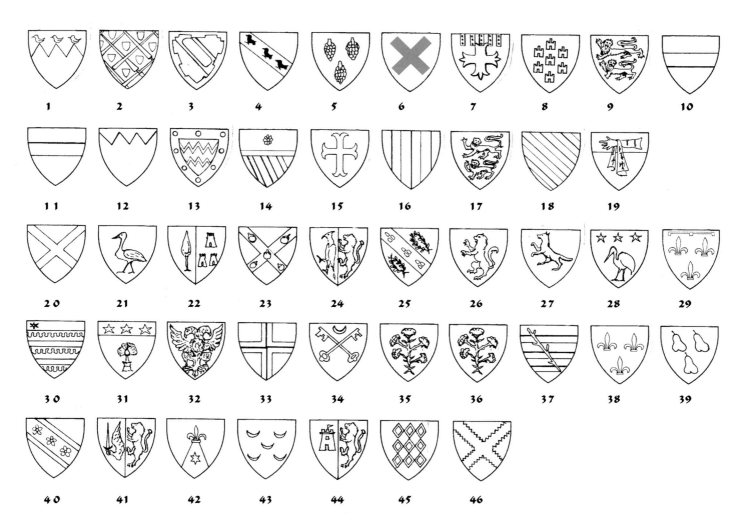

1. Foulques de Villaret
2. Helion de Villeneuve
3. Dieudonne de Gozon
4. Pierre de Corneillan
5. Roger de Pins
6. Raymond Berenger
7. Robert de Juilly
8. Juan Fernandez de Heredia
9. Philibert de Naillac
10. Antonio Fluviano
11. Jean de Lastic
12. Jacques de Milly
13. Raimundo Zacosta
14. Giovan Battista Orsini
15. Pierre d'Aubusson
16. Emery d'Amboise
17. Guy de Blanchefort
18. Fabrizio del Carretto
19. Philippe Villiers de l'Isle Adam
20. Pietrino del Ponte
21. Didier de Tholon Sainte Jalle
22. Juan de Homedes
23. Claude de la Sengle
24. Jean Parisot de la Valette
25. Pietro Ciocchi del Monte
26. Jean l'Evesque de la Cassiere
27. Hugues Loubenx de Verdale
28. Martin Garzes
29. Alof de Wignacourt
30. Luis Mendes de Vasconcellos
31. Antoine de Paule
32. Jean-Baptiste Lascaris de Castellar
33. Martin de Redin y Cruzat
34. Annet de Clermont de Chattes Gessan
35. Rafael Cotoner y de Oleza
36. Nicolas Cotoner y de Oleza
37. Gregorio Carafa della Roccella
38. Adrien de Wignacourt
39. Ramon Perellos y Rocafull
40. Marcantonio Zondadari
41. Antonio Manoel de Vilhena
42. Ramon Despuig
43. Manuel Pinto da Fonseca
44. Francisco Ximenez de Texada
45. Emmanuel de Rohan de Polduc
46. Ferdinand von Hompesch

Military Engineers & Architects who worked on the Fortifications of the Order

Name	Period	Country of Origin	Employer	Status	Major project/s
Bartholino de Castilion	1506-?	Italy	Order of St John	Resident	Forts in the Dodecanese
Basilio della Scuola di Vicenza	1519-21	Vicenza	Emperor Maximillian	Visiting	Rhodes
Mastro Zuenio	1520 (?)	Italy	Order of St John	Resident	Rhodes
Gabriele Tadini da Martinengo	1522	Martinengo	Order of St John		Siege of Rhodes 1522
Nicola Flavari	(?)/1530 -43	Rhodes	Order of St John	Resident	
Piccino	1532-35	Florence.			
Antonio Ferramolino	1535 / 1541	Bergamo	Viceroy of Sicily	Visiting	Cavalier of Fort St. Angelo
Pietro Prato	1552	Italy	Viceroy of Sicily	Visiting	Fort St. Elmo
Nicolò Bellavanti	1554-?	Italy	Order of St John	Resident	Senglea
Bartolomeo Genga	1558	Cesena	Duke of Urbino	Visiting	Fortress on Mount Sciberras
Baldassare Lanci	1562	Urbino	Duke of Florence	Visiting	Fortress on Mount Sciberras
Evangelista Menga	1560-67	Brindisi	Order of St John	Resident	Spur of Senglea, Great Siege of 1565
Francesco Laparelli	1566-68 1569-70	Cortona	Pope	Visiting	Valletta
Gabrio Serbelloni	1566	Milan	King of Spain	Visiting	
Giorgio Palearo (Il Fratino)	1566	Italy	King of Spain	Visiting	Valletta
Scipione Campi	1566/76	Pesaro	King of Spain	Visiting	Valletta
Gerolamo Cassar	1567-92	Malta	Order of St John	Resident	Valletta
Pompeo Floriani	1576	Macerata	King of Spain	Visiting	
Giovanni Rinaldini	1599	Ancona	King of France	Visiting	Gozo Citadel and coastal towers
Vittorio Cassar	1590-1607	Malta	Order of St John	Resident	Gozo Citadel
Pietro Paolo Floriani	1635-36	Macerata	Pope	Visiting	Floriana Lines
Francesco Buonamici	1635-59	Lucca	Order of St John	Resident	Floriani's assistant, Marsalforn fortress
Jardin	1636-38	France	Landgrave of Hesse Darmstadt	Visiting	Floriana Lines
Vincenzo Maculano da Firenzuola	1638	Firenzuola	Pope	Visiting	Sta Margherita Lines
Giovanni de' Medici Marquis of St. Angelo	1640	Florence Tuscany	Grand Duke of Tuscany	Visiting	various, Valletta Counterguards
Blaise François, Count de Pagan	1645	France	King of France	Visiting	Gozo Citadel and coastal towers
Louis, Viscount d'Arpajon	1645	France	King of France	Visiting	
Louis Nicolas de Clerville	1645	France	King of France	Visiting	
Giovanni Bendinelli Pallavicino	1645	Italy			
Domenico Guazzo	1645-46	Italy	Grand Duke of Tuscany	Visiting	
Mederico Blondel	1659-98	France	Order of St John	Resident	
Antonio MaurizioValperga	1670	Turin	Duke of Savoy	Visiting	Cottonera Lines, Fort Ricasoli,Floriana outerworks, various proposals
Carlos Grunenberg	1681/87-90	Flanders	Viceroy of Sicily	Visiting	Carafa Bastions, Fort St Angelo
Claude de Colongues	1703	France	King of France	Visiting	
Romano Fortunato	1706-38	Rome	Order of St John	Resident	Notre Dame gate, Cottonera Lines
Johannes Person	1707-09	Germany	Order of St John	Resident	
Johan Hecker	1708	Sweden	Pope		
François Bachelieu	1713	France	Order of St John	Resident	
René Jacob de Tigné	1715/16,23	France	King of France	Visiting	Master Plan - various proposals
Victor-Hyacin d'Artus	1715	France	King of France	Visiting	
Philippe de Vendôme	1715	France	King of France	Visiting	Coastal fortifications
Jean Charles de Folard	1715	France	King of France	Visiting	
Philippe Maigret	1715-16	France	King of France	Visiting	
Charles Françios de Mondion	1715-33	France	Order of St John	Resident	Fort Manoel, Marsalforn Tower, Mdina Sta Margherita Lines, Birgu Landfront, and various other projects
Francesco Marandon	1727-62	Turin	Order of St John	Resident	Fougasse, Fort Chambrai
François Charles Count de Bourlamaque	1761	France	King of France	Visiting	Various proposal
Pontleroy	1761	France	King of France	Visiting	
Balì François-René J. de Tigné	1762-1788	France	Order of St John	Commissioner of Fortifications	Fort Ricasoli, Coastal,
Henry des Mazis	1788-91	France	Order of St John	Resident	
Stephen de Tousard	1791-98	France	Order of St John	Resident	Fort Tigné

Bibliography

AMBROISE, R., *L'Estoire de la Guerre Sainte (1190-1192),* edited and translated by G. Paris (Paris, 1897)

ANDREWS, K., *Castles of the Morea* (New Jersey, 1953).

Atlas of the Crusades edited by J. Riley-Smith (London, 1991)

ARAFAS, M., *Symi:A Greek Island* (Athens, 1989).

ARISTIDOU, E., *Kolossi Castle through the Centuries* (Nicosia, 1983).

AURIGEMMA, S., *I Cavalieri Gerosolimitani a Tripoli negli anni 1530-1551* (Rome, 1937).

AURIGEMMA, S., 'Il Castello di Tripoli di Barberia' *in La Rinascita della Tripolitania* (Rome, 1926).

BALBI, F., *The Siege of Malta,* translated by H. Balbi (Copenhagen, 1961).

BENEVISTI, M., *The Crusaders in the Holy Land* (Jerusalem, 1970).

BILLINGS, M., *The Cross and the Crescent* (London, 1987).

BONACCI, G., 'I monumenti e le fortificazioni di Rodi', *Lettura* (1913).

BOSIO, G., *Dell'Istoría della Sacra Religione et Illustrissima Militia di San Giovanni Gierosolimitano* (Rome, 1629).

BOASE, T.S.R., *Castles and Churches of the Crusading Kingdom* (London, 1967).

BOASE, T.S.R., (ed.), *The Cilician Kingdom of Armenia* (London, 1978).

BOASE, T.S.R., 'Military Architecture in the Crusader States in Palestine and Syria' in *A History of the Crusades,* edited by K.M. Setton, Vol.IV (Madison, 1977).

BORG, V., *Fabio Chigi, apostolic delegate in Malta (1634-1639),* Studi e Testi, no.249 (Vatican City, 1967).

BOTTARELLI, G., *Storia politica e militare del Sovrano Ordine di S. Giovanni di Gerusalemme detto di Malta* (Rome, 1940).

BOWERMAN, H.G., *The History of Fort St. Angelo* (Malta, 1947).

BRADFORD, E., *The Great Siege: Malta 1565* (London, 1961).

BRADFORD, E., *The Shield and the Sword* (London, 1972).

BRAUDEL, F., *The Mediterranean and the Mediterranean World in the Age of Philip II* (London, 1984).

BRICE, M., *Forts and Fortresses* (Oxford, 1990).

BRIDGE, A., *The Crusades* (London, 1985).

BROCKMAN, E., *The Two Sieges of Rhodes* (London, 1969).

BURMAN, E., *The Templars* (Kent, 1986).

BUSTRON, F., *Chronique de L'Ile de Chypre,* edited by R. de Mas Latrie (Paris, 1886).

CAOURSIN, G., *Obsidionis Rbodiae urbisdecriptio* (1482) edited by H.W. Fincham (London, 1926).

Cartulaire general de ordre des Hospitaliers de St. Jean de Jerusalem, **1100-1310** edited by J. Delaville-le-Roulx, 4 volumes (Paris, 1894-1906).

CASSOLA, A., *The 1565 Ottoman Malta Campaign Register* (Malta, 1998).

CATHCART KING, D.J., 'The taking of Le Krac des Chevaliers in 1271' in *Antiquity* (1947).

Chronicles of the Crusades, ed. by E. Hallam (London, 1989).

Chronique d'Ernoul et Bernard le Tresorier edited by L. de Maslabrie (Paris, 1870).

CORMONTAIGNE, L., *L'Architecture Militaire, ou l'Art de Fortifier,* 3 volumes (The Hague, 1741).

CORONELLI, F., *Isola di Rodi geografico storico, antica e moderna coll'altre adiacenti già possedute da Caualieri Hospitalieri di S. Giovanni di Gerusalemme* (Venice, 1688).

CRESWELL, K.A.C., *A Short Account of Early Muslim Architecture* (London, 1989).

CRESWELL, K.A.C., *The Muslim Architecture of Egypt* (London, 1952/59).

CUTAJAR, F., *L'Occupazione Francese di Malta nel 1798* edited by G. Curmi (Malta, 1933).

CUTAJAR, D., & **C. CASSAR,** *Malta's Role in Mediterranean Affairs: 1530-1699, Mid-Med Bank Report* (Malta, 1984).

CUTAJAR, D., & **C. CASSAR,** 'Malta and the 16th-century struggle for the Mediterranean', *Mid-Med Bank Report* (Malta, 1985).

D'ALLECIO, M.P., *I veri ritratti della guerra Dell' Assedio alla lsola di Malta dell'Armata Turchesa l'anno 1565* (Rome, 1582).

DARMANIN, J.F., *The Phoenico-Graeco-Roman Temple and the Origin and the Development of Fort St. Angelo* (Malta, 1948).

DE CURTI, G., *La Città di Rodi assediata dai Turchi il 23 maggio 1480* (Venice, 1480).

DE LUCCA, D., 'The built environment in Gozo: a historical review' in *Gozo: The Roots of an Island,* edited by C. Cini (Malta, 1990).

DE LUCCA, D., 'Architectural Interventions in Mdina following the Earthquake of 1693' in *Mdina and the Earthquake of 1693,* edited by Can. J. Azzopardi (Malta, 1993), 45.

DELUCCA, D., and **J. TONNA,** *Studies in Maltese Architecture, Romano Carapecchia* (Malta, 1975).

DEGIORGIO, R., *A City by an Order* (Malta, 1985).

DELAVILLE-LE-ROULX, J., *Les Hospitaliers a Rhodes jusqu'a la mort de Philibert de Naillac, 1310-1421* (Paris, 1913).

DELAVILLE-LE-ROULX, J., *Les Hospitalliers en Terre*

Sainte et Chypre, 1100-1310 (Paris, 1904).

DESCHAMPS, P., *Les chateaux des Croises en Terre Sainte: I, Le Crac des Chevaliers* (Paris, 1934), 2 volumes.

DESCHAMPS, P., *Les chateaux des Croises en Terre Sainte, II, La defense du royamme de Jerusalem* (Paris, 1939), 2 volumes.

DESCHAMPS, P., *Les chateaux des Croises en Terre Sainte, III, La defense du comte de Tripoli et de la principaute d'Antioche* (Paris,1973), 2 volumes.

DESMOND, S., *The Monks of War* (London 1972).

DESQUESNES, R., R. FAILLE, N. FAUCHERRE, and **P. PROST,** *Les Fortifications du Littoral; La Charente-Maritime* (Chauray, 1993).

DIEHL, C., *L'Afrique byzantine* (Paris, 1896).

DOUKAS, M., *Decline and Fall of Byzantium to the Ottoman Turks,* trans. by H. Magoulias.

DUFFY, C., *Fire & Stone: The science of fortress warfare, 1660-1860* (London, 1975).

EDBURY, P., 'The Latin East (1291-1669)', in *The Oxford Illustrated History of the Crusades,* ed. by J. Riley-Smith (Oxford, 1995).

EDWARDS, R.W., *The Fortifications of Armenian Cilicia* (London, 1990).

EDWARDS, R.W., 'The Crusader Donjon at Anavarza in Cilicia', *Tenth Annual Byzantine Studies Conference* (Cincinnati, 1984).

EDWARDS, E., 'The Knights Hospitalliers and the Conquest of Rhodes', *The Proceedings of the Royal Philosophical Society of Glasgow,* 50 (1918-20), 50-63.

EFTHYMIOY-HADZILACOU, M. *Rhodes et sa Region elargie au 18eme siecle: les activities portuaires* (Athens, 1988).

ELLUL, M., *Fort St. Elmo* (Malta 1989).

ENLART, C., *Les Monuments des croises dans le royamme de Jerusalem; Architecture religieuse et civile* (Paris, 1936/37).

FEDDEN, R., *Crusader Castles: A brief study on the military architecture of the Crusades* (London, 1950).

FINO, J., *Fortresses de la France Medieval* (Paris, 1970),

FIORINI, S. & M. BUHAGIAR, *Mdina, The Cathedral City* (Malta, 1998) 2 volumes.

FLORIANI, P.P., *Difesa et ofesa delle piazze* (Macerata, 1630).

FOREY, A., *The Military Orders* (London, 1989).

GABRIEL, A., *La cité de Rhodes* (Paris, 1921-23), 2 volumes.

GABRIELI, F., (ed.), *Storici Arabi delle Crociate* (Turin, 1963).

GALEA, M., *German Knights of Malta* (Malta, 1986).

GANADO, A, 'A Sixteenth Century Manuscript Plan of Mdina by Gabrio Serbelloni' in *Mdina and the Earthquake of 1693,* edited by Can. J. Azzopardi (Malta, 1993), 77.

GANADO, A, and **M. AGIUS-VADALA,** *A study in depth of 143 Maps representing the Great Siege of Malta of 1565* (Malta, 1994).

GEROLA, G., 'I Monumenti mediovali delle tredici Sporadi', *Annuario Scuola Archaeologica Italiana di Athene,* 1, (Athens, 1914).

GEROLA, G., 'L'Opera di Basilio dalla Scuola per le fotificazioni di Rhodi', *Atti Veneti* 74 (Veince, 1914-5).

GEROLA, G., 'Il contributo dell'Italia alle Opere d'arte militare rodiesi' in *Atti Veneti* 89 (Venice, 1930).

GINNIS, J., *Historic Cyprus* (London, 1940).

GLOSSARIUM ARTIS: *Fortresses, military architecture after the introduction of firearms* (Munich, 1979).

GRAVETT, C., and **HOOK, R.,** *Medieval Siege Warfare* (London, 1991).

GROOT, A.H. De, 'The Ottoman Threat to Europe, 1571-1830: Historical Fact or Fancy', in *Hospitaller Malta, 1530-1798,* edited by Victor Mallia Milanes (Malta, 1993), 199-254.

HALE, J.R., *Rennaissance Fortifications: Art or engineering?* (London, 1977).

HALE, J.R., (ed.), *The early development of the Bastion in Europe in the late Middle Ages* (London, 1965).

HALEVY D., *Vauban: Builder of Fortresses* translated by C. Street (London, 1924).

History of the Fortifications of Malta issued by the General Staff Malta Command (Malta, 1920).

HASLUCK, F., 'Heraldry of the Rhodian Knights formerly in Smyrna Castle', *Annual of the British School of Athens* XVII (1910-1911), 145-150.

HOPPEN, A., *The Fortification of Malta* (Edinburgh, 1979).

HOPPEN, A., 'Military Priorities and Social Realities in the Early Modern Mediterranean: Malta and its Fortifications' in *Hospitaller Malta, 1530-1798* edited by V. Mallia Millanes (Malta, 1993).

HUGHES, Q., *Military Architecture* (Hants, 1991).

HUGHES, Q., *Fortress: architecture and military bistory in Malta* (London, 1969).

HUGHES, Q., *The Building of Malta 1530-1795* (London, 1956).

HUGHES, Q., *Guide to the Fortifications of Malta* (Malta, 1992).

HUGHES, Q., 'Considerazioni e Teorie sulla Difesa Costiera Inglese', *Castellum,* no.25/26 (1986), 25-44.

HUGHES, Q., and **A. MIGOS,** 'Rhodes: The Turkish Sieges', *Fort,* XXI (1993), 5.

INALCIK, H., *The Ottoman Empire:The Classical Age, 1300-1600* (London, 1973).

JAGER, H., 'Die erste aller Grabenwehren', *Fortifikation,* VI (1992).

KARPODINE-DIMITRIADI, E., Kastra Tes Peloponnhsou (Castles of the Peloponnese), (Athens, 1990), Greek text.

KARPODINE-DIMITRIADI, E., *The Greek Islands* (Athens, 1990).

KLONER, A., & D. CHEN, 'Bet Govrin: Crusader Church

and Fortifications', *Excavations and Surveys in Israel*, II (1983), 12-3.

KOLLIAS, E., *The City of Rhodes and the Palace of the Grand Master* (Athens, 1988).

KOLLIAS, E., *The Knights of Rhodes* (Athens, 1991).

LANGE, S., *Architettura delle Crociate in Palestina* (Como, 1965).

LAURENZA, V. 'Malta nei Documenti Angioini', *Archivio Storico di MAlta*, VIII/1 (Malta, 1936-37).

LAWRENCE, A. *'A Skeletal History of Byzantine Fortification'*, *Annual of the British School at Athens* (Athens, 1983).

LAWRENCE, T.E., *Crusader Castles*, edited by D. Pringle (Oxford, 1988).

LAZARD, P., *Vauban, 1633-1707* (Paris, 1934).

LOGHENA, N., 'L'Impresa di Tripoli nel 1510', *Rivista d'Africa* (Rome, 1912).

LOT, F., *L'Art militaire et l'armees au moyen age* (Paris, 1946).

LUISI, R., *Scudi di Pietra: I castelli e l'arte della guerra tra Medioevo e Rinascimento* (Rome, 1996).

LUTTRELL, A., 'Settlement on Rhodes, 1306-1366', in *Hospitallers of Rhodes and their Mediterranean World* (London, 1992).

LUTTRELL, A., 'The Hospitallers of Rhodes confront the Turks', in *Hospitallers of Rhodes and their Mediterranean World* (London, 1992).

LUTTRELL, A., 'Lindos and the Defence of Rhodes', in *The Hospitallers of Rhodes and their Mediterranean World* (London, 1992).

LUTTRELL, A., 'The Military and Naval Organisation at Rhodes: 1310-1444', in *The Hospitallers of Rhodes and their Mediterranean World* (London, 1992).

LUTTRELL, A., 'The Rhodian Background of the Order of St. John on Malta', in *The Hospitallers of Rhodes and their Mediterranean World* (London, 1992).

LUTTRELL, A., '*Appunti sulle compagnie navarresi in Grecia; 1376-1404*', in *The Hospitallers of Rhodes and their Mediterranean World* (London, 1992).

LUTTRELL, A., *Latin Greece, the Hospitallers and the Crusades; 1291-1440* (London , 1982).

LUTTRELL, A., 'The Hospitallers' Intervention in Cilician Armenia, 1291-1375', in *The Cilician Kingdom of Armenia* edited by T.S.R. Boase (Edinburgh, 1978).

LUTTRELL, A., 'The Military Orders, 1312-1798', in *The Oxford Illustrated History of the Crusades* (Oxford, 1995), 338-41.

LUTTRELL, A., 'The Hospitallers at Rhodes 1306-1421', in *The Hospitallers in Greece, Rhodes and Cyprus and the West; 1291-1440* (London, 1978).

LUTTRELL, A., 'The Latin Colonization of Rhodes', in *The Hospitallers in Greece, Rhodes and Cyprus and the West; 1291-1440* (London, 1978).

LUTTRELL, A., 'Venice and the Knights of Rhodes in XIV Century', *Papers of British School of Rome*, XXVI (1958), 195-212.

LUTTRELL, A., 'Girolomo Manduca and Gianfrangisk Abela: Tradition and invention in Maltese Histiography', in *Melita Historica* VII, No.2, 1977, 131.

LUTTRELL, A., (ed.) *Gozo Citadel, Malta*, Report submitted to the Division of Cultural Heritage UNESCO (Malta, 1980).

LUTTRELL, A., *The Later History of the Maussolleion and its Utilization* in *the Hospitaller Castle at Bodrum* (Copenhagen, 1986),

LUTTRELL, A., and **K. JEPESSON,** *The Maussolleoin at Harlikarnassus* (London, 1991).

LYLE KALCAS, E., *Bodrum Castle and its Knights* (Bilgehan Basimevi, 1989).

MAALOUF, A., *The Crusades through Arab Eyes* (London, 1984).

MAGGI, G., & **G. CASTRIOTTO,** *Della fortificatione delle città* (Venice, 1564).

MAIURI, A., 'I Castelli dei cavalieri di Rodi a Cos e a Bodrum (Alicarnasus)', *Annuario Scuola Archaeologica Italiana di Athene*, IV-V (Athens,1921-2).

MALLET, M.E. & **J.R. HALE,** *The Military Organisation of a Renaissance State Venice c.1400-1617* (London, 1984).

MALLIA-MILANES, V., 'Scipione Campi's Report', *Melita Historica* VIII (Malta, 1983), 275-90.

MARCHI, F., *Della architettura militare* (Brescia, 1599).

MARSHALL, C., *Warfare in the Latin East, 1192-1291* (Cambridge, 1992).

MANGION, G., 'Girolamo Cassar architetto maltese del cinquecento', *Melita historica*, VI (1973), 192-200.

Mdina and the earthquake of 1693, edited by Can. J. Azzopardi (Malta, 1993).

MICHALAKI-KOLLIA, M., *All Rhodes* (Athens, 1988).

MIFSUD, A., 'La Milizia e le torri antiche di Malta', *Archivum melitensis*, IV (1920).

MIGOS, A., 'Rhodes: the Knights' Battleground', *Fort* XIX (Oxfordshire, 1990).

MIZZI, E.F., *Le Guerre di Rodi: Relazioni di diversi autori sui due grandi assedi di Rodi* (Torino, 1934).

MONREAL Y TEJADA, L., *Medieval Castles of Spain* (Madrid, 1999).

MONTALEMBERT, M. R., Marquis de, *Le Fortification Perpendiculaire; ou essai sur plusieurs manieres de fortifier* (Paris, 1776-84).

MULLER-WIENER, W., *Castles of the Crusades* (London, 1966).

NICOLLE, D., *Saladin and the Saracens* (London, 1986).

NICOLLE, D., *Medieval Warfare Source Book, Vol I: Warfare in Western Christendom* (London, 1995).

NICOLLE, D., *Medieval Warfare Source Book, Vol II: Christian Europe and its Neighbours* (London, 1996).

O'NEIL, B.H. St. J., 'Rhodes and the Origin of the Bastion', *The Antiquaries Journal* (1954).

Oxford Illustrated History of the Crusades, edited by J.

Riley-Smith (Oxford, 1995).

Palmanova, fortezza d'Europa, *1593-1993,* edited by G. Pavan (Palmanova, 1993).

PARADISSIS, A., *Fortresses and castles of the Greek islands* (Athens, 1982), 3 volumes.

PARKER, G., *The Military Revolution: military innovation and the rise of the West; 1500-1800* (Cambridge, 1996).

PAULI, S., *Codice diplomatico del Sacro Militare Ordine Gerosolimitano, oggi di Malta* (Lucca, 1733-7), 2 volumes.

PERBELLINI, G., 'Le Fortificazioni di Cipro dal X al XVI secolo', *Castellum,* 17 (Rome, 1973).

PORTER, W., *The History of the Fortress of Malta* (Malta, 1858).

POUTIERS, J.C., *Rhodes et ses chevaliers, 1306-1523* (1989).

POUTIERS, J.C., 'Les Establissements des Hospitaliers dans le mer Egee: Villages fortifies et Bourg maritimes', *V Congress International d'Etudes de Sud-Est Europeen,* (Belgrade, 1984).

POZZO, B. DAL, *Historia della sacra religione militare di S. Giovanni Gerosolimitano, detta di Malta* (Verona, 1703).

PRAWER, J., *Crusader Institutions* (Oxford, 1980).

PRAWER, J., *The Latin Kingdom of Jerusalem* (London, 1972).

PRINGLE, D., Introduction to *Crusader Castles* by T.E. Lawrence, 1988 edition (Oxford, 1988).

PRINGLE, D., *The Red Tower (al-Burj al-Ahmar): Settlement in the Plain of Sharon at the time of the Crusades and Mamluks A.D. 1099-1516* (London, 1986).

PRINGLE, D., 'Survey of Castles in the Crusader Kingdom of Jerusalem', *Levant,* XXIII (1991).

PRINGLE, D., and **R. HARPER,** 'Belmont Castle: A Historical Notice and Preliminary Report of excavations in 1986' *Levant,* XX (1988) and XXI (1989).

PROMIS, C., 'Gl'ingegneri militari della Marca d'Ancona che operano e scrissero dall'anno MDI all'anno MDCL' in *Miscellania di storia italiana,* VI (Turin, 1865), 241-356.

PROMIS, C., 'Biografia dei ingegneri militari italiani dal secolo XIV alla metà del XVIII', *Miscellania di storia italiana,* XIV (Turin, 1874).

PROST, P., *Les Forteresses de L'Empire: Fortifications, villes de guerre et arsenaux napoléoniens* (Paris, 1991).

QUINTANO, A., *Ricasoli, Malta: history of a fort* (Malta, 1999).

RANDOLPH, B., *The present state of the islands in the Archipelago sea of Constantinople, and the Gulph of Smyrna, with the islands of Candia and Rhodes* (Oxford, 1697).

'Relation du Pelegrinage a jerusalem di Nicholas da Martoni, notaire Italien 1394-1395' ed. by L. Legrand, *Revue se Orient Latin,* III (1895).

REY, E., *Etude sur les monuments de l'architeture des Croises en Syrie* (Paris, 1871).

REY, E., *Les colonies franques de Syrie aux XIIme et XIIIme siecles* (Paris-1883).

RILEY-SMITH, J., *The Crusades: a short history* (London, 1987).

RILEY-SMITH, J., *The Knights of St. John in Jerusalem and Cyprus c.1050-1310* (London, 1967).

RITHCIE, M.B.H., 'The Fougasses of Malta', *Archivum Melitensis,* VI (1927).

ROSSI, E., 'Il Dominio degli Spagnoli e dei Cavalieri di Malta a Tripoli' in *Storia di Tripoli e della Tripolitania, dalla Conquísta Araba a 1910* edited by M. Nallino (Rome, 1968).

ROSSI, E., *Assedio e Conquista di Rodi nel 1552* (Rome, 1927).

ROCELLE, P., *2000 Ans de Fortification Française* (Paris, 1989), 2 Volumes.

RYAN, F., *The House of the Temple* (London, 1930).

SAILHAN, P., *La Fortification: Histoire et Dictionnaire* (Paris, 1991).

SAMUT-TAGLIAFERRO, A. *The Coastal fortifications of Gozo and Comino* (Malta, 1993).

SANTORO, R., 'Architetti Italiani Operanti alle Difese dello Stato dei Cavalieri di Rodi in Architetti e Ignegneri Militari Italiani all'Estero dal XV al XVIII Secolo', *Istituti Italiano dei Castelli,* (1994), 33-7.

SARNOWSKY, J., Die Johanniter und die Verteidigung Smyrnas: 1344-1402.

SCHERMERHORN, E., *Malta of the Knights* (Surrey, 1929).

SCHNEIDER, A.M., 'The City-walls of Istanbul', *Antiquity* (London, 1837).

SCHNEIDER, A.M., 'The City Walls of Nicaea', *Antiquity* (London, 1938).

SCICLUNA, H., *The Order of St. John of Jerusalem* (Malta, 1969).

SEBASTIANI, F. G., *Viaggio al Archipelago* (Rome, 1687).

SETTON, K., *The Papacy and the Levant: 1204-1547* (Philadelphia, 1976/78).

SIRE, H.J.A., *The Knights of Malta* (New Haven, 1994).

SMAIL, R.C., *Crusading Warfare 1097-1193* (Cambridge, 1989).

SMAIL, R.C., 'Crusaders' Castles in the Twelfth Century', *Cambridge Historical Journal,* X (Cambridge, 1951).

SPAGNESI, P., *Castel Sant'Angelo, La Fortezza di Roma* (Rome, 1995).

SPECKLE, D., *Architectura von Festungen* (Strasbourg, 1589).

SPITERI, S.C., *Discovering the Fortifications of the Order of St. John in Malta* (Malta, 1988).

SPITERI, S.C., *The Knights' Fortifications* (Malta, 1989 and 1990 revised edition).

SPITERI, S.C., *British Military Architecture in Malta* (Malta, 1996).

SPITERI, S.C., 'Fort St. Elmo', *Fortress: The Castles and Fortifications Quarterly,* 10 (Hants, 1991).

SPITERI, S.C., *The Fougasse: The Stone Mortar of Malta* (Malta, 1999).

SPITERI, S.C., *The Palace Armoury: A study of a military storehouse of the Knights of St John* (Malta, 1999).

STERIOTOU, I., *The Fortezza of Rethymno* (Athens, 1989).

STRINGA, P., *Genova e la Liguria nel Mediterraneo* (Rome, 1992).

TATAKI, A.B., *Lindos: The Acropolis and the Medieval Castle* (Athens, l986).

TESTA, C., *The Life and Times of Grand Master Pinto* (Malta, 1989).

TESTA, C., *The French in Malta, 1798-1800* (Malta, 1998).

TOY, S., *Castles* (London, 1939).

TRUTTMANN, P., *Les Dernier Chateaux Forts: les prolongements de la fortification médiévale en France, 1614-1914* (Thionville, 1993).

TURNER, A., *Town Defences in England and Wales* (London, 1968).

VAN CLEVE, T.C., 'The Fifth Crusade', in *A History of the Crusades* edited by K. Setton (Madison, 1969).

VERTOT, L'Abbe de, *Histoíre des Chevaliers Hospitaliers de S. Jean de Jerusalem* (Paris, 1726).

VILLENA, L., 'The Iberian Strategical Castle', IBI Bulletin 47 (1990-1), 59-66.

VIOLLET-LE-DUC, E.E., *Essai sur l'architecture mílitaire au moyen age* (Paris, 1854).

VIOLLET -LE-DUC, E.E., *Military Architecture* (1990 publication of 1860 English translation by M. Macdermott).

VITE, G., A. CADEI, & V. ASCANI, *Monaci in Armi: L'Architettura Sacra dei Templari attraverso il Mediterraneo* (Florence, 1995).

VOLONAKIS, M., *The Island of Roses and her Eleven Sisters* (London, 1922).

WARNER, P., *The Medieval Castle* (USA, 1993).

WARTBURG, M. Von, 'The Medieval cane Sugar Industry in Cyprus', *The Antiquaries Journa* (1983/II).

WETTINGER, G., 'The Castrum Maris and its suburb of Birgu in the Middle Ages' in *Birgu, A Maltese Maritime City* (Malta, 1993), I, 31.

WILLIAM OF OLDENBURG, 'Peregrinatio', in *Peregrinatores medii aevii quator,* edited by J.C.M. (Leipzíg, 1864).

WILLIAM OF TYRE, 'Historica rerum in partibus transmarinis gestarum', in Recueil des historiens des croisades, Historiens occidentaux, I.

WINTER, F., *Greek Fortifications* (Toronto, 1971).

WISE, T., *The Knights of Christ* (London, 1984).

WISMAYER, J.M., *The History of the Kings Own Malta Regiment and the Armed Forces of the Order of St John* (Malta, 1989).

ZABARELLA. C.S., *Lo Assedio di Malta* (Torino, 1902).

ZACHARUADOU, E., *Trade and Crusade: Venetian Crete & the Emirates of Menteshe and Aydin;1300-1415* (Venice,1983).

Table I : Maltese Money		
6 piccioli or dinieri	=	1 grano
5 grani	=	1 cinquina
2 cinquine	=	1 carlino
2 carlini	=	1 taro
I2 tari	=	1 scudo
30 tari	=	1 oncia or pezza

Table II : Measurements			
12 pulzier (inches)	= 1 palmo	= 0.2619 metres
1 piede (foot)	= 11.167 inches	
8 palmi (xbar)	= 1 canna (qasba)	= 2.095 metres
1 toise		= 1.949 metres
I salma	= 4.444 acres	= 1.798 hectares

References & Notes

Castellans of Outremer (4)

1. Delaville le Roulx, 47.
2. Burman, 50-4.
3. Sire, 16.
4-6. Riley-Smith, 69.
7. Forey, 62.
8. Riley-Smith, 56.
9. *Cartulaire des Hospitaliers,* No. 258.
10. Pringle, *Crusader Castles,* n. 68, 74.
11. Riley-Smith, 58.
12. Ibid., 70.
13. Ibid., 69.
14. Ibid., 66.
15. Ibid., 67.
16. Pringle, *The Red Tower,* 16.
17. Ibid., 130.
18. *Cartulaire des Hospitaliers,* No. 3236.
19-20. Riley-Smith, 131.
21. Ibid., 68.
22-29. Ibid., 428-32.

The Crusader Fortress (8)

1. Pringle, *Crusader Castles,* xxv.
2. Fino, 170-7,
3. Pringle, *The Red Tower,* 15; Edwards, *Donjon at Anavarza, passim.*
4. Smail, *Crusading Warfare,* 230-6; Marshall, 100.
5. Pringle, *Crusader Castles,* xxvii.
6. Creswell, *Early Muslim Architecture,* 163.
7. Ibid., 35-146; Creswell, *The Muslim Architecture of Egypt,* 161-217.
8. A. Lawrence, 171-227.
9. Winter, 193.
10. A. Lawrence, 171-227.
11. Turner, 65.
12. A. Lawrence, 171-227.

Knights and Mercenaries (12)

1. Riley-Smith, 54-5.
2. Marshall, 49-52.
3-5. Marshall, 111-21.
6. Riley-Smith, 124.
7. Marshall, 58-60.
8-9. Smail, *Crusading Warfare,* 111-2.
10. Riley-Smith, 455.
11. Marshall, 120.
12. Marshall, 121; *Cartulaire des Hospitaliers,* No.2213.
13. Marshall, 121.
14. Ibid., 210-56.

15. Riley-Smith, 137.
16. *Les Gestes des Chiprois,* 248-9.
17-18. Marshall, 116.
19. Ibid., 210-56.
20. Gravett, *passim;* Marshall, 212-4.
21. Marshall, 232.
22. Gabrieli, 339.
23. *Les Gestes des Chiprois,* 217-9.
24. Ibid., 244-5.
25. Marshall, 192.
26. Ibid., 121.

Rearguard of the Crusades (16)

1. Bridge, 194-5.
2. Riley-Smith, 109.
3. Pringle, *Belmont Castle,* 102.
4-6. Riley-Smith, 110-1.
7. Ibid., 444.
8. Van Cleve, 389-428.
9. Riley-Smith, 424.
10. Ibid., 136.
11-13. Ibid., 445.
14-15. Luttrell, *Cilician Armenia, passim.*
16. Boase, 169.
17. Ibid.,158.
18-19. Riley-Smith, 131.
20. *Les Gestes des Chiprois,* 236.
21. Riley-Smith, 131.
22. Ibid., 133.
23. Ibid., 129.
24. Ibid., 133.
25-26. Marshall, 115.
27. Ibid., 20-1.
28. Riley-Smith, 429.
29. Ibn Shaddad, quoted in Cathcart King.
30. Riley-Smith, 429.
31. Deschamps, 270-3.
32. Marshall, 117.
33-34. Riley-Smith, 195-6.
35. *Les Gestes des Chiprois,* 243-56.

A New Role in Cyprus (20)

1. On Cyprus, see Edbury, 295-303.
2. Luttrell, *Cyprus, Rhodes, Greece,* 162; Riley-Smith, 198-226.
3. Ginnis, 15-9, 135.
4. Luttrell, *The Military Orders,* 338-41.
5. Luttrell, *Rhodes 1306-1421,* 280.
6. Delaville le Roulx, *Chypre,* 272.
7. Poutiers, 23-8.
8. Luttrell, 'Settlement on Rhodes',273.
9. Zachariadou, 10.

10. Luttrell, *Venice and the Knights,* 195-212; Delaville le Roulx, *Philibert de Naillac,* 10-1.
11-12. Delaville le Roulx, *Chypre,* 272.
13. Luttrell, *Rhodes 1306-1421,* 284.
14. Ibid.; tradition tells of the knights copying the ruse Ulysses played upon Polyphemus; Bradford, 60.
15. Zachariadou, 10-1.
16-17. Luttrell, *Hospitallers at Rhodes,* 284.
18. Brockman, 30.
19. Edwards, *Conquest of Rhodes,* 50-63.
20. Delaville le Roulx, *Chypre,* 260-84; Vertot, I, 493-500.
21. Luttrell, *Hospitallers in Cyprus,* 162.
22. Enlart, II, 654-58.
23. Bustron, 252.
24. *Cartulaire des Hospitaliers,* No.1354

Rhodes and the Dodecanese (23)

1. Volonakis, 243.
2. Luttrell, 'Turks', 86-7.
3. Zachariadou, 13; Luttrell, 'Turks', 8; On Leros, Delaville le Roulx, *Rhodes,* 365-7.
4. Luttrell, 'Turks', 97.
5. Volonakis, 242.
6-7. Luttrell, 'Turks', 85-8.
8-9. Ibid., 273-81.
10. Luttrell , *Lindos,* 317-8; Luttrell, 'Military and Naval organization', 145; AOM 319, f. 299; Luttrell, 'Settlement on Rhodes', 275.
11. Ibid., 136-8.
12. Gabriel, 1-2, 226-7.
13. Lib MS 321, f. 212v; Luttrell, 'Military and Naval organization', 137.
34. Bosio, II, 321.
15. Bosio, II, 350, 261, 274, 326, 396, 398 respectively.
16. Attacks on Leros in Bosio, II, 256, 260, 367, 561, 587-9; Kalymnos, 256.
17-19; Poutiers, 190-6; See also Poutiers, 'Villages fortifies et Bourg maritimes'.
20. Bosio, II, 349-50 gives the villages assigned to the various castles in 1475; *Lindos, Calatto, Pilona, Lardo, Stlepio, Ianadi; Canea* (Lahania), *Tha, Defania, Efgales; Catavia, Messiuagro, Vati; Polochia, Stridio, Porfilia, Arnita; Polona, Laderma; Salaco, Capi, Quittalia; Fanes, Diosoro,Nicorio, Dimilia; Villanouva, Chimedes, Altoluogo,*

Dimitria, Sicegai; Feraclo-Salia, Ianadoto, Malona, Catagro, Camimari; Arcangelo, solo guardare si dovesse. E che nella città di Rhodi ritirare si dovessero le genti de Casali di Fando, di Psito, di Archipoli, d'Arima, di Calaties, e di Demathia; other defence preparations can be found in 321 (1470), 375 (1475), and 387 (1479).

21-22. Poutiers, 190-6; Bosio, II, 387.

23-27. Poutiers, 190-6.

28. Ibid., 583.

29. Luttrell, 'Turks', 88-9.

30. Delaville le Roulx, *Rhodes*, 88-95;

31. Sarnowsky, *passim*.

32. Luttrell, 'Turks', 94-9; Ibid., *Latin Greece, passim*.

33-34. Ibid., 'Turks', 94-9.

35. Ibid., *compagnie navarresi*, chap. VIII, 119.

36. Ibid., 'Turks', 98; Delaville le Roulx, 277-82.

37. Andrews, 141; Luttrell & Jeppesson, 160; Karpodine, 22.

38. Luttrell, 'Turks', 98.

39. Delaville le Roulx, 284-6.

40-41. Luttrell and Jeppesson, 143-61; Delaville le Roulx, 287-90.

42. Bosio, II, 214-5.

43. Hughes and Migos, *Rhodes: the Turkish Sieges* (paper to be published).

44. The bibliography on the first siege of Rhodes is considerable; Bosio, II, 399-426; Brockman, 58-92; Hughes and Migos; Mizzi, 17-88.

45. Bosio, II, 447.

46-47. S. Pauli, 419-30.

48-49. For the second siege of Rhodes, see Bosio, II, 639-707, Brockman, 111-55; Mizzi, 119-202; Hughes and Migos; and Rossi, *Conquista di Rodi, passim*.

From Medieval Castles to Gunpowder Forts (28)

1. Gerola, 'Monumenti mediovali', *passim*.

2. Luttrell, 'Military and Naval organization', 136.

3. Gabriel, I, 43-4.

4. *Infra*.

5. Hughes and Migos.

6. See the chapter on the city of Rhodes, *infra*; Migos, 14.

7. Kollias, *The City of Rhodes*, 68.

8-9. Villena, 59-66.

10. Poutiers, 264-9.

11. For Venetian fortifications, see Perbellini, *passim*.

12. St J. O'Neil, 44-54; Hale, *The Early Development*, 466-94.

13-14. O'Neil, 45.

15. See note 44 in previous chapter.

16. Gabriel, I, 17.

17. O'Neil, 48.

18. See chapter on the fortress of Rhodes.

19. For early Italian military engineers see J.R., Hale, *Renaissance Fortifications, passim*; Santoro, 33-7.

20. Luttrell & Jeppesson, 108:

21. AOM 394, f. 246v.

22. Luttrell and Jeppesson, 169.

23. Bosio, I, 393, 400, 411-2.

24. Bosio, I, 335.

25. G. Gerola, 'Il contributo dell'Italia', 1015-27; Gerola, 'Basilio dalla Scuola', 1159-66; Gabriel, I, 115-6.

26. Bosio, I, 624.

Building the Rhodian Fortresses (35)

1. Bosio, II, 455-56.

2. Especially Rhodes, Lindos, Kos, Bodrum, and, possibly, Nisyros; the lesser islands had smaller vessels.

3. Prawer, 295-300.

4. Luttrell and Jeppeson, 150.

5. Ibid., 166 *et seq*.

6. Marshall, 104-5.

7. AOM 394, ff. 188-9.

8. Luttrell and Jeppeson, 161.

9. A procedure retained and adopted by the Order in Malta after 1530, see Hoppen, *Fortification of Malta*, 129-34.

10. Hoppen, *Fortification of Malta*, 129-34.

11. Bosio, II, 387.

12. Hoppen, *Fortification of Malta*, 130.

13. Gabriel, I, 97-8.

14. Kollias, 64.

15. AOM 420, f.110.

Rhodes under Attack (42)

1. Hughes & Migos, *The Turkish Sieges*, 5.

2. Bosio, II, 214-5.

3. Hughes & Migos, *The Turkish Sieges*, 8

4-6. On sieges of Rhodes, see Borckman, *passim*: Bosio, II, 632 *et seq. chap*.

7-8. Luttrell, 'Military and Naval organization', XIX, 162.

9. Delaville La Roulx, 230-2.

10-11. Luttrell & Jeppeson, 147; AOM 339, ff. 240-1.

12. Bosio, II, 322.

13. Luttrell & Jeppeson, 147.

14. Bosio, II, 357.

15. Luttrell, 'Turks', chap. II, 87.

16. Bosio, II, 237, 256, 22, 275, 290, 551, 558, 650.

17. Ibid., 398.

18. Ibid., 261.

19. Ibid., 256, 260, and 381.

20. Ibid., 256, 260, 367, 561, and 587.

21-22. Ibid., 587-9.

23. Poutiers, 185.

24. Ibid., 187.

25. Bosio, II, 584.

26. Ibid., 644.

27. Ibid., 293.

28. Ibid., 644.

29. Poutiers, 187.

30. Bosio, II, 325.

31-32. Migos, *Knights' battleground*, 22-3.

33. Relief forces arrived on 15 October from Candia (20 men & 4 gunners), on 20 October from Lindos (12 men & 2 master gunners), and on 9 November from Bodrum (12 knights & 100 men-at-arms).

Bulwark of Christendom (49)

1. Bosio, III, 28.

2. Cutajar & Cassar, 30.

3. Bosio, III, 302-5.

4. Bosio, III, 305; AOM 88, f. 106v.

5. Pauli, II, 208.

6. Bosio, III, 325; AOM 88, f. 106v.

7. Bosio, III, 323.

8. Ellul, 21-2.

9. Fiorini & Buhagiar, 441-96.

10. Cutajar & Cassar, 32.

11. Hoppen, *Fortification of Malta*, 28.

12. Bosio, III, 395, 398.

13. Ibid., 454.

14. A summary of the report is found in Bosio, III, 445-6.

15. Braudel, II, 967-1014.

16. Braudel, 1014-26.

17. There is an extensive narrative literature on the Great Siege - see bibliography.

18-20. De Giorgio, 60-75.

21. The chapter general of 1569 decided to transfer the convent from Birgu to Valletta, AOM 289, f. 50; AOM 93, f. 6v.

22. Hoppen, *Fortification of Malta*, 45-55: see also Borg, *Fabio Chigi*.

23. Hoppen, *Fortification of Malta*, 47-8.

24. Chigi, R I 25, f. 329v (with a sketch of

the Floriana land front).

25. Hoppen, *Fortification of Malta,* 50.

26. AOM 256, f. 178v.

27-8. Hoppen, *Fortification of Malta,* 51-5

29. AOM 6554, f. 47.

30. Hughes, *Guide,* 247.

31-2. Hoppen, *Fortification of Malta,*
79-81.

33. Ibid., 90-4.

34. AOM 6554, ff. 94v-98, '... *devono essere
tutte le sue opere talmente disposte che possa
con la gente nella Città e nell'Isola
ordinariamente residente, al nemico benche
potente resistere. Per questo non si devono
multiplicare le difese per non multiplicare il
numero de difensori'.*

The Development of Military Architecture (57)

1. Hale, *Early Development, passim.*

2. Steriotou, 12.

3. *Infra.*

4. Hughes, *Military Architecture,* 102-3;

5. Hoppen, *Fortification of Malta,*15.

6. Hughes, 118-27;

7. AOM 6554, f. 143.

8-9. Hughes; on Vauban, see R. Blomfield,
Sebestien Le Prestre de Vauban, 1633-1707.

10. Hughes, *Military Architecture,*125-6;

11. Ibid., 130-1.

12. Prost, 39-51.

13. Hughes, *Military Architecture,*130-1.

14. Hughes, 'Difesa Costiera Inglese', 25-
44.

Ramparts of Stone (61)

1-4. Hughes, *The Building of Malta,* 191-9.

5. Rossi, *Storia di Tripoli,* 130, n.77.

6. Hoppen, *The Fortification of Malta,* 140.

7. Ibid., 139.

An Island Fortress in the Mediterranean (65)

1. AOM 100, f. 193v.

2. AOM 6554, f. 42.

3. AOM, 256, f. 129v, AOM 257, f. 136v: ,
AOM 6402, f. 146v; Papal permission for
the project was given on 11 September 1643,
AOM 470, f. 266, AOM 257, f. 165.

4. AOM 1012, f. 67.

5. Pozzo, II, 101.

6. Hoppen, *The Fortification of Malta,* 103.

7. On the coastal towers of Malta, Gozo, and
Comino, see Mifsud, 55-100, and Samut-
Tagliaferro, *passim*; See also AOM 101, f.

191; AOM 103, f. 103, 146v; AOM 105, f.
76; AOM 106, ff. 124, 209.

8. Hoppen, *The Fortification of Malta,* 105-
13, 122-5.

9. AOM 267, f. 124v; AOM 1011, f. 38.

10. See AOM 1015, ff. 28, 72, 289.

11. AOM 1015, ff. 389, 392.

12. Lib. Ms. 590, no foliation; AOM 6552,
f. 38, and AOM 6557, f. 187 show lists of
proposed fougasses.

13. Spiteri, *The Fougasse, passim.*

14. AOM 6557, f. 62.

15. AOM 1015, ff. 412-3.

The Last Crusaders (71)

1. For a discussion of the Hospitaller military set-up, see Spiteri, *The Palace Armoury,*
chap. 1-2.

2. For an account of the Great Siege, consult
titles in bibliography.

3. De Groot, 199-254.

4. AOM 105, f. 71v.

5-6. AOM 110, f. 31.

7. Wismayer, 3-18.

8. AOM 265, f. 49

9. Wismayer, 66-9.

10-11. Ibid., 27-34.

12. AOM 1015, ff. 373-4.

13. Testa, *Pinto,* 247-76.

14. Cutajar & Cassar, ' Mediterranean Affairs', 39-71.

15. Wismayer, 73.

16. Hoppen, 'Military Priorities', 414.

17. For an account of the French invasion
see Testa, *The French in Malta.*

Gazetteer

i

Bait Gibrin (77)

1-2. Riley-Smith, *Knights,* 52.

3-4. Sire, 16 .

5-6. Riley-Smith, *Knights,* 104.

7. Marshall, 20-1.

8. William of Tyre, I, 639.

9. Kloner & Chen, 12-3.

10. Benvenisti, 185-8.

11-13. Kloner & Chen, 13.

Belmont (77)

1. Pringle & Harper (1988), 102.

2. Delaville Le Roulx, *Cartulaire,* I, 276-7,

No. 803.

3. Pringle & Harper (1988), 102.

4. Delaville Le Roulx, I, 276-7, No. 803.

5-6. Pringle & Harper (1988), 102.

7. Ambroise, line 6857.

8. Pringle & Harper (1988), 101-18; Ibid.,
(1989), 47-61.

9. Smith, *Crusading Warfare,* 235.

10-12. Description and measurements based
on Pringle & Harper (1988).

13-14. Ibid., 115.

Gibelcar (78)

1. Riley-Smith, 66-7.

2-5. Deschamps, *Terre Sainte,* III, 308.

Touban (79)

1. Deschamps, *Terre Sainte,* III, 407.

2. Ibid., 160

3. Ibid., 21.

4. Ibid., 160.

5. Ibid., 135.

Mont Ferrand (79)

1-4. Deschamps, *Terre Sainte,* III, 321-2.

Forbelet (79)

1.Pringle, *Survey of Castles,* 90.

2. Riley-Smith, *Knights,* 110.

3. Pringle, *Survey of Castles,* 90.

Castrum Rubrum (Qal'aat Yahmur) (80)

1-2. *Cartulaire des Hospitaliers,* No. 519;
Deschamps, *Terre Sainte,* III, 317.

3-4. Measurements based on Pringle, *Red
Tower,* 16-8.

5-6. Deschamps, *Terre Sainte,* III, 317-9.

7. Pringle, *Red Tower,* 18.

8. Lawrence, *Crusader Castles,* 51-5.

Turris Rubea (81)

1. Pringle, *Red Tower,* 88.

2-3. Ibid., 124.

4. Ibid., 100-4.

5. *Cartulaire des Hospitaliers,* No.2141.

6. Pringle, *Red Tower,* 86.

7. *Cartulaire des Hospitaliers,* No. 2482.

8-9. Pringle, *Red Tower,* 86.

Qula (81)

1-2. Pringle, *Red Tower,* 21-2.

Recordane (81)

1-4. Pringle, *Survey of Castles,* 89.

Bordj es-Sabi (82)
1-2. Deschamps, *Terre Sainte,* III, 327-8.

Bordj Arab (82)
1-2. Deschamps, *Terre Sainte,*III, 327-8.

Coliath (83)
1. Deschamps, *Terre Sainte,* III, 311-2.
2. *Recueil des Historiens des croisades, Historiens occidentaux* I, 167.
3. Deschamps, *Terre Sainte,* III, 312.
4. Willbran of Oldenburg.
5. Description of Coliath taken from Deschamps, *Terre Sainte,* III, 311-2.

Belvoir (84)
1-2. Prawer, *Jerusalem,* 300.
3. Delaville Le Roulx, *Cartulaire,* I, No. 317.
4. Excavations on the site of the castle were carried out under the direction of M. Ben-Dov and the plan and report of the excavation were published in *Qamonioth.*
5-6. Prawer, *Jerusalem,* 304.
7. Rey, *Les colonies franques,* 437; Prawer regards it as a great tower but at the same time states that it was lower than the rest of the castle.
8. Prawer, *Jerusalem,* 301.
9. Pringle & Harper (1988), 116.
10-14. Riley-Smith, *Knights,* 110.
15-16. Marshall, 20-1.

Crac des Chevaliers (86)
1. Deschamps, *Terre Sainte,* I, 106-97.
2. Cathcart King, 83.
3-6. Maalouf, 41.
7. Cathcart King, 83.
8. For a narration of the siege, see ibid., 83-92; Deschamps, *Terre Sainte,* I, 132-6.
9. Smail, *Crusading Warfare,* 224-5; Deschamps, *Terre Sainte,* I, 275-305.
10. Deschamps, *Terre Sainte,* I, 204.
11. On Saladin's campaigns, see Nicolle, *Saladin and the Saracens, passim.*
12. Riley-Smith, *Knights,* 192.
13. Prawer, *Jerusalem,* 296.
14. Smail, *Crusading Warfare,* 225: Deschamps, *Terre Sainte,* I, on chapel, 197-202.
15. Cathcart King, 84.
16. Delaville La Roulx, *Cartulaire,* II, 797-8, No. 2727: Deschamps, *Terre Sainte,* I, 130.
17. Cathcart King, 86-8.
18. Deschamps, *Terre Sainte,* I, 177-182.

19. Frà Lorne was constable of Marqab between 1250 and 1254 and presumably of Crac des Chevaliers afterwards.
20. Deschamps, *Terre Sainte,* I, 146-60.
21. Deschamps, *Terre Sainte,* I, 167-72.
22. Ibid., 174-7.
23. Rey, *Etude sur les monuments,* 40.
24. *Cartulaire des Hospitaliers,* No.1602; The words of Andrew, king of Hungary, who made an annual grant of 100 marks from his Hungarian revenues in 1218, which grant was confirmed soon afterwards by Pope Honorius III.
25. Willbrand of Oldenburg, 169.
26-27. Riley-Smith, *Knights,* 137.
28. *Cartulaire des Hospitaliers,* No.3308.
29-33. Cathcart King, 87-92.
34. Deschamps, *Terre Sainte,* III, 169-71.

The Fortress of Marqab (95)
1-2. Deschamps, *Terre Sainte,* III, 269.
3. Sire, 9.
4. *Cartulaire des Hospitaliers,* No.3236: Riley-Smith, *Knights,* 68.
5. Deschamps, *Terre Sainte,* III, 264.
6. *Cartulaire des Hospitaliers,* No.3236: Riley-Smith, *Knights,* 68.
7. Deschamps, *Terre Sainte,* III, 264.
8. *Chronique d'Ernoul,* 254-5.
9. Riley-Smith, *Knights,*131.
10-11. Deschamps, *Terre Sainte,* III, 266-7.
12. Willbrand of Oldenburg, 170.
13. Deschamps, *Terre Sainte,* III, 267.
14. Riley-Smith, *Knights,* 192.
15-16. Deschamps, *Terre Sainte,* III, 270-3.
17. Willbrand of Oldenburg, 170.
18. Riley-Smith, *Knights,*195.
19. Marshall, 233.
20. Riley-Smith, *Knights,*195.
21. Measurements based on Deschamps. 22-26; Deschamps, *Terre Sainte,* III, 277-80.
27. Ibid., 281-4.
28. Willbrand of Oldenburg, 170.
29. *Gestes des Chiprois,* 217-8.

Silifke (101)
1-3. Boase, 18, 25, 119, 180-1

Ascalon (102)
1. Riley-Smith, *Knights,*133.
2. Marshall, 102.
3. *Cartulaire des Hospitaliers,* nos.2031, 2320.

4-6 Marshal, 233-4, 102-4.
7. This is due to the weathering of the surrounding masonry courses.
8. Only the *tell* of the citadel has survived.

Acre (103)
1. Billings, 171-9.
2-3. Riley-Smith, *Knights,* 131.
4. Wilbrand of Oldenburg, 170.
5. *Atlas of the Crusades,* 102-3.
6. Sire, 214.
7. Riley-Smith, *Knights,*193.
8. *Gestes des Chiprois,* 243-56.

Kolossi Castle (104)
1. *Cartulaire des Hospitaliers,* No.1354.
2. Ibid., No.4549; Luttrell, *Hospitallers in Cyprus,* 170.
3. Aristidou, *passim*; Poutiers, 305-8.
4. Wartburg, 301 and 312, and Plates XLIXa and b.

ii

Fortifications of the City of Rhodes (106)
1. Michalaki-Kollia, 5.
2. Ibid., 9.
3. Paradissis, III, 159-74.
4-5. Michalaki-Kollia, 9.
6. Kollias, *Knights of Rhodes,* 9.
7. Kollias, *City of Rhodes ,* 118.
8-9. Bottarelli, 61.
10. Bosio, II, 447.
11. Lawrence, *Crusader Castles,* 51.
12. Gabriel, II.
13. Bosio, II, 85.
14-15. Migos, *The Knights' Battleground,* 17-9.
16. Bosio, II, 249.
17. Migos, *Knights' Battleground,* 18.
18. Kollias, *The City of Rhodes,* 68.
19. Migos, *Knights' Battleground,* 14; see also Lawrence, 44-53.
20. Villena, 65.
21-2. Migos, *Knights' Battleground,* 19; Gabriel, 60.
23. AOM 75, f. 54; Bosio, II, 350.
24-25. Kollias, *Knights of Rhodes,* 170.
26. Bosio, II, 293.
27. Ibid., 399, 402, 407.
28. Gabriel, 79-90.
29-31. Bosio, II, 646-7.
32. Migos, 19.
33. Bosio, II, 399-426; on the first siege of

Rhodes, see also Brockman, 58-92; Mizzi, 17-88.

34. Migos, *Knights' Battleground*, 9.

35. Bosio, II, 335.

36. O'Neil, 49; Hale, *The Development*, *passim*.

37-40. Kollias, *City of Rhodes*, 166-7.

41-2. O'Neil, 48-9.

43-44. Migos, *Knights' Battleground*, 14.

45. Gabriel, 34.

46. Kollias, *The City of Rhodes*, 168.

47. Caoursin, f.175; On the Djem episode, see Pauli, 419-30.

48. Gabriel, 32; Kollias, *City of Rhodes*, 162.

49. Jager, 23.

50. Gabriel, 55-7.

51-53. Bosio, II, 621.

54. O'Neil, 50.

55. Hughes, *Military Architecture*, 60.

56-7. Bosio, II, 624.

58. Gabriel, 115; on the second siege of Rhodes, see Bosio, 639-707; Mizzi, 119-202; Brockman, 111-55.

Pheraclos (126)

1-3. Poutiers, 264-9.

4-5. Ibid., 193.

Lindos (130)

1-3. Tataki, 14-22.

4. Poutiers, 286-8; Bosio, II, 398.

5. Poutiers, 193.

6. Ibid., 288.

7. Tataki, 34.

8. Bosio, II, 47.

Philerimos (132)

1-2. Poutiers, 269-72.

3. Paradissi, 181.

4. Luttrell, 'Hospitallers at Rhodes', 284.

5-6. Bradford, *Shield and the Sword*, 60.

7. Luttrell, 'Hospitallers at Rhodes', 284.

8-9. Bosio, II, 398.

10. Paradissi, 181.

11-12. Poutiers, 269-72.

13. Bosio, II, 399.

14. Luttrell, 'Rhodian Background of the Order of St. John', 9.

Lardos (134)

1. Bosio, II, 143.

2. Poutiers, 284-8; Gerola, 'Monumenti mediovali', 350.

3. In 1479 the people of Lardos were to retreat to the fortress of Lindos, see Bosio, II, 382.

Sianna (135)

1. Poutiers, 291-3; Gerola, 'Monumenti mediovali', 331-2.

Archangelos (136)

1. Bosio, II, 235.

2. Ibid., 312.

3. Poutiers, 253-8.

4. Gerola, 'Monumenti mediovali', 337.

5. Poutiers, 253.

6. See chapters on other castles such as Kritinia.

7. Poutiers, 255.

8. Bosio, II, 362.

9. Ibid., 387.

10. Ibid., 572.

Monolithos (138)

1. Poutiers, 290.

2. Bosio, II, 360.

Askiplion (140)

1. Poutiers, 258-64.

2. Gerola, 'Monumenti mediovali', 328-31.

3-4. Poutiers, 258-64.

Kritinia Castle (144)

1.. Bosio, 329

2-3. Poutiers, 275.

4-5. Gerola, 'Monumenti mediovali', 330-1.

6. Poutiers, 279.

Kremasti (148)

1. Poutiers, 280-3; Gerola, 'Monumenti mediovali', 323; the coat-of-arms of Grand Master Fabrizio del Carretto are recorded as having been once found placed inside this castle.

2. Ibid., 280-3.

3. Bosio, II, 387.

4. Poutiers, 280-3.

Apolakkia (149)

1. Poutiers, 251-3; Gerola, 'Monumenti mediovali', 335.

Villanova (149)

1. Poutiers, 293.

2-3. Bosio, II, 371.

4-5. Poutiers, 293.

6. Bosio, II, 387.

7. Ibid., 396.

8. Ibid., 397.

9. Poutiers, 294.

Kattavia (150)

1-2. Bosio, II, 321.

3. Ibid., 347.

4-5. Ibid., 370-1.

6-7. Gerola, ''Monumenti mediovali'', 354.

8. Bosio, II, 387.

9. Gerola, 'Monumenti mediovali', 354.

10. Bosio, 398.

Fanes (150)

1-2. Gerola, 'Monumenti mediovali', 322.

Coastal Towers (151)

1. Luttrell, 'Settlement on Rhodes', 273-7.

2. Bosio, II, 346.

3. Ibid., 235.

4. AOM 75, ff. 49-v.

5-8. Bosio, II, 360.

9. Ibid., 361.

10. Ibid., 363.

11. Ibid., 371.

12. Poutiers, 272-4.

13. Gerola, 'Monumenti mediovali', 358.

14. Ibid., 320.

15. Ibid., 336.

Kastellorizo (154)

1. Luttrell, 'The Hospitallers at Rhodes', 284.

2. AOM 321, f. 212; Bosio, II, 135.

3. Bosio, II, 135.

4-7. Paradissis, 186-7.

8. Luttrell, 'Turks', 91.

9. Bosio, II, 238.

10. Luttrell, 'Turks', 97.

11. Bosio, II, 214.

12-13. Ibid., 238.

14. Bosio, II, 328.

15-16. Poutiers, 304-405.

17. Paradissis, 187.

Chalki and Alimonia (158)

1. Bosio, II, 350.

2. Ibid., 350, 398.

3. Ibid., 105.

4. Gerola, 'Monumenti mediovali', 6.

5. Bosio, II, 105.

6. Luttrell, 'Military and Naval organiza-

tion', 137.
7. Bosio, II, 353.
8. Ibid., 360.
9. Gerola, 'Monumenti mediovali', 11.
10. Bosio, II, 391.

Symi (161)
1. Bosio, II, 35.
2. Ibid., 82.
3. Ibid., 215.
4. Arfaras, *passim*.
5. Gerola, 'Monumenti mediovali', 4; Poutiers, 314.
6. Poutiers, 314.
7. Luttrell and Jeppeson, 169.
8. See page 43.
9. Gerola, 'Monumenti mediovali', 4.
10. Bosio, II, 217.
11. Ibid., 255-6.
12. Ibid., 490.
13-14. Ibid., 584.

Tilos (164)
1. Coronelli.
2. Gerola, 'Monumenti mediovali', 13-4.
3. Bosio, II, 105.
4-5. Gerola, 'Monumenti mediovali', 14-5.
6. Ibid., 19.
7. Paradissis, 15.
8. Bosio, II, 350, 398.
9. Ibid., 393.
10. Ibid., 397, 584.

Nisyros (167)
1. Bosio, 514.
2. Luttrell, 'Lindos and the Defence of Rhodes', 319.
3. Ibid., 64.
4. Ibid., 82.
5. Gerola, 'Monumenti mediovali', 21.
6. Bosio, II, 204.
7. Gerola, 'Monumenti mediovali', 21.
8. *Relation du Pelegrinage a Jerusalem*.
9. Luttrell, 'The Latin Colonization of Rhodes', 262.
10. Bosio, II, 324.
11-12. Ibid., 326.
13-15. Gerola, 'Monumenti mediovali', 22.

Kos: Narangia (172)
1. Luttrell, 'The Hospitallers at Rhodes', 284.
2. Zachariadou, 13; the Hospitallers had a commandery in Kos by 1337, AOM 280,

f. 39v.
3. Gerola, 'Monumenti mediovali', 28; Bosio, II, 259.
4. Paradissis, 150-1.
5. Delaville, *Rhodes*, 230-231; Bosio, II, 143.
6. Gerola, 'Monumenti mediovali', 36.
7-8. Bosio, II, 246.
9. *Supra*.
10. Bosio, II, 257.
11. Ibid., 275.
12. Ibid., 328.
13. Ibid., 498.
14. Lib MS 77, ff. 110v-5; Bosio, II, 512-3.
15. Bosio, II, 521.
16. Ibid., 558.
17. Ibid., 583.
18. Ibid., 650.

Kos: Paleo Pyli (180)
1-2. Bosio, II, 275.
3-4. Ibid., 512.
5. Ibid., 516.
6. Gerola, 'Monumenti mediovali', 46-9.
7. Apparently this escutcheon was not seen by Gerola for he fails to mention it in his description.
8. Ibid., 46-9.

Kos: Andimacchia (184)
1. Gerola, 'Monumenti mediovali', 50.
2. Bosio, II, 135.
3. Ibid., 255.
4. Ibid., 257.
5. Bosio, II, 512: AO.M. 77, ff.110v-5.
6. Ibid., 512.
7. Ibid., 516.
8. Ibid., 513.
9. Gerola, 'Monumenti mediovali', 21, 51.
10. Another tenaille trace is found at Pheraclos on Rhodes.
11. Poutiers, 308-12.
12-13. Gerola, 'Monumenti mediovali', 21.

Kos: Kefalos (189)
1. Poutiers, 312; Chiffala as in Bosio, II, 275.
2. Gerola, 'Monumenti mediovali', 21, 52.
3. Bosio, II, 583.
4. Luttrell and Jeppeson, 170.
5. Poutiers, 312.

Kalymnos: Choria (190)
1. Stringa, 301.

2. Gerola, 'Monumenti mediovali', 330.
3-4. Paradissis, 148-50.
5. Gerola, 'Monumenti mediovali', 57.
6. Ibid.
7. Bosio, II, 511.
8-9. Gerola, 'Monumenti mediovali', 57.
10. Ibid., 56
11. Bosio, II, 256-7.
12-13. Bosio, II, 261 & 381; The island was given to Grand Master Orsini in 1471, and formed part of the magistral isles, ibid., 330.

Kalymnos: Pothia (194)
1-2. Gerola, 'Monumenti mediovali', 58.
3. Gerola mentions another escutcheon with the arms of Giacomo Geltru.

Kalymnos: Kastelli (196)
1. Gerola, 'Monumenti mediovali', 58-60; Paradissis, 149.
2. Paradissis, 149.
3. Karpodini-Dimitriadi, *The Greek Islands*, 177.

Telendos (197)
1. Paradissis, 149; Gerola, 'Monumenti mediovali', 60; Poutiers, 134.
2. Ibid., 313.

Leros (198)
1. Bosio, II, 35.
2. Luttrell, 'Turks', II, 84.
3. Coronelli, *L'Isola di Rodi*, 349.
4. Stringa, 306.
5. Gerola, 'Monumenti mediovali', 63.
6. Ibid.
7. Bosio, II, 511.
8. Ibid., 257.
9. Ibid., 260.
10. Ibid., 587-9.

Smyrna and Bodrum (204)
1. Luttrell, 'Turks', II, 87.
2. Ibid., 83.
3. Ibid., 86-8.
4. Ibid., 89.
5. Ibid., 91.
6. *Chronicles of the Crusades*, 304.
7. Setton, I, 186,190-4, 208-9, 218, 223.
8. Luttrell, *Cyprus*, V, 203-4.
9-10. Luttrell, 'Turks', II, 92.
11. Bosio, II, 77.
12. Ibid., 80.
13-14. Ibid., 111.

15-19. Ibid., 118.

20. Luttrell, 'Military and Naval organization',, 134.

21. Bosio, II, 131.

22. Lyle Kalcas, 2.

23. Hasluck, 145-150.

24. Efthymioy-Hadzilacou, 233.

25-26. Bosio, II, 138-9.

27. AOM, 327, f. 25.

28. Luttrell, 'Turks', 97.

29. Luttrell & Jeppeson, 143.

30. Bosio, II, 157.

31. Luttrell, 'Turks', 100.

32. Luttrell & Jeppeson, 143-144.

33. Luttrell, *Maussolleion*, 144-5.

34. Doukas, xviii:3-11; xxi:2,3-5; xxii:1.

35-36. Luttrell, 'Turks', II, 102.

37. AOM 339, ff. 230v-1, 245.

38. Luttrell & Jeppeson, 146; text in D. Wilkins, *Concilia Magna Britanniae et Hiberniae* (London, 1737), 131-2.

39. Text given in Luttrell & Jeppeson, 146.

40-41. Ibid., 141.

42-44. Ibid., 147-9.

45. Doukas, xxii:1.

46. Gerola, 'Monumenti mediovali', 29.

47. Luttrell & Jeppeson, 151.

48-49. Ibid., 152.

50. Ibid., 156.

51-52. Ibid., 154-5.

53. *supra.*

54. Luttrell & Jeppeson, 151.

55. Ibid., 156.

56. Ibid., 150; text in G. Fedalto, *La Chiesa Latina in Oriente, iii: Documenti Veneziani* (Verona, 1978), 186-7.

57. Luttrell & Jeppeson, 146.

58. Ibid., text from C. Cepio, *Pietro Mocenici Imperatoris gestorum libris tres* (Venice, 1477), b 2-3 ,quoted on page 185.

59. Luttrell & Jeppeson, 146.

60. Bosio, II, 326.

61. Luttrell & Jeppeson, 166.

62. AOM 339, ff. 240-1; 284, ff. 72v, 74v.

63-55. Bosio, II, 322.

66. Ibid., 325, 349, 498, 558.

67. Galea, 8.

68. Luttrell & Jeppeson, 166; AOM 77, f. 75v.

69. AOM 339, ff. 267v-71v.

70. Luttrell & Jeppeson, 146-7.

71-72. Ibid., 164.

73. Bosio, II, 328, 348.

74. Luttrell & Jeppeson, 151-4.

75. Ibid., 156; AOM 392, ff. 175v-6.

76-77. Bosio, II, 435.

78-79. Luttrell and Jeppeson, 166.

80. Ibid., 165.

81. Ibid., 166 *et seq.*

82. Ibid., 198 *et seq.*

83. Bosio, II, 512.

84. AOM 392, ff. 175v-6.

85. Luttrell & Jeppeson, 158.

86-87. Ibid.; a new bastion was completed in 1504, Bosio, II, 580.

88. Bosio, II, 603.

89. Ibid., 621.

90. Luttrell & Jeppeson, 169.

iii

The Fortress of Tripoli (220)

1. Longhena, 4; Rossi, *Il Dominio degli Spagnoli*, 109-12.

2. Bosio, III, 29-30.

3. Ibid., 67.

4. Ibid., 85.

5. Ibid., 188-9.

6. Map of Tripoli showing a fictitious siege of the fortress by the duke of Medina Celi in 1559, in Biblioteca Nazionale di Firenze.

7. Bosio, III, 161.

8. Ibid., 234.

9. Rossi, *Il Dominio degli Sapgnoli,* 130.

10. Bosio, III., 219.

11-13. Ibid., 309.

14. Ibid., 29.

15-16. Ibid., 309-10.

17-18. Rossi, *Il Dominio degli Sapgnoli,* 129.

19. Also known as *Torre de Rey*; Aurigemma, 79-81, the knights attacked the tower with three cannon and 700 men and captured it for the loss of five soldiers, and razed it to the ground.

20. Rossi, *Il Dominio degli Spagnoli,* 134.

21. Bosio, III, 309-10.

22. Bradford, *Siege of Malta,* 39.

Fort St Angelo (222)

1. A.E. Caruana, *Origine della Lingua Maltese* (Malta, 1896), 69.

2. Luttrell, 'Girolomo Manduca', 131; on the Arabs in Malta, see G. Wettinger, 'The Arabs in Malta', *Mid-Med Bank Annual Report,* 1985, 32.

3. This model is currently at the Museum of Fine Arts, Valletta.

4. Laurenza, 32-5; Darmanin, 16.

5-6. Wettinger, *The Castrum Maris*, I, 54.

7. Ibid., 45.

8. Ibid., 55.

9. AOM 1016, ff. 27.35-6, 116, 229, 303.

10. Wettinger, *The Castrum Maris*, 55.

11. S. Fiorini, extract from NAV R.439/19, f.8v, Notary Bartolomeo Selvagia Devia 3.4.1536.

12. Darmanin. 22.

13. Bosio, III, 140.

14. Ibid.

15. Fiorini, extract from NAV R.439, 19, f. 8v.

16-17. Bosio, III, 198-9, 213.

18. Darmanin, 35 and 127; AOM 87, f. 79.

19. Bosio, III, 223, 245, 293, 475, 587.

20. Darmanin, 36.

21. AOM 262, ff. 123-4, 285-91.

22. AOM 263, ff. 61-3.

23. AOM 1011, f. 3.

Città Notabile (229)

1. Ganado, 77-80.

2. Fiorini and Buhagiar, 441-88.

3. Bosio, III, 727.

4. Dal Pozzo, II, 101.

5. AOM 260, f. 84.

6. AOM 1016, f. 348.

7. Ibid., f. 480.

8. Ibid., f. 481.

9. AOM 6557, f. 62.

10. De Lucca, 'Architectural Interventions in Mdina', 45-67.

11-12. Hoppen, *Fortification of Malta,* 103.

Gran Castello (237)

1. De Lucca, 'The built environment in Gozo', 131.

2. Luttrell, *Gozo Citadel,* 55.

3. See G. Wettinger, *The Jews of Malta in the Late Middle Ages* (Malta, 1985), 25.

4. AOM 441, f. 259

5. Promis, 308.

6-7. AOM 6554, f.258.

8-9. Ibid., f.274.

10. Ibid., f.274v.

11. Dal Pozzo, I, 426.

12. R. Vella Bonavita, 'The Fortifications' in Luttrell (ed.) *Gozo Citadel*, XI iii, 1-8.

13. Ibid.

14. AOM 1012, f. 183.

15. AOM 6554, f. 42.

16. AOM 256, ff. 129v, 257, 136v.

17. AOM 6554, f. 299.

18. Ibid., f. 309.
19. Hoppen, *Fortification of Malta*, 118.
20. AOM 6552, f. 101.
21-22. AOM 6554, f. 317.
23. AOM 6552, f. 34; Hoppen, *Fortification of Malta*, 120.
24. De Lucca, 'The built environment in Gozo', 148.
25. AOM 1012, f. 183.
26-27. Ibid., f. 184.

Città Vittoriosa (244)
1. Bosio, III, 84.
2. Ibid., 140.
3. Ibid., 343, 362, 395, 460.
4. Ibid., 454.
5. Balbi, 105.
6. Ibid., 119.
7. Hughes, *Guide*, 246-47.
8. Balbi, 106-74
9. Ibid., 44-8.
10. Bradford, 181.
11-12. De Giorgio, 66-7.
13. AOM 110, f. 247.
14. AOM 6554, f. 92.
15. Ibid., f. 92v.
16. AOM 6554, f. 37.
17-20. AOM 1016, f. 364.
21. AOM 6554, f. 374; Hoppen, *Fortification of Malta*, 120.
22. AOM 6554, f. 163.
23. AOM 6560, f. 80.

Fort St Elmo (252)
1-2. De Giorgio, 37-39; Bosio, II, 323-5.
3. Ellul, 10.
4. De Giorgio, 13, 18.
5. Ellul, 9.
6. Bosio, III, 128.
7. Ibid., 198.
8. Ibid., 370.
9. Ibid., 323.
10. AOM 88, f. 121.
11. Bosio, III, 323.
12. AOM 1011, f .3.
13. Bosio, III, 353.
14. Ibid., 371.
15. Ibid., 353.
16. AOM 1011, f.3.
17. Bosio, 593.
18. Ibid., 499.
19. Balbi, 48.
20. For a day-to-day account of the Siege, see Balbi, 49-98.

21. Bosio, III, 733.
22. Hoppen, *Fortification of Malta*, 68.
23. AOM 1016, f. 191.
24. AOM 1011, f. 4.

Senglea (262)
1. Bosio, III, 27.
2-3. Scicluna, 97.
4. AOM 88, f. 106v.
5. Bosio, III, 353.
6. Hughes, *Guide*, 195.
7. Balbi, 48.
8. De Giorgio, 66.
9. AOM 439, f. 270v.
10. AOM 110, f. 247v; AOM 111, f. 14.
11-13. AOM 256, f. 128v.
14. AOM 1015, f. 385.
15. Hoppen, *Fortification of Malta*, 83.
16. AOM 6554, f. 80.

Valletta (268)
1. Bosio, III, 198.
2. Ibid., 395 and 455.
3. Ibid., 454-6.
4. Bosio, III, 720-2.
5. Bosio, III, 745; De Giorgio., 73-4.
6. Ibid., 792.
7-8. Hoppen, *Fortification of Malta*, 38.
9. De Giorgio, 144.
10. Speckle, *passim*.
11. Mallia-Milanes, 275-90.
12. AOM 1016, f. 191.
13. Hughes, *Guide*, 231.
14. AOM 6554, f.17.
15. De Giorgio, 182.
16. AOM 6554, f. 49.
17. Ibid., f. 18.
18. Ibid., f. 199.
19. AOM 263, f. 11.
20-21. AOM 6554, f. 281.
22. AOM 1016, ff. 183, 189, 192, 207.
23. AOM 6560, no foliation.

Floriana Lines (281)
1. AOM 111, f. 14.
2. AOM 6554, f. 21.
3. Ibid., f. 25.
4-5. Hoppen, *Fortification of Malta*, 47.
6. AOM 6402, f. 1365.
7. Hoppen, *Fortification of Malta*, 49.
8. AOM 256, f. 101.
9. Ibid., f. 168.
10. Ibid., f. 177.
11. AOM 257, f. 36.

12-13. AOM 6554, f. 69.
14. Dal Pozzo, 387.
15. AOM 6554, f. 115.
16. AOM 261, f. 176.
17. AOM 6551, f. 1.
18. AOM 6554, ff. 71-5.
19. AOM 262, f. 128v.
20-21. AOM 6560, no foliation.
22. AOM 1562, f. 1357.
23-24. Ibid.
25. Cutajar, *passim*.

Sta Margherita Lines (290)
1. AOM 6554, f. 22.
2. Ibid., f. 47.
3. AOM 112, f. 117.
4. AOM 6554, f. 47.
5-6. Ibid., ff .47-9,.
7. Ibid., f. 55.
8. Ibid., ff. 55-61.
9. Ibid., f. 53.
10. Ibid., f. 31; Hoppen, *Fortification of Malta*, 140.
11. AOM 6554, f. 87.
12. AOM 257, f. 14.
13. Hughes, *Guide*, 140-1.
14-15. AOM 6560, no foliation.
16. AOM 6519.
17. AOM 6557, f.62.

Cottonera Lines (295)
1. Hughes, *Guide*, 151-6.
2. Hoppen, *Fortification of Malta*, 79.
3. AOM 6551, f. 45.
4. AOM 261, f. 169v; Dal Pozzo, II, 389.
5. AOM 6551, f. 52; AOM 6402, f. 304.
6. AOM 6554, f. 143.
7. AOM 6551, f. 55v.
8. AOM 6554, f. 143.
9. Ibid., f. 167.
10. AOM 6551, f. 60.
11. Hoppen, *Fortification of Malta*, 81.
12. AOM 6552, f. 40v.
13. Hughes, *Guide*, 151-6.
14-15. AOM 6560, no foliation.
15. AOM 6555; AOM 6519.
16. AOM 6560, no foliation.
17. De Lucca & Tonna, 4, 16, 19.
18. AOM 6557, f. 62.
19. AOM 1011, f. 43.
20. AOM 6558, f. 70.

Fort Ricasoli (301)
1. AOM 100, f.248; AOM 296, f. 146v.

2.   AOM 109, f. 164v.

3.   Hoppen, *Fortification of Malta*, 91.

4.   AOM 6554, f. 75

5.   Hoppen, *Fortification of Malta*, 199.

6.   AOM 6554, f. 81.

7-8. Ibid., f. 85.

9.   Dal Pozzo, II, 388.

10. AOM 261, f. 166.

11. AOM 6554, f. 176.

12. PRO WO MS 55, 1555/1, 231.

13. AOM 6554, f. 176.

14. Ibid., ff.140, 146.

15. AOM 26, ff. 97, 146; AOM 263, f. 279; AOM 1016, ff. 425-6.

16. AOM 6560, no foliation.

17. Lib MS. 1301, f. 57.

18. AOM 6552, f. 40v.

19. AOM 6560, no foliation.

20. AOM 6557, ff. 62, 79.

21. AOM 1054, f. 18.

22. AOM 6558, f. 18.

23. Hoppen, *Fortification of Malta*, 94.

24. AOM 1015, f. 356.

Fort Manoel   (306)

1.   De Giorgio, 123.

2.   Ibid., 125.

3.   Mallia-Milanese, 285-9.

4.   Dal Pozzo, II, 76.

5-6. Hughes, *Guide,* 133.

7.   AOM 6554, f. 129.

8.   Ibid., f.176.

9.   AOM 6560, no foliation.

10. AOM 6552, f. 49v.

11. AOM 1011, f. 44.

12. AOM 1054, f. 19.

13-14. AOM 276, f. 223.

15. Hoppen, *Fortification of Malta*, 96.

16. AOM 6557, f. 89.

17. De Lucca & Tonna, 30.

18. See G. Bonello, *Art in Malta, Discoveries and Recoveries* (Malta,1999), 112-24.

19. AOM 6557, f. 62.

20. AOM 6556, f. 176.

21. AOM 1054, f. 19.

22. AOM 6554, f. 176v: See P. Cassar, 'Malta's Role in Maritime Health under the Auspices of the Order of St John in the 18th century' in *Lombard Bank Ltd. Annual Report,* 1989 (Malta, 1989).

23. Schermerhorn, 259.

Fort Chambrai   (312)

1.   AOM 6554, f. 267.

2.   Ibid., AOM 6556, f. 6.

3.   AOM 276, f. 165.

4.   AOM 6554, f. 253.

5-6. Ibid., f. 309.

7-8. Ibid., f. 331.

9-11. AOM 1012, f. 184v.

12-13. De Lucca, 'The built environment in Gozo', 149.

14-15. AOM 1012, f. 67.

16. Ibid., f. 42.

17. Ibid., ff .29, 30, 41.

18. AOM 271, f. 90v.

19. AOM 6557, f. 9.

20-21. AOM 6558, f. 37v.

Fort Tigné (318)

1.   AOM 6560, no foliation.

2.   AOM 6552, f. 49v.

3.   Lib MS. 590.

4.   Hughes, *Guide,* 233-45.

5-6. AOM 1015, f. 412.

7.   Ibid., f.13.

8-9. Hughes, *Guide,* 235 *et seq.*

10. From description by Gen. Pasley, see Hughes, *Guide to the Fortifications,* 237.

11. AOM 1015, f. 430.

Coastal Towers   (322)

1.   Mifsud, 55-100.

2-3. AOM 6554, f.253.

4.   See Artillery inventory compiled by Chevalier De Saint Felix Laine in AOM 1061.

5-8. AOM 110, f. 31.

9-10. Ibid., f. 258.

11. Wismayer, 13-5.

12. AOM 1015, f. 382-4.

Coastal Bateries   (333)

1.   AOM 6556, f. 2.

2-3. Ibid., f. 3.

4.   Ibid., f. 9.

5.   Hoppen, *Fortification of Malta,* 110-1.

6.   AOM 6556, f. 11.

7.   AOM 6543, f. 41. This volume gives the details of the costs of construction of the coastal batteries built in   1715-16.

8.   AOM 1015, f. 386; on the artillery of batteries see reports AOM 1015, f. 72 (1769), f. 289 (1783), f. 349 (1791), ff. 357-89 (1792) and f. 393 (1793).

9.   AOM 1015, f. 387.

Coastal Redoubts   (341)

1.   AOM 1015, f. 357.

Coastal Entrenchments   (345)

1.   Vertot, as cited in Samut-Tagliaferro, 237.

2.   AOM 6552, f. 6v.

3.   Ibid., f. 34.

4-5. AOM 6556, f. 3

6.   AOM 1012, f. 183v.

7.   AOM 247, f. 124v.

8.   AOM 1011, f. 45 (3 July 1722)

9-10. AOM 6556, f. 175v.

11. AOM 6557, f. 193.

12. CL, MS OI, item 21.

13. Lib MS 590, report entitled 'Memoria ragionata per le Triniere delle Coste accessibili dell'Isola di Malta dal Bali Chirsulia in Malta in Aprile del 1763', no foliation.

14-19. Lib MS 590; for other reports on the defence of the coastline see Lib Ms 140, 'Osservatione sopra i littorali di ponente dell'Isola di Malta, 1761', f. 142; 'Reflessioni circa la difesa delle marine di Malta', *1761,* f. 182; 'Vantaggi de fossi e trincieri incavate nel rocco, 1762', f. 153.

Fougasse   (357)

1.   For a detailed review of the fougasse, see Spiteri, *Fougasse, passim.*

2.   AOM 6552, f. 38.

3.   Lib. Ms. 590.

4.   AOM 1020, f. 25.

5.   AOM 1015, f. 363.

Index of Place Names & Military Engineers

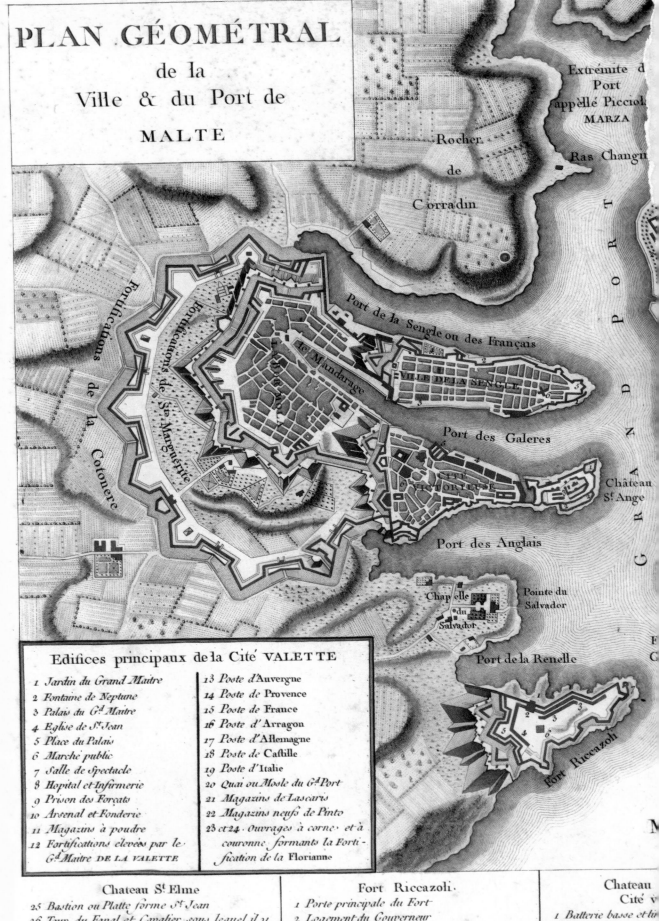

PLAN GÉOMÉTRAL
de la
Ville & du Port de
MALTE

Rocher de Corradin

Extrémité d Port appellé Picciol MARZA

Ras Changi

Port de la Sengle ou des Français

Fortifications de la Cotonere

Fortifications de Ste Marguérite

le Mandarage

VILLE DE LA SENGLE

Port des Galeres

CITÉ VICTORIEUSE

Château St Ange

Port des Anglais

Chapelle du Salvador

Pointe du Salvador

Port de la Renelle

Fort Riccazoli

GRAND PORT

Edifices principaux de la Cité VALETTE

1 Jardin du Grand Maitre
2 Fontaine de Neptune
3 Palais du Gd Maitre
4 Eglise de St Jean
5 Place du Palais
6 Marché public
7 Salle de Spectacle
8 Hopital et Infirmerie
9 Prison des Forçats
10 Arsenal et Fonderie
11 Magazins à poudre
12 Fortifications élevées par le Gd Maitre DE LA VALETTE

13 Poste d'Auvergne
14 Poste de Provence
15 Poste de France
16 Poste d'Arragon
17 Poste d'Allemagne
18 Poste de Castille
19 Poste d'Italie
20 Quai ou Mosle du Gd Port
21 Magazins de Lascaris
22 Magazins neufs de Pinto
23 et 24 Ouvrages à corne, et à couronne formants la Fortification de la Florianne

Chateau St Elme

25 Bastion ou Platte forme St Jean
26 Tour du Fanal et Cavalier sous lequel il y a des Souterrains
27 Caserne et Logement du Gouverneur
28 Porte du Fort
29 Platte forme sous laquelle est un reservoir d'eau
30 Bastion St Georges.

Fort Riccazoli.

1 Porte principale du Fort
2 Logement du Gouverneur
3 Casernes des Soldats
4 Loges ou se font les Cables et les cordages
5 Bastion de la tete, ou ouvrage a couronne
6 Grande Citerne
7 Batteries basses et rasantes

Chateau Cité v

1 Batterie basse et li
2 Batteries rasantes
3 Ancien Palais des
4 Hotel du Général d
5 Arsenal des Galer
6 Grande Caserne de